# The Italian Encounter with Tudor England

The small but influential community of Italians that took shape in England in the fifteenth century initially consisted of ecclesiastics, humanists, merchants, bankers, and artists. However, in the wake of the English Reformation, Italian Protestants joined other continental religious refugees in finding Tudor England to be a hospitable and productive haven, and they brought with them a cultural perspective informed by the ascendancy among European elites of their vernacular language. This original and interdisciplinary study maintains that questions of language are at the centre of the circulation of ideas in the early modern period. Wyatt first examines the agency of this shifting community of immigrant Italians in the transmission of Italy's cultural patrimony and its impact on the nascent English nation; Part 2 turns to the exemplary career of John Florio, the Italo-Englishman who worked as a language teacher, lexicographer, and translator in Elizabethan and Jacobean England.

MICHAEL WYATT, an independent scholar, has previously taught at Northwestern University and at Wesleyan University. He is a fellow of Villa I Tatti, The Harvard University Center for Italian Renaissance Studies.

*Cambridge studies in renaissance literature and culture*

General Editor
STEPHEN ORGEL
Jackson Eli Reynolds Professor of Humanities, Stanford University

Editorial board
ANNE BARTON *University of Cambridge*
JONATHAN DOLLIMORE *University of York*
MARJORIE GARBER *Harvard University*
JONATHAN GOLDBERG *Johns Hopkins University*
PETER HOLLAND *University of Notre Dame, Indiana*
KATE MCLUSKIE *The Shakespeare Institute, University of Birmingham*
NANCY VICKERS *Bryn Mawr College*

Since the 1970s there has been a broad and vital reinterpretation of the nature of literary texts, a move away from formalism to a sense of literature as an aspect of social, economic, political, and cultural history. While the earliest New Historicist work was criticized for a narrow and anecdotal view of history, it also served as an important stimulus for post-structuralist, feminist, Marxist, and psychoanalytical work, which in turn has increasingly informed and redirected it. Recent writing on the nature of representation, the historical construction of gender and of the concept of identity itself, on theatre as a political and economic phenomenon, and on the ideologies of art generally reveals the breadth of the field. Cambridge Studies in Renaissance Literature and Culture is designed to offer historically oriented studies of Renaissance literature and theatre which make use of the insights afforded by theoretical perspectives. The view of history envisioned is above all a view of our history, a reading of the Renaissance for and from our own time.

Recent titles include

Joseph Loewenstein *Ben Jonson and Possessive Authorship*
William N. West *Theatres and Encyclopedias in Early Modern Europe*
Richmond Barbour *Before Orientalism: London's Theatre of the East, 1576–1626*
Elizabeth Spiller *Science, Reading and Renaissance Literature: The Art of Making Knowledge, 1580–1670*
Deanne Williams *The French Fetish from Chaucer to Shakespeare*
Douglas Trevor *The Poetics of Melancholy in Early Modern England*
Christopher Warley *Sonnet Sequences and Social Distinction in Renaissance England*
Garrett A. Sullivan, Jr. *Memory and Forgetting in English Renaissance Drama*

*A complete list of books in the series is given at the end of the volume*

# The Italian Encounter with Tudor England

## *A Cultural Politics of Translation*

Michael Wyatt

CAMBRIDGE UNIVERSITY PRESS
Cambridge, New York, Melbourne, Madrid, Cape Town, Singapore, São Paulo

CAMBRIDGE UNIVERSITY PRESS
The Edinburgh Building, Cambridge CB2 2RU, UK

Published in the United States of America by Cambridge University Press, New York

www.cambridge.org
Information on this title: www.cambridge.org/9780521848961

© Michael Wyatt 2005

This book is in copyright. Subject to statutory exception
and to the provisions of relevant collective licensing agreements,
no reproduction of any part may take place without
the written permission of Cambridge University Press.

First published 2005

Printed in the United Kingdom at the University Press, Cambridge

*A catalogue record for this book is available from the British Library*

ISBN-13 978-0-521-84896-1 hardback
ISBN-10 0-521-84896-2 hardback

Cambridge University Press has no responsibility for
the persistence or accuracy of URLs for external or
third-party internet websites referred to in this book,
and does not guarantee that any content on such
websites is, or will remain, accurate or appropriate.

# Contents

| | |
|---|---:|
| *List of figures* | *page* vii |
| *Acknowledgments* | ix |
| *Note on the text* | xii |

Introduction    1

## Part 1   'A parlar d'Inghilterra': Italians in and on Early Modern England

| | | |
|---|---|---:|
| 1 | The two roses | 15 |
| | A Venetian ambassadorial report | 19 |
| | Italian humanists in Britain | 28 |
| | Italian artists in England | 43 |
| | England and the Roman church | 53 |
| | Italian actors in Henry VIII's 'great matter' | 62 |
| 2 | Reformations | 65 |
| | Italian views of Henry VIII | 66 |
| | Edward VI through one Italian's eyes | 72 |
| | The Italian 'reformation' in England | 84 |
| | Michelangelo Florio and the Tudor interregnum | 98 |
| | Italians and the English Catholic queen | 101 |
| 3 | La Regina Helisabetta | 117 |
| | From Mary to Elizabeth | 118 |
| | Elizabeth, Italian, and Italians | 125 |
| | The status of the 'stranger' in England | 134 |
| | The Italian mercantile presence in England | 140 |
| | The Italian community in England | 146 |

## Part 2   John Florio and the Cultural Politics of Translation

| | | |
|---|---|---:|
| 4 | Language lessons | 157 |
| | Roger Ascham contra Italy | 159 |
| | Language instruction in Elizabethan England | 163 |
| | John Florio's language pedagogy | 165 |
| | The poetic 'lie' in the service of language learning | 170 |
| | Proverbial lessons | 174 |

v

vi    Contents

|  |  |  |
|---|---|---|
| | Instruction in courtesy | 180 |
| | The Italian book, made in England | 185 |
| | A Shakespearean language lesson | 199 |
| 5 | **Worlds of words** | 203 |
| | Alessandro Citolini and the Italian 'language question' | 204 |
| | Grammars | 210 |
| | Instruments of cultural control in early modern Italy | 218 |
| | Florio the lexicographer | 223 |
| | Readings through Florio's dictionary | 231 |
| | Gender and the language arts | 244 |

| | |
|---|---|
| *Appendix I* | 255 |
| *Appendix II* | 262 |
| *Notes* | 265 |
| *Bibliography* | 341 |
| *Index* | 366 |

# Figures

| | | |
|---|---|---|
| 1 | Pinturicchio, fresco of Enea Silvio Piccolomini and James I in Scotland, Piccolomini Library, Duomo, Siena. Reproduced courtesy of Scala Archivio/Art Resource, NY. | 30 |
| 2 | Pietro Carmeliano, first page of *Carmen* in honor of Mary Tudor and Charles of Castille. Reproduced by permission of the British Library. | 33 |
| 3 | Gubbio *Studiolo*, Garter of Federico da Montefeltro. Reproduced courtesy of Metropolitan Museum of Art. | 36 |
| 4 | Baldassare Castiglione, first page of *Ad Henricum Angliae Regem epistola*, Amherst Ms. B3, n. 3. Reproduced courtesy of Amherst College Archives and Special Collections. | 38 |
| 5 | Giovanni Michele Nagonio, miniature of Henry VII in *Carmen*, York Minster Ms. XVI N2. Reproduced by kind permission of the Dean and Chapter of York. | 45 |
| 6 | Pietro Torrigiano, tomb of Henry VII and Elizabeth of York, Westminster Abbey. Reproduced courtesy of Scala Archivio/Art Resource, NY. | 48 |
| 7 | John Foxe, *Acts and Monuments*, Woodcut. Reproduced courtesy of Department of Special Collections, Stanford University. | 52 |
| 8 | John Haidt, Painting of Edward VI, John Laski, and the Elders of the Church of Austin Friars. Reproduced by permission of the United Reformed Church History Society, Westminster College, Cambridge Theological Federation. | 99 |
| 9 | Giovanni Alberto Albicante, frontispiece of *Il sacro et divino sponsalitio*. Reproduced by permission of the British Library. | 110 |
| 10 | Alessandro Magno, drawing of St. Paul's, Folger Shakespeare Library Ms. V.a.259. Reproduced by permission of the Folger Shakespeare Library. | 120 |

| | | |
|---|---|---|
| 11 | The 'Moorfields' section of the 1559 copperplate map of London. Reproduced courtesy of the Museum of London. | 149 |
| 12 | Title page of John Wolfe's edition of Machiavelli, *I discorsi*. Reproduced by permission of the British Library. | 190 |
| 13 | John Hole, Engraving of John Florio in *Queen Anna's New World of Words*. | 253 |

# Acknowledgments

One of my most accomplished students generously acknowledged in the preface to his senior thesis several years ago that all valuable intellectual work is collaborative, and I roundly second his judgment. This book owes an infinitude of debts: to my teachers; to the libraries where I have worked and whose staffs have worked indefatigably for me; to the institutions in which I have been formed and those for which I have taught; and to the inestimable support of colleagues, friends, and family.

Thomas Howard introduced me to Renaissance studies over twenty-five years ago at Gordon College, and while he may not recognize some of what he will find in these pages, their genesis began in his course on seventeenth-century English prose and poetry. John Florio first came to my attention in Marcel Tetel's National Endowment for the Humanities Summer Seminar for School Teachers dedicated to French Renaissance humanism at Duke University in 1990; I deeply regret that Marcel did not live to see the fruits of that enormously stimulating experience in the form of this book. Penn Szyttya, Bruce Smith, and Anthony Hecht at Georgetown University each made valuable contributions to my understanding of literary culture and helped to refine my critical reflection about it, while Catherine Belsey opened my eyes to the utility of contemporary theoretical approaches to cultural production in a seminar at the Folger Shakespeare Library Institute in 1991. The paleography seminar conducted by Armando Petrucci and Franca Nardelli at the Newberry Library in the summer of 1993 introduced me to working with manuscripts, documents, and early printed books, the beginning of an on-going exchange that has, with regard to this book, saved me from a number of historical and philological infelicities. Louise George Clubb has been indispensable in furnishing a model of how to negotiate differing cultural and linguistic traditions, and as a professor at the University of California, Berkeley while I was a doctoral student at Stanford, she always welcomed me into her graduate seminars and was generous in the time she devoted to helping me find my comparatist's voice. Stephen Orgel has been *il personaggio chiave* for this project from its inception, and I am enormously grateful for his encouragement and manifold forms of support even in the face of my tortoise-like progress; his is an emblematic form of direction, generously enabling his students to develop scholarship that frequently comes to be articulated in ways quite different from his own work.

For their close reading of the entire manuscript I am particularly obliged to Albert Ascoli, Ronald Martinez, and the anonymous readers for Cambridge University Press. Having read and commented on sections of the book in various stages of completion, I thank Andrew Curran, Peter Davidson, Caroline Elam, Hilary Gatti, Jacques Gres-Gayer, Noah Isenberg, F. A. Kent, Ellen Nerenberg, John Paoletti, Armando Petrucci, Tilde Sankovich, Jeffrey Schnapp, Norman Shapiro, Cinzia Sicca, and Jane Stevenson. Stephanie Jed provided an invaluable critique of the very earliest draft of the project's outline. I am also grateful to Judith Brown, John Freccero, and members of the Bay Area Early Modern Reading Group – particularly Timothy Hampton and Harry Berger – for their help in fine-tuning critical parts of my argument in its infancy.

Joseph Reed and Maurizio Campanelli, playing Matthew Gwinne to my John Florio (see page 337, n. 152), translated a number of thorny passages (and otherwise corrected my translations) from Latin. A number of colleagues have provided other translation assistance, bibliography, and countless useful clues and insights: Peter Bilton, Pier Luigi Ciapparelli, Joseph Connors, Rachel Doggett, Bruce Edelstein, Keir Elam, Giovanni Ercoli, Margaret Gallucci, Paul Gehl, Dilwyn Knox, Bernardo Piciché, Stephen Schloesser, Alan Stewart, J. B. Trapp, Francesco Villani, Laetitia Yeandle, and Dmitrios Zikos.

I particularly grateful to the librarians of Stanford University's Green Library who were unfailingly helpful during the initial phase of research for this book; Mary Jane Parrine, then curator of the Romance Languages collection, assisted enormously in honing my research skills and frequently pointed me in the direction of materials I would never otherwise have known to look for, procuring still others which I needed. Subsequent research was carried out in a number of university, state, and private libraries and archives, and I thankfully acknowledge them and their staffs. In the United States: the Bancroft Library at the University of California, Berkeley; the Newberry Library in Chicago; the Folger Shakespeare Library in Washington, DC; the Library at Northwestern University; Special Collections and Archives at Wesleyan University (especially Suzy Taraba); the Library of the University of Minnesota, Twin Cities; the Horton Library at Harvard University; Archives and Special Collections at Amherst College (particularly Peter A. Nelson); and the Beinicke Library at Yale University. In the United Kingdom: the British Library, the Warburg Institute, and the Library at Lambeth Palace in London; the United Reformed Church History Society, Westminster College,

Cambridge Theological Federation (especially Margaret Thompson); the Library at York Minster; the National Library in Edinburgh; and Queen Mother Library at the University of Aberdeen. In Italy: the Libraries at Villa I Tatti (special thanks to its head librarian Michael Rocke) and the Istituto Nazionale di Studi sul Rinascimento (especially its director, Michele Ciliberto, and head librarian, Vittorio E. Vasarri), the Biblioteca Nazionale, and the Archivio di Stato in Florence; and the Biblioteca Apostolica Vaticana, the Archivio Storico Capitolino, and the Biblioteca Nazionale in Rome.

Thanks to Sarah Stanton, Victoria Cooper, Rebecca Jones, and Jackie Warren at Cambridge University Press; and to Chris Jackson for the careful attention he dedicated to editing a complex manuscript.

Part of Ch. 5 appeared first in *Giordano Bruno, Philosopher of the Renaissance*, Hilary Gatti, ed., and is reprinted here by kind permission of Ashgate.

Very special thanks to Cristoforo Grotta, James Anderson Jr., Francesca Duranti, Marina Perotti, Stephen Smith, Angiolo Pergolini, Patrizia Tanini, Fausta Quarato, Peter Davidson, Jane Stevenson, Edward Brubaker, Mary Brubaker, Giovanni Ercoli, Susan Lair, Douglas Trobough, Curtis Vredenburg, Brad Hinkley, Jonathan Hibbs, and Portia Jones.

I dedicate *The Italian Encounter with Tudor England* to the memory of my mother, Nancy, who unhappily did not live to see it completed, and to those other relatives and friends who have now passed into the great cloud of unknowing: Eula Riley, Patrick Thomas Riley, Pearl Thompson, Igino Cardinale, James Madden, Van Ernst, Jack Frey, Bernard McVeigh, Timothy Wyatt, and Marcel Tetel.

# Note on the text

Unless otherwise noted, I cite in my chapter notes the first editions of books printed in England, which during the final stages of the preparation of this book have all been consulted through *Early English Books Online* (hereafter *EEBO*); in the Bibliography, I list modern editions if available, for the benefit of readers without access to electronic resources.

For the sake of simplicity, in the chapter notes I have abbreviated the titles of Florio's principal works under consideration in this volume as follows:

*FF*: *Florio His Firste Fruites: which yeelde familiar speech, merie Proverbes, wittie sentences, and golden sayings. Also a perfect introduction to the Italian and English tongues.* London: Thomas Woodcock, 1578.

*SF*: *Florios Second Frutes, To be gathered of twelve Trees, of divers and delightsome tastes to the tongues of Italians and Englishmen.* London: Thomas Woodcock, 1591.

*WW*: *A Worlde of Wordes, or most copious and exact Dictionarie in Italian and English.* London: Edward Blount, 1598.

*QA*: *Queen Anna's New World of Words, or Dictionarie of the Italian and English Tongues.* London: Edward Blount and William Barret, 1611.

Other abbreviations utilized in the chapter notes are as follows:

BL: British Library
*DBI*: *Dizionario biografico degli italiani.* Rome: Istituto della Enciclopedia Italiana, 1960–present.
*DNB*: *Dictionary of National Biography.* Leslie Stephen and Sidney Lee, eds. London: Smith and Elder, 1885–1901.
*OED*: *Oxford English Dictionary Online*: www.dictionary.oed.com
*Grove*: *Grove Art Online*: www.groveart.com
*STC*: *A Short-Title Catalogue of Books Printed in England, Scotland and Ireland, and of English Books Printed Abroad, 1475–1640,* A. W. Pollard and G. R. Redgrave, eds. (revised by

W. A. Jackson and F. S. Ferguson, and Katherine F. Pantzer). London: Bibliographical Society, 1976–1991.

For the spelling of English names, I have followed the usage of the *STC* and the *DNB*; for names in Italian, the forms found in the *Sistema bibliotecario nazionale* [*SBN*] and *Il censimento delle edizioni italiane del XVI secolo, EDIT 16* – both from the *Istituto centrale per il catalogo unico* [*ICCU*] – and the *DBI*. Regarding centuries, I have used the Italian form 'cinquecento' in discussing issues specific to the Italian context, and 'sixteenth century' otherwise.

Interpolations of my own in citations, as well as translations into English where not in closed quotes or indented, are indicated [in brackets].

Early Italian, neo-Latin, and English texts have been only minimally corrected in order to facilitate their legibility. Titles of books printed in England and available through EEBO retain their original form in my notes and bibliography in order to facilitate searching, while they are corrected in the main body of my text (the *Lasino doro*, or *L'asino d'oro*, of Machiavelli, for example).

# Introduction

> It is not the literal past, the "facts of history", that shape us, but images of the past embodied in language.
>
> Brian Friel, *Translations*

Translation functioned in the "long" sixteenth century as both a practice and a metaphor. The period saw an explosion of translation between European vernacular languages, a significant development which did much, in concert with other forces, to vitiate the powerful authority of classical culture, even as translations from Greek and Latin continued to abound. But translation also comes to describe in an increasingly suggestive manner the various modes of cultural transmission which constituted a central dimension of early modernity.

Translation – *tradurre* in Italian, *vertere* and *translatio* in Latin – is defined by John Florio as "to traduce, to transpose, to bring or leade over, to bring, to convay, to remove from one place to another. Also to translate from out of one tongue into another."[1] Susan Sontag, in a recent essay on translation, evokes these and several other senses of the term as "to circulate, to transport, to disseminate, to explain, to make (more) accessible."[2] Translation serves as a means of recovering access to the material culture of the past and its effects that the term "Renaissance" has denoted since Jules Michelet, Jacob Burckhardt, John Addington Symonds, and other scholars of the period took it up in the nineteenth century: retrieving the past, however, through a process mediated by the critical language of the present.[3] Translation is as well a process that re-situates the cultural phenomena of a period variously demarcated – within the parameters of this study, the early fifteenth through the early seventeenth centuries – in a dynamic relation with the future characterized by the more recently coined "early modern."[4] Fundamental to both taxonomies – the one looking back, the other ahead – is the operation of displacement that Florio identifies with his work of translating the *Essais* of Montaigne:[5] "What doe the best then, but gleane after others harvest? borrow their colours, inherite their possessions? What doe they but translate? perhaps, usurp? at least, collect?"[6] This nexus of terms neatly encapsulates Florio's career as a language teacher, lexicographer, and translator, serving to situate him as an emblematic representation of this compound understanding of translation and anticipating many of the concerns of this book.

Italian commerce with England is traceable from the thirteenth century, and by the early fifteenth century Italians other than merchants and bankers began to make their presence felt there. The earlier history of the Italian encounter with England forms a crucial component for understanding the context out of which Florio's later accomplishments emerged. We consequently turn in the first part of this study, *'A parlar d'Inghilterra': Italians in and on Early Modern England*, to a consideration of these relations in three historical chapters organized initially around the consolidation of Tudor power after the Wars of the Roses, but looking back to the first Italian humanists in England and moving forward through the period of Henry VIII's divorce trial.[7] Ambassadorial accounts, the effort to introduce a reasonable approach to English historical narrative, the significance of Italian ecclesiastical representation in the English church, and the presence of Italian artists in pre-Reformation England are matters we shall examine in the first chapter, "The two roses," forming as they do useful instances of the discrepancies and synergies which characterized the earliest notable phase of the conjunction of Italian and English interests. We then turn – in "Reformations" – to the arrival of the Reformation in England in the latter part of Henry's reign, its consolidation under Edward VI, and the short-lived Catholic reform of the Marian era. These decades of variously contrary reformations competing for control of English polity as well as for the minds and souls of the English people came to be registered in a diverse range of Italian literary, diplomatic, and religious writing (produced both in England and in Italy) – literature that will provide us with windows onto this transitional period often different (at times surprisingly so) from standard English accounts of the same history. The third chapter, "La Regina Helisabetta," offers a variety of Italian images of the Tudor monarch most closely associated with Italian vernacular culture and presents a further assortment of Italians – merchants, a prominent aristocrat, musicians, and a new generation of religious refugees – active, but not always fully assimilated, in Elizabethan England.

The second section of the book, *John Florio and the Cultural Politics of Translation*, looks first – in "Language lessons" – at Florio's work as a language teacher and author of two language-learning dialogue books, *Firste Fruites* (1578) and *Second Frutes* (1591), situating this activity within the wider implications of Italian *translatio* for Elizabethan cultural politics. The final chapter, "Worlds of words," explores Florio the lexicographer, considering his unique contributions in this arena in relation to the contemporary Italian debate over the character of the Italian language, and with regard to the censorship of Italian books in light of the successive versions of the Catholic *Index librorum prohibitorum* or Index of Forbidden Books (beginning in 1559), the temporal parameters of this account encompassing both the first and second editions of Florio's dictionary, published first as *A Worlde of Wordes* in 1598 and subsequently as *Queen Anna's New World of Words* in 1611. I shall argue, as Frances Yates did in her first published monograph, that Florio and others like him have been mistakenly relegated to the sidelines of early modern cultural history, for though he produced no plays, poetry, or narrative prose of his own, Florio's work as a language merchant in Elizabethan and early Stuart England placed him squarely within the most important cultural currents of the period, and his achievements represent the culmination of a long and complex trajectory.[8]

The meaning of Florio's identity as an English-born Italian is of particular importance for understanding both his professional activities and the significance of the Italian presence in early modern England. Born in London to a mother of uncertain origins and an Italian father, Michelangelo, who had served as the first pastor of the Italian Protestant congregation in London, the younger Florio's early life is almost completely a matter of speculation. Shortly after John's birth, the family fled to Protestant Switzerland at the time of Mary Tudor's accession to the English crown, when the welcome that Edward VI had extended to continental Protestants was abruptly withdrawn.[9] Whatever might be made of the scanty traces of the young John Florio, a number of issues about his early formation must necessarily remain open to question, not the least of which for our purposes is where to situate him linguistically, and hence culturally.[10]

Discussing the translation of Montaigne, Yates maintains that Florio "was translating from a language not his own into a language not his own,"[11] assuming that Italian was his mother tongue, but as Florio's mother could have been English he may well have grown up using both languages. His subsequent fluency in both Italian and English would seem to argue in favor of a sustained acquaintance with both,[12] but it is apparent in a number of respects that Italian was the language in which he found himself most at ease. As the son of an exiled heterodox Protestant minister, Florio would have had neither the opportunity nor the means to travel to or study in the urban centers of the Italian peninsula,[13] and thus to a very high degree the cultural program that he did so much to advance in early modern England was acquired at a considerable distance from the context in which its various elements had developed.

As we shall see, this "virtual" aspect of Florio's Italian character is a crucial factor for appraising the cultural mediation he practiced in England. Such an identity raises fundamental questions about what it means to "inhabit" a culture, for while Florio moved easily between several linguistic and cultural worlds – never completely a part of any one of them – there is a distinctly performative (and hence artificial) dimension to his polyglot practice. This is not to diminish the significance of studying languages but rather to draw attention to the contingent and conditioned nature of such efforts, recognizing that language and its artefacts consistently resist our Sisyphean attempts to subdue them. Michael Holquist, writing about the centrality of philology to the foundation of Berlin's Humboldt University in 1810, notes that language was initially considered essential to that institution's pedagogical mission:

because in the study of foreign tongues students best learned the humility that comes from never forgetting that we are signs. The necessity to negotiate the otherness of the world that accompanies struggling to master alterity in other languages had... the capacity to provide students two gifts that any education should strive to give: positive knowledge of other cultures and a critical stance toward one's own.[14]

But Holquist also cautions that the task of the language teacher is to remember "the ineluctable foreignness of language itself (even when we think we are speaking our mother tongue),"[15] a point as apposite for the early modern history we shall be examining as it is for our contemporary world menaced by the narrow and frequently mistaken use of words which has resulted equally in horrific acts of terrorism and the continuing oppression of entire classes of people due to their differences from normative ideologies.[16]

Philology, the history of words, is a far cry from the irrelevancy it is too often dismissed as being. It retains its power to provoke critical insights, and we ignore its lessons at our peril, as Edward Said compellingly argues in the new introduction to the twenty-fifth anniversary edition of *Orientalism*, prepared shortly before his death. Praising Erich Auerbach's ground-breaking comparative study, *Mimesis* (1946), Said notes that:

the main requirement for the kind of philological understanding Auerbach and his predecessors were talking about and tried to practice was one that sympathetically and subjectively entered into the life of a written text as seen from the perspective of its author. Rather than alienation and hostility to another time and culture, philology... involved a profound humanistic spirit deployed with generosity, and if I may use the word, hospitality. Thus the interpreter's mind actively makes a place in it for a foreign "other." And this creative making of a place for works that are otherwise alien and distant is the most important facet of the interpreter's mission ... humanism is the only, and I would go so far as to say the final, resistance we have against the inhuman practices and injustices that disfigure human history.[17]

# Introduction

An affirmation of the potential of words to allow us into a space different culturally or historically from our own, Said's reassertion of humanist values is a welcome reminder of why and how much a considered understanding of the operations of language does indeed matter.

A study engaged with philology should make as clear as possible the significance of the terminology which it employs repeatedly. In addition to words already noted, I use three others (and their derivatives) throughout the book in the following ways:

"Language"
*Lingua*, in one of Florio's digressive definitions, is "a tongue in general. Also a language or speach. Also the word given among soldiers. Also a little spattle or languet to take salves out of a boxe. Also a narrow piece of land or long ridge running into the Sea like a tongue lolling out of the mouth. Also a kind of hearbe good against the falling of the haire called Adders-tongue."[18] Jonathan Goldberg sheds further light on the word in suggesting that "*language* ... subsum[es] such terms as *writing, discourse* [or, in the context of my fourth and fifth chapters, also 'speaking'], *literature*, and *representation* [which should be understood here as also encompassing the 'visual']."[19]

"Politics"
*Politica* in Florio is "a book of Policie or civill government of a State,"[20] and for Goldberg "*politics* ... refer[s] to those social processes in which relationships of power are conveyed [and additionally, following Florio's lead, the 'communities' and 'institutions' which give them shape]."[21]

"Culture"
*Cultura* for Florio is "husbandrie, tillage, manuring, ploughing,"[22] and these horticultural associations of the word nicely complement its early modern figural sense associated with what the *OED* defines as "the cultivating or development of the mind, faculties, manners, etc.; improvement or refinement by education and training," as well as its nineteenth-century evolution into "a particular form or type of intellectual development. Also, the civilization, customs, artistic achievements ... of a people, especially at a certain stage of its development or history."[23]

The question of philology in early modern Europe is an especially loaded one, given the degree to which the region's principal conflicts throughout the sixteenth and well into the seventeenth centuries can be characterized as the result of the struggle to define or redefine certain words. Three factors contributed to England's linguistic instability in this period: the relative poverty of sixteenth-century English in comparison with the more developed vernacular languages and cultures of Italy, France, and Spain; the vitality of languages other than English in the Three Kingdoms; and the continuing utility of Latin as both a spoken and written language among the learned and professional classes.[24]

The presence of such "strangers" as Florio was a reminder, uncomfortable for many even otherwise sophisticated Englishmen, that theirs was a language used only in England (and not even universally there), as suggested by two of Florio's interlocutors in *Firste Fruites* 27 [50r][25]:

| | |
|---|---|
| *Che vi pare di questa lingua inglese, ditemi di gratia.* | What thinke you of this English tongue, tel me, I pray you? |
| *E una lingua che vi farà bene in Inghilterra, ma passato Dover, la non val niente.* | It is a language that wyl do you good in England, but passe Dover, it is woorth nothing. |
| *Dunque non è praticata fori in altri paesi?* | Is it not then used in other countreyes? |
| *Signor no ...* | No sir ... |

For our modern world in which English has so pervasively colonized the globe it is increasingly difficult to imagine a moment when this was anything but the case. The Italian philologist and former minister of education, Tullio De Mauro, has suggested about the recent intrusion of English into the Italian lexicon that "now and again I would so like to hear ... that Italian has 'invaded' the English language."[26] In the second half of the sixteenth century it had, at least at the level of elite culture, though the proverbial English aversion to foreign languages is perfectly caricatured in that period by Florio in *Firste Fruites* 27 [51r]:

| | |
|---|---|
| *Pochi di questi Inglesi si dilettano di far imparar lingue ai figlioli, la qual cosa mi dispiace. Io quando arrivai in Londra, non sapendo parlar Inglese, scontrai piu di cinque cento persone, inanzi che io sapessi trovar uno, che mi sapesse dire in Italiano o Franzese, dove stava la Posta.* | Few of these Englishmen delight to have their chyldren learne divers languages, which thing displeaseth me. When I arrived first in London, I coulde not speake Englishe, and I met above five hundred persons, afore I coulde finde one, that could tel me in Italian, or French, where the Post dwelt. |
| *E che cosa voresti che loro facessero? Imparare lingue?* | And what would you have them doo? learne languages? |
| *Signor, si, & alenare i loro figlioli bene, & insegnarli a leggere, scrivere, & parlar diverse lingue ...* | Yea sir, and bring up their children well, and have them taught to reade, write, and speake divers languages ... |

The distance between popular English resentment of what were considered to be alien interlopers and the distinctly Italianate culture of the Elizabethan court and its circles delineates a space within which to locate Florio's work and its relation both to the foreign community of which he was a part and the privileged Elizabethan world to which he aspired but would reach only as it was passing into history with the accession of the first Stuart king. A number of terms or concepts can be employed to describe such a space, and this project is an attempt to tease out as wide a range of them as might render the Italian encounter with Tudor England intelligible.

Italy's rich cultural tradition remained unanchored in the cinquecento by any stable unifying political force, a fact of tremendous importance for the circulation of Italian culture in England in this period. Florio promoted a cultural system that in traveling beyond the Italian peninsula achieved a degree of coherence which it did not entirely enjoy on its native soil through its translation into a radically different political context via the mediating continental Protestant culture he brought with him to England. The prominence accorded Italian vernacular culture by the Elizabethan elite called attention to the inadequacy of the English language and its literary culture, but the valorization of Italian models (among others) also, paradoxically, contributed to the process through which England expanded its linguistic, cultural, and political scope. The Italianate Englishman perhaps initially felt that he had been:

born into the wrong tribe, taught to play the wrong language game ... worried that the process of socialization which turned him into a human being by giving him a language may have given him the wrong language, and so turned him into the wrong kind of human being.[27]

Through the appropriation of other languages and their cultures, England tacitly acknowledged the scarcity of its own cultural capital but in so doing enabled the appropriating mechanisms that would provide one among the many diverse factors that came to advance its growing sense of a "national" character and facilitate its global ambitions.

The idea of Italy – an idea that has continued to exercise a powerful hold on the English imagination – took on a life of its own during the years that Elizabeth I occupied the English throne. This process occurred through the agency of members of an actual community, but its result was a fictive specter of political and cultural authority that contributed to the legitimizing rationale for English imperialist ideology. Florio's first published translation, *A shorte and briefe narration of the two navigations and discoveries to the northwest partes called Newe Fraunce* (1580), was of Jacques Cartier's account of his first two voyages to the New World (translated from Ramusio's Italian translation of Cartier's French text). Though possibly commissioned by Richard Hakluyt – it was later included in his great collection of colonizing narratives, *The Principal Navigations, Voyages and Discoveries* (1589) – Florio first had the work published himself, prefacing it with what Yates describes as one of the earliest summonses to would-be colonizers written in English:

> Here is the description of a country no less fruitful and pleasant in all respects than is England, France, or Germany, the people though simple and rude in manners, and destitute of the knowledge of God or any good laws, yet of nature gentle and tractable, and most apt to receive the Christian religion, and to subject themselves to some good government ... al which opportunities besides many others might suffice to induce our Englishmen, not only to fall to some traffic with the inhabitants, but also to plant a colony in some convenient place, and so to possess the country without the gainsaying of any man.[28]

Besides its obvious meaning, this exhortation can also be read as registering what in fact was already happening in England, as its dominant culture absorbed – even as they were passing out of fashion in Italy – the axiomatic Renaissance Italian lessons of *sprezzatura*, *virtù*, and *petrarchismo* to which Florio and the other purveyors of Italian culture in England afforded them access.[29]

The introduction into the English monarchy of "stranger" elements with the translation of James VI into James I in 1603 – a Scots king with a marked francophone tilt inherited from his mother, possessed of formidable theological and humanist learning (he was skilled equally in Greek and Latin), and married to a Danish consort – effectively rewrote the coordinates of the Italian encounter with early modern England. Florio's translation of Montaigne's *Essais* was prepared in the waning years of the Elizabethan era, but the elaborate encomiastic apparatus of its first edition was clearly directed at the incipient Stuart age, published as it was early in 1603, just as Elizabeth I was dying. The transition from the Tudor to the Stuart periods was thus marked for Florio by a conspicuous turn not only from Italian to French, but more significantly by the practice of translation into English on a large scale, a maneuver that to a very great extent rendered mute his original advocacy of learning foreign tongues in order to negotiate the cultures they represented. The distinctiveness of the early Stuart era in relation to the period immediately preceding it is, consequently, best considered on its own terms, and I intend to return to the later period of Florio's career in a separate volume that will deal with the diminishing prospects in the Jacobean world for the particular form of cultural arbitration Florio had earlier performed so singularly in Elizabethan England.[30]

It should be understood from the outset that this is a study of the circulation of Italians, their language, and culture in Tudor England and does not seek, except tangentially, to tell the story of the English in Italy in this period. I am likewise unconcerned here with the question of Shakespeare and his Italian sources, though a scene from *Henry V* does

# Introduction

come into consideration in the conclusion to "Language lessons" (Ch. 4), where the issue of linguistic difference in England is addressed.[31] And while it is abundantly clear that other vernacular cultures in England played similar roles to what is examined here with regard to Italian, it would be far outside the scope of this project (and my expertise) to deal with this analogous history in detail.

In this study otherwise focused on the figural senses of translation in the Tudor period – those represented by the first part of Florio's definition of the term – a word is in order regarding the considerable amount of translated material to be found in these pages. It has been one of my objectives throughout this project to bring together in one place, and in English, a variety of primary texts written in Italian and neo-Latin as well as critical literature written in Italian hitherto largely unregistered by English-language scholarship. But given the enormous differences in emphasis and style between (to take three disparate examples) a humanist and papal diplomat such as Francesco Chiericati (Ch. 1, pages 56–58), a literate merchant the likes of Alessandro Magno (Ch. 3, pages 118–122), and the modest literary talent that was Petruccio Ubaldini (Ch. 2, pages 72–84 and Ch. 3, pages 127–128), my approach has been to aim for legibility while reproducing in English as much of the particular flavor of a given author's language as possible, even if the result is not always an especially lovely one. I have made my own interpolations only when the sense of a passage might otherwise be unclear, as I have done for instance in several places with the magnificently excessive letter that Pietro Aretino addressed to Henry VIII in dedicating the second volume of his collected letters to the English king in 1542 (Ch. 2, pages 68–69), and in the loopy epithalamium by Giovanni Alberto Albicante celebrating the 1554 marriage of Mary Tudor and Philip II of Spain (Ch. 2, pages 109–112).[32]

The questions addressed in this book necessarily cut across disciplinary and linguistic boundaries, but the task of negotiating between Italian, neo-Latin, and English has been further complicated by the hostilities which tenaciously persist between scholarly disciplines even more than half a century after the comparative critical innovations of Aby Warburg, Frances Yates, and Erich Auerbach paved the way for new ways of thinking about the inter-connectedness of disparate modes of cultural representation.[33] Though the most recent English-language scholarship dealing with early modern England is widely known in Italy (in part thanks to a booming translation industry), it is not so widely imitated there, for the great majority of Italians who study the same material as their native-English-speaking colleagues do so from within a tradition considerably more grounded in "old" history, philology, and close reading. The little substantive exchange thus generated across language differences within the same field is multiplied exponentially when we move from the English situation in the period under consideration to contemporary Italian culture and its political coordinates. *La questione della lingua* [the language question] in early modern Italy, to which I devote the initial section of "Worlds of Words" (Ch. 4), has been largely ignored in estimations of the significance of Florio's dictionary. This has been as true of Anglicists who have failed to address the *questione* – such a debate about the specific character of a "national" language never having occurred in quite the same way in English – as it has been of Italianists, reluctant to recognize that a "virtual" Italian could have produced a vocabulary at the end of the sixteenth century in a context far from the Italian peninsula which might have something consequential to say about the contentious native debate over the Italian language.[34]

The very real cultural divides which work against a more truly comparative cultural and intellectual history are represented no more clearly in present-day Italy than in its libraries. Though they hold the greatest collections of manuscripts and early books anywhere in the world, there is no single Italian library that can lay claim to the breadth of the British Library, the Bibliotèque Nationale in Paris, the Library of Congress, the German state libraries, or a number of American and British university libraries.[35] The actual condition of many Italian libraries and archives is increasingly alarming – drastically reduced allocations and shrinking staffs effect a deficit that encompasses preservation, acquisition, and consultation – a situation caused not only by the complex demands of maintaining existing collections, but also by the budgetary neglect of recent leftist governments and the outright hostility of the current rightist administration preoccupied more with American business models than with constructively confronting the massive crisis facing all of Italy's cultural institutions. Completing a book of this sort while living in Italy as an unaffiliated independent scholar has consequently posed a sometimes daunting series of challenges, and whatever gaps there might be in my bibliography are to some extent due to these difficulties.

The multiplicity of approaches in literary and historical scholarship today is both a blessing and a curse. My own working methodology is an unapologetically heterogeneous one, assuming that all serious criticism has something potentially useful to bring to the table and that no single critical approach should be considered definitive in itself or necessarily prescriptive of other points of view. Disciplinary boundaries between history and literature, to say nothing of the sub-divisions which have emerged within these fields, had not yet been fixed in the sixteenth century, and I am convinced that the assertion of disciplinary prerogatives – themselves historically conditioned – hinders more than it helps to promote understanding of a period as complex and in so many respects distant from our own concerns as was the time circumscribed by the terms

"Renaissance" and "early modern." Needless to say, no one scholar can hope in this polysemous environment to have gotten it right on every score, and in a study such as this one, which encompasses a diversity of disciplines and issues while employing a wide range of analytic tools, there are certain to be matters which have been addressed with only an approximate degree of clarity. Numerous helping hands have assisted me in navigating these shoals, but clearly whatever errors remain are my own.

*Part 1*

'A parlar d'Inghilterra': Italians in and on
Early Modern England

# 1   The two roses

>   ... remotissimus orbis angulus Anglia ...
>   Boccaccio, *Genealogia deorum gentilium*, XV.vi

Imagine for a moment that you are an Italian merchant newly arrived in England in the late 1570s, speaking no English, and anxious to know something of the lay of the land. You are introduced to an Italian who has himself been in the country for almost ten years, employed as a language teacher but entertaining higher ambitions. He engages you in a dialogue and provides you with the following picture of England: a country where the air is clear, food – bread, meat, eggs, cheese, butter, salted and fresh fish, and fowl – is plentiful, its women beautiful – though later he qualifies this by saying that[1]:

| *ce ne di tutte le sorte ... e pur sono tutte donne* | there is of al sorts ... and yet are all women |

and beer is the beverage of choice; merchants are everywhere to be found, trading in tin, wool, precious metals, saffron, leather, and farm animals. Among these merchants you will find a large number of *stranieri* [strangers, foreigners], who, your guide tells you, are all Protestants. There are ambassadors from Portugal and France. In their leisure time, the English attend plays, dance, and attend or participate in sporting events such as fencing matches, bear-baiting, archery and artillery shooting, as well as boating; the *stranieri*, each according to their "national" affiliation [16r]:

| *ha la sua chiesa, con bon ordine* | hath a church with good order |

There are a great many scholars, and two universities. *Malfattori* [sinners] are as legion as their punishment is harsh: death by hanging, except for traitors, who are drawn and quartered. The queen's justice is a strong deterrent to crime, though she is evidently unconcerned about [16v]:

| *la gente [che] vanno vestiti ... con gran pompa* | the people [who] go wel apparelled ... with great pomp |

merchants dressing as gentlemen, gentlemen as lords, a duke as a king – and so tacitly condones a dubious habit through her indulgence. She is a great friend of Italians, most of her court musicians being from Italy, and [18r]:

| | |
|---|---|
| *si diletta di parlar con loro elegantissamente.* | delightes she to speak with them ... eloquently. |

Prostitutes and scheming women are, regrettably, much in evidence, for [18v]:

| | |
|---|---|
| *il denaro regge ogni cosa* | money ruleth al things |

and the laws, being [18v]:

| | |
|---|---|
| *tutte corrotte* | al corrupted |

do little to stem the tide of moral corruption. The city of London is governed by twenty-four aldermen, from whose number is elected [17r]:

| | |
|---|---|
| *Me Lord Mairo* | my Lord Maior |

for a term of one year; London is beset by plague, which keeps the queen and her court in fear and often outside the city. Your interlocutor concludes by suggesting that you and he go to visit the court in order to speak with one of the queen's councillors, and he tells you that he was there just yesterday speaking with the queen's secretary.

Such is the image of England provided by John Florio in Ch. 15 [14v–19r]:

| | |
|---|---|
| *A parlar d'Inghilterra* | To speake of England |

of his 1578 Italian–English dialogue book, *Firste Fruites*. And so it might have seemed to many Italians first arriving in England early in the first two decades of the reign of Elizabeth I. Though the picture is cursory, it touches upon several aspects of the presence of "strangers" in England – their involvement in commerce, their own Protestant congregations, the queen's affection for Italians – that are of significance for the larger picture this chapter and the next two aim to draw. In several respects, however, Florio skews the picture he presents: many of the merchants remained Catholics, and the Protestant churches were anything but models of good order. *First Fruites* Ch. 40, for instance, entitled [92r]:

| | |
|---|---|
| *Discorso in laude di Henrico ottavo, Re di Inghilterra* | A discourse in prayse of Henry the eyght, kyng of England |

serves as an appendix to Florio's earlier reflections on England while playing into the revisionism typical of so much Elizabethan historiography. Florio's Henry is a paragon of all virtues [92r-v]:

| | |
|---|---|
| *chiaro nella sua vita, puro in conscientia, integro di Nobiltà ... prudente nel disimilare ... sobrio nel vivere ... verace nel suo procedere ... mantenitore della sua parola, fedele ne le sue promesse, liberale verso molti, avaro verso pochi, famoso, in clementia, diligente nell'esaltar virtu, & punir vitio, negligente nel'mantener vitio, & abandonar virtu ...* | in his lyfe cleare, in conscience pure, perfecte in Nobilitie ... prudente in dissembling ... sober in living ... true in his proceedyngs ... a mayteyner of his woorde, faithfull in his promises, liberall towarde many, covetous toward few, famous in clemencie, diligent in exalting virtue, and punishing vice, negligent in mainteinyng of vice, and abandonyng virtue ... |

This comes as no surprise from a "stranger" subject of Henry's younger daughter eager to make a good show of himself in print, but while such exaggerated praise is in sharp contrast to several other Italian estimations of Henry VIII we shall examine in the next chapter, the tenor of these reflections is indicative of an effort at accommodation to English actuality which was characteristic of the "stranger" engagement with early modern England.

The valorization of one culture through the prism of another is the broad subject of this study. Earlier Anglo-Italian scholarship delineated the impact that high Italian Renaissance culture had in the re-invention of England's cultural life in the sixteenth century, but less attention has been paid either to the actual presence in England of Italians mediating this influence or to its extension into many aspects of England's development of a national consciousness. Indeed, neither the contemporary political and religious situation on the Italian peninsula nor the related sense of what it meant to be an Italian in the early modern period have been adequately brought to bear upon the significance of the Italians who functioned in England as humanists, bureaucrats, clerics, theologians, merchants, entrepreneurs, and artists. These first three chapters aim, therefore, to draw an image of the Italian presence in England during the fifteenth and sixteenth centuries from a wide range of disparate evidence, in order to accordingly situate John Florio and his contributions to both English and Italian cultures – the focus of the final two chapters – within the context that provided him with the cachet through which he built his career. Many of the names that figure in these initial chapters will be unfamiliar ones, the role of Englishmen famous during the Elizabethan era for their promotion of Italian culture – Philip Sidney or John Harington, for example – being sufficiently well-known to not require reiteration in a history that aims at establishing the earlier parameters that made such later advocacy of Italian in England possible.

The first prominent figure in English cultural history to heed the siren call of an Italy that has subsequently exercised such a powerful hold on the English imagination, Geoffrey Chaucer, visited the peninsula twice on diplomatic business in the 1370s, evidently learning enough Italian to conduct his duties and to read the manuscripts that he purchased there.[2] He could conceivably have met Boccaccio in Florence or Petrarch in Milan, but despite the absence of convincing evidence that he did, there remains a persistent desire – the starting-point of this study – for the traces of cultural transmission to assume tangible form.[3] That Chaucer's poetics borrowed heavily from Boccaccio and Petrarch in the period following his trips to Italy is a critical commonplace, but to posit actual meetings between the leading fourteenth-century English and Italian *letterati* is to bring complex intellectual issues out of the hermetic realm of the study and into the socialized space of the salon. David Wallace has recently pursued a more promising line of inquiry by situating Chaucer's encounter with the texts of Dante, Boccaccio, and Petrarch as having been so decisive for the development of his literary imagination because of his experience with the actual political communities from which their work emerged.[4]

Italians were slower in demonstrating an interest in the cultural topography of England. Boccaccio's use of *remotissimus* in the epigraph to this chapter expresses a common sentiment among trecento Italians, and given the relatively later codification of English culture, Italian literary attention toward England did not gain a significant advocate until Ugo Foscolo, himself the product of several politically inflected dislocations, settled in London in the early nineteenth century.[5] Boccaccio had, nevertheless, recognized the long-standing economic ties that bound the two regions to one another and set the third *novella* of the *Decameron*'s second day against the backdrop of the failure of the Florentine Bardi-Peruzzi bank in 1345, which had been precipitated at least in part by Edward III's defaulting on a sizable loan.[6]

In the early sixteenth century, Ludovico Ariosto went further than any preceding Italian literary figure had done in appropriating an element of antique English culture, one that came to be of central importance in Tudor efforts to establish its historical legitimacy, when he utilized the legends associated with King Arthur and the Round Table for *Orlando furioso*, bending the Arthurian material to his own purposes in singing the praises of his Este patrons. There is an indicative scene in Canto 33.1–52 in which Merlin foresees the collapse of Italy at the hands of foreign invaders, a prophecy that chronicles not only the actual sequence of historical events that swept through Italy in the late fifteenth and early sixteenth centuries while Ariosto was composing his poem, but, spoken by an often-invoked figure in the Tudor version of British mythography, also anticipates the growing role England would come to play on the European stage as the sixteenth century progressed. It is striking that Ariosto should have chosen Merlin to convey the collapse of Italian Renaissance civilization, for a Celt thus becomes not only the bearer of ill tidings for Italy but, rhetorically, also functions as the custodian of its desecrated culture. England, this study will argue, played a similar role in the later sixteenth century, though by the time that John Harington published his translation of Ariosto's epic poem in 1591, several of the most influential Elizabethan players in the promotion of Italian culture were dead, and England was beginning to redirect its attention inward in the quest for a national culture, a language to rival other continental vernaculars, and a theoretical basis for its government, having for several generations benefitted from the presence in England of Italians who had fled Italy because of its political and religious turmoil. When Ariosto first introduces Merlin, in *Orlando* 3, it is to use him as the oracle who reveals to the warrior-lady Bradamante how her destiny is linked both backward in time to the noble line of the Trojans and forward to the glorious future (Ariosto's present) of the Este clan. Merlin functions in Ariosto's poem much as the idea of Italy operated in Tudor England: as both enchanter and as ideological foil; he is thus an emblematic figure for the web of exchanges that this study aims to detail, a figment of the elite imagination of Tudor England creating itself out of the ruins of the world that Ariosto's Merlin apostrophizes.[7]

"... *per l'ordinario odiano li presenti [re] e laudano li morti* ..."

### A Venetian ambassadorial report

Extensive records accounting for the presence of foreigners in England only began to be kept under Henry VIII, but there is ample earlier evidence that attests to the presence of Italians in England, interested by and engaged in its social, religious, political, and cultural structures.[8] By far the richest source of Italian information regarding early modern Britain is contained in the reports that Venetian ambassadors presented to their government upon returning from tours of duty there.[9] While these *relazioni* and others like them will be cited at several other points in the historical narrative of this chapter and the next two, a close look here at the earliest extant of them will provide a useful point of reference for understanding the idea of England that a well-placed and observant Italian might have formed of the country at the outset of the sixteenth century.

The first trace of Venetian diplomatic representation in England dates from a letter addressed on April 24, 1370 by Edward III to Doge Andrea Contarini recognizing the credentials of a Venetian merchant, Luca Valaresso, though his mission like those that succeeded it for over a century was primarily commercial. In February of 1496, however, Pietro Contarini and another Luca Valaresso, merchants already active in London, were entrusted by the Venetian Senate with gaining Henry VII's adherence to the anti-French Holy League formed in 1495 and consisting of the Papal States, Spain, the Holy Roman Empire, Milan, and Venice. Henry agreed to join the League – "even if only platonically"[10] – on July 18, 1496, and this agreement marked the formal establishment of diplomatic ties between Venice and England that would continue more or less uninterruptedly until (and including) the reign of Edward VI. Following the repatriation of Valaresso and Contarini later that year, Andrea Trevisan was designated their successor. The son of the procurator of San Marco and a member of Venice's Great Council from 1480 onwards, Trevisan arrived in London in August of 1497 and remained in England all through March of 1498; returning to Venice by mid-May, he presented his *relazione* to the Senate on the 31$^{st}$ of that month.[11]

Britain's geographical shape is described by Trevisan as triangular, supposedly similar to that of Sicily, and the climate as "very healthy, and free from many complaints with which Italy is afflicted" [8],[12] winters being more temperate and summers milder, and with practically no spring. The triangular shape of the island is seen to be reflected in its political divisions: Scotland, Wales, and England, each with its own unique geography, customs, and language [12–13].

News of Scotland comes second-hand, from the Spanish ambassador. Though known by the English as "savage Scots" [15],[13] they are, in fact, as gracious as they are numerous. Titled aristocrats reside in houses built of durable materials just as in Italy (and unlike England's wooden structures with thatched roofs), while ordinary citizens work as merchants, with their hands, or in mechanical arts. "Don Pedro also says that all the Scottish nation are extremely partial to foreigners, and very hospitable" [15],[14] an attitude in marked contrast to the English, who "have an antipathy to foreigners, and imagine that they never come into their island but to make masters of it, and to usurp their goods" [23–24].[15] The Scots are fiercely devoted to their monarchs, another factor that distinguishes them from the English, "few of [whom] are loyal. They generally hate their present and extol their dead sovereigns" [32].[16] Independence from England is a point of honor among the Scots, who field an army of which "[the ambassador] never saw anything better appointed ... [a] power never exercised but against the English, their natural enemies, as is commonly the case with neighbors" [16].[17] And though:

all the English chroniclers insist that their king is the supreme lord of Scotland, and that they have changed the kings of Scotland at their pleasure ... the Scots ... pride themselves on having always repulsed the English, regaining possession of their land [17].[18]

The English have managed, however, to gain control of Berwick, the fortress on the River Tweed at the eastern frontier between Scotland and England whose possession had for some time see-sawed back and forth between the two, and peace exists there now principally due to the careful diplomacy of Don Pedro. There are fifteen dioceses in Scotland, two of them archbishoprics. The Scots speak the same language as the Irish, quite different from English, but many of them are said to speak English well, given their frequent contacts at the border.

Trevisan characterizes Wales as the smallest and least developed of the island's three areas, a mountainous region with little agriculture, though there are large dairy farms. Once a land of seven dioceses, these are now reduced to four. Having no large cities, the people reside primarily in the country and:

are generally supposed to have been the original inhabitants of the island ... they themselves say, and it is also believed by the English, that they are descended from the Trojans; and they consider themselves to be gentlemen, and call each other *cosaio*, a word in their language which bears that meaning; nor would they on any account intermarry with the English, of whom they are the most mortal enemies. Their language is different from both the English and the Scots ... Wales was formerly a separate kingdom ... and if the renowned Arthur ever existed at all, it was in this country, according to what I have read in English histories [19].[19]

From the time of Edward III's dominion over the Welsh in 1267, the eldest son of the English king has been designated Prince of Wales, and the current King Henry VII is himself a Welshman.

As a Venetian living through a period of acute trauma for the already politically fragmented Italian peninsula at the end of the fifteenth century, Trevisan would naturally have been sensitive to the potential ramifications of British regional differences as they are registered in the *relazione*. The bulk of the report, however, is dedicated to England:

for she alone is larger and richer than both the other [parts], and everything that I find the island produces is yielded in most abundance there ... diversified by pleasant undulating hills, and beautiful valleys, nothing [is] to be seen but agreeable woods, or extensive meadows, or lands in cultivation; and the greatest plenty of water springing everywhere [20].[20]

The country is represented as overflowing with natural resources – "a quantity of iron and silver, an infinity of lead and tin," as well as "an enormous number of sheep which yield them quantities of wool of the best quality" [11, 10][21] – and with the material wealth that stems from their exploitation. But when it comes to the uses to which these riches are put, a distinct sense of Venetian parsimony can be detected in the tone of the *relazione*, the English being said, for instance, to prefer spending money (or having it spent on them) for a meal than in charitable acts [22], and the titled nobility creating as many as 4,000 parks, entirely enclosed by wooden fences, rather than cultivating their enormous landholdings for agriculture [39].

While Trevisan fails to appreciate to what an extent the English economy was indeed based upon agriculture in this period, he also sounds a note that he repeats elsewhere, the determined self-referentiality of the English, for:

[they are] great lovers of themselves, and of everything belonging to them; they think that there are no other men than themselves, and no other world but England; and whenever they see a handsome foreigner, they say that "he looks like an Englishman," and that "it is a great pity that he should not be an Englishman"; and when they partake of any delicacy with a foreigner, they ask him whether such a thing is made in their country [20–21].[22]

The abundance of English fish and shellfish is praised, particularly salmon and other salt-water varieties; tasty mussels are mentioned, with their small irregular pearls. There is a profusion of meat and game of every imaginable type. Among a wide array of trees none yield olives or oranges; and while there are vines, wine is not made from them but imported from Crete, Germany, France, and Spain. The most popular beverages, however, are produced by:

the common people ... from wheat, barley, and oats, one of which is called beer, and the other ale; and these liquors are much liked by them, nor are they disliked by foreigners, after they have drunk them four or six times; they are most agreeable to the palate, when a person is by some chance rather heated [9–10].[23]

Trevisan offers contradictory evidence with regard to English manners: immediately following the passage about their self-preoccupation, he praises the English for their hospitality but is critical both of their habit of stinting on the wine service at meals and of drinking from a communal cup (a practice Giordano Bruno was later disgusted by); still, he notes, when there is a choice offered between wine and beer, though the English themselves will always prefer beer, they offer it to their foreign guests only if requested [20]. Unlike in Italy, "*donne di onore*/ladies of honor" [*18*, 21] are often seen in taverns, but English men "keep a very jealous guard over their wives, although anything may be compensated in the end by the power of money" [24].[24] Profit from even morally questionable practices is cited at several points as a prevalent English characteristic.

The population of England is said to be thin, a result of the preceding decades' war and the devastation of several bouts of plague [30]. The English class system is already apparent to Trevisan in that "the people are held in little more esteem than if they were slaves" [34],[25] though at the two universities of the kingdom, Oxford and Cambridge, there are colleges founded to support the studies of impoverished scholars; "few, however, apart from the clergy, are addicted to the study of letters" [22].[26]

The longest single section of the *relazione* is dedicated to the English monarchy, initially in a brief discussion of the question of succession by noting that for 600 years the realm has been ruled by kings whose legitimacy is established either through heredity or, in the absence of a clear heir, through "*il mezzo dell'armi*/the force of arms" [*40*, 46], as was the case with Henry VII, who:

in all of his difficulties has shown that even were he to have lost all else, he would still have defended himself with the fortresses; and his fortune has been equal to his spirit, for he has never lost a battle. From the time of William the Conqueror to the present, no king has reigned more peaceably than he has, his great prudence causing him to be universally feared [46].[27]

Trevisan makes Henry out to be a forerunner of Machiavelli's prince *avant la lettre*, over a decade before the elaboration of that treatise and well before the epithet "Machiavellian" was applied to his grand-daughter, Elizabeth.[28]

The bulk of the *relazione*'s discussion of Henry VII is not concerned, however, with his political skills but rather with the seemingly endless sources of his wealth, income derived first of all from the king's own vast land-holdings, and then through a web of estates reverting to the crown, heavy customs duties on all goods leaving or entering the country,[29] vacant ecclesiastical offices (which were, consequently, slow to be filled), other fees extracted from the clergy in various circumstances, and taxes on currency exchange. It would seem from this account that there was hardly a corner of England's economic production untouched by a royal claim to some part of it, and Trevisan also describes the complex bureaucratic network necessary for the regulation and collection of all these fees, whose agents sought to grease the wheels of their own financial self-interest [*41–47*/48–53].

The *relazione* declares emphatically that there is no sign of selfless love demonstrated among the English, either at court or among the people, "whence one must necessarily conclude either that [they] are the most discreet lovers in the world, or that they are incapable of love" [24].[30] English treatment of children confirms this impression for the Venetian ambassador, as he indignantly notes the custom of all social classes of turning their children out of the home between the ages of seven and nine to pursue "apprenticeships" in the homes of others:

few are born who are exempted from this fate, for everyone, however rich he may be, sends his children into the houses of others, while he, in return, receives those of strangers into his own. And on inquiring their reason for this severity, they answered that they did it in order that their children might learn better manners. But I, for my part, believe that they do it because they like to enjoy all their comforts themselves, and that they are better served by strangers than they would be by their own children ... were the English to send their children away from home to learn virtue and good manners, and take them back again when their apprenticeship was over, they might perhaps be excused; but they never return, for the girls are married by their masters, and the boys make the best marriages they can [25].[31]

Whence the cycle begins all over again. The money exchanged in these transactions is also seen in this instance to be a central and corrupting force. But here Trevisan has mistakenly conflated the contemporary practice of committing working-class children to professional apprenticeships with that of the nobility who in this period did, in fact, frequently farm their children out to be raised by others.[32] The *relazione*'s mistake reads like a Dickensian indictment of English social ills grafted onto puzzlement over the similar role of the modern English public school system, but for an Italian of Trevisan's class the idea of separating children from their parents at such an early age for whatever motive could only have been construed as ruinous of the social order. One further consequence of this market in children is the example of a woman left widowed with apprentices in her home who can then in the plenitude of her inheritance decide to marry whichever of them is most pleasing to her, inevitably one "[who] was perhaps not displeasing to her in the lifetime of her husband" [26],[33] he in turn benefitting from her fortune at her death. In this regard, Trevisan reports the emblematic case of:

a very handsome young man of about 18 years of age, the brother of the Duke of Suffolk, who as I understand, had been left very poor, the whole of the paternal inheritance amongst the nobility descending to the eldest son. This youth ... was boarded out to a widow of fifty with a fortune, as I was informed, of 50,000 crowns. This woman knew how to play her cards so well that he was content to become her husband and patiently waste the flower of his beauty with her, hoping before long to enjoy her great wealth with some lovely young lady [27–28].[34]

But lest one think that English widows were always left to live the life of Riley, the *relazione* notes in its survey of the numerous sources of the king's income that any revenues accruing from the estate of one of his deceased feudatory lords devolve directly to the crown, through appropriating the income due to his surviving minor-aged children and/or in so cripplingly taxing his widow that she forgoes her fortune in order to remarry at the king's discretion [50–51].

These consequences of English inheritance law, in such marked contrast to contemporary continental European practice, lead into a discussion of English common law, which Trevisan distinguishes from "the Caesarian code of laws" as having been "given them by their kings" [32].[35] The *relazione*'s focus on common law tends, however, to obscure the vestiges in English jurisprudence of older law (including Roman) and neglects to provide any example of how the ecclesiastical courts – whose canon law was based on the Roman model, and to which one could appeal in the absence of a positive finding in common law courts – functioned. But the centralization and definition of English legal power in judges did indeed originate with the medieval English monarchy, and Trevisan notes several instances of how the system worked at the end of the fifteenth century. He considers the widespread use of juries to be dangerous, though this "*mala consuetudine*/bad custom" [*28*, 32] is said to be particularly advantageous to Italian merchants implicted in a drawn-out trial:

for although the native jurors chosen by the Englishman in the dispute are well fed in advance of their confinement and eager to support him in his cause, they cannot withstand fasting and privation as the Italians who are so accustomed to them can, such that the final judgment is usually given in their favor [32–33].[36]

Apart from the sense of "national" pride registered here (and the swipe at English feebleness), if the account accurately reflects contemporary practice it would confirm that foreigners were not only the subjects of legal causes in early Tudor England, but that they were, unusually, also involved in the actual adjudication of cases involving their "co-nationals." Trevisan says that the use of juries is just as prevalent in criminal cases, though in the event of a guilty verdict the case is remanded to a second jury (which, should it find against the defendant, leads to a death sentence). It appears "the easiest thing in the world to get a person thrown into prison in that country" [33],[37] given the liberal extension of the right of arrest to individuals other than designated officers of the law. But for all of the various mechanisms of justice in England, the *relazione* puzzles over their failure to keep in check the worst impulses of the English and concludes that "there is no country in the world where there are so many thieves and robbers" [34],[38] roaming countryside and city in bands, wreaking social and economic havoc.

Trevisan's failure to address the critical role of canon law in England is a conspicuous omission, for he argues that it is above all the church that determines the course of English polity. The institutions of the English church are criticized for their collusion with criminality and for their inordinate wealth, and the *relazione* ends by suggesting that for all of its vaunted independence, England is in thrall to the Holy See. With regard to crime, two practices are singled out as particularly corrupt. In the first:

> priests have provided that a number of sacred places in the kingdom should serve for the refuge and escape of all delinquents; and no one, even were he a traitor to the crown or had he practiced against the king's own person, can be taken out of these by force [34–35].[39]

Trevisan is hardly exaggerating,[40] for remarks by the Lord Protector in 1483 corroborate this impression, and Henry VII was constrained on several occasions to seek papal intervention to deal with problems issuing from this privilege. The second example pertains directly to the clergy themselves, in that:

> no thief or murderer who can read, should perish by the hands of justice; and when anyone is condemned to death by the sentence of the twelve men of the robe, if the criminal can read, he asks to defend himself by the book; when a psalter, missal, or some other ecclesiastical book is brought to him, if he can read it he is liberated from the power of the law, and given as a clerk into the hands of the bishop [35–36].[41]

This almost Boccaccian confluence of crime, literacy, and the clerical state had its source in Edward III granting the recognition of clerical status in 1352 to any layman who could read; but the practice had grown so widespread, and was subject to just such abuse as the *relazione* records, that an act of parliament was passed in 1499 (after Trevisan's embassy) distinguishing between lay and clerical scholars, the latter of whom still benefitted from an initial exemption from the law in the case of a crime committed – though their heads were branded 'M' for murderer or 'T' for thief – only being subject to the full force of the law in the event of recidivism.

Trevisan reports that wealth tied to English land-holding is shared not only by the crown and the titled nobility, but also by the church, according to a formula worked out by William the Conqueror, after the Battle of Hastings in 1066, through which the church came to control almost one-third of the entire territory [38]. And in addition to their enormous real-estate income:

the lords spiritual ... possess the actual tenth of all the produce of the earth, and of every animal; and anyone living in his own house pays a tithe of everything to the church, besides the third part of every inheritance [40].[42]

Monasteries and convents possess such wealth that the English ironically consider that the greatest marriage imaginable would be between the Abbot of Glastonbury and the Abbess of Shaftsbury, each with annual incomes of 25,000 and 10,000 crowns respectively [40–41].

Ever the sober Venetian, Trevisan subtly but insistently registers a sense of reproach with regard to the riches of the English church, and his criticism sounds a prophetically cautionary note, given the battle over English ecclesiastical identity that would erupt with Henry VIII's divorce proceedings almost three decades after his embassy. The church's financial balance sheet as presented in the *relazione* suggests that for both sides in that later dispute the issues were not simply matters of principle, canon law, or international politics, but also involved the ultimate control of a vast web of material resources. Trevisan ends his *relazione* by calling attention to the financial ties that have bound England to Rome from the moment that William the Conqueror was helped to the English throne by Pope Alexander II, after which time England has subsequently paid regular and sizable financial homage to the Holy See [53–54]. The pay-off of this first incidence of papal interference in English politics thus anticipates one of the most serious consequences for Rome of what would turn out to be the final gesture of papal intervention in England with Henry VIII's excommunication: the sudden end of this pecuniary relationship.[43]

There are several surprising ellipses in Trevisan's *relazione*, most egregiously his failure to account for any aspect of English government apart from the monarchy. But given the typically short period of time that the Venetian ambassadors were in England, it would be unfair to expect that their conclusions should be either comprehensive or entirely reliable, for beyond their own *in situ* observations (and those of their retinue) none of them spoke English,[44] the sources of information they depended upon varied widely, and the mistrust of foreigners almost all of them report meant that certain kinds of knowledge would have been very difficult to come by. Dependable or not, however, the Venetian *relazioni* do share a common point of view, even as their *foci* shift with the developments that each successive embassy was required to confront; they do not possess the rhetorical finesse of contemporary Italian historiographical writing, nor are they as artful as some of the Italian literary texts dealing with England that we shall be considering, but the most alert of them convey an almost journalistic sense of immediacy that provides a pithy outsider's snapshot of early modern Britain.

"... de sacratissimus Britanniae regibus, de dignitate insulae, de hominum antiquissima nobilitate disserebat."

### Italian humanists in Britain

The scarce attention to "letters" that Trevisan found in England at the end of the fifteenth century is earlier lamented by the Florentine humanist Poggio Bracciolini, whose stay in the household of Henry Beaufort – at the time Bishop of Worcester, but later a cardinal and the most powerful of Henry VI's advisors – from 1418 through 1423 was motivated by a search for classical manuscripts on behalf of Italian patrons.[45] Disappointed in his sleuthing and unimpressed with the state of learning in England, Poggio wrote disparagingly of what he found there in his *Liber facetiorum*. In a 1421 letter addressed from London to Niccolò dei Niccoli in Florence, Poggio writes that:

I went traveling with my master [Beaufort] at the time of the great plague here; but the trip afforded me no pleasure, for a number of reasons, but particularly because I found no books. The monasteries here are very rich but only newly founded ... [I found] nothing worthwhile for the study of the humanities, and no wonder. This island was for a long time invaded by foreign nations, so there were many different kings in it, all attacking one another. Not only will you not find old books but not even one trace of ancient times ... you had better give up hope of books from England, for they care little for them here.[46]

The story has generally been considered to have ended there, with Poggio sarcastically shaking the dust from his sandals after abandoning Beaufort's service in 1423 and returning to Italy. But Susanne Saygin has recently drawn a considerably more complex picture of Poggio's English sojourn and its afterlife, situating the Florentine humanist's literary activity as inseparable from his long-term professional ambitions.[47] In this light, far from having been a sterile interlude, the time Poggio passed in England provided him with first-hand knowledge of the issues and key players in that period's English political scene, experience that proved decisive for his admission into the Roman curia in May of 1523. There, as Saygin has established from hitherto unnoted Vatican archival documents, Poggio quickly came to be regarded as the curia's English expert. Responsible for close to 50 percent of curial correspondence with England during his tenure in the papal administration, Poggio maintained good relations with Beaufort and his circle well into the 1440s – the period of Beaufort's greatest influence over the English crown – just as he cultivated links to other power brokers working for and between English, Italian, and related international concerns.

The future Pope Pius II, Enea Silvio Piccolomini, visited England and Scotland in 1435 on a mission to persuade the Scottish King James I to cooperate with a plan of the papal legate to the Council of Arras, Cardinal Albergati, to end the Hundred Years' War between England and France.[48] Piccolomini's charge was to convince the Scottish king to provide diversionary incursions of his troops into England in order to keep the English occupied and out of France while the details of a peace could be worked out. A splendid fresco commemorating Piccolomini's meeting with King James by Pinturicchio in the Piccolomini Library of the Duomo in Siena is perhaps the earliest visual image of an Italian in Britain and a good example of the discrepancy between representation and reality that so often characterizes the translation of one culture's values into another (Figure 1). The painting depicts an elderly James I, seated on a throne at the center of a lavishly decorated chamber, turned to his right to greet the dashing figure cut by Piccolomini. The room is filled with courtiers and several other emissaries, and it opens out onto a verdant, hilly landscape, with another castle in the distance perched above a bay that extends into the sea. Enea's actual experience of Scotland, however, could not have been more at odds with the sunny quattrocento coordinates of this painting. In his *Commentarii*, Piccolomini writes of arriving at Dunbar after a perilous series of misadventures on the North Sea. In thanksgiving to the Blessed Virgin Mary for his deliverance, he describes making a ten-mile pilgrimage to a shrine at Whitekirk dedicated to her; but this bare-footed trek in severely wintry conditions would result in Piccolomini's lifelong struggle with rheumatism in his ankles and feet.[49] He found the Scottish court unworthy of the term, and thought that the king lived more poorly than many European commoners. After arriving in England at the conclusion of his mission he recalls that:

there [in England] it seemed that I was seeing, as if for the first time, a civilized world inhabited by human beings. Scotland and the part of England that borders Scotland are nothing like the world in which we live: horrifying, primitive, and in the winter never touched by the warming rays of the sun.[50]

Piccolomini included lives of James I and Henry V in his *De viris claris*. But he left a rather different vestige of his visit, a *pignus amoris* born to a Scottish girl whom he mentions in a letter to his father, though it seems that the child died soon after her birth.[51]

Another quattrocento humanist sets the stage for the increasingly pervasive presence of Italians in England in the sixteenth century. Tito Livio dei Frulovisi was brought to England and employed by the English humanist Humphrey Duke of Gloucester from 1437 to 1439.[52] In addition to managing Humphrey's extensive Latin correspondence and curating his manuscript collection, Frulovisi composed a heroic poem in honor of his patron, the *Humfroidos*, and may have written two Latin comedies,

*Figure 1* Pinturicchio, fresco of Enea Silvio Piccolomini and James I in Scotland, Piccolomini Library, Duomo, Siena. Reproduced courtesy of Scala Archivio/Art Resource, NY.

*Peregrinatio* and *Eugenius*, while in England.⁵³ His most important work, however, the *Vita Henrici Quinti*, is the first officially sanctioned biography of an English monarch – Humphrey was Henry V's youngest brother, and the *Vita* is dedicated to Henry VI as a further element in Humphrey's educational program for him – and a benchmark in the evolution of historiography in England. Sergio Rossi notes that in Frulovisi's hands:

the dead king ... who had been bound to a feudal mentality and operated within a world that was still completely medieval ... is transformed into a Renaissance prince. The Duke of Gloucester made use of the Italian historian in order to present [an image] of his deceased brother from a perspective that favored his own political designs, and accordingly in the *Vita* we have the first biography of a historic Englishman seen as the central figure around whom a series of events is arranged and no longer as one among many of the actors in a linear historical chronicle.⁵⁴

Frulovisi's biography was reworked into English around 1513–14 by an anonymous translator and augmented with material from Monstrelet's *Chroniques*, Higden's *Polychronicon*, and a now lost memoir of James Butler, the Earl of Ormonde and an acquaintance of Henry V. Concurrently, Thomas More was writing his *Life of Richard III*, and Polidoro Virgilio the earliest version of his *Anglica historia* (discussed below), so Frulovisi's *Vita* in its English adaptation thus contributed to the process of historiographically justifying the Tudor dynasty and, in this form, served for much of the sixteenth century as the standard life of Henry V, "the hero in whom the [subsequent] Tudor era loved to identify itself and reflect its nascent 'national spirit'."⁵⁵ Yet in his edition of Shakespeare's *Henry V*, Gary Taylor dismisses any substantive influence of Frulovisi's *Vita*, finding it enough that Shakespeare had "read both Holinshed and Hall."⁵⁶ What Taylor neglects to take into account is whom these historians themselves had read. Concluding the section on Henry V in his *Chronicles*, Holinshed writes that:

Titus Livius de Foro Luvisiis lived also in these daies, an Italian borne: but sith he was both residant here, and wrote the life of this king, I haue thought good to place him among other of our English writers. One there was that translated the said historie into English, adding (as it were by waie of notes in manie places of that booke) sundrie things for the more large understanding of the historie: a copie whereof I have seene belonging to Iohn Stow citizen of London. There was also about the same time an other writer, who (as I remember) hath followed the said Livius in the order of his booke, as it were chapter by chapter, onelie changing a good, familiar and easie stile, which the said Livius used, into a certeine poeticall kind of writing: a copie where of I have seene (& in the life of this king partlie followed) belonging to master Iohn Twine of Kent, who (as I was informed) meant to leaue to posteritie some fruits of his labors for the due understanding thereof.⁵⁷

As with so much else regarding the impact of foreign cultures in England's early modern development, Frulovisi's influence is refracted and, consequently, obscured through English appropriation of his original work.[58] Together with many of the humanists later active in England, "one can argue about Frulovisi's worth as a literary figure and as an historian ... but not about the value of the contribution he made to the cultural renewal of a country still tied to the medieval tradition but for which the recent Italian humanistic Renaissance was of growing importance."[59]

A Brescian, Pietro Carmeliano, was the first Italian humanist to translate the sphere of his activities definitively to England, which he did in the early 1480s.[60] He was caught up in the events surrounding the end of Edward IV's reign, the brief and unhappy career of Edward V, Richard III's arrogation of the crown, and the enthronement of the Tudors. That he composed and presented long poems in honor of Edward V, Richard's wife Katherine, and the Tudor Prince Arthur over the course of several extremely turbulent years of political upheaval is a sign of Carmeliano's resilience and of his political savvy.[61] In a 1483 manuscript of correspondence dedicated to the conflict between Rome and Venice fought in Ferrara, he describes himself as "Petrum carmelianum poetam laureatum in Westmonasterio." What precisely "poet laureate" might have meant at this point in English history is unclear, but Carmeliano's talents nevertheless served him well as Henry VII turned his attention from the Wars of the Roses to the creation of a sophisticated court culture receptive to foreign influences. But Carmeliano's courtly success, however considerably it benefitted him materially and socially, was financed by an impressive accumulation of benefices – he was ordained a priest while in England – that expose the precarious web of temporal and spiritual relations that would later be tested by Henry VIII's divorce and complicated by the onset of the Reformation.[62] His role as Latin secretary to both Henry VII and Henry VIII put him into regular contact with highly sensitive information, and while aware of the risks run in doing so he frequently passed along intelligence to his native Venetian Republic that he deemed of importance to her interests, covert activity that further enriched Carmeliano's coffers at the same time that it advanced the concerns of his family, who remained in Italy.

Carmeliano contributed the introductory and closing poems appended to a longer Latin prose encomium composed by its publisher, Richard Pynson, to celebrate the formal engagement of Henry VII's daughter Mary to Charles of Castille in 1508.[63] Accompanying the first of these poems (Figure 2), the Tudor rose and Beaufort portcullis, each topped with a crown, are linked with emblematic devices associated with England's royal heritage: in the quartered shield, the three lions of the Plantagenets are

*Figure 2* Pietro Carmeliano, first page of *Carmen* in honor of Mary Tudor and Charles of Castille. Reproduced by permission of the British Library.

joined with the French *fleur de lis* of the Lancastrians. The poem itself extols the unity Henry's Tudor line has established:

> England, the red rose grants you perpetual triumphs,
> a perpetual name, and perpetual grace.
> This fragrant rose of yours grows in a hidden garden,
> and joins both waters with its vessels.[64]
> King Henry VII, wise king and yardstick of morality,
> who possesses a divine talent joined to uprightness,
> has alone, by his vigilance, brought you to such great honors;
> he should, therefore, be duly and freely honored by you.[65]

A typical example of Carmeliano's chameleon-like capacity to adapt to actual English political exigencies, these lines give no clue as to the tortuous route by which Henry VII reached the throne, or of the difficulties he faced in both remaining there himself and ensuring that his heirs would follow in his footsteps. One aspect of Henry's effort to consolidate his family's power was to seek advantageous foreign marriages, hence the engagement of an English princess and a Spanish prince while both parties to the contract were still only children. In the longer poem that closes Pynson's *libretto*, Carmeliano sums up the various elements of this political equation:

> ... the lovely maiden Mary is bestowed upon Charles,

first on the English side by recalling the bond already existing between England and the royal house of Burgundy, again praising King Henry and evoking the blessed memory of his wife, Elizabeth, who:

> ... while she was still alive,
> flourished without an equal among the queens of the world.

Carmeliano then cites the younger Henry:

> ... to whom no prince is a close second,
> [and who] sheds his brilliant rays upon all the world.

and next Margaret:

> mated to the mighty king
> of the Scots, his sister, wise, beautiful, lovely, and comely.

As for the Spanish, Charles is acknowledged as the son of Philip I:

> whom time – ah, all too brief! – stole away:
> Caesar Augustus's one hope, his only son,
> great-hearted, outstanding, vigorous, and mighty

and his mother:

> ... the illustrious Queen Joan,
> undoubted heiress to three kingdoms.

Charles is then encouraged to see Henry VII as a:

> ... new father by the favor of Fortune
> [who] will foster you and your governance,
> placing strong reins on your enemies.
> He it is who can ordain peace for nations and realms
> when he sets his battle-standards in motion.[66]

Beyond the encomiastic commonplaces of these verses, there is a series of projected associations that would have inevitably altered England's political and religious landscape in the later sixteenth century had this marriage actually taken place. Already linked to Spain through Katherine of Aragon (who goes unmentioned here), lately widowed by Prince Arthur, the Tudors hoped to realize a further Spanish, and imperial, alliance with Charles – Katherine's nephew, and the grandson of the Holy Roman Emperor Maximilian – that would have rendered even more problematic Henry VIII's later divorce initiative. Only a single copy of this Latin tribute has survived, surely the embarrassed consequence of the projected marriage of Henry VII's youngest daughter to the man who was to become Charles V falling prey to more pressing political alliances (on the Spanish side of the arrangement).[67] But Carmeliano's poem is also of interest in that it records the relationship effected between England and Scotland in the marriage of Henry's elder daughter Margaret to James IV that later provided James VI with his claim to succeed Elizabeth to the English throne in 1603, spelling the end of the Tudor line.[68]

Baldassare Castiglione's presence in England from November 1506 through January 1507 as Guidobaldo da Montefeltro's proxy at the investiture ceremony in which the Duke of Urbino was made a Knight of the Garter by Henry VII is cited by Castiglione himself as the explanation for his absence from the conversations that constitute his *Libro del cortegiano*.[69] Another projected English royal marriage, one that would have irrevocable consequences for English history, accounts for Guidobaldo's receipt of this honorific: his father, Federico, had been inducted into the Order of the Garter in 1474 by Edward IV – commemorated in the *intarsia* of one of the panels in the *Studiolo* from Federico's palace in Gubbio, now in the Metropolitan Museum in New York (Figure 3) – as a tribute for the services Federico had performed for the English crown as an agent and guarantor of English interests in the papal court before the development of the various forms of papal and royal representation that will be examined in the next section of this chapter. Guidobaldo's principal claim to the

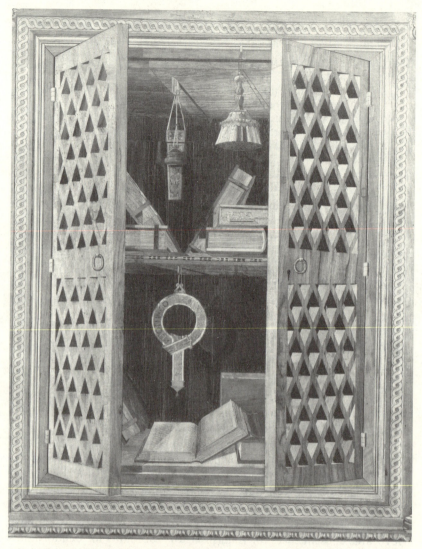

*Figure 3* Gubbio *Studiolo*, Garter of Federico da Montefeltro. Reproduced courtesy of Metropolitan Museum of Art.

Garter was made through advancing his potential utility as a cousin of Julius II (1503–1513), the pope who for several years blocked the dispensation Henry VII sought in order that Prince Henry might marry his widowed sister-in-law, Katherine. Henry VII might well not have understood in the end that Guidobaldo had little or nothing to do with the dispensation that was eventually granted, but at any rate Castiglione was designated to travel to England in order to receive the Garter on the duke's behalf. While there, he was a guest of Edward Hastings, Baron of Huntington, the great-grandfather of Henry Hastings, Earl of Huntington, to whom Thomas Hoby later dedicated his hugely popular and widely influential English translation of the *Cortegiano* in 1561.[70]

In the letters that he wrote from England, Castiglione shows himself to be quite pleased about his visit, for though he was acting as Guidobaldo's surrogate he was treated with great deference by his English hosts, and by the king.[71] Later, writing from Urbino to Henry VII after the death of Guidobaldo in 1508, Castiglione recalls that "as he [the duke] learned from me just how warmly and honorably I was welcomed by Your Majesty, and to what extent I was laden [by you] with dignities and gifts, he could not but with cheerfulness and delight share with everyone all that to which my letters bore witness."[72] Cecil Clough suggests that a detail early in the *Cortegiano* which has bedeviled commentators registers Castiglione's own homage to the courtesy shown him in England: In Book I.9, Bernardo Accolti (also called Unico Aretino, not to be confused with Pietro Aretino) proposes that the friends gathered together for conversation "each say what might be the meaning of the letter that the Duchess wears on her forehead, for though certainly a cunning sign meant to mislead, perhaps some one of you might find an interpretation of it that she has not anticipated."[73] The letter is an *S*, and after the interlocutors decline to determine its significance, Accolti is said to rattle off an explanation that Castiglione does not report but suggests was invented on the spot. Clough's contribution to the discussion makes Elisabetta Gonzaga's *S* one of the S-links in the gold collar awarded to Castiglione by Henry VII (a judge's insignia, similar to the one worn by Thomas More in Holbein's portrait, now in the Frick Collection in New York), detached and presented to the duchess as a gift after his return to Urbino.[74] Accolti mentions *catene* [chains] just before he poses his challenge, so it seems entirely plausible that Castiglione is dropping a hint as to his meaning here, effecting his own sleight of hand by planting in his narrative material evidence of the mission he claims kept him from participating first-hand in the discussions he nevertheless manages to recount.

Castiglione clearly valued the collar, as he "adopted it for his own [coat of] arms, and it [was] found encircling them on the first folio of the manuscript" of *Ad Henricum Angliae Regem epistola de vita et gestis Guidibaldi Urbini Ducis* (Figure 4, here the first page of the earliest surviving manuscript, with its slightly different title, dating probably from 1518).[75] This remarkable letter aspires to more than an obligatory notice to the English

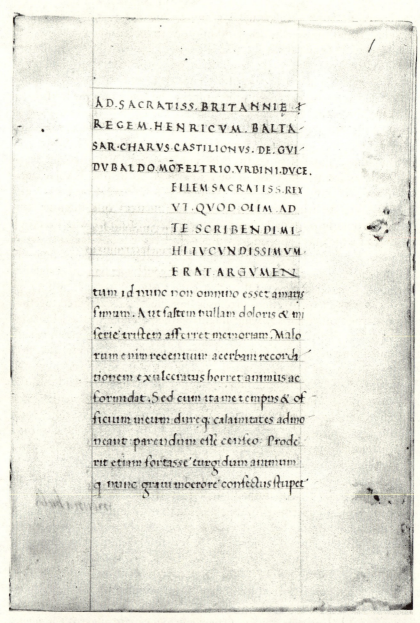

*Figure 4* Baldassare Castiglione, first page of *Ad Henricum Angliae Regem epistola*, Amherst Ms. B3, n. 3. Reproduced courtesy of Amherst College Archives and Special Collections.

king of the death of one of his knights, but the presentation copy of the letter did not arrive in England until after Henry VII's own death in April of 1509. If Clough is correct in speculating that the epistle makes a subtle case for Guidobaldo's designated successor in Urbino, Francesco Maria della Rovere, also being awarded the Order of the Garter, the bid fell on deaf ears, as Henry VIII apparently never acknowledged its receipt and the new duke never received the English honorific. The *Epistola* is significant, however, for two other reasons: for its Latin exposition of a linguistic issue that Castiglione further developed in Italian in the *Cortegiano*; and for the deeply sympathetic portrait of Guidobaldo that it provides, an outpouring of admiration, affection, and grief that readers of the *Cortegiano* would do well to take into account.

Guidobaldo's absence from the *mise-en-scène* of the *Cortegiano* has been interpreted variously as Castiglione's indifferent, equivocal, or hostile assessment of his patron, but given the picture of him that emerges in the *Epistola*, these appraisals bear reconsideration.[76] The image that Castiglione paints of the duke is of a good and learned man, beaten down by early disease and betrayed by political allies (most notably by Cesare Borgia, the son of Pope Alexander VI (1492–1503), and the emblematic hero of Machiavelli's *Principe*) but whose mere ten years at the helm of Urbino endeared him to his people. Guidobaldo's erudition is presented as having been worn very lightly – he is said to have practiced that insouciance that Castiglione would later in the *Cortegiano* coin as *sprezzatura* – but pursued with tremendous dedication, forming in the *Epistola* the key to both the duke's character and his inner life:

he bore a particular love for the study of Greek, of which he acquired such an exact knowledge that he was as apt in speaking it as if it were his native tongue, taking care with its words such that he uttered both their accents and aspirations as a Greek would have. In adolescence he was known as a great reader, an exercise he did not pursue with the same diligence in the last years of his life but in recompense for which he enjoyed such a fortunate and inexhaustible wealth of memory that in this, as far as I can judge, he exceeded all other men. Accordingly, once he had heard something recounted only once or twice he already grasped it so well that he was able to reiterate not only the meaning but each of the words used, in exactly their original order. He had only a summary acquaintance with most poets, but with both Virgil and Homer he was on intimate terms, such that he could precisely identify their figures of speech, their witticisms, and their vast knowledge of all things. He was as thoroughly familiar with as he was admiring of the majesty, abundance and genius of these inspired poets, and he had them so deeply impressed in his memory that only briefly hearing someone recite a passage from either Homer or Virgil, he was able to immediately follow suit, to the enormous satisfaction of his listeners.[77]

Reminiscent of the vivifying colloquies with the ancients of Machiavelli and Montaigne (both of whose political vicissitudes were not so different from his), Guidobaldo's passionate but unpedantic love for words and his facility with them (despite a lifelong problem with stammering that Castiglione notes) are consistently invoked throughout the letter as his defining virtue, one that offsets the unhappy course of both his political life and his physical health.[78]

Castiglione's elegant prose is written in a heterogeneous language that while replete with classical vocabulary makes a compelling case for a modern Latin rhetoric free from the suffocating constraints of the neo-Ciceronianism that his contemporary Pietro Bembo advocated in his own tribute to Guidobaldo and elsewhere in his literary work.[79] Castiglione's unwillingness to be hidebound by linguistic anachronism allows his Latin prose to breathe the diverse cultural air of its own historical moment, and the result he achieves in this regard in the *Epistola* would be put to further use in his elaboration of the similarly eclectic vernacular language of the *Cortegiano*. There is no reason to suppose that the *Epistola* was known in England until the eighteenth century, but in its linguistic practice it anticipates developments in sixteenth-century vernacular linguistic politics that would make possible the semantic liberalism of Florio's Italian–English dictionary.

Castiglione writes Guidobaldo's death scene as the culminating performative moment of his patron's life.[80] As the duke's vitality ebbed away, Castiglione reports that he and several others tried to distract him from thoughts of death, but Guidobaldo responded to their efforts by asking why:

"you begrudge me that good which I have so long desired? Should you not rather concede that my liberation from such an accumulation of intolerable griefs be deemed not only desirable but requisite?" And after (again) lapsing briefly into silence, he turned to me saying, "As long as I am in this life (reciting then the following verses of Virgil):
   ... *surrounding [me], dark slime and misshapen reed of Cocytus, and*
   *the hateful swamp, with sluggish waters*
   *bind [me], and Styx gushing in nine streams*
   *between [the living and the dead].*"[81]

This citation of the Hades that Orpheus confronts in *Georgics* 4: 478–80 is utilized by Castiglione to characterize Guidobaldo's life of suffering, the duke conspicuously made to substitute himself in these verses for the multitude of Virgil's dead souls. But the eruption of Virgil's gnarled syntax into Castiglione's carefully measured prose makes a forceful onomatopoeic point, underscoring Castiglione's eschewal of an anachronistic classicism that would otherwise collapse an ancient sense of death into the decidedly Christian context of the letter as it simultaneously demonstrates the striking utility of rough language that the neo-Ciceronians would have rejected as ugly and unbefitting of humanist discourse.[82]

The centrality of this moment is marked immediately after, when Castiglione writes that "then, little by little, he began to lose his capacity for words, rarely and with difficulty being able to speak. Seemingly quiescent, he remained silent."[83] Guidobaldo is in the letter's formulation a tragic but not a pathetic figure:[84] caught by historical events beyond his power to control, he is distinguished through the pursuit of humanistic learning, but once deprived of the voice through which this erudition has been performed, his life is represented as effectively over. In the closing pages of the *Epistola*, Castiglione evokes the image of the Garter draped over Guidobaldo's casket as he recalls the occasion on which it had originally been conferred, "*Heu! Quam dissimilis pompa!*/Ah! How different that ceremony and this!"[85] The grief of Guidobaldo's people, and particularly that of his wife, Elisabetta Gonzaga, further develops the letter's Virgilian subtext in language that specifically cites both the funeral rites for Pallas in *Aeneid* 11: 42–44 and the netherworld of *Aeneid* 6; at the same time it relies on theatrical tropes that shift between the public and private spheres in their representation of the grieving citizens of Urbino and the grief of the duchess, scenes staged with a sharp delineation of its principal actors within a context of "accentuated illusionistic effects."[86]

Castiglione sought to consolidate Guidobaldo's reputation in his *Epistola* addressed to the English king, a letter whose exposition may have originated in a formal address given by Castiglione within the context of the 1506 Garter ceremony at Windsor, but whose more expansive elaboration as an elegy capitalized upon its author's own learning and his experience in Urbino as a stage-manager of plays and ceremonial events. Despite its late arrival in England and its subsequent neglect, Castiglione's *Epistola* in both its style and substance is the most accomplished Latin literary text composed in this period by an Italian for an English addressee.

Several years prior to Castiglione's visit, and two decades into Carmeliano's tenure at the English court, Polidoro Virgilio arrived in England as the deputy papal collector. Except for several later short periods spent in Italy, Virgilio was to remain in England through the accession of Mary in 1553, serving Henry VII, Henry VIII and Edward VI in varying roles. As Archdeacon of Wells from 1508 on, Virgilio successfully crossed the line into Anglicanism at the time of Henry's divorce and subsequent schism, but his well-disguised sympathies were always to remain with Rome. Virgilio's most important achievement is the

*Anglica historia*, written – initially at the behest of Henry VII – between 1506 and 1513 but not printed until 1534, with a final chapter added in a further edition issued in 1555.[87] A work of substantive historiographical import, the *Anglica historia* aims to give a critical account of English history from its first traces in antiquity to the early sixteenth century, its first edition extending through the reign of Henry VII, then in its subsequent elaboration through that of Henry VIII (this final chapter written toward the end of Virgilio's life with a certain score-settling ferocity). Virgilio set out to write a history that, building on the work of Frulovisi, would go beyond the fact-compiling of earlier English chroniclers. Though his work ultimately assisted the English in coming to regard themselves as constituting a "nation" through providing them with a serviceable guide to their own past, Virgilio also found a great deal of material in English annals that smacked of a nationalistic provincialism he considered abhorrent, an issue that will be of particular interest when we come in the third chapter to consider the meaning of the "stranger" within such an evolving "national" context.

In his study of Polidoro Virgilio's career, Denys Hay notes that there were several key characteristics of the Italian historiographical approach Virgilio sought to bring to his consideration of British history: a distinction between *history* and *annals*, the importance of conveying good example while also inspiring delight, and impartial observation in the service of objectivity, all of which was articulated through the use of Ciceronian rhetorical principles that, however, "contained directions as to manner which could be easily incompatible with ... advice on matter and method."[88] One of the methodological innovations in Virgilio's history was the introduction of an index of places and persons, an important factor in its accessibility. But, as his unrelenting vehemence toward Cardinal Wolsey in the final book of the *Anglica historia* demonstrates, Virgilio was not always as true to his purpose as he might have intended to be. Discussing Wolsey's extraordinary rise to power, he writes that:

> with his arrogance and ambition, [Wolsey] raised against himself the hatred of the whole people and, in his hostility towards nobles and common folk, procured their great irritation at his vainglory. His own odiousness was truly complete, because he claimed he could undertake himself almost all public duties. It was indeed significant to see this fellow, ignorant of law, sitting in court and pronouncing judgment ... the government of Wolsey in the beginning had for the common people a shadowy appearance of justice, which indeed, because it was only a shadow, quickly disappeared.[89]

Hay considers Virgilio's history most reliable in its earlier books, those that deal with events occurring before the late fifteenth century, after which he finds the humanist's judgment often clouded by his experience in England. Sergio Rossi, however, while recognizing the potentially skewed perspective of a historian writing about events through which he has lived, values Virgilio's ability to "make manifest the drama of an era in full decline with no sense yet of what the future might promise."[90]

Virgilio's boldest gamble in trying to establish a surer footing for English history was his dismissal of the mythology of Camelot, an effort for which his posthumous reputation was to pay dearly. The fables associated with King Arthur and the Knights of the Round Table were firmly established articles of ideological faith in early Tudor England, but even if "Henry VII and his son were prepared to accept [Virgilio's skepticism] as part of the price to be paid for having English history presented in humanist form, Englishmen [themselves] reacted violently and attacked Virgilio without respite for his temerity."[91] John Leland, in his *Assertio inclytissimi Arturii* (1544), criticizes Virgilio not only for questioning the veracity of the Arthurian history but also labels him as *Polydorus italus*, this subtly xenophobic tag implying that the Italian "stranger" has no legitimate voice in recounting a history that is not his own. Both John Bale and Holinshed contributed later in the sixteenth century to Virgilio's disrepute by condemning him and aggressively reasserting the veracity of the Arthurian origins of the English monarchy. Just as Ariosto utilized the "Matter of Britain" in *Orlando furioso*, Spenser – entirely ignoring Virgilio's contribution to the issue – came to use Arthurian mythology for similarly ideological purposes in order to subsume Elizabeth and her court into the world of Færie.[92] If by the standards of modern historical scholarship the *Anglica historia* leaves something to be desired, it remains a useful index to a Tudor-sanctioned humanist view of English history and, in spite of the excesses of its final book, still serves as a valuable commentary on the England that Virgilio inhabited for most of his adult life. Resistance to his program of a more historically grounded understanding of the British past anticipates the direction Tudor ideology would subsequently take, from the rewriting of the script of Henry VIII's first marriage, through the fictions propagated in and about the Elizabethan court.[93]

"... *avendo a fare una grande opera al mio Re* ... "

### Italian artists in England

Italian artists were a small but significant presence in early Tudor England, and as P. G. Lindley points out, it was in the illumination of humanist manuscripts that Italian Renaissance visual forms first arrived in England in the mid-fifteenth century.[94] The elaborately decorated page shown in (Figure 5), for example, introduces a volume of encomiastic Latin poetry dedicated to Henry VII by Giovanni Michele Nagonio (Nagonius), an Italian humanist working in England in the last decade of the fifteenth century.[95] The central image, depicting a not especially verisimilar Henry in a triumphant position (its occasion unclear), is accompanied by this epithet:

God watches over you, Henry, sustains you, and snatches you away from the hands of the impious enemy [here represented kneeling in the lower left of the image, subjected to the king's judgment]. Glad [is] your English empire, Henry VII, God preserve you.[96]

Paul Gwynne has noted the originality of this image's iconography with regard to previous representations of English monarchs, drawing as it does upon classical *triumphator* imagery, Petrach's *Trionfi*, and the depiction of Henry VII on the gold sovereign first minted in England in 1489.[97] Given the later precedence accorded word over image that developed after Henry VIII's break with the Roman church, it is noteworthy that among the earliest signs of Italian visual style in England should be not independent works of art but illustrations for a literary collection.

The first Italian sculptor in England was Guido Mazzoni, who had accompanied Charles VIII to France following the French king's military conquest of the Italian peninsula in 1494–96. Working on commissions first from Charles and then from his successor, Louis XII, Mazzoni visited England as early as 1506 to submit a design for the tomb of Henry VII, and the latest evidence for his presence there is in 1507.[98] Mazzoni's design projected a double effigy of the king, one of the figures reposing next to the effigy of Elizabeth of York, and the other kneeling beside them. Henry's own plan for the monument projected a kneeling second figure, but in the instructions he spelled out in his will only a month before his death he intended that this *priant* image, with its crown in hand, be placed upon "a table of silver and gilte ... in the mydds of the Creste of the Shryne of Saint Edward King."[99] The meaning of Henry's design is obvious, establishing, as it would have, an unmistakable inconographic link between the newfangled Tudors and England's preceding regal line. The king likely appropriated Mazzoni's idea of the praying figure for his own design – exploiting its ideological possibilities – while rejecting the rest of the Italian's plan, but in the end, by the time that Pietro Torrigiano finally realized Henry VII's tomb in Westminster Abbey by 1519, this second effigy of the king had been eliminated from the monument.

*Figure 5* Giovanni Michele Nagonio, miniature of Henry VII in *Carmen*, York Minster Ms. XVI N2. Reproduced by kind permission of the Dean and Chapter of York.

Torrigiano's reputation has until recently been largely determined by Vasari's sharply negative appraisal. Blaming the sculptor for having broken Michelangelo's nose sometime prior to 1492, Vasari dismisses Torrigiano's gifts as an artist, asserting that they were fatally compromised by haughtiness and pride.[100] Benvenuto Cellini writes in his *Vita* of having met Torrigiano, who had come to Florence:

from England, where he had lived for many years, and because he was a good friend of my master's he came to visit him each day. Upon seeing both my designs and my finished work, he said to me: "I am in Florence to find as many young artisans as I can, given that I would like the help of my fellow Florentines on a big project that I am to undertake for my king. As your method of working and your designs are more those of a sculptor than a goldsmith, and this work of mine shall be a bronze-cast, I could simultaneously make you a skilled artist and a rich man."

Cellini goes on to say how much he initially admired Torrigiano's physical appearance and his audacity; seemingly more a soldier than a sculptor he inspired awe in his gestures, through his booming voice, and in a fearsome frown, frequently boasting of "his exploits among those English beasts." But when the conversation turned one day to Michelangelo, Torrigiano definitively lost his potential apprentice by boasting that:

"As young men, Buonarotti and I used to go to draw in Massaccio's chapel in the Church of the Carmine. And because Buonarotti had the habit of making fun of the others drawing there, one day I got fed up with his attitude. More angry than usual, I clenched my fist and punched him in the nose so hard that I felt its bone and cartilage crumble as if it were a cookie. So marked by me he shall remain his whole life." Given my esteem for the works of the divine Michelangelo, these words generated such a hatred in me that not only could I not imagine accompanying Torrigiano to England, but I couldn't even stand to see him any longer.[101]

Michelangelo did indeed sport a deformed nose as an adult, but he did not evidently nurse the grudge against Torrigiano that his partisans did, for as late as 1506, when Torrigiano left Italy for northern Europe, the two men maintained something of a professional relationship.[102]

Exactly when Torrigiano arrived in England is unclear, as the earliest documentation of his presence there dates from 1511, when he signed the contract for Lady Margaret Beaufort's tomb.[103] But he was almost certainly active in England with other royal projects as early as 1509. The first documentary evidence of Torrigiano's link to the Tudor court is in 1510, when Margaret of Austria, Regent of the Netherlands, arranged for him to repair a (now lost) terracotta bust of Mary Tudor then in Bruges that had been made at the time of her engagement to Margaret's nephew, Charles of Castille. Several art historians have suggested that Torrigiano was not only the restorer of the piece but its original sculptor,[104] and if so this would have marked the second Italian contribution to Mary's ephemeral espousal to Charles.

Three terracotta busts – of Bishop John Fisher, Henry VII, and Henry VIII – form a group of works that establish Torrigiano's presence in England from the period immediately following Henry VII's death in 1509. C. Galvin and P. G. Lindley have determined that the craftsmanship involved in Henry's funeral effigy – which is extant, though badly damaged by water after Westminster Abbey was hit by a bomb in 1941 – could have been executed only by an Italian of Torrigiano's skill, and the similarities between the effigy's head and the bust of Henry VII are so striking as to warrant the attribution of both pieces to him.[105] The identification with Fisher of the bust now in the Metropolitan Museum of Art in New York has occasioned several dissenting voices,[106] but his close relationship with Lady Margaret – Fisher had been her confessor – and his involvement in the negotiations with Torrigiano for her tomb help to account for his presence with two Tudor kings in Torrigiano's terracotta triptych, as it was through Margaret Beaufort that the Tudors made their somewhat precarious claim to the English throne.[107] The three terracotta busts could well have served as Torrigiano's portfolio in his bid to be awarded the commission for Lady Margaret's tomb, which because of its dynastic implications was of the utmost importance for the political face that her Tudor progeny wished to present to the world. The project as it came to be realized, however, was marred "by the medieval collaborative process ... which resulted in an unbalanced design and created a not wholly successful visual tension between the northern Gothic tabernacle (the work of the London painter Maynard Vewick), reminiscent of other late Gothic English tombs, and Torrigiano's new Italianate-inspired tomb chest."[108]

His patron, however, was pleased with the result, and in 1512 Torrigiano was entrusted by Henry VIII with the design and execution of the monument for his parents in the Chapel of Henry VII at Westminster Abbey that John Pope-Hennessy deemed "the finest Renaissance tomb north of the Alps" (Figure 6).[109] He was awarded the sum of £1,500 to "make and worke, or do to be made and wrought, well, surely, clenly, workemanly, curiously and substancyally ... a tombe or sepulture of whit marbill and of black touchstone wt. ymags, figures, beasts and other things of cuppure gilt."[110] The effigies of Henry VII and Elizabeth of York are placed atop a tall, typically English, sarcophagus adorned with the same sort of classical decorative figuration – here grotesques, garlands, birds, and acanthus-leaf – that Raphael and his assistants were using to great effect in several Vatican fresco projects

*Figure 6* Pietro Torrigiano, tomb of Henry VII and Elizabeth of York, Westminster Abbey. Reproduced courtesy of Scala Archivio/Art Resource, NY.

in the same period. There are seated angels at each of the four corners of the monument, bearing the Tudor arms and an epitaph, with six roundels linking relief images of the king's twelve patron saints whose presence is meant to guarantee the royal couple's eternal future. While Elizabeth's features are idealized, Henry's head is clearly fashioned from a mask, probably the same one used in Torrigiano's previous representations of the king. Apart from its several English elements – the height of the tomb, its gilding and articulation – Torrigiano's work reflects a more thoroughly Italian approach than does the Beaufort monument, demonstrating a more expert grasp of bronze-casting than the contemporary English standard (though he did follow the English custom of using almost pure copper, mixed with a very small percentage of other metals) as well as his absorption of several quattrocento artists' practices and styles, most notably those of Pollaiuolo (whose tomb for Pope Sixtus IV provided Torrigiano with his principal inspiration), Donatello, Verrocchio, and Ghiberti.

Torrigiano was subsequently awarded the commission for an enormous tomb for Henry VIII and Katherine of Aragon in 1519, the project for which he had sought Cellini's help in Florence. Other young Italian artists proved more eager to join Torrigiano in England, among whom the painter Antonio Toto del Nunziata, and the sculptors Giovanni da Maiano and Benedetto da Rovezzano; the latter two would continue to work in England after Torrigiano's departure, utilizing his workshop and foundry at Westminster Abbey.[111] But this monument never got beyond the planning stages, and by sometime in the early 1520s Torrigiano had settled in Spain, possibly having accompanied Charles V there after his visit to England in 1522. Little is known about Torrigiano's actual life in England, though he did live until 1514 in the household of the Florentine banker Giovanni Bardi, and he had other contacts with prominent members of London's Italian merchant and banking community. Besides the large-scale projects for the English monarchs – there was also an altar for the Henry VII chapel in Westminster, destroyed in 1644 but rebuilt in the 1930s – Torrigiano and his workshop produced the wall-tomb of Dr. John Yonge in the Rolls Chapel, Chancery Lane, that Darr characterizes as "the first entirely Renaissance-style monument in England," and a number of other smaller-scale pieces.[112] Torrigiano died in a Spanish prison in the summer of 1528, apparently sent there by the Inquisition, having destroyed a statue of the Virgin and Child after a financial dispute with its patron.

Two phantom sculptural projects by Italians in this period are of particular interest, given both their projected scope and the relationship that each of them bears to Henry VIII's unrealized ambitions regarding his own funerary monument. The first is mentioned by Paolo Giovio in his biography of Leo X (1513–1521), where he writes that the pope, having contracted a terrible fever at his country villa, returned to Rome on November 30, 1521 only to find:

a terrible omen of his imminent death upon entering the room, for an artist was awaiting him there in order to present the wooden model of a beautiful marble tomb which he was then sculpting for King Henry of England.[113]

The very next day Leo was dead. It could well be that Giovio is engaging in literary license here, for this *vita* was written sometime after the events it recounts and was not published until 1549: by associating the figure of Henry VIII with this premonitory event so close to the pope's death, Giovio might well be anticipating Henry's later nettlesome presence for the pontificate of Clement VII (1523–1534), Leo's illegitimate cousin and the pope who would refuse Henry his divorce. But even if the timing of the model exhibition is open to question, other documentation establishes that Leo did intend to subsidize a magnificent tomb for the English king, that a wooden model of it was actually produced, and that its sculptor was to be Baccio Bandinelli.[114] Giovio mistakenly assumes in his account that work on the monument was actually underway, for there is no evidence to suggest that the project was ever initiated. A letter from Leonardo Sellaio to Michelangelo dated December 14, 1521 identifies Bandinelli as the model's artist, and also notes its gargantuan proportions, including what were to be 142 life-sized figures, the king seated on horseback, and bas-relief panels, all in bronze, the gilding of which alone was expected to cost 40,000 gold *ducati*; he says that Giovanni Cavalcanti, a banker active in London and Rome, was instructed by the papal datary – the curial official responsible for (among many other things) the pope's personal expenses – to have Bandinelli create the model, but he also predicts that the monument will never be built. A much more elaborately detailed description of a tomb-model for Henry VIII is given in John Speed's *History of Britain* (1623), and a comparison with Sellaio's letter suggests that they are describing the same object, though the later account leaves out all reference to the Italian and papal origins of the model.[115] It would appear that from both sides of the divide that was created by Henry's divorce this commodity became simply too hot to handle.[116]

Vasari confuses Bandinelli's model with Benedetto da Rovezzano's entirely unrelated work on a tomb for Thomas Wolsey,[117] a monument that the cardinal himself had played a significant role in designing and which Benedetto had evidently gone quite far in realizing by the time of Wolsey's fall in 1529.[118] The scale of the tomb was on a par with its patron's ego and was meant to rival, if not actually exceed, the scope of Torrigiano's monument for Henry VII and Elizabeth of York. Enclosed in an area 9 feet long and 8 feet deep and surrounding the tomb itself with the cardinal's effigy situated atop, there were to be at each of its four corners 9-foot high pillars, each topped with standing angels holding candelabra, four angels kneeling at the base of the tomb and another kneeling atop it, with two naked children positioned at Wolsey's head and two at his feet bearing his coat of arms; there were also to be emblems linked to Wolsey's status as a churchman, twelve figures of saints, a crucifix, and a myriad of decorative elements. The materials utilized ranged from black touch and white marble for the base and sarcophagus, to fully gilt and burnished copper for the pillars and all of the various figures involved. After Wolsey's fall from power, Benedetto prepared an inventory in two different lists of what he had already realized, one of items linked specifically to the figure of Wolsey himself and the other detailing those pieces of the monument that could be recycled, for Henry VIII meant to plunder Wolsey's tomb (just as he had appropriated his palace at Hampton Court) in order to finally initiate work on his own monument at Windsor; the former items were probably melted down for reuse, but Benedetto and Giovanni da Maiano set to work in late 1530 with the remaining components on a project that never came to term.[119] Four of Wolsey's candlesticks wound up in a church in Ghent, the marble base and sarcophagus were moved in 1808 to St. Paul's Cathedral, where they were utilized for Lord Nelson's tomb, but everything else has vanished.

Few Italian artists were active in later Tudor England.[120] Following Henry VIII's divorce and the ensuing iconoclasm of the early Anglican period, the fashion for Italian Renaissance art seems to have passed, one factor that could partially account for the king's tomb remaining unrealized. A woodcut in Foxe's *Acts and Monuments* (Figure 7) vividly illustrates the prevailing attitude in Edwardian England toward the kind of ecclesiastical art earlier promoted there by Italian artists. Above two symbolic scenes of the reformed church's new axes – the king's authority linked to the Bible on the left, and two of the retained sacraments, baptism and the eucharist, balanced by a sermon being preached to an attentive congregation on the right – there are three moments in the attendant denudation of English churches depicted: on the left, a statue is about to be pulled out of its niche just as books and several objects are being carried out of a church; in the middle, a bonfire consumes some of this material; and on the right, what remains is being loaded onto "The Ship of the Roman Church" so as to be sailed safely away from England. That this latter image is not merely polemical is borne out by a 1547 Florentine document in which Pier Riccio, a canon of the cathedral in Florence, writes of a Florentine entrepreneur, Giorgio Dati,[121] then in Antwerp, who reported that:

ships had arrived in certain Flemish ports loaded with beautiful altar tables, reliquaries, and images of saints for sale, having been brought from London where, considered idolatrous objects created in the workshops of priests, they had been stripped from churches.[122]

*Figure 7* John Foxe, *Acts and Monuments*, Woodcut. Reproduced courtesy of Department of Special Collections, Stanford University.

As has been suggested, there was a powerful economic component in the reform of the Anglican church following Henry's divorce, seen at work here in turning a profit from the discarded artefacts of the old religion.

The lower half of Foxe's woodcut demonstrates the unmistakable valorization of word over image, an opposition that in various forms marks the transition into the early stages of a distinctly Protestant cultural politics in England. English taste for extravagant display would find other subsequent outlets, particularly in Elizabethan public spectacle, but the evanescent character of those later pageants – whose words are frequently the only surviving traces of them – is in striking contrast to the enduring contributions to England's artistic patrimony made by Italian artists working there early in the sixteenth century.

*"Inghilterra non è senza qualche subiettione ... della Santa Sede."*
### England and the Roman church

Polidoro Virgilio had originally come to England in the role of deputy papal collector, and the significant part that Italian clerics in England played as representatives of the papacy in several different offices during the early Tudor period requires some explanation.[123] The papal collector was originally a Roman curial official resident in a country such as England, responsible for the collection and dispatch of the manifold fees and taxes owed to the papacy by the reigning monarch, bishops and their dioceses, priests and their parishes, and religious orders. The function of papal collector by the late fifteenth century had in a number of instances been grafted onto the newly designated role of papal nuncio (or ambassador), who served as the pope's eyes and ears within "national" contexts, gathering intelligence on both secular and religious issues as well as researching and making recommendations to the pope regarding the appointment of bishops. By the early sixteenth century, these offices were sometimes filled by more than one individual simultaneously, and "two or even three resident ones are frequently found." Monarchs, in turn, appointed their own (usually native) ambassadors, and "the return to Rome of a papal nuncio as an ambassador for the government to which he had been accredited was not uncommon, and the pope [on occasion] sent an ambassador home to serve as papal nuncio."[124]

An additional factor in this mix of clerical offices was the non-resident cardinal protector, the first of whom for any "nation," Francesco Todeschini Piccolomini, was approved by Pope Alexander VI in 1492 to look after English interests within the Roman curia. This position was not strictly speaking either a papal or a royal appointment, the potential protector having proffered his services to a monarch – in the case of Piccolomini, to Henry VII – in exchange for a hefty fee. In return, the monarch could more or less rest assured that in addition to his other official ties to Rome, a highly placed insider would be "protecting" his interests within the hermetic world of the curia.[125] As we shall see, a number of the key Italian players in the drama of Henry VIII's divorce benefitted from one or several of these arrangements. It was through these Italian clerics that early modern England enjoyed its closest relationship with both Italy and the wider continental Catholic context, and it was the rupturing of these bonds following the divorce that simultaneously isolated the country and created the space within which its singularly Protestant culture could develop.

A further aspect of the symbiosis operative in early Tudor English relations with Rome was the succession of Italian bishops who held, *in absentia*, several important dioceses in the English church prior to the schism provoked by Henry VIII's divorce. Giovanni dei Gigli was born in Bruges in 1434 to a prominent Lucchese mercantile family with significant interests in the Belgian city, and it seems that he was educated at least in part at Oxford, obtaining a degree in law. Little is known of his ensuing career, but he was again in England by 1476, serving first as papal collector and as nuncio; he was then named non-resident Bishop of Worcester in 1497, by which time he had returned to Rome, where he was functioning as Henry VII's ambassador.[126] In addition to his ecclesiastical responsibilities in England, Gigli was involved in promoting the revival of English literary culture after the conclusion of the Wars of the Roses. He wrote an epithalamium in celebration of the engagement of Henry VII to Elizabeth of York and subsequently obtained the papal dispensation necessary for the marriage to take place.[127] Henry regarded Gigli's elevation to the episcopate a fitting means of recognition for services already rendered as well as conferring upon his delegate the requisite degree of *gravitas* in the curial duties he continued to perform for the English crown. Though Giovanni only lived to exercise his episcopal prerogatives for just under a year, following his death in 1498 he was succeeded in his appointment to Worcester by his nephew, Silvestro dei Gigli, who had previously worked in England with his uncle but was by then also residing in Rome.[128] Another of Giovanni's nephews, Sebastiano, was in England at the time working as a merchant, and the nephew of Pope Innocent VIII (1484–92), Gianbattista di Girardo Cibò, had earlier been engaged there in diplomatic work for his uncle. As William Wilkie suggests, Italian ecclesiastical representation in early Tudor England was a family affair.[129]

Adriano Castellesi, appointed Giovanni dei Gigli's successor as collector and papal nuncio in 1493 by Pope Alexander VI, was also given the task of reforming the secular clergy in England.[130] He was not long at this latter task, however, for in 1494 he too settled permanently in Rome, effectively serving there as Henry VII's ambassador while his protégé, Polidoro Virgilio, looked after Castellesi's interests as deputy collector in England. A great favorite of the Borgia pope, Castellesi was appointed papal secretary in 1497, awarded the English diocese of Hereford in 1502 upon the recommendation of Henry VII, and raised to the cardinalate in 1503. Castellesi's long experience in England gave him a decisive advantage over the cardinal protector Piccolomini, but after the latter's election to the papacy as Pius III in 1503, both Henry VII and Henry VIII played him off against Silvestro dei Gigli, Castellesi's chief curial rival for the attention of the English king. Castellesi successfully spearheaded the campaign to obtain a dispensation from Pope Julius II for Prince Henry to marry Katherine of Aragon (widow of Henry's brother Arthur) in 1503, though it was Gigli who delivered the dispensation in England, along with other gifts to Henry VII from the pope. Similarly, Castellesi's later efforts to secure a cardinal's hat for Thomas Wolsey were anticipated behind the scenes by Gigli, who in the end got the credit for this coup, reaping its attendant benefits.[131] In a bid to secure his authority in Rome over matters pertaining to England after Julius' election, Castellesi in 1504 deeded his Roman *palazzo* to the English monarchy in perpetuity for use by "royal ambassadors both temporary and resident," but as he had no intention of vacating the property he hoped "to be indirectly acknowledged as the king's representative in the curia simply by occupying his own palace at the king's sufferance. Henry VII, however, even more adroitly accepted the gift without all the accompanying implications."[132] Castellesi abandoned Rome twice in 1507, first in August and then again definitely in early October because of his fears that Julius had discovered the defamatory content of letters he had written to Henry VII regarding the pope. He did not return for six years, until Giovanni de' Medici was elected to the papacy as Leo X, though then his earlier anxieties would be rekindled, initially in the move by Wolsey and Gigli to strip him of the English collectorship he had held *in absentia* for more than twenty years, and then by being implicated in the 1517 assassination attempt on Leo by a group of younger cardinals disillusioned with the direction his papacy was taking.[133] Fleeing Rome once again when it would have been in his best interests to stay to defend himself, Castellesi was eventually deprived of the collectorship and of the wealthy Diocese of Bath and Wells, the former snapped up by Silvestro dei Gigli and the latter by Wolsey. In spite of this run of very bad luck, some of it clearly self-inflicted, Castellesi is of further interest for this study in that he anticipated in a 1507 work entitled *De vera philosophia ex quattuor doctoribus ecclesiae* (published in Bologna and dedicated to Henry VII) the anti-humanistic, scripturally based nominalism of one branch of the Italian movement toward religious reform, some figures of which would find refuge in later Tudor England.[134] Linked to his theological polemics, Castellesi wrote treatises on rhetoric and grammar (another factor that the Italian Protestants in England would in time share with him), and as a Hebrew scholar he translated the first two books of the Old Testament into Latin.

Pietro Griffi, a Pisan, first visited England in 1506 on a papal mission in part to enlist Henry VII's participation in a planned crusade against the "infidel," but he was recalled to Rome at the end of 1506, leaving behind him papal censures provoked by the king's importation of alum from Turkey, the very region Henry had been asked to assist in recuperating.[135] Returning to England in 1509 just at the liminal moment preceding Henry

VII's death, Griffi had been sent by Julius II to take up the English collectorship in the wake of Castellesi's flight from Rome, but it took several months (and three increasingly insistent papal briefs) to compel Polidoro Virgilio to transfer the office to him. Griffi tried to take his responsibilities "more seriously than other collectors, [but] the duties of the office were probably more depressing than onerous, [for] few people paid their dues and the only sums that came in were procurations."[136] Documentation regarding Griffi's time in England and elsewhere is sparse, and "unlike many of his predecessors and successors he did not hold – beyond that of nuncio and papal collector – any other ecclesiastical office or royal appointment, remaining ever the pope's man, detached from official English society."[137] Griffi spent much of his time in England trying to make some sense of the history of the papal collectorship there in order to provide a useful manual for his successors, and though his research was severely limited by the erratic, often non-existent, record-keeping of his predecessors, he produced the first study of papal taxation in England, *De officio collectoris in regno Angliae*.[138] Concluding his career as Bishop of Forlì, Griffi died just shy of his forty-sixth birthday, and for all the sketchiness of the historical record regarding him, he is buried in an impressive tomb in the Church of Sant'Agostino in Rome.[139]

Just prior to Castellesi's renewed Roman difficulties, he succeeded in having Francesco Chiericati appointed nuncio to England in 1515. A native of Vicenza, Chiericati had studied law in Padua, Bologna, and Siena before benefitting from the patronage of Federico Fregoso, Archbishop of Salerno and one of the interlocutors in Castiglione's *Cortegiano*.[140] Through Fregoso, Chiericati entered the circle of Cardinal Francesco Alidosi (who served, but apparently not very attentively, as cardinal protector of England from 1509 until his murder in 1511),[141] and then attracted the attention of Sigismondo Gonzaga, under whose patronage he joined the ranks of the apostolic notaries before moving on to service as orator and Latin secretary for the Swiss Cardinal Mattheus Schinner in Rome. Schinner was among those cardinals who had favored Leo X's election, and Chiericati's fortunes rose accordingly, as he was named a prelate of the apostolic household in 1514. Later that year, after a serious illness, he joined Castellesi, who employed him in a series of delicate diplomatic maneuvers with the French before advocating Chiericati's promotion to the English nunciature, the scope of which was to secure Henry's cooperation with the pope's revived anti-French politics.

While in England, Chiericati was caught in the battle of wills waged between Castellesi and Wolsey, and he sent a series of letters to Isabella d'Este and other Italian acquaintances that offer a sharply etched image of the English court. Writing to Isabella in July of 1517, Chiericati describes several days of elaborate entertainments staged for the reception of "el Re Catholico" on the occasion of the ratification of a coalition consisting of England, Spain, the Holy Roman Empire, and the papacy, which aimed at restraining Francis I's expansionist designs, the impression here and elsewhere being that Henry and his courtiers were given over almost entirely to pleasure, a factor that for the papal nuncio set the English court apart from those of the other European monarchs he knew and accounts for what he perceived to be the total control of the English political scene by Thomas Wolsey:

> Most Reverend York governs all, and of his own accord; nor does his Royal Majesty bother himself with details, all of which are kept in his Most Reverend Lord's breast, as equally those things pertaining to his own state as the other private matters of the Realm, and accordingly it seems that we deal not with a cardinal but with another king ... his Majesty the King is given to nothing but virtuous pleasures, leaving the weighty matters to [Wolsey], and those who would wish to negotiate must do so with the Most Reverend, who rules with consummate authority, integrity, and prudence; his Majesty the King bears [the Cardinal] so much deference that he does not himself speak but through [Wolsey's] mouth.[142]

Whether Chiericati's sense here of the balance of power was due to his inexperience in England or to Wolsey's powers of dissimulation, he was not alone among contemporary Italian visitors (or among curial officials in Rome) in seeing the cardinal's hand as steering the English ship of state.

Chiericati (along with Polidoro Virgilio) shared his patron's disgrace at the time of the plot against Leo X's life and was recalled to Rome in 1517. But before leaving he was eager to make a pilgrimage to St. Patrick's Well, the site of a reputed portal into Purgatory at Lough Derg in Ireland that had been attracting both ardent pilgrims and skeptical detractors for several hundred years.[143] Chiericati's account of Ireland is not the first by an Italian – Virgilio had written about Ireland and the Irish in the thirteenth chapter of the *Anglica historia*, which circulated in manuscript well before its initial publication in 1534[144] – but it is particularly unenthusiastic, this pilgrimage into the Irish interior depicted as a journey into the heart of darkness. At Armagh, the oldest diocese of the island, Chiericati notes its desolation and that there he and his traveling companions "began to encounter beastly people," and further on – beyond the limits of English sovereignty – "thieves and scoundrels,"[145] who traffic in a sort of pearl whose properties were said to be determined by the black vapors prevalent to the area. Finally arriving at their destination in what is now County Donegal, Chiericati and his companions were ferried to an island in the midst of a large lake, where besides five other pilgrims they found three canons as gate-keepers, a church with three bells dedicated to Saints Patrick, Brigitta, and Columba, and a grotto carved out of the rock in which was situated the deep well said to mark the entrance to Purgatory. The ritual visit required ten days, nine of which were spent by the pilgrims ascetically preparing to be locked naked inside the grotto for a culminating twenty-four-hour period. Scared by what he had seen of the place, however, the nuncio absented himself from these rigors, forgoing the first-hand experience he had traveled so far to witness, but he remained stranded there, aware that he would nevertheless have to share the hardier pilgrims' minimal diet of stale bread and water, as well as the other discomforts associated with exposure to the elements. Chiericati's companions emerged from their ordeal seemingly more dead than alive, each having been tormented by visions that the other pilgrims had not shared and about which they were completely unaware. Once the pilgrimage was concluded, each participant inscribed his name and an account of his experience in a book listing all previous pilgrims, and in which Chiericati found that "the first inscribed was Guarino da Durazzo, whose description of the place I had [earlier] believed to be a myth."[146] The nuncio seems to hedge his bets here, however, by then suggesting that an even older parchment manuscript seen at the site confirms Guarino's account, as if to say, "Well, perhaps ... " For this urbane Italian, the testimony of books was to be taken at least as seriously as that of his eyes (or, rather, those of his traveling companions), and his verdict regarding *il pozzo di san Patrizio* remains equivocal. But, for good measure, Chiericati subsequently paid a visit to the tombs of Ireland's three patron saints, hosted there by an Italian bishop said to be 114 years old. Chiericati's view of the Irish, specifically those living away from the eastern coast and the "civilizing" effect of English occupation, was of a people who lived without law or social distinction, and whose fervid religious life was determined largely by superstition. Though he tells Isabella d'Este that both Ireland and St. Patrick's Well are of "little moment," and that he has written to her about them due to her "peregrine curiosity that desires to understand not only the greatest but also the smallest things,"[147] one is left with the lingering impression that Chiericati is unable to fully square his experience in *Hibernia* with the skeptical expectations he brought with him there.

Silvestro dei Gigli proved to be a persistent thorn in Adriano Castellesi's flesh, and during the pontificate of Julius II he showed himself to be a more adept figure in the curial navigation required of the English monarchy's Roman agents. He secured his influence in England living there from 1505 until 1512, consolidating his relations with Wolsey, the king, and those Italians associated with the English court.[148] Though Silvestro was implicated in the 1514 fatal poisoning of the English Cardinal Bainbridge, resident in Rome since 1509 as Henry VIII's ambassador and another of Silvestro's rivals as *in situ* intermediary for the English king, Henry showed little interest in pursuing the matter, and he was finally acquitted of the crime by Leo X.[149] Though the cloud of scandal which this episode generated never entirely dissipated, Wolsey found Silvestro to be a highly reliable confidential agent in his complex engagement with European politics, until Gigli's obstinate designs on a cardinal's hat for himself led Giulio de' Medici, the pope's cousin and later Clement VII, to turn both Leo and Wolsey against him.[150] At the time of Silvestro's's death in 1521, Cardinal Lorenzo Campeggio pressed Wolsey repeatedly to arrange for his own appointment to the Diocese of Worcester – now all but reserved for an Italian – but the king had other plans and offered the see to de' Medici, who had been functioning since 1514 as England's cardinal protector, a role he would maintain until his own election to the papacy in 1523.[151]

As de' Medici was already Archbishop of both Florence and Narbonne, he apparently had some reservations about assuming yet another prominent episcopal appointment and suggested that Gheronimo Ghinucci, then in London as nuncio, be named to the vacant diocese, with the proviso that he (de' Medici) be paid an appreciable stipend and retain the role of diocesan administrator, an arrangement that was not worked out for almost a year. Though he never visited England, both this prebendary arrangement and his work as cardinal protector casts de' Medici's subsequent papal role in Henry's divorce proceedings in a rather embarrassing light. Ghinucci, who had been one of the curial judges in 1518 when charges were brought against Luther, was sent to England in 1520 by an anxious Leo X to look into the Field of the Cloth of Gold summit meeting that at least temporarily effected friendly relations between Henry VIII and Francis I. Whatever financial gains Ghinucci acquired through Worcester were diminished not only by the money due to Giulio de' Medici, but also by Wolsey's imposition of another stipend to be paid to an Italian friend of his, Gian Matteo Giberti, Bishop of Verona.[152] And Ghinucci was ordered by Wolsey to scour Italian libraries for books and manuscripts that might be acquired for the English chancellor's library. He proved useful in a number of other respects to the English crown, particularly during the early 1530s, in conducting archival research and consulting with both Christian and Jewish theologians regarding Henry's by then increasingly tenuous divorce case.

Andrea della Rena, better known as Ammonio, a Lucchese humanist who had spent the early years of his career working in the papal curia – where he developed important relations with the della Rovere cousins of the deceased Sixtus IV and the ascendant Julius II – probably accompanied Silvestro dei Gigli to England in 1505.[153] Little is known of Ammonio's first years in England, but by 1509 he was in the service of William Blount, Lord Mountjoy; in 1511 he was appointed Henry VIII's Latin secretary; and in 1515 he successfully maneuvered to win the deputy collectorship, having blocked Polidoro Virgilio from regaining the office after Pietro Griffi's departure through a protracted and bitter fight during which Ammonio shared with Henry compromising correspondence between Castellesi and Virgilio highly critical of the king. Ammonio was awarded the full entitlements of collector after Castellesi's second Roman disgrace following the assassination attempt against Leo X, but unhappily for him just prior to his own premature death in 1517. Ammonio formed important friendships with the humanists in Thomas More's circle soon after his arrival in England, and he lodged in More's home until the autumn of 1511, when the widowed future chancellor married Alice Middleton, who was evidently uncomfortable with her husband's humanist acquaintances. Through his English friends, Ammonio was introduced to Erasmus during the latter's English visit of 1505–06, and the two developed an immediate and intensely shared bond; it is largely through their epistolary exchanges that we have a sense of Ammonio's character.[154] He would prove to be a crucial link to the papal curia for Erasmus, providing the Dutchman with papal news and gossip, but more substantively intervening to win papal dispensation from potential canonical difficulties – arising either from his illegitimate birth or from his belonging to a religious order – that the expanding collection of benefices through which Erasmus financed his itinerant career might have provoked; acting as Leo X's proxy, Ammonio performed the ceremony of dispensation in April of 1517 in London, though this proved to be the last time that the two friends would meet, Ammonio dying suddenly of the "sweating sickness" on August 17 of that year.

The poem Ammonio composed in 1509, *Elegia de obitu regis Henrici VII et felici successione Henrici Octavi*, is a fine example of skillfully measured neo-Latinity that sustains "a balance between mourning Henry VII and celebrating his son" and also suggests that despite his association with Erasmus and More, Ammonio managed "to stand outside this esoteric circle of cautionary equivocation."[155] Though not a point of view universally shared in other accession verses written at this time, Ammonio extols the continuity between father and son, seeing in Henry VIII's accession the initiation of a Golden Age whose emblem is "*uterque Rosas*/the Two Roses" that Henry VII had brought together in the Tudor resolution to the Wars of the Roses and with which the poem concludes. In common with much of the neo-Latin literature of the period (though not, as has been noted, with Castiglione's work), Ammonio's poem is highly anachronistic, unproblematically situating the new king not merely in parity with the human and divine actors of classical antiquity – his splendid body, represented as the envy of the gods and their lovers, is meticulously catalogued in more than half of the lines dedicated to him – but arousing the expectation that Henry VIII will exceed them all:

> Astraea returns, revisiting the abandoned places
>   and chasing away the evil arts.
> See how the rivers begin to turn white with milk
>   and how the dewy honey issues forth from the cavities of trees.
> Octavius returning, if by some chance you were unaware,
>   brings to the world a new Golden Age. We shall offer every good wish
> For Henry *Octavius*: that he live the years of Nestor
>   And exceed the accumulation of yours, white-haired Sibyl.
> That he might be greater than Nerva, happier than Augustus himself,
>   and surpass Trajan in both strength and authority.
> May Jupiter see that all his undertakings be accomplished in full,
>   and Phoebus nurture the Two Roses, both White and Red.[156]

There is "an intimation of empire" in these concluding verses that is unique to the poem's elegant but otherwise facile onslaught of classical allusion, an *imperio* that recalls "Augustus who presided over the Golden Age of Latin literature, Nerva ... himself a poet, and Trajan to whom Pliny addressed his *Panegyrics*,"[157] the poet thus foreseeing an era of promising opportunity for humanist *letterati* such as himself in a dawning age of enlightened leadership.

Ammonio's extensive official correspondence tells the subsequent story of his wide-ranging involvement in European affairs of state in the second decade of the sixteenth century. As Henry's Latin secretary, he enjoyed unencumbered access to highly sensitive forms of information transmitted to the king, but unlike Carmeliano, his predecessor in the position, he seems not to have buttered his bread on both sides. "Often the first to read confidential and secret dispatches, the fact that he served as intermediary between representatives of English political life such as Richard Foxe, Wolsey and those on the continent gave [Ammonio] considerable social and political influence."[158] It is a sign of Henry so identifying the "nation" with himself and his business that an Italian granted English denizenship, as Ammonio was in 1514, could function in such a capacity, for where one's primary duty was understood as loyalty to the sovereign, one's "national" origins were, if not quite irrelevant, not *de facto* a hindrance in being privy to the complex and sensitive operations of state (though as we shall see, English popular opinion regarding such "stranger" influence was another matter entirely). Italians in the Elizabethan era were in some respects even more conspicuously engaged in what by then can be considered the construction of the English "nation," but none of them, even those reputedly involved in Walsingham's espionage system, enjoyed the freedoms Ammonio briefly exercised under Henry.

*"Quel re che ha ceduto ad 'omnia vincit amor'."*

## Italian actors in Henry VIII's 'great matter'

Though Cardinal Campeggio's earlier standing in England had been made clear when he was denied the diocese of Worcester, he was to become one of the most critical players in the divorce proceedings, for in tandem with Wolsey, Campeggio was delegated the responsibility of adjudicating *in situ* the annulment of Henry VIII's marriage to Katherine of Aragon.[159] Campeggio's actual role in these momentous events has attracted little careful attention, perhaps due to Wolsey's ubiquitous one-upmanship,[160] but it reveals several noteworthy aspects of this turning-point in English history that would redefine the character of the Italian experience in England. One of the most distinguished papal diplomats of his generation, Campeggio was made a cardinal by Leo X in 1517 and served as nuncio in Germany; highly regarded there, he was named cardinal protector of Germany by the Holy Roman Emperor Maximilian in the same year and later reconfirmed in that office by Charles V. His first experience in England was in 1518, as Leo's envoy to Henry VIII, charged with convincing the English king to join in a pan-European *pax Christiana*, a new crusade to both defeat the Turk and prevent any further Muslim incursions into Christian territory. Never content to allow anyone to upstage him on his own turf, however, Wolsey refused to allow Campeggio passage into the country, forcing him to remain at Calais for three months until the English cardinal managed his own joint appointment as papal envoy. Though the mission came to nothing – Henry was considerably more concerned about his relations with France than with the threat of the distant Turk – Campeggio left England as Bishop of Salisbury and with the keys to the Bramante-designed Palazzo Carneto in Rome, having impressed the king and established a good working relationship with Wolsey. For the next ten years, Campeggio was occupied in shuttle diplomacy connected both to the rise of Charles V and to the spread of Lutheranism in Germany; but in 1528 he was again in England, this time as Clement VII's representative in the examination of Henry VIII's claim against his first wife.

Given that Katherine of Aragon was the aunt of Charles V (to whom, as we have seen, Henry's younger sister Mary had been engaged), Campeggio's close relationship to the emperor and his earlier experience in England with both Henry and Wolsey made him the logical choice to carry out the pope's impossible charge to stall for time in the hope that the English king would change his mind or, short of that, convince Katherine to take monastic vows, hence freeing Henry from the marital contract.[161] Campeggio was, contrary to received opinion about his motivations, acting only on the orders he received from Clement VII. He in fact carried with him to England a decretal commission, drafted most likely by Wolsey but ratified by the pope, that spelled out in equivocating terms a resolution of the crisis in Henry's favor. But on only one occasion did Campeggio allow both Henry and Wolsey to see the papally authorized document, after which it was destroyed.[162] As it is clear that the pope never had any intention of allowing Henry to divorce his wife – Clement's precarious relationship with Charles V was of strategically greater importance to him than was a continuing alliance with England, and the issue of undoing the dispensation granted through Castellesi's earlier intervention by Julius II for Henry to marry Katherine in the first place posed troubling questions about papal authority – it is difficult to understand what purpose such a baiting gesture was meant to accomplish other than to buy time, demonstrating that a conciliatory solution was literally at hand, borne by the pope's representative. At any rate, the trial by a general commission entrusted to Campeggio and Wolsey convened in May of 1529 and set out to examine the validity of the original dispensation of Katherine's marriage to Henry's deceased elder brother Arthur. The trial was an unmitigated disaster for the king, from Archbishop Fisher's pointed account of the legitimacy of Henry's marriage to Katherine, to the queen's unfaltering testimony that her first marriage had never been consummated.[163] Once the emphasis had shifted away from the original dispensation to the issue of consummation, Henry found himself in a completely untenable position, and the trial was abruptly adjourned on July 23 by Campeggio, probably to the Italian cardinal's great relief but perhaps even more so to that of the king and his cardinal-chancellor (and possibly with their consent).

Other Italians were then entrusted on several different fronts with the business of determining a resolution to the situation. Gian Matteo Giberti, one of Clement VII's closest advisors, had visited England in early 1522 and thereafter maintained good relations with both Wolsey and Henry, making gifts to the king of several patristic editions published by his own press.[164] Giberti was approached for assistance with the divorce in December 1527, but as his position in the curia had been considerably weakened after the Sack of Rome, he was on the verge of taking up the episcopal see of Verona where, after relaying mixed signals to England for several years, his press published a tract in support of Katherine's position in late 1531 or early 1532. Pietro Vanni, Ammonio's cousin and his successor as Latin secretary to both the king and to Wolsey, accompanied Sir Francis Bryan in November 1528 on an embassy to appeal directly to Clement VII in order that Henry's marriage might be declared void *ab initio* and to convince the pope to abandon his alliance with Charles V.[165]

They were ordered to use whatever means they could muster to gather curial support for the king's position, and they were charged to discover why Campeggio was getting nowhere with the divorce question as well as with researching the authenticity of the document in Katherine's possession nullifying the original defects in Julius II's dispensation for her marriage to Henry. But in the end they accomplished nothing and returned to England empty-handed. As noted, Gheronimo Ghinucci took up the cause in the early 1530s, after the possibility of direct papal intervention had faded. Italian universities were consulted, and through them a number of Italian jurists and theologians weighed in with their opinions on the divorce.[166]

Henry, of course, ultimately took matters into his own hands, and one of the repercussions of the parliament of 1534 that established his supremacy was that Campeggio was stripped of his appointment to the diocese of Salisbury and Ghinucci of Worcester, though from the Roman perspective Henry had no authority in this area after the schism, and these bishops, in title at least, retained their sees.[167] Thus abruptly ended a rich period in the ecclesiastical and political history of early modern England in which Italians were for the last time as Catholics so deeply involved in matters of national and international consequence. Italians in later Tudor England would in several respects be even more critically engaged in the evolution of the English "nation," but their influence was to be mediated through a wider array of means and refracted through the alternative authorities of Protestantism.

# 2    Reformations

> "What hath God wrought!"
>
> *Numbers* 23:23, *King James Bible*

With Henry's divorce and the creation of an autonomous Church of England, Italian intercourse with England entered into a period of disjointure that would continue, except for a brief revival under Mary, through the end of Elizabeth's reign. It is worthwhile, therefore, pausing for a moment to consider the implications of Henry's actions and the subsequent realignment of England's ecclesiastical polity in terms of Anglo-Italian relations. The history detailed in the previous chapter demonstrates a lively and unencumbered stream of high-profile Italian visitors to England over the course of almost a century, some of whom settled there permanently. Following the royal divorce, the variety of Italians who then came to England shifted (with the exception of those involved in commerce) in accord with England's new political and religious orientation. The status of foreigners under Henry VIII was often precarious, the result of xenophobic motives as potent in the sixteenth century as they are in our own era, but at no time were the "strangers" already in England at more of a disadvantage than after the king had severed ties with the Roman church and effectively isolated foreign-born Catholics in an initially ambiguous religious environment.[1] The situation would have been particularly problematic for Italians in England, given the manifold ways in which we have seen that they were inserted into English political and cultural life. Henry's schism raised serious questions of fealty for all Catholics, but for those who saw in the church some locus of communitarian identity, the English king's actions provoked a crisis of political definition that was as profound for Catholic foreigners in England as it was for many of the English themselves.

*"le male acquistate nozze ..."*
## Italian views of Henry VIII

Apart from the veiled outrage of contemporary diplomatic accounts,[2] it is difficult to assess the reactions of other Italians in England to Henry's divorce. Even in the best of times they left erratic records of their reactions to the pivotal events through which they lived, and given the tenuous and shifting legal status of foreigners during Henry VIII's reign it is hardly surprising that the "stranger" population would be reluctant to leave evidence of their opinions of the English king, upon whose largesse many of them depended. There are, however, several contemporary Italian literary readings of the English monarchy at this critical juncture that can be construed as reflecting a range of sentiments representing perspectives that would conceivably have been shared by many of the resident Italians of the mid-Tudor period.

Matteo Bandello, among the most important voices in the elaboration of the sixteenth-century Italian *novella* and a Dominican priest, registers a sharply negative reaction to the behavior of the English king in his *novella* II.37, written around the time of Henry VIII's death in 1547. The story is set in an earlier period and has as its central concern the consuming lust that develops in Edward III for the wife of one of his most dedicated soldiers, an ensign who languishes in a French prison after having been captured there on one of Edward's military campaigns. Bandello appears to have the recently deceased Henry as much in mind as he does Edward when he writes that:

just as it was natural for the Appians to be the enemies of the Roman *plebs* and for Scipioni to conquer Africa, so it seems to me fitting that the English kings should extinguish their own blood-line, persecuting their nobility, butchering clerics, and stealing church property.[3]

Bandello has Edward going to appalling ends in his pursuit of Aelips – an idealized version of Edward's actual and less-than-chaste mistress Alice Perrers – whose virtue in resisting the king's "mal regolato desiderio" is praised by the story teller but scorned both by Edward's courtiers, who are concerned for their futures, given the unpredictable nature of the king's clouded judgment, and by members of Aelips' own family, who eventually convince her that their continued well-being is endangered by her rectitude. Aelips' father stands alone among Bandello's cast of characters in his initial response to Edward's importuning, and though he inevitably capitulates, urging his daughter to think better of her family and less of her chastity, he tells Edward that the plot involving gifts of money, land, and titles with which the king proposes to ensnare the girl brings uneasily to mind the intrigues Edward's mother, Isabella, had been implicated in at the time of the assassination of his father, Edward II. Aelips, on the verge of suicide if Edward refuses to marry her honorably (her husband, in the meantime, having died shortly after his release from French captivity), tells Edward that in raping her:

> your pleasure can endure only a moment, but your infamy shall be proclaimed for all time and in every civilized place. And not only will you be considered guilty, but each of your descendants shall be stained with your shame.[4]

In the end, the king is impressed with Aelips' willingness to die rather than suffer the indignity he had intended to commit and agrees to make her his wife.

In his rendering of this *novella* in *The Palace of Pleasure* I.46 (1566) – actually a translation from Boaistau's French version of the story – William Painter presents a less objectionable Edward, a gallant if overly zealous *innamorato*, "more polished, more refined, more courtly and, even while his passion is raging, less oblivious to the claims of morality."[5] Bandello's Edward, reflecting the not-so-distant scandals of Elizabeth I's father (and perhaps also raising the question of her legitimacy), could not have been allowed to assume in translation an English guise that would reflect badly on the young queen, and Painter's version of this story is a good example of the ideological uses to which translation was often put in the sixteenth century.[6]

But Bandello's *novella* III.62 could not be so handily manipulated, and this explains why the story, based on material from Paolo Giovio's *Descriptio brittanniae*,[7] never appeared in any contemporary English adaptation. In it Henry VIII is openly castigated for demonstrating the same uncontrolled desire that had brought Edward so low. After beginning to list the consequences suffered by Cardinal Wolsey, Archbishop Fisher, and Thomas More for having opposed the king's divorce plans, Bandello breaks off in exasperation:

> were I to make a catalogue of all that the unbridled will of the king had permitted, I would have to write a new *Iliad*, for he has left neither monk nor friar on the island, murdering an enormous number of them, destroying their monasteries, laying waste to their abbeys, bestowing bishoprics according to his whim and without the authorization of the sovereign pontiff ... the great difficulty being that matters marked by such a wicked and vicious beginning can never end well.[8]

He then proceeds with four pages of gossip parading as evidence about the adulterous adventures of Anne Boleyn after marrying Henry, before concluding the story with more sympathetic sketches of the king's other wives.[9]

A radically different perspective is offered by Pietro Aretino, Henry's one prominent Italian supporter, who in his *Pronosticon* (1534) writes approvingly of the king's decision to divorce Katherine, a gesture of solidarity that earned its author 300 *scudi*, "per signo di cortesia" [as a show of courtesy], later that year from Thomas Cromwell, the English Secretary of State.[10] Encouraged by this success, Aretino dedicated the second collection of his epistolary to the English king in August of 1542, begging Pietro Vanni in an obsequious letter included toward the end of the volume to ensure that the book find its way into the king's hands. The dedication likens Henry to:

an Eagle among all other birds, meriting such honour and glory that I aim now to offer you in this my little labour, aware that God has willed that you be generated not as a mere happenstance of Nature (as are all other Princes), but as the issue of great, even Divine, forethought. Here is a subject (finally!) worthy of receiving the influence of the stars, the admirable effects of which, assembled together in your sacred breast and under your eternal crown, move with the same authority that they exercise there above.[11]

Though there is little in these opening sentiments to distinguish Aretino's plaudits from any other similar book dedication of the period, the suggestion of "divine forethought" might well be read as an allusion to "predestination," a notion essential to several of the emerging reformed theological traditions with which Aretino might have intended to situate Henry.[12] Aretino was close to several of the critical figures in the Italian efforts aimed at an internal reform of the church, and the summer of 1542 brought a succession of devastating blows – the death of Cardinal Gasparo Contarini, among the most powerful and influential of the reformers; the establishment of the Roman Inquisition by Pope Paul III; and the subsequent flight beyond the Alps of Bernardo Ochino and Pietro Vermigli, the two most celebrated reform-minded Italian theologians – which effectively ended this promising episode and paved the way for the Council of Trent, from whose deliberations Protestants and their remaining sympathizers were to be excluded.[13] Aretino then immediately cuts to the chase:

Equal to Heaven in imbuing happiness in others, you exceed it in freeing still others from their miseries; for Heaven countenances evil influences, while you purge iniquity from the wicked will. You have earned the title Deity for your service to religion, and the name Divine for your immortal actions. Instruction in religion – while always revering the divine cult – is your domain, wherein you possess a transparent intelligence, the testimony of goodness, the fullness of the law, and the sign of perfection. Ever faithful and subject to the power of Christ, you alone maintain yourself in truth, not its semblance; thus we must seek neither to imitate (which would be impossible) nor envy (which must be eschewed), but rather admire all those who wield dominion over men.

Virtually piling idolatry atop the theological conundrum of a God who permits evil to exist in the world, Aretino asserts that Henry exceeds this divine shortcoming in not brooking the interference of malign forces in the world under his sovereignty. The audacity of this point is somewhat mitigated by subsequently underscoring the English king's submission to Christ, but then redoubled by referring to his commitment to the truth rather than its simulacrum, an unmistakable indictment of the Roman church with which Henry had broken and which Aretino consistently (though rarely so candidly) skewered throughout his literary career. The remainder of the dedication is devoted to accounting for both the singular configuration of qualities that Aretino is so eager to praise and the difficulty with which they come to be esteemed:

Accordingly, I – who anxiously await the joyous day that you accept me as your servant – say that those acts to which the prestige of your great soul gives birth are so numerous and of such great variety that were there one such greater than another I would have to describe as quite small what I have so far said of you in comparison with what I should then be bound to say. You are so constituted that the repute of your name, the shadow of your Majesty, and the miracle of your prudence alone compel the people to venerate your footsteps, to bow before your feet, and to kiss your right hand – the same member that grasping the sword challenges the madness of the infidel, that moving the pen dispels the depravity of heretics, and that in making oaths reassures the minds of the doubtful. As recompense for such merit, this and every future age is obliged to offer the sweat of its brow, the ink of its presses, its progeny, and its best thinking, perpetuating your fame in the language of a celestial homily impervious to earthly emendation, come what may by way of Fortune or time; for although these greet the illustrious assembly of your unfathomable actions with mute stupidity, the course of your proceedings does not follow any ordinary path. Certainly we see that you move with a kind of justice and mercy that come closer to divine than to human attributes. The pity, gentleness, severity, and courtesy with which you reward, punish, welcome, and pardon vary as much as the conditions of such virtues utilized by others, just as the Christian faith, dignity, generosity, and beauty which make you most handsome, most generous, most worthy, and most Christian are different from the circumstances of others' merits. Such that one must affirm that you do not but incline your brow that it is of such a new, profound, and admirable example that one knows not how to, dares not, indeed cannot express its significance. But because all things that bear novelty and marvel daze us before we can truly appreciate them, you must not, SUPREME ARBITOR OF PEACE, AND OF TEMPORAL AND SPIRITUAL WARS, be angered if the Universe does not dedicate temples or consecrate altars to you, as befitting one of the sublime Divinites; for the infinite number of your immense concerns keeps the Cosmos addled, not otherwise than we would be confounded were Nature to wrench the Sun from its proper setting and place it within close reach of our eyes.

Aretino plays with a series of increasingly over-the-top figures here that flirt with irony but which are, in fact, carefully calibrated rhetorical elements deployed with serious purpose. Regarding the metaphor of the king's formidable right hand, for instance, Henry, in fact, forswore participation in any crusade against Islam; he subverted the theological works that had earlier earned him the admiration of Leo X, Erasmus, and others; and by the time Aretino published the second volume of his *Lettere*, the English king had only one month before married Katherine Parr, taking the last of his six matrimonial oaths. Henry's actions could well be construed, consequently, as *incomprensibili*, a term which I have rendered in the positive sense that Aretino surely intends primarily as "unfathomable," but which can also be read negatively as "incomprehensible," a *double-entendre* that Aretino more than likely also meant to suggest to the attentive reader. Perfectly in accord with the strategy of extremity that he employs in his imaginative works in order to expose the limits of the highly artificial worlds of both Renaissance court and church, Aretino's dedicatory epistle to Henry VIII reflects in its complex syntax the fantastic claims he makes about (and for the delectation of) its subject. Aretino's Henry is a corollary to the seasoned prostitutes of his *Ragionamenti* who hoist elite Renaissance culture on its own petard, a pariah whose apparent incongruities are, in fact, the key to his animating genius. The web that Aretino weaves here is meant to be a seduction into a new kind of understanding – certainly one, regarding Henry, unheard of in Italy at the time – that he says will frankly take time to be assimilated, its stunning novelty akin to an otherwise unimaginable reordering of the physical world (and in this final outlandish analogy a hint of the sea change occurring through the "new world" already then under exploration, anticipating as well the provocation of those "new worlds" soon to be posited by early modern science). This dedication thus reads as one of Aretino's more daring exercises in challenging the authority of the Roman church, and by so deliberately endorsing the most prominent heretical monarch of the moment he risked more than contamination by association, a factor that perhaps served as one part of the rationale that relegated his collected works to the Catholic Index of Forbidden Books in 1559, just a few years after his death.[14] Henry, however, appreciated this token of approbation from Italy's most celebrated living literary figure – "il Flagello dei Principi" in Ariosto's celebrated formulation, or "the whip of Princes" as John Florio has it in *Second Frutes*[15] – and made him another gift of 300 *scudi*,[16] a sum that Aretino nevertheless experienced some difficulty in actually collecting.[17]

An amalgam of Italian attitudes toward Henry VIII is found in William Thomas' pamphlet dedicated to Aretino, *The Pilgrim, A Dialogue on the Life and Actions of King Henry the Eighth*, which circulated (in English) in manuscript but was not published until the nineteenth century.[18] By the time that this book was printed in Italian in 1552,[19] Thomas had already been back in England for several years, having lived in Italy from 1545 to 1549, fleeing there after embezzling money from his employer, Sir Anthony Browne. This *libretto* is the purported record of a meeting in Bologna at which Thomas fielded queries about the recently deceased English king from Italian interlocutors:

> Constrained by misfortune to abandon the place of my nativity, and to walk at the random of the wide world; in the month of February, and after the Church of England the year of our Lord 1546, it happened me to arrive in the city of Bonony in the region of Italy; where, in the company of certain gentlemen, known to be an Englishman, I was earnestly apposed of the nature, quality, and customs of my country, and especially of divers particular things touching the estate of our King's Majesty Henry the 8th, who then nearly was departed out of this present life.[20]

Given Thomas' earlier disgrace, his orthodox-Tudor defence of Henry's behavior must have been pitched as a gesture of contrition to attract Edward VI's patronal attention. This it certainly achieved, for as soon as Browne was dead and buried, Thomas promptly returned to England and speedily rose to prominence as a clerk of Edward's Privy Chamber – playing a significant role as political tutor to the king – and also publishing after his return a *Historie of Italie* (culled largely from Guicciardini) as well as the first published Italian–English vocabulary.[21] The chief interest of *The Pilgrim* for this study is that it is the only account, factual or otherwise, of an Englishman close enough to Henry VIII to have witnessed some of the events he discusses, defending the king in Italian to an Italian audience situated in Italy, and at some risk to himself, given that Bologna was in papal territory and that many of the things Thomas has himself saying there would have been grounds for imprisonment or expulsion.[22]

The Italians offer fourteen points of contention, astonished that Thomas is prepared to defend the reputation of "the greatest tyrant that ever was in England."[23] He responds to each accusation in kind, dwelling on the most serious charges at some length. On the rationale for Henry's divorce, Thomas resorts to the Levitical injunction against marrying a sibling's spouse that had preoccupied the ecclesiastical tribunal over which Campeggio and Wolsey presided, but he elides the actual proceedings of the trial and says that Henry, appalled at the Italian cardinal's immorality, threw him out the country, proceeding almost immediately to divorce Katherine, wed Anne, and establish the autonomy of the English church. This hasty chronology and the allegation of Campeggio's contemptible behaviour are unique to Thomas' account, but while there is nothing particularly novel about Thomas' approach to the issues he addresses, I cannot agree with Sergio Rossi that "the book is of scant importance as a historical document,"[24] for its Italian version makes it among the very earliest instances of a text composed by an Englishman to appear in a continental vernacular, foreshadowing the important relationship that would develop between Italian and English in the latter half of the sixteenth century. That Italian can be employed in Henry VIII's defence by an English author – either in its Italian version or in the Italian the reader is to imagine Thomas speaking in the English text – is clear evidence of its signifying capacity in the service of Tudor ideology, a decisive shift from the similarly sighted Latin tributes of Italian humanists examined in the previous chapter.

"... *quanto danno apporti alli stati la Fanciulezza de' Principi* ..."

### Edward VI through one Italian's eyes

In his *Scisma d'Inghilterra*, an account of contemporary English history published in Rome in 1602, Bernardo Davanzati mistakenly situates three epochal deaths within two months of one another in 1546: Martin Luther on February 18, Francis I on March 31, and Henry VIII having preceded them on January 28. But as the French and English kings actually died in the following year, Davanzati's attempt to signal an instance of divine intervention ending an era of perilous trouble for Catholic Italy turns out to be not quite so providential as suggested. By way of eulogy, he has this to say of Henry:

A lover of letters, he favored scholars. He adored the sacrament of the altar and received it in only one species. He would have [remained] a Catholic had he not been libidinous and prodigal. Every beautiful woman whom he met he desired. He had a fine mind, serious judgment, and was frequently drunk ... due to his noxious appetite, from a most handsome youth he became a fat and disgusting man, such that he could no longer enter through doors or climb stairs ... he reigned 37 years, 9 months, and 6 days: 21 [years] as a Catholic, 5 ambiguously, the rest schismatically.[25]

Davanzati was the scion of a patrician Florentine family, a founding member of the Accademia della Crusca, and an estimable translator of Tacitus (a volume among the books listed in the library prefacing Florio's *Queen Anna's New World of Words*); but with no personal experience of (or evident links to) England, he seems a strange candidate to have written such a book.[26] The *Scisma* is, in fact, an abbreviated version of Girolamo Pollini's *Historia ecclesiastica della rivoluzion d'Inghilterra*, printed first in Bologna in 1591 but then reissued in a much-expanded second edition by Davanzati's Roman publisher, Faccioti, in 1594, this latter a quarto volume running to almost 800 pages and itself derived from *De origine ac progressu schismatis anglicani* by the English recusant priest Nicholas Sanders which was completed after his death in 1581 by a fellow recusant cleric, Edward Rishton, and published in Cologne in 1585. Pollini's

*Historia* provoked Elizabeth's fury for its scandalous presentation of both her mother and father, and it was possibly as a response to the English reception of Pollini's volume that Davanzati compiled his much shorter and slightly more sober volume, concluding with the Marian period "so as not to enter into the things of the present queen."[27]

An intermittently more reliable measure of English events following the death of Henry VIII through the middle years of the Elizabethan period is to be found in the successive redactions of Petruccio Ubaldini's *Relazione d'Inghilterra*, the first full version of which dates from 1552 and was likely written for the Venetian Senate, providing the most extensive *in situ* Italian account of the reign of Edward VI. Apparently the illegitimate son of a prominent Florentine father, Ubaldini spent two initial periods in England fighting as a mercenary soldier first for Henry VIII between 1545 and 1547, and then again seeing service in Edward VI's Scottish war in 1549, remaining in England until 1552, when he returned to Italy. A sumptuous copy of the *Cebetis thebani tabula* prepared for Grand Duke Cosimo I's sons, also from 1552, is the last sign of Ubaldini until 1563, when he settled definitively in England just as Elizabeth was consolidating her power. Following upon his early career as a soldier, Ubaldini was "a courtier, a talented miniaturist, in his spare time a poet, a memorialist, and possibly also a spy."[28] He published a number of books of his own dealing with a wide range of topics, as well as serving as an editor for the Italian books that John Wolfe's press issued in the 1580s, and though "he was clearly a man with a fluent pen, he wrote on too many [different] things to excel in any one of them."[29] The *Relazione d'Inghilterra* is the most important of all Ubaldini's original work, but it remained unpublished during his lifetime, its frequently critical tone – particularly evident in the first redaction – doubtless explaining why.[30]

The 1552 *Relazione* differs little in its form from typical Venetian ambassadorial accounts, and it is likely that Ubaldini had seen a version of the report that Daniele Barbaro made to the Venetian Senate upon the conclusion of his 1548–50 mission to England.[31] But given that Ubaldini's initial experience of Britain was as a mercenary soldier, the perspective he brings to his reporting is as different from that of a learned, aristocratic diplomat as is the unpolished language that he employs. Ubaldini's Italian at this stage in his career indeed often makes for difficult reading: despite his expertise as a copyist, it is unlikely that he had enjoyed a typical humanistic education, there being little trace in any of his work of a wider linguistic or literary culture. Later redactions of the *Relazione* reflect a more courtly flair, but the relatively unstudied point of view of the 1552 version, despite its frequent syntactical and rhetorical leaps, has much to recommend it.

The *Relazione* opens with a survey of British geography,[32] showing a closer first-hand knowledge of the subject than does Trevisan's report from half a century before. Ubaldini provides summaries of the reigns of Henry VII [69–72] and Henry VIII [72–76], devoting most of his attention regarding the latter to the divorce and its repercussions. The largest section of the *Relazione* is dedicated to Edward VI [76–100], and after establishing his priority in the line of succession following Henry VIII's death [76–77], Ubaldini turns to the effect of a group of regents ruling England in the king's minority, suggesting that by describing their intrigues readers will perceive "how damaging to states are the childhoods of Princes."[33]

The *consiglieri* are faulted first with so poorly managing Edward's 1549 war with the French, abetted by Scottish troops (fresh from their victory over the English and against whom Ubaldini had fought), that they have lost strategic territories won and fortified by the earlier Tudor monarchs, making concessions "unworthy of the glory of England's previous kings" [78]. The brunt of Ubaldini's critique of the regents is directed at Edward Seymour (who, as brother of Jane Seymour, was the king's uncle), Duke of Somerset and Protector of the Realm; and at John Dudley, Earl of Warwick, and later Duke of Northumberland. As a group, the regents are criticized for having assumed the prerogatives of religious reform through imposing the use of the English vernacular in church ceremony, and by inviting both natives and foreigners to contribute to the various channels through which the Protestant faith is represented as fast overwhelming the country [78].

Edward's regents are seen as so determined to impose their will in the religious arena aided by anyone who will assist them – particularly those "molti da altri Nationi" [many from other Nations, 78] – that they exercise no sense of proportion, compelling foreigner and citizen alike to conform to their new legislation, barely recognizing the rights of foreign ambassadors, and depriving clerics of their livelihoods. Ubaldini here draws attention to one of the distinguishing features of the Edwardian period: the involvement of "stranger" authorities in the elaboration of England's newly vernacular religious politics. He tends to muddle the picture considerably, however, in collapsing together distinct policies and actions, and his univocal impression of the Protector accords little with the image Diarmaid MacCullough has drawn of Seymour as an aggressively earnest evangelical populist, the English people often being made in the *Relazione* to represent negative views of him that MacCulloch ascribes to the other members of the Privy Council. Ubaldini's "people," for instance, see the Protector as:

the cause of each successive disorder: frequently defending himself with the hand of the King in full sight of the people, while in the King's presence obliging him to sign those things that [would] ordinarily be signed by Kings [of their own volition], even if in their minority; and for such motives [the people] proclaimed him a traitor to the Crown.[34]

But in MacCulloch's account of the letters Seymour wrote (or had written) in the summer of 1549 with regard to popular demonstrations in Hampshire, the Protector clearly comes across as the champion of the very people Ubaldini has him so single-mindedly imperious toward.[35]

Seymour did indeed arrogate to himself responsibilities the boy-king could little have dealt with alone, but in the end the Protector was himself poorly equipped for the role that he assumed, for he showed himself to be "personally ambitious and rather haughty in manner ... liberal in ideas and generous in practice ... an excellent general in the field, he proved visionary, short-sighted, and incompetent in politics."[36] Ubaldini's discussion of Seymour's return to the Privy Council after being arrested and incarcerated in October 1549 notes that his rehabilitation was a move opposed by "several of better judgment, who saw in [it] the foreshadowing of future disorder."[37] Here Ubaldini begins to reveal the partiality that he brings to his account, for the original accusations that landed the Protector in the Tower of London in the first place were widely believed at the time to have been leveled by the Catholic minority among the regents along predictable ideological lines,[38] and the *Relazione*'s effort to show that Seymour's fate was determined entirely by pecuniary motives aims to deflect attention from the religious issues driving the agenda through depicting both the accused and his liberator as more concerned with their own prosperity than that of the nation they were meant to be safeguarding.[39] Because Dudley had earlier shown himself to be Seymour's chief opponent among the regents, Ubaldini suggests – and perhaps not entirely without reason – that the only motive for Dudley to have intervened on Seymour's behalf was to take advantage of his relative poverty, forcing upon him a marriage that he would never in other circumstances have consented to:

so that following upon his liberty came the marriage of his eldest daughter with [Dudley's] first-born Son, which girl the Duke would never before have thus wished married, having earlier disdained the ignobility of this Earl; the Duchess of Somerset paying, in addition to all this, a great sum of ill-gotten money to the Earl, almost as a bounty premium.[40]

Neutralized by this series of misfortunes, Seymour survived two further years in which Dudley used him to advance his own program of reform. But in the end, after he was of no further utility (and, to be sure, after plotting against Dudley), Seymour was imprisoned again, this time on trumped-up charges of treason, though in the end he was convicted of a felony – attempting to incite a riot – and was executed in January 1552.[41]

Ubaldini ignores the spurious nature of the indictments, instead seeing in Seymour's fate a just reward:

> he paid with his life the penalty of the broken Religion, the badly administered Realm, and the death of his brother, Mr. Seymour, shortly before (perhaps wrongly) condemned.[42]

Ubaldini's distorting animus toward Seymour is conspicuous in this instance, for Thomas Seymour's attempted insurrection – he had married Henry VIII's widow Katherine Parr, and then after her death set his sights on Princess Elizabeth, with the intention of then leading a full-fledged rebellion in order to seize control of the government – was patently a treasonable act. Dudley was ultimately successful in arguing that Edward Seymour's numerous deficiencies added up in their sum total and effect to treason, but in leaving open the question of Thomas' innocence (whose execution, which actually occurred before Edward's first incarceration, did indeed weaken his brother's position), Ubaldini aims to paint the former Protector into a corner reserved for him alone.

Dudley succeeded in eliminating his principal rival and in the meantime also managed to remove the remaining Catholics involved with the regency, part of a broader strategy that saw the arrest of prominent Catholics and the forfeiture of their titles and property, which Ubaldini notes with bitter reproach [79–80]. William Fitzalan, Earl of Arundel, was the most powerful of the Catholic nobles in this difficult period, and though he fell foul of Dudley's designs after Seymour's execution, he was rehabilitated by the king (and eventually, after Edward's death, served Dudley his own arrest warrant for his role in enthroning Jane Grey), and he was Ubaldini's most important English patron both at this time and after the Florentine's return to England in the early Elizabethan era. It has been widely assumed that Ubaldini's presence in England at this time along with several other prominent Italian Protestants situates his sympathies with the reformers,[43] but given the manner in which he portrays the political consequences of the Anglican reform, the fact that he was still at this early point in his career seeking a permanent *sistemazione* in Italy (possibly with Patriarch Barbaro's assistance), and the fact of Arundel's patronage, there can be little doubt that the 1552 *Relazione* is the work of a Catholic partisan.

Momentarily leaving aside the English political situation, Ubaldini shifts registers in order to discuss the layout of the numerous residences occupied by the English monarch, though much of the information that he reports could only have been gleaned through a well-placed informant. The *Relazione* makes a distinction between the large public rooms and spaces accessible to anyone with business at court [80–81] and a series of smaller, "secret" rooms forming the king's household, to which no one is admitted (including, of course, Ubaldini himself) if he:

is not a gentleman of the Chamber, from which grade many great Lords are excluded. [In the first], the King normally eats; the second is contiguous with this, which the King uses for discussion, and to eat in secret, that is, within sight of very few of his Ministers; the third is used to dress and undress the King, here being another Canopy, as I had mentioned in the public Presence Chamber, together with similar ornaments. In the fourth, lacking the Canopy, is placed a bed for the King, richly decorated; and joined to these rooms are the study, the secret Chapel, and several other rooms, with the Gallery ..."[44]

which opens out onto the public chapel, and from which the king can be observed when assisting at services from his suite.

Following an enumeration and description of the ranks of English courtiers [82–89], and a concise history of the Order of the Garter [90–91], Ubaldini provides a glimpse of the king's day. An early riser, Edward is assisted by four of his Gentlemen of the Chamber, on their knees, as he dresses [93]; they then exercise together in ball games, dancing, riding, bow-shooting, and other sports. Breakfast, eaten alone by the king, is followed by morning prayer, and then two hours of either Greek or Latin with one of his tutors. Meetings with the king's councillors fill the remaining time before lunch [94]. The protocols of the private royal lunch, again eaten alone, are described in precise detail, the king ordinarily consuming twelve courses – each said to be modest – both at mid-day and at dinner [94–96]. Further consultation with the councillors follows, and if there is time afterward, a lute lesson. An hour of French, a language in which Edward "speaks and writes anything that he wishes,"[45] is then followed by another lesson in Latin or Greek. Dinner is preceded by further physical exercise and followed by entertainments, after which the morning's dressing ritual is repeated in reverse and the king retires to bed, one of his gentlemen sleeping in the adjoining dressing room [96]. Apart from the political meetings and fussy formalities, the emphasis on sport and study reminds us that the king was only a teenager (aged fifteen at the time of Ubaldini's report), and that these were the equivalent of his early high school years; the heavy emphasis on languages – five hours a day and including a contemporary vernacular – is another indication of the increasingly logocentric orientation of Tudor cultural politics, a point not lost on Girolamo Pollini, who sees in Edward's language study an inculcation in the grammar of heresy.[46]

For all of his close attention to the minutiæ of the English court, Ubaldini does occasionally disclose some exasperation with its excesses.

Concluding a discussion of the public royal meal, staged in the Presence Chamber, he notes that there is:

> even more ceremonial when one of his two sisters goes to eat with the King ... it is not permitted that they be under the Canopy, nor seated on a Throne, but only on a simple footstool with a cushion; not, to be sure, at the head of the table, but exactly as far from the King as necessary for the Canopy not to be overhead, nor any [of their limbs] inside [it] ... the rituals which they overdo before sitting down at table are almost ridiculous ... I have seen Madame Elizabeth genuflect fives times before sitting, just as they [the sisters] do again when they speak to the King.[47]

Unsurprisingly, this embarrassing and servile image of Elizabeth as well as several other not entirely flattering references to her and to her parentage are omitted from later versions of the *Relazione* rewritten after her accession.

Determined to separate Edward's character from the designs of his regents, in a crucial passage of his report Ubaldini writes that:

> in the King's coming and going from the [ecclesiastical] Offices, or his amusements, it is possible to make petitions to him, and also at times even for him to speak with us; but neither the one thing nor the other is willingly suffered by those who govern him (a plain sign of their wicked behaviour).[48]

Keeping the king from his people – and hence from the actual, unmediated problems of his kingdom – is the central issue in Ubaldini's critique of the *consiglieri*, but the *Relazione* goes on to try to establish that Edward was not so entirely a dupe of his regents as might be supposed, nor his rapport with the people entirely ingenuous. Among the preachers whom the king heard regularly was one who proposed to him the following stratagem: to sit in the gallery opening from his rooms onto the public chapel, from where he could both hear the service and be seen from below by those in attendance. Edward was to have with him a book in which to:

> note something of what seems ... to be said by the Preachers; and because at certain times he has been seen to be writing, recording either facts or rebukes made by them, but not wishing that the people see what he had written, he has given them occasion to hope well of him, to bear him love ... principally because he has begun to settle many things, aiming that all the [attendant] graces be recognized by his living word, and not by particular favours.[49]

In this, one of Ubaldini's more baffling vignettes, what he appears to be arguing is that the king's act of taking notes, writing publically – rendering political a practice normally reserved for the study and consultation that takes place in the palace's "secret" rooms – is meant to be interpreted by his people as a gesture of solidarity in apparently questioning the conclusions of preachers authorized by the regents, a display similar to the king's stopping to interact with his people (and like it, certainly displeasing to his governors, who are made to seem as nervous about what the king might have written in his *libretto* as the people are to be reassured). The entirely staged nature of the gambit, producing such a positive effect in its popular viewers, is linked, however, to the reliability of the king's "living word," for whatever good might issue from this subterfuge, the trustworthiness of the royal word *revealed* is taken here to be vital to the political health of the community.

Along similar lines meant to further differentiate Edward from his advisors, Ubaldini describes three exempla of the young king's political virtue [99]. Each of these anecdotes is intended to reveal an aspect of the king's wisdom, but the third of them rather backfires:

Being another time in a boat, and speaking in the presence of the entire Court with his Falconers, he wished to see a falcon, praised as the very best; and having it, he commanded that it be completely skinned alive, to the great astonishment, however, of all. The Falconer skinned [the bird] and showed it to [the king], who spoke thus: "This falcon, so much more excellent than the others, has been stripped [of its skin], just as I, the first among all others of the Realm, am skinned."[50]

While the incident is apparently meant to be read as illustrating the king's keen sense of his vulnerable political position, it even more palpably shows the streak of cruelty and arrogance that some historians have noted among Edward's unfortunate characteristics,[51] undercutting whatever positive impression might have been intended by the first two examples: one imagines an awkward, even disgusted, silence following the gruesome spectacle of the falcon skinned alive by his trainer to prove a point during a boating party. Nowhere in the *Relazione* does Ubaldini suggest that the difficulties of the Edwardian period lie anywhere other than in the regents having steered England along a truly perilous course in these years, but the agency with which the *Relazione* aims to empower the king never fully convinces, constrained as Edward always is in Ubaldini's eyes by his tender age.[52]

Conversely, the *Relazione*'s close account of the transformation of English religion in this period [125–136] is noteworthy, given the hostility Ubaldini demonstrates in his report regarding Anglican innovations.[53] His careful attention to the specifics of the *Book of Common Prayer* and the *Ordinal* would have proven especially helpful to an Italian audience trying to grasp precisely what the changes wrought in the English church meant in practical terms.

Foregrounding this discussion, Ubaldini revisits the issue of Henry's divorce and second marriage, seeing in them:

the planting of that Tree which so many evils has generated, and not only in that moment over the Religious monasteries but later even more impiously strewn over the heads of all.[54]

Anne Boleyn becomes in this reading a second Eve, and England's subsequent break with the Roman church a reiteration of Original Sin, an extreme but functional analogy, given the biblical parameters of the Anglican reform Ubaldini goes on to describe, directed in all of its particulars by Thomas Cranmer:

> the Archbishop of Canterbury, first in the Realm among Prelates; designated Primate, he vests accordingly; he examines the Preachers, the Doctors of Public studies, priests, and all those who are occupied with speaking in the interest of the Faith, referring all matters to the Royal Council, where they are then deliberated. This is a learned man, much admired among the English in sacred letters, but profanely, for writing and speaking as much as he does he foments their worst [tendencies].[55]

Here we see two distinctive features of the new English faith: its symbiotic relationship to the state, and its propagation through "profane" learning – intended here primarily as "converted from an holie to a base use,"[56] but also anticipating the "vernacular" sense of the term – which makes of religious discourse the menacing preserve of any nominally literate person. The Archbishop of Canterbury's role, always central, is now heightened, given the absence of papal authority, his responsibility being to ensure the uniformity of Anglican belief and practice – that all follow "the same doctrine"[57] – in a clamorous period of transition.

Unlike continental Protestant bodies, the Anglican church sought to retain both the hierarchical structure and liturgical forms it inherited from Rome, but divested of historical accretions unjustified by biblical or patristic precedent. In describing this process, Ubaldini follows the first version of the *Book of Common Prayer*, published in 1549 after being ratified by parliament, the markedly more Protestant tone and drift of the 1552 revision being largely absent from his account (though some of the practices and ideas that inform the later prayer book were already in circulation before its publication and are reported as if belonging to the rubrics of the earlier edition).

Language is the first issue that Ubaldini addresses, for:

> it being obligatory to observe these rules in their native language only in those places where the English language is understood and spoken, Wales and the other islands subjugated to the Realm are not obliged to [follow] the same laws, [but rather] in Latin or in their own languages; [to those] being at Cambridge or Oxford ... only is conceded the right, except during the Sunday supper [of the Lord], to pray in Latin, Greek, or Hebrew, in order to exercise the students in diverse languages.[58]

The pared-down Roman liturgical offices (originally seven separate periods of prayer spaced throughout the day) that form the heart of the new Anglican liturgy in morning and evening prayer [127] are described by emphasizing their elimination of extra-biblical accretions in:

leaving aside the Responses [and] Antiphons, [together] with all those things that in the old Ceremonies were not [to be found] in the Bible.[59]

The entire Bible had been published in Miles Coverdale's English translation in 1535, but it must have been a striking novelty for the still largely illiterate population to hear for the first time in their own language in the 1549 liturgy the wild assortment of narrative, prophecy, proverbs, poetry, and epistolary that constitute the books of the Bible, material that would earlier have been selectively available to them only through paraphrase or artistic representation.[60]

Cranmer endeavoured with this first prayer book to "persuade Catholics to accept it,"[61] and many of the changes it authorizes, apart from the wholesale adoption of English, could have been interpreted to suit a Catholic theological perspective. Several rubrics that Ubaldini notes, however, would not have sat well with Catholics. While most of the principal Catholic feasts days were still to be observed, and the Athanasian Creed had been retained, on Wednesdays and Fridays, when:

the litanies are read, prayers to the Saints are omitted, invoking none other than God the Father, Son, and Holy Spirit, the Blessed and glorious Trinity, following them in the rest as should be done, but adding these words: "from the tyranny and schemes of the Bishop of Rome, deliver us O Lord."[62]

There is no mention of the Feast of Corpus Christi, judged to be idolatrous by Anglican iconoclasm for its reverence of the consecrated eucharistic host, and this tendency is also evident in the new rite for Ash Wednesday, the first day of Lent, for:

instead of Ashes [used by the priest to sign a cross on the forehead], used for public penitence, at a certain point several imprecations from *Deuteronomy* 27 and other books are recited, cursing those who would make statues or simulacra fashioned by an artificer's hand in order to be worshipped.[63]

Thus one of the more palpably physical gestures of the liturgical year comes to be replaced with words that disparage the material representation of faith, a disjuncture demonstrative of the Edwardian valorization of language over image and pointing to the problematic rapport that Anglican theology has often subsequently demonstrated with regard to the sacramental.

Ubaldini provides a survey of the Anglican sacraments, noting that the mass is now called the "Lord's Supper," and that one is allowed to receive communion only once:

the Priest knows in the morning hours the life of whoever intends to communicate; and if it be the case that such a one might scandalize his neighbor, the

Priest shall warn him that he must not take Communion unless he has demonstrated his penitence, amended his life, and satisfied his neighbor; whereby the Priest, should he learn of any fiction [in this regard], can proceed according to several directives.[64]

The accent here on individual accountability could not have been particularly encouraging to a Catholic in the environment that Ubaldini previously describes in his *Relazione*, and the degree of vigilance required of priests needing to ferret out both sinners and wrongful-accusers was certainly not practiced with equanimity.

Ubaldini observes that the rite of baptism is more or less equivalent to its Catholic form, except that the oil used to anoint the baptized is not consecrated, and likewise the oil used for the rites of confirmation and the anointing of the dying [129–130]. There is a detailed description of the "Lord's Supper" [130–133], its principal irregularities being that communion is made by partaking of both the eucharistic bread and wine, and that these elements are not to be reserved but entirely consumed within the course of the ceremony in which they are consecrated; but:

kneeling, making the sign of the Cross with the arms, raising the hands, and beating the breast, are left to the discretion and conscience of who wishes more or less to use them, without admonition or obligation.[65]

Regarding the ordination of Anglican ministers, the rubrics for which are given in the 1550 *Ordinal*, the only unusual practice that Ubaldini singles out is the number of bishops involved for each grade: for the ordination of a deacon, one bishop alone suffices; for a priest, two are necessary; and for a bishop, three, of whom one must be the Archbishop of Canterbury [135–136].

Two economic issues are addressed toward the end of Ubaldini's discussion of the changes in English religious practice. The first concerns the Catholic obligation to eat fish on Fridays, during the four major seasons of the church year, and on certain other feast days:

there being an abundance of fish, and many poor fishermen, meat is saved [for other days], and these [fishermen] can thus live from the earnings of their fishing; wishing, [on the one hand], to displace this abstinence from meat to other days and times, [on the other hand] taken as Papal decrees, the which are detested, they yet wish to rid themselves [entirely] of this bizarre [practice].[66]

One of the distinguishing marks of continental Protestants in the early years of the Reformation was the rejection of Catholic dietary rules, such that eating meat on days designated for fish came to be considered a conspicuous sign of adherence to reformed religion. One dilemma for the Anglican reform was the economic reality of an alimentary culture highly dependent on fish and in which meat was less abundant and more expensive, and the pragmatic solution described here is typical of other compromises the English reformers were constrained to make in order to maintain social order and advance the cause of Anglican independence.

The obligation that one member of each household within a parish receive communion at least each Sunday also had an economic rationale, for the priests Ubaldini had earlier in the *Relazione* described as reduced to penury receive from each communicant:

8 *quattrini*, a part of the income of the priest consigned to him by the Royal Council, which no one fails to pay; [but] because this is not sufficient for [his] salary, much more is given, [money provided by] the Crown, so that he might live, given that the true revenues of the Churches have been confiscated, and alms are [no longer] given for the offices; they come to have no additional [fees] than those received for the dead, which consist of some candles, and a little money for the burial.[67]

From their privileged position in the early Tudor period, clerics in Edwardian England had for all intents and purposes become beggars, dependent upon the charity of their parishioners (and for this reason, not always scrupulous about who would be admitted to the "Lord's Supper") and the altruism of the king. And though marriage may have been held out to the clergy as one of the positive outcomes of the Anglican reform, those who did wed would:

come to regret it, finding themselves with their own and others' children in poverty, and without any quarter from where they might have assistance from others ... [and further] they are only able to have base and poor women, even if similar relations are abhorred in others; whence it follows that any [priest] is praised who does not take [a wife], although for [those] used to [spreading] wicked thoughts, it [might] seem that one can think little good regarding the chastity of these [bachelors].[68]

A more degrading picture of the English clergyman is hard to imagine, finally free to marry but without the material resources to do so with any degree of dignity, and those remaining unmarried suspected of sexual license. This final gratuitous dig aside, the issue of the revenue lost with the seizure of the ecclesiastical properties would continue to be of concern not only to the Protestant reformers in England, but also to Queen Mary and Reginald Pole (as well as to Philip II and Pope Paul IV) in their struggle to re-establish England's Catholic obedience after the death of Edward VI. For Protestants and Catholics alike, a reasonably satisfied clerical class was critical to their competing prospects of religious reform and political stability.

Equal to the debased state of the clergy, for Ubaldini, is the stark appearance of English churches, where there:

are no images in relief, nor pictures, no crosses, no sepulchers raised above the ground ... in place of the altar is a table set with a cloth, but without candles ... and because the walls of the churches, as I have said, are without pictures of saints, on their white [surfaces] are placed many written passages from both the Old and New Testaments, torn [out of context] to suit their purposes, in the middle of which one sees the arms of the King.[69]

Again we witness the emphatic opposition of image to word, though here their contraposition is taken a step further in that the sacred language of the Bible is literally made to supersede images which are henceforth meant to be considered in and of themselves idolatrous; and by inserting the royal arms into the midst of these "word-pictures," the identification of the purified church with a reforming monarchy is meant to be seen as complete. But the malleable form of the word would prove to be a less susceptible target of control than had the statues and paintings that once filled English churches, to a great extent because the English language was at this stage in its development still something of an untamed beast, given to permutations (such as the influx of foreign words) that both destabilized and over-determined the precise meaning of words, and also because the compass of the vernacular was beginning to extend in so many different directions as to render it indomitable.

Petruccio Ubaldini left England in 1552 discouraged by many aspects of his experience there. The encomium to the young English king he included in the manuscript of the *Cebetis thebanae* submitted in his bid for patronage after returning to Italy was meant to demonstrate to Cosimo de' Medici its author's international credentials. But Ubaldini hedges his bets in the verses he included in this elaborately decorated text for Henry Fitzalan, the Earl of Arundel, and for Edward VI, evidently aiming not to burn his English bridges should hope of Italian employment not materialize. The lines addressed to Arundel demonstrate Ubaldini's ties to the English Catholic aristocracy, while those dedicated to the king reinforce the optimistic view of him offered in the *Relazione*.[70] The graphic extravagance of this manuscript suggests, however, that it is to some extent a reaction to the impoverishment of English visual culture subdued under the newly Protestant polity over which the English king presided so precariously.

> "... una certa satietà delle cose Catholiche ..."

### The Italian 'reformation' in England

In the preface to the second of two pamphlets addressed to Edward VI in 1550, Pier Paolo Vergerio – the former Catholic bishop become a Lutheran[71] – extols the geographic and moral divide separating Britain from the European continent that he faults for continuing to harbor the pope, while also noting a development that had already proven to be of signal importance for emerging English Protestant culture. Vergerio promises to detail how badly the recently elected Pope Julius III has been behaving:

> especially [given] the cruelty and rage with which he sends his ministers and executioners into all of the cities of Italy, [where they] diligently aim to persecute and trample upon the pure doctrine of Jesus Christ ... [but] your Majesty will undoubtedly rejoice and thank the heavenly father, through whom to you and to all your Kingdom such happiness has been conceded that you have been able speedily and completely to separate your souls, your religion, and your obedience from all shackles and influence of that true Antichrist ... just as your most fortunate Island is excellently divided and separated from the same.[72]

The persecution of Italians sympathetic to reformed theological ideas that had driven Vergerio from Italy was continuing to force other clerics and lay people to flee the peninsula, and this just as Edward VI and his councillors were attempting their consolidation of the reform of English ecclesiastical life. It was during the Edwardian period that Italian religious refugees, a previously unknown quantity, began to appear in England, and among them Pietro Martire Vermigli and Bernardino Ochino were the earliest and the most prominent.[73] They had been summoned to England in 1547 from Geneva by Archbishop Cranmer in order that they might participate in a projected Protestant council equivalent to the recently convoked Catholic Council of Trent, and though this reformed council never materialized, the two Italian reformers remained in England and exercised a decisive influence on both the initial development of the independent Anglican church and the distinctly Protestant culture that would take shape in England in the latter half of the sixteenth century.[74] In a neat précis of the role that the Protestant "stranger" would come to play in the formation of England's national identity, Hugh Latimer, speaking of the recently invited foreign divines in a sermon preached before Edward VI in 1547, advised the young king that "we ... collect together such valuable persons in this kingdom; it would be the means of ensuring its prosperity."[75]

That there was anything resembling a movement for religious reform within Italy itself in the first half of the sixteenth century often comes as a surprise to those unfamiliar with the heterodox religious history of the period.[76] A full account of the manifold ways in which the Italian experience was translated into the English situation would require far greater consideration than we can dedicate to it here, but a sketch of its principal elements will help to clarify the circumstances out of which developed this new phase in the history of Italian relations with England, one registered not only in the move from Catholic to Protestant polity, but also in the closely related shift from Latin to vernacular linguistic politics that begins at this time to reconfigure the boundaries between elite and popular cultures.

The foundation for what would develop into the diverse, philologically grounded theologies of later reformers was laid by Lorenzo Valla, the mid-fifteenth-century humanist who challenged both the prevailing philosophical and linguistic orthodoxies of his profession while teaching in Pavia, working in the Aragonese chancellory in Naples, and then in the Roman papal curia, while authoring a series of treatises on a range of topics that came to occupy a pivotal position in the intellectual controversies of the sixteenth century.[77] Valla excited the animosity not only of religious authorities – for his negative estimation of matters such as the Aristotelian framework of scholastic theology and its solution of the problem of free will – but also that of his fellow humanists: his painstaking study of the Latin language led him to reject the prevailing view of its immutability, identifying a historical trajectory that clearly proved otherwise;[78] he also opposed its mandate as the learned language of both discourse and writing, maintaining instead that Latin remain henceforth strictly a written language purged of all elements of rhetorical excess:

The demand to speak clearly, to use precise not abstruse definitions, to always bear in mind the full and complete meaning of words to be employed, was nothing other than an aspect of the determination to avoid any compromise with the tradition which [Valla's] adversaries used as a defensive shield, [a sign] of the radicalism necessary to any transformation that aims at having universal value, and a condition for the renewal of ideas through the [rebirth] of language.[79]

These critical values are united in Valla's most widely known work, *De falso credita et ementita Constantini donatione declamatio*, written in 1440 but not edited and published until 1517, in which the authenticity of the document upon which the church had for centuries claimed its temporal authority is demolished.[80] Through carefully establishing that the Latin found in the text is a later form of the language than that dating from the supposed fourth-century period of the deed in which Constantine was made to have handed over his Western kingdom to the church, Valla initiated an innovative way of thinking about language and how it comes to be used in written texts that had a profound impact on the patristic and biblical studies that gained momentum later in the fifteenth and early sixteenth centuries; he was the first practitioner of what would become historically informed philology, paving the way for both orthodox and heretical reformed ideas, as well as providing an early standard for textual integrity in the preparation of printed books.

A legacy of an entirely different kind was bequeathed to Italian reformers by Girolamo Savonarola, the Dominican friar who dominated

Florence's public life in the middle years of the 1490s.[81] In the wake of his feverish activity and brutal execution in 1498, Savonarola's influence extended well into the successive decades of the sixteenth century and provided one of the strands that contributed to the varieties of reformed thinking that developed in Italy in the 1530s and 1540s.[82] In death Savonarola came to be confirmed by his surviving followers and their heirs, the *piagnoni*, as the prophet he had sought to be in life. The political humiliation of Italy by foreign powers culminating in the Sack of Rome in 1527 and the initial spasms of the Reformation seemed to be the fulfillment of Savonarola's conviction – the basis of all of his preaching and writing – that the church would be submitted to a withering chastisement before it could be renewed, and that this purgation was imminent. The period of the second Florentine Republic, re-established immediately following the Sack (given the vulnerability of the Medici pope, Clement VII) and enduring through 1530, saw the most open reassertion of Savonarolan sentiment in Italy, both religiously and politically,[83] but a decade earlier Bartolomeo Cerretani in his *Dialogo della mutazione di Firenze* had identified Martin Luther as the prophetic saviour anticipated by Savonarola, whose:

writings having appeared in Italy, and chiefly in Rome ... suggest that he is most excellent in character, doctrine, and religion; his fitting conclusions appear to us to be in conformity with the thinking and practice of the primitive church militant.[84]

A poem dating from the mid-1530s, the *Stanze di Zanobio Ceffino cittadino fiorentino sopra l'eresia del re d'Inghilterra e sopra la morte di Tommaso Moro gran cancelliero*, is less interesting for its entirely second-hand account of the events leading up to Thomas More's execution than for its framing of the English tragedy in language that, while scant on poetic merit, evokes in its cadence and rhetorical drift the hortatory voice of Savonarola:

> Our Father, eternal Creator,
> True redeemer of human seed,
> If already my faults have caused you to turn
> Your back on my bitterly extreme miseries,
> See fit now my Lord from this inferno
> To raise me up and put me in a higher place
> That I may in your praise and honor
> Make into verse that which I have in my heart.
> Impart to my intellect a mite
> Of that grace that you to Paul did give,
> And in my heart a single spark
> Of that fire that in Stephen you made burn.

> Make of my voice a trumpet
> In order that such a great Case might attest
> To the glory of your holy Faith
> And for the comfort of those who most believe in you.
> And you Fisherman and honor of the church,
> If these my verses you deem worthy,
> Then you shall have understood their subject's
> Tenor, one perhaps such as never heard before.
> So that with Pity love might move you
> To bewail with me the grievous woes
> Of another blessed Thomas of our age,
> Mirror of sanctity and virtue's vessel.[85]

The figures of the martyrs Paul, Stephen, and the new Thomas point to the urgency of exemplary witnesses in the diffusion of the "holy Faith." At the time he composed his poem, Ceffino was a lay functionary in the papal administration of Paul III, married to a niece of the Farnese pope, and his *piagnoni* sympathies suggest that the impetus for reform was beginning to gain a foothold in Rome itself.

The philological imperatives of Valla and Savonarola's clarion-call to spiritual renewal found a common denominator in Juan de Valdés, the Spanish theologian who arrived in Rome in the winter of 1530–31 after fleeing a Spanish Inquisitorial investigation provoked by the publication of his *Diálogo de [la] doctrina cristiana*. This influential text – a synthesis of elements absorbed from the circulation of Erasmus' thinking in Spain, the Spanish tradition of spiritual illuminism (*alumbradismo*), Luther, Melanchthon, and other Protestant theologians – is a good example of why the history of early modern religious ideas must necessarily be addressed in its complexity, not conceived of "as linearly derivative but as creatively sedimentary, with multiple contributing strata."[86] In Italy, Valdés showed himself to be equally receptive to a number of diverse influences, including Ficinian neo-Platonism and humanist civic religion,[87] and this singular fusion of ingredients proved as irresistible to a widely representative cross-section of Italian society as it had in Spain. The Italian public in favour of reform in the 1530s and 1540s was a "sizable group of common people, artisans, teachers, and merchants; but also prestigious intellectuals, acclaimed preachers, gifted clerics and prelates, to say nothing of figures at the top end of the social scale and in political power."[88] As had also been the case in Spain, women were prominent and actively involved participants. Valdés was at first protected in Italy by Clement VII's curia, in which he may have been acting in some political capacity as an agent for Charles V, but after the election of Paul III to the papacy he moved the center of his activities to Naples, from where he skillfully employed a variety of means for the widest possible dissemination of his ideas, through "personal meetings and colloquia, the clandestine circulation of his writings, epistolary exchanges, [and] from the pulpit."[89] As Massimo Firpo has argued, in contrast with earlier commentators, Valdés' theology is not easily classifiable as either Protestant or Catholic; inspired by such a wide range of disparate components it is not reducible to any one of them.[90] Its central focus, on the interior action of the Holy Spirit working in the soul to defeat what Valdés terms *prudenza umana* [fallible human judgment], as well as its indeterminate ecclesiology, makes of the Valdesian approach a closer precursor of the various strains of Anabaptism which similarly developed outside of the Catholic/Protestant struggle to establish the precedence of their respective orthodoxies.

Nevertheless, for our larger story the most interesting consequence of Valdés' impact in Italy is the part his ideas had in compelling Bernardo Ochino and Pietro Vermigli to flee Italy and their well-established positions within the Roman church in order to join the Protestant reform in northern Europe; and in pushing Reginald Pole further into the vanguard of the Italian Catholic reformers, establishing in 1541 (the same year in which Valdés died) the so-called *ecclesia Viterbiensis*, the group of similarly minded clerical and lay reformers that gathered in Viterbo under Pole's ægis and which proved to be the most open, even if short-lived, forum for the experimentation of reformed thinking within the church in Italy.[91]

The *Alfabeto cristiano*, an account of the private theological conversations Valdés held with Duchess Giulia Gonzaga in Naples,[92] is among the books John Florio lists among those he consulted for the compilation of the second edition of his dictionary, and one can discern in Valdés' works a linguistic model for the illumination of the soul, passing from the "alphabet" of spiritual language through to its further elaboration in "grammar" and on to its full expression in "rhetoric".[93] Valdés was himself occupied with linguistic politics, and his defense of the Castilian vernacular, the *Diálogo de la lengua*, was written in Naples in 1535 at the mid-point of the decade of his work as a spiritual catalyst between Spain and Italy. This confluence of systematic concern with language and religious controversy reiterates a pattern evident in the Latin humanist tradition in Valla and Erasmus, but Valdés' Spanish treatise is the harbinger of a specifically vernacular debate about the centrality of language to cultural politics.

Luther and Calvin were, of course, equally concerned with the theological and political implications of words, and the discrepancies between their respective versions of the reformed faith are in several critical instances attributable to nuances of definition (especially with regard to the eucharist). An important pragmatic difference in the repercussions of orthodox and heretical Protestant reassessments of language is apparent with regard to the meaning of the church as a community: though the reformers in their initial efforts maintained a critical view of hierarchical organization, the diverse movements that emerged within the reforming world were very soon obliged to establish institutional structures, both because of the need to deal with growing numbers of adherents and in order to effectively counter the aggressive Catholic response to their challenge. Those who failed to recognize the necessity of some sort of clearly delineated organizational framework – the Huguenots and Anabaptists, for instance – were particularly vulnerable to persecution, and not only from the Catholic side of the ideological equation. For with the new hierarchies came old problems, at no time more evident than with the execution of Miguel Serveto, the Spanish anti-Trinitarian, in Calvin's Geneva on October 27, 1553. This *auto-da-fé*, whose rationale merely substituted new dogmatic words for those they were meant to supersede, was greeted with horror by those of more moderate reformed sentiment, among whom Ochino, who had at the time literally just arrived back in Geneva after his flight from Marian England.[94]

Ochino had earlier spent a period of several years in Geneva, Basel, and Augsburg after abandoning Italy in 1542, and his published sermons from this period testify in their focus on interiority to the influence that Valdés had exercised over his spiritual development.[95] Ochino's defection from the Roman church was considered a seismic event, given his prominence in the Franciscan order that he had joined as an adolescent: he had been named Definitor General of the Observant Franciscans in 1532, and he was elected General of the Franciscan Cappuchins after that monastic reform movement took shape later in the 1530s. As a young monk, Ochino had attended the medical faculty of the University of Perugia with Giulio de' Medici, the future Clement VII; he was a confidant of the poet Vittoria Colonna, and both Pietro Bembo and Pietro Aretino thought highly of him.[96] Renowned for his asceticism, Ochino was considered "a modern Chrysostom,"[97] having acquired a wide following in Italy as a powerful and persuasive preacher, cities from Palermo to the Po Valley clamoring for Lenten and other sequential series of his homilies.

In London, Ochino initially aroused the ire of Italian merchants and bankers, many of whom remained Catholic, for his sharp denunciation of the papacy in public sermons preached in Italian.[98] An immediate success, however, with Archbishop Cranmer, the king, and his regents, Ochino was awarded both a non-residentiary prebend at Canterbury and a royal pension of 40 marks.[99] Lady Anne Cooke (the mother of Francis Bacon) translated into English fourteen of Ochino's sermons on predestination, a topic he is reported to have discussed with Princess Elizabeth, who also translated one of his sermons into Latin.[100]

In addition to treatises dealing with sin and sedition,[101] Ochino's major printed work from his English years is *A Tragedie or Dialoge of the uniuste usurped primacie of the Bishop of Rome, and of all the iust abolishing of the same*, published in John Ponet's English translation in 1549. Ochino's "play" leans heavily on the Latin comedy *Pammachius* (1538) by Thomas Kirchmayer (whom Ochino had met in Augsburg), but baptized in the Thames it takes on a distinctive voice of its own.[102] Its unwieldly length – over 250 pages of text in its only modern edition[103] – as well as the absence of any dramatic *mise-en-scène* render the *Tragedie* unperformable,[104] but as an ambitious and frequently engaging example of Ochino's thinking it reveals perhaps better than any of his other writing from this period both the shape of the religious ideas he brought with him to England and how he sought to translate them into the English Protestant context.[105]

The first of the *Tragedie*'s nine *tableaux* is a dialogue between Lucifer and Beelzebub, recently cast out of heaven with their co-conspirators, in which the two fallen angels plot their revenge against God by creating the papacy in order to undo the redemptive work of Christ:

LUCIFER ... it is necessary that this man be so furnished with all wickedness and iniquity that I may worthily say of him: This is my beloved son in whom is my only delight, hear him; even as the heavenly Father long agone did testify of His Son Christ.
BEELZEBUB Methinketh that I hear the lively image of Antichrist himself, handsomely and properly described of you.
LUCIFER It is even so, indeed, as thou sayest. [10]

Ochino's theme throughout the *Tragedie* is the all-encompassing evil wrought through the primacy of the Roman church, and the pope is made out here, through an inversion of the prophetic dictum about Christ, to be the "beloved son" of the prince of the underworld. Lucifer then further details the ill-effects of the projected papal administration:

LUCIFER ... know ye my brethren, that this kingdom of ours shall be so pestilent and abominable that it shall not only infect and hurt the Church of God, the holy ceremonies and constitutions, true worshipping of God and the sacred Scripture itself, but it shall also destroy and overthrow other liberal arts and sciences.
BEELZEBUB When I consider how short the life of man is, it seemeth to me a thing impossible that one Bishop of Rome, in so short a space, should bring to pass so many mischiefs.
LUCIFER Brother, methinketh that ye be very dull ... [18]

Not only the the full religious life of the church but learning in general comes to be polluted through the meddling of the pope, Beelzebub's incredulity here cleverly mirroring Ochino's suggestion that humanist culture has been compromised by the Renaissance papacy's promotion of it, thus neglecting its theological and spiritual imperatives: the demonic under-secretary shows himself here to be a poorly prepared student.

In the second *tableau* Ochino aims simultaneously (and not altogether successfully) to discredit the temporal power of the Roman church and support the theocracy that the Anglican reformation had effected. To this end, he agrees with some reformed theologians in seeing the beginnings of the pope's temporal authority in the conferral upon Pope Boniface III of the title *caput omnium ecclesiarum* by the Byzantine Emperor Phocas in 607 that established the pope's authority over both the Eastern and Western churches.[106] But Ochino gingerly side-steps the Catholic position supporting the donation of the Western empire to Pope Silvester I by Constantine against which Valla wrote and that Luther dismisses,[107] the open rejection of which would have called into question the Henrician symbiosis of church and state.[108]

The third *tableau* stages a debate between the "People of Rome" and the "Church of Rome" regarding the innovations introduced after Phocas' concession; and the "People of Rome" intervene again at the end of the fourth *tableau*, where they claim to know nothing of the history of Peter in Rome from which the popes deduce their spiritual primacy (a newfangled history proposed just pages before by "Man's Judgment" – a clear Valdesian marker – to be propagated in forged books).

Trust in the superior wisdom of the individual believer alert to the Roman church's fictions is central to Ochino's program of reform, and accordingly the fifth *tableau* consists of news from an ecumenical council convened by the pope and presided over by the emperor (the Council of Trent had only recently convened at the time of Ochino's writing) but reported by the pope's chamberlain to the papal stable-boy. These remarkably learned servants banter back and forth for over eighty pages, the chamberlain recounting a largely scriptural debate in which Ochino assigns the task of explaining his own theological perspective to the "Eastern Ambassador":

> ... in the spiritual church of Christ ... such as have greater light of the Spirit, they be higher and greater. And they that be such, serve all other by the help of the Spirit, as men hath received greater gifts of God, more light of knowledge, more grace, more spirit, and a greater talent ... the power, therefore, and the greatness of the ministers of Christ is altogether spiritual, and standeth wholly in the service and governance of souls' health ... [134–135]

The church represented here as a spiritual reality, vivified by the interior action of the Holy Spirit, further demonstrates Ochino's continuing affinity for Valdesian theology, but by putting these sentiments into the mouth of a Byzantine representative he is also pointing to the wider theological reach of the reformers, whose philological and exegetical scholarship extended beyond the Bible to encompass both the Eastern and Western patristic traditions. Still, at this point in the *Tragedie*, Ochino allows the pope to consolidate his authority as he hastily shuts off debate and suspends the council.

The sixth *tableau* marks Lucifer's final appearance in Ochino's play, he and Beelzebub conferring about expanding the pope's power and prerogatives, perverting the sacraments, and introducing the idea of purgatory into their great design:

I will apply all the powers of my wit that this creature of ours may do much more hurt to the souls of men than Christ Himself did good. And it is not to be doubted that we will make of this Church a very Babylon. True it is that a thing of such holiness cannot be brought in a moment suddenly to the highest degree of abomination; wherefore in this noble mischief we must go forward by little and little, letting no occasion slip and opportunity of time shall offer unto us ... [197–198]

Christ himself appears in the seventh *tableau*, in dialogue with the Archangels Michael and Gabriel, to argue that God has allowed the papacy to develop along such appalling lines in order that:

He would make His glory more notable ... mark, therefore ... that he [the Antichrist/pope] may be destroyed with more ignominy, I will not use my power, but the bare words of my ministers, whereby I will disclose these great mischiefs, and will lighten their minds with the knowledge of the truth ... [200–201]

Building upon the notion of *felix culpa* – the "happy fault" whereby humankind having known sin is even more blessed in the wake of Christ's redemptive work than it would otherwise have remained without the fall from grace – Ochino suggests that the papacy has been permitted to degenerate in order that a purer church might emerge from its ordure, fired by the inspired words of God's true priests.

The *Tragedie* concludes as its action moves suddenly to England, where Gabriel is sent by Christ to mobilize Henry VIII into action against the pope. In the eighth *tableau*, Henry announces to his interlocutor, "Papista," that:

there is a thought entered into our head which we be persuaded cometh of God ... that the Pope, who heretofore hath been taken for a god on earth, is very Antichrist, and if we had certain knowledge that this thing were true, we would, as we are bound, banish him out of all the coasts of our kingdom ... [207]

"Archbishop Thomas" Cranmer subsequently develops, over the course of twenty-four pages, a biblically supported attack on Antichrist, and in the end "Papista" is, of course, defeated. But as Christ had foreseen that

Henry would die before his work was entirely finished, it falls to the young Edward VI to bring the English reformation to its consummation.

In the final *tableau*, Edward begins by comparing himself to Alexander the Great, who as a young man lamented his father's victories thinking that they would deprive him of his opportunity to "compass the dominion of the world by his own wit and industry" [242], but he soon embraces the occasion to "banish out of our kingdom the name of Antichrist, and his jurisdiction" [244]. Edward is made to claim that:

> to drive [Antichrist] out of the hearts of men, it is not needful to use sword nor violence. The sword of the Spirit, that is, the Word of God, is sufficient, whereby Christ overcame and conquered His enemy Satan in the desert ... [245]

Ochino blithely elides the actual bloody history that would contradict such a position, just as he had presented Henry's motivations as entirely upright, but the facts of recent English history seem to him as nothing in comparison with the corrupt history of the papacy. Edward goes on to dismiss the Petrine claims regarding the papacy invented by "Man's Judgment" in the fifth *tableau*, and all of the other "popish" imaginings with which the *Tragedie* is preoccupied, and then says that:

> we must search all about, and get the most faithful ministers of God's Word, which be endued with a great light of the Spirit, in the knowledge and exposition of the Scriptures, with a heavenly eloquence, boldness and liberty, which ministers both can and will print Christ in the hearts of man. [249]

The linguistic ground of reformed theology – represented here by "God's Word" (a figure throughout the New Testament for Christ) expressed in the actual language of the Bible, and figurally "printed" in the hearts of believers – thus comes to be the instrument of England's spiritual and political purification, and (if his reader had hitherto missed the point) Ochino writes himself specifically into the realization of this agenda, for Edward concludes by acknowledging that:

> if we cannot find enough such men within our own dominions, they must be sought for, wheresoever they may be found; good learning must be made much of, and promoted forward; good wits must be nourished, and provoked to learning and study, that the heavenly philosophy of Christ may reign always in our kingdom. [249]

Linked to the renewal of the church's life, the "cleansing" of the various channels of learning fouled by the papacy will, in Ochino's judgment, be accomplished by just such men as himself.

One not entirely transparent consequence of the religious history that we have been considering is its uneasy relationship with Italian Renaissance vernacular culture, the legacy of which came to be transmitted to later Tudor England largely through the agency of the Italian

Protestants who found refuge there.[109] While Renaissance philology had provided an indispensable methodology for the innovations of reformed theology, the actual content of Italian Renaissance texts – their polymorphous representations of sexuality, as well as their celebration of "pagan" culture, and their often open disregard for religion – was as problematic for a Protestant culture of containment as it was for increasingly conservative Catholic cultural politics.[110] The turn to Protestantism in England represented a turn toward a culture oriented around the dangerous power of words, and as such John Florio's life and career there represents the most manifest example of the course of these trends. But already at the end of the *Tragedie* the problematic authority of an ideology organized around the "word" makes itself manifest when Edward's "Councillors" respond enthusiastically to his program of renewal by arguing that:

[God] endowed subjects with a certain natural fear towards their liege lords that they may reverently obey them. Wherefor if a prince or king intend a thing, and then declare the same to be his mind and pleasure with a certain effectualness and authority, by and by they all obey ... neither is it to be doubted that the Gospel should breed any tumult in these dominions, or cause any sedition or looseness of liberty, for Christ doth approve and confirm chiefly the power and authority of princes and magistrates, and causeth men to think humbly and lowly of themselves, and to love peace and quietness; and therefor, as though they were gentle lambs, it shall be an easy thing, and no great pain, to rule them. [250–251]

The "Gospel" thus conceived and practiced, however, produced in some quarters anything but the anticipated effect. The Edwardian attempt to impose English liturgical language in Devon and Cornwall – provinces in which many people still did not speak English – was disastrous, provoking an insurrection that, ironically, was contained only "with the help of Spanish, German, Italian, and Flemish mercenaries, paid with funds loaned by Jews."[111]

By the time of his return to Geneva in 1553, Ochino's theology had taken a decidedly anti-Trinitarian turn,[112] and he explored this and other heterodox questions in the *Triginta dialogi*, which caused a furor among the Zurich clergy after its publication in 1563. Given the recently concluded Council of Trent and the accordingly redoubled efforts of Catholic persecution, "the gravity and the audacity of the questions proposed" in this work – among them the potential legitimacy of polygamy – were taken to be "impertinent and dangerous,"[113] and they provoked Ochino's expulsion from Protestant Switzerland.[114] He would have been well advised had he accepted one of Elizabeth's several offers to return to England following her accession, for the last period of his life was an impoverished and itinerant one, Ochino having become a pariah in the eyes of orthodox

Protestantism and in Poland running afoul of the papal nuncio. Ochino evidently contracted the plague in Moravia and died there late in 1564.

Pietro Martire Vermigli's legacy is a more sober matter, even as much of his career followed a course seemingly parallel to Ochino's. After his student years as an Augustinian monk in Padua during the early years of Luther's agitation in Germany, Vermigli was designated an itinerant preacher of his order, an office he held first while based in Brescia, and then in Bologna, while also teaching theology and studying Hebrew. Appointed Prior of Spoleto in 1525, a monastery with a particularly decadent reputation, Vermigli energetically moved to reform the community, and it was during this time that he was invited to participate in the meetings convened by Cardinal Contarini in 1536 and 1537 at Pope Paul III's behest to explore the eventuality of an internal reform of the church.[115] As Prior of San Piero ad Aram in Naples in the late 1530s, Vermigli came into contact first with Ochino, and then through him with Juan de Valdés. Vermigli's introduction to the Valdesian understanding of the idea of justification by faith alone proved to be an overwhelming experience, for:

acceptance of this vital doctrine entailed so drastic a reorientation of heart and mind that it amounted to a conversion ... [it] would revolutionize his understanding of the Bible and the sacraments ... and render him independent of a sacrificing priesthood. It would open his eyes to abuses which he had never questioned, and bring him more and more into conflict with Roman orthodoxy. It would entail an agonizing reappraisal of Catholic soteriological and sacramental theology ... and would begin a lifelong dedication to the doctrine of the Eucharist. It was a light that would lead him step by step to the sanctification and priesthood of all believers.[116]

In an age of modern skepticism, it is almost impossible to reconstruct the powerful sensation such a revelation would have provoked in its recipient. Given the association of this theological notion with destabilizing Protestant trends elsewhere in Europe – though Valdés' formulation of the idea of justification was somewhat different from Luther's and Calvin's – acceptance of its implications was tantamount to what the affirmation of political dissidence or sexual difference within a repressive socio-political context might signify today (minus, obviously, its transcendent aspect). From a personal encounter with what one believes to be the truth – about God, the political order, or one's own self – to the ostracizing actions of those whose values are deeply embedded in the *status quo*, the sixteenth-century heretic and the contemporary dissident or sexually different subject share something of the same experiential trajectory. While much has been rightly made in recent early modern European cultural history of the social anxiety about sodomy in the period, in the middle years of the sixteenth century doctrinal "heresy was the anti-social crime *par excellence*,"[117] and in England the two categories later came to be regarded by some as manifestations of the same problem.[118]

At the time of his decision to flee Italy, Vermigli was the Prior of San Frediano in Lucca, a city that as we have seen had enjoyed in the late fifteenth and early sixteenth centuries important ties to England, and in the subsequent period of religious foment became one of the centers of reforming activity in Italy.[119] Vermigli initially spent five years in Strasbourg, where in addition to teaching Hebrew he published his first doctrinal study, an exposition of the Apostle's Creed. During the years he spent in England from 1547 to 1553, he advanced the cause of English reform in a way that "was not only greater, but also of a more positive and 'Catholic' nature than is recognized by many Anglican writers."[120] In spite of his lack of English, Vermigli was involved in the gestation of the *Book of Common Prayer* in both its 1549 and 1552 versions, defining the *Articles of Religion*, and contributing to the never-enacted *Ecclesiastical Laws*.[121] He was the second occupant of the Regius Chair of Theology at Christ Church, Oxford,[122] but he was dismayed by the poor state of scholarship he found there and blamed the university's decline on a poor standard of learning still hide-bound to tired scholastic formulæ. Many at Oxford were, in turn, shocked that the formerly celibate Augustinian monk brought his wife with him to Christ Church, a sign that the split with Rome was still relatively recent (and in many people's minds temporary).[123] Vermigli chose *First Corinthians*, one of the most hotly contested letters in the New Testament vis-à-vis the major points of contention in reformed thinking,[124] as the subject of his inaugural lectures at Oxford. Paul's epistle serves as the Catholic scriptural authority in support of the church's positions on purgatory, clerical and monastic celibacy, and the doctrine of the eucharist, and having already gotten himself into trouble in Naples in 1540 with his exegesis of the Pauline passage used to justify the existence of purgatory, Vermigli clearly understood that in tackling the issue again he was courting controversy.[125] He was eventually drawn into a public disputation with his Catholic-tending colleagues on the nature of the eucharistic presence and was compelled to articulate his understanding of "real presence" as opposed to the "mere sign" of the more extreme voices of the continental Reformation, a definition that left a permanent imprint on Anglican eucharistic theology.[126] By the time he joined the other foreign Protestant refugees and some of their English supporters in fleeing the resurgent Catholicism of the Marian era, Vermigli had perhaps done as much as anyone short of Cranmer himself to establish the *via media* between Catholic and Protestant doctrine and practice with which Anglicanism has since the Elizabethan era sought to distinguish itself from other Christian churches.

*"S'io vo, chi sta? S'io sto, chi va?"*
### Michelangelo Florio and the Tudor interregnum

The "stranger" Protestant congregations that John Florio mentions in the fifteenth chapter of *First Fruites* originated during the Edwardian era, were suppressed under Mary, and reinstituted after Elizabeth came to the throne. An eighteenth-century painting by the Moravian John Haidt (Figure 8) commemorates Edward VI's gift of the Church of Austin Friars to John Laski (or à Lasco), a Polish reformer who had come to England in August of 1548,[127] and provides an albeit posterior visual clue to the structure of these disparate "stranger" churches:[128] though there were several distinct congregations, each organized according to the language utilized in worship, they all met in the same place, at staggered times, and were administered, under Edward, by a synod of elders representing each group and presided over by Laski.[129] The Augustinians had yielded many of the seminal figures of reformed thinking – Egidio da Viterbo, Erasmus, Luther, and Vermigli, among others – and so it was especially fitting that the former Augustinian church should have hosted the various continental Protestant communities. We shall return to the history of the Italian congregation when we come in the next chapter to examine the Italian colony in Elizabethan London, but for now it is enough to note that those advising the English monarch recognized the need for "strangers" resident in London to have a house of worship distinct from the Church of England – though in doctrinal and canonical affinity to it – where they could celebrate their own versions of the reformed religion, and that Michelangelo Florio, John's father, served as the first pastor of the Italian congregation.

Michelangelo gained this office through his connections to Archbishop Cranmer and to William Cecil (in whose household he lived) soon after his arrival in England in 1550. Cecil was among the savviest of Edward VI's councillors, initially tied to Edward Seymour (and briefly imprisoned with him) but subsequently shifting his allegiance to John Dudley, and in time to Mary. A superb Greek scholar, Cecil had been educated at Cambridge just at the moment when the university served as the epicenter of English reformed thinking (Roger Ascham was a classmate), and during the Edwardian period he was closely involved in the initial structural changes in Anglican ecclesiology, even hosting at his own home several of the disputations concerning the eucharist.[130] Cecil's resilience through the Marian and into the Elizabethan eras served him and his adherents well, and given his earlier patronage of Michelangelo it is plausible that Cecil

# Reformations

*Figure 8* John Haidt, painting of Edward VI, John Laski, and the Elders of the Church of Austin Friars. Reproduced by permission of the United Reformed Church History Society, Westminster College, Cambridge Theological Federation.

might have played some part in John Florio's return to England in the 1570s.[131]

The elder Florio seems to have come from a line of Tuscan Jews converted to Catholicism, and as a young man he became a Franciscan, falling under the sway of reformed thinking while touring Italy as an itinerant preacher throughout the 1540s.[132] Tortured by the Inquisition and imprisoned in Rome, Michelangelo eventually escaped and made his way across Italy, into France, and finally to England.[133] He appears, temperamentally, to have been an extremely difficult man, and problems quickly developed between pastor and flock. These came to a head in 1551, for just as Michelangelo was making an emphatic denunciation to Cecil of fourteen members of his congregation for papistry, he was himself implicated in the rape of one of his parishioners.[134] Subsequently stripped of his post and his royal stipend, Michelangelo somehow managed in disgrace to retain Cecil's good will. Allowed to remain in England (there was some question of expulsion),[135] Florio took up a second career as an instructor of Italian, and through his political connections found employment with John Dudley, Duke of Northumberland, and Henry Grey, Duke of

Suffolk.[136] Michelangelo's *Regole de la lingua thoscana* (1553)[137] was dedicated to Lady Jane Grey – Suffolk's daughter and Northumberland's daughter-in-law – to whose fortunes his own were by that time very much tied. Following her execution after succeeding Edward to the English throne for only nine days in 1554, and given the subsequent misfortunes of his principal patrons in England, Florio fled with his wife, son, and daughter first to Antwerp and then to Strasbourg, settling into another pastorate in the village of Soglio, in the Grigione region of Switzerland in 1555.[138]

The brief and unfortunate life of Lady Jane Grey found in Michelangelo yet another Italian chronicler willing to take on the dynastic vagaries of the English royal succession. Florio's *Historia de la vita e de la morte de l'Illustrissima Signora Giovanna Graia, gia regina eletta e publicata in Inghilterra e de le cose accadute in quel regno dopo la morte del re Edoardo VI*, written shortly after the author's flight from England in 1554 but not printed until 1607, is the only immediately contemporary account of Jane's brief reign, but it is of equal importance for the sympathetic impression its Protestant author provides of Mary's character.[139] While Florio writes that he had had the highest respect for Edward's judgment, he believes that the decision to reject both Mary and Elizabeth in favour of Jane required more time and consideration than was taken. He suggests that while Mary could conceivably have been considered unfit for the throne because of her Catholic faith, her priority in the line of succession established by Henry VIII was clearly authoritative. As for Elizabeth, he writes that she was of "true piety, holy both in doctrine and habits; she showed herself always to be a clear mirror, example, and legitimate daughter of her father Henry."[140] Florio deplores the manner in which Jane had been compelled into taking the crown, for:

all things measured only according to human wisdom, violence, force or one's own interests displease God and have an unhappy ending.[141]

Of the rebels' efforts to keep Mary from the throne after Jane was put there, Florio writes suggestively that:

it is certain that one could have repeated many times without exaggeration that phrase of the most learned Dante, [when] out of favor with the Florentine Republic, "If I go, who shall remain? If I stay, who shall go?"[142]

Regarding Mary's claim to the throne, Florio says that "the heart of the king is in the hands of God," and that "Mary was of pure Royal blood."[143] He goes on to say of her, speaking to the argument that the Protestant faith ratified in England by Edward must be preserved at any cost, that:

I do not know whether to affirm or deny it. On the one hand, I feel compelled to believe that it were so, given the public acclamation that argued such; but on the

Reformations

other hand, I am pulled in the opposite direction. I confess that being in London I heard the former position held by the majority, though I find myself unconvinced because Mary was a woman generous in nature and greatly talented.[144]

This is a remarkably tolerant position, given all that was personally at stake in the matter for Florio and the other Italian religious refugees in England. But of the people's reaction when Mary overthrew Northumberland and had deposed Jane, he writes:

> that a greater celebration could not be imagined even if a new Christ were to be born into the world. But if the unstable and crazy London rabble had known then what painful and lamentable sufferings lay behind their revels, I am certain that they would have clothed themselves in sackcloth, and with bitter tears, humbly kneeling, would have implored God's mercy rather than sporting in such a joyous fashion.[145]

He faults Bishop Stephen Gardiner, not Mary, for the cruel persecution of Protestants, Gardiner having with Mary's consent hatched a scheme of false religious toleration in order to hunt down heretics; this accomplished, he convinced the queen to obligate all to return to the profession of the Catholic faith [40–42]. According to Florio, Gardiner – one of Henry's chief defenders during his divorce of Mary's mother, and an outspoken critic of the pope – was almost entirely responsible for the tragic turn of events that took place early in the Marian period [56–57]. Regarding Jane's death sentence, he asks:

> who could think Mary so barbarous and cruel that she would have wished to wrong the noble nature, reputation, and innocence of such a close relative? And to do injury to reason itself?[146]

In spite of all that he had lost personally and professionally by the time he wrote his *Historia*, Michelangelo was reluctant to blame Mary for Jane's fate.

> "... in Ciel fia Dea, qual'è Regina in terra ..."

## Italians and the English Catholic queen

Excitement in Italy was palpable at Mary's accession. The incorrigible Pietro Aretino, having taken a pass on Edward VI and ignoring the favours he had exchanged with Henry VIII, produced a letter and this sonnet celebrating the advent of the English Catholic queen:

> Propitious stars, it behooves you all,
>   As well as you bright-shining Sun, and you lustrous Moon,
>   To see that Fortune crown the godly Mary
>   with your variously resplendent rays.
> Make it such that her splendour disperse
>   The night, and the day where shadow obscures

>     And darkens, so that the great World without demur
>     Is ever reflected in her, has her ever in its regard.
> Proud stars, do not dally in concurring,
>     Since the never-erring, eternal God
>     From the blessed and most lovely lights round about Him
> Adorns and binds her with a Diadem,
>     Witnessing to these people and to those,
>     That in Heaven she shall be a Goddess who is Queen on earth.[147]

Times had changed dramatically in both Italy and in England since the end of the Henrician period, and Aretino was no longer so prone to the daring gestures he had practiced little more than a decade before, this sonnet's conventional rhetoric reaffirming the poet's Catholic filiation in the newly vigilant Italian climate. The accompanying letter addressed to Mary is even more polemically Catholic in its survey of the dogma, ceremony, and piety Aretino believed to be restored in England with her accession, and as such it reads more emphatically as self-defense than as a tribute to the new queen.[148] The retrograde character of this fresh bid for English patronage fits well, however, as an epitaph for the Marian era, which would seek with little imagination or success to recover England's Catholic past, though there is no evidence to suggest that this gesture met with the same approbation Aretino's earlier efforts to attract English royal attention had won him.

In the introductory section to the third book of his *Historia ecclesiastica della rivoluzion d'Inghilterra* (1594), Girolamo Pollini weaves a parable of "virile" ladies – Amazons, Cleopatra, Judith, Deborah, and others – who "have honoured this most frail and weak sex with their enterprise ..."[149] and in whose company he aims to situate Mary:

> who having overcome, with Divine assistance and the prudence and valour of her soul, the rage of all the Princes and Barons of the State, admirably vanquishing the whole force of their arms, miraculously gathered together an army of 30,000 men, entered into the Tower of London, and without bloodshed took possession of her Realm. She renounced the title of Primate of the Church, opened the prisons [wherein were kept] all of the Ecclesiastical Prelates and other Catholics, and adjusted the corrupt currency. She severely castigated all of the heretics, chasing some of them out of England, while others necessarily paid the penalty of the fire; she annulled all of their laws and in prejudice of the Catholic Faith restored the Pulpits and University Chairs to Catholic Preachers and Readers, and she had the Mass celebrated according to Catholic custom. She obtained from the Roman Pontiff as Extraordinary Legate Cardinal Reginald Pole, with which means reconciling England to the Roman See, and making [the country] return to Papal obedience, all bonds of heresy and Schism were dissolved.[150]

The compressed chronology here is more or less accurate, though the correction of debased English currency was actually initiated by the economic policies of John Dudley while Edward was still alive, and Mary's financial minister merely confirmed this course.[151] Pollini's conclusion regarding the eradication of Protestantism in England, however, reflects the wishful thinking that still gripped the Roman authorities several decades into the Elizabethan period. Mary was unquestionably acclaimed by her people as England's legitimate ruler, but at the time of her accession more than twenty years of religious turmoil had left their indelible mark, and the four-and-a-half conflictual years of her reign did nothing to resolve the issues raised by Henry VIII's break with the papacy or her brother's attempt to consolidate the English reformation. Mary had lived a sequestered life too long in her father's formidable shadow and its afterlife to fully grasp what would have been required to confront England's manifold contemporary problems, and Reginald Pole, her chief ally and councillor, was even further detached from English actuality, having lived continuously in Italy for over twenty years at the time of his repatriation in 1554.

But for a brief time at the very beginning of Mary's reign, all was rejoicing, nowhere more keenly registered perhaps than in Rome, and Pollini's account of Mary's coronation thus reads as an uncontested celebration the likes of which had not been seen in England for well over three decades. He pays particular attention to one aspect of the coronation festivities that we shall see reiterated, with obviously different inflections, in the subsequent coronation festivities honouring Elizabeth and James: the erection of triumphal arches in different areas of London, two of which were financed by Italian merchants resident in the city. Pollini concentrates most of his attention on the first of the two arches, sponsored by the Florentine merchants, providing a detailed picture of its extravagant architectural and artistic elements [305],[152] as if to proclaim that the period of Edwardian iconoclasm was at an end; and he then goes on to describe the arch's textual program, inspired by powerful women of the past, and summarized in the principal epigraph on its upper facade:

VIRTUTES FAMA REGINAM AD SIDERA TOLLUNT

The virtues and renown of the queen are lifted up to the stars [306].

There is an echo here of *Aeneid* 4.321–323, the moment when Dido confronts Aeneas about his impending departure from Carthage and the betrayal of their love,

>... te propter eundem
>Extinctus pudor et, qua sola sidera adibam,
>Fama prior ...[153]

>     ... due to you,
>  dead are both my chaste honor and its earlier renown,
>  that singular glory through which I was to go among the stars ...

A bizarre choice of literary precedent for readers accustomed to Virgil's account of Dido's story appears in an entirely different light from the perspective of its earlier versions, considered historical in the early modern period, which Stephen Orgel has identified as the source for the "widow Dido" allusion in *The Tempest* [2.1.75] that had so puzzled previous editors of Shakespeare's play.[154] A princess of Tyre, Dido fled her homeland after the murder of her husband by her brother, collected a group of fifty women – who may have been raped by Dido's followers – en route to:

North Africa, where through a combination of shrewd bargaining and deceptiveness she obtained the land to found Carthage. She was an exemplary ruler, famous for her chastity and her devotion to the memory of her murdered husband. She committed suicide to prevent her forced marriage to a local king.[155]

Virgil's innovation was to introduce Aeneas into the narrative, transforming Dido in the process into a sensualist who would indeed be Mary's opposite in almost every respect. If this epigraph were intended to be a legible evocation of Dido, it could only have been meant to be read as such by writing the tragedy out of Virgil's text and restoring to Dido her more ancient emblematic status.[156]

The epigraphs that follow, at any rate, identify Mary unambiguously as triumphing over her enemies:

>                MARIAE BRITANNORUM REGINAE
>                  VICTRICI, PIAE, AUGUSTAE,
>                          FLORENTINI
>                       GLORIAE INSIGNIA
>                           EREXERUNT

The Florentines have erected emblems of glory to the victorious, faithful, majestic Mary, Queen of the British [306]

On the opposite side of the arch, in the upper middle section, there was a portrait of the queen, who in her gestures and appearance looked glorious and triumphant; to one side was the image of Pallas Athena; on the other the story of Tomyris; above was the image of Judith with the head of Holofernes; and under the image of the queen was written:

SALUS PUBLICA                    Salvation of the People

Under that of Pallas one reads:

INVICTA VIRTUS                   Unshakeable virtue

Below the story of which were found these words:

LIBERTATIS ALTRICI                    Wet-nurse of liberties

And under the image of Judith:

PATRIÆ LIBERATRICI                    Liberator of the Nation

[306]

The conventional allusion to Athena identifies Mary with wisdom and as guardian of the law, but the other two more unusual tags are of greater interest, for they establish the queen as the agent of England's deliverance from its enemies by associating her accession with two of the most fiercely independent women of the ancient world.

Herodotus recounts the story of Tomyris, Queen of the Messagetæ, inhabitants of the expansive plain east of the Caspian Sea on which Cyrus, King of the Persians (circa 590/580–529 BC), had set his conquering sights. Cyrus expected to make Tomyris his wife in the process, but when she made it known that she and her people would resist, the Persian king threatened war, kidnapping Tomyris' son after slyly getting the Messagetan army drunk. Tomyris responded by taunting the Persians for this tactic, telling Cyrus to:

> give me back my son, and then you can leave this country without paying for the brutality with which you treated a third of my army. But if you do not, I swear by the sun who is the lord of the Messagetæ that for all your insatiability I will quench your thirst for blood.

Herodotus judges the ensuing battle to have been the "fiercest battle between non-Greeks there ever was", and in the end Tomyris and her troops prevailed, slaughtering most of the Persian army, including Cyrus himself. In order that her earlier admonition be fulfilled, Tomyris:

> filled a wineskin with human blood and searched among the Persian corpses for Cyrus' body. When she found it, she shoved his head into the wineskin, and in her rage addressed his body as follows: "Although I have come through the battle alive and victorious, you have destroyed me by capturing my son with a trick. But I warned you that I would quench your thirst for blood, and so I shall."[157]

Herodotus certainly embellished some aspects of this account, but given the new English queen's subsequently "bloody" reputation, the inclusion of Tomyris among her symbolic progenitors here at the outset of her reign can only be read as eerily prophetic.

The story of Judith attempts to sound a similar note, and as the book in which it is told was not included in the acknowledged canons of either the Hebrew or Protestant scriptures (in both the Tyndale and the King James translations, *Judith* is included among the apocryphal books), its citation in the program of the Florentine arch is a notable reaffirmation of Roman

Catholic biblical parameters in England. Nebuchadnezzar, king of the Assyrians (circa 630–561 BC), sent the chief of his army, Holofernes, to Palestine in order to seek revenge against the Jews – only recently returned from their captivity in Babylon – for having defied him. There, before laying siege to the city of Bethulia, Holofernes is warned of the dangers of attacking the Jews on account of their protective deity. Once the city is under attack, he encounters Judith, who, having slipped away in feigned escape from the city after offering supplication to the God of Israel, tells him:

> if thou wylte doo after the wordes of thy handmayden, the Lorde shall bringe thy matter to a prosperous effecte.[158]

She proves herself a consummate Machiavellian, moving with swift and certain determination to eliminate her people's oppressor: invited to dine and dally in Holofernes' tent, Judith lingers once her drunken host retires to bed; after his servants withdraw, she seizes the moment by decapitating the Persian general with his own sword. Judith is thus depicted as Israel's deliverer, and the book closes by asserting that "so long as she lyved ther was none that troubled Israel, and many yeares also after her death." Though sharing her resolve, Mary lacked Judith's political acumen, and no similar settlement was to be achieved in newly Catholic England. Still, the fusion of religious devotion and patriotic zeal in this biblical narrative must at the time have seemed an irresistible harbinger of the dawning Marian era, sentiment reiterated in the concluding epigraph of the Florentine arch:

> MAGNANIMIS PER TE QUOD PAX SIT PARTA BRITANNIS
> EX ILIO AC REDEANT IUSTITIA, ET PIETAS
> ET VIRGO PRÆSTES, QUOD VIX EFFECERIT ULLUS
> VIR, SUMMUM QUI SIT VECTUS AD IMPERIUM,
> DUM RECIPIT VIRTUS AUGUSTAM RITE CORONAM,
> ET REDDUNT OMNES PUBLICA VOTA DEÆ,
> LAETA TIBI TALEM TRIBUIT FLORENTIA CULTUM
> QUI TAMEN ARCANO PECTORE, MAIOR INEST[159]

For [the fact that] through you peace be procured from Troy for the magnanimous British, justice and true religious devotion return, you, virgin [queen], guarantee what barely any man who were to come to the supreme power could accomplish: while virtue duly recovers the august crown, and all render their public oaths to the saintly [queen], glad Florence pays tribute to you with such public worship that is even more deeply hidden in its inmost breast. [307]

Mary's response to this program of nation-rebuilding goes unregistered, and one cannot help but ask to what extent the account was retouched by its reporter (particularly given Pollini's stinting citation of sources), writing decades after the event. But the conservative invocation of Britain's mythological history and its return to "true" religion are counterbalanced by the suggestion of a powerfully rechannelled feminine sexuality, the queen exceeding in her virginity the assertiveness of any male aspirant to political power. And the public/private parameters of Florence's devotion, playing on the classical notion of "cultum," is a confirmation of England's reasserted Catholic sacramental theology: outward signs simultaneously representing and reproducing an indissoluble relation to hidden ontological realities.[160]

Both the pope and the Holy Roman Emperor had substantive reasons to see England again under the jurisdiction of the Roman church, and Mary played into their conflicting agendas largely because "two things dominated her mind – her religion and her Spanish descent."[161] The queen's insistence that if she were to marry it would only be to a Spaniard complicated the papal/imperial struggle to gain the upper hand in England, because while Pope Julius III was eventually persuaded by Mary that Reginald Pole's presence was indispensable to the restoration of English Catholicism, his return to England was successfully delayed by Charles V in order that the queen and the emperor's son, Philip II, might first celebrate their nuptials (Charles being anxious that Pole, widely but perhaps mistakenly believed to be opposed to the union, might pose a threat to his dynastic plans). The prospect of this marriage was not, however, greeted in England with the same jubilation as the Catholic Tudor queen had initially enjoyed herself, and Pollini provides one explanation why:

heretics as a race of restless, insolent, and shameless men, were unable to accommodate themselves in patience either to marriage with a foreign Prince, so Catholic and powerful, or to the dependence and friendship that they feared with the Apostolic See ... in addition to the particular and hidden deceptions that [they] necessarily used to impiously, and against every legitimate motive, keep Queen Mary from the realm (for which Thomas William, scrivener of the Senate during the reign of Edward VI, was with justly merited death punished),[162] the wicked heretics plotted a new and never before heard of stratagem so as to stir up turmoil among the People, who were already then in ferment and more than ever earnestly inclined to heresy. [359–360][163]

"Heresy" in this reading is synonymous with "opposition," for it was not only Protestants who opposed Mary's Spanish marriage: the lower house of parliament mounted a united and vigorous protest,[164] representing the barely repressed hostility toward the "stranger" in England that had been consistently building in the Tudor period among those outside aristocratic ranks regarding the preference and privileges extended to foreigners, resentment that occasionally erupted into open conflict. Philip was seen by many of the English as an instrument of Spanish and imperial expansionism, and had Mary lived, their fears that England would be turned into a Spanish province might well have been confirmed.

The additional deceit that opponents to the marriage are reported to have devised was a crude prank to further agitate Pollini's excitable "heretics":

> they persuaded a poor simple Girl of eighteen years, no less stained by the poison of heresy than with the greedy cupidity of the corrupted currency, that for a certain span of time she be left to one side in a secure place, hidden between the walls of an apartment house, and via certain well-placed Grooves and Conduits fitted to this purpose, she would emit tremendous and horrible cries, using those accents and words that among commoners would seem normal. The name of the girl was Elizabeth Crust, and the originator of this deceit and Stratagem was a certain Dragon ... [360]

Pollini notes that the girl was an easy target for such manipulation, given her age, poverty, stupidity, and heresy. Once ensconced in the wall, Elizabeth set about successfully frightening the wits out of the Catholics at whom the gambit was aimed, as well as anyone else unaware of the plan, Dragon and his minions working the alarmed crowds by suggesting that the voice was that of a heavenly messenger threatening all manner of personal and communal calamity should the Spanish marriage proceed. The voice also disseminated anti-Catholic propaganda, railing so virulently against the sacraments – a move further "interpreted" for her public by the girl's employers – that Pollini notes the people began to grow suspicious. A magistrate was finally called in to investigate the situation, and when the wall was opened and the girl discovered she confessed everything, after which:

> the inventors and authors of this stratagem fled, but the girl due to her age, and having been by them deceived, was punished lightly. The entire case ended in laughter, [though] in great horror and scorn of heresy, which for the singular wickedness of heretics is sown in the hearts of the simple and ignorant faithful, and with similar stratagems of the devil is easily nourished and maintained. [361]

Pollini equates "heresy" in this vignette with money-grubbing and gullibility, this latter characteristic shared by both the perpetrators of the scheme and those duped by it. While such puerile strategies could not in anyone's wildest dreams have had an impact on marriage negotiations in which the most powerful forces in European statecraft were involved, Pollini's portrayal of the imbecility of the English commoner echoes one of the basic problems that doomed Marian politics from the start: a supreme condescension toward the very people its reforms were intended to assist. As Thomas Mayer notes, among Reginald Pole's "major weakness[es], [was] his elitist belief that the English should be treated as children."[165]

# Reformations

In 1555, Giovanni Alberto Albicante, an obscure Milanese *letterato*, published an oddball poem, *Il sacro et divino sponsalitio del Gran Philippo d'Austria et della sacra Maria Regina d'Inghilterra*, celebrating the English/Spanish marriage alliance and England's reconquest for the Roman faith (Figure 9). Albicante was an active player in Milanese politics during the middle decades of the cinquecento and in that capacity enjoyed good relations with Charles V (to whom the poem seems to be addressed, even if dedicated to the Duke of Alba, commander of the imperial forces in Italy); he was at times a sparring partner of both Anton Francesco Doni and Pietro Aretino; but his most important contribution to Italian literary culture of the period was in seeing Francesco Berni's revision of Boiardo's *Orlando innamorato* through its first edition, printed in Milan in 1542.[166] Such close editorial work likely fuelled Albicante's poetic ambitions and perhaps contributed something to the fantastic, occasionally bizarre, flights of fancy his epithalamium takes.

The *Sponsalitio*'s second-hand description of the marriage rite, conducted (and written out) "in bel latino,"[167] represents in linguistic terms England's return to its Roman religious heritage, in contrast with the remainder of the poem written in Italian. The city of Rome is depicted as euphoric over the royal wedding, its first citizen beside himself with joy:

> How deeply content the Holy Father felt,
> jointly with the cardinals and all of Rome,
> well-vested in his sacred Mantle,
> the Mitre placed o'er his ever-blessed head,
> in jubilant voice and heavenly song
> he now proclaimed that on earth heresy
> was fallen, issuing Bulls of highest charge
> throughout all Italy to celebrate.

The pope and the college of cardinals are shown together in consistory giving thanks for the conjunction of elements that has led to the realignment of England's religious and political coordinates. The ancient city itself is represented as moved to its depths by the events recently unfolded in England:

> From o'er the great Mound of Hadrian
> the cannons gave out their awful thunder,
> and gurgling to itself, thus little by
> little the Tiber murmured dulcetly,
> and from its banks, the city's hills and dales,
> from its *piazze*, its nooks and crannies,
> so much revelry there was, so much joy,
> that even the noblest words fall short.

# IL SACRO ET DIVINO SPONSALITIO
## DEL GRAN PHILIPPO D'AVSTRIA
### ET DELLA SACRA MARIA REGINA D'INGHILTERRA;

Con la vnione & obedienza data alla catholica Chiesa, sedente sommo Pontefice
GIVLIO III.
Dedicato All' Illustrissimo & Eccellentissimo Signore
IL S. DVCA D'ALBA.
Fabricato in ottaua Rima per
L'Albicante Furibondo.

IN MILANO, DAI MOSCHENI.
M. D. LV.

*Figure 9* Giovanni Alberto Albicante, frontispiece of *Il sacro et divino sponsalitio*. Reproduced by permission of the British Library.

> Not so wanting the Holy Father, traveling
> each street and avenue throughout the city,
> showing with graciously generous hand
> his munificence, how grateful he was to all;
> how many of those enclosed in prison,
> whose crimes his goodness bent to pay;
> spending lavishly at his own expense,
> favouring those who to him most gracious proved.
>
> And then he said the Mass, this Good Shepherd,
> to thank most worthily the highest Lord,
> with all the clergy giving thanks to Him,
> united with the pope in solemn prayer;
> each cardinal there of purest heart
> on high his ardent desire lifted up,
> each and all for the great gain rejoiced:
> England again was made servant to Christ.

The poet aims to make of his effort something of the singular give-and-take between actuality and myth that Boiardo initiated and Ariosto perfected in the Italian chivalric epic, but his ambitions were obviously greater than his limited literary gifts would permit. Here, following a brief stab at pastoral tropes applied to the urban landscape, the pope is made out to be an almost comic figure, freeing prisoners for no other evident motives than his elation over the news from England and their ability to flatter his vanity.

Earlier in the poem, following descriptions of the marriage rite and banquet, Albicante unleashes the force of Eros among the gathered wedding guests:

> 'Ere long the god Cupid had spread his wings,
> and removed the blindfold from his eyes,
> amongst the Spanish, several of his
> arrows he let pierce hearts with no repair;
> here were no rivals made for jealousy,
> for in its place reigned reciprocity;
> and so to sweeten the lovers' ardour
> he gave them lovely, sweetly perfumed gloves.

This strategy working its effect through the next three stanzas, the guests pair off, day turns to night as they turn to dancing, but Jove in the end compels Mercury to intervene to send the lovers all chastely to sleep, touching their eyes with a wand previously dipped in the river of forgetfulness. All of this to set up Albicante's most astonishingly inept verses:

> So to fully CONSUMMATE the Marriage,
> the King, with the Queen, entered into her secret place
> and baring to the Lady his lovely idea,

> 'twas infused in her the more-than-blessed thought.
> Oh now how great the glory and peace borne
> to CHARLES the true, honour of all his States;
> and that his joy might be more complete, so
> to honour the world, may a fair Son be born.

Cupid's preliminary activity reads in the light of this stanza as a kind of baroque aphrodisiac, but allowed to play itself out only in the case of the two principal protagonists of the poem (its effect on the other revellers seemingly annulled by Mercury's intervention). But the language Albicante utilizes here to represent this auspicious nuptial coupling is particularly loaded: "in steccato" can stand for a verbal battle – the sort of feisty polemic that the poet was much given to – but in this context it plays off the term's several other senses, namely fencing and fencing weapons, a fenced-in space, as well as the female hymen.[168] Further confusing what is actually represented here is the continuation in the following two lines of the "verbal duel" figure, extended to Mary's receiving Philip's "lovely idea," when clearly what he is meant to be doing is spreading her legs, "pensiero" being a euphesim for the penis common in sixteenth-century *novelle*.[169] Elsewhere there are many such metaphors that do not quite deliver, a pervasive inconsistency of tone, and a curious sense of causality, but in attempting to represent this moment – already laden with significance both for Tudor England and Hapsburg Europe, given the consequences of Katherine of Aragon's unconsummated first marriage – Albicante loses control of his poem by stumbling into an erotic mode, failing to understand (besides the cheekiness of depicting the sexual act in an epithalamium) that a crucial dynamic element in the poetry of Boiardo and Ariosto is precisely the perpetual deferment of erotic consummation in the exploits of their protagonists (whereas in Aretino's literary writing the pornographic is exploited specifically for its potential to make scandal in the service of social commentary). These infelicities aside, however, we are here confronted with a premonition of the shattered hopes the Marian period would in short order bring, for there was to be no "fair Son," the reference to the "joy" of "CHARLES the true" indicative of the only real purpose of this marriage, which it was never to fulfill.[170]

The marriage concluded, Reginald Pole was permitted to cross the Channel to England, having spent more than two decades away, largely in the company of Italy's leading prelates and humanists.[171] A seminal figure in the history of the Roman church in the critical middle years of the sixteenth century, Pole's standing has suffered both from the excessive zeal many of his followers in Marian England exercised in attempting to restore England to the Roman fold, and from his reluctance to restrain them.[172]

It is an unfortunate irony that Pole, who was involved in the most seriously reform-minded circles in Italy – the same environment that had earlier produced Vermigli and Ochino – should be remembered principally as Mary's ideological henchman, when his central role in the promotion of reformed thinking in Italy provoked an Inquisitorial investigation after his return to England, to which he was preparing a response at the time of his death.[173] Pole was at first closely identified with the reforming efforts of Gasparo Contarini; both men had been named to the cardinalate as laymen and to some extent remained outsiders to the clerical culture that accompanied the red hat. It is important to recognize the marked differences that distinguished the approach of these would-be Catholic reformers from that of the Inquisitorial politics that in the end prevailed in Rome, the former cautiously conciliatory and the latter polarizingly prosecutorial.[174] In his few final years in England, Pole attempted to address many of the same concerns, as had Protestant leaders under Edward VI, but from a Catholic position that was compromised by the complex crosscurrents of reform and intransigence fighting for precedence in Rome and at the Council of Trent in the 1540s and early 1550s, forces in relation to which he failed to stake out a clear position. Several of the Italians in Pole's circle accompanied him to England, the Paduan aristocrat Luigi Alvise Pruili the most conspicuous of them,[175] but it was through the English cardinal's own Italian training and experience that the cultural and political ties with the peninsula that had existed for almost a century prior to Henry VIII's divorce and schism were briefly renewed.[176]

Pole's life was first recounted in an Italian biography, the *Vita del Cardinale Reginaldo Polo*, published in Venice in 1563, by Ludovico Beccadelli, a Bolognese literary figure and cleric close to Pole and the other reform-minded prelates originally in Contarini's circle.[177] Beccadelli's portrait of the English cardinal is a warmly personal one, providing details of the most significant incidents and relationships of Pole's eventful life, but as recent scholarship has demonstrated, the *Vita* often veers into hagiography as it rewrites critical episodes in Pole's experience in order to present him in a light that tends to render his actions and choices more coherent and deliberate than they frequently were in actual fact.[178]

Beccadelli begins the *Vita* by situating Pole – born to parents of both Tudor and Plantagenet blood – within the Arthurian tradition of *la tavola ritonda*,[179] thus from the outset suggesting that the cardinal's life was the stuff of legend and setting Pole's personal history apart from the Italian humanist historiography that, as we saw in the previous chapter, sought to discredit such mythography. Pole's own potential claim to the English throne (even if more than several steps removed) explains Henry VIII's particular interest in his early formation and opinions,[180] and coupled with

Pole's repeated candidacy for the papal office his existence was a constant threat to the architects of England's Protestant polity.

Of the 1530 interview Pole may have had with the king, following Henry's request that he elaborate a disposition on the question of the divorce, Beccadelli writes that Pole told the king in no uncertain terms that:

> he could never in his spirit conform to the will of the king, such appearing to him too wicked, and counter to the holy laws of the Church ... Lord Reginald said to me that in that moment the king's face turned red, his disposition went from content to agitated, and he put his hand on a small dagger that he was carrying; but then, hesitating, the king said, "I shall consider your opinion and then reply," dismissing him from the room with scorn.[181]

But, as Mayer points out, it is not clear that the meeting ever took place, Pole's own testimony regarding the incident being as contradictory as evidence from other quarters in which differing versions of the encounter turn up.[182] Pole's later written response to the king's request, *Pro ecclesiasticae unitatis defensione* (or *De unitate*),[183] failed to earn Henry's assent, and it did nothing to mitigate the disastrous consequences this opposition would have for his family. Reginald's mother, Margaret, had been one of Katherine of Aragon's closest friends (she had served as Mary's governess), and for her fealty to the relinquished Spanish queen, sharing her son's objections to Henry's divorce, she lost her life in one of the king's pogroms in 1541, her eldest son, Henry, having been executed in an earlier purge in 1538.[184]

Beccadelli shows himself at times to be more than an authorial accomplice in Pole's self-fashioning. Writing himself into the scene in which the cardinal received news of his mother's death in a letter, but unable to read English, Beccadelli listened as Pole calmly conveyed the terrible news, seemingly unmoved by it. For Beccadelli, the anecdote is a sign of Pole's extraordinary inner strength, a quality that his mother had so instilled in him that even her death at seventy years of age on the express order of her cousin, the English king, could not shake his fortitude. Mayer argues, however, that Beccadelli was far from Viterbo when Pole was informed of the news, and also that a series of letters exchanged with Vittoria Colonna at this time "suggests that Pole took his mother's death much harder than he or Beccadelli wished posterity to believe."[185]

As Beccadelli was not among Pole's Italian circle in England, the *Vita* is of principal interest in charting the English cardinal's life and career in Italy, and in detailing how the shifts in papal power in the years immediately after Pole himself came within one vote of being elected pope in the long conclave of 1549–50 determined, or rather impeded, much of the course that he tried to pursue following his return to England. On this latter score, Beccadelli lays the blame for the ultimate failure of Marian politics (and the attendant loss of England again to Protestantism after the queen's and Pole's premature deaths) squarely on the shoulders of Paul IV, Pole's former colleague in the reform movement in Italy but subsequently the first prefect of the Roman Inquisition. For:

> the demon that is always the enemy of the good, and of our peace, planted the idea in Pope Paul's mind to chase King Philip out of the Kingdom of Naples, and to this end sent his nephew, Cardinal Caraffa, as legate to France in order to compel that crown's army against King Philip. And perhaps fearing that Cardinal Pole might be a powerful tool, as he was with the queen [Mary], in procuring peace between France and Spain, or because of an old grudge, or due to the instigation of the malicious, he recalled the cardinal to Rome, making another Englishman, Friar Peter Peto, cardinal and legate in his stead.[186]

This was an arrangement that Mary was not prepared to accept, and Beccadelli writes that without informing Pole she sealed off the port of Calais to anyone coming there from Rome looking for passage to England, had intercepted any pertinent correspondence, and without speaking either to Pole or to the newly appointed legate, wrote directly to her ambassador in Rome telling him to inform the pope that:

> removing Cardinal Pole, the Anchor of the [English] Catholics, was not the way to keep England Catholic, but rather to turn the country even more heretical than it had been previously; and further that His Holiness should carefully scrutinize whatever he might do, for she would be making her case before God himself for all of the difficulties that were to ensue.[187]

Further moves in this perilous game of Catholic chess were blocked by Mary's sudden illness following the end of a presumed pregnancy; her condition deteriorated rapidly, and she died on November 17, 1558.[188]

Beccadelli gives this brief account of Pole's death, coming only hours after Mary's, and only two months after that of Charles V:

> It was an astonishing thing that the queen died on the morning of November 15, and the cardinal only sixteen hours later, at three the following morning ... he passed away peacefully in the company of the angels, as is to be believed had his holy and Catholic queen, he having lived and worked 58 years and three months in this world.[189]

Pole had almost been elected pope and could under other circumstances have become king of England (either through his own blood line or through wedding Mary), but at the time of his death he was expected in Rome to answer to charges of heresy. With these two deaths, Rome's presumed reacquisition of England came to an abrupt conclusion.

The Catholic queen's unexpected death was greeted with dismay in the same Italian circles earlier so enthusiastic about her accession. In a sermon preached in Naples in February of 1559, Fra Francisco Visdomini prefaces his funeral oration for Mary with a long pæan to Charles V, emphasizing in so doing the unambiguously political tenor of Catholic Europe's concern for England at the same time that it tragically underscores Mary's naive confidence in her Spanish relations. The preacher notes the "holy love" Charles had shown to Mary in uniting her with his son Philip, so as to more perfectly link their Christian objectives. He provides a predictable review of the English succession, cursing the "dolorosa e mostruosa mutatione" [sorrowful and monstrous mutation] initiated by Henry VIII, and claims that, with the sole exception of Mary, the legitimacy of the English monarchy had been fatally compromised. In the time preceding her accession, she was:

> the Sun of Christian truth in that eclipsed Kingdom, [where] the Moon had turned to blood, and the stars in Heaven had fallen ... [in] miserable excommunicated England, in just one Mary could one find the faith and sinew of Catholic truth there where there were no churches, no sacraments, no prayers, no Masses, no rites, neither adoration nor tolerance of the holy Eucharist other than in her impoverished and disconsolate prison cell.[190]

Visdomini's apocalyptic hyperbole deliberately elides the relative freedoms Mary had enjoyed in Edwardian England – though she had been compelled to live for some time in isolation, she was never made to suffer the privations that Elizabeth endured for a period during the Marian era, following the Wyatt rebellion – freedoms that had been won for her by Charles V;[191] and the preacher just as disingenuously expresses his concern for Philip's grief, ending with a prayer that Mary's suffering, already so extended in her earthly life, might soon free her from Purgatory. This homily, preached to a congregation of Spanish colonizers and Neapolitans sensitive to Spanish concerns, reflects both the ambitions of Spanish imperialism (in the case of England, now apparently defeated) and the newly invigorated Roman faith – the twin axes of the queen's political and personal culture – thus providing a sharp contrast with the Protestant cultural politics which were even then taking shape under Mary's younger sister and successor. As Pollini has it:

> by this odious mayorality of darkness, and by the devil that even today has all that unhappy Realm so madly obstructed, England remained entirely and miserably beset.[192]

Or as Nicholas Sanders, Pollini's primary source, had written so much more succinctly:

> mox hora Satanae et potestas tenebrarum Angliam occupant.[193]

> now the hour of Satan and the power of darkness take possession of England.

# 3 La Regina Helisabetta

> The mind is but a barren soil; a soil which is soon exhausted, and will produce no crop, or only one, unless it be continually fertilized and enriched with foreign matter.
>
> Jonathan Reynolds, *Discourses on Art*

The accession of Elizabeth to the English throne initiated what was to be the longest and relatively most stable period in Tudor history. And yet the Elizabethan era was consistently marked by paradox: at no time before had elite English culture been so preoccupied with the world beyond its island limits and never in its recent history had the country been so isolated from the rest of the world; the great colonizing power that England was to become in the later sixteenth century was ruled by a sovereign who seldom traveled more than a hundred miles from London but who nevertheless had an easy command of Italian, French, Latin, and Greek; and despite the queen's formidable intellectual gifts, the culture that she encouraged was characterized by a distinctly anti-intellectual tenor,[1] many of the most distinguished minds of the epoch over which she presided marked more for their distance from court than by their proximity to it. The position of the Italian in England in the Elizabethan period is indelibly marked by the same incongruities, for while one of the queen's closest personal associates was an Italian immigrant, many of the most significant Italian voices in these years registered only slightly, if at all, in the royal ear.

Though Protestant religious refugees returned to England in droves following Elizabeth's coronation – most of them arriving from nearby France and the Netherlands, and many of them remaining only for brief periods – the size of the Italian colony in London always remained small in comparison with the other "stranger" communities there. The various components that constitute the term "Italian" – language, culture, individuals – enjoyed an unmistakably privileged position in England between 1558 and 1603, and yet the actual status of most of the Elizabethan Italians was considerably humbler than that of their predecessors. With very few exceptions, these figures were not significant players in the native Italian cultural, religious, or political life of the latter half of the cinquecento, and in the case of John Florio, who probably never set foot in what we recognize today as Italy, just what constitutes "Italian" identity is itself quite problematic. And while merchants and some others retained substantive ties to the peninsula and traveled more or less freely between Italy and England, many Elizabethan Italians had little or no contact with their homelands.

The final two chapters of this study will detail how two forms of "stranger" cultural influence – language learning and lexicography – became emblematic representations of larger developments in the emerging English nation that were fueled simultaneously by the presence of Italians in England and by the absence of any vital exchange, other than commercial, between the two regions. Here we look at the Italo-Elizabethan world to which John Florio returned as a young man in the 1570s, in order to situate his later contributions within the context that rendered them possible.

"... *qui si vive in tutto e per tutto, quanto alla religione, lutteranescamente* ..."

### From Mary to Elizabeth

Two Italian accounts of England, written roughly ten and fifteen years before Florio set out to establish his credentials as a language teacher in London, provide us with contrasting Italian impressions of the country and its people from the late Marian and early Elizabethan periods. The first was written by the Mantuan representative, Annibale Litolfi, dating from 1557, and the second by a Venetian merchant, Alessandro Magno, who visited England in 1562.[2] Both provide observations of the English scene in the middle of the sixteenth century from visitors who, like their Venetian predecessors, were only temporarily in England and would have been dependent for much of their factual information on resident Italians or Italian-speaking Englishmen.

Of the two, Magno is by far the more optimistic about what he encountered in England, but Litolfi was not physically well during much of his English stay and also suffered the indignities of an inadequate diplomatic stipend.

Magno found London to be:

a very beautiful city, rich and populous. There are abundant supplies of wool and kersey. The circumference of the city is five miles, nine including its lovely suburbs. It has nine gates, eight with suburbs beyond them, and the other has a beautiful common where every Sunday men and women gather to socialize and play. Almost all of the houses (save for those few palaces belonging to the Queen and other noblemen which are of stone) are made of wood.[3]

Litolfi formed a different impression:

> At one end is a fortress called the tower and at the other end is a neighbourhood called Westminster, where the monarch lives. Here there is an enormous and comfortable palace, haphazardly designed, as in general are all the buildings of this country ... the building materials are coarse ... rooms have no order whatsoever to them.[4]

Magno reports the (for him) strange mutations in English religion by noting that at:

> the church of St. Paul ... it is a pitiful thing to see the beautiful marble statues of saints and their adornments broken and ruined because of their heresy ... in the churches they say no masses but sing only psalms in their own language, and they preach there.[5]

He accompanies these remarks with a drawing of old St. Paul's, which is less a representative image of the church than an illustration of the consequences of English heresy in depicting the reconstruction of its central bell-tower (Figure 10), destroyed in a fire during the preceding year (1561), which was widely interpreted as a negative sign of God's judgment on the emerging Elizabethan age:[6]

> I have said that the bell-tower was burned: this seemed to me to be a warning to divert them from the wicked path to the right one, and I want to illustrate this by describing what happened. They say that in that same year, not long before we arrived, there was a flash of lightening that struck the tower and burned it completely, melting the lead that was covering the church. This produced so much heat that the people were afraid of being burned, and their consciences were so pricked that recognizing their sin they began to cry out for mercy. But the fire was quenched and they returned to their earlier errors.[7]

Both Magno and Litolfi are agreed on what they perceive to be the extraordinary freedoms enjoyed by women in England, most notably the ability to socialize on their own with whomever they please. Litolfi sees English women who:

> do as they like, common as it is in all of England for a woman, and most particularly wives, to dine out either alone or in the company of a female friend not only with a fellow countryman but even with a foreigner. And were it to occur that a husband find his wife with such another, he would not only not take offense but would shake the man's hand and thank him for the invitation extended to his wife.[8]

Both accounts call attention to the kissing habits of the English, shocked and titillated as they are by being practiced "in the middle of the street as at home."[9] Magno describes a street game in which young women:

> play with young men even though they do not know them. Often, during these games, the women are thrown to the ground by the young men who only allow them to get up after they have kissed them. Here they kiss each other a great deal, and if a

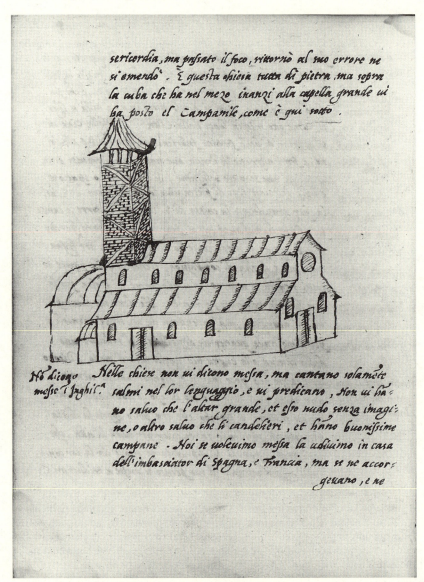

*Figure 10* Alessandro Magno, drawing of St. Paul's, Folger Shakespeare Library Ms. V.a.259. Reproduced by permission of the Folger Shakespeare Library.

foreigner enters a house and does not first of all kiss the mistress on the lips, they think him badly brought up.[10]

Strange that a social custom now associated so much more with the Mediterranean world would have taken Italian visitors by such surprise in England at this time.[11] Litolfi claims that "there are no brothels."[12]

Magno finds English cuisine superb, and he sees the English as sophisticated gourmands. Litolfi takes a more sober view, given that the English "eat often, five or six times a day," and he is taken aback by the quantity of meat consumed, "more than any other thing."[13] Magno gives descriptions of the beef, mutton, chicken, and other birds and game available in English markets; he also provides a lengthy disquisition on fish and shellfish, indicating that:

they have plenty of fish, and among the best are pike and very large flounders. These are cut up into filets and cutlets which they eat grilled. Best of all, however, is the salmon which is similar to Venetian sturgeon. There are warehouses full of a particular kind of dried fish which comes from the Indies and they call stock fish, which in our language would be called "beaten," or "salt cod." There is a street which has many shops on both sides where they do nothing for three days of the week but tie fish into bundles and beat it continuously. This makes the fish very white, tough and flavorless, and they send large quantities of it to Flanders and to Germany. They have and enjoy great quantities of oysters, and on fish days there arrive as many as eighteen to twenty fishing boats, which are about the same size as our merchant ships and have as many as four sails and carracks. There is an excellent market where for one *marcello* one can have a big basket full of oysters. They serve them roasted, fried with butter and in every possible way but prefer to eat them raw before a meal with barley bread – they are delicious.[14]

Magno's pæan to English gastronomy may come as a surprise to some, but this catalogue of raw materials demonstrates that then, as now, England enjoys an enviable natural bounty. Litolfi's praise of English weather, its "mild air ... so exceedingly moderate and pleasant that it could not be better,"[15] might be considered equally surprising, but perhaps not by an Italian accustomed to oppressively muggy summers and the persistent annoyance of mosquitoes.

Both Litolfi and Magno give accounts of the animal-baiting passion of the English public. Magno is particularly taken with the swans on the Thames, protected from harm by force of law, and he describes a kind of royal zoo at the Tower of London, where he saw a leopard and four lions, and where "every monarch places a lion, so they are named after their donor. Hence one can see a Henry, a Philip, a Mary, and an Elizabeth."[16]

But within the context of unflattering remarks about the business practices of English merchants, Magno mentions that "many [of the merchants' clients] find themselves driven to hang themselves, or to throw themselves into a well and drown."[17] Litolfi notes that "there is a prevalent cruelty that masquerades as pity," a practice we would now call euthanasia, and he writes that even if "they not do this with everyone, they do so with very many."[18] It is difficult to know what to make of these observations.[19] In Litolfi's case, they follow comments on reports of the English predilection for dying with a smile on one's face, even when being burned at the stake or hung from a gallows, fates that were, according to an anecdote he relates, the true sign of English nobility. He prefaces these reflections by asserting that "they value death very little, as Petrarch says so well in that verse, 'to which death is no sorrow', speaking of England."[20] Magno's allusion to the prevalence of suicide among the English can possibly be taken in the same light. At any rate, the public spectacle of death in the middle of the sixteenth century in England, as elsewhere in religiously divided and war-torn Europe, was an omnipresent reality, and the Marian persecutions could well have provided Litolfi or his sources with ample evidence of English stoicism in the face of death.

Although the *Relazione* was written in the penultimate year of her life, Queen Mary does not figure in Litolfi's text, but she is mentioned approvingly as having subjugated Ireland, a land of "savage men, different from all other men of law, tradition, and nature,"[21] and for having put in place her own governor there.[22] Writing five years later, Magno has this to say about Mary's successor:

I saw Queen Elizabeth when she was staying at Greenwich, which is a village on the river about five miles from London. She was there with the nobles of her court. The Queen is a very lovely woman, greatly good, benign, affable, and about thirty years old.[23]

This is perhaps the most unassuming description of Elizabeth rendered by an Italian while she occupied the English throne, her other Italian observers being almost without exception extravagant in their praise of the queen.

One further Italian index of the shift in focus that would distinguish the Elizabethan era so decisively from the Marian period is provided in the correspondence of Aloisio Schivenoglia, a Mantuan and a minor functionary of the Gonzagas who resided in London throughout Mary's reign and stayed long enough after Elizabeth's accession to know that England was changing in ways he could never support. In a letter written from London in May of 1556, Schivenoglia had noted the continuing progress of the persecution of Protestants under Mary:

They do not hesitate to continue burning these heretics, having sent into the fire last Friday an old man of 70 who hobbled there on his crutches, willingly, angrily and pertinaciously declaring himself; and also a blind young man whose spirit was perverse and obstinate. Then on Saturday they burned two elderly and two younger women, wives of those others burned about whom I had already written to your Lordship; these went happily to their deaths, without shackles or any other constraints, as if they were going off to be married.[24]

Not yet a month into Elizabeth's reign, in mid-December of 1558, Schivenoglia was already complaining that parts of the liturgy were being celebrated in English, "in the manner of King Edward ... I pray to God that [the situation] not worsen."[25] But things did not improve, as he writes in a letter about the Christmas mass celebrated at court one week later: Elizabeth had made it clear to the celebrant, Bishop Ogelthorpe of Carlisle, that he was not to raise the eucharistic bread and wine at the moment of consecration, but when he responded that this was how he had been taught to perform the liturgy the Queen abruptly departed following the reading of the gospel.[26] Schivenoglia also recalls that on the same Christmas day, Italians he describes as "handcraftsmen and diggers" forcibly entered the church of Austin Friars – formerly and shortly again to be the home of the foreign Protestant congregations in London – and from the pulpit denounced England's recent Catholic history:

saying a thousand terrible things about the reign of Queen Mary of blessed memory and about Cardinal [Pole], calling the people who had believed in them from their error, in such a way that never before had there been seen a more sudden and striking metamorphosis into two scoundrels than what was preached from this pulpit.[27]

By the spring of 1559, Schivenoglia writes that "here as regards religion one lives in and for everything *Lutheranistically*."[28] His ambition in England had been to attain an assignment with the Venetian ambassador, the renewal of those ties having been planned by Reginald Pole, but as Elizabeth was never to be recognized by the Venetian government, Schivenoglia's continued presence in England grew to be irrelevant.

He nevertheless provides us with the most extensive account of Elizabeth's coronation and the events surrounding it that has survived.[29] The document is also of interest for its censorious view of the queen's comportment. The tone in which Schivenoglia's narrative is couched is that of a superior æsthete witnessing elaborate ceremonial he claims to have seen better executed elsewhere, though there are elements in what he reports that do indeed impress him. The January 12, 1559 procession of Elizabeth and her court from Whitehall to the Tower on the Thames brings to mind for Schivenoglia "Ascension Day, as it is celebrated in Venice when the Signoria goes to marry the Sea."[30] But the detailed account of the January 13 nomination and investiture of the Knights of the Bath calls attention to these men appearing at court "dressed in robes of little value,"[31] and there are other signs later in the same ceremony that too little money has been spread around too thinly to make the desired impression, "the border of each horse's bridle was adorned with a tiny cross like those of the Knights of Jerusalem, having spent as little as possible because of their custom of giving everything away."[32]

Elizabeth's ceremonial encounter with the City of London, on January 14, is the only part of Schivenoglia's account that is replicated in the anonymous English description of the coronation festivities. As earlier with Mary and later with James I, an elaborate public pageant was organized for Elizabeth around ceremonial arches constructed in different areas of the city, and on all three occasions an arch was erected at Gracestreet (today Gracechurch St.). Just as Girolamo Pollini had noted the Italian patronage of two arches erected for Mary's coronation, in the later spectacle for James – the *Magnificent Entertainment*, as one of its authors, Thomas Dekker, entitled it – the Gracestreet Arch was sponsored quite conspicuously by the Italian colony in London; but while neither Schivenoglia nor the anonymous English chronicler cite any such specific patronage in Elizabeth's case, it is noteworthy that the ritual entry into London of all three monarchs should have been staged in a part of the city associated with the foreign colonies resident there. The area around Gracestreet was, as we shall see below, the principal locus of the Italian presence in London, and it was here that the foreign Protestant congregations had practiced their hybrid species of continental Protestantism at the Church of Austin Friars under Edward VI, and would soon again be allowed to do so under Elizabeth. As suggestive as the location of the Gracestreet Arch is the attention that Schivenoglia notes Elizabeth paid to both its iconography and its Latin/English text:

> Having arrived at the said arch, from a small balcony over the central portal Her Majesty was greeted by a small boy who briefly interpreted its significance. Her Majesty stopped her progress, giving the lad gracious audience and demonstrating her gladness.[33]

Mary's reaction to the two Italian arches discussed by Pollini is unrecorded, but James was to demonstrate his impatience and boredom with the complicated pageant staged for his coronation, one register of the many facets of his character that separated him from Elizabeth and that decisively demarcated the Stuart from the Tudor era.

The coronation itself, on January 15, is described in considerable detail [85–90]. The queen is pictured as being very much in control of the proceedings and, according to the reporter, oversteps the bounds of proper behaviour in so unabashedly displaying her enthusiasm for them:

> Her Majesty carried in one hand the sceptre and the golden orb, and in the other the Imperial crown; she wore on her shoulders the solemn Royal Mantle; [she was] very

happy, showing good cheer to all present and extending a thousand greetings, such to my eyes that it passed all sign of propriety and seriousness.[34]

There was, in the meals and other festivities, too much indulgence for Schivenoglia's taste. Of the music accompanying these events, he says that "there were various musical entertainments offered, but because none of them were distinguished and myself having heard better it is best to say nothing further of them."[35] This is particularly surprising, given the several generations of Italian musicians who were continuously employed at the English court throughout the Tudor period (to say nothing of the considerable native English talent already evident in these years). Taken together with the letters cited above, the critical tone of Schivenoglia's coronation narrative demonstrates that here was an Italian clearly unsuited for the Elizabethan world to come.

> "... non so se avrò ben parlato in questa lingua italiana, pur perchè io la imparai da fanciulla credo che sì di non avermela scordata ..."

### Elizabeth, Italian, and Italians

Elizabeth had learned to speak and write Italian at an early age, and her fluency in a number of languages was considered remarkable by those who witnessed her linguistic skills in action. Her polyglotism was all the more extraordinary given that she never set foot on the European continent.[36] Her preference for Italian and the prominence she accorded Italian culture can to a high degree be ascribed to the close presence in her life of Giovanni Battista Castiglione, the first sign of whom appears in 1544, when he fought among Henry VIII's troops in France.[37] By 1550 Castiglione had been naturalized as an Englishman, and at some point shortly before or after this time he was made a sort of bodyguard to Elizabeth, and also served as her Italian tutor. When the young princess was imprisoned in the Tower of London after the suppression of Wyatt's rebellion in 1554, Castiglione served as her principal link to the outside world, carrying "her private letters (all of her owne hand) to goe unto King Philip's confessor and to the French ambassador late in the night, concerning her Grace's greate troubles and wronge imprisonment."[38] Twice imprisoned there himself, an experience that left him permanently lame in one of his legs, Castiglione was among the few who would have shared the young Elizabeth's life on such intimate terms (certainly no other foreigners did), and it is a sign of her dedication to him that the culture he opened to her would come to play such a significant role in the era over which she presided. On close terms with both Robert Dudley and William Cecil – besides the queen, among the Englishmen most closely associated with the promotion of the Elizabethan Italianate fashion – Castiglione was instrumental in furthering the activities of other Italians who came to England after Elizabeth's accession.[39] He also played a key role in mediating between them and the competing factions of the court, but unlike most of them he also rose to an established position within the English aristocracy as a wealthy, landed gentleman. Castiglione composed two poems in honor of "la Serenissima Elisabetta Regina d'Inghilterra," and had them printed in the first of the Italian books John Wolfe published in London in the 1580s, Giacomo Aconcio's *Una essortatione al timor di Dio*.[40]

Entertainments performed for the queen often included Italian elements, as in the September 1575 performance at Woodstock of *Hemetes the Hermit* (subsequently translated into Latin, French, and Italian and with the original presented in manuscript to the queen by George Gascoigne in 1585). The anonymous reporter of the revels writes – in the form of a letter to a friend – that "after mentioning certain nosegays presented to Ladies of the Court, 'to every one was annexed a posy of two verses ... one above the rest of greatest price for the Queen's Majesty with her posy in Italian, which because I neither understood it, nor scarce can write it to be understood: I leave also till my next coming to visit you.'"[41] A document from 1573 licensed Italian puppeteers to perform their "Strange-motions" in England, and Susan Young writes that:

there were several theaters established in the region by these companies; in London at Southbridge fair, Holborn Bridge, and in Fleet Street, and also at Eltham. The letter authorizing the establishment of theaters for *marionette* and *burattini* predates by three years the construction of London's first [public] theater, built by Burbage in Shoreditch in 1576.[42]

There were also several Italian acting companies that performed in England in the 1570s. The queen evidently witnessed a play performed by one of them at Windsor or Reading in July of 1574, and descriptions of its pastoral *mise-en-scène* have led to speculation that the piece staged on this occasion was Tasso's *Aminta* (it had been performed for the first time in Ferrara in July of 1573), but there is no conclusive evidence for or against this intriguing possibility.[43]

Despite the conspicuous and much regretted absence of weighty Italian visitors to her court, Elizabeth would have had ample opportunity to use her excellent Italian. Giovan Carlo Scaramelli, the first official Venetian envoy to visit England during the Elizabethan era, writing in 1603, reports that the queen ended their long interview by saying:

non so se avrò ben parlato in questa lingua italiana, pur perchè io la imparai da fanciulla credo che si di non avermela scordata

I do not know if I have spoken well in this Italian language, yet given that I learned it as a girl I do believe that I have not forgotten it

patent evidence – if the envoy's corrective hand has not intervened – that she had not.[44]

Petruccio Ubaldini had returned to England definitively by 1563, and for the remainder of his life he was an ubiquitous, even if decidedly marginal, player in courtly circles.[45] In addition to writing a series of works addressed to aristocratic and political figures – among which a *Vita di Carlo Magno* (1581); *La descritione del regno di Scotia et delle Isole sue adjacenti* (1588); two commentaries on the defeat of the Spanish Armada;[46] *Le Vite delle Donne Illustri del Regno dell'Inghilterra et del Regno di Scotia* (presented in manuscript to Elizabeth in 1576, and printed in 1591), and a collection of *Rime* (1596) – Ubaldini sent regular dispatches to Tuscany regarding events in England,[47] was active as a copyist and miniaturist,[48] worked as an editor for John Wolfe, and continued to supplement and revise the *Relazione d'Inghilterra* that he had initiated during the reign of Edward VI.

In this latter redaction, the *Relazione* takes a broader look at the history of the Tudor monarchy, beginning with Henry VII's ascent to the throne [669–683][49] and providing a version of Henry VIII's career that would be less offensive to his daughter [683–687]; the section dealing with Edward VI is significantly reduced [687–689], and there are brief accounts of Jane Grey [689–690], Mary [690–692], and Mary Queen of Scots [694]; but its most extensive treatment is of Elizabeth's character [692–696] and the practices and institutions of her government [696–757], which updates and expands the similar presentation in the Edwardian version of the *Relazione*.

Ubaldini has this to say about the behaviour of the queen regarding her various suitors:

Elizabeth has never married. Though desired by many, foreigners as well as Englishmen, it seemed to them that in the practice of thus managing her affairs she in the end had rather demonstrated less concern about marrying than in not concluding with them whatsoever by which she might be dispossessed of her liberty of body and mind; and though she might have had any one of them, nevertheless she knew so well how to conceal her intentions that it seems that she had rather desired to know the minds of others than to lay herself open to being known by them; and from this it happened that men of noble stripe came to believe and obstinately proclaim that marriage with her was to follow, but then in failing they revealed so much more their frippery, it being true that human prudence issues from the practice of things accompanied by judgment, and not from the exterior favours often eagerly but unworthily received from Princes.[50]

Here, Ubaldini suggests, is a statesman, a queen worthy of the epigraphs invoking Dido, Tomyris and Judith in the Marian coronation festivities, equal to them in her bold but subtle dissimulation and in her prudent self-protection. Elizabeth deploys these tools, the *Relazione* further notes, by being:

> most cunning in the art of persuasion and insinuation. Because of her not inconsiderable grasp of history, given her knowledge of the Latin and Greek languages as well as Italian and French, she also uses an admirable finesse with foreigners, through whom she can gain praise beyond the Realm for her shrewdness and eloquence.[51]

The focus on the ends to which the queen's learning is put is especially striking in these passages, for in addition to speaking foreign languages Elizabeth knew how to use them to her advantage, a critical point lost on many of the other admirers of her linguistic facility.

These skills found a very specific purpose in 1592, after Elizabeth and her councillors had had occasion to learn what Girolamo Pollini had written in the first edition of his *Historia ecclesiastica della rivoluzion d'Inghilterra* (1591) regarding her parentage:

> among those of Henry's concubines still living, Anne [Boleyn] was the daughter of one of them, and sister of another. Furthermore (an infinitely worse matter, although it seems an incredible and unbecoming thing to be written, being so abominable), she was judged to be – and not without the most manifest and clearest evidence – the actual daughter of the same King Henry.[52]

This making Elizabeth not only a bastard (declared such by her father after Anne's execution, though consistently considered so by Catholics, given that Katherine of Aragon was still alive at the time of her birth) but also the issue of an incestuous union. Pollini here repeats an anecdote related by Sanders (earlier proposed by William Rastell, in his account of the trial and death of Thomas More),[53] consequently "naturalizing" English recusant slander in Italian, bringing full circle a process initiated with the queen's excommunication in 1570 by Pope Pius V, and the appointment to the cardinalate in 1586 of William Allen, the most eminent of the recusants exiled in Rome and the dedicatee of Pollini's history.[54] As Pollini was a Florentine subject, a Dominican friar of the monastery of Santa Maria Novella, once news of the *Historia* reached England there was an initial series of exchanges – first *in situ* through the mediation of Thomas Darcy and Henry Wotton (both at the time in Florence) and then in letters – between the Elizabethan government and Ferdinando de' Medici, regarding the Grand Duke's possible suppression of the book. A subsequent letter followed two months later, after the full thrust of the *Historia*'s polemic had been revealed – probably with the arrival of the volume in England – and once it became clear that nothing had been done to impede the book's circulation in Italy. Elizabeth, writing in Italian (who the scribe was is unknown), initially appeals to Ferdinando's past benevolence toward her and to the nobility they share as rulers, but then passes quickly to the matter at hand:

> an infamous scandal, a more than evident falsehood published in Your Highness's Territories against a Prince of such glorious memory, as was our father Henry the Eighth, and against our mother the queen his consort, and finally directing [a] malignant tongue to the injury and denigration of our own government, with as many great calumnies and lies as the author has managed to invent; but just as so very evidently false [these accusations], so very clearly appears to the [entire] world God's blessing over Us, our people, and kingdom with all the signs of prosperity, peace, obedience, riches, strength, and increase of subjects.[55]

The text is identified as having been conceived and written within Ferdinando's jurisdiction, and Pollini is named as its author. The queen then reviews the progression of her knowledge about the book, at first aware only of a libellous work directed against her state, but now fully informed as to its contents, such that:

> every single one of its pages is filled with the most extreme falsehoods, innumerable scandals, and the most wicked slander. It does not follow that We, given as is fitting to the office of every Prince or State, to say nothing of an Absolute Sovereign, should in such a guise by defamatory libels be defamed; as again given the great friendship between us received and appreciated; and given that it has pleased the Omnipotent God to make us heirs of such a great Father and Glorious King, whose fame was unequalled in his time, and to have us as Sacred Queen of these Christian Kingdoms, the which we by Divine Grace rule with great prosperity and honour, against the hatred of no Small Princes, we come to ask of your Highness – who by the grace of the same God possesses such a great State to be called of it Grand Duke of Tuscany, and being a Prince of great dignity, that as you have under your power the aforementioned Friar Girolamo, a Florentine – that you might wish to show us, for all of the previous considerations, an effect worthy of a Princely friend towards an absolute Princess and Queen, as we are, to suppress and condemn to flame all those books that might be found in your Dominions, and to castigate as your subject that wickedly infamous person their author, for having composed and published such horrible calumnies and lies against such great Princes living and dead.

There is a contrast made here, perhaps emphasized just a hair too much, of Elizabeth's absolute sovereignty with respect to Ferdinando's status, which the queen's keen knowledge of history would have informed her was due to the coup effected by his father, Cosimo I, in 1537, as well as to the subsequent despotic measures taken and advantageous marriages made to turn the Medici into a European dynastic power. For all of her vaunted admiration of Italian culture, whether or not Elizabeth would have truly recognized Ferdinando as an equal is an open question, but under the circumstances suggesting that she did was tailored to this particularly urgent request. The only mention of measures Ferdinando might have taken in response to this appeal is a brief note in a history of Dominican writers referring to the book as having been burned to satisfy Elizabeth's anger over it.[56] Two Italian biographical notes about Pollini mention a bonfire in London of the *Historia* complete with an effigy of its author and presided over by the queen, but neither gives a date and I have found no corroboration of such an event in any English sources.[57] Extant copies of the 1591 edition of the *Historia* are, at any rate, extremely rare, while the second edition, published in Rome in 1594, is widely represented in the rare book collections of European and American research libraries. Though Pollini did leave Santa Maria Novella, it is unlikely that this was the result of punitive action against him; if so, it was negligible, for he was then appointed prior of the Dominican monastery in San Gimignano, a move out of Florence but a promotion in rank. One tangible effect of Ferdinando's intervention, however, could well have been Bernardo Davanzati's *Scisma d'Inghilterra*, printed in 1602, the year after Pollini's death. Though published in Rome, this other Florentine account of English ecclesiastical history in the sixteenth century (which concludes with the death of Mary) was printed by the same Roman press, Facciotti, that had issued Pollini's second edition. Given the absence of control over publishing beyond his territories, Ferdinando might have wished to address Pollini's second, even more defamatory, edition by encouraging one of his most literate and distinguished subjects to take up the matter, publishing – with the same printer whom Pollini had obviously used to circumvent whatever Tuscan interdict there might have been against his work – a history entirely leaving Elizabeth out of the picture and considerably (though, as we saw in the previous chapter, not entirely) softening the image of her father. If so, Elizabeth's rhetorical skills in this case turned out to be enormously persuasive.[58]

There was just one prominent Italian welcomed to the Elizabethan world, in January of 1601, and the background to his visit reads like a classic *novella* plot. Virginio Orsini was through his mother a nephew of Grand Duke Ferdinando, but as Isabella de' Medici-Orsini had been strangled in a fit of jealous rage by Virginio's father in 1576, the boy was raised in the heady world of the Florentine Medici court.[59] After his father's death he inherited the title of Duke of Bracciano and in 1589 married the niece of Pope Sixtus V. Virginio was evidently engaged in an affair with his cousin, Maria de' Medici, when she was designated in 1600 to marry the French King Henri IV[60] – an alliance crafted by Ferdinando and Pope Clement VIII to consolidate Medici power in France at the same time that it served to shore up the papal front against Spain. When Maria set out to travel to France, Orsini accompanied her, informing Ferdinando that he was making the trip only after having already left Italy, never requesting permission for the voyage from the pope (Bracciano was in this period still a papal dependency), and leaving a pregnant wife behind at home. If traveling to England had been part of Virginio's plan from the outset, it might have been as a ruse to divert attention from the actual motives for the trip: a lingering farewell to Maria; the slim hope that he might be offered employment by the French king; or the possibility of renewing ties with Spain (seemingly unaware of the difficulties this would have caused with both his Medici uncle and the pope). Political acumen was clearly not Virginio's forte,[61] and while he almost certainly did not visit England with any intention of playing a political role there, his English hosts – as well as Jesuit spies close to the Elizabethan court, reporting back to Rome – were more attuned to Orsini's potential political instrumentality. So too were the Hapsburgs – whom Virginio visited in Brussels on his return to the continent – anxious as they were for the confirmation of any opening to seize England after the disgrace of the Armada and the death of Philip II.

William Cecil had met Orsini on his visit to the Grand Ducal court in September of 1600, and given the extensive network of informants Elizabeth and her councillors maintained throughout Europe, they would have been well apprised of their distinguished visitor: cousin of the queen of France, nephew of the Tuscan Grand Duke, and through marriage related both to the previous pope and to Alessandro Peretti, among the most influential contemporary curial cardinals. Elizabeth issued very specific directives regarding all of the particulars of Virginio's brief stay in England.[62]

Orsini was overwhelmed by his reception at court, and the dazzling images he took away with him soon dampened the wishful thinking of his imperial hosts in Belgium, who fully expected to hear that Elizabeth was at death's door and the country thrown into a crisis that only they could resolve. In two letters to his wife, Flavia Peretti-Orsini, Virginio details the extraordinary lengths to which the Elizabethan court went to welcome the only Italian of his station it was ever to see.[63] His host in London was Filippo Corsini, one of the most prominent of the Italian merchants in England and a Medici agent, through whom Orsini's visit was coordinated. Virginio's audience with the queen, though "not [to be] quite as private as I had hoped,"[64] was set for Tuesday, January 6, the Feast of the Epiphany, and in the two intervening days Elizabeth saw to it that her visitor was kept handsomely entertained.

After attending mass on Sunday at the residence of the French ambassador, because "in London [it] is said in no other place,"[65] he received a succession of aristocratic callers. On Tuesday, Lord Rutland came in an impressive carriage to accompany Orsini to Whitehall, where he found an apartment reserved for his use, and beyond which in a succession of other ceremonial rooms he was introduced to:

damsels ... ladies and gentlemen ... the Knights of the Garter, all dressed in white, as was the entire court that day, but with so much gold and so many jewels that it was a marvelous thing. These all came to greet me, the greater part of them speaking Italian, many French, and several Spanish. I responded to each in the way that I knew, in the language that I felt like speaking, and I am certain that I at least made myself understood. I found only two gentlemen who spoke nothing but English and with these I used others as interpreters.[66]

Impressed as he was with the sophistication of the court, Virginio was amazed when the queen herself appeared, "speaking Italian so well and relating such lovely ideas that I can [honestly] say that I have been taking lessons from Boccaccio or at the Academy."[67] Orsini was a member of the Accademia della Crusca, the Florentine linguistic institution about which there will be more to say in the next chapter, but here it is enough to note that Elizabeth's mastery of Italian was validated by one of the language's Florentine custodians.[68] He writes that he was equally stunned by the weight of the jewels the queen wore, wondering how she could even move under the burden.

When the moment arrived for the celebration of the Epiphany service, rather than directly entering the church Orsini paused in a small balcony room from which he was able to witness the liturgy without actually participating in it (probably the same space from which Ubaldini had depicted Edward VI observed while taking notes of the chapel preachers). He describes the music as having been "stupenda" [stupendous]. Afterwards, Virginio was conducted into the queen's dining room, where he observed the elaborate ceremonial carried out in anticipation of her arrival, a table set there for Grigori Ivanovic Mikulin, the representative of Czar Boris Gudonov, and his small entourage also visiting the court at this time, it "being the custom in Moscow that were he not seen to eat in the presence of the queen, his Grand Duke would have his head cut off."[69] Orsini ate lunch, splendidly, in an adjoining room, and then accompanied the queen as far as her private rooms. A musical entertainment prepared for him followed, with "several instruments as far as I know never heard in Italy, but miraculous."[70] Dinner was served afterward in the rooms set aside for him, in the company of Edward Somerset, Earl of Worcester, and George Clifford, Earl of Cumberland, after which Virginio was again ushered into the queen's presence, to the accompaniment of more music, and then:

a comedy mixed with music and dance ... the Russian ambassador was not present, I was always at Her Majesty's side, who commanded me to keep my head covered and had a stool brought for me, commanding me a thousand times to sit, though I never wished to obey her.[71]

As proud as he was that the Russian representative was not invited to this latter festivity,[72] Orsini was even more gratified about the queen's deference shown both by the hat that she insisted remain on his head and the singular place he occupied at her side, she continuing to talk with (perhaps even translating for) him throughout the entire performance. It is possible that the comedy performed by Shakespeare's company, the Chamberlain's Men, that evening was an early version of *Twelfth Night*, but if so the play Virginio witnessed and the one we know diverge in at least one significant respect: had the male protagonist of this entertainment staged in Orsini's presence actually borne his name, we might reasonably suppose that there would be some mention of such a gesture in the correspondence otherwise so filled with details of the attention this Italian visitor attracted in England.[73]

Virginio saw the queen on two other occasions. The first was at another party at court, on January 9, during which he reports that "Her Majesty was happy to dance, which is the greatest honour that she could give me, according to the word of this court, for they confirm that for the last 15 years [she] has not danced at all."[74] The following morning, Orsini was told that Elizabeth wished to see him privately, and following lunch he was taken by two gentlemen of the court by carriage to a garden entered through a secret door where the queen awaited him. About this final royal interview, Virginio wrote to his wife that "I seemed to have become one of those paladins traveling among enchanted palaces."[75] The following morning he departed London on the river, accompanied by Lord Rutland and a flotilla of royal skiffs as far as Gravesend, where he inspected the queen's navy before sailing for the Belgian coast.

The visit had lasted only a week, and though absolutely nothing of substance had been transacted it was to have serious unanticipated consequences for Orsini and his two traveling companions, for they had dared to pay homage to a woman declared in the 1570 papal bull of excommunication, *Brutum fulmen*, to be:

a heretic and favourer of heretics, and her adherents in the matters aforesaid to have incurred the sentence of excommunication and to be cut off from the unity of the body of Christ. And moreover, (we declare) her to be deprived of her pretended title to the aforesaid crown and of all lordship, dignity and privilege whatsoever.[76]

Less than a year had passed since the public execution of Giordano Bruno in Rome, and it has been suggested that in addition to the cosmological views which provoked his death sentence, Bruno's two-and-a-half years in Elizabethan England were considered by his Inquisitorial judges to have decisively contributed to the heterodox turn his thinking had taken.[77] England was from the Roman perspective now a contaminated space, and association with it was tantamount to contracting an infectious disease (which, of course, in this period was often fatal). The Jesuit priest Anthony Rivers, writing from London to his fellow English Jesuit Robert Parsons in Rome soon after Orsini's departure, reports that Elizabeth had invited the duke to follow the Epiphany service from:

> her closet over the chapel, having before given order that the Communion table should be adorned with basin and ewer of gold and evening tapers and other ornaments; some say also with a crucifix, and that all the ministry should be in rich copes. The Duke, of curiosity, accompanied her, and she was very pleasant thereat, saying she would write to the Pope not to chide him for that fact, with other discourses; and so, service ended, they returned. But herewithal many Papists are much scandalized.[78]

Upon his arrival in Florence in May of 1601, Virginio was informed by the nuncio to the Grand Ducal court that he and those with him in England were in the process of being excommunicated, news that came as a total shock to him, apparently never having imagined that he was running any risk whatsoever in traveling to England.[79] The disingenuous excuse he offered in his defense – that his cousin-in-marriage, Cardinal Peretti, as Vice-Chancellor of the Roman curia should have known of, and informed him about, any potential difficulties – was as compromising for the cardinal as it was for Orsini: for it had evidently never occurred to the cleric that his cousin's trip could be in the least bit dangerous, and in the two extant letters they exchanged during Virginio's absence from Italy Peretti wistfully wishes he were in his cousin's shoes. Far from warning Orsini to keep away from England, the cardinal made a request that Virginio bring back with him two prized dogs, about which he had heard wonderful things.[80] The excommunication crisis dragged on through the early summer, but given Orsini's weighty connections he finally managed to obtain his own absolution on July 1, and that of his companions on July 15. It seems that Elizabeth, the "heretic pretender," never wrote to the pope on Virginio's behalf, and just as well, for had she done so it might have made matters considerably worse for him.

"... *bisogna veder a chi si vende, e de chi si vende* ..."

### The status of the 'stranger' in England

Schivenoglia's disappointment regarding the musical dimension of the events surrounding Elizabeth's coronation is plainly contradicted by

Orsini's impressions of music at the English court. He was in an excellent position to judge, for he had supported the work of Luca Marenzio and Giulio Caccini, two of the greatest Italian composers of the period, and he was a promoter of the new form of music drama that would develop into opera in the seventeenth century. One of Virginio's traveling companions was, in fact, Garzia di Montalvo, who had played the chitarrone at the first performance of Jacopo Peri's *Euridice* in Florence in February of 1600.[81] Among musicians whom the Italian visitors would have heard perform during their time at court were members of the Bassano family, a dynasty of Italian musicians in England – wind instrumentalists and makers, as well as composers – whose father, Gieronymo, is first recorded in 1502 as an organ tuner in Bassano del Grappa, near Venice, and who later played in the wind band of the doge. Three of his sons – Jacopo, Zuane, and Antonio – served briefly in Henry VIII's sackbut consort in 1531.[82] Jacopo and Antonio returned to England in 1538, but as only Antonio was given a royal appointment, Jacopo returned definitively to Venice in the early 1540s, by which time Alvise, Gasparo, Zuane, and Baptista had settled in London, appointed (with Antonio) "brothers in the art or science of music" for the court. Their descendants would supply three generations of English court musicians, ending in 1665 with the death of Henry.[83] Orsini might also have encountered Alfonso (ii) Ferrabosco, the most distinguished of the Italian string players in England and later Ben Jonson's collaborator on masques for the Stuart court (he played the lute for Elizabeth's funeral). His father, Alfonso (i), had performed as a singer and instrumentalist for the French court before arriving in England sometime after Elizabeth's accession. He is listed among the queen's musicians in 1562 (Ubaldini collaborated with him on a court masque in 1572),[84] and he continued to work for the court through 1578, when he returned to Italy with his English wife for what was to have been a temporary visit, leaving their infant children effectively as hostages against his return in the care of a Dutch musician in Elizabeth's flute consort. The queen never allowed the children to rejoin their parents, after it was made clear to her that Alfonso (i) would not be returning to her service. Three of Alfonso (ii)'s sons were musicians: Alfonso (iii) and Henry, both of whom performed at court, inheriting some of their father's prerogatives there; and John, who worked as an organist and composer at Ely Cathedral.[85]

Gieronymo Bassano was most probably a Jew, and the introduction of his sons to England – where they likely continued to practice their Jewish faith in secret – was effected through the recommendation of another Italian wind player, Anthony Symonds, himself almost certainly also a Jew. The qualifiers I use here suggest that the evidence for making these claims is open to interpretation, but Roger Prior has made a persuasive case arguing that a sizable number of the musicians performing for the English court throughout the sixteenth century were indeed Jewish (though not all of them were Italian, as there seem also to have been a number of Spanish and Portuguese viol players, earlier associated with the Hapsburg court in Milan), and that though they might have made changes in their names, their identities were fully known to the monarchs who employed them.[86] Prior offers an intriguing explanation for the formation of this community of Jewish musicians in England, that "it was the particular character of the English Reformation which attracted them. It did so ... because it was both anti-Papal and anti-Lutheran, and the Jews had reason to fear both extremes."[87] While it might be more accurate to define English religion in these years as still in search of a fixed identity, the resulting ambiguities could perhaps have permitted the absorption into protective contexts of Jews who belonged to none of the warring Christian factions even if, as Stephen Orgel has noted with regard to the Lopez case, Jews were frequently taken for agents of the Jesuits.[88]

An incident involving the Bassano in 1584 demonstrates how difficult it can be to get at the facts about a small, largely undocumented, population such as the Italians in early modern England were. In the first version of the story – which demonstrates the brothers' arrogance and the queen's protective indulgence of them – Mark Anthony and Arthur, two members of the family's second generation in England, were found loitering at the gate leading into Aldgate High Street (now Aldersgate St.), and though requested by the sheriff's officers to continue on their way, the two Italians stood their ground; a fight ensued, and they were finally jailed.[89] But the Privy Council immediately summoned both the recorder and sheriff, and an apology was extracted in writing from the mayor and then sent to Francis Walsingham, Elizabeth's Secretary of State. A more elaborate version of the same incident has Arthur, Edward (i), and Jeronimo (ii) watching the "muring up of a gate called Christchurch [which] pretended to be privileged and to be made a harbour for strangers, artificers and other foreigners to the great hindrance of citizens, especially of the poorer sort."[90] When the sheriff, John Spencer, asked them to leave, the brothers, without identifying themselves or revealing their relationship to the queen, said that they had friends in equally important places as he; though they were arrested, there is no mention in this redaction of the story of the swift retaliatory action of the queen's ministers on their behalf, but once it was made known that the brothers were musicians of the queen, they had to be released, as they were immune to prosecution.[91] While ringing somewhat truer, this second account also suggests several issues to which we now turn regarding the status of foreigners in Elizabethan England, for there were reasons the brothers might have been concerned, protected though they were, about those "strangers, artificers and other foreigners" excluded from refuge in Christchurch.

One of the most problematic matters in the consideration of the Italian in early modern England is underlined by the opposition between these "others" and "citizens." I have suggested that the idea of Italian "citizenship" in the cinquecento was fraught with contradictions. There was, to be sure, no tangible sense of Italian "nationhood," political identity then residing in cities or regions, but all "Italians" spoke versions of the same language and prior to the Reformation shared the same faith, authorized by an institution that also governed the largest Italian territory. The portability of such an identity within such a context as Tudor England compounded the ambiguities of citizenship. England was only in the sixteenth century beginning to address the issue of citizenship as it sought a greater role on the stage of international affairs and was forced, partly as a consequence of this ambition, to deal with the sometimes alarmingly huge number of foreigners who flocked to British shores.

Despite the high degree of enthusiasm on the part of the Tudor monarchs for those "strangers" who brought with them to England skills that were otherwise in short supply, the reception given them by the wider English public was often blatantly hostile. There was a considerable amount of resentment that much of the skilled labor practiced in England in the sixteenth century was undertaken by foreigners; the Tudor middle and lower classes were never favorable to them, and several times these tensions erupted into riots aimed at protesting the presence and prerogatives of "strangers."[92]

The periodic censuses made of England's foreign population in the latter half of the sixteenth century were at least partly conducted to assuage public anxiety about the "strangers" among them. Just how well these indices accomplished that goal is open to question. Official English tax, census, and denization records provide a wealth of demographic data but must be used cautiously in drawing any conclusions about the populations they were intended to track. The imprecise methods utilized for collecting information (in the case of the tax and census returns), the opportunistic motives behind normalizing one's status as a foreigner (regarding the records of denizens), as well as irregularities in orthography and the anglicizing of Italian names,[93] all pose exasperating problems in attempting to understand the demographic parameters of the Italian colony. But if the official record is an untrustworthy guide to the specific details of the Italian presence in England, it does provide us with helpful information about its general contours.

We learn, for instance, from the 1571 *Returns of Strangers* that there were just over 3,000 Dutch living in London, compared with 424

Burgundians, 32 Scots, 2 Danes, 138 Italians, 5 Lucchesi and 5 Venetians.[94] This suggests a total of only 148 Italians living in London at the time, but the figure is misleading because it is not always clear that wives, children and servants figured in the tally.[95] The total number of strangers in England listed in the 1571 *Returns* is 4,755; by 1593 the number had increased to 7,113 and in 1618 had dropped to 1,281.[96] The number of foreigners in England throughout the years of Elizabeth's reign often grew dramatically (even if temporarily) in direct proportion to political disturbances on the continent: the St. Bartholomew's Day Massacre in 1572 drove thousands of French Protestants into England, at least briefly, while the Spanish occupation of the Netherlands ensured a steady stream of Dutch refugees and accounts for the Dutch always far outnumbering any other foreign communities in England in the later sixteenth century. My aim here is not to untangle a mass of conflicting statistics that resist any simple conclusions, but to suggest that these numbers make an important point that has often been obscured in efforts to establish the ascendancy of Italian influence as the English Renaissance unfolded: at no time during the Elizabethan period did the Italian community in London exceed more than several hundred persons, and of them only a very small number were engaged at any given time in professions associated with the promotion of Italian culture. This is not to call into question the manifest character of Italian influence in England and its material vestiges; on the contrary, the accomplishments of a genuine minority stand out in even greater relief when viewed in relation to the much larger number of England's Dutch and French immigrants in this period.

This incongruity is symptomatic of the function of Italian culture translated into the structures of the emerging English nation in the Elizabethan period. Speakers or readers of Italian, indeed any appropriator of an element of Italian culture, entered into an imagined relationship with a "nation" that, apart from its language and the culture that gave it a transmissible form, did not, in fact, exist.[97] But unlike Latin, which as the sixteenth century advanced lost ground as the language of learned discourse to the growing vitality of European vernaculars, Italian was particularly well-suited to enabling notions of national identity, being the language of a large population of culturally rich but politically impoverished peoples (almost exactly the opposite situation prevailed in England at the time). In addition to French, Dutch, Spanish, and to a much lesser extent German (though each of these languages was associated with more clearly defined political units), Italian could function for authorizing elites as a tool somewhere between Latin and English with which to facilitate England's aggressive entry into the international community. Both the absence of a politically centripetal force in Italy and the presence in England of a small colony of Italians throughout the Tudor era contributed to the singular status that Italians and their skills enjoyed in the Tudor world. For the Italians themselves, and this is most true during the Elizabethan years, their association with the authoritative voice of the Renaissance granted them in England a privileged status many of them would not have enjoyed in their Italian homelands; but citizenship, or more properly, denizenship was the reward for only a handful of those Italians who enabled English access not only to Italian language and culture, but also to its material resources.

The legal position of the "stranger" in England was "subject to the complex, ever changing, and at times contradictory Statutory Law, Common Law, Lex Mercatoria, Custom of the City, local parish regulations, and so forth. Their position was far from clear even in the eyes of contemporaries, and far less so today when hindsight sometimes helps, but more often blurs the picture."[98] The principal issue in question was the right of a stranger to possess property, and it came to an equivocal resolution in the case of Calvin, a three-year-old Scottish orphan, in 1609. There was some question as to whether or not Calvin, born in Scotland, could legally inherit in England the benefits from freehold tenements in Haggard (or Haggerston, or Aggerston), Shoreditch and other properties in the parish of St. Botolph. After an involved debate by English legal scholars, it was decided that as Calvin was born in Scotland after James I became king of England, his English citizenship was to be considered a corollary of the king's sovereignty there.

Earlier, the situation had been even more ambiguous. Though it was not enacted, a bill was put before parliament in 1580 that would have prevented the English-born children of a first-generation "stranger" – John Florio, for example – from being legally considered English; these second-generation "stranger" offspring were nevertheless submitted to many of the same liabilities as their parents, including a higher rate of taxation on goods and earnings (which the failure to pay led to total forfeiture). Because of the growing success and power of English merchants during the Elizabethan period, foreign merchants found themselves in an increasingly tenuous position.[99] Alessandro Magno had noted the restrictions under which the foreign merchants in England laboured:

No one can set up shop or buy anything from foreign merchants if he has not served a seven-year apprenticeship; and if it is discovered that goods have been bought from foreign merchants rather than from an Englishman who has served the required time, the goods are forfeited. If they have been sold but not yet paid for, it is the seller who loses his money, and so one has to be careful to whom one sells and from whom one buys goods.[100]

There were two ways in which to mitigate the disadvantages of being a "stranger" in England: through obtaining either an act of naturalization or a patent of denization, the chief difference between the two residing in their provenance (though acts were generally granted to children born abroad to English parents), the latter issued by the crown or its delegates, and the former by parliament.[101] With a few notable exceptions, the Italians active in the Elizabethan period generally did not take out patents of denization. Few of them ever achieved the social or economic status that would have necessitated protection of their limited legacies, and so the question of their "citizenship" – where they fit into the socio-political world – consequently remained unresolved for all but a handful of the English Italians.

> "... li nostri mercanti la mattina, e la sera si riducono in una strada ... come diciamo noi a Rialto, e a S. Marco ..."

### The Italian mercantile presence in England

Merchants represent the most uninterrupted sign of the Italian presence in early modern England. Their role in twice witnessing the transformation of England from a Catholic into a Protestant society provides an important link with the pre-Henrician Italian community there, as they were the principal Italians in England with regular, continuing ties to Italy throughout the Elizabethan years.[102] Without them one might be led to think, as some critics have been, that other Italians in England functioned in a kind of sequestration, entirely cut off from their origins. But just as the merchants were for commercial motives in close contact with their Italian families and centers of business, they would have provided – in spite of the many differences that separated them – at least some degree of connection with the peninsula for those in England who could not or would not return there.[103]

Active commerce between Italy and England had existed for more than two centuries when Elizabeth came to the throne in 1558. Beginning in the latter half of the fourteenth century there had been a colony of Italian merchants at Southampton that continued to flourish until it was afflicted by the general decline of Italian mercantile business in England in the late sixteenth century.[104] The demand for Italian products in England, similar to the interest in its culture, had always been more a reflection of elite taste than of any more general or popular need or interest. And though Italian merchants had always done a good deal of their business in exporting English goods, once English merchants found their international bearings in the last quarter of the sixteenth century they invaded markets that had previously been the exclusive preserve of the Italians and effectively appropriated the role these had played not only in England but throughout the established maritime commercial corridors of the period. The expansion of England's mercantile role was, of course, closely linked to its growing colonial ambitions, an area Italians could not possibly have competed in, given the cumulative consequences of the political traumas the Italian peninsula had suffered throughout the sixteenth century.[105]

But the Italian merchants played more than just an economic role in England, a number of them having forged bonds with the central figures in English political, intellectual, and cultural life. The Lucchese merchant Antonio Buonvisi was among the handful of Thomas More's remaining friends after his imprisonment in the Tower of London, ensuring that he had food and wine in his otherwise miserable prison cell and looking after More's family following his execution.[106] The penultimate letter of More's life, written out in coal just days before his death in 1535, is addressed to Buonvisi and testifies poignantly to the depth of their relationship:

> I cannot otherwise ... reckon ... but that it was ordained of God, that you, good master Bonvisi, amongst my poor friends, such a man as you are and so great a friend, should by your consolation assuage and relieve a great part of these troubles and griefs of mine, which the hugeness of fortune hath hastily brought upon me. I therefore my dear friend and of all mortal men to me most dearest do (which now only I am able to do) earnestly pray to Almighty God, which hath provided you for me, that sith he hath given you such a debtor as shall never be able to pay you, that it may please him of his benignity to requite this bountifulness of yours, which you every day thus plenteously pour upon me. And that for his mercy sake he will bring us from this wretched and stormy world into his rest, where we shall need no letters, where no wall shall disever us, where no porter shall keep us from talking together ... thus of all friends most trusty, and to me most dearly beloved, and as I was wont to call you the apple of mine eye, right heartily fare ye well.[107]

For his continuing advocacy on behalf of persecuted English Catholics, Buonvisi was constrained to leave England in 1548 for Louvain, where his household served as a critical focal point for the exiled English Catholic community on the continent until his death in 1558.

Italian merchants were important conduits for the diffusion of luxury goods in England, and their places of business were showcases of contemporary Italian style, as Cinzia Sicca has shown in her study of the London house of the Bardi and Cavalcanti company.[108] The Cavalcanti enjoyed a long ascendancy in Florentine civic life and culture, their duecento poet Guido being one of Dante's early companions and his father, Cavalcante de' Cavalcanti, represented among the shades of the tenth canto of *Inferno*; the marriage of Ginevra Cavalcanti to Cosimo (the Elder) de' Medici's younger brother Lorenzo in 1416 established the line from which issued Cosimo I and his successors as the Grand Dukes of Tuscany. Giovanni de' Cavalcanti first appears in records in London in 1509, in business with Misotto de' Bardi, whose family had been conducting mercantile and banking business in England for almost two centuries. Sicca notes the frequency with which Cavalcanti's name appears in English financial and war provision documents of the period, and his influence in the papal court after the election of Giovanni de' Medici as Leo X was considerable.[109] He was involved in the purchase and renovation of Palazzo Corneto in Rome for Cardinal Campeggio, as well as in the financial arrangements for the monumental tomb planned for Henry VIII and Katherine of Aragon by Torrigiano.

The house of the Bardi-Cavalcanti company was located on Throgmorton Street, in the immediate vicinity of the Church of Austin Friars, where the Florentines had established a chapel dedicated to their patron saint, John the Baptist, in 1509 and where, after the Reformation, the continental Protestant congregations were to meet. The house consisted of nineteen rooms, though only a handful of permanent residents lived there, so apart from providing accommodation for guests, the building functioned primarily as a sort of corporate headquarters. There were two gardens, with a loggia in the Italian fashion giving onto one of them, fitted with canvas curtains painted by Toto del Nunziata (establishing "a link with the fictive fresco decoration of the most avant-garde Roman loggias of the period, namely those in the villa of the Sienese banker Agostino Chigi, where, in the so-called loggia of Galatea, the painted fictive curtains are still visible"),[110] and two or three floors, the ground level consisting of a warehouse space, counting room, and a sizable parlour. Given that the house has not survived, its arrangement is a matter of speculation, but as Sicca suggests, "if central Italian architectural principles were to be applied here, one would envisage the [residential] apartments as being located on the principal story (the *piano nobile*) ranged around [an] upper parlour which would thus act as a *sala*,"[111] and there was a room with a bath located near the loggia.

Eleven Flemish tapestries are known to have hung in various private rooms of the house; Italian paintings of the Adoration of the Magi, and of the Roman hero, Marcus Curtius, adorned two of its public rooms (paintings of other biblical figures graced several of the house's bedrooms).[112] The Bardi-Cavalcanti company had long been affiliated with the Medici, themselves closely associated in Florence with the Confraternity of the Magi; the iconographic significance of a painting of foreign princes bearing costly gifts to the new-born son of God here translated into the context of Italian economic exchange in England would not likely have been lost on visitors to the room in which it was displayed. The image of Curtius, an exemplar of public virtue in his self-offering for the ancient Roman people – as the first son of a noble Roman family, he is said to have leapt into a chasm that had opened in the Forum which seers predicted would consume the city were its most valuable commodity not offered in sacrifice – made an analogous point that could have been read both as a sign of the company's extreme readiness to satisfy its English clients' needs and as an indication of its enduring devotion to Florence, having sent some of its first citizens to live and work for its "national" interests very far from home.[113]

A noteworthy feature of this and other Italian merchant establishments in England and elsewhere in Europe was the absence of Italian women in any of their business or social operations, these companies consisting almost entirely – from clerks on up – of men from within the same families, linked by either patrilineal or matrilineal kinship, a sociological indicator of the high degree of cohesion then as now typical of Italian family structure, here (also typically) extended into the business world. But given the relatively later age at which Italian men married in the sixteenth century, the homosocial world of the merchant household abroad reproduced in many respects the situation at home.

Sketches of two entirely dissimilar Italian merchants in the Elizabethan period illustrate how problematic it is to generalize about an Italian "community" in London. While many of the merchants would have fallen somewhere between these two extremes in terms of their characters and professional dealings, these examples demonstrate the polarities – particularly in terms of class and religion – that divided the Italians in England.

The first of these men, Paolo Gondola, was in London from 1590 to 1592 and worked with Niccolò de' Gozzi, a rival of Filippo Corsini's. Gondola, like many of the merchants, was a Catholic and, as Magno and Orsini had, he describes attending mass at the continental embassies in London. Gondola addressed a number of letters to another merchant, Gualtieri Panchiatichi, who had been in England but by the time of the correspondence had returned to Italy.[114] Gondola, unlike many of the Italians we have met in this history, seems to have earned the opprobrium directed at foreigners by the English populace, recounting in various letters to Panchiatichi his drunken adventures with whores, his excessive gambling, and other spendthrift habits. Though Gondola had hoped, with the help of Corsini, to set up his own business in London, his own boss, de' Gozzi, effectively prevented this from happening.[115] Gondola achieved such a reputation for *scapigliatura*, outrageous and unmeasured behavior, that a representative of the Florentine mercantile clan Gerini traveling to London in 1591 was forbidden by his family to have anything to do with him.[116]

As unseemly as his own conduct was, Gondola rather approvingly describes in one letter just how unruly the English themselves could be: he had heard about a fight that had broken out between a group of students and apprentices in London that left a school building severely damaged and one or two of the apprentices dead; he goes on to report that the same students had accosted a husband and wife on their way home one evening, seizing the woman in order to "fuck her good,"[117] forcing her under a water pump, practically drowning her, then compelling the husband who had witnessed the whole attack to swear to be an accommodating cuckold [36–38]. Gondola also relates that the frequent seizure of English boats at Livorno by the Tuscan Grand Duke had provoked a great deal of popular hostility in London [38–39], but he fails to mention that by the 1590s English pirates were making their own incursions into the Mediterranean, activity that initially only exacerbated commercial tensions between the two regions but which would eventually contribute to English dominance over Italy in the Mediterranean sea trade.[118]

Horatio Pallavicino's profile could not be more different. Born into the merchant aristocracy of Genoa – where, unlike in England, the terms merchant and gentleman were not considered mutually exclusive – little is known of his early life, but by 1576 he was serving as his family's representative in Antwerp, where he came into contact with English merchants and government functionaries. By 1580, Pallavicino had settled in England, where he replaced the recently deceased Thomas Gresham as the Elizabethan government's financial agent in its relations with other European powers. As Lawrence Stone describes it, "for twelve most crucial years from 1580 to 1592, [Pallavicino] played a part in English foreign policy even more important than that played by Gresham in the previous thirty."[119] He was involved in practically every major continental initiative undertaken by Elizabeth's government during this period, both as a diplomatic agent and as a banker.

Without attempting an exhaustive survey, a brief look at several of Pallavicino's responsibilities will help to demonstrate the scope of his engagement with the promotion of English national concerns. Between 1581 and 1585, he was responsible for the costly and complicated financial arrangements connected to keeping the Duke of Anjou – still hopeful that Elizabeth would consent to marry him – and his campaign in the Netherlands against the Spanish afloat, handling loans, extending letters of credit, delivering huge sums of cash, and then, after Anjou's death, renegotiating the terms of these transactions and trying, unsuccessfully, to convince the French King Henri III to assume responsibility for them [101–109].[120] In the immediate wake of the 1588 Armada crisis – he had made a sizable contribution to Elizabeth's war chest – Pallavicino served as the go-between for the survivors of the wreck of the Spanish ship the "Valencera" off the coast of Ireland, and he also intervened in the negotiations to liberate sixty-one Italian and Spanish prisoners held in Ireland

[204–205]. He found himself in the middle of the preparations for Leicester's Netherlands campaign, charged with obtaining "the invasion of France by the largest possible force with the expenditure of the smallest amount of English money" [125]. Pallavicino also shopped for the queen and for her courtiers when on his frequent trips abroad, a charge that sometimes required him to advance large amounts of money for items their English recipients were not always prepared to pay for [186–188].

Like Giovan Battista Castiglione, Pallavicino earned a secure place among the English aristocracy, moving after his retirement from active involvement with the government in the early 1590s from an elegant home in London, at Bishopsgate, to a large country estate, Babraham, several miles south of Cambridge (he had been accumulating properties in Essex, Norfolk, and Cambridgeshire since 1585). At his death in 1600, a commemorative volume was assembled by a number of Pallavicino's literary and academic friends, *An Italians dead bodie Stucke with English Flowers*, one of which begins:

> An Englishe man Italianate
> Becomes a devill incarnate
> But an Italian Anglyfide
> Becomes a Saint Angelifide.[121]

Though he had been initially reluctant to abandon his Catholic faith, the arrest of his brother Fabrizio by Pope Gregory XIII's deputies in 1579 compelled Pallavicino to join the Anglican church, a choice that further consolidated his incorporation into the English gentry. Fabrizio's imprisonment provoked a rare direct appeal from Elizabeth to the pope that, though unsurpisingly never acknowledged, provides further evidence of the esteem Pallavicino enjoyed in England.

One other Italian merchant must be briefly mentioned. Roberto Ridolfi was a prominent figure in the London foreign merchant community from early in the reign of Mary Tudor,[122] though he is much more widely known as the author of the 1570–71 plot to overthrow Elizabeth and her government. The Ridolfi plot is another rare exception to the usual course of Italian sentiment toward the queen in England, but not the only shadow that must have occasionally crossed Elizabeth's mind if she ever stopped to consider the less savoury implications of the Italian presence in her kingdom. Ridolfi had, it turned out, been working simultaneously as an agent for Philip II, Pope Pius V, and for Mary Stuart, whom he hoped to help put on the English throne. The total failure of this initiative – which eventually led to the executions of both the Duke of Norfolk and Mary herself – can be ascribed, as Sergio Rossi has noted, to Ridolfi's basic ignorance of the Elizabethan political apparatus, for "he did not know the contemporary

English political reality thoroughly and was not in a position to understand its new political significance."[123]

The plot had involved an Italian active in the Duke of Alba's army in the Netherlands, Chiappino Vitelli, who had traveled to England in 1569 to negotiate a peace between Spain and England that came to nothing owing to the Northern Rebellion initiated by Catholics aiming to free Mary Queen of Scots, install her in Elizabeth's place, and restore Catholicism to England.[124] In 1572, Vitelli volunteered to Ridolfi to assassinate Elizabeth himself, but by 1575 he had been rehabilitated to the extent that he was in a position to write a letter of introduction for Federico Zuccaro, the Florentine painter, who was eager to work in England for the queen and her circle.[125] The letter was probably addressed to Robert Dudley, and likely delivered in person by the artist when he arrived in London in March of 1574. Zuccaro completed two full-size portraits of Dudley and Elizabeth while in England, but all that survives of them are preparatory drawings, now in the British Museum. As the artist is recorded again in Florence in mid-October of the same year – in a document regarding Zuccaro's eventual completion of the frescoes in the cupola of the Florentine Duomo initiated by Vasari but left incomplete at his death – his visit to England, as Roy Strong has established, could not have encompassed more than six months.

"... [il] Giardin di Piero ..."

### The Italian community in England

Other professionals active during the Tudor period give an idea of the range of the Italian presence in England, but with these as with so many other English "strangers," their names and occupations are often the only traces that survive of them.[126] Glass-blowers from the Venetian island of Murano had come to England during the reign of Edward VI but incurred the wrath of the Venetian Council of Ten for revealing the secrets of Venetian glass-making and eventually returned to unknown fates in their native city. Under Elizabeth, a Venetian by the name of Sebastian Orlanden was a partner in the establishment of a glassworks at Beckley in Sussex, and another Venetian, James Vasselyn, set up a glass furnace at Crutched Friars in London. A Florentine goldsmith, Francis Capone, had worked in England during Henry VIII's reign. Giovan Battista Agnello, an alchemist, was active in England from about 1569 through the early 1580s, his arrival anticipated by the 1566 publication in London of a mystagogical treatise entitled *Espositione sopra un libro intitolato Apocalypsis spiritus secreti*.[127] In 1564, Thomas Baroncelly, described simply as an Italian, and his German business partner received a twenty-year license for a novel method for the production of salt. The sword masters Vincentio Saviolo and Rocco Bonetti both set up schools during the Elizabethan era to instruct the English in the Italian art of fencing.[128] And among several other schools opened by foreigners in London, there was one operated by Francis Maquire (Maquino) and his wife, Levinia, for twenty-four sons of "stranger" parents in Shoreditch, London, in the 1560s.

Giulio Borgarucci, from Urbino, was one of Elizabeth's physicians, possibly as early as 1562, the year in which he was naturalized, but definitively by 1573, when he was named Physician of the Royal Household.[129] During the plague of 1563-64, he played a major role in containing the epidemic, and he is cited in his brother Prospero's *Trattato di peste* (Venice 1565) for his innovative treatment utilizing knobs made from odiferous wood. Borgarucci enjoyed such a close relationship with Robert Dudley, Earl of Leicester, that he earned a place in *Leicester's Commonwealth*, the slanderous Catholic tract published in 1584 that pictured Leicester as the *capo* of a band of accomplices who had together usurped the powers of England's government and forced its people into unwilling bondage to Calvinism.[130] Both this charge and the quarter from which it was leveled are particularly incongruous, given that Borgarucci had faced problems with the Italian Protestant congregation in London, having been excommunicated from that assembly after a false accusation of Catholic sympathies. Abandoned by his first wife, he spent three full years fighting for a divorce in order to legitimately marry again, a solution that the Archbishop of Canterbury, Edmund Grindal – who earlier, as Bishop of London, had functioned as the presiding authority for the foreign Protestant churches and as such was ill-disposed toward Borgarucci – had done everything in his power to block, but which in the end only succeeded in further straining Grindal's already difficult relationship with the queen. She would not, it seems, brook any opposition to her favoured Italians.[131]

When the Bassano brothers first settled in England in the early 1540s, they were granted the Charterhouse property that had belonged to the Carthusian monks in London. Foreigners in Tudor London tended to settle in the vicinity of the monastic properties, both before and after the dissolution of the monastic orders,[132] and from the evidence of the *Returns of Strangers* the majority of Italians were clustered in the neighbourhoods of the Tower and Bishopsgate. Alessandro Magno's *Journal* offers a glimpse of the latter neighborhood:

The Italian merchants gather in the mornings, and in the evenings at nine o'clock, in a street which is closed off at one end with chairs so that neither horses nor carts can enter. They meet, as we would say, "at the Rialto," or "at San Marco," or "at the Rialto hour" ... [and] on Sundays after hearing mass, our merchants gather at the crossroads which is called the four corners, and here they make their deals.[133]

This picture of Italians taking both their social and business lives into the street, turning an otherwise busy London thoroughfare into a *piazza*, is one indication that Italians in England – the merchants, at any rate – maintained a sense of their native cultural identity abroad, and it is one of the only accounts I have come across which actually describes Italians in England among themselves.

One of the earliest extant maps of London, of the Moorfields area, shows the Bishopsgate neighborhood where many of the Italians lived in the sixteenth century. This fragment of the map [Figure 11] shows the area just south of what is now Liverpool Street, with an enclosed space marked "Giardin di Piero," accessed through a gate leading in from the adjoining lane. Unlike other similar gardens represented on the larger map, Piero's contains no trees, flower-beds, or shrubbery; its proximity to "the City 'dogge hous', and the fact that the lane running eastward from Norton Fulgate was long known as 'Bearward Lane', may be taken to support the contention that it was a bear-garden ... [or] a pleasure-ground of some unspecified kind."[134]

Another section of the Moorfields map also includes the Church of Austin Friars, where the several foreign Protestant congregations – Dutch, French, Spanish (for a brief time), and Italian – assembled for worship, the property having been ceded to them first by Edward VI and then again by Elizabeth.[135] The Augustinian parish had also served before the Reformation arrived in England as the principal "stranger" church in the city, as an anonymous Milanese merchant noted in the 1516 journal he kept of a brief visit to the country:

the third church [of London is] the Augustinians where all the foreigners go to Mass and Vespers, for if they were to go to other churches they would be very badly received, and thus all go to the Augustinians and not to other churches... the English do not [usually] go to the Augustinians [but] from time to time, though rarely, they occasionally [also] meet in this place.[136]

One might assume that the Italian congregation in London would be a likely point around which to organize a history of the Italian colony there, but this turns out to be anything but the case.

The history of the Italian church, "one of the most bizarre ecclesiastical institutions of its day,"[137] shows that far from providing a point of reference for Italians in London, it merely replicated many of the same problems that drove reform-minded Italians away from the peninsula in the first place.[138] Its Italian-language services seem to have functioned as

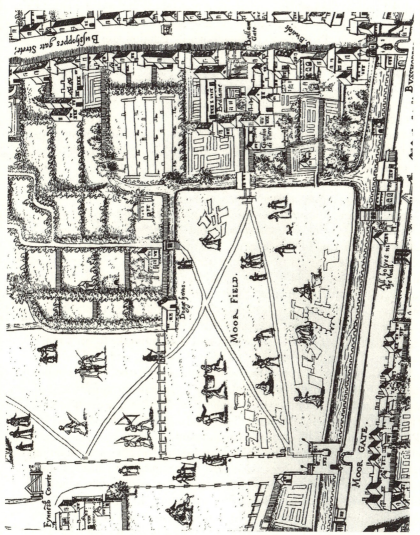

*Figure 11* The "Moorfields" section of the 1559 copperplate map of London. Reproduced courtesy of the Museum of London.

much as a practicum for English polyglots eager to rehearse newly acquired language skills as it served to satisfy the spiritual needs of native Italians; and about half of the regular congregation was Dutch, having abandoned their own congregation for doctrinal and disciplinary reasons.[139] As noted earlier, the foreign Protestant congregations in London were disenfranchised when Mary Tudor reasserted England's Catholic polity, but they were reconstituted under Elizabeth in 1560 and placed under the jurisdiction of the Bishop of London (previously they had been more or less self-governing). There had been some possibility that the Italian church would not be revived, given its tenuous beginnings, but a new pastor, the Sicilian Girolamo Ferlito, was appointed in 1565,[140] and the congregation relocated to the Chapel of the Mercer's Hall. Ferlito found the Italians under his spiritual care just as contentious as those who had troubled Michelangelo Florio, but it was a Spaniard, Antonio del Corro, who was to prove to be the most persistent thorn in his flesh.[141]

One of the more idiosyncratic figures among the foreign religious refugees in Elizabethan England, Corro came into conflict with the "stranger" congregations in London, a case that illustrates how easily Elizabethan officialdom could play its foreign guests off against one another for its own, often inscrutable, motives.[142] Corro had spent ten years shuttling between Protestant continental courts and churches after fleeing the Monastery of San Isodoro, a hot-bed of Spanish reformed thinking near Seville, in 1557. He studied in Geneva but fell out with Calvin; he cultivated the patronage of both Jeanne D'Albert (mother of the future French King Henri IV) and Renée, the Duchess of Ferrara, and her Calvinist court at Montargis; in Antwerp, he refused to sign the Netherlandish confession of faith, insulting the "left-wing" of the Reformation; and he sent a strange letter to Philip II in which he insisted that the Spanish king preside over an ecumenical council that would establish the superior claims of Protestantism over those of the Roman church. Corro was thus a man who arrived in London in 1567 with few friends and a heavy accumulation of political as well as religious baggage that would earn him enemies among the foreign population, explaining his future problematic relations with the "stranger" churches. But he, like Michelangelo Florio before him, was to find a powerful protector in William Cecil, and after another decade of continuing controversy (and after providing Elizabeth's minister with some useful covert services), Corro was settled in an Oxford position, first as reader in theology in 1578, and then as *censor theologicus* in 1581. Several months before his death in 1591 he published the *Spanish Grammar*, the first such instructional manual in English.

Corro's career is germane to the situation of the Italians in England for several reasons: his polyglotism – on at least one occasion, this Spaniard preached in French to the Italian congregation constituted by a large proportion of Dutch members – is representative of the malleable linguistic borders operative in Elizabethan England which will be examined in detail in the second half of this study; and he functioned as a lightning rod for the theological controversies that both divided the various "stranger" churches from one another and continued to play a role in the evolution of the Anglican church. Corro's specific problems with the Italian Protestants also mirror those of one of the most interesting and least known of the English Italians, Giacomo Aconcio, whose name has already been mentioned in connection with Giovan Battista Castiglione.[143]

While Aconcio's limited fame is due almost entirely to his theological work, "it is symptomatic of our ignorance of the history of technology that only one student of Aconcio has noted that he was brought to England in the autumn of 1559 by Elizabeth's new government explicitly because of his skill in fortification."[144] In the mid-sixteenth century, England was far behind its continental neighbors in the development of military technologies. Early in Elizabeth's reign, William Cecil moved quickly to address this problem, first by approaching the Florentine engineer Giovanni Portinari to return to England (he had previously worked for Henry VIII and Edward VI but fell out of favor and returned to Italy to work for the French).[145] At the same time, Cecil made an invitation to Aconcio, having learned of him through Nicholas Throckmorton, then ambassador to France. The defence of Berwick, the principal fortress on the English side of the border with Scotland, was the subject of great concern to Elizabeth and her government, for a French invasion of England by way of Scotland then seemed a distinct possibility. Portinari arrived back in England in 1560 but by the summer of 1563 had made little progress at Berwick, workers there evidently unwilling to take orders from a foreigner in the realization of what was supposed to be a vigorous assertion of England's national sovereignty. In an effort to resolve this stand-off, Cecil (or perhaps Elizabeth herself) established a team of two English engineers working with Portinari and Aconcio. The recommendations of both Italians – fortifying the lower town and the eastern side of the peninsula, strengthening the defences of the bridge over the River Tweed, wider casements, masonry instead of wood for the south-facing defensive walls, and a very thick stone wall for the Scottish-facing side of the fortress – were by and large adopted, and the intact Elizabethan defences of Berwick remain as testimony to their efficacy.

Aconcio also made the first request in England for the granting of a patent, the use of which had been sporadically applied in Italy since the early fifteenth century but never before in England. The patent that was granted in September of 1565 was actually for several inventions: energy-efficient furnaces for the production of beer and dyes, a vertical-axle windmill, and a water-mill utilizing still water. This latter apparatus was "to become one of the favourite perpetual motion devices of the seventeenth century."[146] With the financial support of Castiglione and several other investors, Aconcio also undertook a project in 1563 to reclaim 2,000 acres in the lower Thames tidal basin, a procedure he had observed in use in northern Italy, and though only partially successful his efforts introduced to England the possibility of the reclamation of marshy areas previously considered useless.

The first of Aconcio's two major contributions to the intellectual history of the sixteenth century,[147] the *De methodo, hoc est, de recta investigandarum tradendarumque scientiarum ratione*, was published in Basel in 1558, before his arrival in England. In it he delineates a method with which to organize Renaissance innovations in the arts and sciences. In many respects, this treatise anticipates the Cartesian revolution of the next century, "though in some ways [it is] better balanced, because [Aconcio] does not hang all his philosophy upon inborn ideas like Descartes but declares that our general notions or basic principles are partly innate, partly derived from our early comparisons of sense perceptions."[148] Aconcio's method, confident of the possibility of achieving substantive knowledge of the world we inhabit, provides one contemporary theoretical framework with which to explore the intellectual assumptions of the later sixteenth century, a helpful supplement to some contemporary cultural criticism that too easily identifies in earlier periods its own post-structuralist premises without adequately accounting for the prevailing conceptual assumptions of a given historical moment.[149] The lasting importance of Aconcio's *De methodo* in the early modern period, and its relevance even in the wake of Descartes' *Discours de la méthode*, is attested by later editions published in Geneva (1582), Leyden (1617), and Utrecht (1651).

Soon after arriving in London in 1559, Aconcio met the young pastor of the Dutch congregation, Adriaan van Haemstede, whom he came to regard as a friend and in whose defence he would later risk his own position in England. Haemstede ran afoul of some members of his congregation over the question of admitting believers to their services who denied the dual nature of Christ, he being of the opinion that doctrinal issues were subordinate to the actual practice of the Christian faith. Bishop Grindal, in his capacity as nominal superior of the "stranger" churches, sided with the Dutch parishioners against their pastor, perhaps concerned that he not be viewed as supporting "the excesses which had made certain German Anabaptists seem hostile to all traditional morality and political authorities."[150] Haemstede and other suspected Anabaptists were exiled by Elizabeth in October of 1560, and those "strangers" who had defended them – Giovan Battista Castiglione as well as Aconcio, in the case of

Haemstede – were never thereafter to enjoy the communion of any of the foreign Protestant congregations. The most important consequence of this episode was that Aconcio subsequently set to work on what was to become the first systematic defence of religious toleration written in England, a subject sorely in need of exposition in Protestant territories prone to many of the same injustices the movement toward reform had been intended to dispel.

Aconcio's *Stratagemata Satanae* was printed in 1564, again in Basel, where it appeared shortly afterward in a French translation, but the book was not published in English until 1647 and 1651, as *Satan's Stratagems, or the Devil's Cabinet-Council and Darkness discovered, or the Devil's secret stratagems laid open.* Aconcio dedicated his treatise to Queen Elizabeth, assuming that she was more likely to understand and enact its program of liberal religious democracy than any of the other Protestant princes, though he was taking an enormous risk in assuming that the same monarch who had banished Haemstede from England would welcome an elaboration of the principles the Dutch pastor had favored. The *Stratagemata* is unusual for the balanced tone of its rhetoric and for its pragmatic linking of religious toleration with the notion of good citizenship, for as Aconcio has it, dogma must give way to compassion if the common values of the community are to be served.[151] In Aconcio's view, Protestants are as easily led as Catholics into self-preoccupation, the fundamental human shortcoming and principal "stratagem" of the book's title. Though he recognizes the Bible as the only authoritative voice in Christian discourse, Aconcio anticipates recent biblical scholarship in acknowledging the elasticity and elusiveness of the language in which the sacred books were composed: if this is true of the Bible, he asks, how much more so of subsequent attempts to adumbrate its message? One of the recurring leitmotifs of the book is the question of how to deal with controversy disinterestedly: Aconcio suggests that it is only through careful examination of one's own motives that a fair and honest solution can be determined, and he advises that assuming the point of view of one's opponent is the only way to fully enter into the polyvalence of any serious issue:

This is most manifest in our passing of our judgment concerning writers. For, so far thou wilt praise any Author, as he shal satsifie thy judgment, and so far thou wilt dislike him, as he shal not content thee, so that every mans rule, whereby he measures what is right or wrong, is his own judgment. Which being so, who ever the Controversie be with, suppose he be the most ignorant fellow in the world, and suppose thou takest thyself to be one that speak Oracles; look how ill thou canst bear it, to be contemned by him, as ill wil he take it, to be contemned by thee; and peradventure he will take it so much the worse, by how much he hath bin less ingenuously brought up. Shal I tell thee in a word, how thou oughtest to deal with him, as to avoid bitterness? Imagine the case to be quite contrary; suppose him to be such an one as thou takest thyself to be; thyself to be such as thou deemest him, and then look what behaviour of thine would become each of you, if the case so stood, endeavour with all thy might to express. If thou shalt not thus do, a thousand to one, thou shalt not avoid, insolently to carry thy self.[152]

As unremarkable as this might seem to a modern eye, it was astonishingly enlightened thinking at the time that it was written. Concerning the question of heresy, Aconcio's sympathies are inevitably with the heretic – Origen is the patristic authority whom he cites most frequently – and he characterizes freedom of inquiry, "the complete independence of private judgment," as being "inspired by a desire and an appetite for truth."[153] He feels unequivocally that the state should keep its operations entirely separate from those of the church – a position that did, in fact, make his life in Elizabethan England somewhat problematic – and argues against "any interference of the ruler in matters of conscience."[154]

Aconcio's case is paradigmatic of the situation of the Italian in early modern England: though useful for his varied expertise – he made contributions to two of the most significant developments of the sixteenth century, reformed religious discourse and military technology – he was because of his identity as a "stranger" mistrusted by many of the people he would have worked with, but at the same time he enjoyed the encouragement and protection of the queen and several of her closest advisors.

With Aconcio, who died in 1567 just a few years before John Florio was to arrive back in London, we come to the end of these chapters in which my interest has been to describe the history and shape of the Italian presence in England as well as to delineate the course of Italian sentiment regarding developments there in order to furnish a more fully contextualized sense of the world Florio came to inhabit. The focus has not by any means been strictly literary, but there is nevertheless a distinctly textual character that emerges in much of what I have aimed to elaborate, one of the distinguishing features of the Italian encounter with Tudor England. The remainder of this volume will successively take up matters more closely tied to the transmission of Italian Renaissance linguistic and literary culture and its role in the articulation of both the English nation and its emerging culture through an examination of the teaching of foreign languages in England, and in the development of vernacular dictionaries. We have to this point witnessed the evolution of the Italian engagement with early modern England; we turn now to the technologies of cultural transmission as practiced there in the Elizabethan period by John Florio.

*Part 2*

John Florio and the Cultural Politics
of Translation

# 4 Language lessons

> It seems to me quite absurd that your countrymen should make such a point of speaking Italian well, since, as far as I know, you derive no advantage from them; on the other hand, they derive the greatest from you, and therefore ought to learn your language.
>
> Hubert Languet to Philip Sidney[1]

John Florio returned to London in the early 1570s, a century and a half into the history of Italo-English exchanges outlined in the preceding chapters.[2] Florio's return to England came at an auspicious moment, for the first three decades of the Elizabethan period, the 1560s through the early 1590s, were marked by considerable Italian influence in the English cultural arena, the time in which Florio saw his two language-learning dialogue books, *Firste Fruites* (1578) and *Second Frutes* (1591), published in London. But as conspicuous as was the circulation of Italian culture in this period, its effects were – at least in terms of its native-dress linguistic and literary character – to be rapidly eclipsed as the Elizabethan era drew to an end. The maturation of the English nation, its language and emerging culture, were forces that Italians had to a high degree enabled but were never, as outsiders, in a position to control.

I argue throughout this study that the power of Italian culture in England is mediated during the Tudor era most consistently though textual means, and this is at no time more evident than in the period – little more than one generation – that *Firste Fruites* and *Second Frutes* demarcate. But if Florio's language-learning dialogue books neatly frame this pronounced phase of Italian influence in England, they (and it) are in turn delimited by two English texts published at the beginning and end of the era. Roger Ascham's *The scholemaster* contains a celebrated critique of the Italianate fashion in Elizabethan England: published posthumously in 1570, just shortly before the likely date of Florio's return to England, Ascham's educational manifesto anticipates a program spelled out in *Firste Fruites* that is similar to it in some respects, though the principal pedagogical aim of *The scholemaster* is a reassertion of the authority of classical languages that is clearly at odds with Florio's advocacy of the culture of the contemporary Italian vernacular. Shakespeare's *Henry V*, first staged in 1599 and printed in 1600, provides a fitting valediction to the Italianate decades in England both in its thematic problematizing of the status of language within the English context and through its staging of a typical Elizabethan language lesson, which, though conducted in French, neatly represents the semiotic theater in which Florio and his language-teaching colleagues in England performed.[3]

From the date of the Norman Conquest through the end of the thirteenth century, England's linguistic coordinates had been largely determined by French, which functioned both as the dominant popular and elite language of exchange.[4] This is not, of course, to suggest that English was unspoken in England, but rather to stress its subsidiary position in relation to French, a relationship that held until the early fourteenth century, when English slowly began to establish its importance outside of the institutions of court and state. Chaucer's literary work in the latter half of the fourteenth century provided a major forward thrust to the fledgling English vernacular, though as a courtier he continued to speak and write French in his professional life; and his appropriation and translation of texts of Dante, Petrarch, and Boccaccio introduced England to the culture, if not the actual language, of the Italian vernacular. But French continued to serve as the language of the English court until the middle of the fifteenth century when, during the reign of Henry VI, English finally established its priority.

"By the sixteenth century French was an entirely foreign language at the English court, and it was round the court circles that developed the new and more serious study of [French] which then arose."[5] The study of vernacular languages thus developed in England in the wake of the English language finally asserting its primacy of place. The displacement of French in England, its assuming the status of a language to be learned, consequently opened up a space for other continental vernaculars – Italian first among them – to share some degree of the former influence that French had previously exercised there. For though the English language had by this point progressed to a position of relative independence, it remained through much of the sixteenth century the "rough tongue" that Shakespeare's Henry V rues, even as he insists that his new queen learn it (5.2.227). As the preceding chapters have demonstrated, the Tudors – whose dynastic compass coincides precisely with the emerging trajectory of the English language – were particularly interested in clothing their regal identity with the authority of more established vernacular cultures, and hence the presence throughout the sixteenth century of the small but influential colony of Italians in England whose earlier history has already been detailed.

Clothing will be a useful metaphor to bear in mind as we examine the study of Italian in Elizabethan England, for as both noun and verb it has a wide resonance in positive and negative terms throughout the period. Clothing most obviously evokes the debate over dressing-up on and off the Elizabethan stage, but it also suggests other contemporary English cultural hot-buttons – the controversy over poetry (or fiction) as lying, and the shape of "courtesy" (the notion of "staged" behavior), both issues of Italian pedigree – which are rearticulated in the acquisition of a foreign language, the putting-on of another culture.[6]

*"Inglese italianato è un diavolo incarnato"*
### Roger Ascham contra Italy

Roger Ascham's *The scholemaster* is the first, but in many respects the most substantive, contribution to a series of educational programs outlined during the Elizabethan era. Written in the first decade of Elizabeth's reign – Ascham served during this time as the queen's Latin secretary – but not published until 1570, just after his death, *The scholemaster* proposes general principles for a more humane education of boys than was then commonly the practice in England, as well as a thorough plan for the most expedient way for students to learn Latin. But what concerns us in *The scholemaster* is its categorical denunciation of the English Italianate fashion, a phenomenon Ascham had regretfully observed developing over the course of the Tudor era and from which he wished to see his students protected.

Uncompromising in its association of modern Italy with seduction, corruption and decay, *The scholemaster*'s metaphorical point of reference is the enchantress Circe, who had tempted the "wise in all purposes and ware in all places"[7] Ulysses to linger on Italian shores and is equally poised to make "of a plaine Englishman, a right Italian. And at length to hell, or to some hellish place, is he likely to go from whence is hard returning" [24r–v]. As Ascham sees it, the encounter of a previously innocent Englishman with Italy – the theater of Circe's authority in *The scholemaster* – is inevitably poisonous. Besides citing his own adverse experience in Venice [29r], Ascham offers further proof of Italy's negative valence in Plato's unhappy experience with the Sicilians he had lived among during his service to Dionysius, the tyrannical ruler of Syracuse, as well as the same philosopher's diagnosis of those who yield to Circe's blandishments [25r]: forgetfulness, the abandonment of learning and honesty, the loss of discernment between good and evil, and an arrogant disdain of the good; all leading to "pride in [oneself], and contempt of others, the very badge of all those who serve in Circe's court" [25v].

Ascham adopts an ambiguous strategy in the central section of his critique of the Italianate moment in England when he first quotes the Italian proverb "Inglese italianato è un diavolo incarnato" [26r] – the saying was frequently reiterated by those who opposed both the Italianate fashion and the presence of Italians in England – and then offers this English version of it: "You remaine men in shape and fashion but becum devils in life and condition" [26r]. Having provided a gloss, not a literal translation, of the proverb, Ascham continues for several pages to amplify his interpretation of it, which he claims:

riseth, of that learning, and those maners, which you gather in Italy: a good Scholhouse of wholesome doctrine: and worthy Masters of commendable Scholers, where the Master had rather diffame him selfe for hys teaching, than not shame his Scholer for his learning [26r].

Ascham maintains that the proverb reflects the considered opinion of learned Italians, whom he claims to respect, about the habits of Englishmen who travel to Italy and return to England corrupted in the process. There consequently seem to be two Italies for Ascham, one that has produced a language he ranks only behind Greek and Latin [23r] and that is associated with "wholesome doctrine" and "commendable scholars," and the other to which his compatriots travel and which is disastrously brought back with them to England, this latter "the Religion, the learning, the policie, the experience, the maners of Italy" [26v]. But with regard to the Italian language that he claims to admire so greatly, it is difficult to understand precisely what Ascham could have had in mind, given that he dismisses Petrarch and Boccaccio, says nothing about Dante, condemns Machiavelli, and leaves unmentioned all but one of the other literary figures of the Italian Renaissance.

One text is exempted from this blanket condemnation of contemporary Italian literature, Castiglione's *Cortegiano*, and Ascham commends its 1561 translation into English by Sir Thomas Hoby. And yet, given the role that the idea of courtesy, and particularly Castiglione's notion of *sprezzatura*, would come to play in the English debate over fiction and truth (issues central to the process of acquiring a foreign language, as we shall see), it is surprising that Ascham would be prepared to suspend his critique for the sake of this book, which advocates precisely the values he later condemns as so irremediably depraved. Melanie Ord has argued that Ascham's recommendation of Castiglione's text is equivocal, as if conceding that, were one Italian text to be read in England, it might as well be this one, and if read in the proper didactic light it could prevent the educable from essaying the inevitably corrupting trip to perilous modern Italy:

To ioyne learning with cumlie exercises, *Conto Baldessar Castiglion* in his booke *Cortegiane*, doth trimlie teach: which book, advisedlie read, and diligentlie followed, but one yeare at home in England, would do a yong gentleman more good, I wisse, then three yeares travell abrode spent in Italie. And I marvell this booke, is no more read in the Court, than it is, seing it is so well translated into English by a worthie gentleman Syr Th. Hobbie [20v].

The most problematic aspect of Ascham's argument about Italy is that it reflects little substantive knowledge of the literature that it proscribes. Praising Castiglione, Ascham is actually praising the translator of *The Courtier* for reformulating a text that in its original shape would otherwise have been considered just as dangerous to impressionable English sensibilities as any other instance of contemporary Italian writing. Hoby, in his introduction to *The Courtier*, asserts that Ciceronian linguistic values are fundamental to Castiglione's treatise, and Ascham clearly shares the translator's perspective;[8] but as we have already seen with regard to the letter Castiglione addressed to Henry VII, a very different set of principles informed his writing practices. In Latin as well as in Italian, what Castiglione sought to develop was a style that emphasized expressiveness over uniformity, and the resulting language in each case is a heterogeneous amalgam of complementary elements alien to Ascham's cultural politics. Ascham mistakes Castiglione's text for its English translation, and compounding this incongruity is the fact that Hoby was himself the living contradiction of Ascham's hysteria about Italy: having spent two years studying and traveling there he returned to England none the worse for it.[9]

Ascham is particularly alarmed at the great number of other English translations of Italian books being printed in England, concerned that even those who do not travel to Italy will be exposed to its infestations through reading.[10] Whatever is bad in contemporary Italy – and just about everything about it is – is far too easily absorbed. Ascham emphasizes the symbiotic tactility of language, but whereas direct acquaintance with Greek and Latin effects for him a kind of moral osmosis, contemporary Italian can only bring about ruin, its decadent undercurrents easily transmissible even when turned into English words by the wrong translator. Here as elsewhere in his attack on Italy, Ascham's reasoning is inconsistent, for in worrying that "mo[r]e papists be made, by your mery bookes of Italie, than by your earnest bookes of Lou[v]ain" [26v], he fails to understand (or, perhaps, acknowledge) that the impetus behind the greatest number of sixteenth-century translations – indeed the growing valorization of all vernaculars which his argument implicitly condemns – issued to a great extent from the reformed religious currents whose moral teaching he sought to convey and consolidate through the medium of classical letters. Ascham would have been appalled had he lived to see John Wolfe's press printing Italian editions of Aretino and Machiavelli in London in the 1580s, and he would have been equally shocked by the extent to which Italians made their presence felt in England throughout the two decades following his death.

The presence of the Italian community in London is acknowledged in Ascham's rebuke to Englishmen who have traveled to Italy and, upon returning to England, attend the services of the Italian Protestant congregation, even though:

> they be not of that Parish, they be not of that fellowshippe: they like not that preacher: they heare not his sermons: except sometimes for company, they come thether to heare the Italian tongue naturallye spoken, not to heare Gods doctrine truly preached [28v].

The implication is that Italian is capable of speaking the truths of a just religion for those whose "natural" language it is – though how this can be so, given the cohabitation of Italian reformed religion, the "progressive" philology we shall be examining in the next chapter, and the transmission of the Renaissance culture Ascham rejects, is anything but clear – but for an Englishman to insert himself into this context is to flirt with the same dangers any other unmediated encounter with Italy or its culture necessarily conveys.

Ascham's argument against contemporary Italy is summed up by his lament that while (ancient) Rome has disappeared, the space it occupied remains [23r-v], tragically denuded of the splendor of its classical past. Like the classical languages he championed, however, Ascham's Italian is not a living vernacular but a dead language, void of any other significance than conveying timeless ethical verities. And yet one of the paradoxes of Ascham's indictment of Italian culture is that it depends on a proverb – one of the most colloquial indices of the vitality of a living, and hence still developing, language – to make his case against the contemporary reality of Italy translated to England.

The attack on Italy is something of an anomaly within the framework of what precedes and follows it in *The scholemaster*. Reading only this episode one might form the impression that the treatise is a typical expression of contemporary English xenophobia. But there is much in Ascham's educational program that, given its historical context, is more enlightened than not: his emphasis on educating sons of both the privileged and less-so classes, his support of brilliant and not-so students, and his opposition to the use of corporal punishment. But coming as it does just at the beginning of the most important period of Italian vernacular influence in early modern England, I read *The scholemaster*'s problematic dismissal of what Ascham perceived to be the dangerous threat of Circean Italy as the opening gambit in the culture wars of the decades immediately following its publication, conflicts in which not only pro- and anti-theatricalists, poets and Puritans, fought for the high ground, but when language teachers – implicated in many of the same issues – also waged a fight to establish the legitimacy of their professional (and extra-national) identities. Edmund Spenser would attempt toward the end of this period to effect an English poetics similar in many respects to Ascham's classicizing program, but neither understood, as John Florio did, that languages do not function in isolation from the environments out of which they emerge and in which they are practiced.

"... où allez vous si matin?"

### Language instruction in Elizabethan England

The single most important factor in the creation of a space for the vernacular language teacher in Tudor England was the absence of modern languages, including English, from the curricula of both schools and universities. Several of the most noted Elizabethan language teachers, including Florio, enjoyed early in their careers some tangential relationship to the scholarly communities in Oxford and Cambridge, where important patronal as well as personal relationships were established,[11] but the idea that contemporary culture was a subject worthy of intellectual scrutiny – a conclusion Florio reached early in his pedagogical career and which had enormous consequences for the image of Italy that he brought with him to England – had not yet reached the Renaissance educational system. Given England's rapidly expanding role on the international stage in the sixteenth century, however, knowledge of other vernacular languages was far from superfluous. Indeed the period saw a host of individual language teachers setting up shop, primarily in London, first as private tutors and then, the more successful among them, as masters of small schools located largely in the area of St. Paul's, where many London printers also had their presses.

The most celebrated language teacher in Elizabethan England was Claudius Hollyband (also known as Claude de Sainliens, with variant spellings of both these names). His *French Schoolmaster* (1565) and *The French Littleton* (1566) were, by the standards of the time, runaway best-sellers, the latter title running to ten editions before 1630.[12] A savvy entrepreneur, Hollyband also issued several Italian-language books both before and after Florio had initiated his publishing career: initially *The pretie and wittie historie of Arnalt & Lucenda* in 1575, a parallel translation into Italian and English of a Spanish *novella*, with dialogues, a brief Italian grammar, and a guide to pronunciation, further expanded as the *Italian Schoole-maister* in 1583 (reprinted in 1591, 1597, and 1608); and the *Campo di fior or else The flourie field of foure languages ... for the furtherance of the learners of the Latine, French, English, but chieflie of the Italian tongue*, also published in 1583. While these books do not approach the challenging design Florio pursued through his two dialogue books, their accessibility and modest ambitions were clearly part of their wide appeal.[13] Of Hollyband's two French-instruction books, *The French Littleton* is closest in conception to *Firste Fruites* (it seems likely that Florio used it in planning the first of his Italian–English manuals), and it also reflects Hollyband's experience in opening his school, in the process refining his methodology for teaching French, which remained his principal bread and butter.

*The French Littleton* is arranged – English on the verso page, French on the recto – in a series of modest dialogues, beginning with one that deals with "Scholers and Schoole/Escoliers & Eschole," in which we find the following exchange:[14]

| | |
|---|---|
| . . . whether go you so early? | . . . *où allez vous si matin?* |
| Whether lead your son? | *Où menez vostre filz?* |
| I bring him to schoole, to learne | *Je le conduy à l'eschole pour apprendre* |
| To speake Latine and French. | *à parler Latin et François.* |
| For he hath lost his time till now, | *car il a perdu son temps jusques à present* |
| And you know well that it were better | *et vous sçavez bien qu'il vaudroit myeulx* |
| To be unborne then untaught, | *n'estre point nay, que de n'estre point enseigné,* |
| Which is most true. | *ce qui est tres veritable.* |
| You say true, it is true certainly: but whether goeth he to schoole? | *Vous dites vray, il est vrai certes. Mais où va-il à l'eschole?* |
| In Paules Churche yard, hard by the signe of the Lucrece: there is | *Au cimitiere de Sainct Paul, près l'enseigne de la Lucrece, il y a là* |
| a Frenchman which teacheth bothe the tongues: in the morning till eleven | *un François, qui enseigne les deux langues: le matin jusques à onze heures,* |
| the Latine tongue, and after dinner French, and which doth his duetie. | *la langue Latine, et après diner la Françoise, et qui fait son debuoir.* |

Each of the dialogues is arranged in a straightforward, school-masterly manner, gradated in terms of difficulty with verb conjugations, noun and adjective agreement, and other pertinent grammatical information incorporated into the narrative. The dialogues deal with a conventional series of topics – "Travellers/*Voyagers*," "The Inn/*Du Logis*," "Weight/*Du Poids*," "Rules for Merchants, to buy and sell/*Pour Merchands, Acheter & Vendre*," "Proverbs/*Proverbes*," "Golden Sayings/*Mots dorez*" – and are followed by a number of moral aphorisms, a word-list of basic vocabulary arranged according to parts of the body, family relations, days of the week, prayers, twelve articles of faith, Ch. 5 of the *Acts of the Apostles*; and a treatise against dancing that reveals its author's sober Huguenot sensibility. A guide to pronunciation and a concise grammar follow.[15]

Neither *The French Littleton* nor *The French Schoolmaster* – in both of which the grammar and vocabulary are placed first – aim at taking the language lesson outside the established boundaries of the discipline. There is no mention of French literature, ancient or contemporary, and one has the distinct impression that Hollyband's classroom, like Ascham's, was, insofar as possible, shut off from the actual gritty world that master and student inhabited.

"*E dove volete andare?*"

## John Florio's language pedagogy

Not so Florio's language lesson. With the publication of *Firste Fruites* in 1578 we are confronted with a notably more ambitious contribution to the practice of foreign-language learning in England. Unlike Hollyband, who enjoyed the favor of the court and created a comfortable niche for himself within the aspiring English middle class, Florio evidently remained something of a marginal figure in the circles to which he aspired during the period that his language-learning dialogue books demarcate (recall that his father had actually lived in William Cecil's household during the reign of Edward VI). As Florio admits to Nicholas Saunder, the dedicatee of *Second Frutes*, the dedication of *Firste Fruites* to Robert Dudley had not yielded the recognition or advancement he had sought. Also unlike Hollyband, Florio provoked a great deal of negative sentiment that seems to have been directed at him personally, the nature of which can only be gathered from his aggressive responses to it in the prefatory material in both of his dialogue books and in the first edition of his dictionary.

Besides the xenophobia that foreigners in England had always faced, one of the most telling pieces of criticism that Florio admits to in *Firste Fruites* is the charge that he has no legitimate right to be teaching Italian:

So bene ... che alcuni diranno come puo scriver costui buon Italiano? & non è nato in Italia? A quelli rispondo che considerano bene i fatti suoi, alcuni altri diranno come è possibile che costui sappja dar regole & non è dotto? A quelli non so che dire perche dicono la verità.[16]

I know it well... that some people will say: how can he write good Italian, not being born in Italy? To them I respond by saying that considering clearly their case, others will say: how is it possible that he knows how to teach grammar, not being learned? To all of them I know not what to say, for they speak the truth.

Born in England, raised in Switzerland, more than likely never having visited the political and cultural matrices of cinquecento Italy, Florio was among the first generation of Italians who considered themselves such by dint of their mother tongue; their families having been driven from Italy for reasons of religion, these refugees occupied an ambiguous political space. "Strangers" in their adopted lands, children born to them in exile often suffered the indignity of not belonging (even if the laws of some countries, England included, suggested otherwise) to either their parents' new or abandoned homelands, before the inevitable process of assimilation made citizens of their descendants, wherever they settled. Florio frankly acknowledges the problem – one that any non-native speaker of a language confronts – associated with the topographical specificity of language, but his promotion of Italian language and culture in early modern England is both a rebuttal of the position that language is limited by geography and an assertion of its power to create an imaginative world unlimited, even if deeply marked, by the temporal conditions in which it is exercised.

In his dedication of *Firste Fruites* to Robert Dudley – the most prominent advocate of things Italian in the Elizabethan period[17] – Florio praises the Earl of Leicester for his "liberalità, cortesia, e virtù." These last two qualities, terms associated with Castiglione and Machiavelli, situate Florio's book within the gathering cultural storms that were to play themselves out in the later sixteenth century not only in England, but also on the continent, a preliminary sign that Florio's idea of the language merchant was of a more engaged agent of cultural transmission than most of his contemporary colleagues demonstrated themselves to be.

*Firste Fruites* begins with a substantial amount of introductory material in Italian and English, followed by dialogues arranged in forty-two chapters of varying lengths, a brief vocabulary, prayers, rules for Italians to follow in pronouncing English, and an Italian grammar. My aim here is not a thorough examination of Florio's copiously constructed text – Arundel del Re's 1936 critical edition of *Firste Fruites* impressively serves that purpose – but rather to situate both it and *Second Frutes* more squarely within a cluster of highly charged cultural questions with which early modern language-learning has not usually been associated.

# Language lessons

The first and most important thing to note about Florio's dialogic method is its performative aspect. To speak Italian in England is to be performing a role, assuming another identity in a way similar to the actor taking on another's *persona* on stage. This might seem an obvious point, but it has a wider resonance when we consider that it was in the period Florio was writing *Firste Fruites* that the first public theater in England was opened in London by James Burbage in 1576, and in the years immediately following its publication that the first hostile anti-theatrical tracts began to appear in England. As we shall see, *Second Frutes* perhaps best exemplifies the theatrical structure of Florio's language-learning methodology, but many of the issues taken up in the later book are already present in a less polished guise in *Firste Fruites*.

Stephen Gosson, the author of the most famous of the attacks on the English theater, *The Anatomy of Abuse*, contributed one of the dedicatory sonnets to *Firste Fruites*, a gesture that left Florio open to being associated with the anti-theatrical trend.[18] But Gosson's innocuous poem plays with the metaphors of planting and harvesting in Florio's "pleasant crop" of "fruits" and neither suggests its author's position on the theater nor recognizes that the cultural project Florio (at times haltingly) elaborates in *Firste Fruites* bears a strong resemblance to the feigned theatrical world Gosson would shortly – in 1579 – come to attack.

When Florio first mentions the theater in *Firste Fruites* 1 [1r], one of his interlocutors asks:

| | |
|---|---|
| *E dove volete andare?* | And whither wyl you goe? |
| *Dove piace a voi.* | Where it please you. |
| *Dove anderemo noi?* | Where shal we goe? |
| *A una comedia, al Toro, overo in qualche altro luogho.* | To a play at the Bull, or els to some other place. |
| *Vi piacciono le Comedie à voi?* | Do Comedies like you wel? |
| *Signor, si la festa.* | Yea sir, on holy daes. |
| *Mi piacciono anche a me, ma i predicatori non li vogliono acconsentire.* | They please me also wel, but the preachers wyll not allow them. |
| *Perche, sapetelo?* | Wherefore, knowe you it? |
| *Dicono che non sono bone.* | They say, they are not good. |
| *E perche si usano?* | And wherefore are they used? |
| *Perche ognuno si diletta in esse.* | Because every man delites in them. |
| *Io credo che si faccia di molte furfanterie a queste Comedie, che credete voi?* | I beleeve there is much knaverie used at those Comedies: what think you? |
| *Cosi credo anche io.* | So beleeve I also. |

Even here at the outset of his dialogue-book, Florio makes a bold departure from the practice of his predecessors. Grammatically the passage encompasses the use of *piacere* – ever a stumbling block for native-English speakers – direct object pronouns, the agreement of nouns and adjectives, as well as the present indicative, future, and present subjunctive tenses. This is quite a mouthful for a beginning student, but it reflects a pedagogical approach that values speaking above grammatical precision. Where *The French Littleton* is careful to provide dialogues that progress slowly in difficulty, spelling out grammatical issues within the course of each dialogue, the very first chapter of *Firste Fruites* charges recklessly ahead, assuming that practice – rehearsal of the dialogue – will make perfect, a pedagogical position that squares well with the subject it promotes.[19] But here as elsewhere in *Firste Fruites* the logical course of the narrative is not always clear: the two interlocutors are at first enthusiastic about the idea of going to the theater, but when the issue of *i predicatori* arises, they retreat behind the notion of *furfanterie*, and *FF* 1 ends with the matter unsettled. Florio returns briefly to the idea of attending the theater at the end of *FF* 2, in which a rather forward gentleman courts a defiant *donzella* – one of the *topoi* of both of Florio's *Fruits* – using as his final ploy an invitation, which is accepted, to *veder la Comedia* [*FF* 2, 2r]. Here a visit to the theater is the culmination of a hitherto thwarted seduction.

In *Second Frutes* 2,[20] one of the interlocutors characterizes the English theater as consisting of:

| | |
|---|---|
| *rapresentationi d'historie, senza alcun decoro* | representations of histories, without any decorum |

and though the preceding two passages are the only ones in *First Fruites* that directly address the question of the English theater, there are several other matters taken up in succeeding dialogues which suggest that the issues raised by the anti-theatricalists were ones about which Florio had not yet made up his own mind, an ambivalence that I understand as a consequence of his perhaps unwitting recognition that as a language teacher he was implicated in the same *furfanterie*.

Questions about proper attire are raised in *FF* 3, 4 and 5 [2r–5v]: there are discussions of shopping for a hat, stockings, slippers, and shoes; whether gloves should be perfumed or not, and by whom; the color of garters; and the cost of white shirts.[21] While there is no moral inflection to any of this sartorial talk, when we come to *FF* 15, in the middle of the lengthy description of England, we find this exchange [16v]:

| | |
|---|---|
| *La gente vanno bene vestiti?* | Go the people wel apparelled? |
| *Benissimo, e con gran pompa.* | Very wel, and with great pomp. |

# Language lessons

| | |
|---|---|
| *Un mecanicho vuol esser mercante, un mercante vuol esser Gentilhomo, il Gentilhomo vuol esser Conte, il Conte, Duca, il Duca, Re, tanto che ogni uno cerca di superar l'altro in superbia.* | A handycrafts man wil be a merchant, a merchant wil be a gentleman, a gentleman a Lorde, a Lorde, a Duke, a Duke a King, so that every one seekes to overcome another in pride. |

The unsettling practice revealed here is that individuals with identities apparently fixed by the clothing that it is assumed they should be wearing are in fact pretending to other identities by sporting the clothing of their next higher social superior. But who is to blame for these indiscretions [17r]?

| | |
|---|---|
| *E maraviglia che la Regina non ci trova rimedio.* | It is marveile that the quene findeth not some remedy for it. |
| *Lei e tanto compassionevole, che lassia fare a ciascaduno quello che piu li piace; la libidine, & cupidita sono praticate assai.* | She is so pitiful, that she letteth every one to doo what he pleaseth most; lust and covetousness are practised very much. |

Though Florio probably means here that the queen in her generosity chooses to overlook the sartorial habits of her subjects, there is nevertheless a degree of criticism implied. Because *Firste Fruites* is dedicated to Robert Dudley – who was closer to Elizabeth than anyone else in her inner circle during these years – citing the queen's indulgence in this context could well be construed as symptomatic of Florio's failure to achieve any significant recognition at court during the era over which she presided, though this ambiguous reference is tempered elsewhere in *Firste Fruites* by the effusive praise which was much more typical of Italian estimations of Elizabeth's character.[22] Florio similarly fails to recognize that these clothing-related observations might well have been made of anyone practicing the particular kind of language skills he promoted in England.

There is a brief earlier discussion of the court in *FF* 5 [4v]:

| | |
|---|---|
| *Donde venite signor mio?* | From where come you sir? |
| *Io venga da la Corte.* | I come from the Court. |
| *Come sta la maesta de la Regina, con tutti I Gentilhomini, e Gentildonne a la Corte?* | How doth the queenes maiestie with all the Gentlemen and Gentlewomen of the Court? |
| *Loro stanno benissimo.* | They do very wel. |
| *Mi piace certo.* | It pleaseth me wel certaine. |
| *Quando si remove la Corte?* | When removeth the court? |
| *Non si sa.* | It is not knowen. |
| *Si dice la settimana prossima.* | It is saide the next weeke. |

| | |
|---|---|
| *Ci fara progresso?* | Shal there be a Progresse? |
| *Non si sa anchora.* | It is not knowen yet. |
| *Io voglio esser in paese, se ce ne.* | I wil be in the country, if there be any. |
| *Cosi voglio anche io.* | And so wil I. |
| *Si dice che ce ne fara uno.* | It is said there wil be one. |
| *Io voglio saper brevemente.* | I wil know it shortly. |
| *Ma come lo saperete?* | But how wil you know it? |
| *Io lo sapero benissimo.* | I wil know it very wel. |

As Roy Strong has examined in detail, the royal progress became under Elizabeth "an elaborate ritual ... with which to frame and present the Queen to her subjects as the sacred virgin whose reign was ushering in a new golden age of peace and prosperity."[23] The progress was thus another manifestation of the theatrical impulse in the Elizabethan world and, as such, exercises a palpable fascination for Florio's interlocutors, one of whom self-confidently presents himself as enough of an intimate of the court to know in advance its plans and movements. Florio would certainly have known Italians who could boast of such connections, and though he aspired to a similar position himself he was not to achieve it until after James I acceded to the English throne in 1603. That this first mention of the court in *Firste Fruites* occurs in terms of an eagerly anticipated spectacle, following as it does the opening dialogues about both the actual English theater and clothing, suggests a nexus of concerns that even if rather crudely realized are also linked to a theory of poetic veracity – the status of fictional accounts – that situates Florio's book, and the acquisition of a "foreign" language that it advances, within a literary-critical continuum that stretches from Boccaccio to Sidney.

"... *fizioni varie e maestrevoli* ..."

### The poetic 'lie' in the service of language learning

In *Firste Fruites* 19 [26r], Florio cites an Italian proverb:

| | |
|---|---|
| *Con arte e con inganno, si vive mezzo l'anno, con inganno, e con arte, si vive l'altra parte* | With art and with deceit, halfe the yeere we live: with deceit and with art, we live the other part |

that tersely encapsulates the Circean element in fiction-making at the same time as it underscores the importance of proverbial usage in Florio's pedagogy. This proverb brazenly interprets all human behavior in precisely the light Ascham had feared: through assuming other roles – be they in the theater, the court, or on the street, and through the medium of a fictive persona, wearing inappropriate clothing, or speaking in a "foreign" tongue – one behaves *con inganno*. Gosson, in his *Playes Confuted in Five Actions* (1582), asserts that "the profe is evident, the consequent is necessarie, that in Stage Playes for a boy to put one the attyre, the gesture, the passions of a woman; for a meane person to take upon him the title of a Prince with counterfeit porte and traine, is by outwarde signes to shewe them selves otherwise than they are, and so within the compass of a lye."[24] The argument is easily translated into the realm of language-learning, for "[from the anti-theatrical perspective] the activity [of the theater cannot] be extenuated, like a crime of passion, as a sudden yielding to a natural urge. Theater involves training, rehearsal, and planning on the part of its producers. On the part of audiences it requires a sustained imaginative collusion with the events portrayed by the actors."[25] This trajectory coincides with the shape of the Italianate fashion in Elizabethan England, from the deliberate choice to study Italian, practice it, and then perform its lessons for (admittedly) limited audiences who were themselves its students. A fundamental leitmotif of the opposition to Italian culture in England is its positing – like the English theater to which it made important contributions – an imaginative world that in one formulation can be considered a space "of withdrawal or experiment,"[26] a place similar to that represented by pastoral in both the theater and poetry of the Elizabethan period in which different identities could be tried on and retained or not depending upon their utility.

But to what end? Consideration of the role of Italians in the Tudor construction of national identity has already yielded in these pages a number of different responses, and the critical function that dictionaries and literary canons played in the shaping of early modern "national" consciousness will provide several others in the next chapter. But a constitutive element in this complex process is the acknowledgment of the creative and ideological possibilities of fiction-making, what Boccaccio characterized in the *Trattatello in laude di Dante* as the delight of the poetic fiction. Describing the birth of poetry as the *terminus ad quem* of an ancient history that anticipates Vico, Boccaccio notes that poetry grew out of the need of primitive peoples to address their divinity in a fitting manner, and he suggests that the first poetry was conceived in a language quite apart from that of the spoken vernacular: an entirely new, delightful, and artful (or cunning) form of speech.[27] Both in the *Trattatello* and in his defense of poetry in the fourteenth book of the *Genealogia deorum gentilium*, where he confronts the notion of the poetic "lie," Boccaccio maps out an apology for "pagan" fiction – the diverse corpus of classical mythology – against which he asserts the unassailable truth status of the Bible.

In the *Genealogia*, Boccaccio's poets – fiction-makers – aim to inspire the putting-on of virtue in a manner that shadows but cannot equal that of the sacred scriptures, and – critical for our consideration of the role of "foreign" languages and cultures in early modern England – they are also useful instruments in the service of the ruler. The *Trattatello* describes the procedures necessary to the consolidation of political power as:

[those] things that could not have easily been done without the collaboration of the poets, who, in order to extend their own fame, as well as to win the favor of princes, delight their subjects, and persuade all to act virtuously – which with plain speaking would have been contrary to their actual intentions – made the people believe what the princes wished by masterfully contriving various fictions that are wrongly understood by today's unlettered, to say nothing of that earlier time.[28]

Boccaccio has Virgil in mind here, the poet-ideologue of the Augustan age whose work served to frame in a "delightful fiction" the re-imagined history of the Roman people by way of justifying their contemporary form of government and simultaneously prompting them to virtue, or its political synonyms, conformity and obedience.

Philip Sidney's *Defence of Poesie* was written by the early 1580s (but not printed until 1595), at the conjunction of Florio's early career and the beginnings of the English theater – negative criticism of which was one of Sidney's targets – and it takes up a number of the issues that Boccaccio raises. While it is likely that Sidney knew at least the *Genealogia*, one of the most popular encyclopedic treatments of classical mythology in the sixteenth century, he was certainly familiar with the shape of Boccaccio's poetics as it was refracted through two successive centuries of debate in Italian, French, and Spanish literary circles. That this debate about the truth-status of fiction had finally reached English shores had something to do with the presence there of Italians and of Englishmen under the sway of Italian ideas. But Sidney's contribution to the argument, like Florio's innovations in language learning, challenges the reactionary formulations of cultural definition represented in Elizabethan England by Ascham and Gosson, and in Italy by the far-reaching consequences of ecclesiastical censorship and by the early work of the Accademia della Crusca.[29]

The *Defence* opens with an account of how Sidney, while in Vienna (in 1574–75) with his traveling companion, Edward Wotton,[30] fell under the influence of an Italian riding master, John Pietro Pugliano, who:

according to the fertileness of the Italian wit, did not only afford us the demonstration of his practice, but sought to enrich our minds with the contemplations therein, which he thought most precious. But with none I remember mine ears were at any time more laden, than when (either angered with slow payment or moved with our learner-like admiration) he exercised his speech in the praise of his faculty. He said soldiers were the noblest estate of mankind, and horsemen the noblest of soldiers. He said they were the masters of war and ornaments of peace, speedy goers and strong abiders, triumphers both in camps and courts. Nay, to so unbelieved a point he proceeded, as that no earthly thing bred such wonder to a prince as to be a good horseman. Skill of government was but a *pedanteria* in comparison.[31]

Though the scene is often elided in analysis of the *Defence*, several critics have identified Sidney's encounter with Pugliano as emblematic of the wider implications of his argument about the legitimacy of fiction-making. Catherine Barnes suggests that "the *Defence* succeeds not so much because it convinces as because it beguiles: it wins support for its theory of poetry by means of sophisticated exercises in audience psychology rather than by intellectually cogent argumentation."[32]

If we can identify a method in Florio's language-learning pedagogy, it would be akin to this sort of rhetorical seduction. It is suggestive that Sidney's riding teacher is also an Italian expatriate trading on the "fertileness of the Italian wit," and he goes on to describe in his anecdote about Pugliano just such an attempted sleight of hand:

Then would he add certain praises, by telling what a peerless beast a horse was, the only servicable courtier without flattery, the beast of most beauty, faithfulness, courage, and such more, that if I had not been a piece of a logician before I came to him, I think he would have persuaded me to have wished myself a horse.[33]

Initiating his *Defence* with a negative example – Pugliano fails to persuade his student, breaking Aristotle's rule in the *Poetics* about not going so far in constructing fictions that they are exposed as such[34] – Sidney coyly positions himself at the outset of his treatise as capable of both decoding others' fictive deceptions and practicing them more effectively himself, for:

if Pugliano's strong affection and weak arguments will not satisfy you, I will give you a nearer example of myself, who (I know not by what mischance) in these my not old years and idlest times having slipped into the title of a poet, am provoked to say something unto you in the defence of that my unelected vocation, which if I handle with more good will than good reasons, bear with me, since the scholar is to be pardoned that followeth the steps of his master.[35]

The real point of interest here, as Barnes notes, is that:

the hyperbolic argumentation of the "maister" leads the persona-as-listener [Sidney] to the equally hyperbolic response of "almost" wishing to be a horse, and, thereby, the object of such elaborate praise. In this way, the persona is identified with the same self-interest and eagerness for praise that he observes and mocks in Pugliano ... [Sidney] has himself written a piece that capitalizes on the listener's self-love: it urges the auditor to wish himself "a horse", that is, the object of a poet's praise.[36]

Horsemanship thus requires disciplined mastery, as does learning another language, and so too "the art of poesie – which Sidney sees as his 'unelected vocation.'"[37] Pugliano's respectable status as "esquire in the stable" of the Emperor Maximilian II implies, in Sidney's anecdote, a relationship between the Italian horseman's fabulations and his professional position within the ambit of the imperial court. This is a corollary to Sidney's own higher station within Elizabeth's circle, since both men practiced a politically engaged form of poetizing about which Florio, at this stage in his career, could only dream. The larger argument that Sidney teases out of the implications of his *exordium* exceeds the limits of this study, but its valorizing of fiction-making, written as it was at just the time that Italian vernacular culture exercised its most powerful hold on Elizabethan England, suggests a congruence between the acquisition of foreign vernacular languages and the cultures they represented, and Sidney's defense of what Boccaccio characterizes as the "poetic lie."[38]

> "... cominciate pure i vostri proverby quando che vi piace, che io vi ascoltero attentivamente ..."

**Proverbial lessons**

We can take this argument a step further by noting that Boccaccio in the *Genealogia* locates legitimate fiction even in the fables of a "maundering old woman, sitting with others late of a winter's night at the home fireside."[39] Proverbs are one of Florio's principal fonts for colloquial Italian in his language-learning dialogue books, and this passage from *First Fruites* 6 [6r-v] links their usage with the work of poets:

| | |
|---|---|
| *Io vedo certe persone bizarre che fanno il bravo hoggi, domani sono poveri, altri fanno conto inanzi l'hoste, vogliono fare, dire, che è che no e sono morti.* | I see certain foolish people, that bragge it out today, and tomorowe are poore, others make their account before the host, they wil do, they wil face, and by and by they are dead. |
| *De questi ne vedemo l'esperientia generalmente.* | Of these we see the experience dayly. |
| *Quelli verificano il proverbio.* | These verifie the proverbe. |
| *Che proverbio volete dire?* | What proverbe wil you say? |
| *Quel proverbio che dice, Chi troppo abraccia, poco stringe.* | The proverbe that sayth, Who imbraceth much, little closeth. |
| *Certo questo e bono.* | Certis this is a good one. |
| *Ma sapete come dicea quel altro?* | But know you how the other said? |
| *Come dice lui, vi prego?* | How saith he, I pray you? |

| | |
|---|---|
| *Lui dice, che e sempre bono per uno haver due corde per il suo archo, accio che se una si rompe, lui ne habbia un altra presta.* | He saith, it is always good for one to have two stringes to his bowe, to the ende, that if one breake, he may have an other ready. |
| *Certo colui la intende.* | Certainly he understands it. |
| *E proverbio anticho.* | It is an old proverbe. |
| *Chi pensate che habbia fatto questi proverby?* | Who think you have made these proverbes? |
| *Io credo qualche poeta.* | I beleeve some poetes. |

Proverbs have served for millennia as terse encapsulations of popular knowledge. But as Robert Alter notes, the biblical book of *Proverbs* "is an expression of mainline wisdom activity, concentrating on the honing of received insights, [and] stresses the presupposition that wisdom is a language craft."[40] The oldest collection of Judeo-Christian proverbs is thus closely tied to the accomplished use of language, the poet's mandate, and the language teacher's obligation. We see in these initial verses of *Proverbs* that:

The wise will hear and gain instruction,
the discerning man will gain astuteness,
To understand proverb and epigram,
the words of the wise and their riddles. [1:5–6]

and Alter suggests that "epigram ... could also be translated metaphor, dark-saying, or poem and it is associated elsewhere with a verb that means to interpret or translate."[41] Erasmus too maintained that "proverbs wrap in figurative darkness a hidden truth that must be unfolded or explicated,"[42] though the erudite commentary he developed in the *Adagia* was of a different kind from Florio's proverbial usage. For John Florio, to speak in proverbs – to "lie" as poets do, utilizing figures of speech that conceal their speaker's meaning – necessitates interpretation, or translation, into other more accessible terms (in *Firste* and *Second Frutes* by incorporating them into dialogic exchanges), thus situating the proverb within the larger compass of linguistic activities that constituted his career. The proverb is in this sense a kind of conjuration,[43] urging its auditors to first divine and then practice its meaning.

While neither *Firste* nor *Second Frutes* spells out a coherent theory of the proverb's place within a cultural politics, Florio's copious employment of them – he supplied an appendix to *Second Frutes*, the *Giardino di ricreatione*, which consists of over 6,000 Italian proverbs, arranged alphabetically – provides us with an opportunity to speculate on their importance for his sense of the significance of the Italian vernacular.[44] Prefacing an onslaught of proverbs in the following chapter, Florio's interlocutors have this to say about them in *Firste Fruites* [*FF* 18, 26v-27r]:

| | |
|---|---|
| ... *cominciate pure i vostri proverby quando che vi piace, che io vi ascoltero attentamente.* | ... begynne you youre proverbe when you please best, and I wyl hearken attentively. |
| *Ma guardate di non dormire.* | But take heede ye sleepe not. |
| *Signor, no, non dubitate, cominciate pure.* | No sir, doubt not, begynne, begynne. |
| *Noi comincieremo con quelli che si usano in Italia, e cosi seguiremo in ordine.* | We wil beginne with those that are used in Italie, and so we wil folow in order. |
| *Fate come vi piace.* | Do as you please. |
| *Ma avvertite prima, che un proverbio Italiano á dirlo in Inglese, non puo haver quella gratia, come ha in Italiano, e anche un proverbio Inglese, á dirlo in Italiano, non ha quella gratia, come ha nel suo natural linguaggio.* | But marke first, that an Italian proverb, to say it in English, can not have that grace, as it hath in Italian, and also an English proverbe, to say it in Italian, can not have that grace as it hath in their natural language. |
| *Quello non importa, pur che habbi qualche senso con se, non puo senon dare un certo diletto al ascoltatore.* | That skylleth not, so that it have some sense with it, it can not but yeelde a certaine delight unto the hearer. |

By beginning with those proverbs "used in Italie" and then following "in order" those used elsewhere, Florio draws attention to the cultural specificity of proverbial wisdom. While it is true that a great number of proverbs traveled from one European language – Latin, as well as the various vernaculars – to another, many proverbs are particularly marked by the cultural coordinates of their originating languages. James Obelkevich's assertion that "national distinctions don't exist in proverbs"[45] is true in the early modern period only insofar as "nations," in our modern sense of the term, are not yet strictly defined as such; but this fails to take into account the distinctiveness of the linguistic clothing in which proverbs are expressed, consequently neglecting the manifold ways in which language defines place.[46] For Erasmus, proverbs disclose the *ethos* of a culture; they were, as Henry Peacham says, "the Summaries of maners, or the Images of humane life."[47] Marked as languages are with "cultural residue ... proverbs often make explicit what is elsewhere implicit in a language: the values, beliefs, and aspirations of a community ... the moral, social, or economic world can [thus] be epitomized topographically,"[48] as here in the sixth chapter of *Second Frutes* [106–9]:

S. *In Italia sono troppo feste, troppo teste, e troppo tempeste.*

S. In Italy too many feasts doe raine, too many stormes, too many a busy braine.

P. *Dove faccio pensiere di fermarmi un pezzo, a veder le belle Città di Lombardia.*

P. Where I purpose to stay a while, to view the faire Cities of Lombardy.

S. *La Lombardia è il giardino del mondo.*

S. Lombardy is the garden of the world.

P. *Io voglio trattenermi qualche giorno in Milano.*

P. I will entertaine my selfe a while in Millaine.

S. *Milan può far, Milan può dire, ma non può far di acqua vino.*

S. Millaine may doe, and Millaine may crake, But Millaine cannot wine of water make.

P. *Visto Milano, io vedrò poi quelle tanto belle città longo il Re de' fiumi Po, come Ferrara, Parma, Cremona, Mantoa, & andrò poi a Pavia, & a Brescia.*

P. When I have seene Millaine, then will I see those fayre Cities, scituate alongst the King of floods, Po: Ferrara, Parma, Cremona, Mantoa, and also Pavia, and Brescia.

S. *Tutte le armi di Brescia, non armeriano la paura.*

S. All the armies of Brescia, will not arm feare.

P. *Io vedrò ancora Padoa, Vicentia, Piacentia, Verona, Treviso, & tante altre belle Città.*

P. I will also see Padova, Placentia, Vicentia, Verona, Treviso, and so many other faire Cities.

S. *Pan Padovano, vin Vicentino, carne Furlana, formaggio Piacentino, trippe Trevigiane, e donne Venetiane.*

S. Bread of Padova, wine of Vicentia, flesh of Furly, cheese of Placentia, tripes of Trevise, and women of Venice.

P. *Io non tralasciarei per cosa del mondo di veder quella tanto celebre, & inclita Citta di Venetia, la quale da molti vien detta l'impossibile nel'impossibile.*

P. I would not for any thing in the worlde, omitt the seeing of that renowned citie of Venice, which of many is called the impossible, within the impossible.

S. *Venetia, chi non ti vede non ti pretia, ma chi ti vede ben gli costa.*

S. Who sees not Venice cannot esteeme it, but he that sees it payes well for it.

And a bit further along, we find this proverbial index of the defining characteristics of the major cities of Italy [*SF* 6, 108–9]:

S. *Milano grande, Venetia ricca, Genova superba, Bologna grassa,*

S. Millane great, Venice rich, Genova proud, Bologna fertile,

*Napoli gentile, Fiorenza bella,*  Naples gentle, Florence faire,
*Padova dotta, Ravenna antica, e*  Padoa learned, Ravenna ancient,
*Roma la santa, che gia fu Regina,*  and Rome the holie, which
*& hora è ancilla del mondo.*  whilom was Queene, but now is
 the sillie handmaide of the world.

Lawrence Manley notes "a relationship between cities and poetry which is perhaps timeless, but which enjoyed a special prominence in the work of Renaissance poets, who often contributed directly to the structures of political power."[49] Through the equation of poetry and proverbs, we can make a similar claim that the demarcation of place in the Italian proverb provided a model for the developing English nation in the Elizabethan period; as England was literally learning to define itself through the cultural apparatus of other "nations" (a process that will be examined lexicographically in the next chapter) the democratic proverb provided a point of departure for organizing the circulation of both moral knowledge and political power.[50]

Though proverbs represent various registers from high to low within particular languages, they do not necessarily travel between languages with the same fluidity. Recalling Ascham's gloss on "Inglese italianato/Diavolo incarnato," we can now suggest that to render this saying literally in English would vitiate its sharp impact in Italian; it becomes clear in English only once its implications are spelled out. In a similar vein, we find these disparate versions of the same proverb in *Second Frutes* 1 [12–13]:

N. *Io m'accomodo ad ogni cosa e*  *N.* I apply myselfe to all, and am
*sono come il sacco d'un mugnaio,*  like a millers sack, and not as
*e non come alcuni che fanno tal*  some, who sometimes make it a
*volta conscientia di sputar in*  matter of conscience to spitt in
*chiesa, e poi cacheranno su*  the Church, and at another will
*l'altare.*  betray the altar.

Florio's definition of *cacare*, in *Queen Anna's New Worlde of Words*, "to shite, to cacke, to scummer" [72], situates this proverbial action on an *altare* far from the semantic euphemism of its English equivalent here. Speaking of the translation of proverbs in his prefatory "To the reader" in *Second Frutes*, Florio advises his students to:

rather drink at the wel-head, than sip at puddled streams ... proverbs are the pith, the proprieties, the proofes, the purities, the elegancies, as the commonest so the commendablest phrases of a language. To use them is a grace, to understand them a good. [*SF*, A5v–A6r]

The cautious strategies of learned sixteenth-century French collectors of proverbs, concerned not to infect the developing high style of the French vernacular with too many "low" elements,[51] are conspicuously contrary to Florio's approach not only in his language-learning dialogue books, but in his dictionaries and translations as well.

Kenneth Burke characterizes proverbs as "*strategies* for dealing with situations,"[52] and it is as "equipment for living" that proverbs have traditionally played their singular role in linguistic culture. As true for Greek and Latin antiquity, the neo-Latin revival and vernacular cultures of the sixteenth century as for our own polyglot world, the rehearsal of proverbial knowledge cuts across social boundaries as no other language game can. Ruspa, the servant of Torquato in the first chapter of *Second Frutes*, easily holds his own in proverbial volleying with his master, and following upon a contentious exchange about the location of various articles of Torquato's clothing, we can see in their subsequent dialogue the complications of the mastery/subservience dialectic inherent also in the sort of pedagogical relationship represented by the language lesson [*SF* 1, 6–9]:[53]

R. *Io non so trovar la chiave.*
T. *Dove l'hai posta, trascurato che sei?*
R. *Stamane l'ho messa nella scarsella, o io l'ho.*
T. *Sei tu cosi povero di memoria?*

R. *Io non mi ricordo dal naso alla bocca.*
T. *Tu non farai mai statuti, ne casa da tre solarie.*

R. *Pur che io ne faccia da uno.*

T. *Tre arbori, ti basteranno à far ciò.*
R. *Molti grandi vengono a star in case cosi basse.*
T. *Al corpo di, ch'io non vuo dire, che s'io metto mano ad un bastone, io ti farò ben star in cervello.*
R. *Io non saprei farci altro.*
T. *Tu vuoi che io dij di piglio à qualche pezzo di legno per perstarti le ossa.*

R. I cannot find the key.
T. Where hast thou layd it? Careless as thou art.
R. I put it in my pocket this morning. Oh I have it.
T. Art thou so short of memory?
R. No man more forgetfull than I.
T. Thou wilt never make statutes, nor houses with three stories.
R. I would I would make any with one.
T. Three trees will serve thee doo that.
R. Many great men come to dwell in as lowe houses.
T. By the bodie of, I will not sweare. If I take a cudgell in hand, I will not make thee looke to thy selfe.
R. I cannot doo with all.
T. Thou longest to take a staffe in hand to swadle thy bones withal.

R. *Cio non vorrei gia io.*

T. *Hora vedo che chi l'ha daratura, fin' ala fossa dura.*

R. *Ecco qui una dozzena di camiscie, due di fazzoletti, altretanti collari direnza, otto ghimphe o lattuche, co' loro manichtti lavorati di seta, quatro tovagliuoli, sei sciugatori, otto scuffie, tre paia di lenzuola, ecco poi in questa pettiniera i vostri pettini d'avolio, e di bosso, le vostre forbicette, con i curaorrechie, et le altre cose.*

T. *Hora vedo che tu sei un huomo da bene, hai il tutto.*

R. Nay mary would I not.

T. Now I see what is bred in the bone, will never out of the flesh.

R. Here is a dozen of shirtes, two of handkerchers, and as many falling bands of lawne, eight ruffe bands, with their hand cuffs, wrought with silke, foure towels, sixe wipers, eyght cuoiffes, three paire of sheetes, then in this combe case are your yuorie & boxe combes, your cisors, with your eare pickers, & al your other knacks.

T. Now I see that you are an honest man, thou hast all.

While Torquato's position of mastery – maintained through the strategic use of proverbs – is never really in jeopardy, Ruspa manages both to deflect his master's threats and resolve the little crisis represented here through his own masterly use of language. "*Trovar la chiave*" is as apposite for the correct reading of the master's intentions as it is for finding his *altre cose*. Interestingly, this valorization of clothing in *Second Frutes* signals a departure from the sartorial prudishness that had marked *First Fruites*, for here the disclosure of clothing initially feared to be misplaced or lost marks Ruspa, at its discovery, as *un huomo da bene*.

"*...è meglio sdrusciolar co' piedi, che con la lingua...*"

**Instruction in courtesy**

Making Ruspa speak with equivalent facility in both Italian and English, Florio underlines a further crucial consequence of the language lesson as he practiced it in Elizabethan England (we could say that this is true of all such educational initiatives): the blurring of social distinctions through the acquisition of new learning. A great deal of recent criticism has focused on the courtesy-book, or the manual of *savoir-vivre*,[54] as the literate arena in which English elite anxiety concerning its privileged hold on power in the later sixteenth century played itself out.[55] Francis Yates suggests that "there is something of the Italian courtesy-book in the *Second Fruits*, and Florio probably hoped that an Italian finish would refine away some of the English barbarism of mind and manners which he and [Giordano] Bruno found so trying."[56] But it seems that this finishing-school aspect of the courtesy-book was precisely what those of the English "gentle class" feared its social inferiors would (and did) appropriate, and while "it is striking to see how much the difference of class is talked about [in Elizabethan England]," it is equally noteworthy "how much the gentle class needs to be taught what it takes to be gentle."[57]

The goals of the courtesy-book are thus often at cross-purposes, and this is nowhere more evident than in the gaps in import that open up between Italian treatises such as Castiglione's *Cortegiano* and Della Casa's *Galateo*, and their Elizabethan English translations. In the case of *Galateo*, John Woodhouse argues that the scope of Della Casa's plan has much more to do with satirizing the conventions of the manuals of *savoir-vivre* than with promoting courtly values, and according to Annibale Ruccelai, the treatise's dedicatee, Della Casa had aimed to frame his satire in a Tuscan register intended to prove Italian's lithe and muscular capacity for comedy. All of this disappears in Richard Peterson's English translation, done, as Woodhouse notes, not from the Italian original but from a 1573 French translation printed in Lyons. In Peterson's English, "the *Galateo* becomes a sober, practical manual ... conveying rules of conduct."[58] Similarly, but in a far more accomplished and subtle vein, Hoby transformed the *Cortegiano* from an examination of social values within an enlightened Italian courtly milieu into an elegantly couched assertion of the essentialist priority of the English aristocratic class. Daniel Javitch notes Florio's reference in the "dedicatory epistle of his *Second Frutes* to the Elizabethan who 'hath learnt a little Italian out of Castilions courtier, or Guazzo his dialogues,' [suggesting] that both books were being read as primers of language and conduct."[59]

George Pettie's English version of Guazzo's treatise, *The Civile Conversation* (1581), again made largely from a French translation, introduces a further wrinkle into the translation of Italian courtesy into the English context: for while Guazzo's original text deliberately sets out to counter Castiglione's assumption of an impenetrable noble class of the courteous with a more egalitarian notion of virtue acquired "by insisting ... on the moral implications of verbal style,"[60] Pettie intervenes with a pæan to Elizabeth and at various other points in his translation by providing a space for the courtier whom Guazzo had all but banished from his civilizing colloquy.[61] I note these differences here in order to contrast the notion of courtesy that Florio advances in *Second Frutes* in both Italian and English dress – situated as he is *in* and *between* both linguistic cultures – to suggest that his work as a language merchant encompasses many of the polarities represented by the conflicting agendas of the *Galateo, Cortegiano,* and *La civil conversazione* in their Italian and English versions. Eager to please aristocratic patrons without whose support his career would have floundered, Florio was nevertheless one of the many individuals in Elizabethan England whose upwardly grasping social ambition gave rise to the "apprehension that the democratic motivation of 'equall experience' would erode hierarchy," a fear that "proved, of course, to be prophetic."[62]

The proverbial enumeration of Italian cities cited earlier occurs within the context of a lesson in courtesy consisting of a large number of proverbs proferred by a Paduan to an Englishman soon to make a trip to Italy. Peeter, the Englishman, begins the exchange with this *proemio* [*SF* 6, 90]:

| | |
|---|---|
| P. *Due sono le cagioni che mi muovono a venir' a basciarvi le mani, l'una a visitar v.s. e ringratiarla di tante cortesie che sempre le è piaccuto mostrarmi non solo in parole ma altresi in effetti, per le quali io me le terrò per sempre obligatissimo. La seconda a saper se le piace comandarmi qualche servigio in Italia, o in altro luogo dove io mi trovi; & sapendo che v.s. ha visto buona parte di esso, è riputata da ogni uno molto intendente, pratica, e prudente, io la prego con le maggior forze che io mi trovo a voler darmi qualche buon ricordo, o civil precetto come io habbia a governarmi in questa mia peregrinatione, accio io possa imparar qualche cosa di buono, & alla fine tornar a casa con honore, e non come molti de' nostri che vanno Messeri e tornano Servi.* | P. There are two causes which moove me now to come and doo my dutie to you: the first is to see you, and to give you thankes for so many curtesies that it hath alwayes pleased you to shewe me, not onely in words, but in effect, for which I will at all times acknowledge my selfe infinitely beholding to you. The second is to understand if it please you to command me any service in Italy, or in any other place wheresoever I am. And knowing that you have seene a great part of the world, and by reason of the long experience you have of every part thereof, you are of all men accounted very skilfull, experienced, and wise, I beseech you as hartely as may be, that it will please you to give me some good remembrance, or civil precepts; how I shal behave my selfe in this my travaile, to the end I may learn some good thing, and at last returne with some credit, and not doo as many of our countreymen who goe out maisters and returne clerks. |

The passage reiterates several of the key elements of courtesy literature, its gracious language – in Italian, couched entirely in the formal third person singular and emphasized through its stilted syntax – serves the purpose of structurally mirroring Peeter's designs, for to speak of courtesy requires the use of courteous language. But ironically, given the precedence accorded *parola* elsewhere in both of Florio's *Fruits*, language here is not enough: "*non solo in parole, ma altresi in effetti*" has Stephan demonstrated to Peeter his courteous authority. And Peeter's evaluation of Stephan's character – he is described as "*intendente, pratica, e prudente*" – provides further validation of his choice of advisor, one prepared to give "*qualche buon ricordo, o civil precetto*" and teach how best to "*governarmi in questa mia peregrinatione ... imparar qualche cosa di buono, & alla fine tornar a casa con honore*," in order to avoid inverting the master/servant distinctions so important to the Elizabethan elite which might be threatened by an otherwise unmediated experience of *Italia*. That Peeter could posit such an end here, when Florio's professional activities aimed precisely to transform his own inferior social status into just such a position of authority and influence, is one more indication of the complex interplay of linguistic artifice and social reality in Elizabethan England.[63]

A further indicator of Florio's mixed objectives in *Second Frutes* is his employment of proverbial wisdom in the advocacy of courtesy. As we have already seen, the proverb functions across class distinctions, to some extent confusing them, while the courtesy-book – in its English form, at least – aimed in rhetorical terms to either maintain or pacify established hierarchies. But Stephan's counsel to Peeter is framed not in the careful language of courtesy with which his friend had begun (and that we might expect) but rather in the rough-and-tumble of the proverbial vernacular [*SF* 6, 92–93]:

S. *E se vuoi esser viandante & andar salvo per il mondo, habbi sempre & in ogni luoco, Occhio di falcone, per veder lontano; Orecchio d'asino, per udir bene; Viso di cimia, per esser pronto al riso; Bocca di porcello, per mangiar del tutto; Spalle di camelo, per portar ogni cosa con patientia; e Gambe di cervo, per poter fuggire i pericoli. E non voler mai haver difetto di due sacchi ben pieni, cio è uno di patientia, perche con essa si vince*

S. And if you will be a traveller, and wander safely through the world, wheresoever you come, have always the eies of a Falcon, that ye may see farre, the eares of an Asse, that ye may heare wel, the face of an Ape that you may be readie to laugh, the mouth of a Hog, to eat all things, the shoulder of a Camel, that you may beare any thing with patience, the legges of a Stagg, to flie from dangers: and se that you never want two bagges very full,

| | |
|---|---|
| *il tutto; & l'altro di denari, perche Quegli che hanno ducati, Signori sono chimati.* | that is one of pacience, for with it a man overcomes all things, and another of money, for They that have good store of crownes, are called Lordes, though they be clownes. |

Stephan's advice continues in this mode for seventeen pages, lacing proverbs together in a pedagogical narrative seamless in its homespun orality but deeply conscious, nevertheless, of the role of verbal strategy in the informed version of courtesy it promotes [*SF* 6, 94–95]:

| | |
|---|---|
| *E non vogliate mai dar fede a faremo di Roma, agli adesso adesso d'Italia, a magnana di Spagna, a by and by d'Inghilterra, a warrant you di Scotia, & a tantost di Francia, perche tutte sono ciancie.* | And take heede you never give credite unto the Faremos of Rome, unto the adesso adesso of Italie, to the magnana of Spain, to the by and by of England, unto the warrant you of Scotland, nor unto the tantosts of France, for they are words of small importance. |

Again we see the "nationally" specific character of proverbial wisdom, here calling into question the reliability of some forms of language to convey the truth. And if others can deceive with their words, it is imperative that one guard one's own tongue, for [*SF* 6, 96–97]:

| | |
|---|---|
| *... molte volte le ciancie, riescono a lancie.*<br>*E quantunque la lingua non habbia osso,*<br>*La fa spesso romper il dosso Et è meglio sdrusciolar co' piedi,*<br>*Che con la lingua.* | ... often words do end with swords.<br>And how be it the tongue be without bone,<br>Yet it breaketh many a one; And better it is with foote to slip,<br>Then with the tongue to trip. |

Both proverb and courtesy-book depend upon the careful use of language to effect their respective purposes, as Florio's interlocutor makes clear in this context and as the title of Torquato Accetto's 1641 treatise, *Della dissimulazione onesta*, suggests in another. According to Woodhouse, "every courtesy treatise which I know, with the possible exception of the *Galateo*, aims to teach its reader varying degrees of dissimulation ... prevarication is an important part of the courtier's ability."[64] Learning appropriate linguistic strategies through the acquisition of other languages and the appropriation of the cultures they represent becomes, in this light, both a forceful offensive weapon in the arsenal of the upwardly aspiring and a defensive tool of containment for the ruling class. Paradoxically, the balance of power in the Elizabethan period depended to a great extent upon the skillful manipulation of rhetorical structures whose contingency is exposed by the operations of the language lesson, making it problematic to keep an underling like John Florio in his place.

> "...da me ridotte ne la maniera, ch'egli le compose, e ne la medesima maniera, ch'egli haveva diterminato di farle prima volta stampare..."

### The Italian book, made in England

The period framed by Florio's two *Fruits* is also marked by a phenomenon that the first of them inaugurated: a series of Italian books printed and issued in London by a handful of English publishers in these decades, the course of which follows the rise and decline of the privileged place Italian held there. The first Italian book to appear in England, in 1553, was an isolated case but not incidental to this later history, for it was a translation by Michelangelo Florio of John Ponet's reformed religious instructions, the *Cathechismo, cioe forma breve per amaestrare i fanciulli*.[65] Dedicated to John Dudley, the Duke of Northumberland, and containing an epistle to Edward VI, it represents precisely the sort of schooling in heresy that Girolamo Pollini lamented about the young king's intense focus on the acquisition of foreign languages (his sources may even have had Michelangelo's text specifically in mind).[66]

The 1578 edition of *Firste Fruites*, printed by Thomas Dawson (for Thomas Woodcock),[67] was almost certainly edited and proofread by its author, a practice Florio likely continued to follow throughout his publishing career but which in this initial instance was absolutely necessary, given the lack of any editorial control with regard to books printed in Italian in England at that time. The only printer to establish such consistent oversight was John Wolfe, and though Florio published just one small pamphlet with his press in 1591, a consideration of Wolfe's role in the transmission of Italian print culture is a crucial component for appreciating the contemporary climate which rendered Florio's career in England possible.

Wolfe had served an apprenticeship with the London printer John Day until about 1572 (he would likely have been involved with the production of Ascham's *Scholemaster*, first issued by Day's press in 1570 and reprinted in the following year), traveling to Italy shortly thereafter, where he continued his training with one of the Florentine publishing houses during his stay of several years in the city. While his later career in London is quite well documented, Wolfe's earlier preparation and professional activities are matters of almost complete speculation.[68] Apart from his later, considerable, and expert practice with the publication of Italian books in London in the 1580s, only several pieces of contemporary evidence survive to situate Wolfe in Italy in the preceding decade, the first of which is a *libretto*, published in Florence in 1576 with these words affixed to its title page:

In Fiorenza, ad Istanza di Giovanni Vuolfio, Inglese

In Florence, By Petition of John Wolfe, Englishman

A life of St. Bernard, this pamphlet bears some of the distinguishing marks of the Giunta press, though without its characteristic imprint, while the provenance of a second Florentine book bearing Wolfe's name, a life of St. Stephen Protomartyr, has proved more difficult to identify.[69] Both were aimed at a marginally literate public and they are related generically to other such books pitched to a popular readership. Between 1576 and 1577, Wolfe's name also appears four times in Florentine judicial records related to matters of the book industry, but it is not clear whether he was obligated to make these appearances on his own behalf or as proxy for his employers.

The other piece of evidence linking Wolfe to Italy is found in the introduction to the first Italian book he issued in England, in 1579, Giacomo Aconcio's *Una essortatione al timor di Dio* (apparently printed abroad), which was edited posthumously by Aconcio's friend and supporter in the Elizabethan court, Giovanni Battista Castiglione. In his dedication of the book to the queen, Castiglione writes:

When, most serene lady, Jacopo Aconcio, your faithful servant, passed from this life to the next, among the papers that he left me I found this short treatise in his own hand, and inasmuch as the style permitted me to understand it appeared to me equally a product of his happy genius. The which [as] more and more I read, ever more pleasing to me, was awakened the desire that it should be printed ... and resolute in this intention, through the occasion of a young man of this city recently returned from Italy where he with great industry learned the art of printing, I am even more determined to bring it into the light of day under the most happy and resplendent name of Your Royal Highness.[70]

This modest pamphlet consists of several poems written by Castiglione himself, preceded by Aconcio's essay, which summarizes the principal aims of his thinking, "a reaffirmation of [his] motives ... an appeal for human renewal, and a call to a deeply held religion whose roots are planted in the heart."[71] Wolfe names himself on the title page as "Servitore de l'Illustrissimo Signor Filippo Sidnei," thus situating himself as the beneficiary of patronage extended by two of Elizabeth's favored courtiers. And as early modern religious politics provided one of the principal motives for Wolfe's career as a printer of Italian books, Aconcio's association with ideas that were then anathema to prevailing Catholic ideology makes of the *Essortazione* a fitting first step in the successive decade of Italian printing with which Wolfe's press would distinguish itself.[72]

Wolfe might have been active in Florence by the time that Vincenzo Borghini's edition of Boccaccio's *Decameron* was printed there by the Giunta press in 1573, an effort supported by Cosimo de' Medici to salvage this foundational Tuscan literary text from the Index of Forbidden Books. Wolfe's time in Italy, apart from supplying him with expertise none of his English colleagues could rival, would have impressed upon him the potential in a market left unserved by the void created by books whose publication was then banned in Catholic territories, "a market ... always in the course of renovation under pressure from cultural, political, propagandistic, and economic factors."[73]

When exactly Wolfe returned to England is unknown, but by the late 1570s he was active in London's shadowy underground world of printers engaged in illegally issuing popular and lucrative books such as the Bible, *The Book of Common Prayer*, and school texts which were exclusively licensed to other sanctioned printers by the Stationers' Company, the official state organ that exercised control over printing in early modern England. Wolfe's identity as a renegade printer in rebellion against the Stationers makes his association with Castiglione – the most highly placed Italian in the Elizabethan court – and with Philip Sidney seem particularly incongruous.[74] That Wolfe's activities as leader of the underground print renegades were conducted simultaneously with the initiation of his printing of Italian books – which the Stationers initially claimed no jurisdiction over – suggests some contiguity between these two aspects of his early publishing career. But Wolfe's admission into the Company of Stationers in 1583 is even more significant, for in his newly authoritative role (he became Company Beadle in 1587) he turned informant on his former colleagues, exposing the location of their presses and stopping them in their tracks.[75] We might identify in the shape of these events a pressure, exercised by either an assimilated Italian of Castiglione's rank or an establishment figure such as Sidney, to embrace the *status quo* in order to capitalize upon the alliances such accommodation would generate. Wolfe may have also have been taking a page from the pragmatics of Niccolò Machiavelli, whose two central works his press issued soon after his entry among the Stationers.

Wolfe's editions of Machiavelli's *Discorsi* and *Il prencipe* appeared together in 1584, and the introduction to the *Discorsi* gives us a good picture both of Wolfe's incentive for publishing the text and of how he and his editor(s) went about their work. The printer, in a preface written in the voice of "Barbagrigia Stampatore" [Graybeard the Printer] addressing his "benigno lettore" [benign reader], notes that he had earlier been misled about the character of Machiavelli's work, believing too readily the opinions of those he has since discovered to be enemies of the truth. Advised by a learned friend to undertake a careful reading of all of Machiavelli from beginning to end, he notes that:

> the more [of his works] I read, so much the more they pleased me, and to tell you the truth, each further hour with them new teachings were revealed, marvelous new insights, and new modes of understanding the true means of extracting something practical from the useful reading of histories; and in short, I learned more from them in one day about the governance of the world than I had previously grasped in all of the history I had ever read. I learned to recognize the difference between a just prince and a tyrant, to tell the government of a majority of the greatest good from that of the least evil, and to distinguish between a well-regulated community and a confused and licentious mob.[76]

Already here Barbagrigia's reading shows itself to be considerably more astute than the emerging tendency of Machiavellianism in England and elsewhere, and, accordingly reoriented in his estimation of these works, the printer resolved to dedicate all his resources to publishing them, in order that no deserving reader should be deprived of the extraordinary experience he had had in first encountering them. Barbagrigia goes on to say that the many voices raised against Machiavelli temporarily gave him pause in pursuing his objective – he has in mind the enormously influential anti-Machiavellian distortions of Innocent Gentillet's *Discours sur les moyens de bien gouverner et maintenir en bonne paix un royaume ou autre principauté*, published first in Geneva in 1576 and immediately a run-away hit – but that now he is more resolute than ever in his determination to see that Machiavelli's work be printed in a form as close as possible to its original shape.[77]

Accordingly, the preface also addresses the problem of not having had available for the preparation of this edition the manuscript texts that Machiavelli's earlier Italian editors would have had at their disposal. Barbagrigia is critical, however, of the 1546 Aldine and 1550 Giolito editions of the *Discorsi* (both published in Venice) upon which his is based, anxious that their irregular orthography might be confused with his own practice (a surprising proviso coming from an English printer in a period when one of the only consistencies in contemporary English spelling was its inconsistency); but he then notes that Machiavelli's frequently idiosyncratic usage, "modes of speech totally contrary to the teaching of our grammarians,"[78] has been allowed to remain as is, as have his occasional mistakes in classical attribution, other great writers being noted as having suffered similar slips of memory.

Inviting his reader to take in hand the Venetian editions for a comparison with this new one, Barbagrigia suggests, quite seriously, that the Wolfe *Discorsi* should be considered the most authoritative edition of the text yet printed.

A note following the relatively few printing errata identified at the conclusion of the *Discorsi* leads us to another peculiarity of Wolfe's Machiavelli and Aretino editions:

> The shrewd and reasonable reader will correct for himself the other minor errors ... for [the text] having been entrusted to compositors, Sicilians to whom the Tuscan tongue is unknown, these were unavoidable, even with all their diligence.[79]

As concerned as Barbagrigia is with establishing the truth about Machiavelli's ideas and with producing a philologically correct text, both the *Discorsi* and *Il prencipe* sport busy title pages citing Palermo as their city of origin, and the heirs of Antoniello degli Antonielli as the printers of the two texts (Figure 12). What exactly Wolfe had in mind in creating a false provenance for these, and for his other editions of Machiavelli and Aretino, will never perhaps be entirely settled but clearly has something to do both with the intended audience for such books and the cultural milieu from which they issued. Having criticized Venetian editors of the Florentine Machiavelli in his preface, feigning to publish a superior edition in Palermo – not in the cinquecento, as it later became a noted center of print culture – with an invented press, Wolfe is both playing with and drawing attention to his acquaintance with Italian regional differences, trumping them, however, with the publication of this volume in London.[80] Continental, and particularly Italian, buyers might have been amused but would not have been fooled by the ruse, and yet there is evidence that Wolfe's Italian editions were successfully marketed at the Frankfurt Book Fair.[81] English readers of Italian, not as attuned to the nuances of the Italian cultural situation or its book trade as their continental contemporaries, would nevertheless have understood at least some of the implications of publishing in England books that were outlawed in Italy.

Barbagrigia's other prefaces (together with those that refer to him after his supposed death) and the other fictitious title pages of Wolfe's subsequent Machiavelli and Aretino editions, continue this game of cultural one-upmanship by inventing an alternative print history whose inconsistent chronology, provenances, and fictional presses all aim with varying means to deflect attention from London as their point of origin.[82] The printer's motto on the title page of the *Discorsi*, "Il vostro malignare non giova nulla" – which might be liberally translated as "Sticks and stones may break my bones, but names will never hurt me" – at first glance strikes

*Figure 12* Title page of John Wolfe's edition of Machiavelli, *I discorsi*. Reproduced by permission of the British Library.

an odd professional posture, but in the end fits its subject's heterodox publishing profile like a glove.

The one issue in Barbagrigia's prefaces unambiguously intended to be read at face value is the program they propose that these books aim to accomplish. The 1588 preface to Machiavelli's *L'asino d'oro* – containing the comedies *Mandragola* and *Clizia* as well as several short prose works – points out that the promises made at the conclusion of the preface to the earlier *Discorsi* have been fulfilled, for with the exception of a volume of letters which have eluded the editor's search for them, all of Machiavelli's principal works had by then appeared in print in Italian in England. The same objective for Aretino fell somewhat short, as none of his religious works or a further projected volume of dialogues and selected letters (this latter licensed by the Stationers in October of 1588) were ever printed.

But together with the rehabilitation of Machiavelli, Wolfe's editions of Aretino's *Ragionamenti* (1584 and 1588) and the *Quattro comedie* (1588) had an equally ambitious goal: balancing his appreciation for Machiavelli's pragmatics, Barbagrigia proposes in his preface to the *Prima parte de' ragionamenti* that the publication of Aretino's no-holds-barred exposition of the hypocrisies of the powerful serves not only to realize the text in print according to its author's intentions:

redacted by me in the manner in which he wrote [it],[83] and in the same manner in which he had determined that [it] should be published the first time[84]

but also functions as an emphatic affirmation of the freedom of the press. Aretino is described as the:

great friend of free men, mortal enemy of twisted necks, mighty lover of knowledge, cruel adversary of ignorance, partisan of virtue, and bitter rebuker of vices[85]

and to publish his work in anything but its unexpurgated form would be an offense against that very "benign Nature" already sullied in "this century of mud, not merely of iron."[86] Despite these high-minded sentiments, the Aretino texts Wolfe undertook to publish in Italian raise a number of issues that are addressed only obliquely in Barbagrigia's prefaces, the most crucial of which is their pornographic mode of representation. No such sexually explicit material was printed in English in this period, and indeed there were no complete English translations of Aretino's dialogues or comedies until well into the nineteenth century.[87] Wolfe's liberty to publish what he saw fit to do must consequently be understood in the light both of his secure position within the Company of Stationers and the relatively limited public in England then in a position to decipher Aretino's notoriously difficult language. Had these texts been more readily accessible – as we shall see they became with the publication of Florio's dictionary – Wolfe might well have found his freedoms notably more circumscribed.[88]

None of the other printers of Italian books in England in this period articulated anything like Wolfe's ambitious program, the realization of which would have been unthinkable without the assistance of native-speaking Italian editors, and critical attention has focused on Petruccio Ubaldini and Giacomo Castelvetro as Wolfe's likely collaborators. The image of Ubaldini already formed by this study, and particularly the character of his written Italian, confirms Bellorini's suggestion that he must have worked primarily as Wolfe's proofreader, Castelvetro being thus identified with Barbagrigia's wider-ranging interventions.[89]

Giacomo Castelvetro was in a number of respects John Florio's double, and though they certainly would have known each other in England it is unclear precisely how close their relations were.[90] Born in Modena to a family of religiously heterodox intellectuals in 1546, he passed the most productive years of his life in Britain, working with Wolfe during the decade in which he produced his Italian books, and then from 1591 to 1594 as Italian tutor to James VI and Anne of Denmark, in Edinburgh. Castelvetro subsequently spent several years in Denmark and Sweden before settling for twelve years in Venice, occupied there as an associate of the Sienese printer Giovan Battista Ciotti and as an agent of the English crown. He returned to England in 1612 after having been briefly jailed by the Inquisition, freed by the Venetian Senate through the arbitration of Dudley Carleton, the English ambassador, on condition that he leave Venice definitively.[91]

Giacomo was a nephew of Lodovico Castelvetro – among the most noted Italian humanists of the middle decades of the cinquecento, the first Renaissance editor and commentator of Aristotle's *Poetics* – and the classical humanistic formation that Giacomo received under Lodovico's tutelage, as well as further experience gained working in the print shop of another uncle, Giovanni Maria, in Lyons, prepared him for the extensive editorial contributions he made first to Wolfe's press and later to Ciotti's.[92] Castelvetro's career reiterates the pattern witnessed so frequently in these pages – reformed religious conviction,[93] exile, and professional concern with language – a conjunction of issues that within the context of Wolfe's press provided a decisive ideological framework that helped to situate its work in an advantageous position vis-à-vis the emerging interests of the English nation. For besides the critical role he played in the production of the Machiavelli and Aretino volumes, Castelvetro was also a prime mover behind Wolfe's publication of two other volumes which functioned as contributions to the promotion in print of England's growing colonial ambitions: the unfinished *Columbeid* (1585)

# Language lessons 193

by a young Roman poet, Giulio Cesare Stella, celebrating Christopher Columbus' voyages in Virgilian language and epic form (dedicated, in Wolfe's edition, to Sir Walter Raleigh); and in separate Italian (1587) and English (1588) translations of Juan Gonzalez de Mendoza's *Historia de las cosas mas notables, ritos y costumbres, del gran reyno dela China* (other translations in French, German, and Latin appeared on the continent within a few years), an account of a part of the world unexamined in other such contemporary narratives, based upon first-hand reports relating its wealth and exploitable goods, and feeding the drive for "discovery" and conquest which England came to dominate in the later sixteenth century.[94] Given his religious orientation, literary formation, and typographical experience, Castelvetro was in an excellent position to assist, through Wolfe's press, in England's "missionary ambitions ... to become the natural protector and bellwether of the new Protestant Christianity ... the physiological manifestation of an intensely optimistic society, powerfully conscious of its own energies."[95]

The Italian Protestant cultural coordinates of Wolfe's press had been determined even earlier in the 1580s through the printer's association with Scipione and Alberico Gentili, the sons of a physician from the Marche, Matteo, who was closely linked to the vestiges of the Italian reformed movement during the dangerous period in which the Council of Trent drew to a conclusion and the Roman Inquisition's reach was growing.[96] Alberico pursued legal studies at the University of Perugia from 1569 to 1572 and subsequently served as a judge in his native San Ginesio through 1579, when Matteo fled with him to Lubyjana in order to escape persecution, and they were soon joined there by Scipione. Early in 1580 the brothers traveled to Heidelberg, Scipione matriculating at the university to study philosophy and literature while Alberico continued on to England where, except for a year spent in Germany between 1586 and 1587, he would spend the remainder of his life. Matteo emigrated to England soon after Alberico, practicing medicine in London for almost two decades.[97]

Among the very first books that Wolfe printed in England – a clear early indication of the parameters within which his press would operate over the next decade – were a Latin paraphrase of selected psalms by Scipione, *Paraphrasis aliquot Psalmorum Davidis, carmine heroico* (1581), and a volume of six dialogues, *De iuris interpretibus* (1582), redacted from a series of lectures given by Alberico at Oxford and which represent a dispute central to his legal thinking: the vigorous defense of a Bartolist reading of Roman law – the practical application of legal principles in the real world – over against recent developments emanating from Italy and France initiated by Andrea Alciato (more famous today as the author of the *Emblemata*), and his students Jacques Cujas and François Hotman, who advocated a philologically oriented approach that aimed at the repristination of classical legal texts such as the *Corpus juris civilis* of Justinian and the re-establishment of the institutions they fostered (work which led, in the end, to undermining the validity of Roman law for a contemporary French society so markedly different from that of ancient Rome).[98] For Gentili, "the purpose of teaching civil law [was] to prepare students for practice in modern society. Where, he asked, did the humanist professors expect their students to go after their studies, to Plato's academy, or to Utopia?"[99]

Scipione published three further books with Wolfe: a second volume of psalm paraphrases; a translation into Latin of the first two cantos of the *Gerusalemme liberata*, and another of the fourth, all from 1584; as well as a 1586 Italian commentary on Tasso's epic poem. And while Alberico continued to publish with Wolfe – four more books issued between 1585 and 1589 – he also brought out work with Joseph Barnes, the university printer in Oxford (where he was appointed Regius Professor of Jurisprudence in 1587), and with Thomas Vautroullier in London. Consulted by the Privy Council for his opinion on how to deal with the Spanish ambassador Mendoza's involvement in the plot to assassinate Elizabeth in 1584, Alberico formulated what became one of the very earliest assertions of diplomatic immunity, which spared Mendoza's life but provoked his expulsion from England. Gentili's thoughts on the matter were spelled out first in a public oration at Oxford, then published by Wolfe as *Legalium comitiorum oxoniensium actio* in 1585. Alberico's *De iure belli* was initially issued by Wolfe's press between 1588 and 1589, then subsequently republished in a greatly expanded definitive edition in Hanover in 1598.[100]

*De iure belli* is not only Alberico's major work, it is among the most far-reaching legal treatises written in England in the sixteenth century, laying out the framework for the elaboration of international law which Hugo Grotius completed in the early decades of the seventeenth century. The focus of the text is on how law functions within the context of war, an issue Gentili argues that had not been addressed since the end of the Roman Republic but that, given the profoundly unstable European situation following the Reformation and Catholic response, was in desperate need of rearticulation. By way of defining a just war and its attributes, Gentili concluded that only God was in a position to judge the religious choices of his human subjects, and that heretics could not consequently be legitimately punished even by their own sovereign rulers unless they threatened the communal good. The resulting emphasis in favor of religious tolerance over against religious uniformity links Gentili's work with Aconcio's thinking on the subject, but other dimensions of his argument are closely tied to ideas explored by Machiavelli, particularly in its emphasis on establishing a balance between the pragmatic application of the lessons of history and the *rationes* of given states (a utilitarian rather than an idealistic approach), in its forceful opposition to all forms of tyranny, and in its underscoring of the right of all peoples to live in freedom.[101]

The limited fame Alberico enjoys today is due primarily to his advocacy of academic theater against the Puritan anti-theatricalists.[102] John Rainolds had unsuccessfully opposed Gentili's appointment at Oxford, and between 1591 and 1594 their disagreement over the validity of theatrical fictions – Rainolds contriving to ascribe Gentili's position to his being an Italian, and hence a Machiavellian atheist – was played out both on the public stage of the university and in an exchange of letters.[103]

A related but lesser-known contribution to the literary culture of late sixteenth-century England is to be found in Gentili's treatise, *Commentatio ad legem III codicis de professoribus et medicis*, published by Barnes in 1593.[104] Answering the legal question as to why poets in the *Corpus juris civilis* were not exempted from taxation while grammarians, logicians, and rhetoricians were, Gentili – contending that poets should have been granted a similar privilege – elaborates a theory of poetry that resonates in a number of its particulars with Sidney's defense of poetics: poets create fictions that are not in and of themselves harmful and that can indeed bear moral weight, given that poetry both delights and teaches; there is an analogy made between poetry and painting (painters were also free from ancient Roman taxation), though poets are said to represent a version of the truth while painters depict it as it is; the poet is an honorable figure and has a public function, in that "poetry is an instrument of active, not ... contemplative, philosophy,"[105] purging "the passions and emotions, thus becoming an instrument of the citizen's formation";[106] and this socially transformative potential of poetics is also linked to the didactic possibilities of the stage. Whether or not Gentili and Philip Sidney had actually discussed these issues – they were on very good terms, and several of Scipione's and Alberico's works published with Wolfe were dedicated to Sidney[107] – is of less interest here than that the question of poetry's legitimacy is addressed within a juridical framework, extending even further the constellation of matters linked to the circulation of foreign languages and the cultures that they reproduced in Elizabethan England. Though his work was published entirely in Latin, Alberico was one of the most prominent members of the Italian community in London, and his relationship with John Florio was significant enough to warrant the inclusion of a sonnet addressed by Gentili to Queen Anne in praise of Florio among the prefatory material to *Queen Anna's New World of Words* (the only such intervention by a native-born Italian in any of Florio's published work) three years after Alberico's death.

Giordano Bruno noted in the course of his 1592 trial for heresy that while in Wittenberg, before returning to Italy, he had seen among the Calvinist and Lutheran factions at the university "a doctor named Alberigo Gentile, a native of the Marche, whom I had met in England; a professor of law who had shown me [many] favors and introduced me to the study of Aristotle's *Organon*."[108] Given this earlier association, it might seem logical that when Bruno came to publish his six Italian dialogues in London between 1584 and 1585 he would have chosen to work with Wolfe; instead he turned to John Charlewood, the same printer who had issued Bruno's *Ars reminiscendi* soon after his arrival in England in 1583 but who lacked any experience whatsoever with Italian printing. Tiziana Provvidera's suggestion that Wolfe would have been too busy with his initial Machiavelli and Aretino volumes to take on any further Italian projects at the time seems to be the best explanation for what otherwise appears to be a curious choice of publisher for the most original Italian texts ever conceived and printed in England.[109] Bruno may also have been offended by Wolfe's identification with incipient English colonialism, a tendency to which he had strong objections. As Charlewood published no further books in Italian and so had no other need for the expert help Wolfe required, Bruno served as his own principal editor for these volumes,[110] but as he and John Florio both lived at this time at the London residence of the French ambassador, Mauvissière, forming a close friendship, it seems likely that Florio lent a hand with several aspects of the production of these books (especially regarding dealings with the publisher, given Bruno's lack of English). Such assistance might explain how Florio came to publish a "news" pamphlet, translated from Italian, with Charlewood in 1585, *A Letter lately written from Rome, by an Italian gentleman to a freende in Lyons*.[111]

Wolfe issued several Italian books in which he openly identifies himself as their London printer, the two most interesting of which are a trilingual edition of Castiglione's *Cortegiano* in 1588, which utilizes in parallel columns Thomas Hoby's 1561 English translation and (though unacknowledged) the French translation of Gabriel Chapuis published in Paris in a 1585 bilingual edition, together with the original Italian, one of the first such printed books in early modern Europe (though multilingual dictionaries were produced from the late fifteenth century and enjoyed quite a vogue throughout the sixteenth); and a 1591 edition of Guarini's *Pastor Fido* issued together with Tasso's *Aminta*, plays then only recently published in Italy that were to have an immediate and exceptional impact on the diffusion of pastoral conventions in both English theatrical and poetic forms.

In all, Wolfe issued twenty-five texts in Italian, fourteen in Latin written by Italian authors, and five English translations from Italian.[112]

The Italian and Latin volumes in this catalogue taken together demonstrate a carefully conceived editorial plan, but Wolfe's dedication to the program they articulate ended suddenly and on a startling note with the 1591 publication by Wolfe's press of an anonymously authored English tract entitled *A discovery of the great subtiltie and wonderful wisdome of the Italians*, a text as Italophobic in its point of view as the evidence of the preceding decade of Wolfe's career is so decidedly Italophilic. The pamphlet's dedicatory epistle marks a jarring rupture with the rhetoric Barbagrigia had utilized in his introduction to Wolfe's edition of Machiavelli's *Discorsi*:

> when they perceive how they can set us together by the ears, they know how to invent store of such new obscurities and shifts to trouble us, if we will give them leave little to come in amongst us to our Countries, where they will shew themselves alwais with prophane knowledge to teach us how we shall goe to heaven, or els inflamed with a burning zeale for the publicke good of all our Countrey. Although if we be so wise as to looke well into them, we shall soone discover their mindes, how they doe but seeke to reape some profite out of our ruines, and to make their hand by us. We must then cast our eies upon the good instruction, their nature or rather the Author therof doth set before us visibly; for he having laid and set the Alpes most high mountaines, so firme and permanent on the one side, and the deepe Seas on the other, for bars between us and them, that we should not go to one another, teacheth us, if we will take his instruction, we should dispose of all that concerneth our State apart and shut up from them al accesse or entrance into our Countrey by the reasons and experience of things already past, which shall more amply be dilated in this discourse, prepared for a general remedy of us all, whether we be Catholiques or Protestants, to recover full deliverance and health of these maladies, which so long time have oppressed and troubled us.[113]

The scope of this condemnation of Italy and Italians goes far beyond a Protestant sectarian abhorrence of Catholics (the subject, in fact, of most of the *libretto*), for it is not only those who presume to teach the true religion but also those who impinge on "the publicke good of all *our* Countrey" (here a hint of the text's anti-Machiavellian thrust) who are singled out for castigation, an unmistakable allusion to the prominence accorded Italians during the preceding decades, a process in which John Wolfe's press had until quite recently played no small part. Wolfe's engagement with Italian print culture bears a distinctly theatrical imprint: encompassing its collaborative nature, Barbagrigia's prefatory fictions (his name taken from Annibale Caro's 1543 *Straccioni*, where he represents a kind of Boccaccian/Falstaffian excess in contrast with the high moral tone of the comedy's principals, a figure patterned after a friend of Caro's, the Roman printer Antonio Blado d'Asola);[114] the shifting tableaux of the Machiavelli and Aretino title pages; and the actual theater pieces represented in his catalogue. But this total repudiation of Italy – symbolized by the Creator's having erected natural barriers to keep Italians from the rest of the world – as Wolfe's valedictory gesture to the Italian ambit of his print activities must have struck those Italians in England who had previously enjoyed his confidence in much the same way that Wolfe's alliance with the Company of Stationers would have impressed his earlier London renegade-print colleagues.

How to explain this radical shift in focus? Giacomo Castelvetro had left London for Scotland in 1591, thus terminating his relationship with Wolfe's press, but Petruccio Ubaldini was still active at this time, and there were others – John Florio, chief among them – who could conceivably have assisted Wolfe had he wished to continue issuing Italian books. There might well have been some precipitating event now lost to view, but from this point forward Wolfe occupied himself exclusively with publication in English, to which Florio made a modest contribution through his translation of *Perpetuall and Naturall Prognostications of the Change of Weather* (1591), a sort of early modern *Farmer's Almanac*. Any lingering doubts regarding Wolfe's detachment from his Italian program would have been settled with his edition of John Eliot's 1593 *Orthoepia Gallica, Eliot's Fruit for the French*, a direct attack on Florio (as the allusion in its title implies) and the other language teachers active at the time in England.[115]

The 1570s and 1580s were clearly a period of particularly focused interest in Italy on the part of the Elizabethan elite and its various arms, but by the early 1590s, with both Sidney and Dudley dead, the Italianate moment in England was beginning to lose its luster as the English language and its literary culture rapidly assumed a powerful autonomous identity of its own. The first three books of Spenser's *Faerie Queene* were printed by Wolfe's press in 1590, and John Harington's great translation of Ariosto's *Orlando furioso* was printed by Richard Field in 1591 (reissued in 1607). Both of these books marked a distinctive turn toward an English culture for which direct knowledge of the Italian language was no longer necessary, the lessons of Italian Renaissance culture now available in thoroughly English dress. Wolfe's disengagement from printing Italian books can be ascribed in large part to this shift in emphasis away from Italian itself and toward its appropriation in English through translation.

Field cornered this market in the final decade of the sixteenth century and maintained his hold on it well into the Stuart period, printing translations issued both by his own press and for other publishers, as well as Shakespeare's *Venus and Adonis* (1593) and *Lucrece* (1594), the final installment of the *Faerie Queene* (1596), and James I's *Basilikon Doron* (1603). In addition to Harington's Ariosto, Field reprinted Geoffrey Fenton's *The historie of Guicciardin* (1598 and 1618), and Thomas North's translation from Jacques Amyot's French translation of Plutarch's *Lives* (1595, 1603, and 1612); he printed separately George Chapman's translations of the *Iliad* (1611) and *Odyssey* (1614 and 1615), and then both together (1616, with William Jaggard); there was an edition of the complete works of Virgil in Latin (1616), and a translation of the *Eclogues* by John Brinsley intended for use as a tool for the instruction of English grammar (1620). Field printed six books in Italian in the 1590s, all of them texts by Petruccio Ubaldini, and one of them a reprint of *La vita di Carlo Magno Imperadore* (1599). When the latter was first issued in 1581, Ubaldini had proudly noted in his preface that his was the first Italian book Wolfe had actually printed in England and he foresaw a golden age of opportunity for further such volumes issuing from Wolfe's press;[116] but by the time of its second edition, Ubaldini's life of Charlemagne was introduced by a generic appeal to "Noble and Illustrious Lords, Magnanimous Knights, and other gentlemen of the English nation,"[117] asserting still that Italian books "can be felicitously printed and reprinted in London,"[118] thus both registering but failing to see the writing on the wall, for this was to be one of the last exclusively Italian books published in early modern England.

*"Ie te prie, m'ensigniez, il faut que ie apprend a parlen."*

### A Shakespearean language lesson

Not that foreign linguistic models had by any means entirely played themselves out there by the end of the sixteenth century. Among Richard Field's bestselling books were his multiple reprints of Hollyband's *French Littleton* (1593, 1597, 1602, and 1603) and *French Schoolmaster* (1612 and 1615), which were also issued by other publishers in the same period. The most celebrated Elizabethan language lesson, in Shakespeare's *Henry V* 3.4, echoes several strains of what has been argued in this chapter regarding the circulation of languages in Elizabethan England through its presentation of the almost-conquered French Princess Katherine struggling to gain some rudiments of the English language that she pragmatically assumes she will soon be speaking in England.[119]

KATHE.  *Alice tu as este en Angleterre, & tu bien parlas le Language.*
ALICE.  *En peu Madame.*
KATHE.  *Ie te prie, m'ensigniez, il faut que ie apprend a parlen. Comient appelle vous le main en Anglois?*
ALICE.  *Le main il appelle de Hand.*
KATHE.  *De hand.*
ALICE.  *Et le doyts.*
KATHE.  *Le doyts, ma foy ie oublie, [l]e doyts mays, ie me souemeray le doyts ie pense qu'ils ont appelle de fingres, ou[i] de fingres.*[120]

Here the performative aspect of language acquisition is literally enacted within the theatrical context that Florio's lessons reflect in pedagogical terms. Of equal, if not greater importance, is the scene's clear correlation of linguistic artifice and the practice of political power. Indeed, as Paola Pugliatti has persuasively argued, *Henry V* can be read as an extended language lesson, in which "languages, dialects, styles, and social discursive varieties mark the boundaries (and differentiate the spheres) of [its] various ethnic, national, and social components ... that the many disturbing and disuniting effects of many voicedness are deployed in [a] play in which national unity is celebrated is, to say the least, noticeable."[121] In *Henry IV, Pt. 2* 4.3.68–69, Warwick says of Prince Hal that he "but studies his companions like a strange tongue,"[122] and yet after the subsequent lessons learned, much of *Henry V* turns on language used in ways that confound its auditors: the Archbishop of Canterbury's discourse on the Salic Law, Nym and Pistol's over-determined contentiousness, the malapropisms of the Hostess, and the diversely vacuous threats of Fluellen and MacMorris all contribute to the play's central preoccupation with the intelligibility (or lack thereof) of language and underscore its problematic role in the consolidation of English political power in Henry's victory at Agincourt.

It is not incidental that Princess Katherine's English lesson – conducted entirely in French, the only such scene in a play in which the French normally are made to speak English – is organized around the parts of the human body, for it is her own body that will serve as surety of the English king's conquest of France:[123]

ALICE.   *N'ave vos y desia oublie ce que ie vous a ensignie?*
KATHE.   *Nome ie recitera a vous promptement, d'Hand, de Fingre, de Maylees.*
ALICE.   *De Nayles, Madame.*
KATHE.   *De Nayles, de Arme, de Ilbow.*
ALICE.   *Sans vostre honneur, d'Elbow.*
KATHE.   *Ainsi de ie d'Elbow, de Nick, & de Sin: coment appelle vous les pieds & de roba?*
ALICE.   *Le Foot Madame, & le Count.*
KATHE.   *Le Foot et le Count. O Seigneur Dieu, ils sont le mots de son mauvais corruptible grosse & impudique, & non pour le Dames de Honeur d'user. Ie ne voudray pronouncer ce mots devant les Seigneurs de France, pour tout le monde. Fo! le Foot & de Count! Neant moys, ie recitera un autrefoys ma lecon ensemble: d'Hand, de Fingre, de Nayles, d'Arme, d'Elbow, de Nick, de Sin, de Foot, le Count.*

ALICE. *Excellent, Madame.*
KATHE. *C'est asses pour une foyes, alons nous a diner.*

That the scene is funny, and almost always played for laughs in performance,[124] masks its more serious implications. Juliet Fleming's contention that Katherine's English lesson is to be "understood as an act of political infidelity ... made apparent by the scene that follows it, in which the French nobility are represented as considering themselves emasculated by their military defeat" is certainly one provocative way of reading the scene, as is her parsing of its sexual puns.[125] But following as it does Henry's notorious speech to the citizens of Harfleur, in which he anatomizes their "fresh pure virgins ... pure maidens" [3.3.94, 100] as he alerts them to their impending – and from his perspective, entirely legitimate – rape by his troops,[126] and preceding the king's rather more courtly wooing of his future bride in 5.2.99–270, Katherine's language lesson is also a primer for Shakespeare's audience in the potentially hazardous terms of language usage. More than merely the "modern pornographic fantasy of a woman who has somehow been tricked into displaying her sensuality against her will,"[127] the scene represents a woman who in advance of her compatriots confronts the reality of their defeat and moves on, doing what she must to accommodate herself to what inevitably promise to be her new circumstances. Though she may get many of the specifics wrong, Katherine recognizes the inextricable relationship of language to power.[128]

The scene's comedy is not to be underestimated, however, for it is the parts of the body that are often among the first vocabulary learned by a beginning language student,[129] and this language lesson is as much a send-up of the language pedagogy of men like Florio (who would, however, have appreciated its scabrous implications, as we shall see in the next chapter) and Hollyband as it is an exposé of the limitations of trying to say too much too soon.[130] Florio himself had warned about this latter presumption when he wrote in *Firste Fruites* Ch. 27 [125–126] about those who:

| | |
|---|---|
| ... *cominciano a imparar Italiano, Franzese, & Spagnolo, & come hanno due parole di Spagnolo, tre parole di Franzese, quatro di Italiano, pensano di haver assai, non vogliono studiar piu.* | ... begyn to spake Italian, French, and Spanish, and when they have learned two words of Spanish, three woords of French, and foure words of Italian, they thinke they have enough, they will study no more. |

Katherine's language lesson sets the stage for the next phase of Florio's instrumentality in the transmission to England of Italian Renaissance and early modern cultures. Shakespeare had written *Henry V* by the spring of 1599,[131] not long after the publication of the first edition of Florio's Italian–English dictionary, *A Worlde of Wordes*. Accordingly, we turn our attention now to the question of language codified through the lexicographical practice of collection and definition in order to understand how Florio's representation of the Italian language and the culture that it mediates assumed a character in England different from its native Italian identity, and in so doing established a paradigm against which later assessments of the Italian Renaissance might profitably be read.

# 5    Worlds of words

> One cannot but recollect that when J. Jungmann's Czech-German dictionary was finished in 1839, the nationalist society in Prague gave a ball in honor of the occasion, with the five volumes displayed on a sort of altar as the central ornament of the ballroom.
>
> Ladislav Zgusta[1]

As we have seen, language learning in later sixteenth-century England was engaged in a complex web of transactions that associated it with larger issues of cultural exchange – the theater, the fraught status of poetry, proverbial wisdom, courtesy, and the book trade – extending its significance beyond the boundaries within which it has conventionally been confined by Renaissance scholarship. During the years in which Florio was engaged in the language teaching that led to the publication of *Firste* and *Second Frutes*, he was also involved in a much more ambitious project, one at the heart of his vocation as a language merchant, whose scope reached far beyond the parameters of the language lesson at the same time that it provided a critical tool for the assimilation of language learning. *A Worlde of Wordes* appeared in print initially in 1598, and then again in an expanded second edition in 1611, rechristened as *Queen Anna's New World of Words*. These dictionaries served not only as indices to the lexical range of the Italian and English languages as they had developed by the end of the "long" sixteenth century, but they also enabled readings of the contemporary cultures that these languages represented. In the case of Florio's selection of Italian *voci*:

a voice, a sound, or repercussion of the aire. Also a word. Also a bruit, a report, a tune, a saying[2]

his characteristic expansiveness defined a position that could not have been more at odds with the prevailing cultural politics in force in Italy at the time and expressed, magisterially, in the first edition of the Florentine *Vocabolario degli accademici della Crusca* in 1612.[3]

As the preceding chapter of this study aimed to delineate the exceptional currency Italian enjoyed in Elizabethan England, here the purpose is to examine the shape of the language that Florio advocated and how its notable differences from that officially sanctioned by the Crusca academicians both valorized contemporary Italian usage and delineated a canonical library of Italian Renaissance literature that would only be recognized as such by nineteenth-century historiography. But before turning to Florio's dictionaries, we must first examine the native Italian terrain against which they should be read. It is my argument throughout this study that language is one of the critical constitutive elements of any politics, and this is clearly in evidence in both early modern England and Italy. We have already seen that "stranger" language merchants such as Florio who exercised their vocations within the rapidly changing Elizabethan world contributed, through their mediation, tools that served a crucial role in the formation of a specifically English Renaissance culture. Here we turn to the ways in which dictionaries anticipate developments in the formation of early modern "nations," vernacular languages having staked out the identities of particular communities in a form different from armed conflict, diplomacy, and fixed geographical boundaries.

> "Io voglio starmi ne la Toscana, non come in una prigione, ma come in una bella, e' spatiosa piazza, dove tutti i nobili spiriti d'Italia si riducono."

### Alessandro Citolini and the Italian 'language question'

*La questione della lingua* was an issue that dominated Italian cultural politics throughout the cinquecento, and its consequences extended well into the following century. But because the English language *per se* has never been the subject of such a focused theoretical debate and has given rise to no ostensibly controlling institution equivalent to either the Accademia della Crusca or the Académie Française, the significance of this problem has been largely elided in studies of the confluence of early modern Italian and English cultures.[4] The remarkable expansion of the possibilities of the English language in the late sixteenth and early seventeenth centuries did not, of course, occur *ex nihilo*, and several scholars have recently turned their attention to the various ways in which contemporary English debates about poetry and the theater contributed to a "national" exchange about the status of the language.[5]

The one English Renaissance text that clearly echoes the central preoccupation of the Italian debate over "classical" or "contemporary" forms of language is the "Preface" to Spenser's *The Shepherd's Calendar* (1579), but the archaizing imperatives Spenser proffers there and subsequently put into practice in *The Faerie Queene* were rejected by his contemporaries.[6] Judith Anderson's evocation of the "frozen words" that Rabelais' Panurge and Pantagruel hear melting in the air while on a sea voyage in the *Quart Livre* – words that exist in a heavenly realm in idealized and suspended animation but which periodically fall to earth as a sort of cultural blessing[7] – are as apposite a figure for Spenser's failed linguistic project as they are for the much more influential initiatives of the classicizing voices of *la questione della lingua* against whose species of cultural politics Florio's Italian advocacy was clearly sighted. It is, therefore, of considerable importance that we understand something of the shape of the Italian debate in order to appreciate the singular contribution that Florio's dictionaries made to it, as well as to the burgeoning scope of dissimilarly unconstrained early modern English.

Alessandro Citolini's *Lettera in difesa de la volgar lingua* (Venice 1540) is particularly germane to the *questione della lingua* as it came to be addressed from within the English context, for Citolini was another of the Italian religious refugees in the Elizabethan world. Florio's relations with him (or with his patrons) were such as to have afforded access to the manuscript of Citolini's *Grammatica de la lingua italiana*, which Florio liberally drew on for the grammar appended to *Firste Fruites*.[8] The *Lettera* goes unregistered in either of the libraries prefacing the two editions of Florio's dictionary – Citolini's ambitious linguistic encyclopedia, the *Tipocosmia* (1561), is noted in both and discussed in "The Epistle Dedicatorie" of *A Worlde of Wordes* – but the principles elaborated therein are so close to Florio's own grammatico-lexical practice that his acquaintance with it can reasonably be assumed.

Citolini was a citizen of the Venetian republic, as were the two most prominent vernacular theorists of the early cinquecento, Pietro Bembo and Giangiorgio Trissino.[9] Venice in the middle decades of the cinquecento provides a further point of reference for Citolini's intellectual profile owing to his relations there with the city's leading heterodox religious figures, an association that led in 1568 to his condemnation by the Inquisition, though by that time Citolini had already been settled in England for over two years.[10] The *Lettera* is dedicated to Cosimo Pallavicini, whose brother Giovan Battista, a Carmelite preacher, was at the time of its publication imprisoned in Rome for heresy.[11] The conjunction of linguistic and doctrinal reform which we have so far witnessed in operation in early modern England came in the middle decades of the cinquecento in Italy to be of tremendous concern to the peninsula's cultural and spiritual custodians, for the principal battles of the Reformation's war of words were conducted in vernacular languages which initially proved resistant to ecclesiastical control, before the conservative line in cinquecento Italian philology fell into synchrony with the intellectual climate issuing from the deliberations of the Council of Trent and the increased power of the Roman Inquisition. Citolini's career in Italy developed during this liminal moment, and the work that he produced in these years provided John Florio with one of several theoretical approaches he drew upon in his cultural advocacy and established a link for him between the doubly heterodox native-Italian perspective – philological and religious – he inherited from his father, Michelangelo, and by which he would later be so marked through his friendship with Giordano Bruno.

Two objectives are elaborated in the course of the *Lettera*: the first, to counter the charge that the Italian vernacular is inferior to Latin; the second, to argue that the various permutations of Italian distinct from "classical" literary Tuscan affirm, rather than compromise, the language's vitality. Citolini cites three motives used by advocates of Latin to disparage Italian – that the classical language is "nobler ... richer ... and more universal"[12] – only to appropriate them as issues around which to organize his defense of the vernacular.

By "noble," Citolini asks, do the Latinists mean "most ancient"? If so, Latin fails the test, for Hebrew, Chaldean, Assyrian, Phoenician, and Egyptian are all older languages. And what of earlier forms of Latin: are they to be preferred over those of Cicero, Caesar, and Virgil [1r]?[13] Citolini finds absurd the idea that the birth of the vernacular is ascribed to "barbarian" incursions into Italy, given that Italian bears such a close relationship to Latin, but even if Italian's origins were determined to be the very lowest, many similarly noble things spring from the basest stock, as an enumeration of ancient Roman, Greek, and Biblical examples shows [2r–3r]. And were it to be established that Italian is a corruption of Latin, "who does not know that the corruption of one thing is the generation of another,"[14] including man himself [3r]? This is the most critical question posed in the *Lettera*, for the effective denial of linguistic mutability – faith in "frozen words" – is at the heart of Renaissance classicizing tendencies in both neo-Latin and vernacular languages, and while there were notable exceptions to it, this is the position that prevailed in cinquecento Italy. Citolini fully embraces the reality of contamination, writing of Latin's origins that "it was not born of the Holy Ghost,"[15] but out of the accretion of elements from even more ancient Italian peninsular and other Mediterranean languages; and Italian's mongrel character is to be similarly valorized.[16]

Dante's status for *la questione della lingua* was a vexed one. The usage of Petrarch and Boccaccio – who, with Dante, came to be regarded as the *tre corone* [three laureates] of the early Italian literary canon – served as the more or less constant paradigm for the debate, but concerns about Dante's use of indecorous language had first been raised even before the poet's death, and a squeamishness about certain episodes in the *Commedia* recurs throughout the history of the language question whenever Dante's authority comes to be challenged. Citolini's position is unambiguous, and in the course of his discussion of the relative merits of ancient classical and Italian writers he argues that "any tale of Boccaccio [is] equal to any Greek Poet; [just as] Dante's chapter which begins:

> 'His mouth was raised from that savage meal',
> [is] the equal of all Greek and Latin poetry together."[17]

In asserting that the first great writers in Italian exceeded their ancient forerunners by citing as proof the gruesome scene of Ugolino gnawing on Archbishop Ruggiero's head in *Inferno* 33, Citolini cuts right through the alternately genteel and evasive rhetoric typically used against Dante by detractors unable to completely dismiss his prominence in the Italian literary canon and in the development of the language. While never addressing the contested question of Ugolino's imputed cannibalism of his own sons later in *Inferno* 33, Citolini's strategy in evoking one of Italian literature's most graphic images is aimed rather at establishing Italian's capacity to represent even the otherwise unspeakable than with tackling what two centuries of commentary had yet failed to agree upon.[18] Citolini's appreciation of Dante is grounded in the diverse registers of his poem, the *Commedia*'s mixed language for Citolini the manifest sign of its universality, capable of encompassing the earthly-to-celestial scope of the poet's ambition.

Citolini's most original contribution to the language question is the designation of "living" and "dead" languages which he proposes in the course of answering the second of the queries he makes at the outset of the *Lettera* – how much "richer" is the Italian vernacular than Latin? Citolini cites two errors of the Latinists: that they believe Latin to have always existed "in its happiest state ... that it never had a childhood"; and that "they are unaware that Latin is dead and buried in books, [while] the vernacular is alive."[19] R. Glynn Faithfull first recognized the novelty of this formulation for the valorization of Italian, noting that what constituted "life" for an early modern consciousness as yet uninformed by the modern hard sciences was considerably more expansive than what we would acknowledge today, Citolini's idea thus meant to function as more than merely a metaphor for his contemporary readers.[20]

Italian pulsates with life because "it grows, generates, creates, produces, gives birth, always making itself richer and more abundant."[21] Besides anticipating the copiousness of Florio's dictionary definitions in which the fullest possible range of a word's meanings is supplied, there is an echo here of one idea in Bembo's *Prose della volgar lingua* (1525) that came to be effaced in that text's emphatic promotion of "frozen words." Leaning on Aristotle, Bembo's interlocutor Federigo Fregoso describes the birth of Italian from the commingling of "barbarian" languages and Latin – entirely disparate substances – the latter of which, however, remained the determinant element given its cultivation on Italian soil, as "plants ... brought from far-away countries" are thought not naturally to take root.[22] But whereas Bembo sought to cap Italian's development at a particular historical moment, Citolini utilizes Fregoso's geographic metaphor by transforming it into a substantive, arguing that accretion is the natural history of cultures, as peoples migrate from one place to another and the disparate elements of their various traditions come to be integrated into a pre-existing context:

> men are not sufficient to impose their nature[s] on countries but are rather obliged to assume those country's [native forms]. Therefore, even had all those Barbarians remained in Italy, it would still not have been enough to turn Italy barbarian, for they would have been compelled to become Italians, as one sees had occurred with the Trojans, the Greeks, and other peoples ... who had already come to Italy and remained there, and from whom issued the Roman People, who were [then], however, no longer Trojan or Greek, but Italian ... and were it not too much of a digression, I would have you see that the fruits of today's soil not only equal those of the ancients but, seemingly not content with this, they seek to (and in many things do) surpass them.[23]

This suggestion of a sort of *gestalt* identified with the soil of countries recalls the geographic particularity of proverbial wisdom in *Second Frutes* – and indeed the agricultural metaphor for language-learning implicit in both of Florio's *Fruits* – crucially orienting political identity around being *in* but not necessarily *of* a specific place. Citolini acknowledges the incessant interpenetration of cultures as a fundamental mark of the way that they function, and though like Bembo he privileges the Italian peninsula as the site of a particularly rich succession of cultural systems, he recognizes, as Bembo does not, that the ancient Romans themselves were a genus grafted from exotic foreign plants onto a native stock. Striking for its sensitivity to historical change, the model of cultural translation described here is also a fitting one for the migration of Italians and their culture to England, a process that ended with the similar assimilation of "stranger" Italians into the emerging English nation.

With the third of the categories that Citolini adopts from his Latinist foes, he probes the issue of "universality." First calling attention to the halting diffusion of Latin in the Roman world, Citolini notes that it "began little by little to be considered, known, and used; and thus it slowly grew, gradually moving beyond the confines of Italy, spreading out here and there."[24] The Italian vernacular, he argues, advances in exactly the same way:

> thus we can understand that this is what will happen with the vernacular, signs of which one indeed begins to see: it has already passed beyond the Alps and is known, loved, and cherished by a great many people in France, as you [the treatise's dedicatee, Pallavicini] and I can testify. I hear that it is rather well known in Spain, and that on the island of Majorca there are public schools where it is taught. And I also hear that in Germany, and even in England, one finds more cognoscenti of Italian than of Latin.[25]

Despite the hyperbole – Latin was much more widely known in learned circles in England than Italian throughout the early modern period – this is both the earliest and one of the very rare examples of a contemporary philologist acknowledging from Italy that the Italian vernacular enjoyed a certain currency elsewhere.

Challenging the assumption that the range of Latin is greater than a vernacular with a written culture less than three centuries old, Citolini asserts that:

> with this language we can speak of the divinity; of the angelic nature; of the things of this world; of the birth, procession, and setting of the stars; of the sun and its nature, and of the moon and its cycles; of fire, air, wind, rain, thunder and lightening; of the waters and their motions; of the earth and its nature. With this language we can speak of stones, trees, herbs, metals; of beasts, and of man; of economics, politics, war, peace, and life. With this language we can deal with agriculture, painting, sculpture, music, poetry, architecture, medicine; with religion, health, wickedness, enormities and trifles, pity and cruelty, friendships and hatreds. With this language we can make manifestly evident our spirit.[26]

With this index of Italian's capacity to reproduce the entire gamut of knowledge and experience – anticipating the scope of his *Tipocosmia*, to recreate the world in lexicographical terms – Citolini aims to establish the superior scope of the vernacular over against Latin by emphasizing the promise of a variegated Italian vernacular. But he goes on to say that:

> I do not in any way praise reckless license ... I decry affectation, and willing, tedious servitude. I wish to find myself in Tuscan not as in a prison, but as in a lovely and spacious *piazza*, where all of the noble spirits of Italy meet together.[27]

The generosity of Citolini's vision, a value sorely missing from so much of the rhetoric of *la questione della lingua*, is also an adroit inversion of the highbrow coordinates of the classicizing position. Citolini is confident of the Italian vernacular's capacity to creatively declare its autonomy from crippling models too uncritically tied to the past, thus establishing its authority for a cultural politics in increasingly urgent need of a coherent alternative to the contemporary forces of standardization that threatened the free circulation of ideas. With regard to these issues, Antonio Gramsci noted that "every time the *questione della lingua* surfaces in one way or another, it means that a range of other problems are asserting themselves ... [namely] the reorganization of cultural hegemony."[28] Citolini's philological progressivism coupled with his heterodox religious identity rendered him a pariah in Italy, but both the apparent rejection of his linguistic ideas there and their adoption through John Florio's Italian advocacy in England mark a further pregnant stage in the interplay between "heresy" and the ascendancy of vernacular languages.

"... à cio piu facile vi sia l'intendere questa nostra lingua, parlarla, e scriverla correttamente come se in Thoscana voi foste nato."

**Grammars**

Developing concurrently with the theoretical dimensions of *la questione della lingua* was a series of efforts that aimed at representing the structure of the Italian vernacular so as to render it not only comparable to the great languages of the past but also transmissible. Several of the grammars that came to be utilized in England were actually written there, while others were translated from Italian texts written on the peninsula and adapted to the English context.[29]

Giovanni Francesco Fortunio's *Regole grammaticali della volgar lingua* (1516) provided Bembo with a point of reference in the elaboration of his own analysis of Italian grammar in the third book of the *Prose*.[30] Fortunio's method is deductive, and the *Regole* are thus predicated upon the assumption that the literature of the *tre corone* is so rich in invention and coherent in its various forms that it must needs yield up a similarly congruent grammatical structure, an approach unconcerned with the spoken language and that takes its cues from principles gleaned from analysis of classical Latin literature.[31] Fortunio's title is something of a misnomer, "the design of this grammar" being "extremely meager,"[32] for it focuses more on noting exceptions to rules than on providing a clear structure for conveying the principles of vernacular writing. The *Regole* are, like most of the grammars and first vocabularies that shortly followed it, largely an exposition of passages from the *tre corone* (Dante's language in the *Commedia* here posing no problems),[33] and so Fortunio's manual, like Bembo's *Prose*, contributes nothing to an understanding or appraisal of the Italian vernacular as it was developing in the sixteenth century. But given the more easily digestible schematic form of the *Regole*, and the volume's considerably lower cost with respect to the first edition of the *Prose*, it was largely through Fortunio that Bembist thinking reached its largest audience in the early decades of its diffusion.[34]

The first Italian grammar that sought to teach both speaking and writing was Pier Francesco Giambullari's *Regole della lingua fiorentina*, or (as its printer preferred) *De la lingua che si parla e scrive a Firenze*, written in the late 1540s, printed in 1552, and addressed "by a Florentine to non-Florentines and to the young who wish to learn to speak *first* rather than write in that most sweet language in use in Florence."[35] Giambullari's grammar raised hopes prior to its publication that it would satisfy the need for an authoritative Tuscan grammar, given the failed efforts of Grand Duke Cosimo's Florentine Academy to produce one.[36] Giambullari's approach represented a truly new direction, for while his *Regole* do not challenge the authoritative status of the *tre corone* and indeed make ample use of them, they do validate the concomitant adoption of a "current Florentine usage that is not [too] exceptionably popular." Giambullari's *Regole* also acknowledge "that [while] examples of thirteenth-century literary Florentine and contemporary Florentine locution do not always coincide, [this] does not mean that they are mutually exclusive."[37] This latter point would come to be of great importance for Leonardo Salviati's editorial work and for his role in defining the principles around which the Accademia della Crusca initially rallied, but Giambullari's assertion of the legitimacy of the contemporary spoken voice of the vernacular had no measurable impact at the time of its publication, and his name is hardly mentioned again in the subsequent phases of the language question. It is, however, of no little interest within the context of this study that Giambullari explicitly modeled his grammar after the *De emendata structura latini sermonis* (1524) by the English humanist Thomas Linacre, the only such borrowing from English literary culture on the part of an Italian philologist that I know of in the sixteenth century.[38]

William Thomas' *Principal Rules of the Italian Grammar, with a Dictionarie for the better understandyng of Boccace, Petrarcha, and Dante*, published in London in 1550, had been written in Italy several years before to meet the needs of a compatriot newly arrived in Padua.[39] Its strictly pragmatic goal was to lay out in a clear and uncomplicated format the principles necessary for understanding and using the contemporary Italian vernacular as quickly as possible; and its word-list, of roughly 8,000 *voci*, was intended as an aid in reading the *tre corone*. Thomas based his grammar and vocabulary on three recent Italian works: Alberto Accarisi's *Vocabolario, Grammatica, et Orthographia de la lingua volgare ... con ispositioni di molti Luoghi di Dante, del Petrarca et del Boccaccio* (Cento, 1543) and his *Grammatica volgare* (Bologna, 1536); and Francesco Alunno's *Le richezze della lingua volgare* (Venice, 1543).[40] The popularity of Accarisi's grammar is attested by eight editions through 1561, and its straightforward presentation served Thomas' unpolemical objectives quite well.[41] The *Principal Rules* are organized according to standard grammatical categories, schematizing its sources' narrative presentations, providing little commentary, and giving terse examples in Italian with English translations to illustrate each point, as for instance when explaining the doubling of the first letter of pronouns or articles when they are attached to verbs:

So that the verbe be hole without lackyng any lettre, and have (as I have said) the accent of the last lettre sharpe, than shall the pronowne or article folowyng double his first lettre.
    *Trovòmmi amor del tutto disarmato.*
    Love founde me cleane unarmed.[42]

Besides its didactic clarity, this example also provides one of the earliest bits of Petrarch (*Canzoniere* 3.7) published in English. Thomas falls into several traps – in one case fumbling his account of the different conditions governing the use of unarticulated and articulated pronouns ("di" or "del"), and in another not distinguishing between the subjunctive and conditional forms of the verb[43] – but on the whole his grammar serves as a concise presentation of Italian usage, and subsequent editions of *The Principal Rules* in 1560, 1562, and 1567 are evidence of its enduring value in the period preceding John Florio's return to England. The vocabulary, occupying almost five-sixths of the volume, takes its *voci* more or less evenly from Accarisi and Alunno, and though it usually offers only a basic sense of the meaning of each of its entries, there are occasionally some illuminating glimpses of Thomas' predilections, as in these gastronomic terms (only the first of which is registered, but not defined, in Alunno):[44]

*Lasagne*, a certaine kinde of thinne paste used in Italie to make porraige with.

*Macheroni*, a certeine kinde of paste boiled, and made as it were in fritters to be eaten.

*Raviuoli*, a certain kynd of meate made in little morsels of herbes and grated cheese, with a little rind of paste.[45]

Michelangelo Florio's *Regole de la lingua thoscana* echo to some extent but significantly expand Giambullari's grammatical principles. Written in England no later than 1553, the elder Florio's grammar was never printed in his lifetime, though John Florio freely adapted his father's work when he came to append an Italian grammar to *Queen Anna's New World of Words*.[46] Given the dedication to Elizabeth in 1563 of Michelangelo's translation of Georg Agricola's *De re mettalica*, some scholars have suggested that Michelangelo may earlier have served as Italian tutor to the young princess Elizabeth, but as was noted in Ch. 2, we know that he did fulfill that function for the unlucky Jane Grey, and his *Regole* are dedicated to her.[47] Michelangelo stakes out a position in the *Regole* that could not place him farther from the sentiment that, with the exception of Citolini, Giambullari, and a handful of others, held sway in Italy at the time, for he insists that a written text be comprehensible; that its vocabulary be up-to-date; that its marketability be a factor in its lexical choices; and that its spelling should reflect how words are actually pronounced.[48] In short, an unabashed endorsement of the "living" early modern Italian vernacular.

The influence of Bembo's gravitational pull is felt, nevertheless, in Florio's *Regole*, most particularly regarding the presentation of verb forms and in its general adoption of the terminology and structure of Latin grammar, but the liberal spirit that informs this work is a far cry from Bembo's patrician aesthetic. In the dedication to Jane Grey of one of the two extant manuscripts of the *Regole*, Michelangelo tells his patron that:

> I have gathered together several rules from the best writers of our Tuscan (or, if you like, Florentine) tongue and from our spoken usage so that whoever reads them shall be able easily to learn, possess, and speak it.[49]

Florio strikes a balance here between the benefit of learning from the authorities of the past and validating contemporary practice. There is a strong emphasis in the *Regole* on the relation of sound to sense:

> the earliest framers of our language were not concerned to explain all the parts of grammar in order to best express its order, but rather focused on its beauty and grace; such practice satisfies equally both the ear and the intellect.[50]

And in what is surely a direct challenge to Bembo's position negating the correlation of correct usage and Florentine birth,[51] Florio introduces his presentation of the verb *avere* [to have] by maintaining that:

> I wish to give you here such as we speak, with the variety of its verbs, so that you shall understand more easily our language, speaking and writing it *as if you were born in Tuscany*.[52]

Pellegrini suggests in his introduction to the *Regole* that it is strange that Florio's grammar should make such extensive use of its author's unapologetic anti-Catholic convictions, but as should be abundantly clear by now, there is nothing at all coincidental about the intermingling of language and ideology.[53] Michelangelo is doing more than conveying grammatical information in offering such examples as:

> *S'io ubbidisse al papa, ad anticristo ubbidirei* (regarding the relationship of the subjunctive to the conditional).[54]

If I were to obey the Pope, I would be obeying the Anti-Christ.

and:

> *Il papa dice d'essere vicario di Christo, ma all'incontra lo spirito santo ci mostra che egli è anticristo* (on contrariety).[55]

The Pope claims to be the Vicar of Christ, but contrarily the Holy Spirit shows us that he is the Anti-Christ.

Here the grammatical lesson drives home the confluence of linguistic usage and politics, connecting language practice to the realities of the world in which it functions, a lesson John Florio learned well from his father and applied expansively in the various phases of his linguistic stewardship in England.[56]

One other grammar was issued in England just prior to the publication of *Firste Fruites*, a translation of Scipione Lentulo's 1567 *Italicae grammatices praecepta ac ratio* by Henry Grantham (who in 1567 had also published a translation of a fragment of Boccaccio's *Philocolo, A pleasaunt disport of diuers noble personages*), the original of which Migliorini notes was written specifically with foreigners in Italy in mind.[57] *An Italian Grammer* appeared first in 1575 (reprinted in 1587) and provided a solid basis for the beginner's acquisition of Italian, based as it was upon "the most serviceable among the many [such] works then available in Italy ... it is not only extremely clear but completely unadorned, even more so than Thomas, for the most part schematic, with little commentary or exemplification, to the point that it often seems more a grammatical survey than a grammar."[58] The persistence of Latin modeling, while not surprising for a work originally written in Latin, surprises a modern eye in Grantham's English presentation of Italian nouns, for while the introductory comment recognizes that:

although the Italian tongue (as wee have before declared in the declining of the articles) hath neither cases nor declension of nouns as are in the Latin, and Greke tonges: yet doth it receive all manner of variation: which is such, as doth depende upon prepositions, either by them selves alone, or ioyned with th'articles ...

the noun is presented as if it actually were inflected:

| Nomin.singul. | L'amico | The frende |
| Genit. | Dell'amico | Of the frende |
| Dat. | All'amico | To the frende |
| Accus. | L'amico | The friend |
| Vocat. | O amico | O frende |
| Ablat. | Dall'amico | From the frende[59] |

though obviously the various "cases" here exercise no effect upon its forms.[60] In the grammar appended to *Firste Fruites*, John Florio singles out *An Italian Grammer* for praise in the opening exchange between master and student over pronunciation:

sir, if you please, you may reade the distinction, and pronunciation of these consonants in the Grammar that *Scipio Lentulo* made, and Maister *Henry Grantham* dyd translate, where they are at large set out, and so doing, shal you save me a great labour, and a long study, for I can not doo it better than he hath done ...
I pray you, how like you his Grammar?
Truly sir, I like it wel, and it is good.[61]

Florio seems not to have known the surprisingly lively treatise on pronunciation, *Perutilis exteris nationibus de Ithalica pronuntiatione, et orthographia libellus*, published in Padua in 1569 by Siòn Dafydd Rhys, a Welsh physician then resident in Tuscany.[62] The grammar of Welsh that Rhys published in London in 1592, *Cambrobrytannicæ Cymraecæve linguæ institutiones et rudimenta accurate*, is closely linked to the principles elaborated in his treatise on Italian pronunciation and provides an exemplary counterbalance to the contemporary development of English by not only establishing the independence of Welsh but also in furnishing its first grammar two years before Paul Greaves published his *Grammatica anglicana*.[63] A Latin grammar, the *Regole della costruttione latina*, written in 1566, demonstrates the mastery of the contemporary Tuscan vernacular which enabled Rhys to elaborate his study of its proper pronunciation. Though this is not the place for a close analysis of *De Ithalica pronuntiatione*, a few examples will serve to demonstrate the utility of its suggestions as well as the wit and erudition with which they are presented.

The primary focus of Rhys' treatise is the language spoken in Florence, Siena, and Pistoia – central Tuscany – but there are contrasts made throughout with other Italian regional usages. Rhys initially cautions his readers not to introduce into the pronunciation of Italian sounds peculiar to their own languages, be they German, English, Polish, or Portuguese,[64] and one of the notable features of his work is the knowledge that he demonstrates of contemporary European vernaculars in addition to classical Greek and Latin. The treatise is organized alphabetically, separate consideration given to the sound and orthographical particularities of each letter. Regarding the sound of the soft *c* when combined with *i* or *e* still characteristic of Tuscan pronunciation, he notes that:

*bacio* [kiss], *aceto* [vinegar], *lecito* [permissible], would be written in English: *basho, asheto, leshito*; in Spanish and Portuguese: *baxo, axeto, lexito*; in French: *bacho, asheto, leshito*; in German: *bascho, ascheto, leschito*. But the pronunciation must be somewhat more subtle and compressed, as we noted earlier, with the sound tending toward the whistle characteristic of *s*. In other words, as with *la cima* [the summit], *belli ceci* [lovely chickpeas], *alma Cerere* [the spirit of Ceres], *crede a ciascuno* [he believes everyone], *vinti cinque* [twenty-five], such a value would be rendered in English spelling by *la shima, belli sheshi, alma Sherere, crede a shascuno, vinti shinque*.[65]

Explaining the combination of *g* and *l*, a typical stumbling-block for native speakers of English (less so for those of consonant-heavy Welsh), Rhys has this to say:

the *l* placed between *g* and *i*, or *gli*, is pronounced in a more sweetly liquid manner on account of the pressure of the saliva involved. The Spanish double *ll* and the Portuguese *lh* correspond to such a sound.[66]

And in one of the treatise's most spirited moments, Rhys shows both a superb command of Latin style and a deep knowledge of the Latin literary tradition in the course of describing the trilled *r* characteristic of both Italian and Welsh:

> The canine letter is pronounced by one and all with a violent and vehement effort, with the tongue vibrating and rising to the roof of the mouth near the base of the upper incisors, with its tip agitating the breath while expelling it, and with a kind of trembling force beating out a fragmented and almost frightful sound.[67]

The density of classical allusion in this passage – the formulation "canine letter" coming from the first *Satire* of Persius (1.109–110), the idea itself going back to a fragment of Lucilius in which *r* is the sound made by "a dog, when it is teased," and a further echo to be found in Terentius Maurus, who in describing the pronunciation of *r* notes that "a vibrating dry sound with trembling blows" is required[68] – is worn very lightly, the tone of this passage (as is frequently the case elsewhere in the treatise) playing with both irony and comedy. *De Ithalica pronuntiatione* is the most thorough survey of the pronunciation of Tuscan Italian produced in the cinquecento, and while Rhys' work was written specifically to serve the needs of foreigners in Italy, it also made a seminal contribution to early modern Italy's linguistic culture. Rhys had a prominent patron in Ludovico Beccadelli, Reginald Pole's biographer, his earliest experiences in Italy were in Trent just as the council was concluding its work, and he was involved throughout his time on the peninsula with eminent figures among the various Catholic expatriate communities there. The religious backdrop of Rhys' linguistic work consequently sets it apart from that of the Italian Protestants active in England, and though upon his return to Britain Rhys made a public profession of adherence to the Protestant faith, it seems likely that he remained a Catholic, a factor that might partially explain the apparent lack of circulation of his treatise on Italian pronunciation there and the absence of any reference to it among the English Italianists.[69]

John Florio's praise for the Lentulo/Grantham *Grammer* in his *Necessarie Rules for Englishmen to learne to reade, speake, and write true Italian*, the grammar appended to *Firste Fruites*, is followed by a more muted estimation of William Thomas' work:

> I like it wel too, but yet he left many things untouched, both in his Grammar, and also in his Dictionarie.[70]

The text that goes unmentioned anywhere in Florio's grammar is Citolini's *Grammatica della lingua italiana*, of which Mariagrazia Bellorini has demonstrated Florio's work to be an unacknowledged translation.[71] What might seem an inexcusable case of plagiarism should, however, be qualified in this case (and in general with regard to the issue in this period), for it is not clear to what extent Citolini might have been involved in Florio's use of his work, and as Bellorini points out, Florio's grammar is the adaptation of a work for the English context originally written in Italy for Italians.[72]

As it appears in Florio's version, Citolini's grammar differs little from its predecessors, though a considerable amount of space is initially dedicated to pronunciation and punctuation.[73] While Trissino is not named by Citolini in the dedicatory epistle of the manuscipt of his *Grammatica*, its aim of providing a correct system of pronunciation tied to corresponding graphic markers without introducing letters extraneous to the Italian vernacular is an obvious attempt to improve upon Trissino's earlier failed effort in this direction.[74] The relationship of Citolini's grammatical treatise to the *Lettera* is manifest in this passage from the dedication of the *Grammatica*:

Being that speech is an instrument with which we express the thoughts and concepts of our spirit, that speech is without doubt most perfect which perfectly expresses these thoughts and concepts; thus writing being an instrument with which we express living speech, that writing is without doubt most perfect which most perfectly expresses living speech.[75]

As in the *Lettera*, Citolini's emphasis is on language as a living reality, for "languages are learned from peoples, as even Plato affirms."[76]

Florio put this principle into practice most originally in *Firste Fruites* not in his reworking of Citolini's grammar but in the *Regole necessarie per indurre gli'taliani a proferir la Lingua Inglese*, a guide to English pronunciation for Italians in England new to the language and requiring a practical introduction to its idiosyncracies, which Florio admits are legion:

This English language, to put it bluntly, I believe to be the most confused of all languages, because it is derived from many others, each day taking new words on loan [from them]. Many are taken from Italian, more from German, and still more from French, and an infinite number from Latin, and also some from Greek.[77]

Though the six-page passage of advice on pronunciation which follows is necessarily rudimentary, Florio provides here the very earliest representation of the sound of English in this period. His explanation of the letter *h*, a perennial impediment for Italians in speaking English, illustrates the utility of Florio's approach gleaned from his pragmatic experience of teaching languages:

The *h* is a great ornament in the English language, and it is the most difficult letter for Italians to pronounce due to its great force, particularly in words such as these: *Thou* (tu), *that* (quello), *this* (questo). In order to pronounce such words as they should be, one must as it were hold the teeth almost clenched while supporting the tip of the tongue between them, [then in] speaking immediately pull it back so as to rest it on the palate of the mouth. To pronounce *what* (che cosa), *which* (quale), *who* (qui), *where* (dove), one must make as if to sip, holding the tongue steady in the middle of the mouth without touching anything, starting to speak slowly. But in words beginning with *h* such as *hay* (fjeno), *hat* (capello), *how* (come), *hen* (una gallina), and other such innumerable, one must use a certain tremendous force in pronunciation, particularly when the *h* is pronounced fully and heavily.[78]

With all of the huffing and puffing required to produce it, there is an unmistakable sense here (as elsewhere in *Firste Fruites*) of the inferiority of English vis-à-vis other more established vernaculars, but Florio learned eventually not only to appreciate but to exploit the malleable and expanding possibilities of the English language, his lived experience with which certainly contributed to the shape and the scope of the Italian–English dictionary he was already contemplating by the time of the publication of his first language-learning dialogue book in 1578.

> "... tutti i linguaggi ... o in tutto od in parte si perdono, o s'infettono, e si corrompono."

### Instruments of cultural control in early modern Italy

The political and religious turmoil that rocked Italy throughout the first half of the sixteenth century and that led such individuals as Michelangelo Florio to flee the peninsula for more hospitable environments gave way after the conclusion of the Council of Trent (1545–63) to a period of comparative calm marked, however, by the foundation of institutions aimed at controlling or regulating cultural production, two of which – the *Index librorum prohibitorum* [Index of Forbidden Books], promulgated by Pope Paul IV in 1559, and the Florentine Accademia della Crusca, founded in 1583 – are of fundamental importance for the history of the Italian language, and for the forms in which it came to be expressed in the two editions of Florio's dictionary. Of the seventy-two entries in the library prefacing *A Worlde of Wordes*, twenty-four of the titles had been placed on the Index, and around fifty of the 252 titles consulted for the compilation of *Queen Anna's New World of Words*; and as we shall see in the next section, the range of Florio's lexicon exceeds by more than three times the restricted scope of the 1612 Crusca *Vocabolario*.

The cultural inquiry, recovery, and experimentation that the modern historiographical term "Renaissance" designates suffered a succession of crippling blows, beginning with the invasion of the Italian peninsula by the French King Charles VIII in 1494, and culminating in the Sack of Rome by the troops of the Holy Roman Emperor Charles V in 1527. One can quibble about precisely where to draw the line of demarcation between what constitutes Italian Renaissance culture and the indeterminate period that followed the collapse of its sustaining values, but by the conclusion of the second session of the Council of Trent in 1552 it was already clear that the political climate of Italy was shifting toward a new paradigm in which the church would function no longer as the promoter of cultural innovation but as its judge and regulator. Various nomenclature has been used to describe this historical moment – "Counter-Reformation," "Catholic Reformation," "Confessional Catholicism," and "Early Modern Catholicism"[79] – but the most significant factor here is that the flexible boundaries and wide-ranging exploration of the Renaissance period had by this time given way to something quite different. In the absence of a centralized Italian political authority, the admonitory post-Tridentine church and its various organs came increasingly to fill that void. The fractured character of Torquato Tasso – torn in his allegiances between a literary art out of step with prevailing linguistic orthodoxies and an over-scrupulous sense of his obligation to contemporary ecclesiastical ideology (he denounced himself to the Inquisition, and then disastrously rewrote his *Gerusalemme liberata*) – functions as a telling reminder of the potential effects of such a narrowing of politically acceptable cultural boundaries.[80]

The impulse toward control was not, however, an Inquisitorial innovation, for from the very first decades of print culture numerous initiatives had been launched by ecclesiastical and civic powers to regulate the circulation of information. Paradoxically, Leo X, one of the most literate and libertine of Renaissance popes, approved a series of regulations in the 1515 bull *Inter sollicitudines* which, while addressed primarily to controlling the publication of books deemed threatening to Christian religion and ethics, set the stage for the totalizing ambitions of later cinquecento Catholic censorship.[81] In England, the Bishop of London, taking his cue from this papal document, moved to ban the import of books from abroad and to permit the publication of books within the country only upon permission granted by a commission headed by the Archbishop of Canterbury. After the split with Rome, Henry VIII attempted to divest the Anglican church of its power over the presses, but the situation remained as conflicted as were the religious and political issues that dominated those decades in England, and it was not until Mary licensed the Company of Stationers in 1557 that an official body was constituted to effect a coherent strategy of regulation. We have already seen, however, in the case of John Wolfe how English print culture could be manipulated, and as Mario Infelise notes, "[England] never managed to create a system of surveillance as efficient and wide-ranging as that which operated in Catholic countries."[82]

One of the fundamental premises of the 1559 Index is a radically revisionist poetics in which fictions are taken for dangerous truths, a result the Roman Inquisitor General, Michele Ghislieri (elected Pope Pius V in 1565), evidently could not have foreseen when he wrote just two years before that "to prohibit the *Orlando furioso, Orlandino* [by Teofilo Folengo], the *Cento novelle* and other similar books is more a cause for laughter than anything else, because such books are to be read not in order to be believed but as fictions."[83] Gian Pietro Carafa, by now Pope Paul IV but earlier the first prefect of the Roman Inquisition, did not share such a discriminating view, and the Index that he promulgated represents the most extreme effort to control the means of cultural production and dissemination in the history of the Roman church. Three categories were established for the 1559 Index, designed to encompass the entire scope of non-Catholic literature, religious and otherwise; the profusion of editions, translations, and paraphrases of the Bible (with the particularly insidious proviso that the Inquisition could grant a license for the reading of a vernacular Bible, but not to women or to those who could not read Latin); and a large swath of the most representative texts of the Italian Renaissance, including the works of Boccaccio, Castiglione, Machiavelli, and Aretino, writers whose lexicons are central to John Florio's work of defining the range of the Italian language (others, such as Giordano Bruno, would find their way onto subsequent revisions of the Index). Carafa died later in 1559, before his directives could be implemented – happily for the printers and booksellers whose warehoused stock would otherwise have gone unsold, a situation that could have caused severe economic problems in places such as Venice, whose economy was so deeply invested in the book trade. The Medici pope who succeeded Carafa, Pius IV, sought to modify the centralization of censorship in the Roman Inquisition by relegating much of its authority to local bishops and their chanceries, while also refocusing the primary sights of such control on religious books. Though these principles were endorsed by the Council of Trent and resulted in the revised Index of 1564, the earlier document continued to exercise considerable influence, and so the competing tendencies of extremism and moderation subsequently fought for three decades to gain control of the process. The Index published by Pope Clement VIII in 1596 was a compromise that incorporated elements of both approaches, but the most destructive aspect of Carafa's ideology, an undisguised hostility toward vernacular languages and the cultures they were creating which posed such a threat to the hegemony of Roman religion, would work their damage for generations to come, as Italians would not be permitted again to licitly read the Bible in their own language until 1758, and many of the classics of their literary tradition, if available at all, could only be had in versions distorted to satisfy the exigencies of ecclesiastically legislated censorship.[84]

The most notorious episode in the early modern history of the church's intrusion into the literary realm is a story to which I shall return when I come in a subsequent volume to address the circulation of "stranger" cultures in Stuart England, for Florio's 1620 English translation of the *Decameron* was made with the 1582 revisionist edition of Boccaccio's *novelle* issued by Leonardo Salviati and a committee of Florentine editors under his supervision in one hand, and Antoine de Maçon's French translation for Marguerite de Navarre in the other. Salviati's *Decameron* was an effort to "improve upon" the edition prepared by Vincenzo Borghini and an earlier editorial *équipe*, published in Florence in 1573.[85] But Borghini's edition was judged not to have gone far enough in satisfying the demands of the Roman censors, and Salviati set out to produce one that would. The resulting edition routinely alters plot lines in order to laicize Boccaccio's clerics and religious, to marry otherwise illicit lovers, or give immoral characters their just deserts, and ellipses are introduced to salvage a particularly felicitous turn of phrase where some unacceptable action occurs or an untoward sentiment is expressed. For Salviati what mattered most in the *Decameron* was its rich lexical palette, and he exercised his editorial work in the service of promoting a philologically informed but literarily reckless valorization of Boccaccio's usage refracted through the spoken Tuscan of the late sixteenth century. Though the Salviati edition can be judged a notable editorial failure for the damage it inflicted on the *Decameron*'s narrative coherence, Brian Richardson notes that Salviati was the first Italian editor to take pronunciation into account when addressing questions of spelling,[86] positioning himself against Bembist ideology in this regard, but confirming what we have already seen to be a similar line of thinking in the grammatical work of Giambullari, Citolini, and Michelangelo Florio.[87]

Though not strictly linked to Salviati's work on the *Decameron*, the foundation of the Accademia della Crusca in 1583 can be seen as the progression into a new phase of Florentine linguistic husbandry in which the preceding decade's editorial activity came to be codified in the newly influential form of the dictionary as well as in other editions of classic Tuscan texts. The Crusca sought early on, under Salviati's influence, to reorient the debate around *la questione della lingua* to matters of lexical propriety over grammatical concerns, and this emphasis would turn out to be simultaneously both a blessing – in recuperating the broad range of the Tuscan lexicon as it had developed through the period of the *tre corone* – and a curse – in so severely limiting the scope of its first *Vocabolario* that it could effectively function only as an index to a form of Italian fixed in an increasingly remote historical past.[88]

We have already noted several earlier examples of Italian dictionaries. The 1543 *Vocabolario* of Accarisi, as well as Alunno's 1543 *Richezze della volgar lingua* and his 1548 *Fabbrica del mondo*, were organized primarily to assist in the reading of the *tre corone*.[89] Only one vocabulary had aimed to move beyond the language of the trecento, Fabrizio Luna's 1536 *Vocabulario di cinquemila vocabuli toschi*, which cites Ariosto, Boiardo, Sannazaro, Bernardo Tasso, and (remarkably) two women, Vittoria Colonna and Veronica Gambara; and it also demonstrates an awareness of extra-Bembist thinking about questions of grammar.[90] But Luna's vocabulary is bogged down by a heavily pedantic style and frequent idiosyncratic digressions; it did not have a wide circulation, and his more accommodating criteria would have to wait for a clearer and more comprehensive elaboration in Florio's lexicographical work.[91]

The proliferation of dictionaries and vocabularies of classical languages and European vernaculars in the sixteenth century exercised a pressure to produce a similarly commanding index to its fundamentally conservative sense of the heritage of the Tuscan language, though in the end the *Cruscanti* almost entirely ignored the dictionaries that had preceded theirs.[92] In the introductory address to the reader of the 1612 *Vocabolario*, the academicians note that they had been prompted to produce their dictionary seeing their language rising "every day in higher esteem ... and with the [increase in] the number of its scholars, both in and beyond Italy, grows also the longing to know its beauties."[93] The motto on the frontispiece of the *Vocabolario* announces that "the most lovely flowers [of the Tuscan language] are [here] gathered,"[94] and the address to the reader explicitly identifies the dictionary's parameters "with the judgment of the Most Illustrious Cardinal Bembo, the Deputies of the 1573 corrected Boccaccio, and lastly with Lord Leonardo Salviati."[95] Two notable incongruities are flagged here, for Salviati's lexical principles allowed for the incorporation of whatever could be recovered from the language of the Tuscan duecento which had paved the way for the *tre corone*, a plain rejection of Bembo's substantially more limited parameters; and in identifying their work with the "tidied-up" editions of the *Decameron*, the *Cruscanti* make explicit the detachment of the *voci* which they admit into their linguistic world from the original contexts in which these words were to be located, as if the sense of a word's meaning could legitimately be severed from the manner in which it has been used (a position made even more problematic by the citation of textual passages within the *Vocabolario*'s entries). The introduction goes on to explain that because, with the passage of time, "all languages ... entirely or partially lose their way, or become contaminated, and hence corrupted,"[96] the academicians chose to concentrate their energies principally on "that time ... from the year of our Lord 1300 to 1400, give or take a few years,"[97] adding the name of the chronicler Giovanni Villani to those of Dante, Petrarch, and Boccaccio, judging later writers or translations from Latin into Italian worthy of inclusion only insofar as they had conformed to the earlier, authoritative Florentine standard, the "manner of speaking of this Country [Florence]."[98] Any notion that inevitable linguistic change might have some positive value is here serenely elided.

The work of the academicians was carried out as a private enterprise, with no financial support from the Grand Ducal coffers, and the costs of publishing the volume had to be met by the *Cruscanti* themselves. That the 1612 *Vocabolario* was actually published in Venice says as much about its potentially uncertain reception in Florence as it does about the shift in priorities that Florentine publishers had adopted in response to the tightening of ecclesiastical control over print culture. Despite these local ambivalences, the failure of the *Vocabolario*'s program to fulfill the Bembist aim of unifying Italy linguistically through adherence to a historically and geographically circumscribed standard of selection must be weighed against the consistent and comprehensive result such limitations enabled. I would, nevertheless, challenge Claudio Marazzini's assertion that the 1612 *Vocabolario* is "the first great European dictionary,"[99] not to diminish its importance but rather to more reasonably situate it within, but not by any means make it representative of, a rapidly developing European lexicographical and philological tradition from which the *Cruscanti* believed they could exempt themselves and their dictionary.[100] Severina Parodi has suggested with regard to the perspective of the academicians that "in the texts of Dante and the poetry of Petrarch, educated men deepened their rooted sense of feeling themselves Italian in a manner similar to the development that elsewhere in Europe, in different historical circumstances, was beginning to lead to the affirmation of national states."[101] But the *Cruscanti* did not speak for all Italians (or even all Florentines), though they go so far as to claim that writers who express themselves in anything other than "the most lovely flowers ... seem sooner foreigners to us than our own,"[102] a breathtakingly insular position, though one that in its exclusionary strategy functions in striking counterpoint to the entirely diverse principles employed by John Florio. His career as just such a "foreigner" was developing in England at precisely the same time as the Crusca academicians were realizing their early projects, and it culminated in the production of a vastly different kind of dictionary, to which we now turn our attention.

> "*Vocabolario*, a dictionarie, a register, or denominating of words and names."

### Florio the lexicographer

In the dedicatory epistle prefaced to *A Worlde of Wordes*, talk of authorities heralds the arrival of Florio's dictionary, and with it a recognition of the differences that separate its author from its dedicatees, a more telling prelude than those that had preceded *Firste* and *Second Frutes*, for while there he had sought patronage that had not in the end materialized to the extent hoped for, here Florio proffers the fruits of his most recent labors to patrons whose largesse he has already enjoyed:

> To the Right Honorable Patrons of Vertue, Patrons of Honor, Roger Earle of Rutland, Henrie Earle of Southampton, Lucie, Countess of Bedford[103]

This dedication (Right Honorable and that worthily) may happily make your Honors muse; well fare that dedication, that may excite your muse. I am no auctorised Herauld to marshall your precedence, Private dutie might perhaps give one the prioritie, where publicke respect should prefer another. [A1r]

The confidence of address here should be understood as both a reflection of Florio's surer footing in the aristocratic circles to which he had long aspired and as an indication of the assured authority – this too marking a significant development over the *Fruits* – from which the dictionary had sprung.[104]

Florio had been associated with Henry Wriothesley, Earl of Southampton, at least since 1594, and perhaps for some time before.[105] Though Yates speculates that Florio may have been placed in the Southampton circle as a spy by Robert Cecil, Lord Burghley – in whose household Wriothesley, Roger Manners, and Robert Devereux, later the Earl of Essex, and many other English aristocratic boys were educated – there seems to be no conclusive evidence leading one way or the other. Just as John Bossy has now acknowledged regarding his case supporting Giordano Bruno's supposed career as an Elizabethan spy in the 1580s, the facts are too elusive to provide anything but tantalizing hypotheses.[106] Apart from the dedication of *A Worlde of Wordes*, what evidence we do have of Florio's attitude toward his patron is an incident – reported by both Yates and Akrigg[107] – in which Florio meets the sheriff responsible for the pursuit of the Danvers brothers, friends of Southampton's and harbored by him after one of them had murdered Henry Long, the final episode in a long-standing inter-family feud. If Florio had indeed "threatened to cast the saide [Sheriff] Grose overboord and saide they woulde teach him to meddle with his fellowes, with many other threatening words," it would be consistent with the the blustery personality Yates details and so much in evidence in the prefatory material in his various works. The pæan to Southampton in the dedication to *A Worlde of Wordes* acknowledges Florio's debt to his patron and likens it to Dante's obligations to his two otherworldly guides:

In loyalty I may averre (my needdle toucht, and drawne, and held by such an adamant) what he in love assumed, that saw the other stars, but bent his course by the Pole-starre, and two guardes, avowing *Aspicit unam*. One guideth me, though more I see. Good parts imparted are not empaired. Your springs are first to serve yourselfe, yet may yield your neighbors sweet water; your taper is to light you first, and yet it may light your neighbors candle. I might make doubt, least I or mine be not now of further use to your selfe-sufficiencie, being at home so instructed in Italian, as teaching and learning could supplie, that there seemed no need of travell; and now by travell so accomplished, as what wants perfection? [A1v]

Though eager to praise his benevolent, industrious, and ingenious benefactor, Florio cannot but help himself to a *soupçon* of self-congratulation, for the excellencies he enumerates here are to a large extent the result of his tutelage. Roger Manners gets a proportionately lesser degree of attention:

my most noble, most gracious, and most gracefull Earle of Rutland, well entered in the tongue, ere your Honour entered Italie, there therein so perfected, as what needeth a Dictionarie? [A1v]

The fifth Earl of Rutland was three years' Southampton's junior and his close friend. After a European tour in 1596 that included a visit to Italy, Manners accompanied Wriothesley in 1599 on the disastrous Essex campaign in Ireland without royal permission and was ordered home in disgrace. He would later participate in the Essex plot against the queen, and though both he and Southampton were imprisoned for their roles in this episode they managed to survive and were rehabilitated early in the new reign of James I.[108]

With patrons like these, Florio invariably would have found himself on the wrong side of many critical issues in the Elizabethan period, but with them he too was to find his fortunes redeemed with the dawn of the Stuart era. Apart from Robert Cecil, who engineered so many of the matters related to the royal succession and transition, probably no single individual had more to do with Florio's promotion to the court of Queen Anne than Lucy Harington Russell, Countess of Bedford, wife of Edward Russell (yet another of the Essex conspirators), and niece of John Harington, the translator of Ariosto.[109] It was in the Harington household and at the behest of its ladies that Florio made his translation of Montaigne's *Essais*, the first book of which he dedicated to Lucy and to her mother, Anne, both of whom were part of an embassy of noble English ladies to James VI and Queen Anne in Edinburgh immediately after the death of Elizabeth. Soon having become the new queen's favored lady-in-waiting, Lucy was in a particularly advantageous position to advance the prospects of her Italian tutor in the Stuart court, and though his appointment there was still several years distant at the time of the publication of *A Worlde of Wordes*, Florio concludes its patronal addresses by rhetorically asking her:

if I offer service but to them that need it, with what face seeke I a place with your excellent Ladiship (my most-most honored, because best-best adorned Madame) who by conceited industrie, or industrious conceite, in Italian as in French, in French as in Spanish, in all as in English, understand what you read, write as you reade, and speake as you write; yet rather charge your minde with matter, then your memorie with words. [A1v]

Florio reserves his highest and most specific praise for the Countess of Bedford, whose linguistic skills are complete. She is a student who has so absorbed her language lessons that she has come to appreciate that words are but one aspect of the complex process of understanding.

Two crucial issues are flagged at the outset of the dedication of *A Worlde of Wordes*: the utility of "ambidexterity," being conversant in more than one language, which Florio presents his dedicatees as shining examples of:

> Lame are we in *Platoes* censure, if we be not ambidexters, using both hands alike. Right-hand, or left-hand as Peeres with mutuall paritie, without disparagement may it please your Honors to joyne hand in hand, and so joyntly to lende an eare (and lende it I beseech you) to a poore man ... [A1r]

and the process of metamorphosis, underscored by the citation of the Baucis and Philemon episode in Giovanni Andrea dell'Anguillara's 1561 Italian translation of Ovid's great poem of transformations and indicative of the most significant operative principle of Florio's philological imagination:

> ... like *Philemon* and *Baucis* may in so lowe a cottage entertaine so high, if not deities, yet dignities; of whom the poet testifies.
>
> > Ma sopra ogni altro frutto piu gradito
> > Fu il volto allegro, è l non bugiardo amore.
> > E benche fosse povero il convito,
> > Non fu la volontà povera è l'core.
>
> > But of all other cheere most did content
> > A cheerefull countenance, and a smiling minde,
> > Poore entertainment being richly ment,
> > Pleaded excuse for that which was behinde.
>
> [A1r]

The positioning early on in the dedication of Florio's dictionary of Ovid's account of the humble Baucis and Philemon graciously extending to disguised deities their inadequate hospitality serves simultaneously to emphasize the differences that separate the author from his patrons and to anticipate a happy conclusion not unlike that of Ovid's generous though impoverished couple, unforeseen in the dictionary's first edition but fully realized by the time of the second with Florio's assimilation into Queen Anne's court. But patrons are not Florio's only concern in the prefatory material to *A Worlde of Wordes*, for "the dedication and the address 'To the Reader' clearly delineate a figure fully engaged in two complex worlds – one a world of station, privilege, and power that comes from birth, another a world of commerce variously populated, where power comes from the pen, press, and sales."[110] Florio's dictionary thus aimed both to serve as a gesture of gratitude to powerful supporters and was intended for the marketplace, a world of words whose scope was not only the delectation of an aristocratic elite but that sought also to cast a wider net.

Florio launches *A Worlde of Wordes* with a discussion of its ambitions,[111] immediately defining a position that places his work at odds with the direction pursued by the majority of his Italian contemporaries:

Yet heere-hence many some good accrewe, not onelie to trauntlie-scollers, which ever and anon runne to *Venuti*, and *Alunno*; or to new-entred novices, that hardly can continue their lesson; or to well-forwarde students, that have turned over *Guazzo* and *Castiglione*, yea runne through *Guarini, Ariosto, Tasso, Boccace*, and *Petrarche*. But even to the most compleate Doctor, yea to him that best can stande *All'erta* for the best Italian, hereof may rise some use, since, have he the memorie of *Themistocles*, of *Seneca*, of *Scaliger*, yet is it not infinite in so finite a bodie. And I have seene the best, yea naturall Italians, not only stagger, but even sticke fast in the myre, and at last give it over, or give their verdict with an *ignoramus. Boccace* is prettie hard, yet understood; *Petrarche* harder, but explained; *Dante* hardest, but commented, some doubt if all aright. *Alunno* for his foster-children hath framed a worlde of their wordes; *Venuti* taken much paines in some verie fewe authors; and our *William Thomas* hath done prettilie. And if all faile, although we misse or mistake the worde, yet make we up the sence. Such making is marring. Naie all as good, but not all as right. And not right, is flat wrong. One says of *Petrarche* for all: A thousand strappadas coulde not compell him to confesse, what some interpreters will make him saie he ment. And a Judicious gentleman of this lande will uphold, that none in England understands him thoroughly. How then ayme we at *Peter Aretine*, that is to witte, hath such varietie, and frames so manie new words? At *Francesco Doni*, who is so fantasticall, & so strange? At *Thomaso Garzoni* in his *Piazza universale*; or at *Alessandro Citolini* in his *Typocosmia*, who have more proper and peculiar words concerning every severall trade, arte, or occupation for everie particular toole, or implement belonging unto them, than ever man heretofor either collected in any booke, or sawe collected in any one language? How shall we understand *Hannibal Caro*, who is so full of wittie jests, sharpe quips, nipping tantes, and scoffing phrases against that grave and learned man *Lodovico Castelvetro*, in his *Apologia de' Banchi*? Howe shall the Englishe Gentleman come to the perfect understanding of *Federico Grisone*, his *Arte del Cavalcare*, who is so full of strange phrases, and unusuall wordes, peculiar onely to horse-manship, and proper but to *Cavalarizzi*? How shall we understande so manie and so strange bookes, of so severall, and so fantasticall subjects as be written in the Italian toong? How shall we, naie, how may we ayme at the Venetian, at the Romane, at the Lombard, at the Neopolitaine, at so manie, and so much differing Dialects, and Idiomes, as be used and spoken in Italie, besides the Florentine? [A1v–A2r]

The characteristically free-form cascade of Florio's prose reveals several critical elements of his lexicographical practice. The first is his reliance on earlier word-books, vocabularies, and dictionaries. Five dictionary-makers are named here: Alunno; Filippo Venuti, author of the 1578 *Dittionario volgare & latino*; William Thomas; Citolini, whose *Tipocosmia* provided an expansive and experimental model for the inclusion in Florio's lexicon of scientific and technological terms outside the parameters of orthodox contemporary Italian usage;[112] and Tommaso Garzoni, himself much indebted to Citolini, who furnished in his *Piazza universale* a further index to the vocabulary and conceptual language of over 500 professions.[113] A number of other dictionaries are mentioned in the catalogues of books consulted in the preparation of Florio's dictionaries that preface both *A Worlde of Wordes* and *Queen Anna*, including the 1571 Spanish–Italian *Vocabolario de las dos lenguas toscana y castellana* of Cristóbal de las Casas. One of the dictionaries Florio drew on most extensively was Thomas Thomas' 1570 Latin–English *Dictionarium Linguae Latinae et Anglicanae*, and the fact that he does not cite this book as a source – Thomas is mentioned, however, along with Sir Thomas Elyot, Bishop Cooper, John Rider, and the Stephanus [Estienne] brothers, as an authoritative dictionary writer against which his own work can be judged – earned the opprobrium of several earlier scholars of Florio's dictionaries. De Witt T. Starnes established that Florio had taken many of his English definitions directly from Thomas' dictionary, concluding that such unacknowledged borrowing seriously diminished Florio's achievement and called into question the extent of the reading his book catalogues imply.[114] But as David Frantz pointed out in a corrective response to Starnes, Florio was simply following conventional practice in making whatever use he deemed helpful of others' work.[115] All of the dictionaries he does cite had been compiled in a similar fashion: Thomas Thomas leaned heavily on Thomas Cooper's 1565 *Thesaurus Linguae Romanae et Britannicae*, Venuti having utilized Calepino's multi-language dictionary, William Thomas basing his vocabulary on those of Alunno and Accarisi, and so on, echoing Stephen Orgel's assertion that "most literature in the [early modern] period must be seen as basically collaborative in nature,"[116] and Jonathan Green's suggestion that "there is a good case for regarding the history of lexicography as the history of an infinite palimpsest."[117]

But if many of Florio's definitions come from other sources, he alone established the remarkably expansive range of the words he chose to include in his dictionaries, some 46,000 entries in *A Worlde of Wordes*, grown to 74,000 in *Queen Anna*[118] (compared with the roughly 28,000 *voci* of the 1612 Crusca *Vocabolario*), bringing us to the second aspect of Florio's dictionary-making referred to in the preface to *A Worlde of Wordes*: the tremendously wide reach of its research and reading.[119] In addition to clarifying the nature of Florio's "plagiarism," Frantz identifies a number of words defined in *A Worlde of Wordes* that could only have been acquired through a personal acquaintance with the books from which they come.[120]

Italian literature and translations of the sixteenth century provide the greatest number of sources among the 72 titles listed in *A Worlde of Wordes* and *Queen Anna*'s 252 – Guarini, Tasso, Doni, Citolini, Castelvetro, and

Caro are among the authors cited in the preface to *A Worlde of Wordes* and ignored in the 1612 Crusca. Though neither Dante nor Ariosto is cited in the catalogue of books prefacing *A Worlde of Wordes*, they are both mentioned in the dedicatory epistle, and at least eleven Dantean terms are defined in the first edition of Florio's dictionary, among them:

Ita, *hath been used of* Dante, *in the latine sense, yea, yes.*[121]

Four comedies of Aretino and Ippolito Salviani's *La ruffiana* are the only plays that *A Worlde of Wordes* acknowledges, but there are thirty *commedie*, four *tragedie*, four *pastorali*, and two additional texts dealing with spectacle and stagecraft listed in *Queen Anna*. Florio's preparatory reading amounts, in fact, to much the same sort of catalogue produced by nineteenth-century historiographers who, it has been fashionable in recent decades to suggest, "invented" the Renaissance. Florio's dictionary libraries already anticipate all of the major and many of the minor texts that would embody that later critical tradition. Such a consensus could never have been reached in contemporary Italy (nor for a very long time into the future), and though Florio apparently worked alone, the choices he made in this regard were anything but idiosyncratic, suggesting that the nature of canons is perhaps not so entirely arbitrary as some recent cultural criticism has attempted to establish.[122]

Not that Florio's books are entirely without their unusual choices: there are cookbooks, represented by *Dell'arte della cucina* of Cristoforo Messi Sbugo (banquet master for the Este during Ariosto's career at the Ferrarese court), cited in both *A Worlde of Wordes* and *Queen Anna*, and the *Libro nuovo d'ordinar banchetti, et conciar vivande* found only in *Queen Anna*; twelve texts deal with arms and the practice of warfare, again only in *Queen Anna*; there are eight volumes of letters in *A Worlde of Wordes*, nineteen in *Queen Anna*; the *Herbario inghilese* of Giovanni Gerardi and the *Herbario spagnuolo* of Dottor Laguna are included in both dictionaries, as is Corrado Gesnero's natural science, *Degl'animali, pesci, ed uccelli, tre volumi*. Noted only in the dedicatory preface to *A Worlde of Wordes* is Cavalarizzi's *Arte del cavalcare*, from which Florio was able to indulge his passion for horses (few pages go by in either edition of the dictionary without the definition of a term in horsemanship, and Florio describes his work as a lexicographer in the dedication to *A Worlde of Wordes* as that of a stirrup-holder). The impression such an eclectic collection of material leaves is that of a modern polymath's library, a selection far from the deliberately limited range of texts cited in the 1612 Crusca *Vocabolario* that marks its begrudging admittance of contemporary voices under the heading: "Autori moderni citati in diffetto degli antichi" [modern authors cited for want of the ancients].

Florio's aim was to provide as extensive a survey of both past and contemporary Italian usage as his reading could afford him, a method that in spite of its limitation to printed material provided his readers with a close approximation of the heterogeneity of several centuries of Italian linguistic practice. The point Florio makes in the dedicatory epistle to *A Worlde of Wordes* regarding the necessity of supplementing Florentine usage to encompass Venetian, Roman, Lombard, and Neopolitan voices was not to be fully implemented until the revisions that led to *Queen Anna* were complete, but this recognition of the legitimacy of other forms of Italian in his effort at reproducing the language – a factor effectively erased in the course of the debate over *la questione della lingua* – substantiates Florio's bold claim in *A Worlde of Wordes*' address "To the Reader" to stand alone in his work of dictionary-making within the context of the Italian language. And though he is not incapable of modesty – Florio recognizes the protean nature of language, more powerful in its operations than those who try to control it, and he "hope[s that] no man that shall expend the woorth of this worke in impartiall examination, will thinke that I challenge more then is due it" – *A Worlde of Wordes* and *Queen Anna* represent a notably more polyvalent approximation of sixteenth-century Europe's most diverse and accomplished vernacular than was then possible in those centers of Italian cultural production in which the language continued to develop, just beyond the horizon of those "naturall Italians" who assumed the mantle of its codification.

The full range of Florio's linguistic work – as language teacher, lexicographer, and translator – also had a marked effect on the tracking of the English language, as illustrated in this example from the *Oxford English Dictionary*:

**masturbation**, n ...
The scanty evidence suggests that this word replaced MASTUPRATION *n.* as the usual term during the early 18th cent. In form *maisterbation* in quot. 1603 at sense 1a perh. remodelled after *maister*, variant of MASTER *n.*1]
I. Simple uses. **1. a.** The stimulation, usually by hand, of one's genitals for sexual pleasure; the action or practice of masturbating oneself or (less commonly) another person; an instance of this.
**1603** J. **FLORIO** tr. Montaigne *Ess.* II. xii. 340 Diogenes in sight of all, exercising his Maisterbation, bredde a longing desire ... in the by-standers ... [123]

John Willinsky has demonstrated Florio's importance as a source for some 3,843 English words in the second edition of the *OED*. Of these, Florio is responsible for the earliest appearances of 1,149 words (as in the example above),[124] 173 of which are unique citations (*hapax legomena* or *h.l.*) so far found nowhere else, as in this example:

**tastesome**, a.
*Obs. rare.*
[f. TASTE *n.* + SOME]
Pleasant to the taste; 'tasty', toothsome.
**1598** FLORIO, *Gustevole*, smacking, **tastesome**, tasting well.[125]

Florio ranks eleventh in this regard behind first-place Chaucer, who has 2,012 of the earliest words cited, 132 *h.l.* (11,906 entries in total); and third-place Shakespeare with 1,969 of the earliest citations, and 284 *h.l.* (out of his 33,205 words in total). These statistics provide a striking picture of the manner in which Florio's work both registered and contributed to the development of English, a further indication of the multi-directional consequences of his philological stewardship.

FRATE:  Se voi vi volessi confessare, io farò ciò che voi volete.
DONNA:  Non per oggi; io sono aspettata; e' mi basta essermi sfogata un poco, così ritta, ritta ...

### Readings through Florio's dictionary

In order to understand the wide-reaching significance of Florio's lexicography for the history of the Italian language and for the dissemination of Italy's early modern print culture, we turn now to several texts written by authors whose lexical range was of tremendous importance for the contemporary scope of *A Worlde of Wordes* and *Queen Anna*: Pietro Aretino's *Ragionamenti*; Niccolò Machiavelli's comedy *Mandragola*; and Giordano Bruno's Italian dialogues – all works printed in Italian in London during the 1580s, the first two by John Wolfe (condemned in the 1559 Index) and the others by John Charlewood (and condemned by the Inquisition in 1600 before being placed on the Index in 1603).[126]

Aretino's infamous reputation in Elizabethan England seems to have been acquired more through hearsay and the assimilation of a small part of his work in that of English literary figures like Thomas Nashe than through direct contact with his writing. There were no English translations until later in the seventeenth century, and those English readers of Italian in the sixteenth century who did obtain copies of Aretino in Italian – as we have noted, John Wolfe published the first two books of the *Ragionamenti* (or *Sei giornate*) in 1584, a third group of dialogues in 1589, and a volume of four comedies in 1588 – would have been hard-pressed to follow a great deal of the Aretine lexicon before the appearance of *A Worlde of Wordes* in 1598, and *Queen Anna* would have helped them even further when it was published in 1611.[127]

The first book of the *Ragionamenti* (1534) consists of a dialogue in which Nanna, a seasoned prostitute, instructs a younger woman,

Antonia, about the lives of nuns, drawing on her own considerable experience with the clerical and monastic worlds. Aretino's depiction of ecclesiastical debauchery is perhaps more surprising for modern readers than it would have been for his contemporaries, accustomed as they were before the Council of Trent to a different standard of ecclesiastical behavior, though many of the targets of Aretino's savage satire – most notably Pope Clement VII – did not respond kindly to his demotic send-up of their privileged hypocrisy.[128]

Of the roughly 350 lexical or syntactical difficulties identified by Angelo Romano in the notes accompanying Aretino's first dialogue in his edition of the *Sei giornate*, almost 300 are defined in *Queen Anna* (though Romano acknowledges Florio's dictionary as a source for identifying only two of these terms). Of them, *Queen Anna* fully defines twenty-five out of sixty-one specifically sexual terms and euphemisms, citing ten other words but missing their sexual connotations, and entirely failing to note sixteen others, a slight advance over *A Worlde of Wordes*' twenty, eight, and sixteen respectively. Both of Florio's dictionaries recognize, for instance, "la *Priapea* di Virgilio"[129] as:

*all manner of filthy or bawdy verses touching privities of men* [400][130]

and offer this further illucidation of "Priapismo":

*priapise, pricke-pride, lust-pride, colts-evell, of or pertayning to a mans yard, the standing of a mans yard and yet without lust or desire, if it come with panting of the yard. Physicians call it* Satiriasi *or* Tentigine. *Also the office of the God of gardens.* [400]

And though both *A Worlde of Wordes* and *Queen Anna* neglect to note the significance of "uccello" (a euphemism for the penis, typical of a surprisingly frequent oversight – there are no such definitions of "franguello," "archeto," "formaggio," "arpione," "lusignolo," or "cane" – given Florio's otherwise expansive sexual vocabulary), *Queen Anna* does register the sexual sense of "uccellare":

*to bird, to fowle, to hawke, to catch birds. Also to cozen, to cunnie-catch, to cheate, to crosse-bite, to catch in some snare. Also to goe sneakingly a wenching.* [589]

Practically none of this immodest material is registered in the 1612 Crusca *Vocabolario*, and though it promotes itself as, among other things, an index to Boccaccio's lexicon, we find this entry regarding "Usignolo":

Uccelletto noto per la dolcezza del suo canto. Lat. *luscinia*. Bocc. n.44.7 E udendo cantar l'usignuolo, e avendo luogo più fresco, molto meglio starei. Fav. Esop. Cominciò la lusignuolo dolcemente a cantare.

[Small bird noted for the sweetness of its song. Latin: *luscinia*. Boccaccio, *Decameron*: Hearing the nightingale sing in a cooler place, the better I would be. Æsop, *Fables*: The nightingale began sweetly to sing]

While the *Cruscanti* cite the passage in which the nightingale represents the male member, *Decameron* IV.4, the tale of Ricciardo and Caterina, their definition completely elides the term's sexual resonance.

Unlike the Crusca *Vocabolario*, Florio's definitions rarely note the morphology or the textual location of a word, though occasionally he will cite an author's name in a definition, as we saw above with Dante, or indicate that a term is in use in a specific place, such as Naples. Despite these *lacunae*, Florio's definitions are often substantially more extensive than those we find in the Crusca, providing a fuller sense of the gamut of terms with multiple meanings.

We turn now to an excerpt from the first book of the *Ragionamenti* as one of Florio's readers might have been enabled to do using *Queen Anna's New World of Words* to identify lexical difficulties, and in order to compare Florio's practice with that of the *Cruscanti*.[131] In the pages just preceding this passage, the seasoned prostitute Nanna has explained to her much younger apprentice Antonia that, visiting a certain monastery, she had discovered a chink in the wall of her cell and through it was able to eye the erotic games of a religious superior, three of his younger friars, and four young nuns, one of whom the *padre generale* had singled out for particular attention:

ANTONIA: Adunque il padre generale consumò il giorno in contemplazioni, ah?
NANNA: Nol consumò miga: che posto il suo pennello nello scudellino del colore, umiliatolo prima con lo sputo, lo facea torcere nella guisa che si torceno le donne per le doglie del parto o per il mal della madre.[132]

Neither dictionary registers the sexual sense of "pennello":

*A Painters pencil. Also a phane or weather-cocke to shew the wind* [366]

Strumento che adoprano i dipintori a dipingere.
[Tool that painters use to paint]

nor "scudelino del colore," a painter's dish "that here alludes to the anal cavity."[133] But Florio's definition of "torcere":

*to wrest, to wreath, to bend, to bow, to retorte, to make crooked. Also to twist, to wrap, to winde in or wherle about. Also to wring, to presse or squeeze out, also to crisp, to curle or frizle. Also to torture or torment* [568]

comes closer here than the Crusca's:

Cavar che che sia della rettitudine, contrario di dirizzare, piegare.
[To extract whatsoever might pertain to rectitude, the opposite of "to raise up," "to fold"]

to the violent sense of Aretino's verb. And though Florio's "male di madre":

*a disease in many women* [296]

does not clarify that the "disease" is "hysteria,"[134] the Crusca fails to cite the term at all.

NANNA: E perchè il chiodo stesse più fermo nel forame, accennò dietrovia al suo erba-da-buoi, che rovesciatoli le brace fino alla calcagna, mise il cristeo alla sua Riverenza *visibilium*; la quale tenea fissi gli occhi agli altri dui giovanastri che, acconce due suore a buon modo e con agio nel letto, gli pestavano la salsa nel mortaio ...[135]

Neither dictionary notes that a "chiodo" is a penis, but Florio alone registers the sexual sense of "forame":

*any kind of hole, an arse* [192]

and his "accennare":

*to nod, to becken, to make a signe, to give an inkling. Also by some signe to glance at anie thing afar of by speech or action* [5]

captures the action at this moment more dynamically than the Crusca's:

far cenno.
[to mention]

Neither Florio nor the *Cruscanti* do particularly well with the following sequence of events, entirely missing "erba-da-buoi," a handsome lad[136] (or boy-toy), whose "cristeo" is certainly not in this context:

*a glister, a suppository* [131]

or a:

serviziale, cocitura d'erbe, con altri ingredienti, che si mette in corpo per la parte posteriore
[an enema, an herbal concoction mixed with other ingredients that one applies to the posterior of the body]

but the young man's "pennello," pressed into service after having "rovesciato" [as "riversare"]:

*to reverse, to overturne, to turn the inside outward, to topsie-turvy*

(a fitting anticipation of the act about to be committed) the *padre generale*'s pants down to his 'calcagna':

*the heele of a man* [74]

la parte deretana del piè.
[the hindmost part of the foot]

But meanwhile, occupied even as he was, the father superior had his eyes on the other two young monks, themselves "acconce":

*a dighting, a making fit or readie, handsome, setled, drest, convenient* [7]

affettato, accomodato
[hastened, placed]

with two of the other sisters on a single bed, who then set out to "pestare la salsa nel mortaio." Florio, while neglecting to note the obvious sexual euphemism in his definition of the phrase:

*to punne sauce in a mortar* [373]

registers it in his definition of "pestello":

*a punner or pestell of a mortar, a stamper that Paviers use, a rammer that Gunners use. Also taken for a mans toole or privities* [373]

and though the Crusca again lists the verb and cites its appearance in Boccaccio in just this form – where it means precisely what it does here in Aretino – the academicians elide its sexual sense.

NANNA: ... facendo disperare la loro sorellina; che per esser alquanto loschetta e di carnagion nera, refutata da tutti, avendo empito il vetriolo bernardo di acqua scaldata per lavar le mani al messere, recatasi sopra un coscino in terra, appuntando le piante dei piedi al muro della camera, pontando contra lo smisurato pastorale, se lo avea riposto nel corpo come si rispongono le spade nelle guaine.[137]

Nanna then turns her attention to the fourth sister. Ignored by all the others for being "loschetto":

*some-what dim-sighted, or pur-blinde* [289]

– Florio expands his definition under "losco," in which form we find the Crusca's more restricted entry:

*one that seeth some-what by day-light, worse after Sunne-rising, and no whit at night. Also squint or bleare eyde, or having but one eye* [289]

Quegli che per sua natura non può veder, se non le cose d'appresso, e guardando ristringe, e aggrotta le ciglia
[Those who by nature cannot see anything other than what is near, and looking, strain and frown] –

and di "carnagion nera," she literally took things into her own hands, using the "vetriolo bernardo," a glass dildo (unregistered by either Florio or the *Cruscanti*) she had initially filled with water in order to wash the *padre generale*'s hands but now in her solitary position appropriated for her own pleasure, positioning her body, back to the floor and legs pushed up against the wall, so that the "smisurato":

*unmeasurable boundlesse* [504]

senza misura
[measureless]

"pastorale" – in Florio:

*pastorall, rurall, belonging to Swaines or Shepheardes. Also a pastorall Comedie treating of Shepherds or Swaines. Also a verge or crosier carried before Prelates. Also a mans toole* [361]

but merely:

Di pastore, da pastore, o attenente a pastore, in senso di prelato.
[Of, by, or belonging to a pastor, that is a prelate]

in the Crusca – lodged or "riposto":

*laide, up, set by, placed to be reserved and kept. Also as* Ripostiglio, *a place where things are laid up and kept, a store-house to keepe things in, as a Buttery, a Lardery, a Pantry, a Cupboard, a Wardrobe, a Warehouse, any hiding corner. Also a side table or presse* [443]

Il riporre. Por di nuovo, rimettere e collocar la cosa dov'ell'era prima ... luogo ritirato da riporvi.
[Placement. Put again, replace and place a thing where it was originally ... any enclosed storage place]

inside her body as snugly as "le spade" in their "guaine":

*any sheath or scabbard* [222]

Strumento di cuoio, dove si tengono, e conservano i ferri da tagliare, come coltelli, forbici, spade, pugnali, e si fatti
[Leather instrument in which cutting irons such as knives, scissors, swords, daggers, etc. are kept and protected]

After all of the excitement she had witnessed, Nanna tells Antonia that:

Io all'odore del piacer loro struggendomi più che non si distruggono i pegni per le usure, fregava la monina con la mano nel modo che di gennaio fregano il culo per i tetti i gatti.[138]

Florio marks the polyvalent force of "struggere":

*to destroy, to ruine, to consume. Also to melt or thaw. Also to weare away. Also a melting or thawing. Also to weare away and faint. Also to array, to build, to compact, to frame or set in order* [541] in contrast to the Crusca's:

Liquefare ... Per metaf. Bocc. n.43.20. Egli si struggeva tutto d'andarla ad abracciare. E nov. 80.11. Al quale pareva, che costei si strugesse tutta per suo amore [Liquefy ... as a metaphor. Boccaccio, *Decameron* 43.20: He ruined everything in going to embrace her. And *Decameron* 80.11: To which it seemed that he destroyed himself for his love]

Nanna avails herself of an economic metaphor, "distruggere i pegni per le usure," "pegno" being defined by Florio as:

*a pawne, a gage, a pledge, a baile, a suertie, a sure signe, a wager, a bet, a stake at gaming. Also a stresse or distresse* [364]

and by the Crusca as:

Quel che si da per sicurtà del debito in mano di creditore.
[What one gives as collateral for a debt in the hand of a creditor]

in order to further describe her state of arousal, and finally, nothing else left to do, she "fregava":

*to rub up and and down, to frigle, to frig, to claw, to frit. Also to chase one. Also to cogge and foist, or gull one* [196]

Leggiermente stroppiciare ... per fare qualche ingiuria al alcuno, o con inganno, o senza rispetto.
[Lightly rub ... in order to do injury to someone, or with deceit, or without respect]

her 'monina', in *Queen Anna*:

*A pretty pug or iakeanapes. Also a womans geare or quaint* [310]

but unaccounted for by the *Cruscanti*.[139]

Though Florio misses some crucial words and allusions in this vivid *tableau*, it is clear from what he does define that a contemporary reader consulting his dictionary would have been enabled to more than follow the drift of Aretino's narrative. The piling-up of meanings in several of his definitions – "torcere," "accennare," "rovesciato," "riposto" – extends the scope of individual words at the same time that it situates them more capaciously in the contexts in which they are to be found. Looking to the Crusca for help in this regard is a futile exercise, for its model of lexical significance is determined, as we have seen, by values that excluded such irreverent and "obscene" satire from its consideration.

Machiavelli's lexicon, closer in many respects than Aretino's deliberately provocative language to the spoken Florentine of the early sixteenth century, is also helpfully explicated in Florio's dictionaries, as a short scene from the comedy *Mandragola* illustrates. Here Fra Timoteo – a priest whose antecedents populate the *Decameron* and whose satirical portrait is considerably more subtle than that of Aretino's pornographic clerics – first demonstrates the capacity for complicity that will subsequently enable him to set into motion the comedy's principal intrigue, in which he will assist an enterprising young man in seducing the virtuous younger wife of an unpleasant and sterile "vecchiaccio":

*a filthie old man* [590].

The scene is often ignored in analysis (and performance) of the play, but as Florio will assist us in seeing, it foregrounds several of the larger issues of sexual politics with which the *Mandragola* is concerned.

FRATE:  Se voi vi volessi confessare, io farò ciò che voi volete.
DONNA: Non per oggi; io sono aspettata; e' mi basta essermi sfogata un poco, così ritta, ritta.[140]

The crucial terms in this opening exchange are "sfogata" and "ritta," defined respectively in *Queen Anna* as:

*to vent, to wreake or burst foorth as fire doth being closely raked up* [495]

and:

*right, upright, iust, even, direct, streight. Also stiff-standing* [448].

The allusions to fire and stiffness suggest that there is more going on here than meets the eye, and one of the play's recent editors confirms "a note of elusive eroticism in this witty exchange, since 'sfogarsi ritto' could allude to consummating the sexual act while standing up."[141] The lady comes from out of nowhere, her excitability unexplained here at the outset of the scene, and is never seen again in the course of the comedy, so it seems that she is introduced teasingly to hint that Fra Timoteo's evidently longstanding relationship with her has been something more than merely confessional.

DONNA: Togliete ora questa fiorino, e direte dua mesi ogni lunedì la messa de' morti per l'anima del mio marito. Ed ancora che fussi un omaccio, pure le carne tirono: io non posso fare non mi risenta, quando io me ne ricordo ...[142]

Florio notes that the significance of adding the suffix "-accio":

*to any positive noun ... makes it grèat unhandsome, ruinous, as* Homaccio, cavalláccio, casaccia, donnaccia [6]

and provides one of his more expansive definitions for "tirare":

*to draw, to pull, to hale, to plucke, to tug or attract unto or towards oneselfe. Also to withdraw or retire. Also to shrinke in. Also to stretch in or out. Also to throw, to cast, to sling, to hurle, to shoote, to darte, to sling or pitch from one. Also to yarke, to kicke or winze with ones heeles as a horse doth. Also to protract, to wire-draw, to prolong, to drive off, or draw in length. Also to entice, to perswade or draw and bend unto. Also to draw or portray.* [564]

The lady cannot but "risentire":

*to recover feeling or sence againe, to heare, to feele or smell againe. Also to resent, to feele or shew a motion, an offer, a remembrance or effect of some wrong received or revenge for it, to revenge or at least to offer to be revenged* [445]

her absent monster of a husband, though "le carne" continue to "tirare," explaining her presence in this scene with the *frate*. Revenge for a previous wrong committed could well be at hand. But what offense specifically?

DONNA: ... credete voi che sia in purgatorio?
FRATE: Sanza dubbio.
DONNA: Io non so già cotesto. Voi sapete pure quel che mi faceva qualche volta. Oh, quanto me ne dolsi io con esso voi! Io me ne discostavo quanto io potevo; ma egli era sí importuno! Uh, nostro Signore![143]

The lady's concern about her dead husband's afterlife is another of the means through which Machiavelli signals the sexual subtext of this scene, in that her question about Purgatory recalls *Decameron* 3.8, where a similarly clever abbot who has his eye on a married lady convinces her gullible husband that he is in Purgatory after consuming a powder that left him for dead. In that story, the husband "returns from the dead," whereas in this one the status of the departed spouse in the other world serves to anticipate the central issue of the scene, "quel che mi faceva qualche volta," about which the lady had earlier so many times "dolsi":

*to ake, to smart, to paine, to grieve. Also to waile and be sorrowful* [160]

to the *frate*. That this protestation reveals an inverted sense of the confessional relationship – normally based on what the one confessing has done, not what has been done to the confessing subject – suggests further evidence of an intimacy between the *frate* and the lady that exceeds both the surface of the text and the licit parameters of a strictly spiritual relationship.

This framework again echoes Boccaccio, this time *Decameron* 3.3 (the same numerical division of this scene),[144] in which the confessional is used to effect a seduction (though there it is the *frate* who serves unwittingly as pandar, not as beneficiary), the unnamed lady's dissimulating words of complaint about her supposedly importunate lover having provided Machiavelli with his lady's protest here:

– Come – disse il frate – Non s'è che egli rimaso di darti più noia?
– Certo no – disse la donna – anzi, poi che *io mi ve ne dolsi* quasi per un dispetto, avendo forse avuto per male che io mi ve ne sia doluta ... [145]

*Mandragola*'s friar responds:

Non dubitate, la clemenzia di Dio è grande: se non manca a l'uomo la voglia, non gli manca el tempo a pentirsi[146]

with another allusive reference to sexual desire,[147] citing the 'voglia':

*a will, a desire, a list, a wishing or extreme longing for* [607]

to repent, which suggests in the terms of this twisted exchange an invitation to future "confessions".

DONNA: Credete voi che 'l Turco passi questo anno in Italia?
FRATE: Se voi non fate orazioni sí.
DONNA: Naffe! Dio ci auiti, con queste diavolerie! Io ho una gran paura di quello impalare. – Ma io veggo qua in chiesa una donna che ha certa accia di mio: io vo' ire a trovarla. Fate col buon dí.
FRATE: Andate sana.[148]

In response to the lady's final question, the *frate* makes one last sexual pun, on "orazioni" [prayers], which goes unregistered in Florio but, once again, turns up repeatedly in Boccaccio in just this sense. The lady's greatest fear, however, "quello impalare," is defined quite specifically by *Queen Anna*:

*to empale, to enstake, to empole, to empalisado, to fortifie with poles or stakes, to raile or paile in. Also to underset with poles or stakes, as they doe Vines and Hops. Also to put bread in an oven with a peele. Also to put to death with a stake as Turkes doe Christians putting a sharpe stake in at the fundament which comes out at the mouth, and so fixe the other end into the ground.* [237]

So the scene turns out to be about sodomy, fear of a possibly impending Turkish invasion – this a legitimate threat in 1518 (a possible date for the composition of the play, given the allusion)[149] – helping to make sense at its conclusion of at least two earlier scattered threads: it clarifies what had provoked the lady's excitement at the outset of the scene and also reveals what her husband had so importunely insisted on doing to her. We are evidently to presume that the *frate* does not indulge in such fearsome practices, but the scene ends with the lady having spotted another woman in the church who "ha certa accia di mio." While the intrepid peruser of Florio's dictionary will not find "accia" defined as anything other than:

*anie yarn to be woven, any spinning, or statute yarne in skeanes. Also a hatchet, an axe, a chip-axe, or chopping knife* [6] a search of topically related terms would turn up:

Facitrice della fusa storta, *a woman that makes or spins crooked spindles, that is maketh her husband cuckold* [177][150]

which can be read in the context of Machiavelli's scene, I would suggest, in either of two ways: that the lady alludes to her "confessional" time with the friar, cuckolding her possibly Purgatory-bound husband; or, that she has other seeds to sow in others' gardens, anxious as she is to stave off the arrival of the impaling Turk. Either way, it is Florio's dictionary that alerts us to the further resonance of a term in the same subject field as "accia," further enriching our reading of this under-appreciated but seminal scene in Machiavelli's comedy of disrupted sexual manners.

As noted in the previous chapter, Giordano Bruno's six *Dialoghi italiani* were written and published in London in 1584 and 1585 during Bruno's residence with the French Ambassador, Michel de Castalnau de Mauvissière, at the same time that Florio was employed "as tutor to [Mauvissière's] daughter, as interpreter, and in other capacities."[151] A renegade Dominican priest, Bruno's peregrinations in flight from the controlling authority of the Inquisition brought him into contact with the intellectual circle around the French King Henri III, and then in England with Philip Sidney and his cadre. The strong and lasting impression Bruno made on Florio is registered both in the large number of words from the *Dialoghi* that Florio included in both editions of his dictionary and in the defense of translation included in Florio's preface to his English translation of Montaigne, published three years after Bruno's execution in Rome in 1600. Florio himself figures as a minor character in the first of Bruno's dialogues, *La cena de le ceneri*, the account of a debate at the residence of Sidney's friend Fulke Greville to which Bruno was summoned, accompanied by Florio and his friend Matthew Gwinne.[152]

In his edition of the *Cena*, Giovanni Aquilecchia pays generous homage to Florio's importance for the interpretation of Bruno's text.[153] From both editions of the dictionary, *Firste* and *Second Frutes*, and the *Giardino di ricreatione*, Aquilecchia identifies scores of words and phrases in Bruno's lexicon for which Florio is the earliest authority. The character of "Frulla," one of the *Cena*'s interlocutors, is suggested by this definition from *Queen Anna*:

*a lisp or clack with ones fingers ends as Barbers doe give. Also a flurt, a toy, a iest or matter of nothing* [199]

and Theophilo, Bruno's stand-in, is defined by Florio as:

*a lover of God, loving god* [563]

in keeping with the notion developed throughout the *Cena* that the enlightened mind renders the human form divine. Bruno chooses the medium of Italian to communicate many of his most important ideas because, as Hilary Gatti translates a crucial passage in *Lo spaccio della bestia trionfante*, "here Giordano ... names things freely, gives its proper name to that which nature has given its proper being."[154]

Though long separated from his native Nola, near Naples, Bruno identified the language of his childhood with his capacity to "describe things and persons 'as they are'."[155] But as far-removed from the simple speech of children as it frequently is, Bruno's vernacular usage expresses his belief that Italian can reproduce the nature of things and persons by being skilfully employed to both catalogue the cosmos and expose the falsity that he sees as undermining the human community while parading under deliberately obscurantist linguistic clothing. Such a position renders his relationship with Florio particularly important, for it is clear that Florio found in Bruno not only a tangible link to one of Italy's liveliest dialects but also a fellow wordsmith who had thought long and deeply about the very questions that animated his own cultural agency.

Bruno was merciless with language employed speciously, and the attack on the tradition of Petrarchism in poetry that punctuates the "Argomento" of the *Eroici furori*, the last of the six Italian dialogues, provides a further telling link between Bruno's linguistic praxis and Florio's own solution to *la questione della lingua*.[156] What might at first appear to be an incongruous, misogynistic tirade – entirely out of keeping with the elevated pursuit of a spiritualized love elsewhere in this dialogue tied inextricably to the beauty of the human body – turns out to be a forceful critique of the fetishized language of a love poetry that transforms women into abusive and unobtainable objects of masochistic desire.

Bruno here employs Petrarchan tropes only to then obliterate them: which acts, he asks, in this *teatro del mondo* are more laughable than the thoughts, contemplations, constancies, and adulations of lovers so entirely dedicated to their own destruction?[157] What a waste of insignia, emblems, mottos, sonnets, epigrams, books, prolix *scartafazzi*, defined in *Queen Anna* as:

any scroule or waste paper. Also an odd corner to throw writing paper in [472, as *scartabello*].

And what useless ruminations over eyes, cheeks, busts, these white and those ruby lips, tongues, teeth, foreheads, dresses, cloaks, gloves, shoes, this *pianella*, in Florio:

a woman's pantofle [378].

All of which leads to that *martello*, defined by Florio as:

a hammer, a sledge, a carpenter's mallet. Also jealousy or suspition in love, panting or throbbing of the heart, an earnest desiring of things absent. *Sonare le campane a martello* to ring the bels backward as in times of warre, of danger or of fire [302].

Thus far, a faithfully Petrarchan vocabulary, but suddenly Bruno shifts registers, introducing a cruder, more forcefully mimetic language derived from Francesco Berni:[158]

*schifo* – coy, quaint, nice, skittish, fond, peevish, puling, awkwarde or froward. Also queasie, nastie, lothsome, odious, to be shunned, eschewed or avoided, disdainfull [475].
*cesso* – yeelded, resigned. Also a privy or close stoole. Also a scroule of paper [95].
*mestruo* (*menstruo* in Florio) – a womans monthly termes, issues, fluxes, sheddings, or flowers. Also quicksilver among Alchimistes [309].
*fantasma* – a ghost, a hag, a spirit, a hobgoblin, a robin-good-fellow. Also the night-mare or riding-hag [179].
*orinale* – a urinall, a pisse-pot [345].
*piva* – any kind of pipe or bag-pipe. Also a Piot, a Pie or Iay. Also a Butterflie. Also used of a mans privy members [385].
*fava* – a beane. Also used for the prepuse or top of a mans yard [184].
*nimfa* – any kind of Nimph, Elfe, or Faerie. Also a Bride, or new maried wife. Also a thicke ruffe-bande, as women or effeminate fellows weare about their necks. Also the void space or hollownesse in the neather lip. Also the cup of any flowre gaping and opening itselfe. Also a little piece of flesh rising up in the midst of a womans privities, which closeth the mouth of the necke, and driveth cold from it. Also the water-rose. Also young Bees before they can fly [352].

One clear consequence of Florio's practice of *copia* – the layering-on of definitions which functions to provide as full a sense of a particular word's meanings as possible – is an opening-up of the potential of language to represent a multitude, we might almost say an infinity, of possible significations, a clear indication of Florio's relationship to the de-centered parameters of Bruno's philosophy.[159] This forceful anti-Petrarchist critique, an attack on the character of Petrarchan love but also a frontal assault on the very language in which that love is imagined, served as yet another model for Florio in his alternative to the conservative linguistic politics of cinquecento Italy.

In striking contrast to the parody of feminine virtue represented by Petrarchism are Bruno's several extended passages of praise for the English queen. The second dialogue of the *Cena* represents Elizabeth as illuminating the entire world with her *giudicio*:[160]

a judgement, a sentence, a doome. Also a place or seat of judgement. Also wit, discretion, learning, or skill. Also opinion, deeming, supposing, or estimation [212].

She exercises:

*sagezza* – wisdom, sagenesse, vigilancie [458]
*consiglio* – counsel, advice, direction. Also a place or chamber of counsel [118]

and:

*governo* – government, rule, sway. Also moderation, administration or care, and looking unto [216].

Practiced in the arts and sciences, Elizabeth is evoked throughout the passage in scientific terms, one of them referring to the *arctico parallelo*:

*arcturo* – a star by the taile of Ursa Minor [37]

or:

*artico* – the Pole articke Northward [41].

The queen's linguistic skills were for Bruno the outward sign of her singular constellation of qualities, permitting her to unlock the world's secrets by making its learning her own while also rendering herself an open book in her capacity to communicate with almost any representative of the "civilized" world of the time.

Though this is obviously an idealized image of Elizabeth – Bruno more than likely observed the queen only from a distance during his English sojourn – and he seems to deliberately disassociate her from the troubling aspects of Elizabethan domestic policy and global aspirations about which he would have been well informed, living as he did in the household of the French ambassador.[161] But if the actual reality of the Tudor queen fell somewhat short of Bruno's estimation of her, the values she is made to represent in the *Dialoghi italiani* did find a receptive audience in John Florio. The titles and the scope of both editions of Florio's dictionary are indelibly marked by the program Bruno articulated through his Italian dialogues: the "worlds" of Florio's linguistic universe, so importantly signed by Bruno's presence, encompass the copious range of words contained in *A Worlde of Wordes* and *Queen Anna's New World of Words*, which in turn entail the political and cultural spaces of Italy and England, the demotic specificity of Bruno's Nola, and the unbounded parameters of the cosmos Bruno sought to delineate.

> "*Le parole sono femine, & i fatti sono maschij ...*"

### Gender and the language arts

Bruno's several apotheoses of Elizabeth draw attention to one further aspect of Florio's linguistic stewardship that we must address before concluding this study of Italian *translatio* into the world of Tudor England. Unlike English, Italian is a language in which gender distinctions are a fundamental aspect of its grammatical character, and in the dedicatory material prefacing *A Worlde of Wordes* Florio describes his dictionary as making a singular contribution to this gendered identity:

> Some perhaps will except against the sexe, and not allowe it for a male-broode, sithens as Italians saie, *Le parole sono femine, & i fatti sono maschij,* Wordes they are women, and deeds they are men. But let such know that *Detti* and *fatti,* wordes and deeds with me are all of one gender. And though they were commonly Feminine, why might not I by strong imagination (which Phisicions give so much power unto) alter their sexe? Or at least by such heaven-pearcing devotion as transformed *Iphis,* according to that description of the Poet.[162]

> > *Et ogni membro suo piu forte e sciolto*
> > > *Sente, e volge alla madre il motto, e'l lume.*
> > *Come vero fanciullo esser si vede*
> > > *Iphi va con parole alme, e devote*
> > *Al tempio con la madre, e la nutrice*
> > > *E paga il voto, è l suo miracol dice.*
>
> > Feeling more vigor in each part and strength
> > > Then earst, and that indeede she was a boy.
> > Towards hir mother eies and wordes at length
> > > She turnes, and at the temple with meeke joy
> > He and his nurse and mother utter how
> > > The case fell out, and so he paid his vow.

> And so his strength, his stature, and his masculine vigor (I would, naie I coulde saie vertue) makes me assure his sexe, and according to his sexe provide so authenticall testimonies.[163]

The passage is remarkable for a number of reasons, not least of which being that it signals such a dramatic departure from Florio's earlier elaboration of the matter.[164]

In the final dialogue of *Second Frutes,* influenced by a similar moment found at the end of the first dialogue of Bruno's *De la causa, principio et uno,*[165] the interlocutors Pandolpho, a shameless misogynist, and Silvestro, who aims to defend the dignity of women, engage in a debate over gender. Here Florio first cites the proverb reiterated in the dedication to *A Worlde of Wordes* [*SF* 12, 176–177]:

| | |
|---|---|
| S. *Parole, parole, senza sugo,* *l'amor ci dà la vita, et in vita & in morte tutto amor governa.* | S. All these are but words, by love we live with doubled breath, living in others after death: and love is all in all. |

| | |
|---|---|
| P. *Le parole sono femine, & i fatti sono maschii. E delle parole, le buone ongano, & le cattive pongono, io vi dico, che chi non vuol periclitare, non si dee metter' ad amare, perche amore nel principio dolcemente applaude, poi esse di nascosto inganno e fraude.* | P. Nay words are Feminine, & deedes are Masculine, and of words the good anoynt & oyle us, the bad anoy & spoile us: I tel you who list no dangerous harmes to prove, must alwayes feare to fall in love for at first love like a Siren sings, but in the end he closely stings. |

Silvestro's proto-feminist perspective is buttressed with a wide array of ancient and modern literary sources skillfully marshaled. Pandolpho, on the other hand, appeals to no authority other than his own unhappy experience with women, and he consequently comes across as nothing other than [*SF*, 198–99]:

| | |
|---|---|
| ... *un'uomo ingegnoso & acuto* [*che*] *nel mal dire mantiene contra le donne* ... | ... a sharpe-witted man [who] in ill speaking holds against women ... |

Silvestro anchors his argument in an appeal to grammar, presenting an expansive list of feminine nouns whose range is both as particular and as universal as the vernacular Bruno advocated (and for which Alessandro Citolini had earlier argued), suggesting an intrinsic relationship between the gender of words and the things that they represent.[166] Beginning with the spiritual realm [*SF* 12, 198–199], the list descends to the terrestrial by first noting how many of the parts of the body are feminine, among which [*SF* 12, 200–201]:

| | |
|---|---|
| *la lingua (instrumento), la voce, & parola (effetto della lingua)* ... | his tong (instrument), his voice, & word (effect of the tongue) ... |

The facing texts here reveal a discrepancy, however, in the relationship between the two languages, evident first in that Florio is compelled in English to use the masculine personal possessive pronoun to translate what in Italian is meant throughout the passage to apply to both men and women equally, and then in the fact that these English nouns bear no gender distinctions. Silvestro continues along these lines for several pages [*SF* 12, 200–204], enumerating the extent to which both the things and the values that positively constitute the human world are in Italian feminine. Such an accumulation compounds Bruno's considerably more succinct contrasting of negative masculine and positive feminine substantives in *De la causa,* Florio making explicit here through melding grammatical and biological gender what Bruno implies at the conclusion of his dialogue with yet another passage of praise for Elizabeth. Words in this regard do more than merely stand in for what they describe, they bear social, indeed political, weight and meaning. The ethical character of language that emerges from such a conclusion – that what one is able to say, and how one is enabled to say it, determines the shape of the community that language gives rise to – is of fundamental importance for understanding why *la questione della lingua* was so much more than merely a debate about taste. The presentation of the issue in *Second Frutes* lacks the philosophical context of Bruno's argument, but Florio cleverly subverts the scholastic topos that maintained women were imperfect men by wedding two fundamental scholastic categories, "material" and "form," in utilizing such a basic grammatical signal as gender for his defense of women. And while Bruno consistently uses the term "grammarian" to contemptuously dismiss the stale Aristotelian pedantry he had encountered at Oxford and at Fulke Greville's table, Florio fashions himself here through Silvestro as quite a different type of "grammarian," one dedicated to the potential of language for opening up entirely new horizons.[167]

What might otherwise be read as a simplistic or over-determined identification of the gendered character of Italian and gendered social reality, Florio's grammatically inflected argument should be read in tandem with what has come to be characterized as the Renaissance *querelle des femmes*, a debate carried out for the most part (and, from the perspective of *Second Frutes*, not coincidentally) in Latin and its Romance offspring as a corrective challenge to the pervasive misogyny of early modern European cultures.[168] Florio certainly knew Agrippa von Nettesheim's treatise on the nobility of women published in Latin (1529), French (1529), Italian (1530), German (1540), and English (1542), for in its etymological association of Adam with the gross "earth" and Eve with "life" there is the foregrounding of a position quite similar to what we see in *Second Frutes*, and justified along similiar lines:

there is no cause why this shulde be called a feble argument, to gyve iugement of thynges by the names. for as we knowe, that the hyghe artyficer and maker of things and names, fyrst dyd knowe the thynges, before he named them, which for as moch as he could not be decyved, for thys purpose he made the names, that it might expresse the nature, propertye, and use of the thynge. for the trouthe of antyque names is suche, as the verye Romayne lawes testyfye, that the selfe names are consonant to the thinges, and manifest significations of them. Therfore an argument of the names of thinges amonges dyvynes and lawyars, is of great weyghte.[169]

Recalling Bruno's symbiosis of words with what they represent as well as the ancient Hebrew association of naming and the essence of the thing named, Agrippa's assertion of the correspondence between words and things was one of the cardinal points of conflict between a Protestant reformed emphasis on evolving vernacular languages capable of representing the whole range of human experience in the world and a Catholic theological perspective expressed in a much less responsive language increasingly far-removed from a world dominated by a rapidly accelerating trajectory away from the medieval intellectual traditions that informed its certainties. However naive we might be tempted to brand the valorization of women essayed in *Second Frutes*, it is a perfectly consistent outgrowth of the Protestant cultural politics Florio inherited from the continental framework of his early life and brought with him as a young man to England. But in addition to these various affirmations of the egalitarian possibilities of a vernacular with a strongly gendered character, Florio would have found further authority for such thinking in a number of the Italian literary texts he drew on for his dictionaries.[170]

Teodolinda Barolini notes that Boccaccio first signals in the "Proemio" to the *Decameron* a distinction between feminine nouns, *parole*, and masculine verbs, *detti*, before then demonstrating in the ninth *novella* of the Second Day how through grammar a courageous and wily female protagonist, Zinevra, is portrayed as skillfully negotiating both gendered polarities when, as "she changes her clothes and her name ... Boccaccio changes the gender of his participles, moving from the one sentence's 'col quale *entrata* in parole' [with whom (a Catalan gentleman) *she spoke*] to the next sentence's 'di miglior panni *rimessi* in arnese [*he was fitted out* in more becoming clothes]'."[171] The early modern English theater was capable of only the first of these transformations, its asexual language ineffectual in completing the picture a change of clothing and name initiates. Zinevra's transvestism is effected in order to re-establish her integrity, impugned at the outset of the *novella* by a too-little-trusting husband, but her return to the realm of *parole* and domesticity by the *novella*'s end would mistakenly be construed as an erasure of the ground she had gained in returning from whence she had come, for she effects through her itinerary what is, in fact, even today, a powerfully (if not always transparently) operative dimension of gendered roles in the cultures of the European Mediterranean: women fulfilling men's roles as capably as men do themselves.

If not more so. The singular moment in the third book of Machiavelli's *Discorsi* in which Caterina Sforza outmaneuvers the murderers of her husband is a telling case in point: "several conspirators from the town of Forlì killed their lord Count Giralamo,"[172] taking his wife and children prisoners. But as the conspirators were aware that there would be no future for their cause without control of the fortress, and the gate keeper being unwilling to yield it to them, Caterina convinced her captors that if she were allowed to return there she would see that it be handed over to them.

Leaving her children behind as ransom, Caterina stunned the conspirators when she appeared on the ramparts of the citadel furiously berating them for:

the death of my husband, [and] threatening them with every imaginable vendetta. And to demonstrate that she paid little heed of her own children, she exposed her genitals to them, saying that there were more where the others had come from.[173]

Here, as John Freccero has suggested, Caterina stands for history itself, the potentiality of future generations who "would proceed in sufficient numbers to overwhelm their oppressors."[174] She is a "fierce caricature of those images of divine maternity found on medieval walls and city gates, welcoming outsiders and offering sanctuary to those within,"[175] and for Machiavelli:

the importance of the use of the Italian feminine plural for a neuter Latin noun, *membrum*, is that it signifies a collectivity: specifically, the unity of a body with a plurality of members ... the body's gender is crucial ... for the *membra* of a woman's body include the future as well as the past. Caterina stands for such a collectivity.[176]

Florio's catalogue of the parts of the body in his survey of feminine nouns in *Second Frutes* should be read in precisely this light.

Perhaps the most complex female figure in the early modern Italian literary canon is Ariosto's Bradamante, the progenitrix of the Este clan in the *Orlando furioso* and the only one of its principal characters who never departs from the path of her destiny once it is spelled out for her in the third canto of a poem otherwise dominated by a stable of male protagonists and one other woman, Angelica, the one shared value among whom is a wildly fluctuating inconstancy. Like Boccaccio's Zinevra, the end of Bradamante's long but constant road is apparently a domestic one, though as Deanna Shemek has persuasively argued, the conclusion of Bradamante's quest in the *Furioso* can neither be easily dismissed as her straightforward assimilation into the governing categories of a patriarchal society, nor can her identity as a warrior – consistent throughout the poem – be assumed to be simply cast off with her marriage to Ruggiero and subsequent motherhood.[177] One episode in particular, Bradamante at the Castle of Tristan at the end of Canto 32, demonstrates Ariosto's (and Italian's) capacity to mix it up both in terms of gendered roles and the gendered language in which they are represented. Bradamante arrives at the castle late on a brutal winter evening only to learn that she will be obliged, according to the rule of the place, to fight the male guests who had preceded her there in order to win lodging for the night. She, of course, handily defeats her opponents, but only after vanquishing them does she remove her helmet, exposing her long hair to those who had witnessed her prowess as a warrior. As Shemek notes, the evident disclosure of Bradamante's gender at this point renders her public literally speechless, just as similar revelations had done earlier and would do again later in the poem.[178] Here would seem to be the very triumph of *detti* over *parole*, but an ensuing development confounds Bradamante's easy martial victory, for now, taken as a woman, she is obliged to confront the other house rule, according to which the beauty of any newly arrived lady must be judged against any others present. Bradamante again easily wins this second contest, though unlike with her earlier vanquished male foes she takes pity on Ullania and insists that the other woman not be turned out into the harsh night, asserting that proof of her own feminine identity has not yet been definitively established. Throughout the episode Ariosto is quite sparing in his employment of the third-person feminine pronoun in relation to verbs describing Bradamante's actions, thus accentuating her gendered ambiguity, and in the culminating octave of her verbal defense he has her claim that:

> *Io ch'a diffender questa causa toglio,*
> *dico: o più bella o men ch'io sia di lei,*
> *non venni come donna qui, né voglio*
> *che sian di donna ora i progressi miei.*
> *Ma chi dirà, se tutta non mi spoglio,*
> *s'io sono o s'io non son quel ch'è costei?*
> *E quel che non si sa non si de' dire,*
> *e tanto men, quando altri n'ha a patire.*[179]

> I who toil to defend this cause
> say that though more or less lovely be I than she,
> I neither came here as a woman, nor do I wish
> that as a woman my advantage should be judged.
> Who shall say, short of me disrobing,
> that I am or am not that which she is?
> What is not known should not be told,
> and even less when others might suffer for it.

Having proven her ability as a paladin, Bradamante knows that no one among her auditors would dare to compel the naked revelation of her sex, and such swaggering confidence enables her to maintain through an equivalent verbal dexterity the enigmatic parameters of the female soldier that she is. John Harington's version of this episode in his 1591 translation of the *Furioso* tends – often necessarily, given the grammatical character of English – to fill in the blanks that Ariosto deliberately left as such, typically supplying the feminine pronoun where it had been omitted in Italian and thus making Dame Bradamant more of a lady than Ariosto normally concedes; but in one of his more brilliant adjustments to the poem,

Harington opens the octave following the one cited above with Bradamant asking:

Who can say precisely what I am?

In this instance, far from a surfeit of gender-specifying pronouns, Bradamant is rendered even more ambivalently than in the original, her identity in all its complexity completely up for grabs.[180]

This unsettling question is effectively the same query Florio aims to put to rest with regard to the gender of his dictionary in the preface to *A Worlde of Wordes*. Florio's earlier endorsement of women on the basis of their identification with *parole* that re-present the values which build and sustain the human community was a reflection of his understanding of a language he had believed to interpret the world differently from what he found to be the case in English. But as Patricia Parker has shown, the copiousness so fundamental to Florio's philological practice was associated negatively throughout the early modern period with women and with effeminacy.[181] In collapsing *parole* into *detti*, imagining his dictionary into a man-child, Florio appears to be rewriting both his grammatical take on the *querelle des femmes* and the terms of his cultural mediation, translating its Italian coordinates into those of an English culture whose neutered language tends by default to favor masculine discourse, given that there is nothing in its grammatical structure to privilege the feminine.[182]

Florio seems to discount his earlier work when he writes at the outset of the preface to *A Worlde of Wordes* that those:

two overhastie fruites of mine some yeeres since, like two forewarde females, the one put her selfe in service to an Earle of Excellence, the other to a Gentleman of Woorth, both into the worlde to runne the race of their fortune. Now where my rawer youth brought foorth those female fruites, my riper yeeres affoording me I cannot say a braine-babe *Minerva*, armed at all assaies at first hours but rather from my Italian *Semele*, and English thigh, a bouncing boie, *Bacchus*-like ...[183]

Such a reversal, now accusing his dialogue books of having functioned as trawling female flirts but auguring an upright masculine future for his dictionary, suggests that Florio was at this stage in his career caught in the grammatical gap between Italian and English, the citation here of Bacchus an effort to transform feminine into masculine excess. But this reference, to a god frequently represented in classical literature as a dangerously effeminized male, as well as the allusion to Minerva, the most manly among the ancient pantheon of goddesses, suggests some degree of confusion as to where exactly Florio considered his reformed gender politics to be headed.

The citation of Ovid's tale of gender-switching Iphis in Florio's dictionary preface should, nevertheless, be considered representative of a dramatic turn in his thinking, and indicative of a change – either already effected or still hoped for – in his experience of England, a divergence echoed by Montaigne's account of the sudden transformation of the country girl Marie Germaine into a man in *Essais* 1.21, "De la force de l'imagination" (1.20 in Florio's translation):

Ce n'est pas tant de merveille, que cette sorte d'accident se rencontre frequent; car si l'imagination peut en telles choses, elle est si continuellement et si vigoreusement attachée à ce subject, que, pour n'avoir si souvent à rechoir en mesme pensée et aspreté de desir, elle a meilleur compte d'incorporer, une fois pour toutes, cette virile partie aux filles.[184]

It is no great wonder, that such accidents doe often happen, for if imagination have power in such things, it is so continually annexed, and so forcibly fastened to this subject, that lest she should so often fall into the relaps of the same thought, and sharpeness of desire, it is better one time for all, to incorporate this virile part unto wenches.[185]

The sense in both translation and dictionary dedication is so close that we can see how Florio's overlapping engagement with the two projects had a determinate effect on the manner in which the question of gender came to be articulated in presenting his lexicon to the world.[186] If dictionaries begin as feminine collections of *parole*, then collecting, classifying, and codifying words in order to give voice to the culture that they represent turns out, for Florio, to be equivalent to the classical Galenic version of "anatomical history, [in which] we all begin as female, and masculinity is a development out of and away from femininity."[187] The selection of *parole* for Florio's compendium of the Italian language clearly established him as an innovator in terms of the contemporary Italian debate over *la questione della lingua*, but the corresponding turn away from the feminine marked, through the transformation of Florio's linguistic child into a young man, his acquiescence to the gendered polarities of early modern English cultural politics.

Unlike Montaigne's Marie Germaine, however, this change was not to prove definitive. The image projected of Florio in William Hole's engraving of him in *Queen Anna's New World of Words* (Figure 13) is the confident picture of a man at the top of his game.[188] But the place that Florio won in Anne of Denmark's court after the accession of James I to the English throne would return him to the feminine realm of words, largely isolating him from any substantive engagement with the activities of the king's governing circle, and the 1611 edition of his dictionary bearing the queen's name conspicuously excludes any talk of Bacchus-boys-once-girls.

*Figure 13* John Hole, engraving of John Florio in *Queen Anna's New World of Words*.

Much more seems to have divided the Stuart king and queen than united them in England, and by 1607 they were leading relatively separate lives.[189] From Denmark House in London and the palace at Greenwich, Anne encouraged so many of the elements that have come to be identified with the Jacobean period that her conspicuous cultural patronage has often mistakenly been taken as a sign of her active involvement in early Stuart statecraft. Florio's professional profile is inextricably linked to the simultaneously marginal character of Anne's court and the oversized ambitions of Stuart self-presentation that emanated from it, the dedications of the second editions of both Florio's dictionary and his translation of Montaigne bearing the same claustrophobic self-referentiality of the Stuart masques that James was apparently so bored by. The communities of influence that had given rise to both volumes' first editions – manifest in the six dedications to prominently oppositional Elizabethan ladies in the 1603 *Essayes* as well as in the expansive reach of *A Worlde of Wordes* – are blithely erased in their second editions rededicated to the queen, a revealing encapsulation of the trajectory of Jacobean cultural politics. Anne's ambivalent religious convictions – which likely made a considerable impression upon her Italian tutor and personal secretary in the sixteen years of their association[190] – would have made her participation in renewed English relations with dissident Italy embarrassing at the very least, and would have rendered Florio's participation in the most significant event in Anglo-Italian relations in nearly a century, the publication of the Venetian Fra Paolo Sarpi's incendiary *Storia del concilio tridentino* in London in 1619, problematic indeed. Far from being thrust into the heart of James I's *realpolitik*, Florio appears to have been entirely uninvolved in the Stuart opening to Italy.[191]

There is, then, one final implication of Florio's citation of the Iphis episode in his 1598 dictionary preface with regard to Montaigne's essay on the imagination:

the subject of impotence already appears in the 1580 version [of the essay], several years before the insertion of Marie Germaine ... if Ovid's Iphis is provided just in time with the consummating instrument of virility, Montaigne's essay moves from the transformation of Iphis to anecdotes that tell a very different story – that of the failure of men on their wedding night to possess the use of this virile part.[192]

Florio's turn toward the masculine in his dictionary, followed by his subsequent re-assimilation into the previously superseded feminine space of *parole*, carried with it the potential for an analogous disappointment, one borne out in the final decades of his career in the strange new world of early Stuart England.

# Appendix I

**Pietro Carmeliano,** *Carmen*. **London: Richard Pynson, 1508, A1ᵣ and E4ᵣ.**

Anglia, perpetuos tibi dat rosa rubra triumphos,
perpetuum nomen perpetuumque decus.
Hec tua celateis redolens rosa crescit in hortis
atque aquam lignis iungit utranque suis.
Septimus Henricus, sapiens rex, regula morum,
celeste ingenium cum probitate tenens,
ad tantos solus vigilans te vexit honores,
ergo abs te debet iure volente coli.

*****

   Festa dies fulget cunctis mortalibus evi
      et solito Titan clarior orbe micat.
   Vir bonus et prudens et quisquis pacis amator
      gaudeat et supero det pia thura Deo.
   Anglia Burgunde domui domus inclyta clare
      sanguinis eterno federe iuncta manet.
   Ecce datur Karolo Maria speciosa puella,
      virtute insignis, moribus atque nitens.
   Septimus Henricus rex inclytus est pater illi,
      qui gemma est regum precipuumque decus.
   Regina Hellisabet mater, dum viveret, orbis
      inter reginas floruit absque pari.
   Henricus frater, princeps cui nemo secundus,
      conspicuum toto fundit in orbe iubar.
   Margareta soror, regi coniuncta potenti
      Scotorum, sapiens pulchra venusta decens.
   Defunctos taceo fratres simul atque sorores
      qui leti in celo regna beata tenent.
   At Karolo genitor fuerat rex ille Phillipus
      quem brevis – ah nimium substulit hora sibi,
   Cesaris Augusti spes unica filius unus
      magnanimus prestans strenuus atque potens.
   Sed regina sibi est genetrix preclara Joanna

>   heres regnorum non dubitata trium.
>   Ipse tamen tanto princeps orbate parente
>   rursus habes patrem sorte favente novum.
>   Hic est Henricus qui te et tua jura fovebit
>   hostibus imponens fortia frena tuis;
>   Hic est qui pacem, sua cum vexilla movebit,
>   gentibus et regnis imperitare potest.
>   Ast igitur laudes supero dominoque potenti
>   reddamus, nobis qui bona tanta dedit.
>   Utque salutiferum sit nobis omnibus istud
>   coniugium, demus nocte dieque preces.
>   Laus deo.

**Pietro Aretino, *Lettere*, vol. II, Francesco Erspamer, ed. Parma: Ugo Guanda, 1998, 3–6.**

Da che voi, Re inclito, per simigliare ne la eccellenza di tutte le virtù a l'Aquila signoreggiante ogni uccello, meritate onore e gloria, ecco ch'io vengo a onorarvi e a glorificarvi con l'offerta di questo mio piccolo parte. E onorandovi e glorificandovi per cotal mezzo, mi accorgo, insieme col mondo, che Dio ha voluto che la Natura vi produca non a bel caso, come il resto de i Principi, ma a sommo studio. E ciò gli parve però che le stelle sue avessero un suggetto capace a ricevere la grandezza de le loro influenze. I mirabili effetti de le quali, essendo raccolti nel sacro petto de la eterna corona vostra, movano con la medesima autorità che esse mostrano lassuso. Onde circa il potere infondere in altrui le grazie de la felicità, sete equale al Cielo; ma nel conto del volere che altri sia libero da gli ostacoli de le miserie, lo avanzate. Questo dico perché egli tolera la insolenzia de gli influssi maligni, e voi stirpate la nequizia de la volontà prave. Tal che vi si conviene il titolo di Deitade, come di religione; vi si debbe il cognome di Divo, a causa che tuttavia fate gesti immortali; e appartienvisi la insegna di religioso, conciosia che sempre riverite il divino culto. Avenga che il farlo è clarità d'intendimento, testimonio di bontade, plenitudine di legge, e segno di perfezione. Ma perché solo voi (oltre il confessare con la fede e con l'opere di esser suddito a la potenza di CHRISTO) vi mantenete giusto in verità, e non in apparenza, voi solo denno non imitare, che è impossibile, né invidiare, che non si dee, ma ammirare tutti coloro che hanno imperio ne gli huomini. Intanto io (che preporrò il giorno che mi accettarete per servo, a quanti ne potessi avere di letizia) dico che gli atti che vi partorisce la prestanzia del grande animo, sono cotanti e sí diversi, che se ci fusse cosa maggiore de le predette, direi esser poco ciò che io ho di voi parlato, a paragone di quel che debbo parlarne. Conciosia che sete sí fatto, che solo co la riputazion del nome, solo con l'ombra de la Maestà, solo col miracolo de la prudenzia, isforzate le genti a venerare le vostre orme, a inchinarsi a i vostri piedi, e a basciar la vostra destra. Di quella intendo, che ne lo stringere de la spada spaventa il furore de gli infedeli, nel mover de la penna disperge la rabbia de gli eretici, e nel dar de la fede rassicura le menti de i dubbiosi. Per guiderdone del qual merito, e questa età presente, e ogni secolo futuro, si obliga a offerirvi i sudori, gli inchiostri, gli anni, e i pensieri, tenendovi ognor la fama ne le lingue d'una predicazione in modo celeste, che non sarà bastante a nuocerle nulla alerazion terrena, veruno intoppo di Fortuna, e niuna antichità di tempo. Per benché il preclaro collegio de le vostre incomprensibili azioni da esser compreso dal muto de lo stupendo silenzio, avenga che gli andari loro non participano punto de le qualità ordinarie. Certo che noi vi vediam procedere con una sorte di giustizia, e con una spezie di misericordia, e a la giustizia, divina, che a l'umana. La pietà, la mansuetudine, la servitade, e la cortesia con cui premiate, punite, accogliete, e perdonate, variano tanto da le condizioni di cotali virtù, usandole altri, quanto la cristianità, la degnità, la generosità, e la venustà, che vi fa venustissimo, generosissimo, degnissimo, e cristianissimo, è differente da la circunstanze de i pregi altrui. Sí che bisgona affermare che non volgete ciglio che non sia di sí nuovo, di sí profondo, e di sí mirando essempio, che non si sa, non si ardisce, e non si puote esprimere. Ma perché tutte le cose che portono seco novità e maraviglia, ci smarriscono prima che agradino, non dovete, O SOVRANO ARBITRO DE LE PACI, E DE LE GUERRE TEMPORALI, E SPIRITUALI, però sdegnarvi se l'Universo non vi dedica i templi, e non vi dirizza gli altari, come a uno de i più sublimi Numi conciosia che il numero infinto de le vostre faccende immense, lo tien confuso, non altrimenti che ci confonderebbe il Sole, se la natura, toltolo dal suo luogo, ce lo ponesse in sul vicino conspetto de gli occhi. Di Vinezia il primo d'Agosto. M.D. XXXXII.

Zanobio Ceffino, *Stanze di Zanobio Ceffino cittadino fiorentino sopra l'eresia del re d'Inghilterra e sopra la morte di Tommaso Moro gran cancelliero*. **BL Additional Ms. 21982, transcribed by Alberto Castelli in "Un poemetto inedito del secolo XVI in onore di San Tommaso Moro,"** *Aevum* **12 (1938): 235.**

O Padre nostro o' Chreatore eterno
O'vero redentor del'human seme
Se i miei delitti gia voltar to ferno
Le spalle a laspre mie miserie estreme
Degnati hor Signor mio da questo inferno
Levarmi e pormi in parte piu supreme
Tanto chio possa a tua laude e honore

Mettere in versi quel chio' nel core.
Fondi nel mio intelletto una scintilla
Di quella gratia c'ha Paol fondesti
E nel mio Core una sola favilla
Di quel calor c'ha Stefano accendesti
Fa che la voce mia doventi squilla
Accio tanto gran Caso manifesti
A' esaltation de la tua santa Fede
E per conforto di chi piu di chrede.
E tu Pescia e de la chisa honore
S'aquesti versi miei ti degnerai
Poi c'haverai del suggetto il tenore
Intenso e forse untal' sentito mai
D'he con la Pieta muovati lamore
A pianger meco i lacrimosi guai
Dunaltro in quest'eta d'aquin Tommaso
Specchio di santita di virtu vaso.

**Girolamo Pollini,** *Historia ecclesiastica della rivoluzion d'Inghilterra.* **Rome: Facciotti, 1594, 359–360.**

... gli heretici come mala razza d'huomini inquieti, insolenti, e sfacciati, non potendo arrecarsi in paztienzia il parentado con un Principe forestiero, tanto Cattholico e potente, ne la dependenza e amicizia d'Inghilterra, che temevano con la Sedia Apostolica ... oltre a gl'inganni particolari e privati, che usarono gli heretici, per far forza, d'impedire empiamente, e contro a ogni ragion di giustizia, il reame all reina Maria (onde Tommaso Guglielmo scrivano del Senato, in vita d'Eduardo Sesto, fu con dovuta e meritevol morte punito) tramarono gli empi e malvagi, un nuovo, e non mai più udito stratagemma, per metter garbuglio nel Popolo, il quale all'ora era al tumulto, e all'heresia dedito molto e più che mai inchinevole.

Persuasero adunque una semplicetta e povera Fanciulla d'Anni diciotto, non meno co'l veleno d'heresia machiata, chè per qualche spazio di tempo, se lasciasse racchidere, in un cantone e luogo sicuro, nascoso fra due mura d'un Casamento, e per Canali, e Condotti ben composti, e accomodati a questo fine, traesse grandissime, e horribil grida, formando quegli accenti, e quelle parole, che da loro le sarebbero ordinate. Era il nome della giovane, Lisabetta Crosta, e lo'nventore di questo inganno e Stratagemma, fu un certo Drago. ... fuggirono glí inventori, e autori di questo stratagemma, la femmina per essere fanciulla, e da costoro ingannata, fu gasigata leggiermente, il fatto fu risoluto tutto in risa, e in maggiore horror, e scorno dell'heresia: la quale per singolar malvagità de gli heretici, si semina ne'cuori de' semplici, e ignoranti fedeli, e con somiglianti strattagemmi del diavolo agevolmente si nutrice e si mantiene.

# Appendix I

**Giovanni Alberto Albicante, *Il sacro et divino sponsalitio*.
Milan: Moscheni, 1555.**

Quanto gaudio, ne sente il Padre Santo
E tutti i Cardinali (et) tutta Roma,
Et ben vestito del suo sacro Manto
La Mitra si vi pon sopra la chioma,
E'n voci altere, di celeste canto,
Disse hor, l'heresia qui in terra toma,
Et manda Bolle, d'alta commissione,
Per tutta Italia a far processione [35v]

\*\*\*\*\*

Et sopra la gran Mole d'Adriano,
Le bombarde gettar horrendi tuoni,
Et mormorando in se, così pian piano,
Il Tebro in l'onde fè suovi suoni,
E tutti i colli, per le rive, eàl piano,
Fuor per le piazze, e tutti i suoi contorni,
Mostrano tanta festa, (et) tanto giuoco,
Ch'ogni gran stile, a dir saria puoco.

Non puoco, il Padre Santo, in ogni via,
Per Roma andando, a tutte le contrade;
Mostrò, con larga mano cortesia,
Quanto sia grata a ognàun la largitade;
Et quanti, n'eran chiusi, in prigonia,
Volse pagar suoi danni, sua bontade.
Sparse dennari anchora alle sue spese,
Per avanzar qual fosse più cortese.

Di poi disse la Messa, il buon Pastore,
Per meglio ringraziar, il sommo IDDIO;
E tutto'l clero a quel facendo honore,
Con alta devotion seco s'unio;
Et ogni cardinal qui di buon core,
Haveva al ciel levato il bel desio,
E tutti s'allegrar, del grande acquisto,
Dell'Inghilterra fatta serva a Christo [35v].

\*\*\*\*\*

Fra tanto il Dio Cupido apperse l'ali
E tolse via da gli occhi la sua benda,
E fra Spagnuoli spinse, alchun suoi strali,
E li percosse al core senza emmenda;
Non si scoprivan quivi già rivali,
Anzi si davan loco a vicendaò

E per far meglio i dolci inamorati,
Donavan guanti belli profumati [20v].

*****

Per CONSUMAR il Matrimonio intero,
Il Re, con la Regina andò in steccato,
E aprendo alla Regina il bel pensiero,
S'infuse quel del Re, più che beato.
O quanta gloria hor nasce a CARLO vero,
Et la quiete, d'honor d'ogni suo Stato
Et questo suo gioir, sia più giocondo,
Che nasca un bel Figliol, c'honori il mondo [21v].

**Archivio di Stato Firenze, Fondo Mediceo del Principato, f. 4183, 30r–32v. Transcribed by Piero Rebora in "Uno scrittore toscano sullo scisma d'Inghilterra ed una lettera della regina Elisabetta."** *Archivio storico italiaro* **93 (1935): 249–252.**

Elizabeta per gratia di Dio Reina d'Inghilterra, di Francia et Irlanda Difenditrice della fede etc. All'Illmo. et Eccmo. Gran Duca di Toscana. Illmo. et Eccmo. Prencipe,

Se ci arrechiamo a considerare la buon'amicitia, con la quale ci siamo scambievolmente riguradanti sin dal principio che Vostra Altezza venne al suo stato, non solo con esteriori dimostrationi, ma etiandio con sincera voluntà infra di noi manifesta, et che nella continuatione di quella siamo per ragione amendoi obligati di non comportare alcuna attione, la quale per via diretta o indiretta, secreta o palese, tenda a biasmo di nostri honori, persone ovvero governi. Certamente ci pare ch'al presente ci sia data una occasione, la qual non possiamo a meno communicarla a Vostra Altezza, mentre massime che rimane in noi l'oppinione della predetta sua costante benevolenza, ciò è un infame scandolo, una falsità più che manifesta pubblicata nelli Stati di V. A. contro un Prencipe di così gloriosa memoria, come è il re Henrico Ottavo nostro padre, et contro la Reina nostra madre sua consorte, et finalmente tendendo la maligna lingua al biasmo et alla denigrazione del nostro proprio governo, con tutte le maggiori calumniè et buggie ch'il scrittore si sia saput' immaginare, ma tanto evidentemente false, quanto chiarissimamente apparisce al mondo la benedittione di Dio sopra di Noi, del nostro popolo, et regno con tutte le più certe marche di prosperità, di quiete, d'ubbidienza, di ricchezze, di forze et d'augumento de sudditi. Cotest'attione intanto sì falsa sì maligna et sì diabolica, è stata, com'intendiamo, concepita et esseguita nel stato del V. A. mediante un libro scritto e pubblicato dalla pestifera mano et lingua di un suo suddito, Gierolamo Pollini, professore nel convento di Santa Maria Novella, del quale noi hebbemo prima notitia pochi mesi sono, per le lettere di un de' baroni del nostro regno nominato il signor Darcie, il quale secondo il debito suo per se stesso si mosse a fare che V. A. ne fusse informata et richiesta che fusse suppresso, alla qual cosa, sì come egli ci scrisse, Ella consentì molto volontieri, et Noi all'hora per nostre particolari lettere le ne resemo, un mese fa, i dovuti ringratiamenti, non sapevamo nondimeno altro in quel tempo, se non in generale ch'ei fusse un famoso libello contro il nostro stato. Ma adesso essendo più a pieno informate di tutta l'opera, et non sapendo di V. A. n'habbi avuto, et dall'altra parte essendo certificate che tutto quel libro, anzi ciascheduna paggina di esso è ripiena d'estrema falsità, d'infiniti scandali et di malignissime calomnie, ne segue che Noi, sì in rispetto che è convenevole all'offitio di ciaschedun Prencipe o Stato molto meno un Absoluto Sovrano d'esser in tal guisa per diffimatorij libelli diffamato, com'ancora per rispetto della buon'amicitia infra di noi ricevuta et apprezzata, et etiandio in rispetto ch'egli è piaciuto all'Omnipotente Dio di farci heredi di cosí grande Padre et Glorioso Re, di cui nessun'altro fu nel suo tempo di più alta famma, et di esser noi Sacra Reina di questi Christiani Regni, gli quali noi per Divina Gratia con grande prosperità et honore reggiamo, contro la nemicitia di non Piccioli Prencipi, venghiamo a richiedere a Vostra Altezza, la quale per gratia dell'istesso Dio possede sì grande Stato d'esserne chiamata il Gran Duca di Toscana, et esser Prencipe di gran dignità, che poi ch'ella ha in suo potere il predetto frate Gierolamo fiorentino, voglia mostrarci per tutte le predette considerationi un effetto degno di Prencipe amico verso un'assoluta Principessa et Reina, come noi siamo, di far supprimere et condannare al fuoco tutti gli predetti libri, che si potrano truovare nelli suoi Dominij, et di far castigare come suo suddito quella maligna infame persona auttor di essi, per haver composto et pubblicato cosí horribili calomnie et menzogne contro cosí grandi Prencipi passati et presenti. In che noi richiediamo a V. A. cosa la quale ella può esser sicura voler noi esser prontissime di far verso di Lei in simigliante caso, se giamai nelli nostri Regni alcun'offesa fusse commessa contro di Lei et del Stato suo. Et cosí fermamente aspettandoci faremo fine desiderandole longa et felicissima vita.

Dalla Nostra Reggia di Westmynster alli 6 d'aprile 1592
Vostra Affetionatissima Cognata Elizabetta R(egina)
(a tergo)
Al gran Duca di Toscana Cugino et Amico nostro Carissimo.

# Appendix II

This list has been checked against Huffman's list of John Wolfe's publications provided in the Appendix to *Elizabethan Impressions*; the only disparity is an annotated translation of *Lamentations* by Immanuel Tremellius which I have been unable to locate in either the *STC* or *EEBO*.

In Italian

*Una essortazione al timor di Dio con alcune rime Italiane, nouamente messe in luce* (1579)

*La vita di Carlo Magno Imperadore, scritta in lingua italiana da Petruccio Vbaldino cittadin fiorentino* (1581)

*Atto della Giustizia d'Inghilterra, esseguito, per la conservatione della commune [e] christiana pace* [trans. of Willliam Burghley's defense of the execution of Edmund Campion] (1584)

*Discorsi di Nicolo Machiavelli, sopra la prima deca di Tito Livio* (1584)

*Il Prencipe di Nicolo Machiauelli* (1584)

*La prima [seconda] parte de ragionamenti di M. Pietro Aretino* (1584)

*Itinerario di Marc Antonio Pigafetta gentil'huomo Vicentino* (1585)

By Italians/From Italian

*Paraphrasis aliquot Psalmorum Dauidis, carmine heroico. Scipio Gentili Italo auctore* (1581)

*Alberici Gentilis De iuris interpretibus dialogi sex* (1582)

*Scipii Gentilis Solymeidos libri duo priores de Torquati Tassi Italicis expressi* (1584)

*Scipii Gentilis in XXV. Dauidis Psalmos epicae paraphrases* (1584)

*Plutonis concilium* [Torquato Tasso] (1584)

*Alberici Gentilis. Legalium comitiorum Oxoniensium. Actio. Francisco Bevanno docturae dignitatem suscipiente* (1585)

*Scipii Gentilis Nereus siue De natali Elizabethae illustriss. Philippi Sydnaei filiae* (1585)

*Iulii Caesaris Stellae nob. Rom. Columbeidos, libri priores duo* (1585)

## Appendix II

*La vita di Giulio Agricola scritta sincerissimamente. Da Cornelio Tacito suo genero. Et messa in volgare da Giovan Maria Manelli* (1585)

*Annotationi di Scipio Gentili sopra La Gierusalemme liberata di Torquato Tasso* (1586)

*Avviso piacevole dato alla bella Italia, da un nobile giovane Francese, sopra la mentita data del serenissimo re di Navarra a Papa Sisto V* [François Perrot] (1586)

*Esamine di varii giudicii de i politici* [Giovan Battista Aureli] (1587)

*Libro dell'arte della guerra di Nicolo Machiauelli cittadino, et secretario fiorentino* (1587)

*Historie di Nicolo Macchiauelli, cittadino, et secretario fiorentino* (1587)

*L'historia del gran regno della China, composta primieramente in ispagnuolo da maestro Giouanni Gonzalez di Mendozza, monaco dell'ordine di S. Agostino: et poi fatta vulgare da Francesco Auanzi cittadino Vinetiano* (1587)

*Esempio d'una lettera mandata d'Inghilterra a Don Bernardo Mendozza ambasciatore in Francia per lo re di Spagna* [trans. from William Burghley by Richard Leigh] (1588)

*Lasino doro di Nicolo Macchiauelli* (1588)

*Quattro comedie del diuino Pietro Aretino* (1588)

*Descrittione del regno di Scotia, et delle isole sue adiacenti di Alberici Gentilis I. C. Professoris Regij. Condicionum Liber I* (1587)

*A true and perfect discourse of three great accidents that chaunced in Italie within twentie and sixe dayes* (1588)

*Alberici Gentilis I. C. professoris regij De iure belli commentatio prima* (1588 and 1589)

*Alberici Gentilis I. C. professoris regij De iure belli commentatio secuda* (1588 and 1589)

*Alberici Gentilis I. C. professoris regij De iure belli commentatio tertia* (1589)

*A true and perfecte description of a straunge monstar borne in the city of Rome in Italy, in the yeare of our saluation 1585* (1590)

*Refutatio cuiusdam libelli sine auctore cui titulus est, de iure magistratum in subditos, & officio subditorum erga magistratus* [Giovanni Beccaria] (1590)

*Perpetuall and naturall prognostications of the change of weather* (1591)

*De furtiuis literarum notis vulgo. de ziferis libri IIII* [Giambattista della Porta] (1591)

*The history of the warres betvveene the Turkes and the Persians* [trans. from Giovanni Tommaso Minadoi by Abraham Hartwell] (1595)

*Vincenzo Saviolo his practise* (1595)

*Petruccio Vbaldini cittadin Fiorentino* (1588)
*The courtier of Count Baldessar Castilio* (1588)
*La terza, et vltima parte de Ragionamenti del diuino Pietro Aretino* (1589)
*Lettera di Francesco Betti gentilhuomo Romano.*
*All'illustris. & eccellentiss. S. Marchese di Pescara. Nella quale da conto a S. Ecc. della cagione, che l'ha mosso a partirsi dal suo seruigio, & vscir d'Italia* (1589)
*Le vite delle donne illustri* (1591)
*Il pastor fido tragicomedia pastorale di Battista Guarini* (1591)
*L'Aminta, di Torquato Tasso, favola boscherecchia* (1591)

# Notes

### Introduction

1 *QA*, 570.
2 Sontag 2003, 13.
3 Both (lower-case) *rinascimento* and *rinascita* were used by Vasari in a limited sense in *Le vite de' più eccellenti pittori, scultori e architettori*; see vol. I, 13, 31, and 274, Rosanna Bettarini and Paola Barocchi, eds. (Florence: Sansoni–S. P. E. S., 1966–97); for Vasari's sense of the terms, see Garin 1975. *Rinascimento/renaissance* had a wider diffusion in its religious sense during the sixteenth century in both Italian and French, as Florio registers in *QA*, 440, by defining the word as "a new birth or a regeneration." The French (upper-case) *Renaissance* does not appear until 1840, in Michelet's *Histoire de France*; Burckhardt's *Die Kultur der Renaissance in Italien* was issued in 1860; and Symonds' seven-volume *Renaissance in Italy* was published in 1875 and 1876. One might say, then, that the use of the term was incidental during the period it came eventually to describe. Walter Pater – cited in the *OED* entry for "Renaissance" – notes that "the word 'Renaissance' is now generally used to denote ... a whole complex movement of which that revival of classical antiquity was but one element or symptom." Huizinga 1952, 103–104, writes, however, that the term *renascentia* "crops up repeatedly in [the] work [of Erasmus]," noting five typical examples from his letters. For Erasmus, *renascentia* refers primarily to the recovery of classical textual culture, whereas in nineteenth-century historiography the term is applied to the great flowering of vernacular, and particularly Italian, cultures from the mid-fourteenth through the early sixteenth centuries.
4 The *OED* provides no definition of "early modern," though the term is employed in hundreds of examples, especially with regard to "early" forms of vernacular languages. Starn 2003, 296, describes the by now almost ubiquitous use of the term as "early, partly, sometimes, maybe modern ... early modernity is a period for our period's discomfort about periodization." While Starn's cautionary critique is a valid one, a range of nomenclature best suits the time-frame and aims of this project. Though "early modern" is used more frequently here, this has more to do with what I see as the progressive thrust of vernacular cultures in this period than with settling scores with the scholarship of the past.
5 See Cheyfitz 1991, 72.
6 Michel de Montaigne, *The Essayes, or Morall, Politike and Millitarie Discourses*, John Florio, trans. (London: Edward Blount, 1603), A5r.
7 For these historical chapters, Lewis Einstein's *The Italian Renaissance in England* (New York: Columbia University Press, 1902) has provided an invaluable point of reference.

8 My work owes an enormous debt to Yates' pioneering work, *John Florio: The Life of an Italian in Shakespeare's England* (Cambridge: Cambridge University Press, 1934), an excellent survey of Florio's life and career which this study makes no pretense to superseding, though there are many gaps to fill and questions – raised by Yates, but not always fully answered – to be addressed. For a critical assessment of Yates' scholarly career, see Delpiano 1993, 180–245, which is particularly good at orienting Yates' intellectual profile within the formative early years of the Warburg Institute in London between the two world wars.
9 See Yates 1934, 12–14.
10 Yates 1934, 19–26, suggests that after being educated by his father in Soglio, in the Swiss Alps just east of Italian Chiavenna, Florio spent a period of time under the tutelage of Pier Paolo Vergerio, the former Bishop of Capodistria and papal nuncio to the German states, who had converted to the Lutheran faith and late in life established an academy of humanistic studies at Tübingen. According to Yates' chronology, Florio might have returned to England in the company of the Earl of Sussex, after an exploratory mission regarding the projected marriage of Elizabeth I to Archduke Charles of Austria in 1567–68 had come to a conclusion. While Florio is himself uncustomarily silent about his early life and education, indications in both *FF* and *WW*, as well as the *Returns of Aliens Dwelling in the City and Suburbs of London from the Reign of Henry VIII to that of James I*, 4 vols., E. F. Kirk and R. E. G. Kirk, eds. (Aberdeen: Aberdeen University Press, 1900–08), suggest that he arrived back in England no earlier than 1570, and no later than 1571; see Arundel del Re's edition of *FF* (Formosa: Taihoku Imperial University, 1936), pt. 2, x.
11 Yates 1934, 239.
12 As we shall see, this distinguished Florio from many of the other foreigners in England at the time. The Dutch poet Constantijn Huygens was considered a prodigy in the early seventeenth century for having learned English; see Davidson and van der Weel 1996, especially 195–218, which gives Huygens' works in English and discusses his relationship to contemporary English literature.
13 As Yates 1934, 21, maintains. There are few records of him traveling anywhere except perhaps to Tübingen as a young boy, to Scotland, and possibly to Ireland, and there is no sure sign of first-hand knowledge of contemporary Italy in any of his works.
14 Holquist 2002, 78–79.
15 *ibid*.
16 Consider two telling cases: the 1986 document issued by the Vatican Congregation for the Doctrine of the Faith, *The Pastoral Care of Homosexual Persons*, and especially its little-noted Paragraph 10, which argues that while "it is deplorable that homosexual persons have been and are the object of violent malice in speech or in action," such violence is nevertheless to be considered understandable given the "intrinsically disordered" moral character of homosexual activity; and the September 11 kamikaze pilots' expectation of "houris", which they evidently understood to mean a paradise filled with accommodating "virgins" or "angels" in return for the sacrifice of their lives and those of their victims, but which, in fact, signifies a rare form of white grape.

17 Said 2003, 6.
18 *QA*, 286; only the first part of the definition is pertinent to this study, but I cite it in its entirety here to give an idea of the inclusive ambition of Florio's philological imagination, one of the keys to his importance, as I shall argue.
19 Goldberg 1983, xi.
20 *QA*, 388. Florio obviously refers here to Aristotle's *Politics*.
21 Goldberg 1983, xi.
22 *WW*, 94. The *OED*, second edition, misattributes the earliest appearance of this formulation to the third edition of Robert Cawdry's *Table Alphabeticall* in 1613, also omitting Florio's 1598 "manuring" and "ploughing."
23 For a relevant discussion of the implications of this term, see Sacks 1988, 465–488.
24 See Waquet 2001, for a fine account of the persistence of Latin well into the modern era. It will be helpful for what follows to bear in mind that Latin did serve to ease "national" cultural distinctions in the period under consideration here for those who benefitted from a humanistic preparation; though their numbers were infinitesimal in relation to the general population, the numbers of the Latin "literate" included many of those who held the reins of power in its various early modern guises.
25 Though I cite the original edition of *FF*, del Re's 1936 facsimile edition provides an exemplary critical introduction and notes to Florio's text, taking issue occasionally with Yates' speculations about Florio's career; see *Florio's 'First Fruites'*, Arundel del Re, ed. (Formosa: Taihoku Imperial University, 1936). Silvio Policardi plagiarized entire sections of del Re's introduction, translating literally, with no acknowledgment, in his *Giovanni Florio e le relazioni culturali anglo-italiane agli albori del xvii secolo* (Venice: Montuoro, 1947).
26 See De Mauro 2003.
27 Adapted from Rorty 1989, 75, where the description of the ironist as one "who has radical and continuing doubts about the final vocabulary she currently uses, because she has been impressed by other vocabularies, vocabularies taken as final by people or books she has encountered" makes for a suggestive definition of the Italianate Englishman in the Tudor period.
28 Jacques Cartier, *A shorte and briefe narration of two Navigations and Discoveries to the North west partes called Newe Fraunce*, John Florio, trans. (London: H. Bynneman,1580), B1r-v; on this translation, see Yates 1934, 55–58.
29 Terms associated, respectively, with Baldassare Castiglione (studied nonchalance), Niccolò Machiavelli (virile determination), and (Francesco) Petrarca (hereafter referred to as Petrarch), the trecento master of the sonnet form.
30 In addition to the clear-cut dynastic shift, there is a great deal of "stranger" evidence which distinguishes the Stuart and Elizabethan eras. The circulation of foreign cultures – particularly French – in the Scotland into which James VI was born will figure significantly in this subsequent study, as will the presence in Stuart Scotland and England of such other Italians as Pietro Bizzarri and Giacomo Castelvetro. And in addition to the *Essayes*, I shall be examining Florio's other translations made in this period: of James I's *Basilikon Doron* into Italian; and of both Boccaccio's *Decameron* (1620) and a number of Troiano Boccalini's *Ragguagli di Parnasso* into English (this latter the first book of Willliam Vaughan's *The New-founde Politicke*, 1626).

31 Mary Augusta Scott's study, *Elizabethan Translations from the Italian* (Boston: Houghton Mifflin, 1916), remains the point of departure for any consideration of the circulation of Italian textual culture in the sixteenth and early seventeenth centuries in England.
32 Original primary texts are provided in the chapter notes (except when I cite an already published translation); for longer prose passages and verse longer than the fourteen lines of a sonnet, see Appendix I.
33 The work of John Hale, another associate of the Warburg Institute, has provided an admirable exception to this trend, and his *The Civilization of Europe in the Renaissance* (New York: Atheneum, 1994) has been a constant point of reference throughout the elaboration of this project.
34 Scholars of Giordano Bruno such as Vincenzo Spampanato, Giovanni Gentile, and Giovanni Aquilecchia are notable exceptions; and Marcel Tetel 1995, 179–180, provides a refreshing valorization of Florio's importance for the *questione* from the perspective of a French *seizièmiste*.
35 Specialized collections such as those of the national academies in Rome, as well as the Istituto Nazionale di Studi sul Rinascimento, the Kunsthistorisches Institut, and the Villa I Tatti in Florence, are obvious exceptions to this rule, though these libraries are organized according to very specific criteria and stray very little outside their defined parameters.

# 1   The two roses

1 *FF*, 18r (and hereafter in brackets preceding the text).
2 Whatever Chaucer's knowledge of Italian, Latin would certainly have played a significant part in his Italian experience.
3 Howard 1987, 190–193, spells out a plausible but entirely conjectural case that Chaucer could have met Boccaccio, while remaining more skeptical regarding a meeting with Petrarch. Chaucer's own silence about these projected encounters, at any rate, seems telling.
4 See Wallace 1997, 9–64. This rich account of Chaucer's exposure to the entirely diverse political cultures of trecento Florence and Milan offers an analogous image to the one I aim to provide here of the Italian encounter with early modern England. For another recent approach to Chaucer and Italy, see Kirkpatrick 1995, 24–79, and particularly 26–31 and 39–51, for a reading of Chaucer's appropriation of Dante, two authors conspicuously unaccounted for in early modern English literary taste.
5 *Il paradiso perduto*, the 1728 translation of the first six books of *Paradise Lost* by Paolo Antonio Rolli, one of Handel's operatic librettists, is the earliest example I have found of an English literary text translated into Italian. The first Shakespeare play in Italian was not published until 1756, a version of *Julius Caesar* translated into prose by Domenico Valentini, a professor of ecclesiastical history at the University of Siena. The first complete Italian edition of Shakespeare's plays, also in prose, was not published until 1838 by Carlo Rusconi; see Rebora 1936, 191–198, which includes a useful evaluation of Shakespeare's first Italian translators.

6 Previous accounts of this Florentine banking collapse have tended to exaggerate the role that the English default had on the wider European economic crisis of the mid-fourteenth century; see Hunt 1990.
7 The interface between Britain and Italy in the *Furioso* is a vast subject worthy of a book-length study entirely its own. In addition to the central role of Arthurian mythology, Astolfo, the English duke and cousin of Orlando and Rinaldo, is one of the poem's principal actors: it is he who travels to the moon to recover Orlando's wits in Cantos 34 and 35, a mission that once accomplished in Canto 39 restores a fundamental equilibrium in Ariosto's topsy-turvy world that had been displaced by Orlando's madness. Several of the poem's most dramatic episodes occur in the British Isles: the stories of Ariodante (Cantos 5–6); Angelica and the Orca (Cantos 9–11); and Lucina and the Orco (Cantos 17–18).
8 Two brief studies by de Cossart from 1984 provide a useful survey – though short on analysis – of Italo-English relations in the period preceding Henry VIII's break with the Roman church (see de Cossart 1984a and 1984b). S. Rossi 1969 and 1984 also deals with a number of important aspects of the early history of Italians in England.
9 A complete edition of the extant *relazioni* written in this period can be found in *Relazioni di ambasciatori veneti al Senato, vol. I: Inghilterra*, Luigi Firpo, ed. (Turin: Bottega d'Erasmo, 1965).
10 "... sia pur solo platonicamente ..." *Ambasciatori veneti in Inghilterra*, Luigi Firpo, ed. (Turin: UTET, 1978) xii, from which I have drawn this summary.
11 The ambassadorial *relazione* was always presented orally to the Venetian Senate upon the completion of a mission, though its final written version was not always composed by the diplomat himself. The history of the written text of Trevisan's *relazione* is a complex one, recounted by Firpo in *Ambasciatori*, xv–xviii, and briefly here: Firpo's corrected and annotated text, 3–49, is based on an earlier edition – an annotated English translation, with the Italian provided at the bottom of each page – by Charlotte Augusta Sneyd, *A Relation or rather a True Account of the Island of England* (London: Camden Society, 1847) and also reproduced in *Relazioni di ambasciatori veneti al Senato*. The Italian manuscript of the *relazione* had been purchased by Walter Sneyd, an Anglican priest and presumably a relative of Charlotte's, when the library of the Venetian Jesuit Matteo Luigi Canonici was dispersed between 1817 and 1836; W. Sneyd's own collection was auctioned off in 1903, and the Trevisan manuscript disappeared at that point. Firpo suggests, on the basis of the Italian text which C. Sneyd provides, that its author was a Venetian aristocrat with a good humanistic preparation who served as Trevisan's amanuensis in England, but given the strong presence of Tuscan elements in the language of the transcription this original text must have been, as Firpo puts it, "dipped in the Arno" late in the sixteenth century. For what follows, I cite C. Sneyd's translation in the main body of my text (with page numbers indicated [in brackets]), correcting it where necessary from Firpo's corrected Italian text in *Ambasciatori*, which I provide in the chapter notes. Given the anonymity of the author, for convenience I refer to him here as Trevisan.

12 *Ambasciatori*, 4: "L'aere ... è molto salubre e manca di molte egritudini, delle quali l'Italia è tribolata."
13 *ibid.*, 13: "... Scoti selvatici ..."
14 *ibid.*, 13: "Dice ancora don Pedro, che tutta la gente scotiana è assai amatrice de' forestieri e molto ospitale."
15 *ibid.*, 20: "Sono inimici de' forestieri e pensano che non passi in quell'isola alcuno, se non per farsi patrone e usurpare i loro beni."
16 *ibid.*, 28: "... pochi sono quelli Inglesi che sieno fedeli al re loro; per l'ordinario odiano li presenti e laudano li morti."
17 *ibid.*, 14: "mai più vidde cosa meglio ordinato. Tanto potenzia non è mai esercitata se non contra gl'Inglesi, loro naturali inimici, come è usanza de' vicini."
18 *ibid.*: "tutte le croniche dell'Inghilterra dicono che il re loro è supremo signore di Scozia e che a suo piaccimento ha mutato il re di Scozia; e li Scoti ... si gloriano di aver sempre ributtato gl'Inglesi e di nuovo possedere la terra loro."
19 *ibid.*, 16: "[Gli abitatori di Wallia] per commune giudizio sono li primi uomini che abitorno l'isola, come da loro vien detto; e dagl'Inglesi è creduto che essi sieno discesi da Troia, e tutti si reputano gentilomini e si chiamano l'un l'altro *cosaio*, che nella loro lingua altro non vuole significare, né [per] cosa del mondo contrarrìano matrimonio con Inglesi, de' quali, sono mortalissimi nemici. Hanno questi lingua diversa da la inglese e dalla scozzese ... fu già Wallia un regno separato ... e se il tanto nominato Arturo fu mai al mondo, fu egli in questo paese, per quanto ho letto nelle istorie inglesi."
20 *ibid.*, 17: "... pure lei sola è la maggiore e la migliore di tutte l'altre, e tutti li beni che io ritrovo nascere nell'isola nascono in abbondanzia in Inghilterra ... è tutta distinta in picciole e piacevole collinette e in belle vallette, non vi si vedendo altro che amene selve o praterie grandissime o cultivazione, e per tutto sorge grandissima abondanzia d'acque."
21 *ibid.*, 10 and 7: "... ferro e argento assai, piombo e stagno infinito ... [hanno] grandissima quantità di pecore, delle quali cavano infinita e ottima qualità di lana."
22 *ibid.*, 17: "... gl'Inglesi sono molto amatori di sé medesimi e d'ogni loro cosa, né credono che si trovino altri uomini che loro, né altro mondo che l'Inghilterra; e quando pur veggono qualche bel forestiero, usano di dire che è pare uno Inglese e che gli è gran peccato che egli non sia inglese; e quando mangiono qualcosa di buono insieme con un forestiero, domandono se di quella tal cosa se ne fa nel paese del convitato."
23 *ibid.*, 6: "... i paesani fanno due bevande di frumento, orzo, e vena, l'una delle quale è nominata *birra* e l'altra *ala*, e tale bevanda molto piace loro, né meno dispiace a' forestieri, quando però n'abbino bevuto quattro o sei volte, e questa è assai più grata al gusto quando l'uomo per qualche accidente è alquanto riscaldato."
24 *ibid.*, 20: "... tuttavia gl'Inglesi guardano le donne di casa loro con molta gelosia, riducendosi però infine ogni cosa nella forza del denaro."
25 *ibid.*, 29: "Il popolo è in poco maggiore stima che se fosse servo."
26 *ibid.*, 18: "... pochissimi, eccetto li preti, attendono all'esercizio delle lettere."

27 *ibid.*, 40: "... in ogni suo affanno ha mostrato di volersi difendere con le fortezze, quando bene si fosse perso il resto, e a l'animo suo ha conrisposto la fortuna, imperò che non perse mai alla campagna. Né dal re Guglielmo Conquestatore fino a questi tempi alcuno ha regnato più pacificamente che il presente, il quale per la sua gran prudenzia è temuto universalmente da tutti."
28 *Il principe*, written in 1512–13 but not published until 1532, may have been known in England in manuscript form before it was available in print. Though the notion of dynasty is inimical to Machiavelli's thinking, these bookend Tudor monarchs each in their own way represent perhaps the most consistent version of the Florentine Secretary's political thinking ever realized. The issue of Machiavelli's influence in early modern England is an important one, but while I can only deal with it episodically – as it is mediated through the Italian presence in England – Kahn 1994a has explored the diffusion of Machiavelli's thinking and reactions to it there.
29 Though, as C. Sneyd mentions, 117, Italian merchants in England had until 1488 paid a double tax on their imports and exports; Henry's relaxation of this burden had a great effect on increased trade between England and the Italian peninsula.
30 *Ambasciatori*, 20: "... onde è necessario dire cio che gl'Inglesi sieno i più segreti amatori del mundo, overo che non abbino amore."
31 *ibid.*, 20–21: "... pochissimi nascono tanto che sieno esenti da questa sorte. Imperò che ciascuno, quanto si voglia ricco, mette li suoi figli in casa d'altri, sì come lui in casa sua prende degli alieni. E domandandogli per che ragione fanno questa rigidità, rispondono di farlo a ciò che li figlioli imparino meglio a vivere. Ma io, per me, credo che lo faccino perché voglino loro godersi ogni comodità e perché meglio siano serviti de li stranieri che non sariano delli figlioli medesimi ... se gl'Inglesi mettessero li figlioli loro fuori di casa a fine che imparassero le virtù e le buone creanze, e poi ripigliassero, passato il tempo della servitù, forse sariano scusati; ma non torneriano mai, perché le fanciulle sono maritate da patrone e li maschi prendono moglie il meglio che possono."
32 See C. Sneyd's note, 75–76, where she transcribes a contract between Edward Stafford, Duke of Buckingham and Mrs. Margaret Hextall, with whom his children were to be raised.
33 *Ambasciatori*, 21: "... il quale forse in vita del marito non gli era dispiaciuto."
34 *ibid.*, 22: "... un bellissimo giovane di età d'anni diciotto in circa, fratello del signor duca di Sofolk, il quale intesi che era rimasto poveretto, perché l'eredità paterna tra baroni rimane al primogenito. Questo giovane ... fu adocchiato da una vedova di cinquanta anni, ricca, per quanto intesi, di cinquantamila scudi. E tanto seppe fare l'astuta e sagace vecchia, per quanto mi fu referito, che il garzone fu contento d'essergli marito e con pazienzia perdere con lei la sua tenera bellezza, sperando presto di godere la sua gran richezza con una galante damigella."
35 *ibid.*, 28: "... ogni legge cesarea ... gli danno li re loro."
36 *ibid.*, 28: "... quantunque gli arbitri isolani eletti dallo Inglese *etiam* prima che si riserrino sieno bene pasciuti e voglino sostenare la parte del suo principale, pure non possono durare al paro delli Italiani, che sono assuefatti alli digiuni a alli disagi, a tal che infine il più delle volte il giudizio segue a favore delli Italiani."

37 *ibid.*, 29: "E la minor fatica del mondo è il mettere gli uomini in prigione."
38 *ibid.*: "... non è paese al mondo dove sieno più ladri e più malandrini."
39 *ibid.*: "... li preti hanno proveduto che nel regno siano molti luoghi sacri per rifugio e scampo d'ogni loro delinquente. E se bene colui avesse trattato contra la corona o contro la persona stessa del re, non può essere levato, per forza di franchigia."
40 See C. Sneyd's extended note, 86–89.
41 *Ambasciatori*, 30: "... alcuno ladro overo omicidio che sappia leggere sia morto per mano di giustizia. E quando per giustizia delli dodici uomini di manto sia alcuno condennato a morte, se il reo sa leggere, domanda che si vuole difendere con il libro; onde se gli porta o il psalmista o il messale o qualsivogli altro libro ecclesiastico, e sapendo leggere, viene liberato de la forza e, come clerico, è dato nelle mani del vescovo."
42 *ibid.*, 34: "li signori spirituali ... hanno la vera decina d'ogni frutto terrestre, come anco di qualunque animale. E se uno abita nella sua propria abitazione, del tutto paga la vera decina alla chiesa, dico oltra quella terza parte ... che le perviene di tutte le eredità."
43 In the early months of 1527, just before the sack of Rome and as Henry was preparing the way for his divorce initiative, Clement VII asked for 30,000 crowns to address an urgent cash-flow problem in the papal coffers; Henry satisfied the request, but this may have been the last such payment in English history; see M. Mitchell 1971, 189.
44 It is unclear to what extent the early Venetian representatives could have relied upon Latin in England, particularly given that the merchant class from which many of them came in this period generally did not learn classical languages. Trevisan, 18, did glean enough about English to suggest, however, that the language, like Dutch, is "tedesco alterato ... pure lassata quella naturale durezza, usano ora la pronuncia assai soave" [derived from German ... has lost its natural harshness, and they now use a pleasing pronunciation].
45 On Poggio and other Italian humanists in England during the first half of the fifteenth century, see Summut 1980, Saygin 2002, and Rundle 2003 (Petrina 2004 has come to my attention too late to be taken into consideration here).
46 Poggio Bracciolini, *Two Renaissance Book Hunters: The Letters of Poggius Bracciolini to Nicolaus de Niccolis*, Phyllis W. G. Gordan, trans. (New York: Columbia University Press, 1974), 48.
47 For this new account of Poggio's English experience, see Saygin 2002, 237–254.
48 For Piccolomini's visit to Britain, see Ady 1958; R. J. Mitchell 1962, 65–73; and Naville 1984, 166–169.
49 See *I Commentarii*, vol. I, Luigi Totaro, ed. and trans. (Milan: Adelphi, 1984), 22–31, for Piccolomini's own account of his visit to Scotland and England.
50 *ibid.*, 28–29: "Ibi primum figuram orbis et habitabilem terrae faciem visus est revisere. Nam terra Scotia, et Angliae pars vicina Scotis, nihil simile nostrae habitationis habet: horrida, inculta, atque hyemali sole inaccessa."
51 See R. J. Mitchell 1962, 71.
52 Humphrey had earlier tried unsuccessfully to persuade Leonardi Bruni, the Florentine Chancellor and widely acknowledged dean of early quattrocento humanism, to come to work in England, but Humphrey did convince Bruni to

undertake a Latin translation of Aristotle's *Politics* as a companion piece to Lydgate's *The Fall of Princes* as part of his educational program for the young Henry VI; see Saygin 2002, 65–67. A great deal of misunderstanding has been generated about Humphrey's relations with Bruni (see, for instance, Weiss 1967, 46–49), but Saygin, 67 n. 50, argues that the mutual lack of comprehension between late feudal and early republican mentalities explains why Humphrey would have thought it "infinitely more honourable" for Bruni to take up employment under an English aristocrat than continue to work as "a city-clerk," and why Bruni would not have wished to do so. Saygin, 228, similarly accounts for Humphrey's troubled relations with Pier Candido Decembrio, one of several middlemen the English duke employed in Italy, given that "different conventions regulated literary patronage in Italy and England ... in England money and reward were difficult subjects to broach in the relations between a patron of letters and his client ... in most cases a literary patron offered his good lordship to his client rather than remunerating his services in financial terms." Humphrey likewise would have considered the prestige his patronage conveyed as sufficient payment for Bruni's translation of Aristotle, but in withdrawing his dedication to Humphrey and redirecting the *Politics* to Pope Eugenius IV, Bruni clearly signaled who – from his perspective – had better appreciated the material implications of his work.

53 While both plays are set in England it is not clear that they were ever staged there, and Saygin 2002, 256–257 n. 73, suggests that "they have only a superficial bearing on the English context." Frulovisi's previous five Latin comedies, written in Venice, are nevertheless the first examples of "purely secular plays [which] imitated classical playwrights, yet drawing their themes from contemporary life and character [and which were] known to really have been performed"; see Tito Livio da Forlí, *Opera hactenus inedita T. Livii Frulovisiis de Ferraria*, C. W. Previté-Orton, ed. (Canterbury: Academic Press 1932), xx. For an Italian perspective on Frulovisi's dramatic work, see Sabbadini 1934, 55–81.

54 S. Rossi 1969, 19; see 19–25 for Rossi's reading of the *Vita*. Saygin 2002, 69–80, provides an account of how and why the *Vita* came to be written; and 254–259 explains Frulovisi's career trajectory, which after leaving England in 1439 led him away from humanism and into medicine.

55 *ibid.*, 24.

56 Shakespeare, *Henry V*, Gary Taylor, ed. (Oxford: Clarendon Press, 1982), 29.

57 *Holinshed's Chronicles*, vol. III, Henry Ellis, ed. (London: J. Johnson, 1808), 136. Patterson 1994, 131 and 133–134, acknowledges the difficulty of pinpointing Holinshed's sources but recognizes Frulovisi's importance for later English historiography and distinguishes between his original Latin history and its anonymous English adaptation.

58 Kingsford 1911, xlvi, writes that "though Tito Livio's *Life* remained in manuscript till 1716 [it has not been republished since], it had through the writing of Stow and Holinshed given colour to all subsequent opinion [of Henry's reign], and not least it had supplied much of the ultimate basis for the historical, as distinct from the legendary, account embodied in the plays of Shakespeare." The anonymous translator's accretions to Frulovisi's history account for many

of these "legendary" aspects: Henry's rejection of his former friends in the final scene of *Henry IV pt. 2*, for example; see Kingsford, lvi.
59 S. Rossi 1969, 25.
60 On Carmeliano's role as Latin secretary, see *DBI*, vol. xx, 410–413; Trapp 1991, 31–32; and Wilkie 1974, 14–15.
61 On these early poems of Carmeliano, and on his agility in negotiating the treacherous English political scene in this period, see Carlson 1993, 37–59; see 20–36, for a useful guide to the way that the English system of humanist patronage operated, and for a look at another Italian humanist, Filippo Alberici, who tried unsuccessfully to peddle his wares in England in 1506 or 1507.
62 For an idea of the scope of the problem, consider that Carmeliano accumulated benefices from the Cathedral of Worcester, the Priory of Christchurch, the Abbey of Hyde, the Cathedral of Southwark, Compton Bishop, Chisenbury and Chute, the Abbey of Ampleforth, St. Stephen's Westminster, Cublington, and the Cathedral of Gloucester; see *DBI*, vol. xx, 411.
63 The English version of the poem issued at the same time, *The solemnities and triumphes doon and made at the spousells and Mariage of the Kynges daughter the Ladye Marye to the Prynce of Castile Archeduke of Austrige*, does not contain Carmeliano's verses; see Carlson 1987, 500. For the full text of Carmeliano's opening and concluding verses, see Appendix I, pages 255–256.
64 A reference to Henry's transaltantic ambitions: after failing to sign onto Colombus' initial journey to the new world, Henry sponsored Henry Cabot's voyage to Labrador in 1497 that initiated England's commercial and colonial relationship with America.
65 Pietro Carmeliano, *Carmen* (London: Richard Pynson, 1508), A1r.
66 Carmeliano, *Carmen*, E4r.
67 Henry VII had earlier made a bid himself to marry Charles' widowed mother, Joan, in 1506, though "the scheme was not seriously entertained on either side"; see *DNB*, vol. IX, 526. She was widely believed to have gone mad following the death of her husband, Philip, and in spite of her "three kingdoms" was detained under guard by her father, Ferdinando, at Tordesillas, where she died in 1509.
68 The question of Carmeliano's value as a poet was raised by Erasmus and by Thomas More, who in one of his Latin epigrams, "In stultum poetam" [On a stupid poet], cited what he viewed as absurdities in Carmeliano's Latin style; see *The Latin Epigrams of Thomas More*, Leicester Bradner and Charles Arthur Lynch, eds. (Chicago: University of Chicago Press, 1953), 65–66 and 185. Carlson 1987, 495, also notes that while Carmeliano "was probably the most materially successful poet of the early Tudor period ... artistic success may be a different matter." Whatever aesthetic judgment one might make about Carmeliano's poetic gifts, however, the absence of his name in Burrow 1999, 793–820, is typical of the short shrift that foreign literary figures active in England in this period have received.
69 See *Il libro del cortegiano*, Walter Barberis, ed. (Turin: Einaudi, 1998), I.2,17. While set in this earlier period, Castiglione's treatise was not published until 1528, following the sack of Rome and the deaths of many of the friends after whom he crafted his interlocutors.

70 For the occasion and circumstances of Castiglione's visit to England, see Clough 1981c, XI, 202–218. In another essay, Clough points out that Polidoro Virgilio (about whom see below, pages 41–43) made the link between Guidobaldo's proposed advocacy with the pope on Henry VII's behalf and his Garter investiture in an early draft of his *Anglica historia*, but later eliminated this material so as not to cause Henry VIII embarrassment in the wake of his divorce, thus rendering Henry VII's gesture toward Guidobaldo entirely magnanimous; see Clough 1981b, XIII, 780–782.

71 For an account of Castiglione's time in England, see Cartwright 1908, vol. I, 179–187. Clough initially maintained that Raphael's *St. George and the Dragon*, now in the Louvre, was taken to England by Castiglione as a gift to Henry VII from Guidobaldo, but he later came to the conclusion that there is no evidence the painting was ever even in the Tudor collection; see Clough 1981c, XI, 202.

72 Baldassare Castiglione, *Ad Henricum VII*, in *Le lettere di Baldassar Castiglione*, Guido La Rocca, ed. (Milan: Mondadori, 1978), 173: "Cum vero me tam humaniter tam honorifice a Tua Maiestate susceptum intellexisset, dignitate ac muneribus auctum, non poterat quin omnibus summa hilaritate et gaudio meas hisce de rebus litteras ostenderet." For the full text of the letter, with a (not always reliable) Italian translation, see 164–198.

73 Castiglione, *Cortegiano*, 31: "... che ognun dica ciò che crede che signifchi quella lettera, che la signora Duchessa porte in fronte; perché avvenga che certamente questo ancor sia un artificiale velame per poter ingannare, per avventura si gli darà qualche interpretazione da lei forse non pensata ..."

74 See Clough 1981c, XI, 217.

75 Hereafter referred to as *Epistola*. The earliest manuscripts of the letter – the presentation copy for Henry VII, and the one used for the 1513 print edition published in Fossombrone (of which only five copies are extant) – have disappeared, though not before J. Anstis, in his 1724 *Register of the Most Noble Order of the Garter*, noted the presence of Castiglione's collar on the title page of the copy he had consulted; see Clough 1981a, XIV, 232 n. 16. The not entirely completed manuscript seen here, Amherst College Library Ms. B3 n. 3, was copied by the ducal librarian in Urbino, Federico Veterani, as a personal gift to Castiglione; see Clough 1981a, XIV, 238–240.

76 The only passage in the *Cortegiano* in which Guidobaldo is explicitly discussed, I.3, forms an impression of the duke that understandably leads to these varying takes on Castiglione's attitude toward him, but the *Epistola* provides a much fuller account of both the challenges Guidobaldo faced – suggesting that they were on a different scale from those that his father had confronted – and the early accomplishments that he achieved. The assertion by Kinney 1989, 99, that "at their best, Guidobaldo's actions mock Federico's," is simply untenable in the light of the *Epistola*. Written during the period of mourning following the duke's death, Castiglione's letter issues from an immediacy to the history it recounts that is entirely missing from the *Cortegiano*, the temporal distance in this latter text a potentially distorting effect that Castiglione is clearly anxious about in it; see Berger 2000, 132.

77 *Epistola*, 175: "... sed Graecarum letterarum praecipuo tenebatur amore, eiusque linguae tam exactam adeptus erat cognitionem, ut non minus quam

patriam in promptu haberet; curavit voces propriis accentibus ac aspirationibus graecanico more proferre. In adolescentia assiduae lectionis fuisse traditur; extremo autem tempore, non satis multum, sed felici ac inexhausto memoriae thesauro iuvabatur, qua omnes homines (mea quidem sententia) superavit. Quicquid enim semel aut iterum audivisset, adeo tenaciter percipiebat, ut non modo sensum, sed et verborum seriem ipso quo erant ordine scripta memoriter continuo referret. Poetas summatim attigit: Virgilium tamen Homerumque familiarissimos habuit; dicendo figuras, lepores, variamque in eis rerum omnium scientiam, maiestatem, abundantiam, divinamque ingenii vim inspiciebat, exacteque pernoscebat ac admirabatur. Atque adeo feliciter omnia memoriae mandaverat, ut quodcumque ex ipsis carmen audiret, caetera ipse subsequeretur ad satietatem usque audientium."

78 Javitch 1983, 18–21, has suggested that the verbal games of the *Cortegiano*, far from excluding Guidobaldo, are actually directed at his physically absent but authoritatively present self.
79 For a discussion of these opposing styles and aims, see D'Ascia 1989, 51–69.
80 Berger's suggestion that Castiglione, in writing of Urbino in the *Cortegiano*, is "writ[ing] its death ... [engagaing in] an act of thanatography," further underscores the utility of reading the later treatise in tandem with the *Epistola*; see Berger 2000, 165.
81 *Epistola*, 187: "Quid, inquit, mihi, exoptatissimum bonum invidetis? Nonne quicquid me ab hac dolorum congerie atrocissima liberaverit, id optimum fateamini necesse est?" Et cum rursus paulum conticuisset, ad me conversus, Virgilii carmina haec pene subiciens: "Dum hanc, dixit, vivo, vitam,

> Me circum limus niger et deformis harundo
> Cocyti tardaque palus inamabilis unda
> Alligat et novie[n]s Stix interfusa coercet."

82 See D'Ascia 1989, 68–69, whose astute reading of this scene I follow closely here.
83 *Epistola*, 187: "Paulatim itaque deficiens coepit rarum ac difficilem habere sermonem. Sed quiescenti similis obticebat."
84 In contrast to the picture of Guidobaldo in *Cortegiano* I.3, where it might be appropriate to argue (as Berger 2000, 165, does) that Guidobaldo's heroism is "alien to the values of courtiership," this is a judgment more problematic to sustain within the context of the *Epistola*.
85 *Epistola*, 194.
86 D'Ascia 1989, 68.
87 Hay 1952, 1–20, provides a précis of Virgilio's career in England and a thorough discussion of the *Anglica historia*, 79–168. Hay also produced a critical Latin text and English translation of the last two books of Virgilio's history, with an introduction: *The Anglica historia of Polydore Vergil A.D. 1485–1537*, Denis Hay, ed. (London: Royal Historical Society, 1950). For a more recent appraisal of the *Anglica historia* from an Italian perspective, see Gabrielli 1986; and for Virgilio's career in general, see Ruggeri 1992 and 2000.
88 See Hay 1952, 150.

89 *Anglica historia*, 231. The sentiments expressed here were deeply felt, for Virgilio was actually imprisoned in the Tower of London for eight months in 1515 at Wolsey's command, a result of both Virgilio's dogged determination to regain the deputy collectorship and Wolsey's effort to use the office as one of the inducements in the course of his ultimately successful bid for a cardinal's red hat; see *Anglica historia*, ix–x. For a critical assessment of Virgilio's appraisal of Wolsey as well as of the Italian's account of the early English Reformation, see Guy 2003.
90 S. Rossi 1969, 39.
91 *Anglica historia*, xxxiv. S. Rossi notes that Virgilio also demonstrates that the myth of Brutus, supposedly descended from Aeneas and the progenitor of the English royal line, was in fact the twelfth-century invention of Geoffrey of Monmouth; see S. Rossi 1969, 37, and 37–38 n. 16.
92 An Italian astrologer active in the early Tudor court, Gulielmus Parronus Placentius, had earlier suggested that the Cornish belief in Arthur's imminent return was as ridiculous as the conviction of those who still believed that Edward V and his brother had survived Richard III's reign of terror; see Armstrong 1960, 433–454. Anglo 1992, 49–56, argues that the significance of Tudor Arthurianism has been grossly exaggerated, but if this were so it would be difficult to account for the reaction to Virgilio's deliberate exclusion of the Arthurian material from the *Anglica historia* and, most tellingly, entirely ignores later Tudor developments that culminate in Spenser's *Færie Queene*.
93 See Higham 2002, 236–237, for an assessment of Virgilio's anti-Arthurianism and its reception in Tudor England.
94 See Lindley 1991, 261–262, n. 3.
95 The only full-scale study of Nagonio is Gwynne's 1990 unpublished PhD dissertation; Wormald 1951, 118–119, provides a list of extant works.
96 York Minster Library Ms. XVI N2, written between 1496 and 1502, contains three books of poems addressed primarily to the king, including a *pronosticon* of 1,320 hexameters, with several shorter pieces dedicated to Prince Arthur.
97 See Gwynne 1992.
98 Meyer 1976, 358–367, assumes that Mazzoni arrived in England after Henry's death in 1509, but Galvin and Lindley 1988, 892–902, argue – based on documentary evidence that Meyer apparently misread – that Mazzoni's design was submitted to the king before his own ideas had been formulated. I follow Meyer's description of the design but the chronology of Galvin and Lindley.
99 Cited by Meyer 1976, 358–360.
100 See Vasari, *Le vite*, vol. IV, 123–128. Vasari's judgment about Torrigiano's value as an artist should be taken with a grain of salt, however, given that he never saw any of the work that Torrigiano produced in England or Spain.
101 Benvenuto Cellini, *La vita*, xii–xiii, Guido Davico Bonino, ed. (Turin: Einaudi, 1973), 26–27: "... veniva di Inghilterra, dove era stato di molti anni; e perché egli era molto amico di quel mio maestro, ogni dí veniva da lui; e veduto mia disegni e mia lavori, disse: 'Io son venuto a Firenze per levare più giovani che io posso; ché, avendo a fare una grande opera al mio Re, voglio, per aiuto, de' mia Fiorentini; e perché il tuo modo di lavorare e i tua disegni son più da scultore che da orefice, avendo da fare grande opere di

bronzo, in un medesimo tempo io ti farò valente e ricco' ... sue bravurie con quelle bestie di quegli Ingilesi ... 'Questo Buonarotti e io andavamo a 'mparare da fanciuletti innella chiesa del Carmine, dalla cappella di Masaccio: e perché il Buonarotti aveva per usanza di uccellare [befare] tutti quelli che disegnavano, un giorno in fra gli altri dandomi noia il detto, mi venne assai più stizza che 'l solito, e stretto la mano gli detti sí grande il pugno in sul naso, che io mi senti' fiaccare sotto il pugno quell'osso e tenerume del naso, come se fusse stato un cialdone: e così segnato da me resterà insin che vive.' Queste parole generono in me tanto odio, perché vedevo continuamente i fatti del divino Michelangelo, che non tanto ch'a me venissi voglia di andarmene seco in Inchilterra, ma non potevo patire di vederlo."

102 See Darr 1992, 112. Darr has also uncovered documentation clarifying significant aspects of Torrigiano's early work in Tuscany and in Rome, see 109–121; for his relationship with Francesco Piccolomini, one of England's cardinal protectors (later, briefly, Pope Pius III), and who very likely played a role in Torrigiano's English career, see 110.

103 For a chronology of Torrigiano's English experience, see *ibid.*, 121–126.

104 See Galvin and Lindley 1988, 900–901, and 901 n. 39.

105 *ibid.*, 895–899, provide a technical discussion of their evidence regarding the effigy, whose face mould they argue was also used for the bust of Henry VII. The translation of such a face mask into a life-sized terracotta piece would have involved choosing between a technique to reduce the shrinkage of the clay in drying and firing it, or compensating through advance calculation for the loss of mass, but "whichever technique Torrigiano adopted, it is apparent that he had mastered it to a high degree of accuracy," 899.

106 See *ibid.*, 901.

107 Margaret was the great-granddaughter of John of Gaunt, Duke of Lancaster, one of Edward III's sons. Her marriage in 1455 to Edmund Tudor, Earl of Richmond and half-brother of Henry VI, provided her with a further link to the English royal line.

108 Darr 1992, 122; for a discussion of the extant documentation regarding the design of the Beaufort tomb, see Darr 1979, 182.

109 Pope-Hennessy 1972, 219. For this description of the monument, see Darr 1992, 122; Darr, Torrigiano entry in *Grove*; and Darr 1979, 177–184.

110 Cited by Darr 1992, 122.

111 Darr 1992, 122 and 125. Two sculptors, Antonio di Piergiovanni di Lorenzo da Settignano and Giovanni Luigi di Bernardo di Maestro Jacopo da Verona, were also recruited by Torrigiano, but I have found no further information about either of them. For Toto del Nunziata, none of whose work survives, see Mary Edmond's *Grove* entry. Toto and another Florentine, Bartolomeo Penni, worked regularly for Henry VIII, Toto being promoted to 'Sarjeant Painter' in 1544; he continued to be employed by Edward VI in designing court revels, dying in London in 1554.

112 Darr *Grove*, which also provides a complete account of the extant works in England convincingly attributed to Torrigiano. Coe 1972, 514, adds an item to the catalogue: a portrait medal of Federico da Montefeltro, made in London in 1509, one of the very few Renaissance medals cast there; Coe does not account for

the occasion of the medal, however, which, given the recent death of Guidobaldo da Montefeltro in 1508 (Federico had died in 1482), seems incongruous.

113 Paolo Giovio, *In vitam Leonis decimi*, in *Opera*, vol. VI, Michele Cataudella, ed. (Rome: Istituto Poligrafico e Zecca dello Stato, 1987), 103: "pessimumque omen immentibus mortis in ipso cubiculi limine accepit in quo constiterat architectus ligneam offrens sepulchri effigiem, quod tum insigni marmoris caelatura Henrico regi in Brittania parabatur."

114 See M. Mitchell 1971, 178–196, which I have relied on for what follows here.

115 For a transcription of Sellaio's letter and the relevant passage from Speed, see *ibid.*, 201–203.

116 There is no mention of the monument in the *Memoriale* of Bandinelli's career, long thought to be his own writing but now ascribed by Waldman 2001, 235, to the sculptor's grandson, Baccio the Younger. Darr 1992, 124–125, notes that "until now, no other references for this monument and tomb (or tombs) were known. The discovery of new references written between September 1522 and January 1523 recording the delivery in London of three models for Henry VIII's tomb is, therefore, highly significant." Sicca 2002, 170–174, suggests that the papal project for Henry's tomb follows upon Torrigiano's having abandoned it, a plausible (though conjectural) hypothesis; she also discusses the documents related to two of the tomb models which arrived in London from Italy.

117 See Vasari's entry on Bandinelli, see *Le vite*, vol. V, 245; and M. Mitchell 1971, 185.

118 For details here, I follow Lindley 1991, 263–278; see 272–273 for drawings of a "conjectural reconstruction" of the tomb.

119 On Giovanni da Maiano's subsequent career in England, see *ibid.*, 280–288.

120 Nicholas Bellin da Modena, who may have studied with Giulio Romano in Mantua, was perhaps the most important Italian artist resident in England from the 1540s through his death in London in 1569. Having worked closely with Primaticcio at Fontainebleu before going to England, Bellin executed similarly fine stucco-work for the palaces at Whitehall and Nonsuch. On Bellin, see Martin Biddle's *Grove* entry; for Federico Zuccaro's brief visit to England, see Ch. 3, page 146.

121 On Dati, see *DBI*, vol. XXXIII, 29–31. From a prominent Florentine family, Dati was at this time in exile for having participated in anti-Medicean pranks, including the burning of the Villa at Careggi; but by 1542 he had returned to Florence rehabilitated, where he assumed a succession of minor regional political offices and translated Tacitus. He participated with Bernardo Davanzati in the Florentine discussions over *la questione della lingua* that led to the establishment of the Accademia della Crusca, about which see Ch. 5, pages 221–223.

122 Pier Riccio, Letter, November 3, 1547 (Florence: Archivio di Stato, Fondo Mediceo del Principato) 1176, 3, 489v: "... qui a certi porti di Fiandra erano venuti vascelli dove erano su tavole d'altari bellissime et reliquieri et imagini di sancti che si vendevano et erano venduti da Londra, spogliatene quelle chiese, come cosa idolatria, et botteghe di preti."

123 See Saygin 2002, 88–97, for a useful discussion of the significant role that Piero Da Monte, papal collector and nuncio in England from 1435 to 1440, played

in the power struggle between Humphrey, Duke of Gloucester and Henry Beaufort over control of the English political situation under Henry VI.
124 Wilkie 1974, 9–10; see 5–11 for my general account of the varieties of papal representatives. Wilkie's study is the most thorough examination of the role of the cardinal protectors and early Tudor England.
125 Two of England's cardinal protectors, Piccolomini and Giulio de' Medici, went on to be elected pope, as did one of its nuncios, Gianpietro Caraffa; Galeotto della Rovere, a nephew of Pope Julius II, served as cardinal protector from 1505 to 1508.
126 On Giovanni dei Gigli, see *DBI*, vol. LIV, 674–676; and for what follows here regarding him and other Italian clerics as English bishops, see Creighton 1902, 202–234. For a sampling of the dispatches that Gigli sent from England to Innocent VIII and Alexander VI, see Pelisser 1901, 479–480 and 588–594; and on Gigli's literary activity, see Carlson 1988, 284–285.
127 Wilkie 1974, 14.
128 On Silvestro, see *DBI*, vol. LIV, 690–693.
129 Wilkie 1974, 14–15.
130 See *DBI*, vol. XVII, 665–671, for a summary of Castellesi's life and career.
131 Wilkie 1974, 29 and 49.
132 *ibid.*, 30.
133 *ibid.*, 106–108.
134 Castellesi's treatise is discussed at length in D'Amico, 1983, 169–188; for a brief treatment of it, see Cantimori 2002, 21–22.
135 The most thorough study of Griffi's life and work is the first part of Michele Monaco's edition of the *De officio collectoris in regno Angliae* (Rome: Edizioni di Storia e Letteratura, 1973), 2–22; for Griffi in England, see 42–51 and 54–75, which is also of interest for its discussion of papal representation in England. For an earlier overview of Griffi's activities in England, see Hay 1939, 118–128.
136 *ibid.*, 123.
137 Introduction to Griffi/Monaco *De officio*, 19.
138 For which see *ibid.*, 237–396; the original is Vatican Ottoboniano Latino Ms. 2948; another copy is BL Add. Ms. 15386.
139 About which, see Asher 2002, 315–330.
140 For a summary of Chiericati's life, see *DBI*, vol. XXIV, 674–681; the only monographic study of his career is Morsolin 1873.
141 See Wilkie 1974, 37.
142 Letters to Isabella, March 28 and April 15, 1517 (cited in Morsolin 1873, 25–26 n. 3): "El Reverendissimo Eboracense governa el tutto solo; nè la Maestà Regia se impazza in cosa alcuna; tutto [che] è rimesso in petto de Suo Reverendissimo Signore tanto pertinente al stato suo, quanto a le altre cose private del Regno; intanto che a noi altri non par di tractar con un Cardinale ma con un altro Re ... la Maestà del Re non se impazza in cosa alcuna, se non in darsi a' piaceri virtuosi et lassa tutto el cargo a lui, et quelli che hanno a negotiar, bisogna, che il tutto se faccia cum el Reverendissimo, el qual cum summa autorità, integrità et prudentia governa el tutto; et tanta observantia li porta la Maestà del Re, che non parla, se non per la bocca sua."

143 Greenblatt 2002, 73–101, discusses this site, but Chiericati's description of his visit to *il pozzo di San Patrizio* differs in many respects from Greenblatt's account of the textual history associated with the place, in that it is framed in decidedly anti-chivalric terms as critical of the Irish as it is anxious about its findings at Lough Derg. That a representative of Pope Leo X could visit the site as late as 1517 and find it still fully operative – Alexander VI having issued a bull in 1497 authorizing the destruction of the shrine on Saints Island (the nexus of activity was then transferred to Station Island, one of ten other islands in the lake) – suggests more about the enduring power of the imagination in popular piety than it does about the vicissitudes of ecclesiastical power. Greenblatt's conclusion, 101, citing a letter of the Bishop of Clogher – whom the English government had sent to suppress the site in 1632 – as "a sober enactment of a secular ritual of disenchantment, the transformation of a sacred space back into a mute heap of stones and dirt," nicely fits his thesis but not the history of the place, for there has remained a continuous Catholic presence at the site, even as its locus of activity shifted to the neighboring island, away from the idea of an actual opening into Purgatory to the experience of a purgative pilgrimage that Seamus Heaney represents in his cycle of poems, *Station Island*.
144 About which, see Haywood 2003.
145 Letter to Isabella, August 28, 1517, cited in Morsolini 1873, 88: "... comminciamo a trovar la gente bestiale ... ladri et ribaldi ..."
146 *ibid*., 90: "Il primo descripto fu Guarino da Durazzo, qual io cressi esser fabule." I have been unable to trace anything relevant to Guarino da Durazzo's identity or to this account of his visit to Lough Derg.
147 *ibid*., 91–92: "... le qual anche che sieno di pocho momento ... conoscendo il suo peregrino ingegno, che non sol vol intendere le cose grande, ma anche le minime."
148 Antonio Buonvisi, another Lucchese, may have traveled to England in Silvestro's company. A merchant dealing primarily in wool and jewels, Buonvisi also functioned as a banker to Henry VIII and developed excellent relations with Cardinals Wolsey and (later) Pole, and with Thomas Cromwell. Though he transferred the seat of his activities to Louvain in 1548, he continued to be involved financially with the English monarchy until his death there in 1558; see *DBI*, vol. XV, 295–299.
149 See Creighton 1902, 212–217, on Gigli's possible role in Bainbridge's death.
150 Wilkie 1974, 108–109.
151 Though de' Medici dismissed "England in general as a nation of which he possessed no great knowledge, and which he thought would not have required so much experience 'as France and other countries' "; see *ibid*., 117. As Clement VII, he later came to regret not having taken the English more seriously.
152 About whom, see below, pages 63–64.
153 On della Rena, see Pizzi 1956; and *DBI*, vol. XXXVII, 236–241.
154 Letters the two friends exchanged during the period when Erasmus was teaching at Cambridge give a good indication of their rapport; see Desiderius Erasmus, *Erasmus and Cambridge: The Cambridge Letters of Erasmus*, D. F. S. Thompson, trans., and H. C. Porter, ed. (Toronto: University of

Toronto Press, 1963), 107–108, 112–119, 123–128, 131–152, 157–159, and 166–175.
155 Rundle 1995, 74.
156 Andrea della Rena [Ammonio], *Andreae Ammonii carmina omnia*, Clemente Pizzi, ed. (Florence, Olschki, 1958), 19; for the full text of the poem, see 16–19.

> Neglectasque diu terras Astraea revisat,
>    Et profugas artes cogat abire malas.
> Cernis ut incipiant fluvii candescere lacte,
>    Arboribusque fluant roscida mella cavis.
> Aurea, si nescis, rediens Octavius orbi
>    Saecula restituit. Fausta precemur ero:
> Octavius Pylios Henricus vivat ad annos
>    Et cumulum supereat, cana Sibylla, tuum.
> Sit melior Nerva, Augusto felicior ipso,
>    Robore Traianum praestet et imperio.
> Quicquid agat, summis fortunet Iupiter, Albas
>    Puniceasque colat Phoebus uterque Rosas.

157 Rundle 1995, 74.
158 *DBI*, vol. XXXVII, 238.
159 For a survey of Campeggio's career, see *DBI*, vol. XVII, 454–462. For further details of his role in adjudicating Henry's marital crisis, see Gwyn 1990, 522–530, 539–540, and 587–589.
160 In *The Life of Henry VIII*, Shakespeare's Cardinal Campeius is, typically, entirely eclipsed by Wolsey.
161 Though for Campeggio this obligation must have come at a particularly inopportune moment, following closely on the heels of the heavy burdens he principally shouldered in dealing with the aftermath of the May 1527 Sack of Rome by troops of Charles V, Clement having fled the city for Orvieto in December; see Wilkie, 178–179. According to several not entirely reliable Italian Catholic accounts that we shall take up in the next chapter, Wolsey was pushing Henry to marry Marguerite d'Angoulême, the sister of Francis I (later the author of the *Heptameron*, she was at the time still married to Henri de Navarre); see Bernardo Davanzati, *Scisma d'Inghilterra* (Rome: Guglielmo Faccioto, 1602), 8–10. Campeggio had also earlier suggested that Mary Tudor be married to her bastard half-brother, Henry Fitzroy.
162 Gwyn 1990, 522–523, observes that "a decretal commission enabled the pope to pronounce sentence upon a particular case, conditional only upon certain facts being established by those to whom the commission was granted. In the decretal commission for Henry's case, the 'facts' under scrutiny were three, all related to the original dispensation granted so that Henry could marry his sister-in-law: Had the marriage between Henry and Katherine been necessary to preserve the peace between England and Spain? Had Henry agreed to the marriage in order to preserve this peace? Had Henry VII, Isabella, or Ferdinand died before the dispensation went into effect? The questions were so posed that not only was it easy to arrive at the factually correct answers, but the answers themselves would be precisely those that would most effectively undermine the validity of the dispensation ... it was to be laid down in the

decretal commission that it required the facts in only one of the three matters to be investigated to prove inconsistent with what was stated in the dispensation for the marriage to be declared invalid." Since the document was destroyed, it is impossible to determine how far Clement went along with this ruse, but given that it was destroyed by papal order one can safely assume that the solution it contained was in the king's favor.

163 Gwyn 1990, 526, notes that "in his younger days, apparently, Henry had been inclined to boast that he had found his wife a virgin. Now, this was the kind of thing that any husband might want to boast about, even in the special circumstances of a marriage to one's brother's widow, and anyway the boast might well have been untrue. Still, it was very awkward that he had made it and, worse, that it probably was true."

164 On Giberti, see *DBI*, vol. LIV 623–629; and Carley 2002, 99–128. For a concise review of the course of events regarding the divorce after the adjournment of the trial until Henry's excommunication by Clement in 1533, see Carley, 102–104. Giberti was involved in Reginald Pole's futile 1537 embassy to win Henry back to Rome, for which see Mayer 2000, 64. And Giberti was also an agent in the Roman scandal over the erotic engravings of Marcantonio Raimondi (whom Giberti had imprisoned) after Giulio Romano and Pietro Aretino's accompanying sonnets, which excited a great deal of interest in Elizabethan and Stuart England; see Ch. 4, page 321 n. 87.

165 On Vanni, see Pizzi 1956, 7–13; Bullock 1939, 53–55; and *DNB*, vol. XX, 134–135. Vanni, like Polidoro Virgilio, successfully negotiated the transition from Catholic priest to Anglican but, uniquely, repeated the whole process a second time, living through the Marian period – he also served as Edward VI's and Mary's ambassador to Venice from 1550 to 1556 – and well into the Elizabethan era, dying in 1563.

166 Among them Mariano Sozzini the Younger, who argued that the original dispensation for Henry to marry Katherine was invalid, the king thus being free to marry Anne Boleyn; see Grendler 2002, 463. On the Italian universities and Henry's divorce, see Surtz 1974; for the contributions of all the major European universities made to the controversy, see Bedouelle and Le Gal 1987; and for a profile of another of the Italians who wrote in Henry's favor, Giacomo Calco, see *DBI*, vol. XVI, 530–532. For his efforts, Calco was richly rewarded by Henry upon his arrival in England, but his early death in 1532 cut short a promising ecclesiastical career within the new English context.

167 Campeggio continued to hope that Henry would be reconciled with Rome, and after the death of Anne Boleyn he undertook a private initiative through his brother Marcantonio to this end; see Wilkie 1974, 226–233, on this ultimately unsuccessful mission.

## 2  Reformations

1 "The contemporary concept of a 'stranger', an 'alien' as defined by Coke, was 'one born in a strange country, under the obedience of a strange prince or country ... or as Littleton saith ... out of the leigeance of the King.' But he

that is born 'within the King's liegance is sometimes called a denizen ... the King's liegeman ... for *ligeus* is often taken for a natural subject' "; see Scouloudi 1985, 1. Though Coke's formulation is late (1628) for the parameters of this study, the reality that it aims to define is essentially the same.

2 Carlo Cappello's 1535 *relazione* to the Venetian Senate, in *Ambasciatori*, 53–58, provides a representative example, criticizing the new English legal and political arrangements: "In questa izola sono molto cative legi e constituzioni, non si regendo per lege imperiale, ma per lege a suo modo" [There are many bad laws and consitutions in this island, where they rule not by Roman law but by laws they have devised themselves]; he thinks little of Cromwell, whom he describes as a "persona bassa e di vil condizione" [a base person, possessing a vile character] but who is "ora il Gran Secretario e il primo apresso il re" [now the Secretary of State and the first in the king's circle]; of the king, Cappello notes that he is "dotati di singulari parti de l'animo e del corpo, come è bellezza, inzegno, lettere ecc. Ed è cosa maravegliosa come sia entrato in tanti errori e cattive opinioni" [gifted with very singular parts of both soul and spirit: handsome, talented, learned, etc. It is thus to be wondered at that he should have made so many mistakes and formed so many unfortunate opinions]. Cappello took his leave of the English king only the day before Henry's formal break with Rome.

3 Matteo Bandello, *La seconda parte de le novelle*, Delmo Maestri, ed. (Alessandria: Edizioni dell'Orso, 1993), II. 37, 310: "come agli Appi fu nativo d'esser nemici de la plebe romana e agli Scipioni vincer in Africa fu natale, così mi pare che di questi regi inglesi sia proprio d'estinguer quelli del sangue loro e perseguitar la nobiltà e far macello d'uomini ecclesiastici e rubar i beni de le chiese."

4 *ibid.*, 314: "un atamo di questa vostra gioia a pena occuperà, ove la infamia in ogni luogo abitato e in ogni tempo sarà predicata. Né solo sarete biasimato voi, ma tutti i vostri discendenti macchiati ne resteranno."

5 Pruvost 1937, 158.

6 See Kirkpatrick 1995, 242–246, for a discussion of Painter's collection.

7 Giovio's history is a jumble of unreliable sources, though as Pruvost argues, 150, "the *Descriptio*'s idealized portrait of [Reginald] Pole and his mission [in 1537, to win Henry back to the church] suggests a propagandistic intent unusual for Giovio and may have been his way of seeking to undo the harm done by Clement VII. It may also be evidence of a deeper connection between Giovio and reforming circles than might otherwise be thought."

8 Bandello, *Novelle,* II.62, 288: "Ma se io vorrò far il catalogo di quelli che a le sfrenate voglie del re non volsero consentire, io farò una nuova *Iliade*, perciò che non lasciò né monaci né frati ne l'isola, e infiniti n'ammazzò, disfacendo tutti i monasteri e guastando tutte le badie e dando i vescovadi a modo suo, senza autorità del sommo pontefice ... ma grandissima difficultà è che le cose comminciate con tristo e cattivo principio buon fine sortiscono già mai." Three other Bandello *novelle*, II.34, III.60 and IV.10, as well as the introduction to II.43, deal with figures in Henry's circle and with issues related to the king.

9 Kirkpatrick 1995, 235, suggests that "the narrative interest [of the story] wholly derives from a High Renaissance court and the lurid details of Henry's six marriages"; for a general discussion of Bandello and the *novella*, see Kirkpatrick 233–239.

10 Defending Henry's actions in the immediate wake of the English king's severing ties with the Roman church, Aretino notes Clement VII's hypocrisy in having granted a divorce to Duke Federico Gonzaga and having himself abandoned a lover whom he then relegated to a convent; the *Pronosticon* is found in a volume including Aretino's *Cortegiano*, Angelo Romano, ed. (Milano: Biblioteca Universale Rizzoli, 1989), 294–295; and see Larivaille 1997, 175.
11 Aretino, *Lettere*, vol. II, Francesco Erspamer, ed. (Parma: Ugo Guanda, 1998), 3–6; for the full Italian text, see Appendix I, pages 256–257.
12 But if so, Aretino may not have been well-informed as to Henry's current theological inclinations, as the earliest rapprochement between the newly aligned English church and continental reformers tended more toward the Lutheran position the king had previously written so pointedly against, and for which Aretino nursed a particular hatred. The notion of predestination is central to the Calvinist line of the Reformation, which would find its way into England partly through the presence of Italian Protestants under Calvin's sway and which had a determinate impact on the development of English ecclesiology during the Elizabethan period. But it was also a much-discussed topic, along with the attendant questions of justification and free will, among the Italian reformers, many of whom were well known to Aretino; see Thomas Mayer, *Reginald Pole, Prince and Prophet* (Cambridge: Cambridge University Press, 2000), 105–113.
13 This conjunction of events in the summer of 1542 is noted by Fulvio Tomizza in his historical novel about Pier Paolo Vergerio, *Il male viene dal nord* (Milan: Mondadori, 1984), 202. Vergerio was another of the Italian reformers – earlier a papal nuncio and then a Catholic diocesan bishop – whose extensive preparatory work among the German principalities for an ecumenical council to be convened with both Protestant and Catholic participation was among the chief casualties of the collapse of the reformed movement in Italy. Yates' suggestion, 1934, 20–21, that John Florio may have studied with Vergerio in Augsburg before returning to England as a young man is neither confirmed nor denied by Tomizza's richly documented novel.
14 An even more blatant indictment comes in a letter published in the first volume of Aretino's *Lettere* in 1538: "... et è miracolo maggiore che 'l Vergerio sendo orattore del Papa sia uomo da bene, fia come prima, che non è il matrimonio consumato dal re de Inghilterra senza aver invitato sua santità alle nozze" [... it is to be considered a greater miracle that [Pier Paolo] Vergerio being the pope's nuncio remains the decent man he was [before assuming the office], than that the King of England has consummated his new marriage without having invited His Holiness to the ceremony]. Aretino subsequently purged this passage, evidently having concluded that the path of rhetorical obfuscation exhibited in the dedicatory letter to Henry VIII was a more prudent strategy; see *Lettere*, vol. I, Francesco Erspamer, ed. (Parma: Ugo Guanda, 1995), 90–97, for both the original text of the letter and its published form.
15 *SF* 12, 189.
16 Though Aretino had hoped for an even more substantial reward: one of the numerous ecclesiastical benefices Henry had at his disposal after the suppression of the monasteries; see *Lettere*, vol. II, 3 n. 1.

17 Fragments of this story are recounted in a series of Aretino's letters, pieced together in Giammaria Mazzuchelli, *La vita di Pietro Aretino* [1763], and reprinted in *Lettere sull'arte di Pietro Aretino*, vol. III.1, Ettore Camesasca and Fidenzio Pertile, eds. (Milan: Edizioni del Milione, 1959), 48–49: Advised early in 1547 by a friend in London of the imminent payment to be made through Henry's representative in Venice, Edmund Harwell (about whom I have been unable to learn anything further), Aretino grew impatient, thinking that Harwell was trying to appropriate the money for himself, and imprudently put into circulation a story to this effect. Upon hearing the slanderous imputation, Harwell confirmed it through spies and then set out with armed guards to beat up on Aretino, which, once done, left the writer with a broken arm and Venice's gossip machine abuzz. Uncharacteristically, Aretino responded to this attack with a reserve that eventually won him, in 1548 and well over a year after Henry's death, both his money and an apology from Harwell. Aretino was understandably a bit touchy about the subject of English money, given that two years earlier a young man with whom he had enjoyed a sexual entanglement, Ambrogio Eusebi, had abandoned him only to then trade on Aretino's name in several European courts as far as his powers of persuasion could take him; he managed to elicit a gift of 200 *ducati*, allegedly on Aretino's behalf, in forged letters to Thomas Cromwell and Henry VIII. Eusebi never returned to Venice, but Aretino did receive a final letter from him in 1544 or 1545 from Paraguay, recounting fabulous and improbable adventures; see Larivaille 1997, 310–311.

18 This more temperate English version of the original title – *Il Pellegrino Inglese ne'l quale si defende l'innocente & la sincera vita de'l pio & religioso re d'Inghilterra Henrico Ottavo bugiardamente calonniato da Clemente VII & da gl'altri adultatori de la Sedia Antichristiana* – was published by J. A. Froude in 1861 from the copy of the *libretto* in the British Library, with a series of appendices that provide a useful overview of continental diplomatic reaction to Henry VIII's actions; see William Thomas, *The Pilgrim, A Dialogue on the Life and Actions of King Henry the Eighth*, ed. J. A. Fronde (London: Parker, Son, and Bourn, 1861). Explaining his dedication, Thomas writes to Aretino that Henry "hath remembered thee with an honourable legacy by his Testament, the which his enemies pretend proceeded from the fear that he had lest thou shouldest, after his death, defame him with thy wonted ill speech ... ", Thomas/Froude, *The Pilgrim*, 1, and missing from the Italian printed version; there is no evidence, however, that Aretino received any further payment from England beyond those previously collected.

19 Concolato 1995, 474, says that the book was printed in Paris and suggests that Thomas was not responsible for the Italian version, but she does not explain why or who might have been; the copy in the British Library is catalogued as having been published in Zurich.

20 Thomas/Froude, *The Pilgrim*, 3, and *Il Pellegrino Inglese ne'l quale si defende l'innocente & la sincera vita de'l pio & religioso re d'Inghilterra Henrico Ottavo bugiardamente calonniato da Clemente VII & da gl'altri adultatori e de la Sedia Antichristiana* (Zurich, 1552), A1v: "Essendo costretto per mia disgratia di abbandonare la dolce patria, & ricercare paesi forestieri non prima da me conosciuti, ne'l mese di Febraio. 1546. gionsi in Bologna famosa, & nobilissima

città d'Italia, la dove accompagnatomi con molti gentilhuomini, & essendo egualmente conosciuto da tutti per Inglese, fui strettamente interrogato de la natura, de la qualità, & de costumi de'l mio paese. Et particolarmente oltre ad ogn'altra cosa, con grand'ansietà fui richiesto circa lo stato de la Maiestà de la felice memoria de'l pio & religioso Re Henrico ottavo, già più giorni passato di questa vita."

21 On Thomas, see Adair 1924, 133–160; and Griffith 1961, 56–65. We shall return to his grammar and vocabulary in Ch. 5, pages 211–212.

22 S. Rossi 1966, 303–306, maintains that the English version preceded the Italian, but the precedence of either text is not really the central question here. The relevance of *Il Pellegrino* as a plausible index of Italian attitudes regarding Henry's divorce – even if the text does reflect a familiar Tudor spin to the issues surrounding it – rests on whether or not the points of contention to which Thomas responds are entirely of his own invention. Given the lack of evidence to the contrary, I assume here that, as an Englishman residing in Italy in the wake of Henry's divorce, Thomas would have encountered similar arguments to those he assigns his questioners, reflecting Italian Catholic concerns about the English king's conduct.

23 Thomas/Froude, *The Pilgrim*, 9, and *Il Pellegrino*, A7r: "Et già tutto' mondo l'ha conoscuito, & notato pe'l maggiore tyrano, che mai sia stato in Inghilterra."

24 S. Rossi 1966, 306.

25 Davanzati, *Scisma*, 72–73: "Amò le lettere, favorì gli scienziati; il sagramento dell'altare adorò, e prese in una specie; sarebbe Cattolico stato, se non era libidinoso, e prodigo; ogni donna che punto bella fosse, voleva; era di sottile ingegno, grave giudizio, spesso ebbro ... per la dannosa gola, di bellisimo giovane, si grassò, e sconcio uomo divenne, che non entrava per le porte, ne saliva la scale ... regnò 37 anni, 9 mesi, 6 giorni: 21 cattolico, 5 ambiguo, gli'altri scismatico."

26 On Davanzati, see *DBI*, vol. XXXIII, 97–103; and Enrico Bindi's introduction to an abridged edition of *Lo scisma d'Inghilterra* (Milan: Casa Editrice Bietti, 1933), 11–56.

27 Davanzati, *Scisma*, 4: "per non entrare ne' fatti della vivente ... " We shall return to Pollini later in this chapter when we come to Mary – the most balanced section of his book, and the least dependent on Sanders – and again in the next chapter, along with Davanzati, to discuss Elizabeth's condemnation of the *Historia*.

28 See Pellegrini's introduction to his edition of the *Relazione d'Inghilterra*, in *Un fiorentino alla corte d'Inghilterra, Petruccio Ubaldini* (Turin: Bottega d'Erasmo 1967), 9: "... uomo di corte, miniatore di non poco talento, a tempo perso poeta, memorialista, e forse anche spia." Pellegrini, *Relazione*, 7–55, fills out the picture of Ubaldini's career outlined in the *DNB*, vol. XX, 1–3, though he does little to situate Ubaldini's report against the historical record of the Edwardian period.

29 Bugliani 1991, 161.

30 There are at least three distinct versions of the *Relazione*, represented by eleven manuscripts copied in various hands, and now in archives scattered throughout Europe; see Maria Crinò's introduction to her edition, *La 'Relatione*

*d'Inghilterra' di Petruccio Ubaldini* [1583], in *Annali della Scuola Normale Superiore di Pisa, Classe di Lettere e Filosofia*, serie 3, vol. IX:2 (1979), 649–668. Bugliani 1991, 167–168, provides an account of this complex manuscript history and helpfully characterizes Ubaldini's text as an "instant book," written and rewritten as circumstances dictated. For the moment we shall be considering only the version of the *Relazione* transcribed by Pellegrini, as it alone contains the extensive treatment of the reign of Edward VI.

31 See Ubaldini/Pellegrini, *Relazione*, 50–54, for a discussion of Barbaro's *Relazione*, the scope of which, he argues, is more limited than Ubaldini's and markedly more polemical; Barbaro, also co-adjutant Patriarch of Aquileia and a forceful voice at the Council of Trent, was Ubaldini's most prominent Italian patron.

32 Ubaldini/Pellegrini, *Relazione* (as all citations here [within brackets]), 62–69.

33 *ibid.*, 77: "... quanto danno apporti alli stati la Fanciulezza de' Principi ...".

34 *ibid.*, 79: "... come causa di ogni disordine seguito; difendendosi egli però molto con la propria mano del Rè appresso de' popoli, mentre che egli havendolo seco gli faceva sottoscrivere quelle cose che sono in uso esser sotto scritte da i Rè, benche Pupilli; et per tal causa lo pubblicarono traditore della Corona."

35 The remarkable series of concessions granted in these letters, recognizing the legitimacy of the protesters' grievances, provided significant fodder for Seymour's downfall; see MacCulloch 1999, 42–51.

36 Elton 1963, 203; see 204–205 for a discussion of Seymour's undoing of several important Henrician legal restraints and the ensuing disastrous consequences, ammunition that Ubaldini fails to employ in his assault on Somerset.

37 Ubaldini/Pellegrini, *Relazione*, 79: "alcuni di miglior giudicio, et del futuro disordine presaghi."

38 See Elton 1963, 208; and Loach 1999, 92–93.

39 The idea that Seymour bought his freedom is flatly contradicted by Loach 1999, 93, who shows that he had paid an inital £10,000 as recognizance upon release from the Tower to house-arrest, but that three weeks later he was freely pardoned by the king.

40 Ubaldini/Pellegrini, *Relazione*, 79: "così come la sua libertà seguì per il Matrimonio di una sua Primogenita nel suo primo Maschio, la qual fanciulla il Duca prima non haveva mai così voluta maritare, havendo rispetto alla ignobilità di esso Conte; pagando, oltre ciò la Duchessa di Somerset gran somma di danari mal' acquistati al Conte, quasi che premio di una debita taglia." Loach 1999, 101, cites BL Add. Ms. 48023, fol. 350, which suggests that Dudley, fearing a plot against his life, did not even attend the ceremony.

41 See Loach 1999, 101–102.

42 Ubaldini/Pellegrini, *Relazione*, 79: "pagò la pena della guasta Religione, et del male amministrato Regno, et della morte del sig.or Semer suo fratello, poco avanti (forse à torto) condannato." See Loach 1999, 103–104, for a discussion of BL Harleian Ms. 2194, fols. 19–20 (used by John Hayward in his *Life and Raigne of King Edward the Sixth*) which calls into question the lack of feeling historians have generally ascribed to Edward regarding the death of his uncle: the regret Edward expresses here may be what "the early seventeenth-century

historian believed Edward ought to have felt, rather than compelling evidence that he did feel such emotions. And yet the possibility remains that Hayward or the author of the Harleian Ms. was drawing on credible memories."
43 See, for instance, Bugliani 1994, 175.
44 Ubaldini/Pellegrini, *Relazione*, 81: "se non è gentilhuomo della Camera, del qual grado molti gran Signori sono esclusi; et qui usa ordinariamente il Rè mangiare; la seconda è questa contigua, della quale il Rè si serve per parlare, et per mangiare in secreto, cioè, in vista di pochi suoi Ministri; la terza serve per vestire, et spogliare il Rè, havendo questa la Ombrella, come nella sala di Presenza dissi, essere, insieme con gli altri ornamenti. Nella quarta, che manca di Ombrella, è posto un letto per il Rè, riccamente ornato; essendo congionta à queste Camere la scuola, la Capella segreta, et alcune altre stanze, et Poggiuoli."
45 *ibid.*, 96: "parla e scrive quello che vole."
46 See Girolamo Pollini, *Historia ecclesiastica della rivoluzion d'Inghilterra* (Rome: Facciotti, 1594), 205; in the first edition (Bologna, 1591), 224–227, this accusation is made of the educational system in general.
47 Ubaldini/Pellegrini, *Relazione*, 98: "usasi ancora molte ceremonie, quando alcuna delle due sorelle và a mangiar seco ... a quelle non è lecito stare sotto l'ombrella, nè sedere sopra Cadrega, ma solamente sopra un semplice scabello, con un cuscino, non già nella testa della tavola, ma appunto tanto lontano dal Rè, quanto basti, che l'ombrella non gli soprastia, et dalla parte pur di dentro ... le ceremonie, che troppo usano avanti che si mettino à tavola, quasi sono ridicole; perchè ho veduto cinque volte inginocchiarsi Madama Helisabeth avanti che la sedesse, come le fanno ancora quando, che gli parlano."
48 *ibid.*, 98: "Nell'andare ò tornare il Rè da gli Uffici, ò solazzi, segli può porgere suppliche, et anche qualche volta parlarci; ma l'una cosa, et l'altra è patita mal volontieri da chi lo governa (indicio appunto de' loro cattivi portamenti)."
49 *ibid.*, 98–99: "nota qualcosa, di quello, che gli par detto da i Predicatori à proposito; et perchè à certi tempi, ò dati, ò riprensioni, fatte da quelli, è stato veduto scrivere, et poi non volendo si vegga quello, che dentro habbia scritto, ha dato occasione à popoli di sperar bene di lui, et di portargli amore ... massime perche hà cominciato à volere spedire molte cose; et vuole che tutte le gratie siano riconosciuto dalla sua viva parola et non da i particolari favori."
50 *ibid.*, 99: "Essendo un'altra volta in un barco, et parlando in presenza di tutta la Corte con suoi Strozzieri, volse vedere un falcone, lodato per il migliore di tutti, et havutolo, comandò che così vivo fosse tutto pelato, con meraviglio però di ciascuno; pellolo lo Strozziero, et gnene rimostra; et egli così disse. Questo Falcone così buono sopra gli altri è spogliato, così io maggior' de'gli altri del Regno sono concio."
51 Elton 1963, 202, is typical in this regard.
52 The compelling portrait that MacCulloch 1999 paints of the young king seriously and increasingly committed to a radical religious reformation he came to understand deeply is a far cry from what Ubaldini sought to praise about Edward.

53 Other well-informed sections of the *Relazione* that cannot be reasonably addressed here deal with English law [100–112]; a description of London [113–116]; the military [116–124]; royal accounts and expenditures [136–143]; and a perceptive consideration of the English temperament [143–152].
54 Ubaldini/Pellegrini, *Relazione*, 126: "la pianta dell'Arbore, che tanti mali hà generato, non solamente all'hora sopra tutti i monasteri Religiosi, mà di poi più empiamente sparsi sopra la testa di ciascuno."
55 *ibid.*, 127: "... l'Archivescovo di Cantauria, primo del regno frà i Prelati, et però nominato Primate; il quale veste habiti consueti, et esamina li Predicatori, li Dottori degli studi Publici; i sacerdoti, et tutti quelli, co' quali s'habbia à parlare dell'interessi della Fede, riferendo ogni cosa al Consiglio Regio, dove si fà poi deliberatione. Questo è huomo dotto, et molto da loro stimato nelle sacre lettere, ma profanamente, poichè egli scrivendo, et assai parlando da fomento alla loro pessima conditione."
56 As Florio defines "profano" in *QA*, 403.
57 Ubaldini/Pellegrini, *Relazione*, 135: "l'istessa dottrina."
58 *ibid.*, 127: "dovendosi osservar queste regole nella loro lingua natia, solamente in quei luoghi, dove la lingua inglese s'intende, et si parla, peroche la Wallia, et l'altre Isole sottoposte al Regno, non sono ubligate à leggere le medesime leggi, se non latine, ò vero nella loro lingua, essendo in Cantbrigge, et in Ossonia ... solamente concedute le prece nelle stesse forme latine, grece, et hebraiche, fuor che la cena dominicale; et questo per essercitare gli scolari alle diverse lingue."
59 *ibid.*, 127: "lasciando i Risponsi, Invitatorij, con tutte quelle cose, che nelle vecchie Ceremonie, non erano tutte nella Bibia."
60 Graff 1987, 151–163, notes that even in the wake of the Reformation, illiteracy in England remained quite high in this period; advances in literacy varied widely between regions but were clearly tied to the more privileged classes (women's literacy remained behind the level of male manual laborers); see also Cressy 1980 and 1981. For the impact of Tyndale's biblical translations on the literate, see Greenblatt 1980, 96–97.
61 Elton 1963, 206.
62 Ubaldini/Pellegrini, *Relazione*, 128: "si leggono le litanie, levatone le prece à i Santi, non invocando altro che solo Dio Padre, Dio Figliuolo di Spirito Santo [the relationship among the persons of the Trinity is one of the most controversial issues in early Christian theology – it remains today at the center of the schism between the Orthodox and Roman churches – and because Ubaldini clumsily stumbles into the breach here, in my translation I have straightened out his formulation, surely a careless mistake rather than a theological statement], Santa Benedetta, et gloriosa Trinità, seguendole nel resto come debbono stare, aggiungendovi poi queste parole: dalla tirannia et insidie del Vescovo di Roma liberaci o Signore."
63 *ibid.*, 128: "in luogo della Cenere, accomodata per la pubblica penitenza, et si recitano à un certo tempo alcune maledittioni del Deuteronomio al cap. 27, et altre di altri luoghi, si maledicono coloro che faranno statue, ò simulacri per man di artefice, per adorarli."
64 *ibid.*, 128–129: "il Prete sappia circa l'hore mattutine la vita di chi s'habbia à cumunicare, la quale se sarà di sorte, che possa scandalizzare, il Prete lo

avvertirà, non debba prendere la Communione se non habbia mostra la sua penitentia, et emendata la sua natura, et sodisfatto al prossimo dove il Prete, conoscendo fintione alcuna, può secondo alcune constitutioni ... procedere."
65 *ibid.*, 132–133: "L'inginocchiarsi, il far la Croce con le braccia, l'alzar le mani, e il batter il petto, si lascia alla discretione, et coscienza di chi vole più o meno usarle senza riprensione, ò carico."
66 *ibid.*, 135: "essendovi molto pesce, et molti pescatori poveri, le carni si conservino, et quelli possino invece vivere del guadagno della pescagione; havendo però opinione di voler mutare tutte queste astinentie della carne in altri tempi, et in altri giorni. Però che tenendole per ordinationi delli Papi i quali odiano, vorriano anchora cavarsi questa altra bizzarria."
67 *ibid.*, 135: "... quattrini otto; et questa è parte dell'entrata del prete, consegnatali dal Consiglio Regio, però nessuno manca di mandare; al qual prete perchè quella non basta, per provisione si dà molto di più, di quello della Corona, che possa vivere, essendo le vere entrate delle chiese confiscate, et non si usando per le Chiese dar limosine per gli uffici; non vengono ad havere altri straordinarij, di quelli, che per li morti ricevono, che consistono in qualche torcia, et in pochi soldi per la sepoltura."
68 *ibid.*, 135: "ne' fa la penitenza, trovandosi co' figliuoli suoi ed di altri in povertà, et senza parte alcuna dove s'habbia da altri ad haver devotione ... non si potranno havere se non donne ignobili, et povere, perchè pur si abhorisce simil sorte di parentela dagli altri; onde avviene che da ciascuno sono lodati quelli, che non la prendono; benchè per uno uso causato da' cattivi pensieri, paia che poco bene si possa pensare della castità di questi."
69 *ibid.*, 134 and 136: "non sono imagini di rilievo, nè pitture, non croci, non sepolchri alti da terra ... luogo dell'altare è posta la mensa apparecchiata con una tovaglia, et senza lumi ... et perchè le mura delle chiese, come io hò detto, sono senza pitture di santi, per le bianche facciate di quelle sono poste in scrittura molte sentenze del testamento vecchio, et nuovo, al loro proposito tirate, nel mezzo delle quali si vede lárme del Rè."
70 See Ubaldini/Pellegrini, 17–18; and Ch. 3, page 307 n. 48.
71 See Introduction, page 266 n. 10.
72 Pier Paolo Vergerio, *Al Serenissima Re d'Inghilterra Edoardo sesto. De portamenti di Papa Giulio III. Et quale habbia ad essere il concilio, che egli intende di fare* (1550), 1–2: "specialmente con quanta crudeltà & rabbia, egli per tutte le città d'Italia mandi fuori ministri & cernefici, i quali con ogni studio attendano a persequitare, & conculcare la pura dottrina di Giesu Cristo ... [ma] ella senza dubbio si rallegrerà, & ringratierà il celeste padre, il quale a lei, & a tutto il suo Regno, tanta felicità ha concesso di haversi potuto sbrigare, & in tutto dalle catene, & soggestione di quel vero Antichristo separati con gli animi, con la religione, con la obedientia si come ella ne è ... la sua fortunatissima Isola ben divisa, & separata."
73 Ubaldini/Pellegrini, *Relazione*, 136, negatively notes the presence in England of foreign theologians: "il Bucero, Alemanno, Bernardino da Siena, Pietro Martire, ò altri, di più nome, et di più scelerata vita" [Bucer, the German, Bernard of Siena, Peter Martyr, and still other even more wicked luminaries]. A third Italian, Emmanuele Tremellio, accompanied Vermigli to England at

Cranmer's invitation: he had been born to a Jewish family in Ferrara in 1510, studied ancient languages (including Syriac and Chaldean) in Padua, was converted to Catholicism by Reginald Pole sometime around 1540, and then fell under Vermigli's sway while teaching Hebrew in Lucca, accompanying him on his flight from Italy in 1542; he was appointed to the chair of Hebrew at Cambridge, but returned to the continent, again in Vermigli's company, after the death of Edward VI. Tremellio's translation of the Bible into Latin, published first in Geneva and Frankfurt, appeared in a quarto edition in London in 1580 and saw numerous editions well into the seventeenth century; this translation had the unique distinction of being accepted as authoritative by English and continental Protestants as well as by the Catholic theologians of Louvain and Douai; Philip Sidney, in *An Apology for Poetry* [or *The Defence of Poesy*] [1595], R. W. Maslen, ed. (Manchester: Manchester University Press, 2002), C2r, notes that "Tremellius ... entitle[s] the Poeticall part of the scripture, against [whom] none will speak that hath the holie Ghost in due holie reverence." A thorough study of this significant figure is long overdue, but in the meantime see *DNB*, vol. XIX, 1113–1114; and Becker 1887.

74 See Ruggeri 2003 for a discussion of Polidoro Virgilio's account of the early Anglican reform in his *Anglica historia*, which Ruggeri argues provided a pragmatic framework for Cranmer and his associates to follow.
75 Cited by M. Anderson 1975, 89.
76 To a striking extent, many of the most influential twentieth-century voices in Italian Renaissance historiography began their careers studying the Italian reformation, among them Benedetto Croce, Federico Chabod, Delio Cantimori, and Carlo Ginzburg. For the most comprehensive bibliography regarding the penetration of reformed religious thinking in Italy, see Tedeschi 2000, with an extensive introductory essay on the historiographical treatment of the issue by Massimo Firpo.
77 For a brief sketch of Valla's life and career, see Cantimori's entry in the *Enciclopedia italiana*, vol. XXXIV, 923–924.
78 Regarding the principles of Valla's philology, see Camporeale 1972, 101–146.
79 Cantimori 2002, 16.
80 Valla's treatise circulated extensively in manuscript before its appearance in print. For an English translation of selected passages, see *The Profession of the Religious, and the Principal Arguments from 'The falsely-believed and forged Donation of Constantine'*, Olga Zorzi Pugliese, trans. (Toronto: Centre for Reformation and Renaissance Studies, 1985), 63–74; the complete Latin text, with an abbreviated English translation, can be found in *De falso credito et ementita Costantini donatione declamation*, Christopher B. Coleman, ed. and trans. (Toronto: University of Toronto Press, 1985); and for a concise discussion of Valla's argument and its reception, see Stinger 1998, 248–254. Ginzburg 1999, 54–70, has written about the Donation and its significance for the historiographical tradition.
81 Just as this book was going into production, J. B. Trapp brought to my attention a manuscript in the British Library, Harley Ms. 554, which I have so far been unable to study carefully: *The boke of the lyf of Wedows, made by frere Hierome Savonarole of Ferrare, of Seynt Domynik's Ordre, at the desire &*

*contemplacion of many devoute wedows*. Dating from the 1490s, this translation is thus among the very earliest examples of an Italian text made into English and demonstrates the contemporary immediacy of English interest in Savonarola's reforming work.
82 For a full account of Savonarola's impact on Italian reform, see Polizzotto 1994.
83 See Albertini 1970, 136–140.
84 Bartolomeo Cerretani, *Dialogo della mutazione di Firenze*, Giuliana Berti, ed. (Florence: Olschki, 1993), 7: "gli scritti del quale sendo comparsi in Italia et maximamente a Roma ... fanno argumento che costui debbe essere per costumi, dottrina, e religione prestantissimo e parci che le sue conclusioni sieno molto proprie e conforme all'opinione et vita della primitiva chiesa militante." On Cerretani, see *DBI*, vol. XXIII, 806–809; Cantimori 2002, 34–35; and Polizzotto 1994, 164–167, who argues that among the *piagnoni* Cerretani's enthusiasm for Luther was not universally shared.
85 Castelli 1938, 225–252, provides a discussion and transcription of the entire poem; see Appendix I, pages 257–258, for the original Italian; on Ceffino, see *DBI*, vol. XXIII, 321–323.
86 M. Firpo 1998, 88.
87 See *ibid.*, 72; and 61–81, for what follows here regarding Valdés.
88 *ibid.*, 64.
89 *ibid.*, 73.
90 See M. Firpo's introduction to his edition of Juan Valdés' *Alfabeto cristiano*, (Turin: Einaudi, 1994), particularly cxii-cl; and also Dell'Olio's review of this edition, 1995, 878–881. Firpo's essay, vii-cl, provides an excellent general introduction to Valdés' thinking.
91 Regarding the influence of Valdés on Pole's circle in Viterbo, where the English cardinal served as papal governor from 1541 to 1545, see M. Firpo 1993, 120–139; and 1990, 135–155; see Mayer 2000, 103–133, for a more general discussion of the *ecclesia Viterbiensis* and its principal actors; and on the ultimate failure of reform in Italy, see Cantimori 2002, 456–462.
92 In his unfinished "Michael Angelo" from 1893, Henry Wadsworth Longfellow takes up the spiritual friendship of Valdés and Giulia Gonzaga, making much of what he sees as their self-conscious heresy; see Nieto 1970, 25–26.
93 Dell'Olio 1995, 883.
94 Benedetto Croce defended Calvin's condemnation of Serveto on the grounds that the Spaniard's religious position subverted the new political order then developing; see Prosperi's introduction to Cantimori 2002, xxxvi–xxxviii; for Cantimori's own entirely different understanding of Serveto's fate, see 180–187.
95 See *ibid.*, 128–134, for a discussion of the development of Ochino's thinking in the period between 1542 and 1547, before accepting Cranmer's invitation to England.
96 Bainton 1941 remains the standard monograph on Ochino's career. Other helpful work on Ochino can be found in Campi 1994; Tedeschi 1973, 289–301; and Nicolini 1970. Recent editions of Ochino's writings include *Patterns of Perfection: Seven Sermons Preached in Patria*, John McNair, trans. (Cambridge: Anastasia Press, 1999); *Seven Dialogues*, Rita Belladonna, trans.

(Ottawa: Dovehouse Editions, 1988), and *I 'Dialogi sette' e altri scritti del tempo della fuga*, Ugo Rozzo, ed. (Turin: Claudiana, 1985).

97 "un Crisostomo moderno," in Philip McNair's felicitous phrase; see 1981, 231.

98 See the letter of Charles V's ambassador to England, François Van der Delft, in *Calendar of Letters, Despatches, and State Papers, Spain, 1547–1549*. Martin A. S. Hume and Royal Tyler, eds. (London: His Majesty's Stationery Office, 1912), 253, where the extent of Ochino's unpopularity is, however, likely exaggerated.

99 Van der Delft, *ibid.*, 266, characterizes Ochino and Vermigli as Cranmer's "pet children." Bainton 1941, 92, notes that Vermigli was granted the same royal pension.

100 Lady Cooke's translations were printed in two editions, in 1548 and 1551, and they were included in a slightly larger collection of Ochino's translated sermons published in 1570. On Elizabeth's translation, see Gabrielli 1983, 151–165; and 165–174 for his transcription of the text.

101 About which, see McNair 1981, 234.

102 McNair 1981 equivocates about the *Tragedie*, describing its perspective at one point as completely English, 235, and then later as a work of plagiarism, 239. Ochino obviously appropriated the structure and much of the substance, if not the actual language, of Kirchmayer's play, translating the German's Latin comedy by adapting its particulars to the English situation; in this, Ochino's "plagiarism" is little different from the practice of many, if not most, early modern imaginative writers.

103 *The Tragedie by Bernardino Ochino*, Constance E. Plumptre, ed. (London: Grant Richards, 1899), from which all citations [in brackets] within my text come. The original Latin text has not survived; see McNair 1981, 236–237.

104 There is no evidence that Ochino's play was ever staged, even partially, while Kirchmayer's *Pammachius* had been performed in Latin at Christ's College, Cambridge in 1545, and was shortly thereafter translated into English by John Bale (soon to be another of Ochino's acquaintances, and like him later to run into trouble over the question of polygamy) as *King John*; see McNair 1981, 240, and Bainton 1941, 96.

105 As MacCulloch 1999, 26–30, notes, Ochino's text was in Edward VI's library and manifestly influenced the young king's treatise written in French against papal supremacy between December of 1548 and August of 1549. (MacCulloch cites a second edition, also from 1549 but printed after Seymour's fall – and so with positive references to him omitted – which evidently lacks *A Tragedie* in its title.)

106 See Ostrogorsky 1968, 71–72.

107 See Martin Luther, *Address to the Christian Nobility of the German Nation Respecting the Reformation of the Christian Estate*, C. A. Bucheim, trans., in the *Harvard Classics* edition of Machiavelli, *The Prince*, etc. (New York: P. F. Collier, 1910), 310.

108 See Bainton 1941, 96.

109 See Tedeschi 1986, 127–151, as well as an expanded version of the same article, 1987, 19–61; and Cantimori 1975.

110 A telling example of the difficult cohabitation of Reform and Renaissance dates from 1529: Alfonso de Valdés – Juan's elder brother and Latin secretary

to Charles V – put into circulation in the Spanish court the manuscript of his own *Diálogo de las cosas ocurridas en Roma*, arguing both that Charles was essentially innocent of the atrocities committed by his troops in the Sack of Rome and that God had willed the catastrophe as "a just punishment of the corrupt clergy ... and for the good of humanity." The papal nuncio then in Spain, Baldassare Castiglione, reacted with uncustomary fury to Valdés' provocation, demanding that the work be destroyed. The resulting correspondence between Castiglione and Valdés reveals two increasingly divergent humanist tendencies: the Italian papal diplomat – whose *Cortegiano* had finally been published only the year before, in Rome – employing his rhetorical skills to defend the Catholic *status quo* (even while well aware that Clement VII's almost complete lack of political acumen had already rendered useless his mission in Spain); and the Spaniard utilizing his similar humanist training in order to make a call for radical change; see Fucelli 1989, 51–57.

111  See Bainton 1941, 98–99. Ubaldini neglects to mention this insurrection in his discussion of the English liturgy in non-English-speaking territories, perhaps unaware that in many areas of England itself the English language was still unevenly assimilated. See Loach 1999, 70–78, for a discussion of the "Western uprising."

112  The anti-Trinitarianism of the sixteenth century was a distant relative of Arianism, the fourth-century doctrinal controversy that denied the divinity of Christ and anticipated the full rejection of all earlier Christian dogmatic formulation in Unitarianism; see *The Oxford Dictionary of the Christian Church* (1974), 67–68 and 1408–1409, for useful summaries of the anti-Trinitarian and Unitarian positions.

113  Cantimori 2002, 252. The controversy over the publication of the *Triginta dialogi* is another example, like the burning of Serveto, of how quickly Protestant orthodoxy moved to adopt Catholic defensive strategies, in this instance only four years after the creation of the Index of Forbidden Books (about which see Ch. 5, pages 218–219). Ochino wrote these dialogues originally in Italian, and when he was informed by the official clerical censors of Zurich that he was not to publish them – and, additionally, that any further printing of his work would be subject to their approval – he went ahead anyway and issued the book in Latin, in Basel. This translation, by Sebastiano Castelliano, had already been in preparation for eight months when Ochino received word of the restriction on his freedom to publish, but he must have known he was asking for trouble in arguing that he was unaware the measure extended to any other Swiss city; see Cantimori, 250–259, for a discussion of both the publication controversy and the book's principal arguments.

114  For a discussion of Ochino's problematic position in the Swiss context, see Taplin 2003.

115  See McNair 1967, 127–136, and in general for the Italian context of Vermigli's later thinking.

116  *ibid.*, 179. James 1998, 151–187, argues that Vermigli himself had a forceful impact on Valdés' understanding of predestination, an idea that appears in the Spaniard's work precisely at the time of his meeting with Vermigli in Naples in 1538.

117 Schenk 1950, 152. With regard to the category of "heresy," I share Massimo Firpo's position in his review of Thomas Mayer's *Reginald Pole, Prince and Prophet* (Cambridge: Cambridge University Press, 2000) that the opposition between "orthodoxy" and "heterodoxy" is not, as Mayer maintains, an "unhelpful" distinction in this period; see Firpo 2001, 861. It is indeed absolutely fundamental to understanding the transformation of religious ideas and practice in the sixteenth century, but equally for appreciating the wider political and cultural implications of the Reformation and the Catholic reaction to it.

118 Similarly, in late sixteenth-century Spain heresy and sodomy were collapsed into the same charges brought against Antonio Perez; see *The Fugger Newsletters, 1568–1605*, Victor von Klarwill and Pauline de Chary, eds. (London: John Lane, 1924), 193.

119 On Vermigli's period in Lucca, see Adorini-Braccesi 1994, 109–143.

120 McNair 1980, 87, citing McLelland.

121 Latin would have served as the principal *lingua franca* of both Ochino and Vermigli with most of their English interlocutors. See M. Anderson 1975, 127–154, for a thorough examination of both Vermigli's influence on Cranmer and his specific contributions to Anglican liturgical, doctrinal and canonical developments under Edward VI.

122 Christ Church was, as McNair has observed, one of the first uniquely Protestant institutions in England, having been created by Henry VIII in 1546, and thus free of any prior papal association, though Vermigli's predecessor at Oxford, Richard Smith, was a convinced Catholic and lost the position as a result of his intransigence; see McNair 1980, 85–105. For further recent work on Vermigli, see Di Gangi 1993; Vermigli, *The Life, Early Letters and Eucharistic Writings of Peter Martyr*, J. C. McLelland and G. E. Duffield, eds. (Appleford, UK: Sutton Courtenay Press, 1989); and Kingdon 1980.

123 Having died and been buried in Oxford, Catherine Dampmartin Vermigli's remains were exhumed by deputies of Cardinal Pole during the Marian era and thrown "on a dung heap because of [their] proximity to the bones of St. Frideswyde in Oxford," an overly literal response to new burial regulations that Pole had enacted. An Elizabethan ecclesiastical commission later ordered Catherine's body reinterred in a grave *with* St. Frideswyde's relics; see M. Anderson 1975, 84.

124 On the combustible mix of issues in *First Corinthians* for Vermigli, see McNair 1980, 99–101.

125 See McNair 1967, 149–157.

126 For a full exposition of this issue, see Corda 1975. M. Anderson 1975, 97, notes that in its printed form Vermigli's Oxford debate on the eucharist was issued in five separate Latin editions before 1581, having appeared in English, Italian, and French translations in the 1550s. Foxe's *Book of Martyrs* also preserves a record of the debate, ensuring that its conclusions would be considered by several succeeding generations of English readers; see M. Anderson, 137–138. Aiming always at simplicity of form and expression, Vermigli summarized his position on the eucharist by saying that "we verily partake of the Thing of the

Sacrament, that is, the Body and the Blood of Christ; but so that I hold, that this is done by the mind and by faith"; translation cited in M. Anderson 105.
127 Erasmus had sold his personal library to Laski shortly before his death in 1536; see Huizinga 1952, 186.
128 The painting was long thought to have been a seventeenth-century "propaganda piece in the struggles between the Puritans of the Church of England and Archbishop Laud, who sought to close the Dutch Church in 1636," Orchard (forthcoming), thus legitimizing religious communities in England other than the official English church vis-à-vis the example of the first fully Protestant English king's donation of Austin Friars to the foreign Protestant congregations. But Orchard has determined that the painting was actually commissioned by Count Zinzendorf, patron of the Moravian Brethren, who established a center for the Moravian community at Lindsay House in London after securing legal recognition for the Moravians in England through an act of parliament in 1749. In this context, Haidt's representation of the royal gift of Austin Friars still served an ideological function, as Orchard shows, shoring up the doctrinal claims of the Moravians in response to a later phase in English ecclesial one-upmanship similar to the earlier Laudian crisis.
129 Italians had long been associated with Austin Friars, as is clear from the reference Matteo di Niccolò Corsini makes in his *Ricordanze*, writing in February of 1349 that two of his brothers, Duccio and Bartolomeo di Niccolò, having died in London in the 1348 plague, were buried there; see *Il libro di ricordanze dei Corsini*, Armando Petrucci, ed. (Rome: Istituto Storico Italiano, 1965), 4.
130 See Graves 1998, 13–19, for a discussion of Cecil at Cambridge and his subsequently moderate but influential role in the diffusion of Protestantism in England through the Anglican "solution."
131 Though, as has been noted, the documentary trail regarding John's early years back in England is thin. Yates 1934, 53, suggests that Florio *fils* might have met John Lyly through Cecil, Lyly's patron, and she notes the strong influence of the proverbial rhetoric of Lyly's *Euphues* on *FF*.
132 It has been suggested in the past that the family was originally Sienese and possibly Jewish, but the *DBI* entry on Michelangelo, vol. XLVIII, 379–381, suggests that they were Florentine; I have found no documentation supporting or disproving either claim; for Michelangelo's equivocating position regarding his family's Jewish origins, see *Regole de la lingua thoscana*, Giuliano Pellegrini, ed., in "Michelangelo Florio e le *Regole de la lingua thoscana*," *Studi di filologia italiana* 12 (1954), 81.
133 See Yates 1934, 1–4; and L. Firpo 1959, 317–318.
134 The names of the accused are given in Burn 1846, 227–228.
135 See del Re's introduction to *FF*, vii.
136 See L. Firpo 1959, 318–323. Yates 1934, 5–7, deals with Michelangelo's behavior more obliquely than Firpo does, though she suggests, 13, that John Florio was the issue of this "moral lapse"; this could well be true and might at least partially account for the younger Florio's apparent detachment from the Italian congregation after he returned to London as an adult.
137 See Ch. 5, pages 212–213, for a discussion of the elder Florio's grammar.

138 Yates 1983, discusses the period Michelangelo and his family spent in Strasbourg *en route* to Switzerland after they had fled Marian England. On Michelangelo's activism within the Swiss Protestant context, see Taplin 2003, 217–221; and Vischer 2000.
139 Yet neither Michelangelo nor the *Historia* warrant any mention in Mathew's 1972 biography. Florio's text contains a good deal of matter extraneous to Jane's brief reign and its consequences, but the *Historia* deserves some place in the history of sources about this short-lived but significant crisis in the history of the Tudor monarchy. Citations are from the 1607 edition of the *Vita*.
140 M. Florio, *Historia*, 30: "vera pietà, di dottrina, e di costumi santi; fu sempre un chiaro specchio, et esempio, e figliuola legittima giustissimamente del suo padre Arrigo."
141 *ibid.*, 30: "tutte le cose misurate da soli giudizi humani, o da la violenza, o da la forza, o da gl'interessi proprii, dispiaccion à Dio, e hanno un doloroso fine."
142 *ibid.*, 37: "ma sia pur certo ognuno, che senza fallo più volte fra se stesso disse quella sentenza, che già messe il Dottissimo Dante in disgracia de la republica Fiorentina; cio è, S'io vo, chi sta? S'io sto, chi va?" The attribution is mistaken, for it was Boccaccio in his *Tratatello in laude di Dante* who put these words into Dante's mouth – "Se io vo, chi rimane, se io rimango, chi va?" – as he pondered a proposed embassy to Pope Boniface VIII conceived to convince the pope to accept Henry VII of Luxembourg as Holy Roman Emperor; see *Il tratatello in laude di Dante*, in *Opere in versi*, Pier Giorgio, ed. (Milan: Riccardo Ricciardi Editore, 1965), 625.
143 Florio, *Historia*, 30–31: "il cuor del Re è ne le mani di Dio ... Maria era di pur sangue Reale."
144 *ibid.*, 34: "io non so che affermare, o negare. Da l'una parte io sento spronar à creder che così fosse, da la publica fama che n'andava attorno; e da l'altra tirato à dietro. Io confesso che trovandomi à Londra, l'udì da più persone, ma io non posso ben persuadermi, che così fosse; perche Maria era pur donna di generosa natura, e d'alto ingegno."
145 *ibid.*, 39: "che se un Christo novello fosse nato al mondo, maggior feste non si poteva fare. Ma se l'instabile, e pazzo volgo di Londra saputo havesse, che doloroso e lamentevol digiuno dietro a queste feste venir dovea, io son certissimo, che più tosto di sacco, et di cilizio si saria vestito, e con amarissimi pianti inginochiato a dimandar misericordia à Dio, che far tal'allegrezza."
146 *ibid.*, 63: "chi è quello che voglia pensare che essa Maria fosse stata si barbara, e crudele, che ella havesse voluto far torto à la sua nobilissima natura, à la sua buona fama, à l'innocenzia d'una si stretta sua parente? e poi finalmente à la ragione istessa?"
147 This sonnet was evidently to have been printed by Tommaso Giunta together with the letter, but I have found no trace of any such edition; they were evidently first printed in *Il primo-sesto libro delle lettere* (Paris: Matteo il Maestro, 1609), vol. VI, 1r-3r [letter] and 243v [sonnet]:

> Stelle propitie a voi tutte conviensi,
>    Anco a te Sole, e a te folgente Luna,
> Il far' sì ch'incoroni la fortuna,
>    L'aurea Maria dei vostri raggi immensi.

> Fatelo acciò che'l suo splendor dispensi
> La notte, e'l giorno ù l'ombra oscura, e imbruna,
> Tal'che il gran' Mondo senza noia alcuna,
> Sempre si specchi in lei, sempre in lei pensi.
> Sì che non indugiate altere stelle
> Da che l'eterno Dio, che mai non erra,
> De l'alme luci, ch' intorno ha piu belle
> D'un Diadema l'adorna, & riserra,
> Che testimonia a queste genti e a quelle,
> Che in Ciel' fia Dea, qual'è Regina in terra.

148 See Aretino, *Lettere*, vol. VI, Paola Procaccioli, ed. (Rome: Salerno, 2002), 15–17, for the full text of the letter.

149 Pollini, *Historia*, 287: "hanno con l'imprese loro questo fralissimo, e debol sesso honorato..." Here and in the other examples in this section dealing with Mary, I cite Pollini's amplified second edition from 1594.

150 *ibid.*, 288: "... la quale, superata con l'aiuto Divino, e prudenza e valor dell'animo suo, la rabbia di tutti i Principi e Baroni del Stato, e tutta la forza dell'armi loro mirabilmente vinta, raccolto miracolosamente un Esercito di trentamila persone, entrò nella Torre di Londra, e senza spargimento di sangue, prese possesso del suo Reame. Rifiutò 'infame Titolo del Primato della Chiesa, aperse le Prigioni a tutti i Prelati Ecclesiastici, e altri Cattolici, aggiustò le corrotte monete. Gastigò severamente tutte gli heretici, parte cacciandone fuori d'Inghilterra, parte con la dovuta pena del fuoco, annullò tutte le leggi loro, in pregiudizio della Fede Cattolica, rese i Pulpiti, e le Cattedre a' Predicatori, & Lettori Cattolici, & le Messe secondo l'usanza de' Cattolici fece celebrare. Ottenne dal Pontefice Romano il Cardin. Reginaldo Polo Legato da Latere, col cui mezzo riconciliando l'Inghilterra alla Sedia Romana, e faccendola tornare all'ubbedienza del Pontefice, la sciolse da qualunque legame d'heresia e di Scisma." Of Pollini's books dealing with each of the sixteenth-century English sovereigns, the one dedicated to Mary seems to be the least reliant on Nicholas Sanders' *De origine ac progressu schismatis anglicani* (Rome: Bartolomeo Bonfadini, 1586). Though the first edition of Sanders' history was published in Cologne in 1585, the Roman edition is likely to have been the one Pollini would have known; its section on Mary comprises only 31 of 500 pages, whereas Pollini dedicates 117 of his nearly 800 pages to her. Little of what I note here is to be found in Sanders, but Pollini only rarely reveals any of his sources.

151 See Elton 1963, 209–210.

152 Citations within brackets in my text referring to Pollini are from the 1594 *Historia*.

153 Virgil, *Aeneid*, in *Eclogues, Georgics, Aeneid I-VI*, G.P. Goold, ed. (Cambridge, MA: Harvard University Press, 1999), translation mine.

154 Shakespeare, *The Tempest*, Stephen Orgel, ed. (Oxford: Oxford University Press, 1987), 40–43.

155 *ibid.*, 41.

156 As Orgel notes, *ibid.*, a number of Elizabethan writers emphasized that Dido's given name was Elissa, providing "an easy analogue for Elizabeth; and by

1595, the name in Charles Stephanus' *Dictionarum historicum*, a standard source-book for the age, had become Eliza. 'Dido' ... usually explained as meaning 'valiant' ... was an epithet that came to be applied to [the Carthaginian queen] after her death."

157 Herodotus, *The Histories* I.212, Robin Waterfield, trans. (Oxford: Oxford University Press 1998), 93–94.
158 I quote from the Tyndale translation, which would have been the one most familiar to the literate English, even if at this time again newly Catholic.
159 The Florentine arch is described by Pollini in the *Historia*, 305–307; a briefer account of the arch sponsored by the Genovese merchants follows, 307–308.
160 On Mary's determination to re-establish the sacramental character of the coronation proceedings, see McCoy 1990, 218–219.
161 Elton 1963, 214.
162 Pollini gets William Thomas' name backwards and also mistakes his political role during the Edwardian era: as noted earlier, Thomas served as one of the clerks of the Privy Council after his return from Italy in 1550; on his part in the Wyatt rebellion, allegedly having written a series of objections to Mary's impending marriage which led to his arrest and execution in 1554, see *DNB*, vol. XIX, 675–676.
163 For the Italian text of this passage, see Appendix I, page 258.
164 See Elton 1963, 217.
165 Mayer 2000, 253.
166 Seven years after Berni's death, and a decade after he had abandoned the *rifacimento*. On Albicante, see *DBI*, vol. II, 1–2; and Sabatini 1960.
167 Giovanni Alberto Albicanti, *Il sacro et divino sponsalitio* (Milan: Moscheni, 1555), 16–17 [and hereafter in brackets following the text]; see Appendix I, pages 259–260, for the Italian text of this and the following stanzas.
168 The former are typical definitions, but for the latter inflections, see the entry for *steccato* in Boggione and Casalegno 2000, 566–567.
169 See *ibid.*, 397, where the definition of "pensiero" cites this passage from Pietro Fortini, *Giornate dei novizi*, III, 17, 35: "Ed egli con il pensiero ritto a quella n'andò, e abbracciatola, con molte villanesche parole la salutò ..." [He with his stiff dick went in, and embracing her, with many rough words, he fucked her ...] Fortini was a Sienese *letterato* in the middle years of the sixteenth century, whose novelle were published only partially in the period owing to their unabashed obscenity and satiric stance regarding religious life.
170 While Charles had renounced his title as Holy Roman Emperor in 1553 in favour of his brother Ferdinand I, his abdication was not formally accepted until 1558, the year of his death; he similarly gave up his claims to the kingdoms of Spain, the Netherlands, and the Spanish Americas in favour of Philip II in 1555–56; see *Chambers Biographical Dictionary* 1996, 294.
171 Like many of the characters who populate nineteenth- and twentieth-century English novels set in Italy (and indeed as in many of the expatriate communities which inspired them and which still exist today), Pole had been very slow to learn Italian, relying on French and Latin until well into the 1540s; see Mayer 2000, 138.
172 See Schenk 1950, 149–153. In all "nearly 300 people were burnt in the course of not quite four years, but they suffered a few at a time or singly, in many

places ... under many authorities, and for a variety of reasons. No one ever decided that there must be a holocaust of heretics; we are faced with a series of haphazard proceedings, not a planned campaign"; see Schenk, 149. This is not to deny Pole's (or Mary's) culpability, but rather to suggest that it has been blown out of proportion, particularly when compared with the considerably more determinate loss of innocent life under Henry VIII.

173 See *Nuovi documenti su Vittoria Colonna e Reginald Pole*, Sergio M. Pagano and Concetta Ranieri, eds. (Città del Vaticano: Archivio Vaticano, 1989). As these Inquisition archival materials demonstrate, a massive amount of information had been collected on both Colonna and Pole, who were close friends, originally by order of Cardinal Caraffa, the first prefect of the Inquisition in Rome and later – during Pole's years back in England – Pope Paul IV. On Pole's friendship with Colonna, see Schenk 1950, 89–105 (which also provides a discussion of the years 1541–45, during which these Catholic reformers saw their early hopes shattered).

174 It is also equally important to acknowledge the various differences that separated the Catholic reformers from each other: Pole, for instance, eventually moved in a direction divergent from Contarini; see Mayer 2000, 107–111.

175 *ibid.*, 442–451, argues that they were lovers, but at any rate the relationship was intimate and longstanding.

176 *ibid.*, 323–330, provides a brief but interesting discussion of Pole's Italianate additions to Lambeth Palace.

177 On Beccadelli, see *DBI*, vol. VII, 407–413.

178 Pole's ambivalences have most recently been examined by Mayer, an important study that, while rich in previously unedited documentary evidence, tends at times to reach conclusions grounded more in post-structuralist theory than in the historiography it aims to challenge.

179 Ludovico Beccadelli, *Vita del Cardinale Reginaldo Polo*, in *Monumenti di varia letteratura tratti dai manoscritti di Monsignor Lodovico Beccardelli*, pt. 2 [1799] (reprinted Farnborough: Gregg Press Limited, 1967), 177.

180 There were earlier suggestions from various fronts that before his elevation to the cardinalate Pole would have made a suitable spouse for Mary, and Charles V had been one of this strategy's earliest proponents; see Beccadelli, *Vita*, 277.

181 *ibid.*, 287: "non puotè mai nel suo animo entrar spirito di conformarsi al voler del Re parendogli troppo iniquo, et contro le santi leggi della Chiesa ... a me ha detto il Sig. Reginaldo, che in quel ragionamento vide il Re tutto cambiarsi nella faccia, et farsi di lieto turbato, mettendo la mano su d'un pugnaletto che portava; pur ritenutosi senza far altro, gli disse: Io considerò questa vostra opinione, et poi risponderò; et licentiatolo di camera con sdegno."

182 See Mayer 2000, 59–60.

183 *ibid.*, 14–30, provides a critical overview of the argument of *De unitate*.

184 Mayer 2000, 46, notes that from a Yorkist perspective, Henry Pole had a better claim to the throne than did Henry VIII, given that his mother Margaret's father George, the Duke of Clarence, had been the brother of Edward IV.

185 The latter part of this conclusion suggests a troubling tendency in Mayer's book: the relentless effort to problematize Pole's motives. While it is noteworthy that Beccadelli seems to have rescripted this dramatic *peripeteia*, it is

not clear in this instance why Pole himself should be implicated in the subterfuge – the *Vita* was published almost a decade after the cardinal's death, and the biographer's program should not *ipso facto* be taken to represent his subject's point of view. If Pole did, in fact, wish to put a more stoic face on his grief, it is difficult to see why he should be faulted for doing so; see Beccadelli, *Vita*, 328–330; and Mayer 2000, 111–113.

186 Beccadelli, *Vita*, 317: "Ma il Demonio sempre nimico del bene, et della nostra pace, mise in cuore a Papa Paolo di cacciare il Re Filippo del Regno di Napoli, et per questo mandò il Cardinale Caraffa suo nipote Legato in Francia per far movere l'armi a quella corona contro il Re Filippo, et forse temendo ch'il Cardinale Polo non fosse instrumento potente, com'era apresso la regina, che tra quelle Maestà procurava la pace, oppure per odio vecchio, o per instigatione de' maligni, rivocò il Cardinale a Roma, et fece un'altro Inglese detto Fra Pietro Peto Zoccolante, Cardinale, et Legato in Inghilterra ... "

187 *ibid.*, 317–318: "questa non era la via di conservar quel Regno Catholico, ma di farlo più heretico che prima, levandogli il Cardinal Polo, ch'era in quello l'Anchora de' Catholici; et però che guardasse bene Sua Santità quel che faceva, perch'ella si protestava innanzi a Dio di tutti gli inconvenienti, che fossero per succedere."

188 Pollini, *Storia*, 396, suggests that Mary had been a lovely young woman, but that she lost her beauty through the sufferings imposed by both her father and brother. Antonis Mor, who painted the most famous portrait of Mary Tudor, is sometimes taken to be Italian, but he was born in Utrecht around 1520 and pursued his career under the ægis of the Spanish Hapsburg dynasty; see Woodall 1991, 192–224.

189 Beccadelli, *Vita*, 321: "Gran cosa fu, che la Regina alli 15 Novembre, morì la mattina, et la sera a tre hore di notte il Cardinale, ne altro intervallo vi fu di 16 ore ... se ne passò quietissimamente in compagnia degli Angioli, com'è da credere con la sua Catholica, et Santa Regina Maria, havendo vivuto, et travagliato in questo mondo anni 58 et mesi sei." The discrepancy in the date of Mary's death is Beccadelli's mistake; Pole died on the same day, some twelve hours after Mary had.

190 Francisco Visdomini, *Oratione funebre fatta in Napoli nell'hon. essequie della serenissima regina d'Inghilterra* (Naples: Raymondo Amati, 1559), A3r: "già il Sole della Christiana verità, in quel Regno eclisso, la Luna insanguinata, le stelle della Ciel cadute ... [nella] misera Inghilterra scommunicata, in una sola Maria tutta la fede & tutt'il nervo della Catholica verità si stava altrove non era chiesa, non santi, non Sacramenti, non voti, non Messa, non ceremonia, altrove non s'adorava, anzi non pur si tolerava la sacratissima eucharistia che nella povera & sconsolata cella, anzi prigione di Maria."

191 On Charles V's earlier intervention with Edward VI and his counsellors on his grand-niece's behalf, see Pollini, *Storia*, 219–223; Loach 1999, 130–134; and MacCulloch 1999, 36–38.

192 Pollini, *Storia*, 395: "[acciochè] ... da questa odiosa podestà delle tenebre, e del diavolo che hoggi ha tutto quell'infelice Reame furiosamente ingombrato, tutta l'Inghilterra restasse miseramente occupata."

193 Sanders, *De origine ac progressu*, 359.

## 3 La Regina Helisabetta

1 See Stevenson (forthcoming).
2 For the text of Litolfi's memoir, see Annibale Litolfi, *Relazine sull'Inghilterra. La Diplomazia Gonzagesca*, Romolo Grazzo, ed. (Milan: Istituto per gli Studi di Politica Internazionale, 1941), 57–70; and for a summary of Litolfi's career, see D. S. Chambers 1990, 73–99. For the Italian text of Magno's journal cited in my footnotes, I have used Folger Ms. V.a.259; in the main body of my text, with some modifications, the translation made by Barron, Coleman, and Gobbi, *London Journal* 9 (1983), 136–152 (which also includes a critical assessment of the work).
3 Alessandro Magno, *Travel Journal*, 165v: "Londra è assai bella citta, ricca, populosa, et abondante de buonissimi panni di lana, e carisee. Circonda il circuito delle mura miglia cinque, et nove con li borghi, quali ha bellissimi. Ha nove porte, otto delle qual hanno li suoi borghi, et l'altra ha inanzi una bellisima praderia, ove si riducono ogni domenica a giocar insieme huomeni, e donne. Ha quasi tutte le case (fuora che alcuni pochi palazzi della Regina, e gl'altri signori, quali son tutti di pietra), fabricate di legname." The *OED* defines "kersey" as "A kind of coarse narrow cloth, woven from long wool and usually ribbed." It was exported in large quantities and was especially associated with making stockings before knitted stockings came in during the reign of Elizabeth. *Love's Labor's Lost* 5.2.413–414, Peter Holland, ed. (New York: Penguin Books, 2000), 94–95, plays on the material's non-luxury status: "Henceforth my wooing mind shall be expressed/In russet yeas and honest kersey noes."
4 Litolfi/Guazzo, *Relazione*, 60 and 62: "Da un capo ci è un castello detto la torre e dell'altro capo è un borgo detto Vasamestre ove abitano i Re. Quivi è un palagio grandissimo e comodissimo di stanze, ma senza molta architettura, sì come sono in generale tutte le fabriche di questo paese ... la materia di fabbricare è molto grossa ... quanto alle stanze non ci è un ordine al mondo."
5 Magno, *Travel Journal*, 167v: "La chiesa di S. Polo ... è degna di compassione veder le belle figure de santi scolpite in marmo, et li adornamenti d'essa per la loro heresia rovinate, e guaste ... nelle chiese non vi dicono messa, ma cantano solamente salmi nel lor linguaggio, e vi predicano."
6 See Aitkins and Matthews 1957, 137–144, for an account of the fire of 1561 that includes an anonymous narrative describing the fire and its specific damage to St. Paul's, as well as the differing interpretations of its significance; Catholics, like Magno, saw a clear indication of God's displeasure with the Elizabethan Protestant settlement, while Protestants saw a sign of their God's judgment of the government's laxity regarding the eradication of remaining Catholic elements in England.
7 Magno, *Travel Journal*, 167r–v: "Ho detto che il campanile si abbruggiò, ma parendomi che sia stato miracolo, e per dimostrare quanto sia difficil cosa el riddure uno dalla cattiva alla buona via voglio dire il modo. Dicono che l'istesso anno poco inanzi el gionger nostro venne una salta dal cielo, e dato in esso lo abbruggiò tutto, e disfece insieme el piombo che era posto sopra la chiesa per coperta, rendendo tanto calor per tutta la città, che dubitando il populo di abbruggiarsi mosso da la lor coscienza, e conoscendo il suo pecato si messe a cridare misericordia, ma passato il foco, rittornò al suo errore ne si emendò."

8 Litolfi/Guazzo, *Relazione*, 63: "fanno ciò che piace loro, essendo introdotto per tutta Inghilterra questa libertà e usanza che una donna massimamente delle maritate anderà sola o con una sua compagna a mangiare non solamente con uno del paese, ma con uno forestiero, e se avverà che il marito la trovi con quel tale, non solo non l'avrà a male, ma gli toccherà la mano e lo ringrazierà dello invito fatto a sua moglie."

9 *ibid.*, 62: "nel mezzo della strada come in casa."

10 Magno, *Travel Journal*, 170v: "si pongono a giocare con diversi giovani anchor che a loro incogniti, e spese molte giocando son gettate a terra da essi, quali basciandole le lasciano levare, e tornano al gioco, et hanno per uso questo atto, e lo tengono a favor grande, et se alcuno forestiero entra nelle case loro, et a prima gionta non bacia la patrona in bocca lo tengono per male accostumato."

11 In his *Commentarii*, vol. I, 22, Enea Silvio Piccolomini had noted that in Scotland "viros statura parvos et audaces, fœminas albas et venustas atque in venerem proclives. Basiationes fœminarum minoris illic esse quam manus in Italia tractiones" [the men were small and brazen, the women fair-complexioned and ready for love-making. To kiss a woman there is of as little moment as in Italy to take a lady's hand].

12 Litolfi/Guazzo, *Relazione*, 64: "luoghi pubblici di disonestà non ci sono."

13 *ibid.*, 64–65: "mangiano molti 5 e 6 volti il giorno ... più che nissuna altra cosa."

14 Magno, *Travel Journal*, 174r–v: "Hanno pesci assai, e buonissimi far quali vi è in stima il luzzo, e la passera che è molto grande tagliata in sonde, over brezuole si mangia sopra la gradella, ma sopra tutti il salomon, che è come a Venezia il sturione. Vi sono magazeni pieni di un certo pesce secco che viene dalle Indie, e chiamano stofis, che vien a dire in nostra lengua battuto, et altramente si chiamano Bacalari, e ci è una strada che ha molte boteghe da una banda, e dall'altra ove altro non si fa tre giorni alla settimana che tenendone in mogio batterli continuamente, e vengono bianchissimi, ma molto duri da mangiare, e senza gusto, e di essi ne passa quantità grande nella Fiandra, e nell'Allemagna. Hanno, e pigliano gran quantità di ostree, et li giorni da pesce ne vengono dischotto, e venti botti (che son navilij di grandezza delle nostre marcinave, e navicono con vele alla quarta) carichi, e ne è si buon mercato che per uno marcello se ne ha ogni gran corba piena, e le cucinano aroste, alesse, fritte co 'l botiro, et ad ogni modo, ma per lo piu usano mangiarle crude inanzi pasto con pan di orzo, e sono buonissime."

15 Litolfi/Guazzo, *Relazione*, 65: "benignità dell'aere ... tanto moderato e buono che non potria essere migliore."

16 Magno, *Travel Journal*, 166v: "ogni Re è tenuto mettervene uno, e quello lo chiamano poi da 'l suo nome. Quelli che vidi alhora erano Henrico, Felippo, Maria, et Helisabet."

17 *ibid.*, 172v: "molti si trovano che da se stessi tratti da certo destino o s'appicano, o se gettano nelli pozzi, e s'aniegano."

18 Litolfi/Guazzo, *Relazione*, 66–67: "ci è di più una crudeltà, la quale usano per una gran pietà ... non si fa questo con tutti, si fa però con molti."

19 Dobson 1997, 243–245 and 254, for instance, cites only a handful of suicides in her otherwise exhaustive study of death in early modern England. A passage in

Lodowick Bryskett's translation of Giraldi's *Tre dialoghi della vita civile, A discourse of Civil Life* (1605), notes the ancient Roman tradition of suicide in the face of shame or servitude but resolutely rejects the practice; see Wymer 1985.

20 Litolfi/Guazzo, *Relazione*, 66: "della morte non fanno stima, come ben dice il Petrarca in quel verso: a cui morir non duole, parlando dell'Inghilterra." Petrarch likely refers in *Canzoniere* 28.50 to northern Europe in general, or to Germany or Scythia in particular; England is mentioned in 28.36.

21 *ibid.*, 69: "uomini molto selvaggi e diversi da tutti gli altri uomini di legge, costumi e natura."

22 Litolfi had evidently prepared a companion piece to his descriptive essay that was to have served as a historical survey of English political life from Henry VII to Mary, but all that survives of this text is an undeveloped series of vignettes about the English Reformation; see D. S. Chambers 1990, 94.

23 Magno, *Travel Journal*, 171r: "Vidi la Reina Helisabet, qual alhora stava a Granuch villa sopra 'l fiume, e longi da Londra miglia 5. Et era con honoratissima corte, donna bella, grande honestamente, benigna, affabile, e di età quasi di anni 30 in cerca."

24 Cited in Bellorini 1980, 66–67: "Non mancano ancora di brusciar questi heretici del Sacramento, havendone spediti venerdì doj, un vecchio di 70 annj che andava con le ferle, et che volontariamente sè ito ad accusarsi, et pertinace è morto nel fuoco; et un cieco giovane, ma molto perverso et ostinato nel suo mal animo. Sabbato poi brusciorno quatro donne due vecchie e 2 giovinij, che furono moglij delli già brusciati che scrissi a Vostra Signoria alli di passati, quali vanno tanto allegramente alla morte, senza ligarli et senza altro sforzo che pare vaddino a nozze."

25 Litolfi/Guazzo, *Relazione*, 67: "al modo del re Eduoardo ... prego Dio faccia che non peggiorano."

26 Even as a young woman Elizabeth had been keenly interested in religious issues, translating (in addition to Ochino) Marguerite de Navarre's *L'âme pecheresse* for her step-mother Jane Seymour and composing a private prayer book with original prayers in English, French, Italian, Latin, and Greek. For this latter, see Elizabeth I, *Elizabeth I: Autograph Compositions and Foreign Language Originals*, Janel Mueller and Leah S. Marcus, eds. (Chicago: Chicago University Press, 2003), 129–149; and for English translations of these prayers, see Elizabeth I, *Collected Works: Elizabeth I*, Leah Marcus, Janel Mueller, and Mary Beth Rose, eds. (Chicago: University of Chicago Press, 2000), 310–321. These useful volumes, regrettably, do not include the translations Elizabeth made from Latin, French, and Italian, which constitute a crucial aspect of the queen's literary activity.

27 Litolfi/Guazzo, *Relazione*, 67: "meccanici e zappattieri ... dicendo mille cosazze del tempo della felice memoria della regina Maria et del cardinale, con far chiamare in colpa il popolo dell'error che comissero credendo a essi, di maniera che mai fu visto la più bella metamorfosi di due mascalzoni ad un tratto in un pulpito predicare."

28 My emphasis; *ibid.*, 69: "qui si vive in tutto e per tutto, quanto alla religione, lutteranescamente."

29 Schivenoglia's report of Elizabeth's coronation festivities is the most detailed of any of the extant records. Bellorini 1980, 70–74, makes a convincing case that

there is no relationship between the Italian account and the anonymous English narrative, *The Quenes Maiesties Passage through the Citie of London*, given their totally different points of view and the considerably wider range of Schivenoglia's coverage; for the complete Italian text, see 74–92. Bellorini also notes, 70, the jingoistic tone of the English report, which expresses "the conviction that the advent of the young sovereign signalled the end of all foreign influence, Spanish in particular, and consequently effected the recovery of a vigorous nationalism in the especially close rapport between Elizabeth and her people," a point of view entirely at odds with the assumptions of this study, which argues that the appropriation of foreign cultures was closely tied to the rise of English nationalism, particularly under Elizabeth. McCoy 1990, 220, dismisses Schivenoglia's narrative, citing Bayne 1907, who dubiously privileges the anonymous English account over a mere fragment of Schivenoglia's text printed in the *Calendar of State Papers, Venice, 1558–1580*, 16–17.

30 Bellorini 1980 [and in brackets thus as follows], 75: "il giorno dell'Assensione, che si suol fare a Venezia quando la Signoria va a sposare la Mare."
31 *ibid.*, 76: "... vestiti con robbe di non molto valore."
32 *ibid.*, 77: "ciascun cavallo havea nella frontiera della briglia una piccola croce adorata della sorte delli cavalieri hierosolimiti havendo fatto manco spesa che potero per il costume di donar via tutto."
33 *ibid.*, 81: "Accostata Sua Maestà al predetto Arco su un piccolo poggiolo di sopra della porta di mezzo venne un fanciullo, che interpretò brevemente tutt'il sugetto del significato, et Sua Maestà si fermò donandolo grattissima audienza et monstrando molta contentezza."
34 *ibid.*, 88: "Sua Maestà portava nelle mani il sceptro et la palla d'oro, con la corona Imperiale in mano, et il Gran Manto d'oro Regale et sollenne indosso, et ritornava molto allegra, mostrando buonissima ciera a tutti et facendo mille accoglienze, a tale che a me parve passasse il segno del decoro e della gravità."
35 *ibid.*, 89: "furno fatte diverse musiche ma perché non vi fu cosa segnalata et haverne io udito di migliore, meglio è tacerle."
36 Elizabeth's translation of the first ninety verses of Petrarch's *Trionfo dell'eternità* is, for instance, more artfully done than the earlier translation of the entire cycle of *Trionfi* by Henry Morley, one of Henry VIII's courtiers.
37 For this and what follows on Castiglione, see Bellorini 1974, 113–132; and *DBI*, vol. XXII, 82–84.
38 Cited in Bellorini 1974, 116.
39 Gabrieli 1983, 162, suggests that Bellorini is too categorical in asserting the primacy of Castiglione's role in Elizabeth's acquisition of Italian, even though he acknowledges both John Foxe and Pietro Bizzari as providing evidence for Bellorini's position, and he fails both to name other candidates and to take into account the singular position Castiglione occupied in Elizabeth's personal world.
40 See the appendix to Bellorini 1974, 133–136, for the text of Castiglione's poems; we shall return to Jacopo Aconcio later in this chapter, pages 151–154; for Wolfe, see Ch. 4, pages 186ff.
41 George Gascoigne, *The Queen's Majesty's Entertainment at Woodstock, 1575*, A. W. Pollard, ed. (Oxford: Daniel and Hart, 1910), vii. Besides the brief verses

performed in Italian at Woodstock, Gascoigne's polyglot version of the *Entertainment*, BL Royal Ms. 18A.xlvii, was prepared after the fact and presented to the queen on January 1, 1576.
42 Young 1996, 9.
43 On the Italian actors in England, see E. K. Chambers 1923, 261–265.
44 Bellorini 1974, 114; for the full text of Scaramelli's *Relazione*, as well as the report of four earlier Venetian visitors to England in 1576, see *Ambasciatori*, 61–76. Despite a concerted effort, Elizabeth was never able to convince the Venetian government to recognize her as the legitimate queen of England, and the rupture of formal diplomatic relations lasted precisely the length of her reign.
45 See Pellegrini's introduction to Ubaldini's *Relazione*, 22–25, for a discussion of his presence at court.
46 In the introduction to her edition of these two accounts, *La disfatta della flotta spagnola* (Florence: Olschki Editore, 1988), 8–9, Anna Maria Crinò notes that Ubaldini made one of his typical political miscalculations in sending a copy of them as a gift to the Tuscan Grand Duke Ferdinando I on the occasion of his marriage to Christine of Lorraine in 1589: Ferdinando had lost one of his best galleys, the "San Francesco" (re-christened "Florentia" by the Spanish), to Philip II's sequestration of foreign ships in his territorial waters at the time of the build-up leading to the Armada; the ship was never returned to Livorno, and Ferdinando's laconic acknowledgment of Ubaldini's gift suggests that he would rather not have been reminded of the episode. Crinò, 13, also notes that Ubaldini's imprecise knowledge of ships made for numerous errors in his account of how the Spanish navy came to be defeated by the English.
47 Collected together by Crinò in *Avvisi di Londra di Petruccio Ubaldini fiorentino, relativi agli anni 1579–1594, connotizie sulla guerra di Fiandra* (Florence: Olschki 1969).
48 As Crinò suggests with regard to the exquisite craftsmanship of the copy of the *Cebetis thebanæ* prepared for Cosimo I, this was the area in which Ubaldini really excelled; see Ubaldini/Crinò, *La relatione*, 642–645. Perhaps the central irony of Ubaldini's career was that he tried, rather unsuccessfully, to make his mark through the printed book when his greatest talent was in the decoration of manuscripts.
49 Page numbers here and below refer to Crinò's edition.
50 *ibid.*, 695: "Elisabetta non s'è mai maritata, benché la sia stata desiderata da diversi in matrimonio, sì forestieri come inglesi, e gl'è parso che nelle pratiche di così fatti maneggi ella alfine habbia più tosto dimostro di curarsi meno di maritarsi che di concluderne cosa alcuna per la quale ella si spotestasse della libertà del corpo et dell'animo, et come che la potesse haver havuto più un oggetto che un altro, nientedimeno ella ha saputo coprire così bene questa parte che par più presto che essa habbia desiderato di conoscer gl'animi altrui che di lasciarsi dagl'altri conoscere; et di qui è avvenuto che huomini di grado honorato si sono creduti et hanno ostinatamente conteso che sarebbe seguito qualche matrimonio di lei, il che poi non essendo riuscito, hanno fatto conoscere tanto meglio la loro leggerezza, essendo vero che la prudenza dell'huomo nasce dalla pratica delle cose accompagnata dal giudicio, et non dai favori esteriori, che si ricevono bene spesso indegnamente dai Principi."

51 *ibid.*, 695–696: "nell'arte del persuadere e insinuare è artificiosissima, e perché non ha poco cognitione delle historie havendo la lingua latina e la greca et le due italiana e franzese familiari, usa anche un'arte mirabile coi forestieri, dai quali ella possa guadagnare fuori del Regno lode di accortezza et di elloquenza."
52 Pollini, *Historia* (1591), vii: "delle concubine del Rè Arrigo, le quali erano ancor'vive, Anna era figliuola d'una, e sorella d'un'altra. Anzi chè (quello che è cosa infinitamente peggiore, avvengachè paia forse cosa incredibile e indegna più tosto d'essere scritta per essere tanto abominevole) ella era stimata, non senza manifesti, e chiarissimi indizi, propria figliuola dello stesso Rè Arrigo." The 1594 edition reads even more emphatically: "Anna era senza dubbio [without a doubt] figliuola d'una e sorella d'un'altra."
53 See Sanders, *De origine ac progressu*, 94–98, where he turns the argument regarding consanguinity between Henry and Arthur (in relation to Katherine of Aragon) on its head by asserting that it was common knowledge that Henry had had sex with Mary Boleyn – he writes that the king had confessed as much in a letter to Clement VII – and that he was hence the father of Anne Boleyn. Rastell's original English text is not extant, but there is a contemporary Latin translation of it by Gerardo Moringo, *Ordo condemnationes Thomæ Mori*: see *Acta Thomæ Mori*, Henri de Vocht, ed. (Louvain: Humanistica Lovaniensia, 1947).
54 For what follows here, see Rebora 1935, 233–254.
55 For the full Italian text of the letter, see Appendix I, pages 260–261; the original is preserved in the Archivio di Stato in Florence, Mediceo del Principato 4183, 30–32.
56 See Rebora 1935, 251.
57 See Inghirami 1844, 154; and Negri 1722, 200.
58 The letter concludes with Elizabeth's assurances that were the Grand Duke ever to find himself similarly slandered by one of her subjects, she would return the favor, but she did not live long enough to do so. When Robert Dallington published his *Survey of the Great Duke's State of Tuscany* (1605), a hateful rant against Florentines in general and Ferdinando in particular, the Grand Duke protested to James I through his representative in London, Ottaviano Lotti, and the king agreed to publically burn whatever copies of the book could be found and imprison Dallington. The book continued to circulate, however, and its author was threatened only with detention; see Rebora 1935, 234–235; and Gargano 1923, 61–64.
59 Some versions of this story lay the blame for her murder with Isabella herself, accusing the lady of a libertine sexuality which her justly angered husband avenged and for which he was then forgiven under the rubric *delitto d'amore* [crime of passion]. But Paolo Giordano-Orsini was the actual reprobate, and his involvement with Vittoria Accoramboni – the murder of whose husband he was almost certainly involved with – led to Isabella's murder so that he would then be free to marry his lover. When Paolo died in 1585 and Vittoria inherited almost his entire estate, she was in turn murdered shortly afterward by her dispossessed Orsini in-laws; see Micheletti 1983, 126–134. John Webster used this material for *The White Divel* in 1612, and Stendhal's 1837 novella, *Vittoria Accoramboni*, is based on two different Italian manuscript accounts of the story. For documentary evidence regarding the case, see Gnoli 1890.

60  In the absence of a smoking gun, Zapperi 1993, 14–15, suggests that a succession of letters addressed by both Virginio and Maria to the potentially offended parties – Henry IV, Flavia Peretti-Orsini, and Ferdinando – form a strategy intended to deflect any such conclusion but that rather tends to confirm it. I follow Zapperi's introduction closely here, which qualifies in a number of respects Leslie Hotson's 1954 account of Orsini's life and the circumstances surrounding his trip to England.

61  At the entry into Florence of the papal delegate to the wedding of Ferdinando and Christine of Lorraine in 1589, Orsini took offense at the priority in protocol extended to Cardinal Aldobrandini and attempted to usurp his place; when called off by Ferdinando himself, Orsini abandoned the ceremony. A letter from the English agent in Lyons, Ralph Winwood, to the English ambassador to France, then in London, suggests that this contretemps was the motive for Orsini's voyage; see Hotson 1954, 62.

62  For the details of which, see *ibid.*, 179ff.

63  Here I follow Zapperi's transcription of the letters dated January 18 (the 8th, according to the Julian calendar still in use in England at this time) and January 31 (the 21st), 1601, 60–68, which correct a number of errors in the letters transcribed for Hotson's use.

64  Zapperi 1993, 61: "non tanto privata quanto io desideravo."

65  *ibid.*, 61: "poi che qui in Londra non si dice in altro loco messa."

66  *ibid.*, 62: "damigelle ... dame e cavalieri ... i cavalieri della giarrattera, tutti vestiti di bianco, com'era quel giorno tutta la corte, ma con tanto oro e gioie che era cosa maravigliosa. Questi tutti mi vennero a salutare, parlando la più parte italiano, molti franzese et alcuni spagniolo. Io risposi a tutti nel modo che sapevo, nella lingua che mi sentivo parlare e sono certo che almeno mi sono fatto intendere. Non ho trovato altro che dui cavalieri che non sappino altra lingua che l'inglese e con questi ho adoperato altri cavalieri per interpreti."

67  *ibid.*, 62: "parlando così bene italiano e dicendo tanti belli concetti che io posso dire d'aver preso lezioni dal Boccaccio o nella Accademia."

68  On the Crusca, see Ch. 5, pages 232–237.

69  Zapperi 1993, 64: "essendo il costume di Moscovia che se egli non fussi stato visto mangiare dalla regina, il suo granduca gl'averia fatta tagliare la testa." John Stow records both Orsini's and the Russian's visit in his *Annales, or, Generall chronicle of England* (London: Thomas Adams, 1615), 815.

70  *ibid.*, 65: "alcuni instrumenti, a mio credere non mai sentiti in Italia, ma miracolosi." Zapperi 1993, 126, notes that these were orphalions, a stringed instrument similar to the lute.

71  *ibid.*, 66: "una commedia mescolata con musica e balli ... l'ambasciatore moscovito non fu presente, io stetti sempre appresso a Sua Maestà, la quale mi comandò di coprire e mi fece portare uno sgabello e se bene mi comandò mille volte di sedere, non volsi però mai ubbidirla."

72  Orsini considered the man to be a buffoon, writing to his wife that he will regale her with stories about the ambassador's "costumi ridicolosi" [ridiculous habits], *ibid.*, 64, but he (typically) failed to understand the strategic significance of the Russian's visit: with the question of the English succession still theoretically unresolved at this point and the alliances forged in the Baltic region by James VI

with his marriage to Anne of Denmark, Elizabeth was anxious to secure an even more formidable ally farther to the east; see Hotson 1954, 19–22.
73 In which case, Shakespeare's subsequent change of his duke's name to Orsino could then be ascribed to Orsini's presence at court on Twelfth Night in 1601, perhaps intentionally making fun of the recent Italian visitor.
74 Zapperi 1993, 73: "Sua Maestà fu contenta di ballare, che è il maggiore honore che ella mi potessi fare, secondo il detto di questa corte, poiché m'accertano che sono 15 anni che Sua Maestà non ha ballato."
75 *ibid.*, 74: "mi parve di essere diventato uno di quei paladini che andavano in quei palazzi incantati."
76 An English translation of this document, dated April 27, 1570, can be found at: http://tudorhistory.org/primary/papalbull.html.
77 The Inquisitorial court that tried Bruno's case in Rome was particularly concerned that he had in his published works praised heretical monarchs. Bruno's response was that "io ho lodato molti heretici, et anco principi heretici; ma non li ho lodati come heretici, ma solamente per le virtù morale che havevano" [I have praised many heretics, and even heretical princes; though I have not praised them as heretics, but only for the moral virtue which they possessed]; see L. Firpo 1993, 188. Such a distinction was lost on the Inquisitors, however, for no heretic in their view could have possessed "moral virtue."
78 Cited by Zapperi 1993, 71, but originally published in *Records of the English Province of the Society of Jesus*, vol. I, Henry Foley, ed. London: Roehampton, 1877), 5.
79 See *ibid.*, 23–26.
80 See Peretti's letter of January 13, 1601, in *ibid.*, 57–58.
81 See *ibid.*, 10.
82 For a glimpse of the importance of music in the Henrician period, see Holman 1991, 104–106; see Stevens 1961, for music in the early Tudor period in general. In addition to these and the other references which follow, see Ashbee, Lasocki, Holman, and Kissy 1998 for an exhaustive bibliography of musicians at the early modern English court.
83 On the Bassano, see David Lasocki's article in *The New Grove Dictionary of Music and Musicians Online*, http://www.grove.com. In Lasocki's fuller treatment of the family, 1995 (with Roger Prior), the extensive documentary evidence he offers regarding the professional activities and living arrangements of the Bassano is the strongest part of the study; but when Prior utilizes some of the same material for more speculative purposes – as he does in attempting to prove that Baptista's daughter Emilia (married to Alfonso Lanier) is the "Dark Lady" of Shakespeare's sonnets – the book takes an unfortunate turn; for a more useful sketch of Emilia's life and two examples of her poetry, see Stevenson and Davidson 2001, 100–108.
84 See Ubaldini/Pellegrini, *Relazione*, 21.
85 On the Ferrabosco, see Field in the *New Grove Dictionary of Music and Musicians Online*, http://www.grove.com; and Lucio De Grandis 1980, 539–547.
86 See Prior 1983.
87 *ibid.*, 262.

88 See Orgel 2003, 149–151. Prior recognizes that Jews in sixteenth-century England did not enjoy unlimited liberties and even those in royal employ were occasionally subject to the shifting political winds of the period, as when Henry VIII – wishing to draw closer to Charles V in 1541–42 – imprisoned a group of Portuguese Jews, among whom turned out to be several of his own viol players; see 259–262.
89 For this first version of the story, I follow Izon 1958, 333–344.
90 Lasocki and Prior 1995, 243.
91 *ibid.*, 243–244.
92 See *Letters of Denization and Acts of Naturalization for Aliens in England, 1509–1603*, William Page, ed. (Lymington: The Huguenot Society of London, 1893), vii, x–xi, and xxiii. The "Evil May-Day" riots of 1517 were the first in a series of such disturbances during the reign of Henry VIII (there had been similar uprisings in 1456–57), which culminated in an act passed by parliament in 1540 that severely restricted the rights of "strangers"; its provisions were so drastic that many foreigners in the service of the king who had been resident in England for generations seriously considered fleeing the country before the Privy Council finally intervened and suspended the measure. On Polidoro Virgilio's account of the 1517 riots in his *Anglica historia*, see Dillon 2003, 168–177.
93 After Cecil's 1567 *Account of Strangers in the several parts of London*, in which Italians were identified as such along with the neighborhoods where they resided, it becomes progressively more precarious determining the "national" affiliation of the aliens counted by Elizabeth's government.
94 *Returns of Aliens Dwelling in the city and suburbs of London from the Reign of Henry VIII to that of James I. London*, E. F. Kirk and R. E. G. Kirk, eds. (Aberdeen: Aberdeen University Press, 1900–08), xiv.
95 Page suggests that the official numbers be multiplied by five, assuming that they account for only the heads of households, though other household members had been (erratically) counted in Cecil's *Account*. There are a number of Italians who turn up in the 1571 *Returns* listed as having lived in England for many years who did not appear in the prior survey. Similar problems arise in comparing the earlier data with the 1593 *Returns of Strangers*.
96 See Scouloudi 1985 for the most recent and accessible analysis of the data gathered by the later Tudor and early Stuart governments regarding England's foreign populations.
97 I owe this discussion to B. Anderson 1991, 1–36.
98 Scouloudi 1985, 1; and 1–13 for what follows here; for a detailed analysis of the "Calvin affair" and its consequences, see Marienstras 1985.
99 In this regard, Scouloudi 1985, 3, discusses the case of the French merchant Stephen Belott, a former apprentice of Christopher Mountjoy and husband of Mountjoy's daughter Mary, and a friend of William Shakespeare's: a promised dowry never having been paid to him, Belott sued Mountjoy and called Shakespeare as a witness on his behalf (providing one of the few examples of Shakespeare's signature); the debt seems never to have been settled.
100 Magno, *Travel Journal*, 173r: "Non puo alcuno levar botega, o comprar robba da mercanti forestieri se non è stato prima sett'anni credo con altri, e se li sono

trovate robbe che habbino compro che da Inglesi, che habbino servito el sopradetto tempo li sono tolte come contrabandi, e se fussero vendute, e non ancora pagate el danno è del venditor, e pero bisogna veder a chi si vende, e de chi si vende."

101 Scouloudi 1985, 3–8, describes the process of obtaining these acts and patents, their cost, prevalence, and implications.

102 To leave such matters to social and economic historians, as a great deal of Anglo-Italian cultural scholarship does, is to fail to see the critical line of contiguity between the uninterrupted foreign mercantile presence in England and issues of cultural transmission. See, for instance, S. Rossi 1984, 55: speaking of merchants and bankers, Rossi suggests that these are "individuals whose history I do not intend to chronicle here, it being sufficient to note them only when their presence emerges from the anonymity of micro-history to assume a specific value." The "specific value" of the Italian merchants in England lies in their having, as resident foreigners, weathered the shifts in religious and political alignments which defined such significant dimensions of the English experience in the middle of the sixteenth century.

103 Even if a number of merchants took out patents of denization, there was a tendency among them to resist assimilation. See Brachtel 1980, 597: "The Italian merchants might form some personal and cultural relationships with their European neighbors. They might act in business with English merchants, and become godfathers to their children. The measure of their separateness lies less in their more natural tendency to live and worship apart, but in a host of suggestive remains. Again and again the Italian merchant appears who is in England 'for the time being'; recurrently in wills drawn up for sick men in London there is the plain hope, against present indications, of a proper burial in Italy."

104 See Ruddock 1951, for a full account of this other significant colony of Italians in England. There were also Italians at Sandwich, on the east Kent coast, but little is known about them.

105 On the decline of the Italian merchants in England and the corresponding rise of the English, see Rapp 1975, 499–525; and Ramsay 1973, 22–49.

106 About whom, see Ch. 1, page 281 n. 148.

107 Thomas More, *Selected Letters*, Elizabeth Frances Rogers, ed. (New Haven: Yale University Press, 1961), 255–256.

108 See Sicca 2002, which I follow closely here.

109 *ibid.*, 169.

110 *ibid.*, 177.

111 *ibid.*, 178.

112 For the 1522 inventory of the contents of the Bardi-Cavalcanti house, see Sicca 2002, 187–200.

113 *ibid.*, 181.

114 These letters form the material transcribed by Gargano 1928, 17–47, which I follow here.

115 De' Gozzi employed several other Italians: Giuseppe Simonelli, Orazio Franciotti, and Mauro Berti. This latter turned out to be a Jesuit, and Gondola claims that Berti was responsible for cutting three fingers off of the

hand of one of the women in his (Gondola's) household, an act for which he was stiffly fined; see *ibid.*, 24–25.
116 *ibid.*, 31.
117 *ibid.*, 36: "futeronla bene."
118 The Venetian envoy, Giovan Carlo Scaramelli, had also complained about English piracy during his audience with the queen in February of 1603; see *Ambasciatori*, 73–74.
119 Stone 1956, 5; the *DNB* entry on Pallavicino, as Stone indicates, mistakenly identifies him as the papal collector under Mary and has him renouncing his Catholic faith only to then deposit the revenues he had collected in his own pockets.
120 Page numbers in brackets refer to Stone 1956. Religious barriers did nothing to impede the flow of credit in war-torn Europe in the latter half of the sixteenth century. While a heretic could lose his or her life for challenging the authority of the Roman or Calvinist churches, others who were economically of use to countries on the wrong side of their religious convictions suffered no loss to their businesses; see Stone, 141–142. On Pallavicino's alum monopoly, see Stone, 41–64.
121 *An Italians dead bodie Stucke with English Flowers, On the death of Sir Horatio Pallavicino*, Theophilus Field, ed. (London: Andrew Wise, 1600), B2v.
122 A document in *Returns of Aliens*, 384–385, suggests that Ridolfi exercised some sort of leadership role in the loosely connected foreign merchant community in England. This "*Certificate* by the Italian Merchants residing in London of their having elected to the office of Postmaster one Godfrey Mareschallj, a Fleming" indicates that the election took place at Ridolfi's house and was validated by the authority of the Spanish Ambassador (with whom Ridolfi, of course, had other dealings). Twenty-eight Italians signed the document, as well as sixteen Dutch merchants, several Germans and Spaniards, and one Portuguese.
123 S. Rossi 1984, 68.
124 On the Northern Rebellion, see Perry 1995, 148–149.
125 See Strong 1959, 359–360.
126 Here, except where noted otherwise, I follow Page's introduction to *Letters of Denization*, xliv–xlix.
127 On Agnello, see *DBI*, vol. I, 431–32; and Jones 1955, 242–247. Aquilecchia 1960, 123, notes that John Kingston's press published an Italian text in 1566, but while he does not identify its title it must be this.
128 On Saviolo, see S. Rossi 1990, 165–175, which argues that John Florio is the likely author of the sword-fighting manual attributed to Saviolo. On Bonetti, see Aylward 1956, 39–49.
129 On Borgarucci, see Bellorini 1968, 251–271; and *DBI*, vol. XII, 565–568.
130 The original 1584 title was *Copie of a Leter Wryten by a Master of Arte at Cambridge to his friend in London*; *Leicester's Commonwealth*, by which the document is now more generally known, was adopted in 1641.
131 Another Italian physician, Cesare Adelmare, had emigrated to England in 1550, but little is known about him. He evidently served as Mary's doctor, and continued in some sort of medical role with Elizabeth; he was arrested in 1566

as a partisan of Lady Margaret Douglas, the Catholic pretender to the throne. One of Cesare's sons, Giulio (Julius Caesar), was born in 1557 or 1558; he rose to a respectable level within the Elizabethan government bureaucracy and was elected to parliament from Windsor; named chancellor and under-treasurer of the exchequer under James I, Giulio sat on the king's Privy Council and enjoyed a close friendship with Francis Bacon. On Cesare, see the limited entry in *DBI*, vol. I, 265; for Giulio, see *DNB*, vol. III, 656–669.

132 See Page in *Letters of Denization*, xli.

133 Magno, *Travel Journal*, 173r: "Li nostri mercanti la mattina, e la sera si ridducono in una strada, qual all'hora si richiude da una parte, e l'altra con cathene accio con esse sia impedito el transito alli cari, i cavalli, e lo riddussi come diciamo noi a Rialto, e a S. Marco, et esser hora di Rialto ... la festa similmente udita la messa si ridducono in una croce di via, qual chiamano quattro canti, et in questi lochi fanno li loro mercati."

134 Holmes 1963, 19–20.

135 For a description of this area of the map, see *ibid.*, 22–23. A later and considerably less detailed map of "Londra" was drawn by an Italian, Francesco Valesio, and included in "a collection of map-views of European (chiefly Italian) cities published about 1595 in Venice. At Mantua there is a fresco with the same title which was probably copied from the engraving soon after 1600"; see Darlington and Howego 1964, 19.

136 *Journal of a Milanese Merchant* [1516], BL Additional Ms. 24180, 24r: "la terza li Augustini ove tutti li forestieri vano ad mesa et vespero et si andasino ad altra giesa seriano molto mal vedutti et perho vano tutti a dicti Augusttini et non in altri giese ... li Anglesi non vano in dicti Augusttini et hoc ordinarie pur aliquando sed raro conveniunt." The author's habitual but casual interjection of Latin phrases into what is primarily a vernacular text was common practice for even the modestly literate Italian in the cinquecento.

137 Tedeschi 1986, 137.

138 L. Firpo 1959, provides the most comprehensive account of the London Italian congregation.

139 *ibid.*, 315, notes that "merchants, bankers, court musicians, book illuminators, artisans, or mercenaries, the London Italians often declared themselves in the periodic censuses to be extraneous to any church."

140 There is no *DBI* entry for Ferlito, and I have been unable to locate any further information about him.

141 After Ferlito's death in 1570, Giovan Battista Aureli[o] was appointed to succeed him and moved decisively to address the endemic problems afflicting the Italian church, but a number of measures he initiated only served to alienate his Dutch parishioners. After Aureli[o]'s death, the Italian elders recognized by 1598 that finding a suitable successor was going to be impossible, effectively marking the end of the Italian congregation.

142 On Corro, see L. Firpo 1959, 343–355; and Hauben 1967, 6–7.

143 On Aconcio, see *DBI*, vol. I, 154–159; and P. Rossi's concise 1952 monograph.

144 White 1967, 427; and 425–444 for what follows here.

145 See *ibid.*, 431, on Portinari; and Merriman 1983, 57–67, for other Italian engineers who had preceded Aconcio.

146 White 1967, 434, where a description of this device is also provided.
147 Aconcio copied out an essay in 1564 on the utility of history, *Delle osservationi et avvertimenti che haver si debbono nel legger le historie*, dedicated to Robert Dudley and probably intended to remain in manuscript form. Completely theoretical in approach, without examples, the chief interest of Aconcio's essay is in its orienting the lessons of history toward an ethical finality, in sharp contrast to Machiavelli's pragmatic reading of history, about which there was so much heated interest in England at this time. For a brief discussion of Aconcio's text, see P. Rossi 1952, 23–24; for a critical edition of the text, see *Acontiana. Abhandlungen und Briefe des Jacobus Acontius*, Walther Köhler and Erich Hassinger, eds. (Heidelberg: C.Winters, 1932), 4–17; the original is in the Public Record Office, State Papers, Elizabeth, Domestic vol. 34, n. 53; and parts of it were used in an English adaptation by Thomas Blundeville, *The true order and Methode of wryting and reading Hystories, according to the precepts of Francisco Patricio, and Acontio Tridentino* (London: William Seres, 1574).
148 Briggs 1976, 483, where he goes on to spell out the implications of Aconcio's position: "Although we perceive particular objects, these single things could not give us real knowledge unless we studied them in relation to other things which appear to be their causes or effects, and which in turn lead us to compare them with other things of similar causation or results. We thus proceed from the known to the unknown, discovering species, classes and general notions which are nearer to the 'cognitio integra' or whole knowledge which we desire, than are our perceptions of single things. Experience and painstaking analysis of each step in our experience is essential for the avoidance of error, so Aconcio lays most emphasis upon three analytical procedures: from general ideas to the particular, from composite things to their constituents, and from the ends of things to those which serve as their means."
149 Though Toulmin 1990 does not discuss Aconcio, the general thrust of his argument that Descartes' successors effectively silenced the more flexibly responsive skeptical humanism of a figure like Montaigne is of some relevance here; see particularly 36–44. Toulmin encourages a form of cultural criticism that takes into account assumptions closer to the actual moment and means of early modern cultural production.
150 Briggs 1976, 485.
151 On the *Stratagemata Satanae*, see *ibid.*, 487–495; and Jordan 1932, 303–365.
152 Jacopo Aconcio, *Darkness Discovered: Satans Stratagems*, R. E. Field, ed. (Delmar: Scholars' Facsimiles & Reprints, 1978), 61–62.
153 Jordan 1932, 358 and 360.
154 *ibid.*, 350. For his liberal sense of religious freedom, Aconcio was placed among those of "first degree" on the (Catholic) Index of Forbidden Books in 1596.

# 4   Language lessons

1 Philip Sidney, *The Correspondence of Philip Sidney and Hubert Languet*, Stuart A. Pears, trans. (Boston: The Merrymount Press, 1912), 35. Writing to Sidney, then in Padua, Languet instead recommends that he learn German,

given that "you English have more intercourse with the Germans than with any other people, and their authority and power as a nation is already the greatest in Christendom, and no doubt will yet be increased by the folly of my own country and other neighboring states." Sidney evidently chose to ignore this advice – in his response to Languet he avoids the issue – and there was, in fact, little attention paid to German in early modern England.

2 See Yates 1934, 13–27; and del Re's edition of *FF*, viii–ix.

3 An antecedent factor that links Shakespeare's play to the cultural history of Italians in England is Tito Livio da Frulovisi's *Vita Henrici Quinti*, see Ch. 1, page 31. In its restaging of Babelic linguisitic confusion, *Henry V* also serves as a link to the next chapter, which explores grammars and dictionaries as indices of "national" consciousness and identity.

4 The most recent study of the relationship of French and English cultures is Williams 2004, but Lambley 1920 remains an important touchstone for any consideration of the subject. Latin, of course, occupied a central position in legal, ecclesiastical, and university contexts, though the language of English civil law would remain for quite some time shaped by Old French; on this latter point, see Watson 1909, 402–403.

5 Lambley 1920, 61.

6 For the extensive ramifications of English concerns about clothing, see Jones and Stallybrass 2000. Hentschell 2002 examines the implications of the importation of fabrics into England from France, Spain, and Italy, a process with many echoes of what will be developed here regarding the circulation of foreign languages in England.

7 Roger Ascham, *The scholemaster* (London: John Day, 1570), 24r [hereafter cited in brackets in my text].

8 See Ord 2002, 211.

9 Hoby saw more of Italy than most other English visitors to the peninsula in this period, which according to Ascham's argument would have rendered him even more susceptible to Circe's dangerous magic: in addition to studying in Padua and Siena, Hoby spent a considerable period in Rome – he was there for the long conclave that almost elected Reginald Pole pope in 1549–50 – stayed in Naples, and traveled as far south as the Sicilian cities of Taormina, Catania, and Syracuse; see Grayson 1985, 140–142.

10 Whether intended or not, Ascham's invocation of Circe in *The scholemaster* would have recalled a popular translation from Italian (by Henry Iden) of Giovanni Battista Gelli's *Circe*, published in London by John Cawood (the royal publisher during the Marian period) in 1557 and reissued in 1558.

11 See Simonini 1952, 32–33; and Yates 1934, 53–55.

12 The first integral text on English law, Thomas Littleton's *Treatise on Tenures* was printed in 1481 or 1482 in London and written in Law French. All previous English law books had initially appeared in Latin and were dependent on Roman (civil) law. Though Hollyband's book does not deal directly with the law, its title is clearly playing off of the continuing importance of Littleton's text, appealing perhaps to lawyers or law students in need of a French education.

13 For all their sophistication, neither of Florio's *Fruits* saw second editions, which might well be read as a sign of the limits of English interest in gaining

the thorough grounding in Italian they offered, or – as I shall argue later in this chapter – as a confirmation of the passing of the Italianate moment in Elizabethan England, Hollyband's lighter approach being sufficient for anyone requiring a basic knowledge of the language. See S. Rossi 1969c, 93–117, for a useful discussion of Hollyband and the other language teachers in England; and 118–139, on Florio's language pedagogy.

14 Claudius Hollyband, *The French Littleton* (London: Thomas Vautraullier, 1566), B4v–B5v.
15 *ibid.*, B5r–B6r.
16 *FF*, **iii.
17 See Rosenberg 1976, 55–58 and 286–293, on Dudley's pivotal role in promoting Italians in England.
18 Yates 1934, 42–45, suggests both that Florio's attitude toward the theater is ambivalent and that he came to realize his early association with Gosson had been a strategic mistake in his pursuit of patronage and fame.
19 Florio considered the acquisition of grammar as a late step in the process of learning a new language, and accordingly our examination of the formal vernacular grammars that appeared late in the fifteenth and throughout the sixteenth centuries will be postponed until the next chapter, where we shall consider the history of the vernacular dictionaries to which they were often appended.
20 *SF* 2, 22–23.
21 See the similar discussions in *SF* 1 and 7.
22 Florio's praise of Elizabeth in the preface "To the Reader" in his *WW*, B1v, reveals a more seasoned view of the Queen: "That well to know Italian is a grace of all graces, without exception which I ever exemplifie her gracious highnes; whose due deserved-praises to set forth aright I may rightly say, as a notable Italian writer saide earst of her most-renowned father of famous memorie, *Che per capir le giuste lodi della quale converebbe o che cielo s'inalzasse, o ch'il mondo s'allargasse* [That to understand the worthy praises most becoming of him, either the heavens would needs be raised even higher or the world wider]; or as the modern Italian Homer saide of a Queene far inferiour to her thrice-blessed Majestie, *Che le glorie altrui si esprimono scrivendo e parlando, quelle di sua Serenissima Maestà si possono solo esprimere maravigliando e tacendo* [While the glories of others are expressed in writing and speaking, those of Her Most serene Majesty can only be conveyed silently marveling]. Of whose innumerable excellencies, if not the fore-most, yet most famous I have heard, and often have had the good hap and comfort to see, that no Embassador or stranger hath audience of hir Majestie, but in his native toong; and none hath answerd but in the same; or in the common toongs of Greeke and Latin, by hir sacred lips pronounced."
23 Strong 1977, 114.
24 Stephen Gosson, *Plays Confuted in Five Actions*, in Arthur F. Kinney, ed. *Markets of Bawdrie: The Dramatic Criticism of Stephen Gosson* (Salzburg: Institut für englische Sprache und Literatur, 1974), 177.
25 Barish 1981, 81.
26 Berger 1988, 12. My effort to re-imagine the conceptual space occupied by Italian in Elizabethan England owes a great debt to this brilliant early essay of Berger's.
27 See Boccaccio, *Il trattatello*, particularly 614.

28 I cite the translation, *The Life of Dante*, Vincenzo Zin Bolletino, trans. (New York: Garland, 1990), 37.
29 For which, see the next chapter, pages 218–223.
30 The elder half-brother of Henry Wotton, later James I's ambassador to the Venetian Republic.
31 Philip Sidney, *The Defence of Poesie* (London: William Ponsonby, 1595), B1r-v.
32 Barnes 1971, 422.
33 Sidney, *Defence*, B1v.
34 See Koelb 1984, 3: "Aristotle clearly believes that the power to excite wonder which *to alogon* [the irrational] gives to language is something that the poet will prize and try to make use of; but he also believes that the poet must take care lest that same power destroy the foundation of his poem ... the poet who wishes to take the risk of using *aloga*, then, must *hide* them, must engage in whatever deception is necessary to make the *aloga* seem *eikota* [plausible] ... what must be avoided at all costs is the audience's disbelief, the presentation of that which is *perceived* as unbelievable (*apithana*), whether it be so or not."
35 Sidney, *Defence*, B1v.
36 Barnes 1971, 425.
37 Doherty 1991, 7; in the midst of a good deal of talk of horses in *SF* 3, 42–43, we learn that in the diversity of a particular horse's colors "*si trova la confusione Babelica*/You may finde the Babilonian confusion."
38 Matz 2000, 77–79, sees the scene as simply poking fun at Pugliano, but such a reading is in my view too literal a take on the surface of Sidney's text.
39 I cite the translation, Charles Osgood, trans., *Boccaccio on Poetry* (New York: Bobbs Merrill, 1956).
40 Alter 1975, 167.
41 *ibid.*
42 See Manley 1985, 250–251. Davis 1975, 234, notes that "to his contemporaries who wanted to make the proverb into a hieroglyph that only an elite could fully decipher, Erasmus pointed out that many proverbs were not dark enigmas. Some of them were clear, and they were widely known and commonly said."
43 This too recalls Sidney's *Defence*, for, as Barnes 1971, 426, notes at its conclusion, "after solemnly recapitulating his arguments, the speaker puns on 'conjure' ... and then rehearses some of Poetry's claims to virtue. The pun ... is a surprisingly accurate description of the speaker's technique of mesmerizing his listeners through word associations, implications, veiled denigrations, and imagistic appeal." The operations of the "pun" as described here are precisely those of both the proverb and the effective language teacher.
44 See Gamberini 1970, 101–129, for a general discussion of the Italian proverb in sixteenth-century England, and for an analysis of Florio's proverbial sources in both of his dialogue books and the *Giardino*. Gamberini notes, 63, that the "proverbs [in] the Italian of the dialogues [of *SF*] are starred to indicate that they are listed among the ... proverbs collected in the *Giardino*." See also Rossi 1969c, 129–139, on the *Giardino*.
45 Obelkevich 1987, 50.

46 "The genius, wit, and spirit of a nation are discovered in its proverbs" is frequently attributed to Francis Bacon, but I have been unable to trace this aphorism in any of his works.
47 Manley 1985, 251. Davis 1975, 234, notes that "context could be so important that Erasmus admitted 'some proverbs have this peculiarity, that they need to be quoted in their native tongue, otherwise they lose much of their charm; just as some wines refuse to be exported.'" Erasmus' *Adagiorum collectanea* was first published in Paris in 1500, but much of it had been assembled in England and was dedicated to William Blount, Lord Mountjoy. The book owes a significant debt to Polidoro Virgilio's *Proverbiorum libellus* (1498) which, together with another of his grouping of proverbs, *Adagiorum liber* (1528), was (like Erasmus' collection) expanded and republished in successive editions through the middle of the sixteenth century; see Ruggeri 1992, 27–50.
48 Manley 1985, 251. Gamberini 1970, 111ff, notes how Florio sometimes tends to homogenize the regional specificity of Italian proverbial language.
49 Manley 1985, 247.
50 Portia's weary enumeration of her suitors' national markers in *The Merchant of Venice* 1.2 reads as a negative instance of this proverbial mapping.
51 See Davis 1975, 236–237, on the proverb collections of Charles de Bouelles.
52 Kenneth Burke 1973, 296.
53 The other actor in the scene is named Nolano, and Longworth de Chambrun 1921, 63, was the first to suggest that this figure represents an image of Giordano Bruno.
54 As Woodhouse 1994, 11, characterizes the genre.
55 Whigham 1984 remains the fullest examination of the conflicted reception of courtesy literature in Elizabethan England.
56 Yates 1934, 138.
57 Steppat 1994, 27.
58 Woodhouse 1994, 14 and 11.
59 Javitch 1971, 181.
60 *ibid.*, 187–188.
61 *ibid.*, 196–197. While Javitch notes that both Guazzo's and Castiglione's original texts would have been available to English readers, as were Chapuis' French translations of both as well as a Latin translation of the *Cortegiano*, a further look at the slippage between these various versions would render even clearer the specific purposes that translation served in this period. Javitch's useful term, "courtly anti-courtliness," 195, nicely sums up Pettie's interventions in Guazzo's text, one of the ways in which the otherwise apparently antithetical positions of Guazzo and Castiglione came to be reconciled in Elizabethan approaches to conduct.
62 Steppat 1994, 32, referring to John Kepers' translation of Annibale Romei's *Discorsi cavallereschi, The Courtiers Academie* (1598), in which Kepers notes his anxiety that through his work of translation, a "lofty original" will be exposed to "malignant eies ... knowledge being an ornament, most befitting those noble or honorable, who command ... it is therefore requisit (they say) that high wisdom, and excellent workes, shuld be concealed from common sight, lest through equall experience, and knowledge in things (according to the ordinary conditions thereof) puffed up, shake off likewise that humility of

spirit which shuld comprehend them under the obedience of laws and magistrates."
63 C. Freccero 1992, 259–279, has examined the collision of the master/servant dialectic and the literature of courtesy; though Freccero's focus is on the Italian context of Castiglione's text, the discrepancies noted in Castiglione's idealized courtly values are entirely apposite to the threat individuals such as Florio posed to English hierarchies through their mastery of cultural systems that, when enacted in pedagogical terms, inverted the social equation by rendering aristocratic students servile.
64 Woodhouse 1994, 11–12.
65 For a discussion of other Italian books published in the late sixteenth and early seventeenth centuries in England, see Aquilecchia 1960, 106–108.
66 See Ch. 2, page 77.
67 *SF* together with *Il Giardino di Ricreatione* were also issued by Woodcock in 1591, but printed by Thomas Orwin.
68 On Wolfe's initial period in London, see Hoppe 1933, 241–243.
69 For this and what follows concerning Wolfe's Florentine period, I follow Bertoli 1995, 579–582.
70 Jacopo Aconcio, *Una essortatione al timor di Dio con alcune rime Italiane, nouamente messe in luce* (London: [but printed abroad] for John Wolfe, 1579), 3–4: "Quando, serenissima Madamma, M. Iacomo Aconcio già servitor di V. M. S. da questa a l'altra vita fece passaggio, tra alcuni scritti ch'egli mi lasciò, trovai una operetta di sua mano scritta, e secondo che da lo stile mi parve potersi comprendere, dal suo felice ingegno parimente composta. La quale da me più e più volte letta, e sempre più piacendomi, in me destò un desiderio grande di mandarlo a la stampa … e così risoluto di fare, massimamente con l'occasione d'un giovane di questa Città venuto di nuovo d'Italia, ov'ha con molta industria appreso l'arte de lo Stampare, mi son risoluto anchora di mandarlo in luce sotto il felicissimo e clarissimo nome di V.S.M."
71 P. Rossi 1952, 34.
72 On Aconcio's essay, see Huffman 1988, 24–27.
73 Bellorini 1971, 43.
74 Wolfe's connection to Sidney might well have been established in Florence, where, as Stewart 2000, 125–126, notes, Sidney made a visit during the course of his ten-month stay in Italy in 1573–74.
75 See Hoppe 1933, 246–253, on this initial phase of Wolfe's career in London; and 263–265 for Wolfe's activities as Beadle.
76 Niccolò Machiavelli, *I discorsi di Nicolo Machiavelli, sopra la prima deca di Tito Livio* (Palermo [London]: Appresso gli heredi d'Antoniello degli Antonielli [John Wolfe], 1584), A2v: " … piu mi piacevano, & a dirti il vero, ogni hor piu in loro scopriva nuova dottrina, nuova acutezza d'ingegno, & nuovi modi d'apprendere la vera via di trarre alcuno utile dalla giovevole lettura delle historie & in brieve conobbi d'havere piu in un giorno da loro imparato, de governi del mondo, che non haveva fatto nel resto della mia passata vita, da tutte le historie lette. Imparai a punto a conoscere qual differenza sia da un prencipe giusto, ad un Tiranno, dal governo di molti buoni, a quello di pochi malvagi, & da un commune ben regolato, ad una moltitudine confusa, & licentiosa."

77 For Gentillet's impact on Machiavelli's reception in early modern England, see Kahn 1994, 539–560.
78 Machiavelli, *Discorsi*, A3v: "maniere di dire tutte contrarie agli'insegnamenti de nostri grammatici."
79 *ibid.*, 200r: "L'aveduto, & discreto lettore ammendera da se gli altri minori errori, & questi anchora, per donandogli a componitori, i quali per essere eglino Siciliani, & per non saper la favella toscana, con tutta la loro diligenza non gli hanno potuti schifare."
80 For the history of the identification of the Machiavelli and Aretino editions with Wolfe by Bongi, Gerber, and Sellers, see Bellorini 1971, 31, n. 30.
81 See Huffman 1988, 6, and Hoppe 1933, 244. Precisely what sort of diffusion Wolfe's editions had in Italy in the cinquecento is impossible to determine, but each of them is represented today in only a handful of libraries throughout the country, the one exception being Aretino's *Quattro comedie* (1588), which can be found in seventeen libraries (with three copies alone in the Biblioteca Nazionale in Florence).
82 See Bellorini 1971, 31–41, for a detailed look at the narrative these prefaces spin out.
83 A claim tempered by an extended note at the conclusion of the *Quattro comedie*, where the lack of authorial manuscripts is again regretted.
84 Pietro Aretino, *La prima parte de' ragionamenti di M. Pietro Aretino* (Bengodì [London: John Wolfe], 1584), P2r: "da me ridotte ne la maniera, ch'egli le compose, e ne la medesima maniera, ch'egli haveva diterminato di farle prima volta stampare."
85 *ibid.*, 2v: "amicissimo de gli huomini liberi, nimico mortale de colli storti, amator grandissimo del sapere, crudele aversario de l'ignoranza, seguace de la virtu, & agro rimorditore de vizi."
86 *ibid.*, 2v–3r: "benigna Natura ... secolo di fango, non che di ferro."
87 The *STC* lists three works published between 1661 and 1663 with *The wandring-whore* in their titles, but the text from which these were translated is mistakenly attributed to Aretino. *La puttana errante* is by Lorenzo Venier, and it was published along with three other scatological works (also his) – *Il trentuno della zafetta*; *Il manganello*; and *Processus contra ser Catium Vinculum* – in a volume (its date contested) with Aretino's sonnets written to accompany Marcantonio Raimondi's engravings after the original drawings of Giulio Romano which have come to be known as *I modi*; see the notes to Aquilecchia's edition of these sonnets in Aretino, *Poesie varie*, Giovanni Aquilecchia, ed. (Rome: Salerno 1992), 290–298, for the clearest account of their history; though unacknowledged, Lawner 1984 based her work upon an earlier version of Aquilecchia's edition. *La putt.errante* is listed among the books Florio consulted for the compilation of *QA*; see Talvacchia 1992 for a discussion of the circulation of Aretino's sonnets in England, and for their resonance in Hermione posing as the Giulio Romanesque statue in the final scene of *The Winter's Tale*.
88 Among prominent Elizabethans interested in Aretino was William Cecil; his copy of the 1584 *Ragionamenti* is now in the British Library.
89 See Bellorini 1971, 33–4; and Ottolenghi 1982, 39–43. A simple comparison of the language of Ubaldini's *Relazione*, or that of any of his three texts Wolfe

published during this period – the *Vita di Carlo Magno Imperadore* (1581), the *Descrittione del Regno di Scotia* (1588), and *Le vite delle donne illustri del Regno d'Inghilterra* (1590) – is enough to establish that the same author could not have been responsible for the lively, clear, rhetorically sophisticated, and frequently ironic style adopted by Barbagrigia.

90  Yates 1934, 76–79, mentions a letter by Castelvetro sent to Florio to be translated and passed along to a certain Alexander Fougli (though why Fougli, who wrote to Florio in Italian in 1606, should have required Florio's services as a translator in an exchange with Castelvetro is unclear). Yates mistakenly identifies two Castelvetros in England, one each in the Elizabethan and Stuart periods, as these were indeed the same individual.

91  For a concise overview of Castelvetro's life and career, see the *DBI*, vol. XXII, 1–4; In addition to Ottolenghi's brief monograph, De Rinaldis 2003 has made a thorough study of Castelvetro's work as a translator.

92  Lodovico spent 1561–64 in Chiavenna after fleeing Italy for religious reasons, while Michelangelo Florio was pastor in nearby Soglio; he returned there again in 1567–69, organizing a private humanist academy where John Florio may have studied for a time.

93  Though Castelvetro apparently had nothing to do with the Italian congregation in London; see Ottolenghi 1982, 19–20.

94  See Rosenberg 1943, 121–135, for a discussion of the *Columbeid*, and particularly Richard Hakluyt's role in the dedication to Raleigh in Wolfe's edition of the poem as publicity for Raleigh's Virginia initiative; and 135–138 for the ways in which Mendoza's *Historia* played into English interests. Castelvetro was also responsible for Wolfe's publication in 1589 of Thomas Erastus' treatise on excommunication, which served other English interests of the moment.

95  Ottolenghi 1982, 21.

96  For an assessment of the diffusion of reformed thinking in the Marche, then part of the Papal States, see van der Molen 1968, 23–27; and in general for the most thorough treatment of Alberico's life and career in English. Panizza 1981 provides the most recent study, updating a number of aspects of van der Molen's book.

97  See *DBI*, vol. LIII, 245–251, on Alberico; 268–272, on Scipione; and 262–265, on Matteo; unlike Castelvetro (or, it seems, John Florio), both Alberico and Matteo were actively involved in the Italian congregation in London until the time of its dissolution in 1598.

98  For an excellent summary of the development of civil law out of the *Corpus juris civilis*, see Grendler 2002, 431–434.

99  Stein, 1999, 86; and 71–86 for a succinct discussion of the vying Bartolist and humanist perspectives represented in Gentili's dialogues.

100 Huffman 1988, 30; see 30–34 for a précis of *De jure belli*'s principal arguments. For more detailed analysis, see van der Molen 1968, 113–158; and Panizza 1981, 89–128.

101 See Panizza 1969.

102 On the relationship between this controversy and the law, see Binns 1990, 350–354.

103 For which, see Alberico Gentili, *Latin Correspondence by Alberico Gentili and John Rainolds on Academic Drama*, Leon Markowicz, trans. (Salzburg: Institut für englische Sprache und Literatur, 1977), originally printed as an appendix to *Th'overthrow of stage-playes, by the way of controversie betwixt D. Gager and D. Rainoldes* (Middleburg, 1599).
104 For both a critical edition of Gentili's text and an English translation of it, see Binns 1972; his introduction, 224–228, provides a summary of Gentili's argument.
105 *ibid.*, 226.
106 Bellorini 1994, 143.
107 Bellorini discusses the significance of the relations between Sidney and the Gentili brothers, *ibid.*, 145–155. Of particular interest in this regard is an unedited manuscript of twenty-five psalms translated into Italian, Bodleian Library Bodleian Ms. 13, which Alberico presented to Robert Bodley soon after his arrival in England in 1581. Bellorini notes suggestive similarities between this work, Scipione's two Latin psalm collections, and Sidney's translation into English of forty-three psalms, completed after his death by his sister Mary.
108 Cited in L. Firpo 1993, 162: "uno dottore che si chiamava Alberigo Gentile marchegiano, il qual havevo conosciuto in Inghilterra, professore di legge, che mi favorì [et me] introdusse a leggere una lettione dell'Organo d'Aristotele."
109 Provvidera 2002 provides a reconstruction of Charlewood's circle of associates and acquaintances, which included several of the key figures in this Italianate period in England; but his other work connected to Italian was issued entirely in translation, a phenomenon that I shall argue represents a move into quite a new phase of the English encounter with Italy. We shall return to Bruno's Italian dialogues in the next chapter with regard to their impact on Florio's dictionary.
110 See Aquilecchia 1960, 125–127.
111 Actually several letters compressed into one, dealing with the death of Pope Gregory XIII and the election of Sixtus V; see Yates 1934, 79–83.
112 See Appendix II, pages 262–264 for a complete list of these publications.
113 *A discovery of the great subtiltie and wonderful wisdome of the Italians whereby they beare sway over the most part of Christendome, and cunninglie behave themselues to fetch the quintescence out of the peoples purses: discoursing at large the meanes, howe they prosecute and continue the same: and last of all, convenient remedies to prevent all their pollicies herein* (London: John Wolfe, 1591), A3v.
114 Though even here there is a mystery, if Wolfe's Barbagrigia is indeed to be identified as Giacomo Castelvetro: Lodovico Castelvetro had been engaged from 1553 until his death in 1571 in an acrimonious fight with Caro, launched initially by the circulation of what was intended to be Castelvetro's private but sharp criticism of an encomiastic poem Caro had written in honor of the French royal family; the substance of the disagreement was linguistic – Castelvetro highly critical of Caro's non-Petrarchist usage – but through its numerous circumambulations led eventually to Caro's technically unrelated denunciation of Castelvetro to the Inquisition for heresy, a charge that stuck

and led to his flight from Italy (Florio lists the *Apologia d'Annibale Caro contra Lodovico Castelvetri* among the books he had used to collect the *voci* for *QA*); see *DBI*, vol. XXII, 13–15; and for a detailed account of the dispute and its consequences, see Ploncher 1879, especially 22–62. As the feud was unresolved at the time of Lodovico's death, the choice of Caro's Barbagrigia as Giacomo's *nom de plume* must be read as either deeply ironic or simply inexplicable.

115 See Yates 1934, 147–173.
116 See Huffman 1988, 8–9.
117 Ubaldini, *La vita di Carlo Magno Imperadore* (London: John Wolfe, 1599), 2r: "Ai Nobili, et Illustri Signori, et Magnanimi Cavalieri, & altri gentil'huomini della natione Inghlese."
118 *ibid.*, 2v: "si possono stampar & ristampar felicemente in Londra."
119 For a discussion of issues connected to language learning as represented in Shakespeare's and Ben Jonson's plays, see Simonini 1952, 81–109. There is an anachronism imbedded in this scene, however, for anyone the historical Katherine came to deal with at the English court would have spoken French, and many English nobles of the period would still have preferred it to English.
120 I use the uncorrected text of the scene reproduced in *The Norton Facsimile, The First Folio of Shakespeare*, Charlton Hinman, ed. (New York: W. W. Norton, 1968), 433. Modernizations of Shakespeare's (or his redactor's) French do not accomplish exactly the same thing here as editing his English usually does, for it is not only spelling and syntax that thus comes to be regularized but also grammar.
121 Pugliatti 1993, 242, and in general for what follows here. See also Williams 2004, 217–219, for a shrewd reading of the linguistic politics of *Henry V*.
122 *Henry IV, pt. 2*, 234.
123 On the analogy of the human body and the body politic, see Hale 1994, 464–465.
124 Mullaney 1988, 87, sees "Catherine's scene of instruction [as] indeed borrowed from French farce, and as such is nearly unique in Elizabethan drama."
125 Fleming 1989, 43–44, where she also notes several terms that Gary Taylor misses in his edition of the play: "*le pied* and *la robe* were used in England to mean respectively one who commits buggery (from pied, meaning variegated), and a female prostitute. *Foot* sounds to Katherine like *foutre* (to copulate), while *count* would have been recognized as *cunt* by the audience. *D'elbow* sounds like *dildo*, *neck* and *nick* were synonyms for *vulva*, and *sin* was a euphemism for fornication. Finally, *excellent* had lewd connotations, and was especially associated with buggery, as was *assez*, understood to mean ass-y enough."
126 See Shakespeare *Henry V*, Anthony Brennan, ed. (New York: Twayne's, 1992), 55–58; and 59–60, for a brief but intelligent reading of the language lesson vis-à-vis the play's further concerns with language. Orgel notes in the introduction to his edition of *The Tempest*, 41, that "imperial mythology [referring to the rape of the Sabines by the Romans], in which rape is essential to the foundation of empire, offers yet another context for Caliban's designs on Miranda."
127 Fleming 1989, 45.

128 Though the play does not represent Henry's actual conquest of Katherine, Poggio Bracciolini wrote to a friend in February of 1421 that he was going to delay returning to Italy in order to remain in London for her coronation; see Bracciolini, *Two Renaissance Book Hunters*, 48.
129 Half of the brief vocabulary appended to the end of Florio's translation of Cartier is dedicated to English/Native American terms for parts of the body.
130 Florio's first survey of the parts of the body, in *FF* 43, 100r–v, is decidedly prudish about anything approaching the "obscene," but as we shall see the dictionaries take a very different tack.
131 See Taylor's introduction in Shakespeare, *Henry V*, 4–7.

# 5  Worlds of words

1 Zgusta 1992, 14.
2 *QA*, 607.
3 Della Valle on Florio 1993, 42, is typical of the scant attention Italian scholarship has paid to Florio's work: while she does admit that *WW* "deserves at least to be cited" in a very brief survey of sixteenth-century bilingual dictionaries, there is no sign that she has actually looked at it, and *QA* is not even mentioned.
4 Grayson 1985, 167–169, notes the entirely diverse trajectories of the English and Italian vernaculars: due to England's early political unity, the continuing dominance of French well into the fifteenth century, and the centralizing pull of London, regional dialects never survived in England as they did on the politically fragmented Italian peninsula.
5 See especially Palmer 2001; Ginzburg's consideration of English treatises on rhyme, 2000, 25–42; J. Anderson 1996, particularly 101–231; and Helgerson 1992, 21–59.
6 Most pointedly by Sidney, to whom the *Calendar* was dedicated, arguing in the *Defence of Poesie*, H3v, that though Spenser's poem "hath much Poetry in [its] Eclogues, [and is] indeed worthy the reading ... that same framing of his style to an old rustic language, I dare not allow, since neither Theocritus in Greek, Virgil in Latine, nor Sannazaro in Italian, did affect it." Shakespeare's canonization in the *OED*, albeit a late development, is the clearest equivalent to the position that Dante, Petrarch, and Boccaccio assumed for the cinquecento Italian debate about language; see Willinsky 1994, 57–75, for a discussion of the development of Shakespeare's linguistic and cultural dominance in the English-speaking world.
7 See J. Anderson 1996, 9–32; Rabelais' frozen/melting words are, however, anything but uniform or conventional.
8 The huge aggregate of primary and critical literature in Italian dealing with *la questione della lingua* resists any simple summary, but we turn to Citolini – the *Lettera* has not yet had a modern printed edition and is little known in Italy – for an introduction to several of the debate's principal concerns. Migliorini's foundational study of 1960 (see Migliorini 1994) – also available in an abridged English translation by Griffith (Migliorini 1984) – furnishes a synthesis of the entire range of Italian linguistic history which remains unsurpassed

in its comprehensive (and comprehensible) vision of the language. For detailed studies of the *questione* in the early modern period, see Tavoni 1992b on the quattrocento; Trovato 1994 on the first half of the cinquecento; and Marazzini 1993b on the second half of the cinquecento and the seicento.

9 While both of these works also go unnoted in Florio's dictionary libraries, he was certainly more than familiar with them. Oppositional figures, Bembo represents the conservative and ultimately prevailing line in cinquecento philology, while Trissino attempted to articulate a more open and flexible approach to the *questione*. In addition to the general studies already cited, see Tavoni 1992a on Bembo; and for Trissino, see Morsolin 1894, and the introduction to Giangiorgio Trissino's *Scritti linguistici*, Alberto Castelvecchi, ed. (Rome: Salerno, 1986).

10 On Citolini, see the *DBI*, vol. XXVI 39–47; and Fessia 1939–1940, 213–243. Della Giustina 1999, 63, notes that the only extant copy of Citolini's Inquisitorial sentence is contained in the records of the trial of Jacopo Brocardo, whose apocalyptic writings exercised a great influence over Giordano Bruno's final Italian dialogue, *Gli eroici furori*.

11 For Citolini among the Venetian "heretics," see M. Firpo 2001a, 96–99.

12 Alessandro Citolini, *Lettera in difesa de la volgar lingua* (Venice: Francesco Marcolino da Forlì, 1540), 1v: "più nobile ... più ricca ... e più comune."

13 *ibid.* (and [thus] for citations of Citolini in my text).

14 *ibid.*, 3r: "chi è che non sappia che la corrotion di una cosa è la generation d'un'altra?"

15 *ibid.*, 3v: "non è nata di Spirito Santo."

16 A later contribution to the issue of "corruption" was made by Celso Cittadini in two works: the *Trattato della vera origine e del processo e nome della nostra lingua* (Venice: Giovanni Battista Ciotti, 1601); and *Le origini della volgar toscana favella* (Siena: Salvestro Marchetti, 1604), this latter cited among Florio's library of books prefacing *QA*. Cittadini argues that Italian was an entirely new language, having emerged from the altered linguistic situation following the end of the Roman empire, but that the "barbarian" invasions had had nothing to do with its development. Almost exactly Florio's contemporary, Cittadini (1553–1627) was the second "lettor di toscana favella" [professor of the Tuscan language] at the University of Siena, the earliest such position dedicated to a vernacular language in a European university, established in 1588–89 by Ferdinando de' Medici. On Cittadini, see Marazzini 1993b, 195–197; and on the "alternative" direction of vernacular studies emanating from the Sienese academy just at the time that the Accademia della Crusca was first active, see Maraschio and Poggi Salani 1991, 204–232.

17 Citolini, *Lettera*, 15v: "... che ogni favola del Boccacio valeva, quanto un Poeta Greco: e' che quel capitolo di Dante, che comincia:

> La bocca si levò dal fiero pasto,
> valeva, quanto tutto l'Poema Greco, e' latino insieme."

18 Durling provides a concise summary of the Ugolino controversy in an extended note appended to his and Martinez's commented translation of the *Inferno* (New York: Oxford University Press, 1996), 578–580.

19 Citolini, *Lettera*, 4v: "in quel suo più felice stato ... che non mai fusse picciola ... non s'aveggono che la latina è morta e sepolta ne' libri; e che la volgare è viva." Citolini's one serious mistake is to treat the Latinists as if they represented a single point of view, though we have already seen in the first chapter of this study how a humanist like Castiglione sought to bring to his use of Latin the same flexibly eclectic principles he used for his writing in Italian. But the fact of Latin increasingly frozen in time as the cinquecento advanced meant that the language grew progressively incapable of representing and responding to a world so drastically transformed from that of classical Rome at its cultural apogee; for a concise discussion of this issue, see Rowland 1998, 199–211.

20 See Faithfull 1953, 280–284, where Citolini's formulation is situated within the notable influence of Claudio Tolomei's philological work (Thomas Hoby, translator of Castiglione, had also studied with Tolomei in Padua); see Grayson 1985, 140.

21 Citolini, *Lettera*, 5r: "crescie, genera, crea, produce, partorisce, e sempre si fa più ricca e più abondante."

22 Pietro Bembo, *Le prose della volgar lingua* I.viii [1525], in *Trattatisti del Cinquecento*, vol. I, Mario Pozzi, ed. (Milan: Riccardo Ricciardi, 1996), 69: "piante ... di lontan paese portate"; and see Faithfull 1953, 282–283.

23 Citolini, *Lettera*, 4r: "gli huomini non son bastanti, à dar la lor natura à i paesi, ma son bene sforzati à pigliarla da quelli. Per tanto, ancór che tutti que Barbari fussero rimasi in Italia, non sarebbon però stati sofficienti à far diventare barbara l'Italia, ma essi sarebbono stati sforzati à diventare Italiani, si come si vede, che avenne de Troiani, e' de Greci, e' de l'altre genti ... che già vennero in Italia, e' ci rimasero [e] da quali ne uscì poi il Popolo Romano, il quale non fù però ne Troiano, ne Greco, ma fù Italiano ... e', se non fusse per uscir troppo del sentiero, vi farei vedere che i frutti d'hoggi di questo terreno non solo agguagliano gli antichi ma, par che non possano star contenti à questo, ma cerchino di passarli, & in molte cose li passano."

24 *ibid.*, 12v: "cominciò à poco à poco ad esser considerata, conosciuta, & adoperata; e' così pian piano crebbe, e' pian piano fuor de' termini de l'Italia uscendo, quà e là si distese."

25 *ibid.*, 12v: "si può comprendere che così interverrà de la volgare, e' già se ne cominciano à veder segni: ella ha pur già passate l'alpi & è in Francia da moltissimi conosciuta, amata, & havuta cara, si come voi & io ne possiamo esser testimoni. Per la Spagna ancóra, io odo, che ella è assai ben conosciuta, e' che ne l'isole di Maiolica vi sono di lei le publiche scuole. & odo che ne la Magna, e' perfino ne l'Inghilterra, vi trovano piu conoscenti di questa, che di quella."

26 *ibid.*, 14r: "Con questa lingua noi possiamo parlar de la Divinità; de la natura angelica; de le cose del mondo; del cielo; de nascimenti, corsi, e tramontar de le stelle; del Sole e de la sua natura; de la Luna, e de le sue mutationi; del fuoco; de l'aria; de venti; de le piove; de tuoni; de baleni; de l'acque e de' motti loro; de la terra e de la sua natura. Con questa lingua noi possiamo parlar de le pietre, de gli alberi, de l'herbe, de metalli, de gli animali bruti, de l'huomo, de l'Economia, de la Politica, de la guerra, de la pace, de la vita. Con questa lingua noi possiamo trattar de l'agricoltura, de la pittura, de la scoltura, de

la musica, de la poesia, de l'architettura, de la medicina; de la religione, de la sanità, de le sceleragini, de le grandezze, de le picciolezze, de la pietà, de la crudeltà, de le amicitie, de gli odii. Con questa lingua noi possiamo far veder palese tutto l'animo nostro."

27 *ibid.*, 10r: "Io non lodo la sfrenata licentia nó ... biasimo l'affetatione, e' la volontaria, e' noiosa servitù. Io voglio starmi ne la Toscana, non come in una prigione, ma come in una bella, e' spatiosa piazza, dove tutti i nobili spiriti d'Italia si riducono."

28 Cited in Marazzini 1993a, 232, who further notes, 232–233, that the struggle registered in terms of class difference for control of the forms of linguistic expression. This was a battle played out not only in the early modern era but again in the period preceding the peninsula's unification in the nineteenth century, "an integral part of the cultural history of [Italy], [that weighs] more than one has realized on the formation of literary figures and intellectuals, on cultural and scientific discovery, and thus on all the forms of the circulation of knowledge." Woodhouse 1985, 175, characterizes Gramsci's view as too narrowly ideological, but one does not have to be a Marxist to appreciate that language reflects the enormous complexity of the social fabric of which it is part. The struggles of cultures as they seek to define themselves inevitably come to be articulated in languages that register this complexity in diversely conflicted ways.

29 Lucilla Pizzoli's study of Italian grammars in England (2004) has, regrettably, come to my attention too late to be taken into consideration here.

30 The two had worked together on editions of Dante and Petrarch published by Aldo Manuzio [Aldus Manutius], and while there are similarities in their respective approaches to the Tuscan language, Fortunio was much more casual about allowing inside his boundaries *voci* which belonged to northen Italian dialects and to the quattrocento; see Trovato 1994, 92–95. Bembo reacted sharply to charges that he had plagiarized Fortunio in the *Prose*, for if anything, the opposite was more than likely the case, as Bembo's early consideration of the question of grammar in his 1505 *Asolani* seems to have been adopted wholescale in Fortunio's *Regole*; see Trovato, 91–92.

31 See Patota 1993, 102.

32 *ibid.*

33 See Marazzini 1993a, 243.

34 See Trovato 1994, 95–96, where he also notes that Fortunio's grammar saw eighteen editions in the forty years following its initial appearance in 1516.

35 Cited in Patota 1993, 111: "da un fiorentino ai non fiorentini e ai giovani, che vogliono imparare a parlare prima che a scrivere nella 'dolcissima' lingua in uso a Firenze" [emphasis mine].

36 About which, see Trovato 1994, 163–166.

37 Patota 1993, 111.

38 See Trovato 1994, 166–168.

39 Grayson 1985, 143, notes that Thomas Hoby also prepared an *Epitome della lingua italiana* for Henry Sidney in 1550, now lost; considering that this text had been written by Hoby in Padua, where he knew Thomas, it might have been the case that their grammars – both intended for an English audience – were collaborative projects.

40 On Thomas's linguistic work, see Gamberini 1970, 61–68; Griffith 1961, 65–80; and Simonini 1952, 42–45.
41 Gamberini 1970, 65, cites Orazio Lombardelli writing at the end of the sixteenth century in praise of Alunno's grammar, which is noted as having been of particular use to "forestieri."
42 William Thomas, *Principal Rules of the Italian Grammar, with a Dictionarie for the better understandyng of Boccace, Petrarcha, and Dante* (London: Thomas Berthelet, 1550), C2r.
43 Gamberini 1970, 62 and 64; though regarding this problem, Gamberini acknowledges that the distinction between the subjunctive and the conditional had not yet at this point been fully settled by Italian grammarians.
44 *ibid.*, 66–67.
45 Thomas, *Principal Rules*, S2v, T2v, Dd1r.
46 Gamberini 1970, 69, notes the sophistication of Michelangelo's grammar in contrast with Thomas', suggesting that Florio *père*'s text was intended not for beginners but as a reference work for those who already had a good grasp of the language; this might explain why John waited to utilize his father's work until the second edition of his dictionary, where it could serve just such a purpose.
47 See Florio/Pellegrini, *Regole*, 88. I am skeptical about Elizabeth's early connection to Michelangelo, particularly given the very limited success John Florio had with the Elizabethan court.
48 *ibid.*, 89, n. 27.
49 *ibid.*, 102: "Ho raccolto da migliori scrittori della nostra lingua thoscana (ò volete fiorentino) e dall'uso del parlar'nostro alchune regole, con le quali chiunque le leggerà, potrà facilmente impararla, possederla, e parlarla."
50 *ibid.*, 157: "I primi ordinatori di questa nostra lingua, non pur' attesero à dargli tutte le parti de l'orazione, à cio qualunque concetto de l'anima ella meglio isprimere potesse, ma alla bellezza, e leggiadria sua; la quale fa che l'orecchio non meno che l'intelletto sodisfatto ne resta."
51 See Bembo, *Prose* I.xvi, 99: "l'essere a questi tempi nato fiorentino, a ben volere fiorentino scrivere, non sia molto vantaggio" [being born Florentine in these times is no advantage in writing the Florentine language well].
52 Florio/Pellegrini, *Regole*, 178: "Voglio qui darlavi tal quale la lingua nostra l'usa, con la varietà delle voci di detti verbi, à cio piu facile vi sia l'intendere questa nostra lingua, parlarla, e scriverla correttamente come se in Thoscana voi foste nato" (emphasis mine).
53 See Florio/Pellegrini, *Regole*, 103.
54 The example is preceded by this explanation, *ibid.*, 170: "posta la verità de la prima che è condizionata, la seconda necessariamente nasce" [given that the first [construction] is conditional, the second is necessarily born], suggesting that this distinction which had hitherto troubled Italian grammarians was finally settled by the time of Michelangelo's writing.
55 *ibid.*, 186.
56 While Pellegrini argues that Bembo's *Prose* had a greater impact on Michelangelo's grammar than he acknowledged, Gamberini 1970, 71, suggests that the *Regole* "represent the mature fruit of a whole tradition of linguistic studies."

57 See Migliorini 1994, 346, where he writes that Latin being the language common to many foreigners in Italy, both Lentulo and Eufrosino Lapini (in 1574) produced grammars addressed to this public.
58 Gamberini 1970, 71.
59 Henry Grantham, *An Italian Grammer, Written in Latin by Scipio Lentulo a Neapolitane, and Turned into Englishe* [1575] (Menston: Scolar Press, 1968), 31–32.
60 Michelangelo Florio and Citolini also present the noun in this way, and John Florio does the same in his appropriation of their grammars.
61 *FF*, "Necessarie rules,"108v.
62 Also known as John David Rhys and as John Davies. Griffith 1961, 5–6, cites Wood (1721) on Rhys: "John David Rhys ... was born in *Lanfaethley* in the Isle of *Anglesea*, elected Student of *Ch[rist] Ch[urch]* after he had been conversant among the *Oxonians* for three or more years, in the month of December, 1555, aged 21, traveled beyond the Seas before he took a degree in this University, became Doctor of Physic of *Senes* or *Sienna* in *Tuscany*, and public Moderator of the School at *Pistoia* in that Country, whose language there, which is Italian, he understood as well as any Native. Afterwards he returned to his Country, where he practised his Faculty with admirable success, and was held in high esteem by learned Men, for his excellent knowledge in all kinds of literature, especially for Physic, Poetry, the Grammatical part of the *Welsh* Tongue, and curiosity in various criticisms; yet by the generality, he being not understood, his rare parts and curious Learning was in a manner buried where he lived ... he died a *Roman Catholic* (as he lived) at, or near *Brecknock* (where he mostly dwelt and practised Physic) in the Reign of K. *James I scil.* about sixteen hundred and nine." Maraschio improves upon this useful but limited sketch by providing a rich picture of Rhys' formation in Wales and England, his lengthy sojourn in Italy, and his subsequent career in Britain; see Rhys, *De Italica pronuntiatione*, Nicoletta Maraschio, ed., in *Trattati di fonetica del Cinquecento* (Florence: Accademia della Crusca, 1992), 257–264, and Maraschio 1980, 5–18.
63 Grayson 1985, 171, notes that Bullokar's *Brief Grammar for English* (1586) is the very first such effort in English, but it is a modest pamphlet-length treatment in comparison to the systematic studies of Rhys and Greaves. Rhys also wrote an unedited defense of ancient Welsh traditions, BL Peniarth Ms. 118, in response to Polidoro Virgilio's attack on the Welsh in Bk. 27 of his *Anglica historia*; see Griffith 1953, 75.
64 See Rhys/Maraschio, *Ithalica, 101r* (in Latin)/195 (in Italian translation).
65 *ibid., 109v-110r*/199: "bacio, id est, 'osculum', aceto, id est 'acetum' lecito, id est 'licitum'. Anglus sic scriberet basho, asheto, info: leshito. Hispanus verò ac Lusitanus sic baxo, axeto, lexito. Gallus bacho, acheto, lechito. Germanus bascho, ascheto, leschito. Nisi quòd aliquanto subtiliùs, & coasctiùs, ut antea diximus, esseri debeat, vergente scilicet sono ab sibilum ipsius s. In diversis dictionibus, ut la cima, id est, 'summitas seu fastigius', belli ceci id est, 'pulchra cicera', alma Cerere id est, 'alma ceres', crede a ciascuno id est, 'credebat unusquique', vinticinque id est, 'viginti et quinque'. Anglis in hunc modum scriberetur talis facultas, la shima, belli sheshi, alma sherere, crede a shascuno, vintishinque."

66 *ibid.*, *188v*/239: "Verum posita inter G & I, sic gli, dulciùs esseri solet atque liquidiùs ob saliva interclusae compressionum. Huic sono respondet Hispanicum & Gallicum ll geminatum, & Lusitanorum lh."
67 *ibid.*, *29r-v*/223: "Litera canina impetuoso nisu & concitato pronunciatur ab omnibus. Lingua crispante, & ab oris coelum iuxta primorum dentium radices se exitante, ac sui cuspide elisum spiritum vibrante, ictuque quodam tremulo fragosum & veluti horrificum sonum expellente."
68 For Lucilius, see *The Twelve Tables*, in *Remains of Old Latin*, vol. III, Eric Herbert Warmington, trans. (Cambridge, MA: Harvard University Press, 1938), 2–3: "*r* littera inritata canes"; and for Maurus, see *Grammatici latini*, Heinrich Keil, ed. (Leipzig: B. G. Teubner, 1855–1880), vol. VI, 332: "vibrat tremulis ictibus aridum sonum."
69 Extant copies of *De Ithalica pronuntiatione* are extremely rare.
70 *FF*, 109r.
71 See Bellorini 1965, 281–296.
72 Bellorini suggests that Citolini's frequent recourse in his *Grammatica* to diverse Italian dialects would make little sense had it been intended for an English public and that the text likely remained unpublished in Italy owing to its unusual orthographic proposals. And while not entirely letting Florio off the hook (noting that Claudius Hollyband did acknowledge Citolini's grammar in his *Pretie and wittie Historie of Arnault and Lucinda*), Bellorini also recognizes that he rendered the work functional for English readers, drawing on his experience as a language teacher and on his knowledge of English; see 283–285 and 288–289.
73 *FF*, 106r–115r; and 1–13 (out of 74 folio pages) in Citolini's still unedited manuscript, BL Arundel Ms. 258.
74 For Citolini on pronunciation and writing, see Cali 1997, 240; on Trissino's orthographic reform, see Floriani 1980.
75 Cited in Fessia 1940, 238: "Imperochè sendo il parlare uno strumento col quale noi esprimiamo i pensieri e i concetti de l'animo nostro quel parlare è senza dubbio più perfetto, che perfettamente esprime essi pensieri e concetti [de l'animo]; così essendo la scrittura uno strumento col quale noi esprimiamo il vivo parlare; quella scrittura senza dubbio è più perfetta che più perfettamente esprime il vivo parlare." For the full text of Citolini's dedicatory epistle to Christopher Hatton (written in an ink different from and considerably more faded than that of the grammar itself, a factor in determining the earlier Italian context of the work's composition), see 236–238.
76 *ibid.*, 236: "le lingue s'apprendano dai popoli, come anche Platone afferma."
77 *FF*, 160r: "Questa Lingua Inglese, à dirla schjetta, credo che sia la pju confusa Lingua de tutte le altre, percjó che ella é derivata da molte altre lingue, e ogni di va togljèndo delle parole in prestito. Molte ne piglia da la Italiana, pju da la Todesca, assai pju da la Franzese, & infinite da la Latina, & anche taluna da la Grèca."
78 *FF*, 161r–v: "L'*h* é di grand'ornamento á la lingua Inglese, & si é la pju dificile lettera per gli Italiani da proferire, perche é di gran forza, massime in simile parole come queste: *thou*, tu, *that*, quello, *this*, questo. Per proferir simile parole come vanno proferite, bisogna come sarebbe a dire tenir i denti quasi insieme

con apoggiarvi la punta della lingua tra mèzzo, e parlando subitamente ritirarla indjetro, e apoggarla al palato della bocca: á proferire *what*, che cosa, *which*, quale, *who*, chi, *where*, dove, bisogna fare come se volessi suppjare, & tenir la lingua ferma nel mezzo della bocca, senza toccar njènte, e comincjar á proferir lentamente. Ma ne le parole che comincjano con *h*, come *hay*, fjeno, *hat*, capello, *how*, come, *hen*, una gallina, & simile altre innumerabile, bisogna usare una certa gran forza nel proferirle: massimamente ne l'*h* é proferirlo pjeno, e grasso."

79 For this latter term, see O'Malley 2001.
80 Prosperi, cited by Infelise 2001, 28, notes that in Italy "it was well instilled ... [by] the late cinquecento that the intellect needed to be supervised, educated, directed, even so far as intervening with painful operations such as eliminating certain damaging and dangerous modes of thought, [in order to] make the root of the intellect grow in proper directions."
81 *ibid.*, 3–12.
82 *ibid.*, 20.
83 Cited in Longo 1986, 980.
84 See Infelise 2001, 31–42, for a fuller account of what I have necessarily summarized here. Longo 1986, 967, suggests a provocative way of reformulating the traditional triad of writer, text, and reader under these circumstances, substituting in their place "the censoring authority, the censored text, and the castrated or absent reader: the author ends by mattering only with regard to a fame already acquired or that is acquired after being consigned to the *Index*; he is no longer, however, the *artificer* of his own linguistic invention."
85 See Richardson 1996, 155–173, for the best recent account in English of this later cinquecento print history of the *Decameron*.
86 *ibid.*, 169.
87 The edition of Luigi Groto – also known as Cieco d'Adria, whose other works figure prominently in Florio's *QA* library – published in Venice in 1588 (reprinted in 1590 and 1612) but having been completed in the late 1570s or early 1580s, was an attempt independent of the Florentine efforts to save the *Decameron* from the Index. Groto took an even more problematic approach to Boccaccio's text, however, such that one critic concluded that "one could define the work of Borghini as serious, Salviati's semi-serious, [but] that of Groto half-crazy"; cited in Tschiesche 1987, 260; see *ibid.* 236–269 for the history and character of Groto's edition.
88 See Malkiel 1985, 11; on the early history of the Crusca through the publication of the first edition of its *Vocabolario*, with transcriptions of relevant documents, see Parodi 1983, 11–47.
89 See della Valle 1993, 35–37 and 38–40, for a discussion of these two early lexicographers.
90 *ibid.*, 37–38.
91 On Luna, see Olivieri 1942, 102–108; and in general for the development of the Italian dictionary in the cinquecento.
92 See Marazzini 1993b, 176.
93 *Vocabolario degli accademici della Crusca*, from the introductory "A lettori", on-line at http://vocabolario.biblio.cribecu.sns.it/Vocabolario/html/index.html:

"ogni giorno in più stima ... e col numero degli studiosi di quella, sì dentro, come fuora d'Italia, crescere insieme la vaghezza di conoscer le sue bellezze." The reference to "studiosi ... fuora d'Italia" raises the question of whether Florio's 1598 dictionary might have come to the attention of the *Cruscanti*. Boucher 1991, 124, notes a letter, Public Record Office SP 99/18, 52, from an acquaintance of the Venetian ambassador Nicolò Molin, Ventura Cavalli, which demonstrates that by 1604 a copy of *A Worlde of Wordes* was in Molin's possession in Venice.

94 *Vocabolario*: "Il più bel fior ne coglie."
95 *ibid.*: "col parere dell'Illustrissimo Cardinal Bembo, de' Deputati alla correzion del Boccaccio dell'anno 1573, e ultimamente del Cavalier Lionardo Salviati."
96 *ibid.*: "tutti i linguaggi ... o in tutto od in parte si perdono, o s'infettono, e si corrompono."
97 *ibid.*: "qual tempo ... dall'anno del Signore 1300 al 1400 poco più, o poco meno."
98 *ibid.*: "manier[e] di parlare di questa Patria." Heller 1985, 110–111, notes, however, that "the work of professors Nencioni and Parodi has identified different strata in the articles even of the first and second editions [of the *Vocabolario*]: that of the *lemma* [entry] itself, officially registered by the Crusca; that of the metalanguage of definition in which the living (and sometimes colloquial) usage of the compilers surfaces; and that of the literary citations in which many terms occur that are not, however, included in the *Vocabolario*."
99 Marrazzini 1993b, 179.
100 The only dictionary of the period that would merit the global aspirations of the designation "European" is the vocabulary of Ambrogio Calepino, first published as *Dictionarium ex optimis quibusque authoribus* in 1503 but reprinted in numerous editions, with an ever-expanding range of European vernaculars added by other contributors, throughout the sixteenth century. The 1585 edition, with eleven languages represented, for the first time included the exotic vernaculars Hungarian, Polish, and ... English. See Green 1996, 49–52, for a useful précis of the history of this extraordinary dictionary.
101 Parodi 1983, 117.
102 *Vocabolario*: "il più bel fior ... forestieri più tosto ci sembrano, che nostrali."
103 Akrigg 1968, 53, notes that in 1596 Southampton's name alone was registered together with Florio's "when the bookseller Edward Blount made an entry in the Stationers' Register reserving for himself the right to publish" *WW*.
104 About voices raised against Florio in the period preceding the publication of *WW*, see Yates 1934, 193–94.
105 See *ibid.*, 124–126, 188–192, 215–218. Simonini 1952, 101 (citing Longworth de Chambrun), notes that through Southampton, Florio would have known the young Shakespeare, and that the two had earlier shared a common patron in Robert Dudley, as they did later in William Herbert, Lord Pembroke.
106 The allegations (and flimsy accompanying paleographical evidence) are presented in Bossy's *Giordano Bruno and the Embassy Affair* (1991), but Bossy has since identified another candidate for the extraordinary multi-tasking that he

assigns to Bruno in this book; for the revisited case, see his *Under the Molehill: an Elizabethan Spy Story* (New Haven: Yale University Press, 2001).

107 Akrigg 1968, 45; and Yates 1934, 125.
108 See *DNB*, vol. XVII, 940–941.
109 On Lucy's role in Queen Anne's circle after the accession of James I, see Lewalski 1987, 52–77.
110 Frantz 1997, 21.
111 There is no equivalent discussion in *QA* of the principles around which Florio constructed his dictionaries. Though *QA* is an exponentially larger dictionary, and its title is a particularly suggestive one, given the acceleration of England's colonial ambitions during the time of its elaboration, *WW* remains the innovator that determined the parameters within which Florio's later dictionary developed.
112 On which, see Della Giustina 1999, 63–87 (where Citolini's innovative role in the encyclopedic genre is emphasized as anticipating the contributions of both Francis Bacon and the later French *philosophes*); Antonini 1997, 161–231 (in which Citolini's *Lettera* is also briefly discussed, 204–206); and Marcato 1991, 259–264.
113 See Cherchi 1997, 121–157, on Garzoni's encyclopedia; it was a surprise runaway bestseller, within the course of the next 100 years seeing "25 editions ... it was translated into German and Latin (by a German) and was adapted in Spanish."
114 Starnes 1965, 407–422.
115 Frantz 1979, 48.
116 Orgel 1991, 87.
117 See Green 1996, 19; and 19–24 for a discussion of the question of "plagiarism" between dictionaries.
118 See Yates 1934, 265.
119 For a fuller treatment of Florio's library, see my annotated bibliography, 2003 and S. Rossi 1969c, 192–212.
120 See Frantz 1979, 148–151.
121 *WW*, 195. The others are "accismare", "appulcrare," "attuiare," "inculare," "lulla," "lurco," "piorno," "roffia," "rubecchio," and "turgere;" I owe this information to a marginal note in the copy of *WW* in Wesleyan University Library's Special Collections.
122 Though Florio does not cite Anton Francesco Doni's *Libraria* in his own library, he must have known it, given the representation of Doni's other works among the books prefacing *QA*. But unlike Florio's library, Doni's collection – published initially in two separate volumes in 1550 and 1551, and then together in 1557 – grandly aims at representing all books then in print in Italian, though "in the pages of *La libraria* ... every hierarchical order among the various specializations gives way, even if the quantitative priority still belongs to the vast ranks of the literary; other categories are well represented here, from horse-shoeing to fencing, mathematics to falconry, architecture to travelogues, concluding with embroidery manuals and musical texts"; see Vanni Bramanti's introduction to his edition of Doni's *La libraria* (Milan: Longanesi, 1972), 36. "Libraria" could have meant in the cinquecento either

"library" or "bookstore" (its primary modern sense), and Doni's booklists appear to have more to do with a modern index such as *Books in Print* than they do with the very specific choices represented by Florio's library.

123 *OED Online*, New Edition. As we shall see, sexual taxonomy merits a high degree of attention in both editions of Florio's dictionary, though erotic terminology has had a strange history in English-language lexicography; Green 1996, 30–31, notes, for instance, that with the exception of the *Random House College Dictionary*, American college dictionaries have routinely omitted "sexual intercourse."

124 See Willinsky 1994, 221. Citing Jurgen Shäfer's work on the first edition of the *OED*, however, Willinsky notes the provisional nature of these statistics in that up to one-third of first-occurrence citations of Shakespeare and Thomas Nashe can be determined to have antecedents at least several decades earlier; Willinsky also writes that James Murray, the first editor of the *OED*, admitted in an 1884 address to the Philological Society that upwards of three-quarters of the earliest-occurrence citations in the first fascicle of the dictionary could be similarly antedated; see Willinsky, 72.

125 *OED Online*, Second Edition.

126 See Bujanda and Canone 2002, 467–468; the same 1603 edict prohibited the *Opera omnia* of Alberico Gentili.

127 Aretino stayed out of the formal debate over *la questione della lingua*, an interesting stance, given that so many of its polemicists were Venetians concerned with the status of a largely Tuscan language and he was a Tuscan who spent the greater part of his adult life in Venice; but Aretino's aggressive views regarding the possibilities inherent in the vernacular were worked out imaginatively rather than theoretically.

128 For a concise analysis of Aretino's rhetorical strategy in this text, see Aquilecchia 2000, 453–462; and on Aretino's use of pornography as social commentary, see Talvacchia 1992, 94–100.

129 Aretino, *Sei giornate*, Angelo Romano, ed. (Milan: Mursia, 1991), 28.

130 All citations from Florio's dictionary in this section are from *QA*, in brackets following the definition.

131 Almost all of the terms defined here were earlier listed in *WW*, but I cite *QA* because its definitions tend to be somewhat more expansive, and in some instances note nuances the earlier dictionary had missed. It should be added that the *Cruscanti* clearly had no intention that their *Vocabolario* function as a means of decoding sixteenth-century linguistic practice; my comparison of Florio's lexical range with theirs serves, however, to demonstrate the limitations of the Crusca's operative principles. Citations from the *Vocabolario* are from the Crusca's on-line site: www.accademiadellacrusca.it/Vocabolario_1612.shtml.

132 Aretino/Romano, *Sei giornate*, 44: "ANTONIA: So the father superior spent his day in contemplation, eh? NANNA: No, I wouldn't say in the slightest that he 'spent' it, for sticking his paintbrush, first having mortified it, into her colored saucer, he made her writhe as women do when giving birth or suffering from the mother's malady." For the full Italian text of this episode, see *ibid.*; I provide Raymond Rosenthal's translation, *Aretino's Dialogues* (New York: Ballantine Books, 1971), 28, somewhat modified, here in the footnotes as a point of reference.

133 Aretino/Romano, *Sei giornate*, 44 n. 135.
134 *ibid.*, n. 136: "isteria."
135 Aretino/Rosenthal, *Dialogues*, 28: "NANNA: And so as to be certain that the nail would be driven more firmly into its hole, he motioned behind him to his preferred boy-toy who then yanked his pants down to his heels and placed his own cock against his Reverence's backside; the Father Superior all this while kept his eyes fixed on the other two bad boys, who having nicely prepped the sisters by settling them onto a bed were now pounding the sauce in the mortar."
136 Aretino/Romano, *Sei giornate*, 44 n. 137: "... bel fanciullone."
137 Aretino/Rosenthal, *Dialogues*, 28: "NANNA: ... the youngest nun was in great despair, for being somewhat squint-eyed and dark-skinned she had been ignored by the others. So she filled the glass dildo with heated water she had intended for washing the mister's hands, placed herself on a pillow on the floor, pushed the soles of her feet against the wall of the cell, thrusting herself onto that enormous crozier and burying it inside her body as a sword in its sheath."
138 *ibid.*: "Intoxicated by the fragrance of their pleasures, I was even more overwhelmed than are pawns by usury, and I began rubbing my little monkey with my own hand just as cats in January rub their asses on roofs."
139 Frantz 1979, 151, identifies twenty-nine terms in *WW* for "*a womans privie parts* ... of these, fifteen are to be found in Florio alone ... [and] of the remaining fourteen terms only six are included in the dictionaries of William Thomas and/or Thomas Thomas."
140 "FRIAR: If you feel like confessing, I'm ready and willing to serve you. LADY: Not today. I'm expected elsewhere. It's enough that I blow off a little steam, standing up." For the Italian text of the scene, see Machiavelli, *Teatro: Andria, Mandragola, Clizia*, Guido Davico Bonino, ed. (Turin: Einaudi, 2001), 97–98.
141 *ibid.*, 97 n. 1; on the erotic undercurrents of this scene, see also de Grazia (1989), 140–141.
142 "LADY: Take this florin now and say a Requiem Mass every Monday for two months for the soul of my dead husband. Even if he was a monster, still the flesh is weak. I can't help but feel that whenever I remember him ... "
143 "LADY: But do you think that he is in Purgatory? FRIAR: No doubt about it. LADY: I'm not so sure. You know perfectly well what he used to do to me. Oh, how I complained about it to you! I did what I could to keep him at arm's length, but he was so insistent. Ugh, dear Lord!"
144 Unlike much of the literature of the early modern English theater, the division into acts and scenes of Italian plays of the period was typically made by their authors.
145 Boccaccio, *Decameron*, Cesare Segre, ed. (Milan: Mursia, 1987), 195: "'What!' said the friar, 'it isn't that he is still bothering you?' 'He most certainly is!' said the lady, 'indeed ever since I complained to you about him he seems to have taken offense at my having done so ... "
146 FRIAR: "Not to worry! God's mercy is great. Where there's the will, there's always time to repent."
147 Again confirmed by Davico Bonino, in Machiavelli, *Teatro*, 97 n. 8: "*La voglia*: sexual desire."

148 "LADY: Do you think that the Turk will invade Italy this year? FRIAR: If you don't say your prayers, yes. LADY: Good grief! Lord save us from these devilish devices. I'm scared to death of that impaling. But I see here in church a woman was has some spindled thread of mine, and I'm going to go find her. Good day! FRIAR: And good health to you!"

149 Francesco Guicciardini, *Storia d'Italia*, in *Opere*, vol. III, Emanuella Scarano, ed. (Turin: UTET, 1981), 1297–1302, confirms that in 1518 there was a real fear in Italy, shared by Pope Leo X, that a Turkish army under the leadership of Saladin Selem would invade the peninsula, though little enthusiasm could be mustered among European princes for a coalition to block such an assault, and in the end the threat came to nothing; for the disputed dating of the play, see Davico Bonino's introduction, Machievelli, *Teatro*, x–xi.

150 While Florio's dictionary is arranged alphabetically, and this had become more or less the norm by the later sixteenth century, there were other systems of organizing words to be defined, as in the topical format of Citolini's *Tipocosmia*, and contemporary readers may well have been accustomed to other forms of searching through wordlists; regarding the ambivalence in this period toward alphabetical organization, see J. Anderson 1996, 58–62.

151 See Yates 1934, 61; for her full account of Florio's relationship with Bruno, see 61–123.

152 Each of Bruno's *Dialoghi italiani* is dedicated to a distinct philosophical issue, though there is a great deal of cross pollination in the concerns, and ultimately in the trajectory, of the six texts. The *Cena* is a spirited defense of Bruno's cosmology which builds upon Copernicus' heliocentrism in order to posit not only the contingent position of the earth and its movement around the sun but also an infinity of worlds. The debate Bruno stages in this dialogue takes place in the presence of both sympathetic listeners – members of Sidney's circle – and pedantic opponents, representing the closed world of the English academy Bruno had encountered at Oxford. Gwinne was a friend of Florio's from the 1570s and played a decisive role in Florio's negotiation of Montaigne's classical citations in the *Essais*, helping to interpret them and also translating from Latin and Greek.

153 Giordano Bruno, *La cena de le cenere*, Giovanni Aquilecchia, ed. (Turin: Einaudi 1955).

154 See Gatti 1989, 126. This examination of Bruno's English career provides a much-needed corrective to Yates' influential but problematic work on Bruno; Gatti's discussion of Bruno's formative experiences in England, 25–34, is particularly useful for helping to understand both his apparent iconoclasm, and the harsh estimation he made of some elements of the Protestant Reformation.

155 *ibid*, 127. For a discussion of Bruno's choice of Italian for his philosophical dialogues – anticipating by almost half a century other significant philosophical and scientific work published in vernacular languages – see Wildgen 1996, 169–185; and for an overview of Bruno's linguistic practice, see Ciliberto 2000, 208–232.

156 In many respects the *Furori* has proven to be the most elusive of Bruno's Italian texts. Hilary Gatti argues in a forthcoming essay against what has

hitherto been the prevailing position by suggesting that Bruno maintained rhetorical control over the *Dialoghi* to the very end, effecting through the apparently apocalyptic ending of the *Furori* a moving-beyond the philosophical and proto-scientific terms utilized throughout the series into an affirmation of radically new forms of knowledge.

157 See Giordano Bruno, *I dialoghi filosofici italiani*, Michele Ciliberto, ed. (Milan: Mondadori, 2000), 755–762, for the passage discussed here.
158 See the note appended to this passage, *ibid.*, 1350 n. 9.
159 See the rich discussion of the "infinite" possibilities of Bruno's lexical and syntactical innovations in Ordine 1987, 138–149. I take issue, however, with Ordine's assertion of the "outdated" character of Bruno's anti-Petrarchism, for while the Petrarchist vogue had played itself out in Italy by the late cinquecento, it was just coming into its own in England in this period and would continue to exercise a hold on the English poetic imagination well into the early decades of the seventeenth century.
160 Bruno, *Dialoghi*, 51.
161 On Bruno's fierce anti-colonialism, see Bolzoni 2002, 125–131.
162 Ovid, cited again by Florio in Anguillara's translation of the *Metamorphoses*.
163 *WW*, A4v.
164 Fleming 1994, 300, notes that "Florio had worked throughout his career to associate himself with the interests of women, and to link those interests with the status and practice of the European vernaculars."
165 See Bruno/Ciliberto, *Dialoghi*, 202–204; Yates 1934, 118–123, discusses the passage, noting that Spampanato 1924, 246–247, had first identified this link between *SF* and the *Causa*.
166 For the earlier history of this relationship in the classical and medieval Italian traditions, see Cestaro 2003, particularly 1–76.
167 As such, Yates' suggestion 1934, 335, that the pedantic Holofernes and the wind-bag Armado of Shakespeare's *Love's Labor's Lost* both reflect elements of Florio's character might have been true at the level of popular Elizabethan reception of the "stranger" language teachers – a prejudice Shakespeare may well have exploited for comic effect – but the larger questions this play sets into motion (and leaves largely unresolved) with regard to the complex operations of language seem to me much more pertinent to the actual substance of Florio's work.
168 One tangible index of the more visible position of women in Italian vis-à-vis their status is England is demonstrated by the 17 English as opposed to the 225 Italian authors listed in the catalogue of women writers in Erdmann 1999, 199–200 and 206–221; even taking into account the differences in population between the two regions, these divergent statistics are significant.
169 Cornelius Agrippa, *A treatise of the nobilitie and excellencye of woman kynde, translated out of Latin into englysshe by David Clapam* (London: Thomas Berthelet, 1542), A3r. I prefer Clapam's idiomatic translation to the more accurate but prosaic language in Cornelius Agrippa, *Declamation on the Nobility and Preeminence of the Female Sex*, Albert Rabil Jr., trans. (Chicago: University of Chicago Press, 1993); for the original text, see the edition of Charles Béné et al., *De nobilitate praecellentia foeminei sexus: edition*

*critique d'apré le texte d'Anvers 1529*, R. Antonioli, Charles Béné, O. Saurage, eds. (Geneva: Librarie Droz, 1990), 50.
170 On Agrippa's sources and his relationship to the *querelle*, see the introduction to Rabil's translation, *Declamation* 18–27. Florio might also have known Lodovico Domenichi's 1549 *La nobiltà delle donne* or its English adaptation in William Barker's *The Nobylytye of Women* (which circulated in manuscript in the period). In general, for the English response to the *querelle* through the end of the sixteenth century, see Isenberg 1983, 51–71. Florio may have first encountered Agrippa's work through his own father, given Michelangelo's sympathies with the radical wing of the Protestant reform, or through Bruno, who would have been familiar with Agrippa's interest in the occult sciences; about both of which, see Zambelli 1976, 69–103. Paolo Giovio initiated a legend regarding Agrippa and the devil which in the German tradition subsequently developed into Goethe's Faust; see *ibid.*, 69–70.
171 Barolini 1993, 176 and 179–180.
172 Machiavelli, *Discorsi sopra la prima deca di Tito Livio* 3.6.18, Corrado Vivanti, ed. (Turin: Einaudi, 2000), 248: "Ammazzarono alcuni congiurati forlivesi il conte Girolamo loro signore."
173 *ibid.*, 368: "la morte del marito e minacciògli d'ogni qualità di vendetta. E per mostrare che de' suoi figliuoli non si curava, mostrò loro le membra genitali, dicendo che aveva ancora il modo a rifarne."
174 See J. Freccero 1993, 171.
175 *ibid.*
176 *ibid.*, 177.
177 See the chapter on Bradamante in Shemek 1998, 77–125.
178 See *ibid.*, 94–95, 97, and 108.
179 Ludorico Ariosto, *Orlando furioso* 32.102.1–8, Emilio Bigi, ed. (Milan: Rusconi, 1982), 1369–1370.
180 John Harington, *Orlando Furioso in English Heroical Verse* 30.96.1 (London: Richard Field, 1591), 265. For a discussion of Harington's gender politics in his translation of Ariosto – a task Harington claims was imposed upon him by Elizabeth after he had initially translated and circulated at court the scurrilous episode of Jocondo which comprises all of Canto 28 – see Scott-Warren 2001, 26–38.
181 See Parker 2000. The crux at the outset of *King Lear* turns these values inside out, Cordelia maintaining – to her imminent destruction – that *detti* speak more honestly than the *parole* with which her sisters trick their father into favoring them: here words speaking falsehoods are mistaken for the truth, while deeds are rendered entirely mute and pointless.
182 Baron 1986, 90–111, discusses the efforts of early modern grammarians to establish gender marking in English, an initiative that gained no momentum until well into the eighteenth century, when it took some particularly circuitous (and ultimately fruitless) twists and turns.
183 *WW*, A3r.
184 Michel de Montaigne, *Essais*, vol. I, Alexandre Micha, ed. (Paris: GF Flammarion, 1969), 144.

185 Montaigne, *The Essayes, or Morall, Politike and Millitarie Discourses*, John Florio, trans. (London: Edward Blount, 1603), 41.
186 The *Essayes* was entered with the Stationers' Company in 1600 but not printed until 1603. Boucher 1991, 275–276, argues that Florio had not begun his translation until 1599, a judgment based upon Samuel Daniel's prefatory poem dated that year, but more problematically assuming that the period of work on the translation can be established according to the various French editions of Montaigne from 1598 onwards (though Boucher admits that differentiating between the 1595 and 1598 editions is practically impossible). Given the resonance between the preface to *WW* and Montaigne's essay on the imagination (Yates cites several others – see Yates 1934, 213–214 – which Boucher finds dubious), I suggest that it is more than likely that Florio was already by the time of the dictionary's publication familiar with the 1595 edition of the *Essais* published after Montaigne's death and edited by Marie Gournay, even if his actual work of translation had not yet begun. And as Tetel 1995, 177, has pointed out, Florio knew the 1590 Italian adaptation of Books 1 and 2 of the *Essais* by Girolamo Naselli, plausibly to be considered among those noted in Florio's address "To the courteous reader" of his translation as one of the "seven or eyght of great wit and worth [who] have assayed but found these Essayes no attempt for French apprentises or Littletonians" (the claim is not limited to translations into English), A6r. The full title of Florio's Montaigne, *Essayes or Morall politike and millitarie discourses of Lo. Michaell de Montaigne*, at any rate, translates literally Naselli's *Discorsi morali politici et militari del molto illustre sig. Michiel di Montagna*.
187 Orgel 1996, 20.
188 A contributor to other monumental cultural projects of the period, Hole also designed the title page for the folio edition of Ben Jonson's works (1616) and made a frontispiece engraving of George Chapman for the edition of his complete English Homer (1616).
189 See Stewart 2003, 181–184.
190 Besides the various evidence regarding Anne's conversion to Catholicism, it is difficult otherwise to account for the significant amount of Catholic devotional literature among the titles in the library prefacing *QA*.
191 A comparison of the relative positions of Florio in the Jacobean world and Andrea della Rena in the administration of Henry VIII (see Ch. 1, pages 60–62) is telling. This is a point of view at odds with one of the central claims in Boucher 1991, the only recent extended study of Florio, from which I have nevertheless learned a great deal. Briefly, Boucher argues that Florio's career evolved along an axis that ran directly from the classical Latin rhetorical treatises essential for humanist pedagogy to Montaigne's *Essais*, and that from out of this typical humanist preparation Florio successfully fashioned himself into a "scholar-diplomat." As I shall argue in a future study of Florio in the Stuart period, my own reading of Florio's classical humanist credentials is somewhat more skeptical, and my sense of this final stage of his professional life is considerably more circumspect.
192 Parker 1993, 343.

# Bibliography

**Primary Sources**

Aconcio, Jacopo. *Darkness Discovered: Satan's Stratagems*, R. E. Field, ed. Delmar: Scholars' Facsimiles & Reprints, 1978.
*Delle osservationi et avvertimenti che haver si debbono nel legger le historie.* In *Acontiana. Abhandlungen und Briefe des Jacobus Acontius*, Walther Köhler and Erich Hassinger, eds. Heidelberg: C. Winter, 1932: 4–17.
*Una essortatione al timor di Dio con alcune rime Italiane, nouamente messe in luce* (London: [but printed abroad] for John Wolfe, 1579). In *Acontiana*: 77–85.
*A discovery of the great subtiltie and wonderful wisedome of the Italians whereby they beare sway over the most part of Christendome, and cunninglie behave themselues to fetch the quintescence out of the peoples purses: discoursing at large the meanes, howe they prosecute and continue the same: and last of all, convenient remedies to prevent all their pollicies herein.* London: John Wolfe, 1591.
Agricola, Giorgio. *L'arte de' metalli tradotto in lingua toscana da Michelangelo Florio*, Luigi Firpo, ed. Turin: Bottega d'Erasmo, 1969.
Agrippa, Cornelius (von Nettesheim). *A treatise on the nobilitie and excellencye of woman kynde, translated out of Latin into englysshe by David Clapam.* London: Thomas Berthelet, 1542.
*Declamation on the Nobility and Preeminence of the Female Sex*, Albert Rabil Jr., trans. Chicago: University of Chicago Press, 1993.
*De nobilitate et praecellentia foeminei sexus: édition critique d'après le texte d'Anvers 1529*, R. Antonioli, Charles Béné, O. Sauvage, eds. Geneva: Librarie Droz, 1990.
Albicante, Giovanni Alberto. *Il sacro et divino sponsalitio.* Milan: Moscheni, 1555.
Alighieri, Dante. *De vulgari eloquentia*, Stephen Botterill, trans. Cambridge: Cambridge University Press, 1996.
*Inferno*, Robert Durling and Ronald Martinez, trans. New York: Oxford University Press, 1996.
*Ambasciatori veneti in Inghilterra*, Luigi Firpo, ed. Turin: UTET, 1978.
*An Italians dead bodie Stucke with English Flowers. On the death of Sir Oratio Pallavicino*, Theophilus Field, ed. London: Andrew Wise, 1600.
*A Relation or rather a True Account of the Island of England*, Charlotte Augusta Sneyd, trans. London: Camden Society, 1847.
Aretino, Pietro. *Aretino's Dialogues*, Raymond Rosenthal, trans. New York: Stein and Day, 1971.

*Il primo-sesto libro delle lettere.* Paris: Matteo il Maestro, 1609.
*Lettere*, vol. I, Francesco Erspamer, ed. Parma: Ugo Guanda, 1995.
*Lettere*, vol. II, Francesco Erspamer, ed. Parma: Ugo Guanda, 1998.
*Lettere*, vol. VI, Paola Procaccioli, ed. Rome: Salerno, 2002.
*Lettere sull'arte di Pietro Aretino*, vol. III.1, Ettore Camesasca and Fidenzio Pertile, eds. Milan: Edizioni del Milione, 1959.
*Quattro comedie.* London: John Wolfe, 1588.
*Poesie varie*, Giovanni Aquilecchia, ed. Rome: Salerno, 1992.
*La prima parte de ragionamenti di M. Pietro Aretino.* Bengodì [London: John Wolfe], 1584.
*Pronosticon.* In *Cortegiano*, Angelo Romano, ed. Milan: Biblioteca Universale Rizzoli, 1989: 294–295.
*Sei giornate.* Angelo Romano, ed. Milan: Mursia, 1991.
Ariosto, Ludovico. *Orlando furioso*, Emilio Bigi, ed. Milan: Rusconi, 1982.
*Orlando Furioso in English Heroical Verse*, John Harington, trans. [1591], Robert McNulty, ed. Oxford: Clarendon Press, 1972.
Ascham, Roger. *The scholemaster* [1571]. New York: AMS Press, 1967.
Bandello, Matteo. *La seconda parte de le novelle*, Delmo Maestri, ed. Alessandria: Edizioni dell'Orso, 1993.
Beccadelli, Ludovico. *Vita del Cardinale Reginaldo Polo.* In *Monumenti di varia letteratura tratti dai manoscritti di Monsignor Lodovico Beccardelli*, pt. 2 [1799]. Farnborough: Gregg Press Limited, 1967.
Bembo, Pietro. *Le prose della volgar lingua* [1525]. In *Trattatisti del Cinquecento*, vol. I, Mario Pozzi, ed. Milan: Riccardo Ricciardi, 1996.
Blundeville, Thomas. *The true order and Methode of wryting and reading Hystories, according to the precepts of Francisco Patricio, and Acontio Tridentino.* London: William Seres, 1574.
Boccaccio, Giovanni. *Boccaccio on Poetry*, Charles Osgood, trans. New York: Bobbs Merrill, 1956.
*Decameron*, Cesare Segre, ed. Milan: Mursia, 1987.
*Geneologia deorum gentilium*, 2 vols., Vincenzo Romano, ed. Bari: Laterza, 1951.
*Il trattatello in laude di Dante.* In *Opere in versi*, Pier Giorgio Ricci, ed. Milan: Riccardo Ricciardi Editore, 1965: 565–650.
*The Life of Dante*, Vincenzo Zin Bolletino, trans. New York: Garland, 1990.
Bracciolini, Poggio. *Two Renaissance Book Hunters: The Letters of Poggius Bracciolini to Nicolaus de Niccolis*, Phyllis W. G. Gordan, trans. New York: Columbia University Press, 1974.
Bruno, Giordano. *I dialoghi filosofici italiani*, Michele Ciliberto, ed. Milan: Mondadori, 2000.
*La cena de le cenere*, Giovanni Aquilecchia, ed. Turin: Einaudi, 1955.
*Calendar of Letters, Despatches, and State Papers, Spain, 1547–1549*, Martin A. S. Hume and Royal Tyler, eds. London: His Majesty's Stationery Office, 1912.
Carmeliano, Pietro. *Carmen.* London: Richard Pynson, 1508.
Cartier, Jacques. *A shorte and briefe narration of two navigations and discoveries to the northweast partes called Newe Fraunce*, John Florio, trans. London: H. Bynneman, 1580.

Castiglione, Baldassare. *Ad Henricum Angliae Regem epistola de vita et gestis Guidibaldi Urbini Ducis*. Amherst College Ms. B3 n. 3.
*Ad Henricum VII*. In *Le lettere di Baldassar Castiglione*, Guido la Rocca, ed. Milan: Mondadori, 1978: 164–198.
*Il libro del cortegiano*, Walter Barberis, ed. Turin: Einaudi, 1998.
Ceffino, Zanobio. *Stanze di Zanobio Ceffino cittadino fiorentino sopra l'eresia del re d'Inghilterra e sopra la morte di Tommaso Moro gran cancelliero*. BL Additional Ms. 21982, transcribed by Alberto Castelli. In "Un poemetto inedito del secolo XVI in onore di San Tommaso Moro." *Aevum* 12 (1938): 235.
Cellini, Benvenuto. *La vita*, Guido Davico Bonino, ed. Turin: Einaudi, 1973.
Cerretani, Bartolomeo. *Dialogo della mutazione di Firenze*, Giuliana Berti, ed. Florence: Olschki, 1993.
Citolini, Alessandro. *Grammatica della lingua italiana*. British Library Arundel Ms. 258.
*Lettera in difesa de la volgar lingua*. Venice: Francesco Marcolino da Forlì, 1540.
*Tipocosmia*. Venice: Vincenzo Valgrisi, 1561.
Cittadini, Celso. *Le origini della volgar toscana favella*. Siena: Salvestro Marchetti, 1604.
*Trattato della vera origine e del processo e nome della nostra lingua*. Venice: Giovanni Battista Ciotti, 1601.
Corsini, Niccolò. *Il libro di ricordanze dei Corsini*, Armando Petrucci, ed. Rome: Istituto Storico Italiano, 1965.
Davanzati, Bernardo. *Scisma d'Inghilterra*. Rome: Guglielmo Facciotti, 1602.
*Lo scisma d'Inghilterra*, Enrico Bindi, ed. Milan: Casa Editrice Bietti, 1933.
Della Rena, Andrea [Ammonio]. *Andreae Ammonii carmina omnia*, Clemente Pizzi, ed. Florence: Olschki, 1958.
Doni, Anton Francesco. *La libraria*, Vanni Bramanti, ed. Milan: Longanesi, 1972.
Elizabeth I. *Collected Works: Elizabeth I*, Leah Marcus, Janel Mueller, and Mary Beth Rose, eds. Chicago: University of Chicago Press, 2000.
*Elizabeth I: Autograph Compositions and Foreign Language Originals*, Janel Mueller and Leah S. Marcus, eds. Chicago: Chicago University Press, 2003.
Letter to Ferdinando de' Medici, April 6, 1592. Archivio di Stato Florence, Fondo Mediceo del Principato, 4183, 30r–32v.
Erasmus, Desiderius. *Erasmus and Cambridge: The Cambridge Letters of Erasmus*, D. F. S. Thompson, trans., and H. C. Porter, ed. Toronto: University of Toronto Press, 1963.
Florio, John. *Florio's 'First Fruites'*, Arundel del Re, ed. Formosa: Taihoku Imperial University, 1936.
*Florio His Firste Fruites: which yeelde familiar speech, merie Proverbes, wittie sentences, and golden sayings. Also a perfect introduction to the Italian and English tongues*. London: Thomas Woodcock, 1578.
*Second Frutes* [1591], R. C. Simonini, ed. Gainesville, FL: Scholars' Facsimiles & Reprints, 1953.
*Queen Anna's New World of Word* [1611]. Menston: Scolar Press, 1968.
*A Worlde of Wordes* [1598]. Hildesheim: Georg Olms Verlag, 1972.
Florio, Michelangelo. *Historia de la vita e de la morte de l'Illustrissima Signora Giovanna Graia, gia regina eletta e publicata in Inghilterra: e de le cose accadute*

*in quel regno dopo la morte del re Edoardo VI.* Middleburg: Richard Shielders, 1607.

*Regole de la lingua thoscana*, Giuliano Pellegrini ed. In "Michelangelo Florio e le sue *Regole de la lingua thoscana.*" *Studi di filologia italiana* 12 (1954): 72–201.

*The Fugger Newsletters, 1568–1605*, Victor von Klarwill and Pauline de Chary, eds. London: John Lane, 1924.

Gascoigne, George. *The Queen's Majesty's Entertainment at Woodstock, 1575*, A. W. Pollard, ed. Oxford: Daniel and Hart, 1910.

Gentili, Alberico. *Commentatio ad legem III codicis de professoribus et medicis.* In J. W. Binns, "Alberico Gentili in Defence of Poetry and Acting." *Studies in the Renaissance* 19 (1972): 229–272.

*Latin Correspondence by Alberico Gentili and John Rainolds on Academic Drama*, Leon Markowicz, trans. Salzburg: Institut für Englische Sprache und Literatur, 1977.

Giovio, Paolo. *In vitam Leonis decimi.* In *Pauli Iovii Opera*, vol. VI, Michele Cataudella, ed. Rome: Istituto Poligrafico e Zecca dello Stato, 1987: 5–106.

Gosson, Stephen. *Playes Confuted in Five Actions.* In Arthur F. Kinney, ed. *Markets of Bawdrie: The Dramatic Criticism of Stephen Gosson.* Salzburg: Institut für Englische Sprache und Literatur, 1974: 139–200.

Grantham, Henry. *An Italian Grammer, Written in Latin by Scipio Lentulo a Neapolitane, and Turned into Englishe* [1575]. Menston: Scolar Press, 1968.

Griffi, Pietro. *De officio collectoris in regno angliae*, Michele Monaco, ed. Rome: Edizioni di Storia e Letteratura, 1973.

Guicciardini, Francesco. *Storia d'Italia.* In *Opere*, vol. III, Emanuella Scarano, ed. Turin: UTET, 1981.

Herodotus. *The Histories*, Robin Waterfield, trans. Oxford: Oxford University Press, 1998.

*Holinshed's Chronicles*, vol. III, Henry Ellis, ed. London: J. Johnson, 1808.

Hollyband, Claudius. *Campo di fior or else The flourie field of foure languages ... for the furtherance of the learners of the Latine, French, English, but chieflie of the Italian tongue.* London: Thomas Vautraullier, 1583.

*The French Littleton* [1566], M. St. Clare Byrne, ed. Cambridge: Cambridge University Press, 1953 (based upon 1609 edition).

*The French Schoolmaster* [1565]. Menston: Scolar Press, 1972.

*The Italian Schoolemaister.* London: Thomas Purfoot, 1597.

*Journal of a Milanese Merchant* [1516]. British Library Additional Ms. 24180.

*Letters of Denization and Acts of Naturalization for Aliens in England, 1509–1603*, William Page, ed. Lymington: The Huguenot Society of London, 1893.

Litolfi, Annibale. *Relazione sull'Inghilterra. La Diplomazia Gonzagesca*, Romolo Guazzo, ed. Milan: Istituto per gli Studi di Politica Internazionale, 1941: 57–70.

Lucilius. *The Twelve Tables.* In *Remains of Old Latin*, vol. III, Eric Herbert Warmington, trans. Cambridge, MA: Harvard University Press, 1938.

Luther, Martin. *Address to the Christian Nobility of the German Nation Respecting the Reformation of the Christian Estate*, C. A. Bucheim, trans. In the *Harvard Classics* edition of Machiavelli, *The Prince*, etc. New York: P. F. Collier, 1910: 276–397.

Machiavelli, Niccolò. *Discorso intorno alla nostra lingua*, Paolo Trovato, ed. Padua: Antenore, 1982.
*Discorsi sopra la prima deca di Tito Livio*, Corrado Vivanti, ed. Turin: Einaudi, 2000.
*I discorsi di Nicolo Machiavelli, sopra la prima deca di Tito Livio;* published together with *Il prencipe*. Palermo [London]: Appresso gli heredi d'Antoniello degli Antonielli [John Wolfe], 1584.
*L'asino doro di Nicolo Macchiavelli con tutte laltre sue operette*. Rome [London]: John Wolfe, 1588.
*Teatro: Andria, Mandragola, Clizia*, Guido Davico Bonino, ed. Turin: Einaudi, 2001.
Magno, Alessandro. *Travel Journal* [1562]. Folger Library Ms. V.a.259.
Maurus, Terentius. In *Grammatici latini*, Heinrich Keil, ed. Leipzig: B. G. Teubner, 1855–1880, vol. VI.
Mazzuchelli, Giammaria. *La vita di Pietro Aretino* [1763], reprinted in *Lettere sull'arte di Pietro Aretino*, vol. III.1, Ettore Camesasca and Fidenzio Pertile, eds. Milan: Edizioni del Milione, 1959.
Montaigne, Michel de. *Essais*, vol. I, Alexandre Micha, ed. Paris: GF Flammarion, 1969.
*The Essayes, or Morall, Politike and Millitarie Discourses*, John Florio, trans. London: Edward Blount, 1603.
More, Thomas. *Selected Letters*, Elizabeth Frances Rogers, ed. New Haven: Yale University Press, 1961.
*The Latin Epigrams of Thomas More*, Leicester Bradner and Charles Arthur Lynch, eds. Chicago: University of Chicago Press, 1953.
Nagonio, Giovanni Michele (Nagonius). *Carmen*. York Minster Ms. XVI N2.
*Nuovi documenti su Vittoria Colonna e Reginald Pole*, Sergio M. Pagano and Concetta Ranieri, eds. Città del Vaticano: Archivio Vaticano, 1989.
Ochino, Bernardino. *I 'Dialogi sette' e altri scritti del tempo della fuga*, Ugo Rozzo, ed. Turin: Claudiana, 1985.
*Patterns of Perfection: Seven Sermons Preached in Patria*, John McNair, trans. Cambridge: Anastasia Press, 1999.
*Seven Dialogues*, Rita Belladonna, trans. Ottawa: Dovehouse Editions, 1988.
*The Tragedie by Bernardino Ochino*, Constance E. Plumptre, ed. London: Grant Richards, 1899.
Piccolomini, Enea Silvio. *I Commentarii*, 2 vols., Luigi Totaro, ed. and trans. Milan: Adelphi, 1984.
Pollini, Girolamo. *Historia ecclesiastica della rivoluzion d'Inghilterra*. Bologna: 1591.
*Historia ecclesiastica della rivoluzion d'Inghilterra*. Rome: Facciotti, 1594.
Ponet, John. *Catechismus brevis Christianae disciplinae summam continens, omnibus ludimagistris authoritate Regia commendatus*. London: Reynold Wolff, 1553.
*Cathechismo, cioe forma breve per amaestrare i fanciulli*, trans. Michelangelo Florio. London: Mierdman, 1553.
Rastell, William. *Ordo condemnationes Thomæ Mori*, Gerardo Moringo, trans. In *Acta Thomæ Mori*, Henri de Vocht, ed. Louvain: Humanistica Lovaniensia, 1947.
*Records of the English Province of the Society of Jesus*, vol. I, Henry Foley, ed. London: Roehampton, 1877.

*Relazioni di ambasciatori veneti al Senato, vol. I: Inghilterra*, Luigi Firpo, ed. Turin: Bottega d'Erasmo, 1965.

*Returns of Aliens Dwelling in the City and Suburbs of London from the Reign of Henry VIII to that of James I*. London, 4 vols., E. F. Kirk and R. E. G. Kirk, eds. Aberdeen: Aberdeen University Press, 1900–08.

Rhys, John David. *De Ithalica pronuntiatione*. In Nicoletta Maraschio, ed., *Trattati di fonetica del Cinquecento*. Florence: Accademia della Crusca, 1992: 91–264.

Riccio, Pier. Letter, November 3, 1547. Florence: Archivio di Stato, Fondo Mediceo del Principato 1176b, 3, 489.

Sanders, Nicholas. *De origine ac progressu Schismatus Anglicani*. Rome: Bartolomeo Bonfadini, 1586.

Sarpi, Paolo. *Considerationi sopra le censure della santità di papa Paolo V contro la republica di Venezia*. Venice: Roberto Meietti, 1606.

*A fvll and satisfactorie answer to the late vnadvised bull thundred by Pope Paul the Fift, against the renowmed State of Venice: being modestly entitled by the learned author, Considerations vpon the censure of Pope Pavl the Fift against the Common-wealth of Venice*, trans. unknown. London: John Bill, 1606.

Shakespeare, William. *Complete Pelican Shakespeare*, Stephen Orgel and A. R. Braunmuller, general eds. New York: Penguin, 2002.

*The First Folio of Shakespeare*. Charlton Hinman, ed. New York: W. W. Norton, 1968.

*Henry V*, Anthony Brennan, ed. New York: Twayne's, 1992.

*Henry V*, Gary Taylor, ed. Oxford: Clarendon Press, 1982.

*Henry IV, pt. 2*, René Weis, ed. Oxford: Clarendon Press, 1998.

*King Lear*, Stephen Orgel, ed. New York: Penguin, 2002.

*Love's Labor's Lost*, Peter Holland, ed. New York: Penguin Books, 2002.

*The Merchant of Venice*, A. R. Braunmuller, ed. New York: Penguin, 2002.

*The Tempest*, Stephen Orgel, ed. Oxford: Oxford University Press, 1987.

*The Winter's Tale*, Frances E. Dolan, ed. New York: Penguin, 2002.

Sidney, Philip. *An Apology for Poetry* [or *The Defence of Poesie*, 1595], R. W. Maslen, ed. Manchester: Manchester University Press, 2002.

*The Correspondence of Philip Sidney and Hubert Languet*, Stuart A. Pears, trans. Boston: The Merrymount Press, 1912.

Stow, John. *Annales, or, Generall chronicle of England*. London: Thomas Adams, 1615.

Thomas, William. *Il Pellegrino Inglese ne 'l quale si defende l'innocente & la sincera vita de 'l pio & religioso re d'Inghilterra Henrico Ottavo bugiardamente calonniato da Clemente VII & da gl'altri adultatori de la Sedia Antichristiana*. Zurich, 1552.

*The Pilgrim, A Dialogue on the Life and Actions of King Henry the Eighth*, ed. J. A. Froude. London: Parker, Son, and Bourn, 1861.

*Principal Rules of the Italian Grammar, with a Dictionarie for the better understandyng of Boccace, Petrarcha, and Dante*. London: Thomas Berthelet, 1550.

Tito Livio dei Frulovisi. *Opera hactenus inedita T. Livii Frulovisiis de Ferraria*. C. W. Previté-Orton, ed. Canterbury: Academic Press, 1932.

Tomizza, Fulvio. *Il male viene dal nord*. Milan: Mondadori, 1984.

Trissino, Giangiorgio. *Scritti linguistici*, Alberto Castelvecchi, ed. Rome: Salerno, 1986.

Ubaldini, Petruccio. *Avvisi di Londra di Petruccio Ubaldini, fiorentino, relativi agli anni 1579–1594, con notizie sulla guerra di Fiandra.* Florence: Olschki, 1969.
— *La disfatta della flotta spagnola,* Anna Maria Crinò, ed. Florence: Olschki Editore, 1988.
— *La 'Relatione d'Inghilterra' di Petruccio Ubaldini* [1583], Anna Maria Crinò, ed. In *Annali della Scuola Normale Superiore di Pisa, Classe di Lettere e Filosofia,* serie 3, vol. IX:2 (1979): 641–757.
— *La vita di Carlo Magno imperadore.* London: John Wolfe, 1599.
— *Relazione d'Inghilterra* [1552]. In *Un fiorentino alla corte d'Inghilterra, Petruccio Ubaldini,* Giuliano Pellegrini, ed. Turin: Bottega d'Erasmo, 1967.
Valdés, Juan. *Alfabeto cristiana,* Massimo Firpo, ed. Turin: Einaudi, 1994.
Valla, Lorenzo. *De falso credito et ementita Costantini donatione declamation,* Christopher B. Coleman, ed. and trans. Toronto: University of Toronto Press, 1985.
— *The Profession of the Religious, and the Principal Arguments from 'The falsely-believed and forged Donation of Constantine',* Olga Zorzi Pugliese, trans. Toronto: Centre for Reformation and Renaissance Studies, 1985.
Vasari, Giorgio. *Le vite de' più eccellenti pittori, scultori e architettori* [1550 and 1568]. Rosanna Bettarini and Paola Barocchi, eds. Florence: Sansoni–S. P. E. S., 1966–97.
Vergerio, Pier Paolo. *Al Serenissima Re d'Inghilterra Edoardo sesto. De portamenti di Papa Giulio III. Et quale habbia ad essere il concilio, che egli intende di fare.* 1550.
Vermigli, Peter Martyr. *The Life, Early Letters and Eucharistic Writings of Peter Martyr,* J. C. McLelland and G. E. Duffield, eds. Appleford, England: Sutton Courtenay Press, 1989.
Virgil, *Aeneid.* In *Eclogues, Georgics, Aeneid I-VI,* G. P. Goold, ed. Cambridge, MA: Harvard University Press, 1999.
Virgilio, Polidoro. *The Anglica historia of Polydore Vergil A.D. 1485–1537,* Denis Hay, ed. London: Royal Historical Society, 1950.
Visdomini, Francisco. *Oratione funebre fatta in Napoli nell'hon. essequie della serenissima regina d'Inghilterra.* Naples: Raymondo Amati, 1559.
*Vocabolario degli accademici della Crusca* [1612]. www.accademiadellacrusca.it/Vocabolario_1612.shtml

**Secondary Sources**

Adair, E. R. 1924. "William Thomas: A Forgotten Clerk of the Privy Council." In *Tudor Studies, presented by the Board of Studies in History in the University of London to Albert Frederick Pollard, being the work of twelve of his colleagues and pupils,* R. W. Seton-Watson, ed. London: Longmans: 133–160.
Adorini-Braccesi, Simonetta. 1994. *'Una città infetta', la Repubblica di Lucca nella crisi religiosa del Cinquecento.* Florence: Olschki.
Ady, C. M. 1958. "Pius II and his Experiences of England, Scotland, and the English." *English Miscellany* 9: 39–49.
Aitkins, W. M. and W. R. Matthews. 1957. *A History of St. Paul's Cathedral.* London: Phoenix House: 137–144.

Akrigg, G. P. V. 1968. *Shakespeare and the Earl of Southampton*. London: Hamish Hamilton.
Albertini, Rudolph von. 1970. *Firenze dalla repubblica al principato, storia e coscienza politica*. Turin: Einaudi [*Florentinische Staatsbewusstsein im übergang von der Republik zum Prinzipat*, 1955].
Alter, Robert. 1975. *The Art of Biblical Poetry*. New York: Basic Books.
Anderson, Benedict. 1991. *Imagined Communities: Reflections on the Origin and Spread of Nationalism*. New York: Verso.
Anderson, Judith. 1996. *Words that Matter: Linguistic Perception in Renaissance English*. Stanford: Stanford University Press.
Anderson, Marvin W. 1975. *Peter Martyr: A Reformer in Exile, 1542–1562*. Nieuwkoop: B. De Graaf.
Anglo, Sydney. 1992. *Images of Tudor Kingship*. Guildford: Seaby.
Antonini, Anna. 1997. "La *Tipocosmia* di Alessandro Citolini, un repertorio linguistico." In *Repertori di parole e immagini, esperienze cinquecentesche e moderni 'data bases'*, Paola Barocchi and Lina Bolzoni, eds. Pisa: Scuola Normale Superiore: 161–231.
Aquilecchia, Giovanni. 1960. "Lo stampatore londinese di Giordano Bruno e altre note per l'edizione della *Cena*." *Studi di filologia italiana*, 18: 101–161.
— 2000. "Aretino's *Sei giornate*: Literary Parody and Social Reality." In *Women in Italian Renaissance Culture and Society*, Letizia Panizza, ed. Oxford: Legenda/ European Humanities Research Centre: 453–462.
Armstrong, C. A. J. 1960. "An Italian Astrologer at the Court of Henry VII." In *Italian Renaissance Studies: A Tribute to the late Cecilia M. Edy*, E. F. Jacob, ed. London: Faber and Faber: 433–454.
Ascoli, Albert. 1987. *Ariosto's Bittersweet Harmony: Crisis and Evasion in the Italian Renaissance*. Princeton: Princeton University Press.
Ashbee, Andrew and David Lasocki, with Peter Holman and Fiona Kirsby. 1998. *A Bibliographical Dictionary of English Court Musicians, 1485–1714*, 2 vols. Aldershot: Ashgate.
Asher, Yoni. 2002. "Form and Content in some Roman Reclining Effigies from the Early Sixteenth Century." *Gazette des Beaux Arts* 139: 315–330.
Aylward, J. D. 1956. *The English Master of Arms from the Twelfth to the Twentieth Century*. London: Routledge and Kegan.
Bainton, Roland H. 1941. *Bernardino Ochino, esule e riformatore senese del Cinquecento*. Florence: Sansoni.
Barish, Jonas. 1981. *The Antitheatrical Prejudice*. Berkeley: University of California Press.
Barnes, Catherine. 1971. "The Hidden Persuader: The Complex Speaking Voice of Sidney's *Defence of Poetry*." *PMLA* 86, May: 422–427.
Barolini, Teodolinda. 1993. "*Le parole sono femmine e i fatti sono maschi*: Toward a Sexual Poetics of the *Decameron* (*Decameron* II. 10)." *Studi sul Boccaccio* 21: 175–197.
Baron, Denis. 1986. *Grammar and Gender*. New Haven: Yale University Press.
Bayne, C. G. 1907. "The Coronation of Queen Elizabeth." *English Historical Review* 22: 650–673.

Becker, Wilhelm. 1887. *Immanuel Tremellius: ein Proselytenleben im Zeitalter der Reformation*. Breslau: Druck und Kommissions-Verlag von C. Dülser.
Bedouelle, Guy and Patrick Le Gal. 1987. *Le 'Divorce' du Roi Henry VIII: Etudes et Documents*. Geneva: Librairie Droz.
Bellorini, Mariagrazia. 1965. "La *Grammatica de la lingua italiana* di Alessandro Citolini." *English Miscellany* 16: 281–296.
— 1968. "Un medico alla corte di Elisabetta: Giulio Borgarucci." *English Miscellany* 19: 251–271.
— 1971. "Le pubblicazioni italiane dell'editore londinese John Wolfe (1580–1591)." *Miscellanea, pubblicazioni dell'Università di Trieste, sede di Udine 1:* 17–65.
— 1974. "Giovan Battista Castiglione, consigliere di Elisabetta I." In *Contributi dell'istituto di filologia moderna, Serie inglese*, Sergio Rossi, ed. Milan: Pubblicazioni della Università Cattolica del Sacro Cuore: 113–132.
— 1980. "Da Londra a Mantova: Immagini di vita e di cultura inglese nella corrispondenza di Aloisio Schivenoglia." In *Studi di letteratura inglese e americana*, Sergio Rossi, ed. Milan: Pubblicazioni dell'Università Cattolica del Sacro Cuore: 57–92.
— 1994. "Note di poesia nell'opera di Alberico Gentili, giurista elisabettiana (1532–1608)." In *Il passaggiere italiano*, Renzo Crivelli, Luigi Sampietro, and Joseph Trapp, eds. Rome: Bulzoni: 139–155.
Berger, Harry. 1988. "The Renaissance Imagination: Second World and Green World" [1965]. *Second World and Green World: Studies in Renaissance Fiction-Making*. Berkeley: The University of California Press: 3–40.
— 2000. *The Absence of Grace, Sprezzatura and Suspicion in Two Renaissance Courtesy Books*. Stanford: Stanford University Press.
Bergeron, David. 1971. *English Civic Pageantry, 1558–1642*. Columbia: University of South Carolina Press.
Bertoli, Gustavo. 1995. "Nuovi documenti sull'attività di John Wolfe a Firenze (1576–1577), con alcune considerazioni sul fenomeno delle stampe popolari." *Archivio storico italiano* 153: 577–589.
Binns, J. W. 1972. "Alberico Gentili in Defense of Poetry and Acting." *Studies in the Renaissance* 19: 224–272.
— 1990. *Intellectual Culture in Elizabethan and Jacobean England: The Latin Writings of the Age*. Leeds: Francis Cairns.
Boggione, Valter and Giovanni Casalegno. 2000. *Dizionario letterario del lessico amoroso: metafore, eufemismi, trivialismi*. Turin: UTET.
Bologna, Corrado. 1986. "Tradizione testuale e fortuna dei classici italiani." In *Letteratura italiana*, vol. VI, *Teatro, musica, tradizione dei classici*, Albert Asor Rosa, ed. Turin: Einaudi.
Bolzoni, Lina. 2002. "Images of Literary Memory in the Italian Dialogues: Some Notes on Giordano Bruno and Ludovico Ariosto." In *Giordano Bruno, Philosopher of the Renaissance*, Hilary Gatti, ed. Aldershot: Ashgate: 121–141.
Bossy, John. 1991. *Giordano Bruno and the Embassy Affair*. New Haven: Yale University Press.
— 2001. *Under the Molehill: an Elizabethan Spy Story*. New Haven: Yale University Press.

Boucher, Warren. 1991. "Florio's Montaigne: Translation and Pragmatic Humanism in the Sixteenth Century." Unpublished dissertation: Queen's College, Cambridge.
  1996. "Vernacular Humanism in the Sixteenth Century." In *The Cambridge Companion to Renaissance Humanism*, Jill Kraye, ed. Cambridge: Cambridge University Press: 189–201.
Brachtel, M. E. 1980. "Regulation and Group-Consciousness in the Later History of London's Merchant Colonies." *Journal of European Economic History* 10: 585–610.
Briggs, E. R. 1976. "An Apostle of the Incomplete Reformation." *Proceedings of the Huguenot Society of London* 22:6: 481–495.
Brown, Peter. 1974. *Lionardo Salviati: A Critical Biography*. Oxford: Oxford University Press.
Bugliani, Francesca. 1991. "La questione ubaldiniana." *Lingua e letteratura* 17: 160–175.
  1994. "Petruccio Ubaldini's Accounts of England." *Renaissance Studies* 8:2: 175–197.
Bujanda, J. M. and Eugenio Canone. 2002. "L'editto di proibizione delle opere di Bruno e Campanella, un'analisi bibliografica." *Bruniana e Campanelliana* 8:2: 451–479.
Bullock, Walter. 1939. "The 'Lost' *Miscellaneae Quaestiones* of Ortensio Lando." *Italian Studies* 2:6: 49–64.
Burdach, Konrad. 1986. *Riforma, Rinascimento, Umanesimo. Due dissertazioni sui fondamenti della cultura e dell'arte della parola moderna* [1935], Delio Cantimori, trans. Florence: Sansoni [*Reformation, Renaissance, Humanismus: zwei Abhandlungen über die Grundlage moderner Bildung und Sprachkunst*, 1918].
Burke, Kenneth. 1973. "Literature as Equipment for Living." *The Philosophy of Literary Form: Studies in Symbolic Action*. Berkeley: University of California Press: 293–304.
Burn, John Southerden. 1846. *The History of the French, Waloon, Dutch, and Other Foreign Protestant Congregations Settled in England from the Reign of Henry VIII to the Revocation of the Edict of Nantes*. London: Longman, Brown, Green, and Longmans.
Burrow, Colin. 1999. "The Experience of Exclusion: Literature and Politics in the Reigns of Henry VII and Henry VIII." In *The Cambridge History of Medieval Literature*, David Wallace, ed. Cambridge: Cambridge University Press: 793–820.
Cali, Piero. 1997. "Per un'edizione della grammatica di Alessandro Citolini." In *Repertori di parole e immagini, esperienze cinquecentesche e moderni 'data bases'*, Paola Barocchi and Lina Bolzoni, eds. Pisa: Scuola Normale Superiore: 235–251.
Campi, Emilio. 1994. *Michelangelo e Vittoria Colonna: Un dialogo artistico-teologico ispirato da Bernardino Ochino, e altri scritti di storia della Riforma*. Turin: Claudiana.
Camporeale, Salvatore. 1972. *Lorenzo Valla: umanesimo e teologia*. Florence: Istituto Nazionale di Studi sul Rinascimento.

Cantimori, Delio. 1975. *Umanesimo e religione nel Rinascimento*. Turin: Einaudi.
2002. *Eretici italiani del Cinquecento* [1939], Adriano Prosperi, ed. Turin: Einaudi.
"Lorenzo Valla." In *Enciclopedia italiana*, vol. XXXIV: 923–924.
Carley, James P. 2002. "Henry VIII's Library and Humanist Donors: Gian Matteo Giberti as a Case Study." In *Reassessing Tudor Humanism*, Jonathan Woolfson, ed. London: Palgrave: 99–128.
Carlson, David. 1987. "Occasional poetry of Pietro Carmeliano." *Aevum* 61:3: 495–502.
1988. "Politicizing Tudor Court Literature: Gaguin's Embassy and Henry VII's Humanists' Response." *Studies in Philology* 85: 279–304.
1993a. "Filippo Alberici, *Cebes' Tablet*, and Henry VII." In David Carlson, *English Humanist Books, Writers and Patrons, Manuscript and Print, 1425–1525*. Toronto: University of Toronto Press: 20–36.
1993b. "Politiking and Manuscript Presentation: Pietro Carmeliano's Development of Publishing Methods, 1482–1486." In David Carlson, *English Humanist Books, Writers and Patrons, Manuscript and Print, 1425–1525*. Toronto: University of Toronto Press: 37–59.
Cartwright, Julia. 1908. *Baldassare Castiglione: The Perfect Courtier, His Life and Letters, 1478–1529*, 2 vols. London: Murray.
Castelli, Alberto. 1938. "Un poemetto inedito del secolo XVI in onore di San Tommaso Moro." *Aevum* 12: 225–252.
Catto, Jeremy. 2003. "Written English: the Making of the Language 1370–1400." *Past and Present* 179: 24–59.
Cestaro, Gary P. 2003. *Dante and the Grammar of the Nursing Body*. Notre Dame: University of Notre Dame Press.
*Chambers Biographical Dictionary*. 1996. Magnus Magnusson, ed. Edinburgh: Chambers.
Chambers, D. S. 1990. "A Mantuan in London in 1557: Further Research on Annibale Litolfi." In *England and the Continental Renaissance, Essays in Honor of J. B. Trapp*, Edward Cheney and Peter Mack, eds. Woodbridge: The Boydell Press: 73–99.
Chambers, E. K. 1923. *The Elizabethan Stage*, vol. II. Oxford: Clarendon Press.
Chartier, Roger. 1988. *Cultural History, Practices and Representations*. Ithaca: Cornell University Press.
Cherchi, Paolo. 1997. "*La piazza universale*: somma di altre somme." In *Repertori di parole e immagini, esperienze cinquecentesche e moderni 'data bases'*, Paola Barocchi and Lina Bolzoni, eds. Pisa: Scuola Normale Superiore: 121–157.
Cheyfitz, Eric. 1991. *The Poetics of Imperialism*. Oxford: The University Press.
Ciliberto, Michele. 2000. *La ruota del tempo, interpretazione e Giordano Bruno*. Roma: Riuniti.
Clough, Cecil. 1981a. "Baldassare Castiglione's *Ad Henricum Angliae Regem*" [1973]. In Cecil Clough, *The Duchy of Urbino in the Renaissance*. London: Variorum Reprints: XIV, 227–252.
1981b. "Federigo Veterani, Polydore Vergil's *Anglia historia*, and Baldassare Castiglione's *Epistola ad Henricum Angliae regem*" [1967]. In Cecil Clough, *The Duchy of Urbino in the Renaissance*. London: Variorum Reprints: XIII, 780–782.

1981c. "The Relations between the English and Urbino Courts, 1474–1508" [1967]. In Cecil Clough, *The Duchy of Urbino in the Renaissance*. London: Variorum Reprints: XI, 202–218.

Cochrane, Eric. 1981. *Historians and Historiography in the Italian Renaissance*. Chicago: The University of Chicago Press.

Coe, Ralph T. 1972. "Small European Sculptures." *Apollo* 96: 514–516.

Concolato, Maria Palermo. 1995. "Aretino nella letteratura del' 500." In *Pietro Aretino nel cinquecentenario della nascita*. Roma: Salerno Editrice: 471–478.

Corda, Salvatore. 1975. *Veritas Sacramenti: A Study in Vermigli's Doctrine of the Lord's Supper*. Zurich: Theologischer Verlag.

Cossart, Michael de. 1984a. *This Little World: Renaissance Italians' View of English Society*. Liverpool: Janus Press.

1984b. *This Sceptred Isle: Renaissance Italians' View of English Institutions*. Liverpool: Janus Press.

Creighton, Michael. 1902. "The Italian Bishops of Worcester." *Historical Essays and Reviews*. London: Longmans, Green and Co.: 202–234.

Cressy, David. 1980. *Literacy and the Social Order: Reading and Writing in Tudor and Stuart England*. Cambridge: Cambridge University Press.

1981. "Levels of Illiteracy in England, 1530–1730." In *Literacy and Social Development in the West: A Reader*, Harvey J. Graff, ed. Cambridge: Cambridge University Press: 105–124.

Cunningham, W. 1897. *Alien Immigrants to England*. London: Swan Sonnenschein.

Dall'Olio, Guido. 1995. Review of Massimo Firpo's edition of Juan Valdés' *Alfabeto cristiana*. *Rivista storica italiana* 107:3: 878–881.

D'Amico, John F. 1983. *Renaissance Humanism in Papal Rome: Humanists and Churchmen on the Eve of the Reformation*. Baltimore: The Johns Hopkins University Press.

Darlington, Ida and James Howgego. 1964. *Printed Maps of London circa 1553–1850*. London: George Philip & Son.

Darr, Alan Phipps. 1979. "The Sculptures of Torrigiano: the Westminster Abbey Tombs." *The Connoisseur* 200: 177–189.

1992. "New Documents for Pietro Torrigiano and Other Early Cinquecento Florentine Sculptors Active in Italy and England." In *Kunst des Cinquecento in der Toscana*, Monika Cämmerer, ed. Munich: Bruckman: 108–129.

(n.d.) "Torrigiano." *The Grove Dictionary of Art Online*. www.groveart.com.

D'Ascia, Luca. 1989. "Bembo e Castiglione su Guidobaldo da Montefeltro." *Giornale storico della letteratura italiana* 106:1: 51–69.

Davidson, Peter and Adriaan van der Weel. 1996. *A Selection of the Poems of Sir Constantijn Huygens*. Amsterdam: Amsterdam University Press.

Davis, Natalie Zemon. 1975. *Society and Culture in Early Modern France*. Stanford: Stanford University Press.

De Grandis, Lucio. 1980. "Famiglie di musicisti nel' 500, i Ferrabosco: da Bologna alla corte di Londra." *Nuova rivista musicale* 14:4: 539–547.

De Grazia, Sebastiano. 1989. *Machiavelli in Hell*. New York: Vintage Books.

Della, Giustina Lisa. 1999. "La *Tipocosmia* di Alessandro Citolini (1561). Nuove forme di enciclopedismo nel XVI secolo." *Archivio storico italiano* 579:1: 63–87.

Della Valle, Valeria. 1993. "La lessicografia." In *Storia della lingua italiana*, vol. I, *I luoghi della codificazione*, Luca Serianni and Pietro Tritone, eds. Turin: Einaudi: 129–192.
Delpiano, Patrizia. 1993. "*Il teatro del mondo*, per un profilo intelletuale di Frances Amelia Yates." *Rivista storica italiana* 105: 180–245.
De Mauro, Tullio. 2003. "Interview." February 16. http://www.repubblica.it.
De Rinaldis, Maria Luisa. 2003. *Giacomo Castelvetro, Renaissance Translator*. Lecce: Milella.
*Dictionary of National Biography*.
Di Gangi, Mariano. 1993. *Peter Martyr Vermigli, 1499–1562: Renaissance Man, Reformation Master*. Lanham: University Press of America.
Dillon, Janette. 2003. "An Italian in England: Cross-Culturism and Racism in Court and City." In *Polidoro Virgili e la cultura umanistica europea*, Rolando Baccielli, ed. Sant'Angelo in Vado: Grafica Vadese: 165–183.
Dobson, Mary J. 1997. *Contours of Death and Disease in Early Modern England*. Cambridge: Cambridge University Press.
Doherty, M.J. 1991. *The Mistress-Knowledge: Sir Philip Sidney's Defense of Poetry*. Nashville: Vanderbilt University Press.
Ebel, Julia. 1964. "Studies in Elizabethan Translation." Unpublished PhD dissertation: Columbia University.
Einstein, Lewis. 1902. *The Italian Renaissance in England*. New York: Columbia University Press.
Elton, G.R. 1963. *England Under the Tudors*. London: Methuen & Co.
Engel, William Edward. 1996. "Knowledge That Counted: Italian Phrase-Books and Dictionaries in Elizabethan England." *Annali d'Italianistica* 14: 507–521.
Erdmann, Axel. 1999. *My Gracious Silence, Women in the Mirror of 16$^{th}$ Century Printing in Western Europe*. Lucern: Gilhofer & Ranschburg.
Faithfull, R. Glynn. 1953. "The Concept of 'Living Language' in Cinquecento Vernacular Philology." *The Modern Language Review* 48:3: 278–292.
Fessia, Lina. 1939–1940. "Alessandro Citolini, esule italiano in Inghilterra." *Rendiconti* 73: 213–243.
Field, Christopher O.S. (n.d.) "Ferrabosco." *The New Grove Dictionary of Music and Musicians Online*. www.grove.com
Firpo, Luigi. 1959. "La chiesa Italiana di Londra nel Cinquecento e i suoi rapporti con Ginevra." In *Ginevra e l'Italia*, Delio Cantimori and Luigi Firpo, eds. Florence: G.C. Sansoni: 308–412.
1993. *Il processo di Giordano Bruno*, Diego Quaglioni, ed. Rome: Salerno, 1993.
Firpo, Massimo. 1990. *Tra 'alumbrados' e 'spirituali', Studi su Juan de Valdés e il valdesianesimo nella crisi religiosa del '500 italiano*. Florence: Olschki.
1993. *Riforma protestante ed eresie nell'Italia del cinquecento: un profilo storico*. Rome: Laterza.
1998a. "Il problema storico della riforma italiana e Juan Valdés." *Dal Sacco di Roma all'Inquisizione, Studi su Juan de Valdés e la riforma italiana*. Alessandria: Edizioni dell'Orso: 61–88.
1998b. "Juan Valdés fra *alumbrados* e Lutero, note su un bilancio critico. *Dal Sacco di Roma all'Inquisizione*: 89–117.

2001a. *Artisti, gioiellieri, eretici: il mondo di Lorenzo Lotto tra riforma e contro-riforma*. Rome: Laterza.

2001b. "Note su una biografia di Reginald Pole." *Rivista storica italiana* 113:3: 859–874.

Fleming, Juliet. 1989. "The French Garden: An Introduction to Women's French." *English Literary History* 56:1: 19–51.

1994. "Dictionary English and the Female Tongue." In *Enclosure Acts: Sexuality, Property, and Culture in Early Modern England*, Richard Burt and John Michael Archer, eds. Ithaca: Cornell University Press: 290–325.

Floriani, Piero. 1980. "Trissino, la *questione della lingua*, la poesia." In *Atti del Convegno di Studi su Giangiorgio Trissino*, Neri Pozza, ed. Vicenza: Accademia Olimpica: 62–64.

Frantz, David. 1979. "Florio's Use of Contemporary Italian Literature in *A World of Wordes*." *Dictionaries, Journal of the Dictionary Society of America* 1: 147–156.

1997. "Negotiating Florio's *A World of Wordes*." *Dictionaries* 18: 1–32.

Freccero, Carla. 1992. "Politics and Aesthetics in Castiglione's *Il cortegiano*: Book III and the Discourse on Women." In *Creative Imitation: New Essays on Renaissance Literature in Honor of Thomas Greene*, David Quint, ed. Binghampton: Medieval and Renaissance Texts and Studies: 259–279.

Freccero, John. 1993. "Medusa and the Madonna of Forlì." In *Machiavelli and the Discourse of Literature*, Albert Ascoli and Victoria Kahn, eds. Cornell: Cornell University Press: 161–178.

Fucelli, Antonietta. 1989. "Umanisti a confronto: annotazioni al margine della polemica fra Castriglione e Valdés." *Studi Umanistici Piceni* 9: 51–57.

Gabrielli, Vittorio. 1983. "Bernardino Ochino: 'Sermo di Christo.' Un inedito di Elisabetta Tudor." *La cultura* 21:1: 151–174.

1986. "L'*Anglica historia* di Polidoro Virgilio." *La cultura* 24: 64–97.

Galvin, C. and P. G. Lindley. 1988. "Pietro Torrigiano's Portrait Bust of King Henry VII." *The Burlington Magazine* 130: 892–902.

Gamberini, Spartaco. 1970. *Lo studio dell'italiano in Inghilterra nel '500 e nel '600*. Messina/Florence: Casa Editrice G. D'Anna.

Gargano, G. S. 1923. *Scapigliatura italiana a Londra sotto Elisabetta e Giacomo I*. Venice: La Nuova Italia.

Garin, Eugenio. 1990. "Il tema della Rinascita in Giorgio Vasari." *Rinascite e Rivoluzioni* (1975). Roma-Bari: Laterza: 39–47.

Gatti, Hilary. 1989. *The Renaissance Drama of Knowledge: Giordano Bruno in England*. London: Routledge.

Ginzburg, Carlo. 1980. *The Cheese and the Worms: the Cosmos of a Sixteenth-Century Miller*, Anne and John Tedeschi, trans. New York: Dorset.

1999. "Lorenzo Valla on the 'Donation of Constantine'." In *History, Rhetoric, and Proof*. Hanover, NH: University Press of New England: 54–70.

2000. "Selfhood as Otherness: Constructing English Identity in the Elizabethan Age." In *No Island is an Island: Four Glances at English Literature in a World Perspective*. New York: Columbia University Press.

Giustina, Lisa Della. 1999. "La *Tipocosmia* di Alessandro Citolini (1561). Nuove forme di enciclopedismo nel XVI secolo." *Archivio storico italiano* 157: 63–87.

Gnoli, Domenico. 1890. *Vittoria Accoramboni: storia del secolo XVI, corredata di note e documenti*. Florence: Le Monnier Editore.
Goldberg, Jonathan. 1983. *James I and the Politics of Literature*. Baltimore: The Johns Hopkins University Press.
Graff, Harvey J. 1987. *Legacies of Literacy, Continuities, and Contradictions in Western Culture and Society*. Bloomington: University of Indiana Press.
Graves, Michael A. R. 1998. *Burghley: William Cecil, Lord Burghley*. London: Longman.
Grayson, Cecil. 1960. "Lorenzo, Machiavelli, and the Italian Language." In *Italian Renaissance Studies: A Tribute to the Late Cecilia M. Ady*, E. F. Jacob, ed. London: Faber and Faber: 410–432.
——— 1983. "Thomas Hoby e Castiglione in Inghilterra." *La cultura* 21:1, 138–149.
——— 1985. "The Growth of Linguistic Consciousness in England." In *The Fairest Flower: the Emergence of Linguistic National Consciousness in Renaissance Europe*, Fredi Chiapelli, ed. Florence: Accademia della Crusca: 167–173.
Green, Jonathan. 1996. *Chasing the Sun: Dictionary Makers and the Dictionaries They Made*. New York: Henry Holt.
Greenblatt, Stephen. *Renaissance Self-Fashioning*. 1980. Chicago: University of Chicago Press.
——— 2002. *Hamlet in Purgatory*. Princeton: Princeton Univeristy Press.
Grendler, Paul F. 2002. *The Universities of the Italian Renaissance*. Baltimore: Johns Hopkins Press.
Griffith, T. G. 1953. "De Italica Pronunciatione." *Italian Studies* 8: 71–82.
——— 1961. *Avventure linguistiche del Cinquecento*. Florence: F. Le Monnier.
Guy, John. 2003. "Polydore Vergil and the Reformation." In *Polidoro Virgili e la cultura umanistica europea*, Rolando Bacciclli, ed. Sant'Angelo in Vado: Grafica Vadese: 185–205.
Gwyn, Peter. 1990. *The King's Cardinal: The Rise and Fall of Thomas Wolsey*. London: Barrie and Jenkins.
Gwynne, Paul. 1990. "The Life and Works of Johannes Michael Nagonius poeta laureatus, c.1450–c.1510." Unpublished PhD dissertation: Warburg Institute, University of London.
——— 1992. "The Frontispiece to an Illuminated Panegyric of Henry VII: a Note on the Sources." *Journal of the Warburg and Courtauld Institutes* 55: 266–270.
Hale, John. 1994. *The Civilization of Europe in the Renaissance*. New York: Atheneum.
Hauben, Paul J. 1967. *Three Spanish Heretics and the Reformation*. Geneva: Librarie Droz.
Hay, Denis. 1939. "Pietro Griffo, an Italian in England." *Italian Studies* 2:7: 118–128.
——— 1952. *Polydore Vergil: Renaissance Historian and Man of Letters*. Oxford: Clarendon Press.
Haywood, Eric. 2003. "La storia dell'Irlanda dell'*Anglica historia*." In *Polidoro Virgili e la cultura umanistica europea*, Rolando Bacciclli, ed. Sant'Angelo in Vado: Grafica Vadese: 143–163.
Helgerson, Richard. 1992. *Forms of Nationhood: The Elizabethan Writing of England*. Chicago: University of Chicago Press.

Heller, Hermann. 1985. "Cosmopolitan versus Parochial Tendencies: The Old and New Crusca." In *The Fairest Flower, The Emergence of Linguistic National Consciousness in Renaissance Europe*, Fredi Chiapelli, ed. Florence: Accademia della Crusca: 109–111.

Hennings, Robert W. and David Rosand. 1983. *Castiglione: The Ideal and the Real in Renaissance Culture*. New Haven: Yale University Press.

Hentschell, Roze. 2002. "Treasonous Textiles: Foreign Cloth and the Construction of Englishness." *The Journal of Medieval and Early Modern Studies* 32:3, Fall: 543–570.

Herman, Peter C. 1994. "Early English Protestantism and Renaissance Poetics: The Charge is Committing Fiction in the Matter of Rastell v. Frith." *Renaissance and Reformation* 18:1: 5–18.

Hibbert, Christopher. 1991. *The Virgin Queen, Elizabeth I, Genius of the Golden Age*. New York: Addison-Wesley.

Higham, N. J. 2002. *King Arthur: Myth-Making and History*. London: Routledge.

Hochsteller Meyer, Barbara. 1976. "The First Tomb of Henry VII of England." *Art Bulletin* 58: 358–367.

Holman, Peter. 1991. "Music at the Court of Henry VIII." In *Henry VIII: A European Court*, David Starkey, ed. London: Collins and Brown: 104–106.

Holmes, M. R. 1963. *Moorfields in 1559: an Engraved Copper Plate from the Earliest Known Map of London*. London: Her Majesty's Stationery Office.

Holquist, Michael. 2002. "Why We Should Remember Philology." *Profession*: 72–79.

Hoppe, Harry Reno. 1933. "John Wolfe, Printer and Publisher." *Library, Fourth Series* 14:3: 241–288.

Hotson, Leslie. 1954. *The First Night of Twelfth Night*. New York: Macmillan.

Howard, Donald. 1987. *Chaucer: His Life, His Works, His World*. New York: E. P. Dutton.

Huffman, Clifford Chambers. 1988. *Elizabethan Impressions: John Wolfe and His Press*. New York: AMS Press.

Huizinga, Johan. 1952. *Erasmus of Rotterdam* [1924], F. Hopman, trans. London: Phaidon Press.

Hunt, Edward S. 1990. "A New Look at the Dealings of the Bardi and Peruzzi with Edward III." *The Journal of Economic History* 50:1, March, 149–162.

Infelise, Mario. 2001. *Libri proibiti*. Bari: Laterza.

Inghirami, Francesco. 1844. *Storia della Toscana*, vol. XIV. Fiesole: Poligrafia Fiesolana.

Isenberg, Nancy. 1983. "Encomio e vituperio: un secolo e mezzo di scritti inglesi sulla donna (1484–1640)." In *Trasgressione tragica e norma domestica, esemplari di tipologie femminili dalla letteratura europea*, Vanna Gentili, ed. Rome: Edizioni di Storia e Letteratura: 51–124.

Izon, John. 1958. "Italian Musicians at the Tudor Court." *The Musical Quarterly* 44: 329–337.

James, Frank A. III. 1998. *Peter Martyr Vermigli and Predestination: The Augustinian Inheritance of an Italian Reformer*. Oxford: Clarendon Press.

Javitch, Daniel. 1971. "Rival Arts of Conduct in Elizabethan England: Guazzo's *Civile Conversation* and Castiglione's *Courtier*," *Yearbook of Italian Studies*: 178–198.

1983. "*Il cortegiano* and the Constraints of Despotism." In *Castiglione: The Ideal and the Real in Renaissance Culture*, Robert W. Hennings and David Rosand, eds. New Haven: Yale University Press: 17–28.
Jones, Anne and Peter Stallybrass. 2000. *Renaissance Clothing and the Materials of Memory*. Cambridge: Cambridge University Press.
Jones, William M. 1955. "Two Learned Italians in Elizabethan England." *Italica* 32: 242–247.
Jordan, W. K. 1932. *The Development of Religious Toleration in England*. Cambridge: Harvard University Press.
Kahn, Victoria. 1994a. *Machiavellian Rhetoric: from the Counter-Reformation to Milton*. Princeton: Princeton University Press.
—— 1994b. "Reading Machiavelli: Innocent Gentillet's Discourse on Method." *Political Theory* 22:4, Nov: 539–560.
Kingdon, Robert M. 1980. *The Political Thought of Peter Martyr Vermigli*. Geneva: Librarie Droz.
Kingsford, C. T. 1911. *The Life of Henry V*. Oxford: Clarendon Press.
Kinney, Arthur. 1989. *Continental Humanist Politics: Studies in Erasmus, Castiglione, Margarite de Navarre, Rabelais, and Cervantes*. Amherst: University of Massachusetts Press.
Kirkpatrick, Robin. 1995. *English and Italian Literature from Dante to Shakespeare: A Study of Source, Analogue and Divergence*. London: Longman.
Koelb, Clayton. 1984. "Aristotle, Boccaccio, and the Problem of the Incredible." *Canadian Review of Comparative Literature* 11:1: 1–11.
Lambley, Kathleen. 1920. *The Teaching and Cultivation of the French Language in England during Tudor and Stuart Times*. Manchester: Manchester University Press.
Larivaille, Paul. 1997. *Pietro Aretino*. Rome: Salerno Editrice.
Lasocki, David and Roger Prior. 1995. *The Bassanos: Venetian Musicians and Instrument Makers in England, 1531–1665*. Cambridge: Cambridge University Press.
—— (n.d.) "Bassano." *The New Grove Dictionary of Music and Musicians Online*. www.grove.com.
Lawner, Lynne. 1984. *I modi nell'opera di Giulio Romano, Marcantonio Raimondi, Pietro Aretino, e Jean-Frédéric-Maximilien de Waldeck*. Milan: Longanesi.
Lewlaski, Barbara K. 1987. "Lucy, Countess of Bedford: Images of a Jacobean Courtier and Patroness." In *Politics of Discourse: The Literature and History of Seventeenth-Century England*, K. Sharpe and S. N. Zwicker, eds. Berkeley: University of California Press: 52–77.
Lindley, P. G. 1991. "Playing Check-Mate with Royal Majesty? Wolsey's Patronage of Italian Renaissance Sculpture." In *Cardinal Wolsey, Church, State and Art*, S. J. Gunn and P. G. Lindley, eds. Cambridge: Cambridge University Press: 261–262.
Loach, Jennifer. 1999. *Edward VI*. New Haven: Yale University Press.
Longo, Nicola. 1986. "La letteratura proibita." In *Letteratura italiana, vol. V, Le questioni*, Alberto Asor Rosa, ed. Turin: Einaudi: 963–991.
Longworth de Chambrun, Comtesse Clara. 1921. *Giovanni Florio: un apôtre de la Renaissance en Angleterre à l'époque de Shakespeare*. Paris: Payot.

MacCulloch, Diarmaid. 1999. *Tudor Church Militant: Edward VI and the Protestant Reformation*. London: Penguin Books.
Malkiel, Yakov. 1985. "Spontaneous Speech versus Academic Constraints in Medieval and Renaissance Europe." In *The Fairest Flower, The Emergence of Linguistic National Consciousness in Renaissance Europe*, Fredi Chiapelli, ed. Florence: Accadamia della Crusca: 9–15.
Manley, Lawrence. 1985. "Proverbs, Epigrams, and Urbanity in Renaissance London." *English Literary Renaissance* 15:3: 247–276.
Maraschio, Nicoletta. 1980. "Sulla formazione italiana del grammatico gallese Joannes David Rhaesus (Rhys)." *Studi di grammatica italiana* 9: 5–18.
Maraschio, Nicoletta and Teresa Poggi Salani. 1991. "L'insegnamento di lingue di Dionide Borghesi e Celso Cittadini: idea di norma e idea di storia." *Studi linguistici italiani* 17:2: 204–232.
Marazzini, Claudio. 1993a. "Le teorie." In *Storia della lingua italiana*, vol. I, *I luoghi della codificazione*, Luca Serianni and Pietro Tritone, eds. Turin: Einaudi: 231–334.
1993b. *Storia della lingua italiana, il secondo cinquecento e il seicento*. Bologna: Mulino.
Marcato, Carla. 1991. "Da *La Tipocosmia* di Alessandro Citolini, note di letture lessicali." In *Saggi di linguistica e di letteratura in memoria di Paolo Zolli*, Giampaolo Borghello, Manlio Cortelazzo, and Giorgio Padovan, eds. Padua: Editrice Antenore: 259–264.
Marienstras, Richard. 1985. "The Near and the Far: the Calvin Affair and the Status of Foreigners under James I of England." In *New Perspectives on the Shakespearean World*, Janet Lloyd, trans. Cambridge: Cambridge University Press: 99–125.
Mathew, David. 1972. *Lady Jane Grey*. London: Eyre Methuen.
Matthiessen, Francis Otto. 1931. *Translation: an Elizabethan Art*. Cambridge, MA: Harvard University Press.
Matz, Robert. 2000. *Defending Literature in Early Modern England: Renaissance Literary Theory in Context*. Cambridge: Cambridge University Press.
Mayer, Thomas. 2000. *Reginald Pole, Prince and Prophet*. Cambridge: Cambridge University Press.
McCoy, Richard C. 1990. "'The Wonderful Spectacle': The Civic Progress of Elizabeth I and the Troublesome Coronation." In *Coronations, Medieval and Early Modern Monarchy Ritual*, János M. Bak, ed. Berkeley: University of California Press: 217–227.
McNair, Philip. 1967. *Peter Martyr in Italy*. Oxford: Clarendon Press.
1980. "Peter Martyr in England." In *Peter Martyr Vermigli and Italian Reform*, J. McLelland, ed. Waterloo, Ontario: Wilfred Laurier University Press: 85–105.
1981. "Bernardino Ochino in Inghilterra." *Rivista storica italiana* 103:1: 231–242.
Merriman, Marcus. 1983. "Italian military engineers in Britain in the 1540s." *English Map-Making 1500–1650, Historical Essays*, Sarah Tyacke, ed. London: The British Library: 57–67.
Meyer, Barbara Hochsteller Meyer. 1976. "The First Tomb of Henry VII of England." *Art Bulletin* 58: 358–367.
Micheletti, Emma. 1983. *Le donne dei Medici*. Florence: Sansoni.

Migliorini, Bruno. 1984. *The Italian Language* [abridged], T. G. Griffith, trans. London: Faber and Faber.

— 1994. *Storia della lingua italiana* [1960]. Milan: Bompiani.

Mitchell, Margaret. 1971. "Works of Art from Rome for Henry VIII: A Study of Anglo-Papal Relations as Reflected in Papal Gifts to the English King." *Journal of Warburg and Courtauld Institutes* 34: 178–203.

Mitchell, R. J. 1962. *The Laurel Tree and the Tiara: Pope Pius II, 1458–1464*. London: Harvill Press.

Molen, Gezina Hermina Johanna van den. 1968. *Alberico Gentili and the Development of International Law* [1937]. Leyden: A. W. Sitjhoff.

Morsolin, Bernardo. 1873. *Francesco Chiericati, vescovo e diplomatico del secolo XVI*. Vicenza: Paroni.

— 1894. *Giangiorgio Trissino*. Florence: Successori Le Monnier.

Mullaney, Steven. 1988. *The Place of the Stage – License, Play, and Power in Renaissance England*. Chicago: University of Chicago Press.

Naville, Charles Eduard. 1984. *Enea Silvio Piccolomini: l'uomo, l'umanista, il pontefice*. Locarno: Analisi.

Negri, Giulio. 1722. *Istoria degli scrittori fiorentini*. Ferrara: Pomatelli.

Nicolini, Benedetto. 1970. *Il pensiero di Bernardino Ochino*. Bologna: R. Patron.

Nieto, Jose C. 1970. *Juan Valdés and the Origins of the Spanish and Italian Reformation*. Geneva: Librarie Droz.

Obelkevich, James. 1987. "Proverbs and Social History." In *The Social History of Language*, Peter Burke and Roy Porter, eds. Cambridge: Cambridge University Press: 43–72.

Olivieri, Ornella. 1942. "I primi vocaboli italiani fino alla prima edizione della Crusca." *Studi di filologia italiana* 6: 65–195.

O'Malley, John. 2001. *Trent and All That: Renaming Catholicism in the Early Modern Era*. Cambridge, MA: Harvard University Press.

Orchard, Stephen. (forthcoming 2005). "What Does the Picture Tell Us?" *Journal of the United Reformed Church History Society*.

Ord, Melanie. 2002. "Classical and Contemporary Italy in Roger Ascham's *The Scholemaster* (1570)." *Renaissance Studies* 16:2: 202–216.

Ordine, Nuccio. 1987. *La cabala dell'asino, asinità e conoscenza in Giordano Bruno*. Naples: Liguori.

Orgel, Stephen. 1991. "What is a Text?" In *Staging the Renaissance: Reinterpretations of Elizabethan and Jacobean Drama*, David Kastan and Peter Stallybrass, eds. London: Routledge: 83–87.

— 1996. *Impersonations, The Performance of Gender in Shakespeare's England*. Cambridge: Cambridge University Press.

— 2003. *Imagining Shakespeare: a History of Texts and Visions*. Houndmills: Palgrave Macmillan.

Ostrogorsky, Georg. 1968. *Storia dell'Impero Bizantino*, Piero Leone, trans. Turin: Einaudi [*Geschichte des byzantinischen Staats*, 1963].

Ottolenghi, Paola. 1982. *Giacopo Castelvetro: esule modenese nell'Inghilterra di Shakespeare*. Pisa: ETA.

*The Oxford Dictionary of the Christian Church*. 1974. Oxford: Oxford University.

Palmer, Patricia Ann Palmer. 2001. *Language and Conquest in Early Modern Ireland: English Renaissance Literature and Elizabethan Imperial Expansion*. Cambridge: Cambridge University Press.

Panizza, Diego. 1969. "Machiavelli e Alberico Gentili." *Il pensiero politico* 2:3: 476–483.

— 1981. *Alberico Gentili, giurista ideologo nell'Inghilterra elisabettiana*. Padua: D. Panizza.

Parker, Patricia. 1993. "Gender Ideology, Gender Change: The Case of Marie Germaine." *Critical Inquiry* 19:2: 337–364.

— 2000. "*Fatti Maschii, Parole Femmine*: Manly Deeds, Womanly Words." In *Sparks and Seeds: Medieval Literature and its Afterlife: Essays in Honor of John Freccero*, Dana E. Stewart and Alison Cornish, eds. Turnhout: Brepols: 291–316.

Parodi, Severina. 1983. *Quattro secoli di Crusca, 1583–1983*. Florence: Accademia della Crusca: 11–47.

— 1985. "L'Accademia della Crusca interprete della coscienza linguistica nazionale." In *The Fairest Flower, The Emergence of Linguistic National Consciousness in Renaissance Europe*, ed. Fredi Chiapelli. Florence: Accademia della Crusca: 113–120.

Patota, Giuseppe. 1993. "I percorsi grammaticali." In *Storia della lingua italiana*, vol. I, *I luoghi della codificazione*, Luca Serianni and Pietro Tritone, eds. Turin: Einaudi: 93–138.

Patterson, Annabel. 1994. *Reading Holinshed's Chronicles*. Chicago: University of Chicago Press.

Pelisser, L. G. 1901. "Catalogue des documents de la collection Podocataro à la Biblioteque Marciana à Venise." *Centralblatt für Bibliothekwesen* 18: 473–598.

Pellegrini, Giuliano. 1954. "Michelangelo Florio e le sue regole de la lingua thoscana." *Studi di filologia italiana* 12: 72–201.

Perry, Maria. 1995. *The Word of A Prince*. Woodbridge: The Boydell Press.

Petrina, Alessandra. 2004. *Cultural Politics in Fifteenth-Century England: the Case of Humphrey, Duke of Gloucester*. Leiden: Brill.

Pizzi, Clemente. 1956. *L'umanista Andrea Ammonio*. Florence: Le Monnier.

Ploncher, Attilio. 1879. *Della vita e delle opere di Lodovico Castelvetro*. Conegliano: Cagnani.

Policardi, Silvio. 1947. *Giovanni Florio e le relazioni culturali anglo-italiane agli albori del XVII secolo*. Venice: Montuoro.

Polizzotto, Lorenzo. 1994. *The Elect Nation: The Savonarolan Movement in Florence 1494–1545*. Oxford: Clarendon Press.

Pope-Hennessy, John. 1972. "The Tombs and Monuments." In *Westminster Abbey*. London: Weidenfeld and Nicolson.

Praz, Mario. 1942a. "Giovanni Florio." In *Machiavelli in Inghilterra, e altri saggi*. Rome: Tumminelli: 165–172.

— 1942b. "Fortuna della lingua e della cultura italiana in Inghilterra." In *Machiavelli in Inghilterra, e altri saggi*. Rome: Tumminelli: 269–328.

— 1944. "The Italian Element in English." In *Ricerche Anglo-Italiane*. Rome: Edizioni di Storia e Letteratura: 1–62.

1966. "Shakespeare's Italy" [1954]. In *The Flaming Heart: Essays on Crashaw, Machiavelli, and Other Studies in the Relations between Italian and English Literature from Chaucer to T. S. Eliot.* Gloucester, MA: Peter Smith: 146–167.

Presa, Giovanni. 1973. "A. Citolini, V. Marcellino e V. Marostica nella vicenda d'una lettera in difesa del volgare (sec. XVI)." In *Studi in onore di Alberto Chiari*, Giuseppe Lazzati, ed. Brescia: Paideia: 1001–1024.

Prior, Roger. 1983. "Jewish Musicians at the Tudor Court." *Musical Quarterly* 69: 253–265.

Provvidera, Tiziana. 2002. "John Charlewood: Giordano Bruno's Printer." In *Giordano Bruno, Philosopher of the Renaissance*, Hilary Gatti, ed. Aldershot: Ashgate: 167–186.

Pruvost, René. 1937. *Matteo Bandello and Elizabethan Fiction*. Paris: Librarie Ancienne Honoré Champion.

Pugliatti, Paola. 1993. "The Strange Tongues of Henry V." *Yearbook of English Studies* 23: 235–53.

Ramsay, G. D. 1973. "The Undoing of the Italian Mercantile Colony in Sixteenth Century London." In *Textile History and Economic History: Essays in Honor of Miss Julia de Lacy Mann*, N. B. Harie and K. G. Ponting, eds. Manchester: Manchester University Press: 22–49.

Rapp, Richard T. 1975. "The Unmaking of the Mediterranean Trade Hegemony: International Trade Rivalry and the Commercial Revolution." *The Journal of Economic History* 35:3: 499–525.

Rebora, Piero. 1935. "Uno scrittore toscano sullo scisma d'Inghilterra ed una lettera della regina Elisabetta." *Archivio storico italiano* 93: 233–254.

1936. *Civiltà italiana e civiltà inglese*. Florence: Le Monnier.

Richardson, Brian. 1996. *Print Culture in Renaissance Italy: The Editor and the Vernacular Text, 1460–1600*. Cambridge: Cambridge University Press.

Rorty, Richard. 1989. *Contingency, Irony, and Solidarity*. Cambridge: Cambridge University Press.

Rosenberg, Eleanor. 1943. "Giacopo Castelvetro, Italian Publisher in Elizabethan London and His Patrons." *The Huntington Library Quarterly* 2: 119–148.

1976. *Leicester, Patron of Letters*. New York: Octagon Books.

Rossi, Paolo. 1952. *Giacomo Aconcio*. Milan: Fratelli Bocca Editori.

Rossi, Sergio. 1966. "Un 'italianista' nel cinquecento inglese: William Thomas." *Aevum* 40: 281–314.

1969a. "Enrico V dalla cronaca alla poesia." In *Ricerche sull'umanesimo e sul rinascimento in Inghilterra*. Milan: Vita e Pensiero (Università Cattolica del Sacro Cuore): 1–25.

1969b. "Profilo dell'umanesimo enriciano: Erasmo e Thomas More." In *Ricerche sull'umanesimo e sul rinascimento in Inghilterra*. Milan: Vita e Pensiero (Università Cattolica del Sacro Cuore): 26–63.

1969c. "'The Only-Knowing Men of Europe', John Florio e gli insegnanti italiani." In *Ricerche sull'umanesimo e sul Rinascimento in Inghilterra*. Milan: Vita e Pensiero (Università Cattolica del Sacro Cuore): 93–212.

1984. "Note sugli italiani in Inghilterra nell'età del Rinascimento." In *Saggi sul Rinascimento*, S. Rossi, ed. Milan: Edizioni Unicopli: 55–115.

1990. "*Vincentio Saviolo his Practise* (1595): A Problem of Authorship." In *England and the Continental Renaissance: Essays in Honor of J. B. Trapp*, Edward Cheney and Peter Mack, eds. Rochester: Roydell Press: 165–175.

Rowland, Ingrid. 1998. *The Culture of the High Renaissance: Ancients and Moderns in Sixteenth-Century Rome*. Cambridge: Cambridge University Press.

Ruddock, Alwyn Amy. 1951. *Italian Merchants and Shipping in Southampton 1270–1600*. Southampton: University College.

Ruggeri, Romano. 1992. *Un amico di Erasmo: Polidoro Virgili*. Urbino: Edizioni Quattroventi.

— 2000. *Polidoro Virgili: un umanista europeo*. Bergamo: Moretti and Vitali.

— 2003. "Polidoro Virgili e la riforma anglicana." In *Polidoro Virgili e la cultura umanistica europea*, Rolando Bacchielli, ed. Sant'Angelo in Vado: Grafica Vadese: 225–240.

Rundle, David. 1995. "A New Golden Age? More, Skelton, and the accession Verses of 1509." *Renaissance Studies* 9:1: 58–76.

— 2003. "Polydore Vergil and the *Translatio studiorum*: the Tradition of Italian Humanists in England." In *Polidoro Virgili e la cultura umanistica europea*, Rolando Baccielli, ed. Sant'Angelo in Vado: Grafica Vadese: 53–75.

Sabatini, Ferdinando. 1960. *Tra i letterati precursori della decadenza ('600), il 'Meschino' Albicante contro il 'Divino' Aretino*. Milan: Gastaldi Editore.

Sabbadini, R. 1934. "Tito Livio Frulovisi, umanista del secolo XV." *Giornale storico della letteratura italiana* 103: 55–81.

Sacks, David Harris. 1988. "Searching for 'Culture' in the English Renaissance." *Shakespeare Quarterly* 39:4: 465–488.

Said, Edward. 2003. "A Window on the World." *The Guardian 'Review'*, August 2: 4–6.

Sammut, Alfonso. 1980. *Unfredo Duca di Gloucester e gli umanisti italiani*. Padua: Editrice Antinore.

Saygin, Susanne. 2002. *Humphrey, Duke of Gloucester (1390–1447) and the Italian Humanists*. Leiden: Brill.

Schenk, W. 1950. *Reginald Pole, Cardinal of England*. London: Longmans.

Scott, Mary Augusta. 1916. *Elizabethan Translations from the Italian*. Boston: Houghton Mifflin.

Scott-Warren, Jason. 2001. *Sir John Harington and the Book as Gift*. Oxford: Clarendon.

Scouloudi, Irene. 1985. *Returns of Strangers in the Metropolis 1593, 1627, 1635, 1639: A Study of an Active Minority*. London: Huguenot Society of London.

Shemek, Deanna. 1998. *Ladies Errant: Wayward Women and Social Order in Early Modern Italy*. Durham: Duke University Press.

Sicca, Cinzia. 2002. "Consumption and the Trade of Art between Italy and England in the First Half of the Sixteenth Century: the London House of the Bardi and Cavalcanti Company." *Renaissance Studies* 16:2: 163–200.

Simoncelli, Paolo. 1977. *Il caso Reginald Pole: eresia e sanità nelle polemiche religiose del Cinquecento*. Rome: Edizioni di Storia e di Letteratura.

Simonini, R. C. 1952. *Italian Scholarship in Renaissance England*. Chapel Hill: University of North Carolina.

Spampanato, Vincenzo. 1924. "Giovanni Florio. Un amico del Bruno in Inghilterra." *La critica* 22: 56–61, 116–124, 246–253.
Sontag, Susan. 2003. "The World as India." *Times Literary Supplement*, June 13: 13–15.
Starn, Randolph. 2003. "The Early Modern Muddle." *Journal of Early Modern History* 6:3: 296–307.
Starnes, DeWitt T. 1965. "John Florio Reconsidered." *Texas Studies in Literature and Language* 6: 407–422.
Stein, Peter. 1999. *Roman Law in European History*. Cambridge: Cambridge University Press.
Steppat, Michael. 1994. "Social Change and Gender Decorum: Renaissance Courtesy." In *The Crisis of Courtesy: Studies in the Conduct Book in Britain, 1600–1900*, Jacques Carré, ed. Leiden: Brill: 27–40.
Stevens, John. 1961. *Music and Poetry in the Early Tudor Court*. Cambridge: Cambridge University Press.
Stevenson, Jane. "The Court Culture of England under Elizabeth I." In *Princes and Princely Culture*, vol. II, Martin Gosman, Alasdair MacDonald, and Arjo Vanderjagt, eds. Leiden: Brill (forthcoming).
Stevenson, Jane and Peter Davidson. 2001. *Early Modern Women Poets*. Oxford: Oxford University Press.
Stewart, Alan. 2000. *Philip Sidney, a Double Life*. London: Pimlico.
   2003. *The Cradle King, A Life of James VI & I*. London: Chatto and Windus.
Stinger, Charles. 1998. *The Renaissance in Rome*. Bloomington: University of Indiana Press.
Stone, Lawrence. 1956. *An Elizabethan: Sir Horatio Palavicino*. Oxford: Clarendon Press.
Strong, Roy. 1959. "Federigo Zuccaro's Visit to England in 1575." *Journal of the Warburg and Courtauld Institutes* 22: 359–360.
   1977. *The Cult of Elizabeth*. Berkeley: The University of California Press.
Surtz, Edward L. 1974. *Henry VIII's 'Great Matter' in Italy: An Introduction to Representative Italians in the King's Divorce, mainly 1527–35*, 2 vols. Ann Arbor: University Microfilms.
Talvacchia, Bette. 1992. "The Rare Italian Master and the Posture of Hermione in The Winter's Tale." *Literature, Interpretation, Theory* 3: 163–174.
Taplin, Mark. 2003. "The 'Ochino Affair' and its Aftermath." In Mark Taplin, *The Italian Reformers and the Zurich Church, c.1540–1620*. Aldershot: Ashgate.
Tavoni, Marco. 1992a. "*Le prose della volgar lingua.*" In *Letteratura italiana, Le opere, volume primo, dalle origini al Cinquecento*, Alberto Asor Rosa, ed. Turin: Einaudi: 1065–1088.
   1992b. *Storia della lingua italiana, il Quattrocento*. Bologna: Mulino.
Tedeschi, John. 1973. "New Light on Ochino." *Bibliothèque d'humanisme et renaissance* 35: 289–301.
   1986. "The Cultural Contributions of Italian Protestant Reformers in the Late Renaissance." *Schifanoia: Notizie dell'Istituto di Studi Rinascimentali di Ferrara* 1: 127–151.

1987. "I contributi culturali dei riformatori protestanti italiani nel tardo rinascimento." *Italica* 64:19–61.

2000. *The Italian Reformation and the Diffusion of Renaissance Culture: A Bibliography of the Secondary Literature, ca. 1750–1997*. Ferrara: F. C. Panini Editore.

Tetel, Marcel. 1995. "Idéologie et traductions de Girolamo Naselli à John Florio." *Montaigne Studies* 7: 169–182.

Toulmin, Stephen. 1990. *Cosmopolis, The Hidden Agenda of Modernity*. Chicago: University of Chicago Press.

Trapp, J. B. 1991. *Erasmus, Colet and More: The Early Tudor Humanists and their Books*. London: The British Library.

Trovato, Paolo. 1994. *Storia della lingua italiana, il primo cinquecento*. Bologna: Mulino.

Tschiesche, Jacqueline. 1987. "Il rifacimento del *Decamerone* di Luigi Groto." In *Luigi Groto e il suo tempo, 1541–1585*, Giorgio Brunello and Antonio Lodo, eds. Padua: Minelliana: 236–269.

Vischer, Lukas. 2000. "Michelangelo Florio tra Italia, Inghilterra e Val Bregaglia." In *Il prostestantesimo di lingua italiana nella Svizzera, figure e movimenti tra cinquecento e ottocento*, Emidio Campi and Giuseppe La Torre, eds. Turin: Claudiana: 67–76.

Waldman, Louis A. 2001. "Bandinelli and the Opera di Santa Maria del Fiore." In *Santa Maria del Fiore: The Cathedral and its Sculpture*, Margaret Haines, ed. Florence: Villa I Tatti/Edizioni Cadmo: 221–256.

Wallace, David. 1997. *Chaucerian Polity, Absolutist Lineages and Associational Forms in England and Italy*. Stanford: Stanford University Press.

Waquet, Françoise. 2001. *Latin, Or, the Empire of a Sign: A Symbol's Empire*. London: Verso Books [*Le Latin, ou, l'empire d'une signe, XVIe-XXe siècles*, 1998].

Watson, Foster. 1909. *The Beginnings of the Teaching of Modern Subjects in England*. London: Pitman and Sons.

Weiss, Roberto. 1967. *Humanism in England*. Oxford: Blackwell.

Whigham, Frank. 1984. *Ambition and Privilege: The Social Tropes of Elizabethan Courtesy Theory*. Berkeley: University of California Press.

White, Lynn Jr. 1967. "Jacopo Aconcio as Engineer." *American Historical Review* 72:2: 425–444.

Wildgen, Wolgang. 1996. "Giordano Bruno come philosophe européen: un essai de morphodynamique dans l'histoire des idées." In *Sciences et langues en Europe*, Roger Chartier and Pietro Corsi, eds. Paris: Ecole des Hautes Etudes en Sciences Sociales: 169–185.

Wilkie, William E. 1974. *The Cardinal Protectors of England, Rome and the Tudors before the Reformation*. Cambridge: Cambridge University Press.

Williams, Deanne. *The French Fetish from Chaucer to Shakespeare*. Cambridge: Cambridge University Press, 2004.

Willinsky, John. 1994. *An Empire of Words: The Reign of the OED*. Princeton: Princeton University Press.

Woodall, Joanna. 1991. "An Exemplary Consort: Antonis Mor's Portrait of Queen Mary Tudor." *Art History* 14:2: 192–224.

Woodhouse, John. 1985. "The Reluctant Academicals: Linguistic Individualism after the Crusca." In *The Fairest Flower, The Emergence of Linguistic National Consciousness in Renaissance Europe*, Fredi Chiapelli, ed. Florence: Accademia della Crusca: 175–184.

———. 1994. "The Tradition of Della Casa's *Galateo* in English." In *The Crisis of Courtesy: Studies in the Conduct Book in Britain, 1600–1900*, Jacques Carré, ed. Leiden: Brill: 11–26.

Wormald, Francis. 1951. "An Italian Poet at the Court of Henry VII." *Journal of the Warburg and Courtauld Institutes* 14: 118–119.

Wyatt, Michael. 2003. "La biblioteca di John Florio, una bibliografia annotata." *Bruniana e Campanelliana* 9:2: 409–434.

Wymer, Rowland. 1985. "Lodowick Bryskett and Renaissance Attitudes to Suicide." *Notes and Queries* 32:4: 480–482.

Yates, Frances. 1934. *John Florio: The Life of an Italian in Shakespeare's England*. Cambridge: Cambridge University Press.

———. 1983. "Italian Teachers in England: John Florio's Father" (1955). In *Collected Essays*, vol. II, *Renaissance and Reform: the Italian Contribution*. London: Routledge and Kegan Paul: 161–164.

Young, Susan. 1996. *Shakespeare Manipulated, The Use of the Dramatic Works of Shakespeare in 'teatro di figura' in Italy*. Madison, NJ: Fairleigh Dickinson University Press.

Zambelli, Paolo. 1976. "Magic and Radical Reformation in Agrippa of Nettesheim." *Journal of the Warburg and Courtauld Institutes* 39: 69–103.

Zapperi, Roberto. 1993. *Virginio Orsini: un paladino nei palazzi incantati*. Palermo: Salerio.

Zgusta, Ladislav. 1992. "History and its Multiple Meanings." *History, Languages, and Lexicographers*. Tübingen: Niemeyer: 1–18.

# Index

Accademia della Crusca
   *Vocabolario* (1612) 221–223, 232–237
Aconcio, Giacomo 151–154
   *De methodo* 152
   *Stratagemata Satanae* 153–154
   *Una essortatione al timor di Dio* 186–187
Adelmare, Cesare 314
Adelmare, Giulio 314
*A discovery of the great subtiltie and wonderful wisdome of the Italians* 197–198
Albicante, Giovanni Alberto
   *Il sacro et divino sponsalitio* 109–112
Alighieri, Dante
   and *la questione della lingua* 206–207
Anne of Denmark, Queen of Scotland and England 252–254
Aretino, Pietro 67–70
   dedication to Henry VIII of *Lettere*, vol. II 68–70, 256
   and *la questione della lingua* 335
   *Pronosticon* 67–68
   *Ragionamenti* (*Sei giornate*) 231–237
   *Sonnetti* (*I modi*) 321–322
   *Sonnetto* for Mary Tudor 101–102
   works printed by John Wolfe (*Ragionamenti* and *Quattro commedie*) 191–192
Ariosto, Ludovico
   *Orlando furioso* 18–19, 249; (translated by John Harington) 198, 250–251
Aristotle, on fictions 173
artists, Italian, and England
   Bandinelli, Bacio 50
   Bellin, Nicholas da Modena 279
   Benedetto da Rovezzano 50–51
   Cellini, Benvenuto 46
   Giovanni da Maiano 279
   Mazzoni, Guido 44
   Torrigiano, Pietro 46–49
   Zuccaro, Federico 146

Ascham, Roger
   *The scholemaster* 159–163, 178, 185
   on Castiglione *Il cortegiano* (translated by Thomas Hoby) 160–161

Bandello, Matteo
   *Novella* II.37 66–67
   *Novella* III.lxii 67
Bandinelli, Bacio 50
Bassano, family of musicians 135, 147
Beccadelli, Ludovico
   *Vita del Cardinale Reginaldo Polo* 113–115
Bellin, Nicholas da Modena 279
Bembo, Pietro
   *Le prose della volgar lingua* 205, 207–208, 210, 212–213, 222, 330
Benedetto da Rovezzano 50–51
Beaufort, Henry 28
Boccaccio, Giovanni
   *Decameron* 18, 187, 233, 248; editions of Vincenzo Borghini and Leonardo Salviati 221, 222; edition of Luigi Groto 332–333
   *Trattatello in laude di Dante* 171–172
   *Genealogia deorum gentilium* 15, 171–172, 174–180
books, Italian, printed in London 185–199
Borgarucci, Giulio 147
Bracciolini, Poggio 28, 325
Bruni, Leonardo 272–273
Bruno, Giordano 196, 224, 241–245, 268, 319
   *De la causa, et principio et uno* 245–247
   *La cena de le ceneri* 241–242
   on Elizabeth I 243–244
   on language in *Gli eroici furori* 242–243
Buonvisi, Antonio 141, 281
Burke, Kenneth 179

Campeggio, Lorenzo 59, 62–63, 64
Carmeliano, Pietro 32–35, 61
   *Carmen* 32–35, 255–256

# Index

Caro, Annibale 197
Castellesi, Adriano 54–55
   *De vera philosophia* 55
Castelvetro, Giacomo, editor for John Wolfe 192–193, 198, 324
Castelvetro, Lodovico 192
   controversy with Annibale Caro 324
Castiglione, Baldassare
   *Ad Henricum VII* 37–41
   association with England 35–41
   *Il cortegiano* (translated by Thomas Hoby) 160–161, 181, 196
Castiglione, Giovanni Battista 125–126, 145, 151, 186–187
Cavalcanti, Giovanni 50, 141–143
Cecil, William 98–99, 131, 150, 151, 165
Ceffino, Zanobio
   *Stanze* 87–88, 257–258
Cellini, Benvenuto 46
Charles of Castille (Charles V) 34–35, 46–47, 62
Charlewood, John
   printer of Giordano Bruno in England 196
Chaucer, Geoffrey 18
Chiericati, Francesco 56–58
   at St. Patrick's Well 57–58
Citolini, Alessandro
   *Lettera in difesa de la volgar lingua* 205–209
   *Grammatica della lingua italiana* (adapted by John Florio) 216–217
   *Tipocosmia* 205, 209, 227, 337
Cittadini, Celso 326–327
Corro, Antonio del 150–151
Corsini, Filippo 131, 143
Council of Trent (1545–63) and its aftermath 218–219
culture, defined 5

Dati, Giorgio 51
Davanzati, Bernardo
   *Scisma d'Inghilterra* 72–73
Della Casa, Giovanni
   *Galateo* (translated by Richard Peterson) 181
Della Rena, Andrea (Ammonio) 59–61
   relations with Thomas More and Erasmus 60
de' Medici, Ferdinando I 128–130
de' Medici, Giulio (Clement VII) 50, 59
de' Medici, Giovanni (Leo X) 49–50, 55
de' Medici, Maria 130–131
dictionaries 227–228
   Citolini, Alessandro
      *Tipocosmia* 205, 209, 227, 337

Florio, John
   *Queen Anna's New World of Words* 1, 5, 178, 195, 203–204, 212, 232–241, 253, 322, 334
   *A Worlde of Wordes* 202, 203–204, 224–230, 245, 251–252, 336
Garzoni, Tommaso
   *Piazza universale* 227
Luna, Fabrizio
   *Vocabulario di cinquemila vocaboli toschi* 222
Thomas, William
   *Principal Rules of the Italian Grammar, with a Dictionarie for the better understandyng of Boccace, Petrarcha, and Dante* 211–212, 216
   *The Pilgrim, A Dialogue on the Life and Actions of King Henry Eighth* 70–72
   *Vocabolario degli accademici della Crusca* 221–223, 232–237
Doni, Anton Francesco
   *Libraria* 335
Dudley, John (Duke of Northumberland) 74, 75–76, 99
Dudley, Robert 165, 166

early modern, defined 265
Edward VI, King of England 20, 74, 77, 78–79
Elizabeth I, Queen of England 23, 78, 122, 123, 125–134, 144, 145
   controversy with Pollini's *Historia* 128–130; letter to Ferdinando I 128–130, 260–261
   excommunication of 133–134
   mastery of languages 125–127, 132
   Florio, John on 317–318
Elizabeth of York 47–49
Erasmus 175, 176

Field, Richard 198–199
Florio, John 1, 2–4, 139–140, 154, 163, 175, 201, 205–206, 265, 297, 317, 322
   books consulted in compiling his dictionaries 228–229
   and Bruno, Giordano 196, 337
   and Citolini, Alessandro 216–217
   cultural identity of 3–4
   early life 266
   language teaching of 165–185
   as lexicographer 223
   in *OED* 230–231
   in the Stuart court 252–254
   on translation 1–2
   *Firste Fruites* 6, 15–17, 165–170, 185, 214

## Index

Florio, John (cont.)
  *Giardino di ricreatione* 175, 319, 320
  *Queen Anna's New World of Words* 1, 5, 178, 195, 203–204, 212, 232–241, 253, 321, 334
  *Second Frutes* 165, 167, 168, 176–180, 245–247, 320
  *A short and briefe narration* (translated from Cartier) 7–8
  *A Worlde of Wordes* 202, 203–204, 224–230, 245, 251–252, 336
Florio, Michelangelo 98–101, 322
  *Cathechismo* (translated from John Ponet) 185
  *Regole de la lingua toscana* 100, 212–213
  *Historia de la vita e de la morte de . . . Giovanna Graia* 100–101
Foxe, John
  *Acts and Monuments* 51–52
Frulovisi, Tito Livio dei 29–32
  *Vita Henrici Quinti* 31

Garzoni, Tommaso
  *Piazza universale* 227
gender and language 244–254
Gentili, Alberico 193–196
  controversy with John Reynolds over theatre 195
  *Commentatio* and a theory of poetics 195
  *De iuri belli* 194–195
  relations with John Florio 195
  relations with Philip Sidney 195
Gentili, Scipione 193–194
Gentillet, Innocent
  *Discours sur les moyens de bien gouverner* 188
Ghinucci, Gheronimo 59, 64
Giberti, Gian Matteo 63
Gigli, Giovanni dei 54
Gigli, Silvestro dei 54, 55, 58–59
Giovio, Paolo
  *In vitam Leonis decimi* 49–50
  *Descriptio brittaniae* 67
Goldberg, Jonathan 5
Gondola, Paolo 143–144
Gosson, Stephen 167
  *Plays Confuted in Five Actions* 171
grammars
  Accarisi, Alberto
    *Vocabolario, Grammatica, et Orthografia de la lingua volgare* and *Grammatica volgare* 211
  Alunno, Francesco
    *Le richezze della lingua volgare* 211
  Fortunio, Giovanni Francesco
    *Regole grammaticali della volgar lingua* 210
  Giambullari, Pier Francesco
    *Regole della lingua fiorentina* 210–211
  Lentulo, Scipione (translated by Henry Grantham)
    *An Italian Grammar* 214
  Thomas, William
    *Principal Rules of the Italian Grammar* 211–212, 216
  Florio, John (adapted from Alessandro Citolini *Grammatica della lingua italiana*) 216–218
    *Necessarie Rules for Englishmen to learne to reade, speake, and write true Italian* 216–217
    *Regole necessarie per indurre gli'taliani a proferir la Lingua Inglese* 217–218
  Florio, Michelangelo
    *Regole de la lingua thoscana* 100, 212–213
Grey, Jane 100–101
Griffi, Pietro 55–56
Groto, Luigi (Cieco d'Adria) 332–333
Guazzo, Stefano
  *La civil conversazione* (translated by George Pettie) 181
Guidobaldo da Montefeltro 35–41

Haemstede, Adriaan van 152–153
Henry V, King of England 31
Henry VII, King of England 20, 21, 23, 32, 35–37, 44, 47–49
Henry VIII, King of England 16–17, 19, 27, 32, 47, 49–50, 53, 66–72
  divorce proceedings 62–64
Hoby, Thomas 160–161, 181, 327, 329
Hollyband, Claudius (Claude de Sainliens) 163–165, 168
  *The French Littleton* 164–165, 168
Holquist, Michael 4
humanists, Italian, and Britain
  Bracciolini, Poggio 28, 325
  Bruni, Leonardo 272–273
  Carmeliano, Pietro 32–35, 61
    *Carmen* 32–35
  Castiglione, Baldassare
    *Ad Henricum VII* 37–41
    association with England 35–41
    *Il cortegiano* 160–161
  Della Rena, Andrea (Ammonio) 59–61
  Frulovisi, Tito Livio dei 29–32
    *Vita Henrici Quinti* 31
  Nagonio, Giovanni Michele (Nagonius) 43, 44

# Index

Piccolomini, Enea Silvio 28–29
Virgilio, Polidoro 31, 41–43, 53, 54, 57, 60, 138–139, 275, 311, 319
  *Anglia historia* 41–43, 331
  critique of Arthurian mythology 43
  on the early Anglican reform 292
Humphrey, Duke of Gloucester 29–31

*Index of Forbidden Books* 187, 218–219
Italian congregation in London 98, 148–150

James VI/I, King of Scotland and England 8, 35

Katherine of Aragon 49, 62–63

language
  clothing and 158–159, 168–169
  defined 5
  English in England 158, 204
  French in England 158
  Italian in England 138–139, 162, 208–209, 311
  learning
    literature of courtesy and 180–185
    the poetic "lie" and 170–174
    role of proverbs and 174–180, 183–184
    theatrical dimension of 167–168, 170–171
  and *la querelle des femmes* 247–248
  *la questione della lingua* [the language question] 10, 204–209
  and religious reform 77, 80, 86, 94
  philology, significance of 4–5
  pronunciation of English
    Florio, John
      *Regole necessarie per indurre gli'italiani a proferir la Lingua Inglese* 217–218
  pronunciation of Italian
    Rhys, Siòn Dafydd
      *Perutilis exteris nationibus de Ithalica pronuntiatione* 214–216
  vernaculars absent from European school and university curricula 163
Languet, Hubert 157
*le tre corone* (Dante, Petrarch, Boccaccio) 206, 325
Litolfi, Annibale
  *Relazione sull'Inghilterra* 118–122
London, Italian neighborhoods 147–148
  map of Moorfields area 148

Machiavelli, Niccolò 23
  *Discorsi* 248–249

*Mandragola* 231
  works printed by John Wolfe (*I discorsi* and *Il prencipe*) 187
Magno, Alessandro
  *Travel Journal* 118–122, 139, 147–148
Manners, Roger, Earl of Rutland 224
Margaret Beaufort 46, 47
Mary I, Queen of England 100–116
  coronation of 103–107
  as Dido 103–104
Mazzoni, Guido 44
Merchants, Italian, in England 140
  Buonvisi, Antonio 141, 281
  Cavalcanti, Giovanni 50, 141–143
  Gondola, Paolo 143–144
  Magno, Alessandro 118–122, 139, 147–148
  Pallavicino, Horatio 144–145
  Ridolfi, Roberto 145–146
Milton, John
  *Paradise Lost* first translated into Italian 268
Montaigne, Michel de
  *Essais* 252, 254
musicians, Jewish, in the English court 135–136

Nagonio, Giovanni Michele (Nagonius) 43, 44
Nettesheim, Agrippa von 247–248

Ochino, Bernardo 68, 85, 89, 90–96
  *A Tragedie* 91–95
Orsini, Virginio 118–122
Ovid
  *Delle metamorfosi* (translated by Giovanni Andrea dell'Anguillara) 226, 245, 254

Pallavicino, Horatio 144–145
Piccolomini, Enea Silvio 28–29
Pole, Reginald 89, 112–115
politics, defined 5
Pollini, Girolamo
  *Historia ecclesiastica della rivoluzion d'Inghilterra* 72–73, 102–108, 116, 128–130, 258, 302
proverbs 162, 174–180
  *Book of Proverbs* 175

Rabelais, François
  *Quart Livre*, "frozen words" 204–205
Renaissance
  defined 265

representatives, foreign, in England
   papal 53–61
      Campeggio, Lorenzo 59, 62–63, 64
      Carmeliano, Pietro 32–35, 61
         *Carmen* 32–35
      Castellesi, Adriano 54–55
      Chiericati, Francesco 56–58
         at St. Patrick's Well 57–58
      Della Rena, Andrea (Ammonio) 59–61
      Ghinucci, Gheronimo 59, 64
      Gigli, Giovanni dei 54
      Gigli, Silvestro dei 54, 55, 58–59
      Griffi, Pietro 55–56
      Vanni, Pietro 63–64, 68
      Virgilio, Polidoro 31, 41–43, 53, 54, 57, 60, 138–139, 275, 311
         *Anglia historia* 41–43
         critique of Arthurian mythology 43, 44
         on the early Anglican reform 292
   Russian
      Mikulin, Grigori Ivanovic 132–133
   Venetian 19–20
      Barbaro, Daniele 73
      Cappello, Carlo
         *relazione* of 284
      Scaramelli, Giovan Carlo 126–127, 313
      Trevisan, Andrea
         *relazione* of 19–27
         English beverages 22
         English church 26–27
         English common law 25–26
         English foodstuffs 22
         English monarchy 23
         English treatment of children 24
         English widows 24–25
         Scotland 20–21
         Wales 21
Romei, Annibale
   *Discorsi cavallereschi* (translated by John Kepers) 320
Rorty, Richard 7
Russell, Lucy Harington, Countess of Bedford 224

Said, Edward
   on Erich Auerbach 4–5
Sanders, Nicholas
   *De origine ad progressu schismatis anglicani* 72, 116, 308
Savonarola, Girolamo 86–88
   *piagnoni* 87–88
Scaramelli, Giovan Carlo 126–127, 313
Schivenoglia, Aloisio 122–125
   on coronation of Elizabeth I 123–125

Seymour, Edward, Duke of Somerset 74–76
Seymour, Thomas 76
Shakespeare, William
   first translated into Italian 268
   *Henry V* 122, 199–202
   status of for the English language 325–326
Sidney, Philip 157, 195, 320
   *Defence of Poesie* 172–174, 318–319, 325
   example of John Pietro Pugliano 172–174
Spenser, Edmund 163, 198
   *The Shepherd's Calendar* 204–205
'stranger' in England
   accounted for (and not) in censuses 137–138
   congregations in London (at the Church of Austin Friars) 98, 148
   defined 283–284
   difficulty of ascertaining facts about 136–137
   English hostility toward 137
   Jewish musicians 135–136
   legal position of 139–140

Thomas, William
   *Il Pellegrino Inglese*/*The Pilgrim* 70–72
   *Principal Rules of the Italian Grammar* 211–212, 216
   relations with Edward VI 71
Tito Livio dei Frulovisi 29–32
   *Vita Henrici Quinti* 31
Tolomei, Claudio 327
Torrigiano, Pietro 46–49
translation, defined 1–2
Tremellio, Emmanuele 291–292
Trissino, Giangiorgio 205, 217

Ubaldini, Petruccio 73, 127–128
   editorial work for John Wolfe 192, 198
   *Relazione d'Inghilterra* (1552) 73–84
   Edward VI
      daily schedule 77
      independence and character of 78–79
      regents of 74–76
      royal residences 76–77
      on the transformation of English religious practices 79–84
   *Relatione d'Inghilterra* (1583)
      on Elizabeth I 127–128

Valdés, Juan de 88–89, 96
Valla, Lorenzo 86
   *De falso credita et ementita Costantini donatione declamatio* 86

Vanni, Pietro 63–64, 68
Vasari, Giorgio 46–49, 265
Venier, Lorenzo
  *La puttana errante* 321–322
Vergerio, Pier Paolo 84–85,
  266, 285
Vermigli, Pietro 68, 85, 89, 96–98
Virgil
  *Aeneid* 40–41, 103–104
Virgilio, Polidoro 31, 41–43, 53, 54, 57, 60,
  138–139, 275, 311, 319
  *Anglica historia* 41–43, 331

critique of Arthurian mythology 43, 44
on the early Anglican reform 292

Wolfe, John 185–198, 262–264
Wolsey, Thomas 42, 50–51, 55, 57, 62–63
Wriothesley, Henry, Earl of Southampton
  224–225

Yates, Frances 8, 180–181, 266, 297, 298,
  316, 317, 319, 322, 324, 334, 337, 338

Zuccaro, Federico 146

*Cambridge studies in renaissance literature and culture*

*General editor*
STEPHEN ORGEL, Jackson Eli Reynolds Professor of Humanities, Stanford University

Douglas Bruster, *Drama and the market in the age of Shakespeare*

Virginia Cox, *The Renaissance dialogue: literary dialogue in its social and political contexts, Castiglione to Galileo*

Richard Rambuss, *Spenser's secret career*

John Gillies, *Shakespeare and the geography of difference*

Laura Levine, *Men in women's clothing: anti-theatricality and effeminization, 1579–1642*

Linda Gregerson, *The reformation of the subject: Spenser, Milton, and the English Protestant epic*

Mary C. Fuller, *Voyages in print: English travel to America, 1567–1624*

Margreta de Grazia, Maureen Quilligan, Peter Stallybrass (eds.), *Subject and object in Renaissance culture*

T. G. Bishop, *Shakespeare and the theatre of wonder*

Mark Breitenberg, *Anxious masculinity in early modern England*

Frank Whigham, *Seizures of the will in early modern English drama*

Kevin Pask, *The emergence of the English author: scripting the life of the poet in early modern England*

Claire McEachern, *The poetics of English nationhood, 1590–1612*

Jeffrey Masten, *Textual intercourse: collaboration, authorship, and sexualities in Renaissance drama*

Timothy J. Reiss, *Knowledge, discovery and imagination in early modern Europe: the rise of aesthetic rationalism*

Elizabeth Fowler and Roland Greene (eds.), *The project of prose in early modern Europe and the New World*

Alexandra Halasz, *The marketplace of print: pamphlets and the public sphere in early modern England*

Seth Lerer, *Courtly letters in the age of Henry VIII: literary culture and the arts of deceit*

M. Lindsay Kaplan, *The culture of slander in early modern England*

Howard Marchitello, *Narrative and meaning in early modern England: Browne's skull and other histories*

Mario DiGangi, *The homoerotics of early modern drama*

Heather James, *Shakespeare's Troy: drama, politics, and the translation of empire*

Christopher Highley, *Shakespeare, Spenser, and the crisis in Ireland*

Elizabeth Hanson, *Discovering the subject in Renaissance England*

Jonathan Gil Harris, *Foreign bodies and the body politic: discourses of social pathology in early modern England*

Megan Matchinske, *Writing, gender and state in early modern England: identity formation and the female subject*

Joan Pong Linton, *The romance of the New World: gender and the literary formations of English colonialism*

Eve Rachele Sanders, *Gender and literacy on stage in early modern England*

Dorothy Stephens, *The limits of eroticism in post-Petrarchan narrative: conditional pleasure from Spenser to Marvell*

Celia R. Daileader, *Eroticism on the Renaissance stage: transcendence, desire, and the limits of the visible*

Theodore B. Leinwand, *Theatre, finance, and society in early modern England*

Heather Dubrow, *Shakespeare and domestic loss: forms of deprivation, mourning, and recuperation*

David Posner, *The performance of nobility in early modern European literature*

Michael C. Schoenfeldt, *Bodies and selves in early modern England: physiology and inwardness in Spenser, Shakespeare, Herbert, and Milton*

Lynn Enterline, *Rhetoric of the body from Ovid to Shakespeare*

Douglas A. Brooks, *From playhouse to printing house: drama and authorship in early modern England*

Robert Matz, *Defending literature in early modern England: Renaissance literary theory in social context*

Ann Jones and Peter Stallybrass, *Renaissance clothing and the materials of memory*

Robert Weimann, *Author's pen and actor's voice: playing and writing in Shakespeare's theatre*

Barbara Fuchs, *Mimesis and Empire: the new world, Islam, and European identities*

Wendy Wall, *Staging domesticity: household works and English identity in early modern drama*

Valerie Traub, *The Renaissance of lesbianism in early modern England*

Joe Loewenstein, *Ben Jonson and possessive authorship*

William N. West, *Theatres and encyclopedias in early modern Europe*

Richmond Barbour, *Before Orientalism: London's theatre of the East, 1576–1626*

Elizabeth Spiller, *Science, reading, and Renaissance literature: the art of making knowledge, 1580–1670*

Deanne Williams, *The French fetish from Chaucer to Shakespeare*

Douglas Trevor, *The poetics of melancholy in early modern England*

Christopher Warley, *Sonnet sequences and social distinction in Renaissance England*

Garrett A. Sullivan, Jr., *Memory and Forgetting in English Renaissance drama: Shakespeare, Marlowe, Webster*

Michael Wyatt, *The Italian encounter with Tudor England: a cultural politics of translation*